W9-DAT-983

# WAHOOLAZUMA!

Created, Written, and Illustrated by
## LARRY MARDER

DARK HORSE BOOKS®

2/16

Dedicated, with all my love, to my wife, Cory.
Your dazzling illumination will always be
the brightest light in my life.

*Editor* Diana Schutz
*Associate Editor* Dave Marshall
*Editorial Assistant* Brendan Wright
*Book Design* Tina Alessi
*Digital Production* Matt Dryer
*Publisher* Mike Richardson

LARRY MARDER'S BEANWORLD™ (Book 1): WAHOOLAZUMA!

Text and illustrations © 1984, 1985, 1986, 1987, 1988, 1989, 2009 Larry Marder. All rights reserved. Introduction © 1989 Scott McCloud. All rights reserved. All other material, unless otherwise specified, © 2009 Dark Horse Comics, Inc. All rights reserved. The Beanworld logo, Beanish, Professor Garbanzo, Mr. Spook, and all characters prominently featured herein are trademarks of Larry Marder. No portion of this publication may be reproduced or transmitted, in any form or by any means, without the express written permission of Larry Marder or Dark Horse Comics, Inc., except for purposes of review. Names, characters, places, and incidents featured in this publication either are the product of the author's imagination or are used fictitiously. Any resemblance to actual persons (living or dead), events, institutions, or locales, without satiric intent, is coincidental. Dark Horse Books, Dark Horse Comics, and the Dark Horse logo are registered trademarks of Dark Horse Comics, Inc.

This volume collects issues one through nine of *Tales of the Beanworld*,
originally edited by Cat Yronwode.

Published by Dark Horse Books
A division of Dark Horse Comics, Inc.
10956 SE Main Street
Milwaukie, Oregon 97222

darkhorse.com

First Dark Horse edition: February 2009
ISBN 978-1-59582-240-6

1 3 5 7 9 10 8 6 4 2
Printed in China

# PREFACE

**WHAT YOU HOLD** in your hands is an artifact of my life.

It started on the day I was born. Apparently I was a difficult birth, and my head came out all smushed to the side. My mother's first words upon seeing me were, "Why is his head shaped like a bean?" Beans became my totem, and I've been associated with the lima bean shape ever since.

In the early '70s, during my run as an editorial cartoonist for my university newspaper, I introduced little minimal-istic characters consisting of a lopsided torso, eyes, and spindly arms and legs. I called them "Beans." As time went by, in a process of trial and error, these simple critters led me to a place I named Beanworld.

For many years, I couldn't quite *see* Beanworld as much as *feel* my way around it. The names, places, and story shards I gathered never fit together snugly into the mosaic I was trying to compose. I was constantly in search of the proper foundation upon which to build Beanworld. This was documented rather well in a letter I wrote to a friend from college around 1978:

*What is Beanworld? Drawings? Stories in my head? Books? Posters? Offset (printing)? Silkscreen? S-F novels? Kiddie books? Relevant? Fantasy? Humor? Color? Black & white? Pencils? Ink?*

I didn't know, but I hoped if I kept plugging away that eventually I might find the right pieces and sense the appropriate patterns.

That moment arrived in 1980, with the discovery of Gran'Ma'Pa as the sole source of food for the Beans. *Wahoolazuma!* It all came together in a blinding flash of clarity. Beanworld stories washed over me like a flooding river. All I had to do was dip my pen into this wild torrent of ideas and transcribe stories onto paper as quickly and efficiently as I could move my hand. Those documentations are the stories in this book.

Nowadays, I can sense the entire *Beanworld* story arc from beginning to end. Parts of it are crystal clear and others still a bit fuzzy. And new ideas pop into my head all the time. It's a lot of fun sorting it all out.

I should note that I took a rather lengthy and unanticipated hiatus from publishing *Beanworld* for fifteen years when I went into the business side of Popular Culture— first as Executive Director of Image Comics and then as President of McFarlane Toys. It was a rather fascinating sidetrack, but, after managing the commercial productivity of others, I've returned to the only endeavor that ever genuinely meant anything to me.

Being the Beanworld guy.

Enjoy your time immersed in these tales of the Beanworld. Believe me, there are a whole lot more where they came from!

With a Hoo-Hoo-HA and a Hoka-Hoka-HEY!

**Larry Marder**
larrymarder.blogspot.com
2009

# THE BEANWORLD GLOSSARY

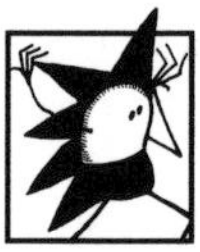

**Beanish:** Artist. Creator of the Fabulous Look·See Show.

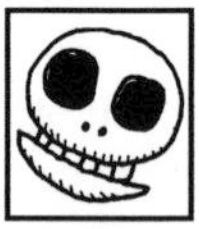

**Bone Zone:** Skull remains of the Hoi-Polloi Ring Herd located underneath the Four Realities.

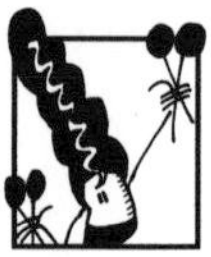

**Boom'r Band:** A hot trio of Beanworld musicians.

**Chow:** A dark stony substance. The Beans eat it, and the Hoi-Polloi use it for money.

**Chowdown:** The act of consuming food.

**Chowdown Pool:** Giant tub used by the Beans as a communal feeding place.

**Chow Sol'jer Army:** They steal Chow from the Hoi-Polloi. Mr. Spook is the leader of the two divisions: Spear-Fling'n-Flank'rs and Chow-Pluk'rs.

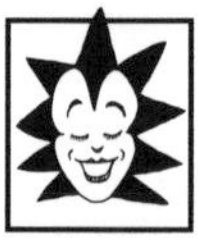

**Dreamishness:** Beanish's secret friend and muse.

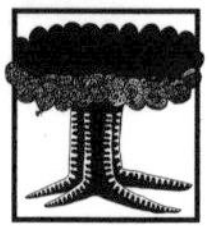

**Gran'Ma'Pa:** Beanworld's spiritual and culinary guardian. Sole source of Sprout-Butts.

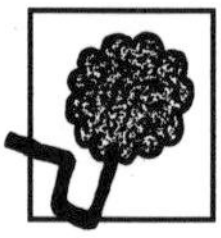

**Gunk'l'dunk:** All-purpose adhesive.

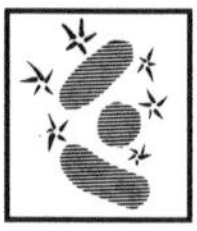

**Float Factor:** When Twinks get near Mystery Pods, both objects transform into a new entity that floats in the air.

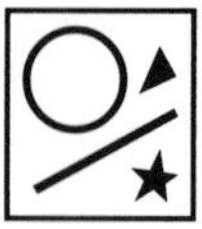

**Four Realities:** Chips, Slats, Hoops, and Twinks. Easily obtainable raw materials for Beanworld arts and industry. For example, a slat and chip can be manufactured into a spear.

**Hoi-Polloi Ring Herd:** General adversaries to the Beans. Greedy gambling folks. The only creatures with the ability to process Sprout-Butts into Chow.

**Legendary Edge:** Departure point from trips to the Four Realities and below.

**Notworms:** What Mr. Spook's fork is made of.

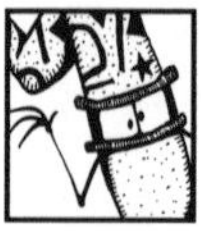

**Professor Garbanzo:** Toolmaker and thinker.

**Proverbial Sandy Beach:** Re-entry point from trips to the Four Realities and below.

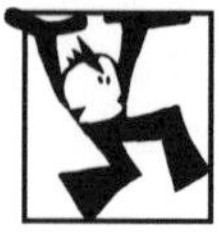

**Mr. Spook:** Hero and leader of the Chow Sol'jer Army.

**Mystery Pods:** Powerful objects of unknown origin. Used in Float Factor.

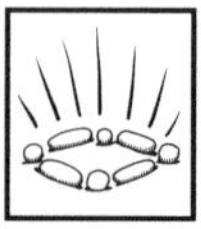

**Secret Sketch:** Circular Float Factor device that mysteriously transports Beanish to Dreamishness for daily midday visits.

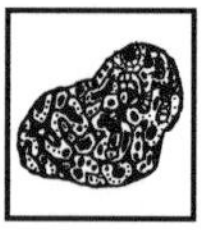

**Sprout-Butt:** Vocal offshoot of Gran'Ma'Pa. Hoi-Polloi convert Sprout-Butts into Chow.

**Thin Lake:** Fresh water that covers the Four Realities.

# MAP OF THE KNOWN BEANWORLD

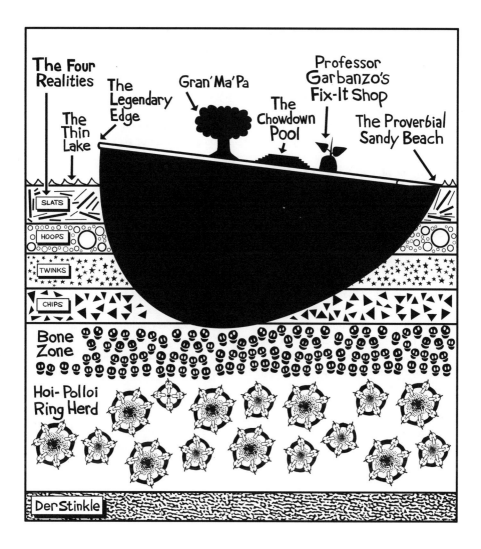

**The Four Realities**

The Legendary Edge

The Thin Lake

Gran'Ma'Pa

The Chowdown Pool

Professor Garbanzo's Fix-It Shop

The Proverbial Sandy Beach

SLATS

HOOPS

TWINKS

CHIPS

Bone Zone

Hoi-Polloi Ring Herd

Der Stinkle

### Hey, what's with this Beanworld anyway?
Beanworld is a weird fantasy dimension operating under its own rules and laws. Beanworld is about the affinity of life. All the characters, whether they are friends or adversaries, understand that ultimately they depend on each other for survival.

### One caution:
Please do not search for scientific or magical explanations; you won't find any. Beanworld is a separate reality. It's not just a *place*, it's a *process*. It is what it is—and th-that's all, folks.

5

# INTRODUCTION

**Y**OU'RE THE FIRST person on earth to read this comic.

Others have been here—thousands, in fact—but they all saw something different, and they all left thinking different things. Of all the people who have ever visited Larry Marder's Beanworld, or who ever will, you're the only one able to see it this way. Your way. The way it is.

*Beanworld* is an all-too-rare experience in comics, or in any medium for that matter—a truly collaborative effort between creator and audience. Stored in Larry's deceptively simple artwork is a treasure chest of ideas and emotion, waiting to be unlocked by the reader. Our experiences and perceptions are the key that unlocks that chest. But each of us has a different key and each key works in a different way, leading us to a different treasure.

In my case, it led me back to my child-hood, a memory of a world in which I

had to start from scratch, where each discovery led to a hundred possibilities and where all the known universe was within my reach. It reminded me of the joy of learning a new language, and how that joy had eluded me lately. Most importantly, *Beanworld* helped change my attitudes about art in general and (my own art in particular) and gave me a renewed sense of purpose and direction.

I can't tell you what you'll discover in these pages. Only you can ever know that. But I guarantee that whatever you find, it'll be worth the search.

I've read thousands of comics since the magic medium caught my eye over fifteen years ago. I have yet to find a comic book as challenging and inventive and downright fun as *Beanworld*. Of all the comics being published today, *Beanworld* is far and away my favorite.

But that's me.

**Scott McCloud**
Boston, Massachusetts
Spring 1989

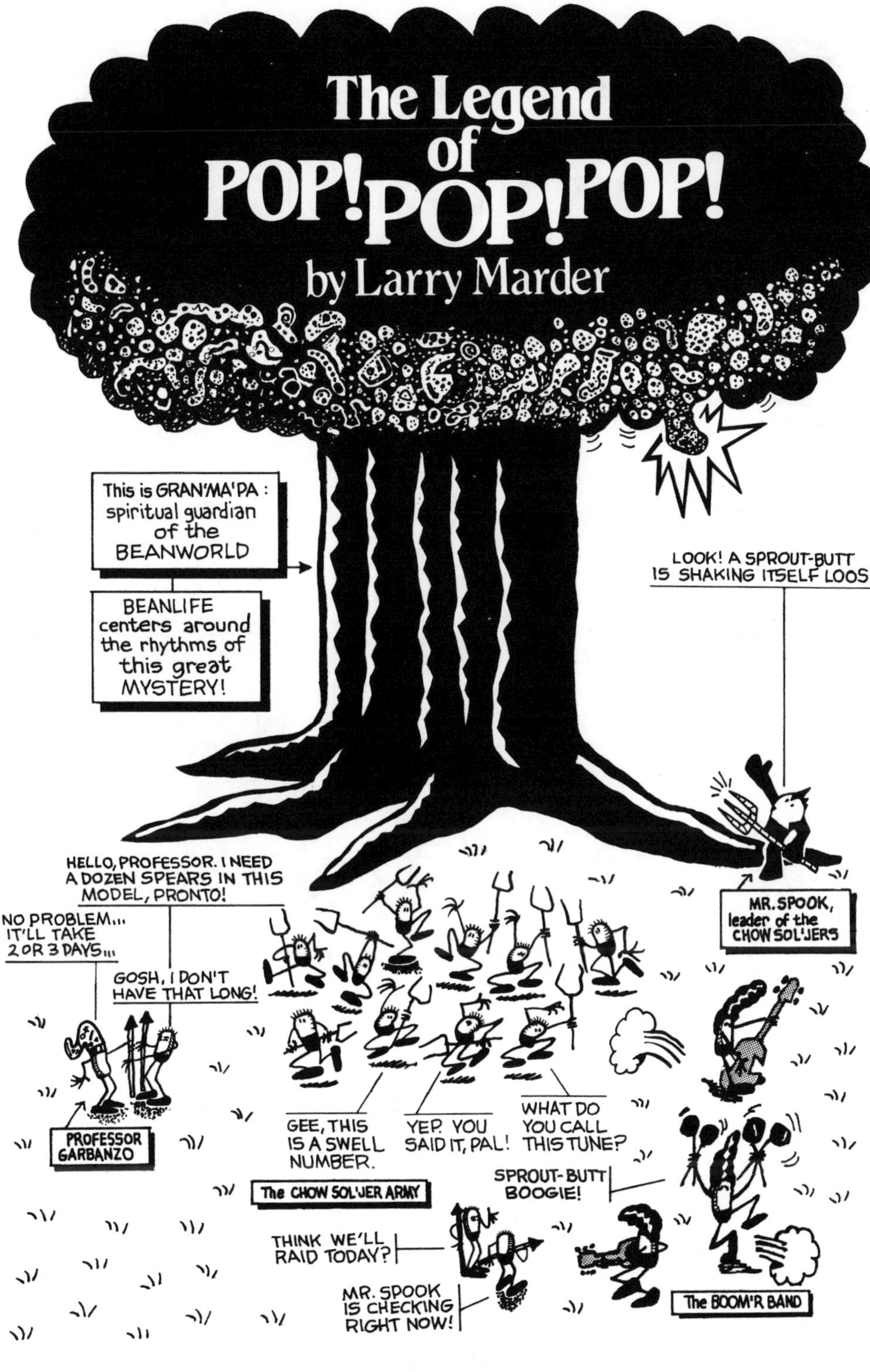

The Legend of POP! POP! POP!
by Larry Marder
This is GRAN'MA'PA : spiritual guardian of the BEANWORLD
BEANLIFE centers around the rhythms of this great MYSTERY!
LOOK! A SPROUT-BUTT IS SHAKING ITSELF LOOSE!
MR. SPOOK, leader of the CHOW SOL'JERS
HELLO, PROFESSOR. I NEED A DOZEN SPEARS IN THIS MODEL, PRONTO!
NO PROBLEM... IT'LL TAKE 2 OR 3 DAYS...
GOSH, I DON'T HAVE THAT LONG!
PROFESSOR GARBANZO
GEE, THIS IS A SWELL NUMBER.
YEP. YOU SAID IT, PAL!
WHAT DO YOU CALL THIS TUNE?
SPROUT-BUTT BOOGIE!
The CHOW SOL'JER ARMY
THINK WE'LL RAID TODAY?
MR. SPOOK IS CHECKING RIGHT NOW!
The BOOM'R BAND

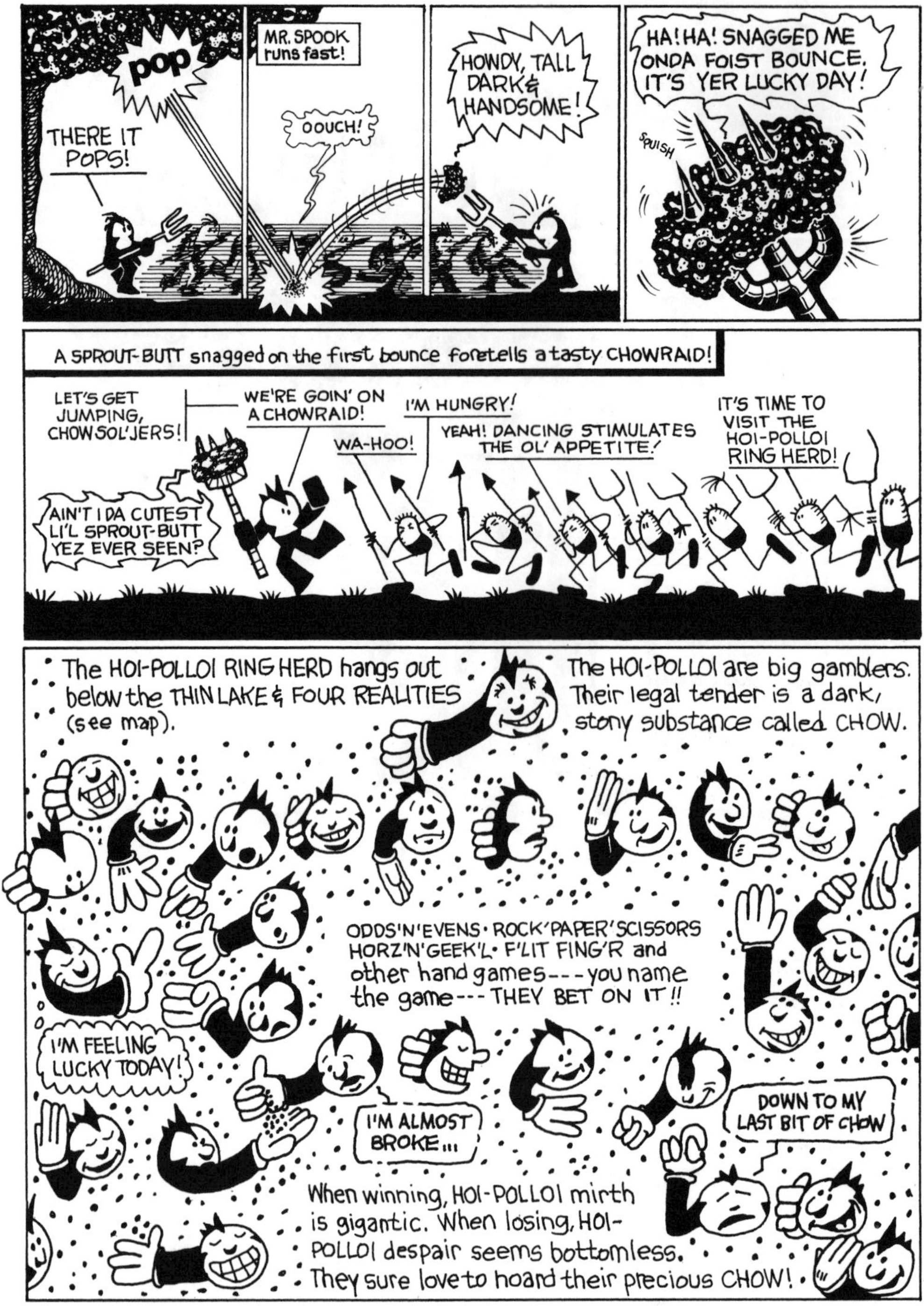

pop
THERE IT POPS!
MR. SPOOK runs fast!
OOUCH!
HOWDY, TALL DARK & HANDSOME!
HA! HA! SNAGGED ME ONDA FOIST BOUNCE. IT'S YER LUCKY DAY!
SQUISH
A SPROUT-BUTT snagged on the first bounce foretells a tasty CHOWRAID!
LET'S GET JUMPING, CHOWSOL'JERS!
WE'RE GOIN' ON A CHOWRAID!
AIN'T I DA CUTEST LI'L SPROUT-BUTT YEZ EVER SEEN?
WA-HOO!
I'M HUNGRY!
YEAH! DANCING STIMULATES THE OL' APPETITE!
IT'S TIME TO VISIT THE HOI-POLLOI RING HERD!
The HOI-POLLOI RING HERD hangs out below the THIN LAKE & FOUR REALITIES (see map).
The HOI-POLLOI are big gamblers. Their legal tender is a dark, stony substance called CHOW.
ODDS'N'EVENS · ROCK'PAPER'SCISSORS HORZ'N'GEEK'L · F'LIT FING'R and other hand games--- you name the game--- THEY BET ON IT!!
I'M FEELING LUCKY TODAY!
I'M ALMOST BROKE...
DOWN TO MY LAST BIT OF CHOW
When winning, HOI-POLLOI mirth is gigantic. When losing, HOI-POLLOI despair seems bottomless. They sure love to hoard their precious CHOW!

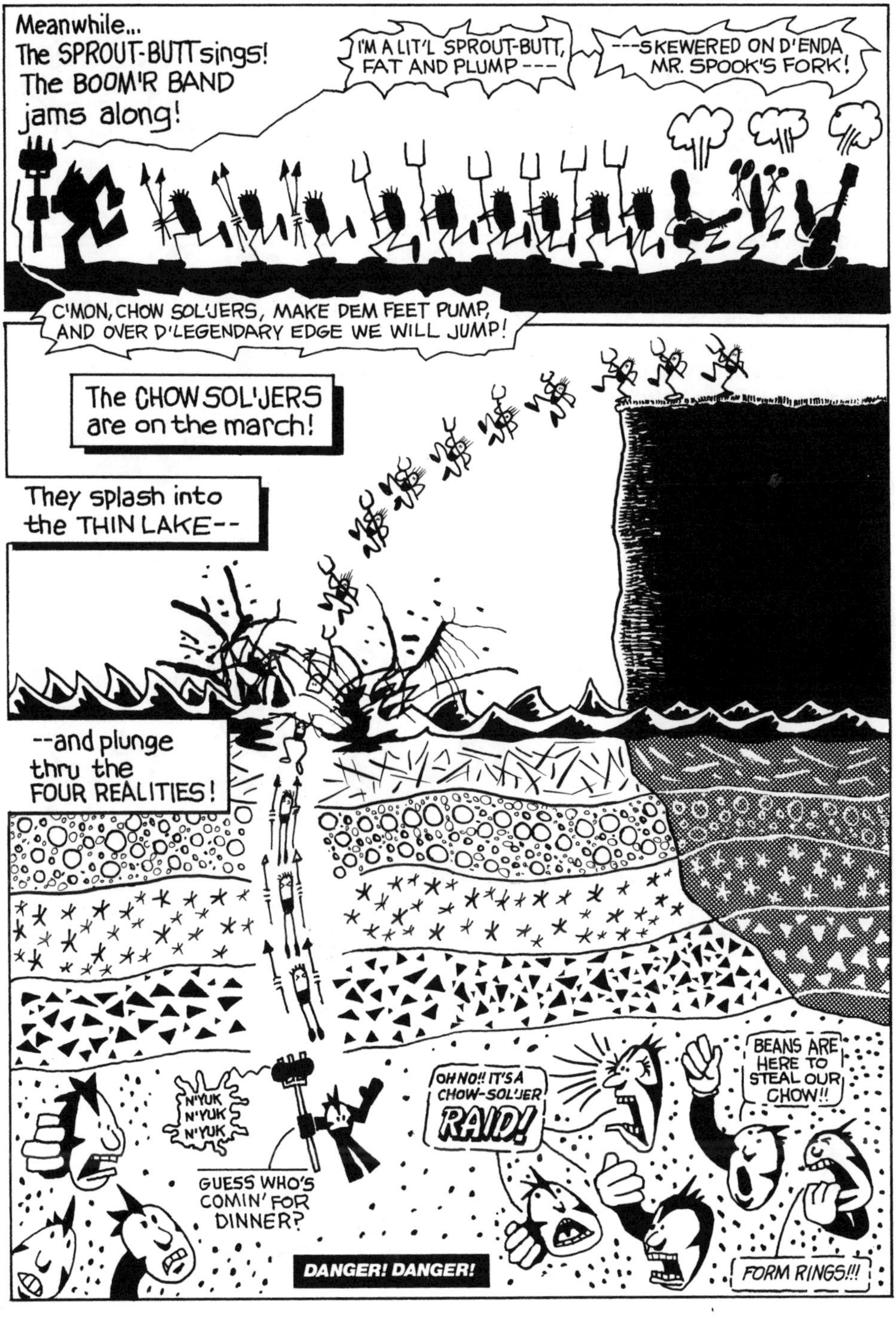

Meanwhile... The SPROUT-BUTT sings! The BOOM'R BAND jams along!
I'M A LIT'L SPROUT-BUTT, FAT AND PLUMP ---
---SKEWERED ON D'ENDA MR. SPOOK'S FORK!
C'MON, CHOW SOL'JERS, MAKE DEM FEET PUMP, AND OVER D'LEGENDARY EDGE WE WILL JUMP!
The CHOW SOL'JERS are on the march!
They splash into the THIN LAKE--
--and plunge thru the FOUR REALITIES!
N'YUK N'YUK N'YUK
GUESS WHO'S COMIN' FOR DINNER?
OH NO!! IT'S A CHOW-SOL'JER RAID!
BEANS ARE HERE TO STEAL OUR CHOW!!
DANGER! DANGER!
FORM RINGS!!!

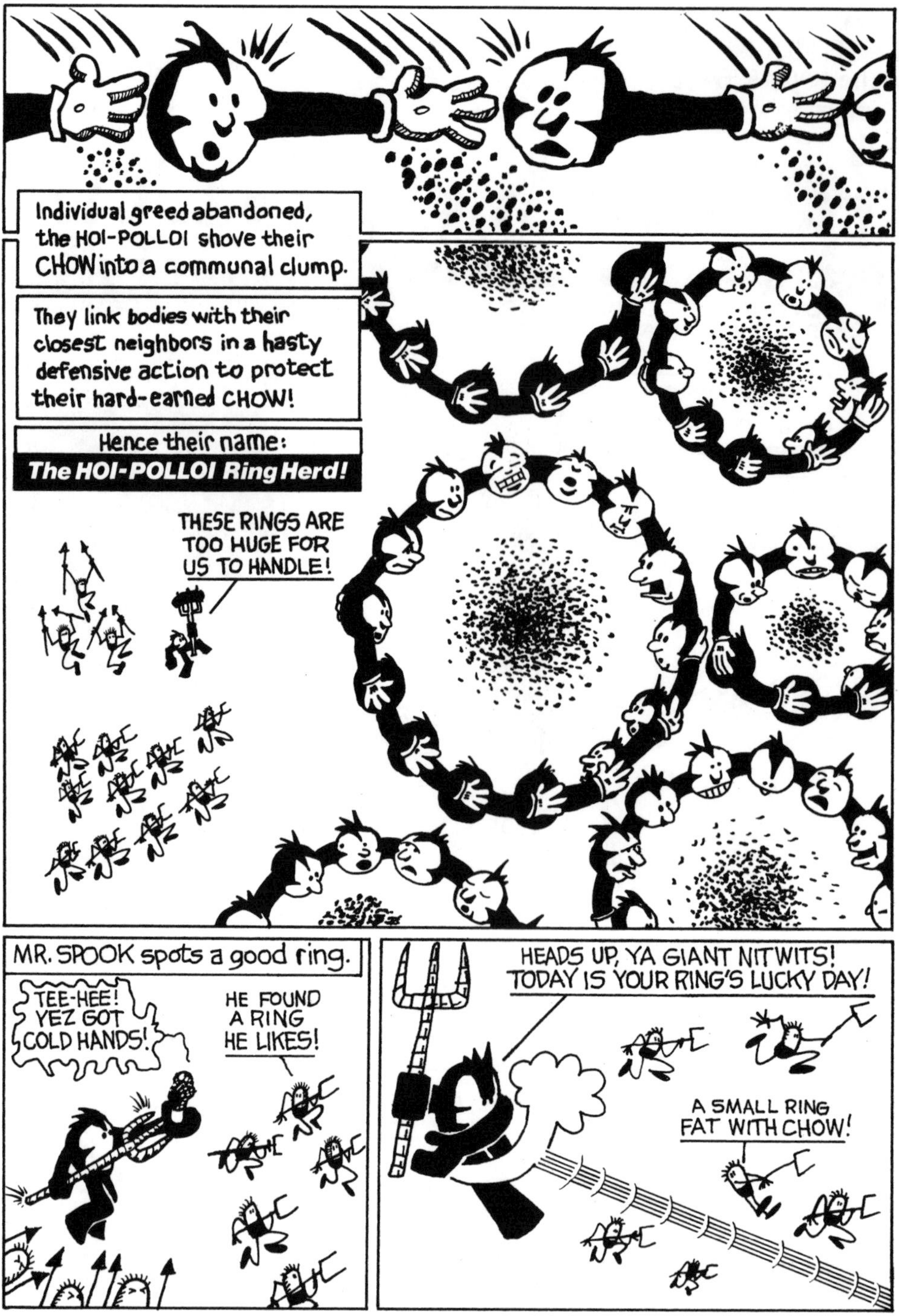
Individual greed abandoned, the HOI-POLLOI shove their CHOW into a communal clump.
They link bodies with their closest neighbors in a hasty defensive action to protect their hard-earned CHOW!
Hence their name:
The HOI-POLLOI Ring Herd!
THESE RINGS ARE TOO HUGE FOR US TO HANDLE!
MR. SPOOK spots a good ring.
TEE-HEE! YEZ GOT COLD HANDS!
HE FOUND A RING HE LIKES!
HEADS UP, YA GIANT NITWITS! TODAY IS YOUR RING'S LUCKY DAY!
A SMALL RING FAT WITH CHOW!

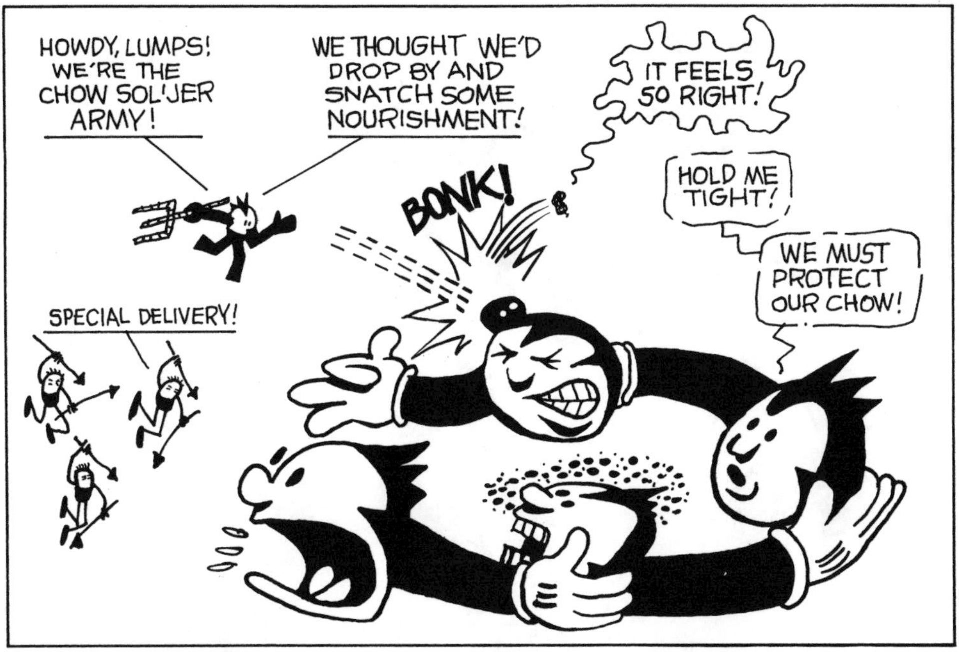
HOWDY, LUMPS! WE'RE THE CHOW SOL'JER ARMY!
WE THOUGHT WE'D DROP BY AND SNATCH SOME NOURISHMENT!
IT FEELS SO RIGHT!
HOLD ME TIGHT!
WE MUST PROTECT OUR CHOW!
BONK!
SPECIAL DELIVERY!

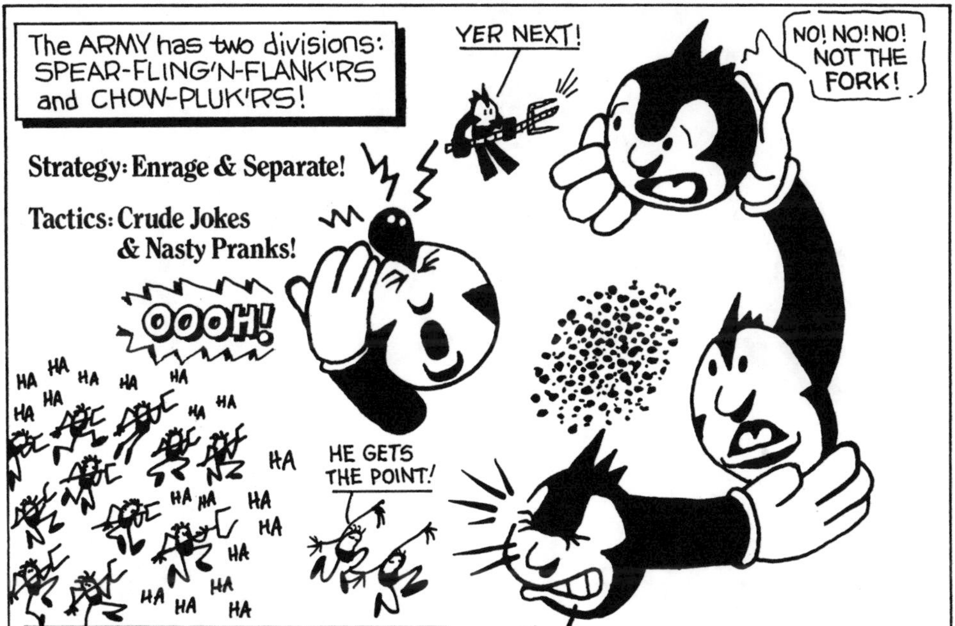
The ARMY has two divisions: SPEAR-FLING'N-FLANK'RS and CHOW-PLUK'RS!
YER NEXT!
NO! NO! NO! NOT THE FORK!
Strategy: Enrage & Separate!
Tactics: Crude Jokes & Nasty Pranks!
OOOH!
HA HA HA HA HA HA HA HA HA HA HA HA HA HA HA HA HA HA HA HA
HE GETS THE POINT!
The SPEAR-FLING'N-FLANK'RS assist MR. SPOOK with the FIERCE OFFENSIVE BLITZ!!
The ring is breached.

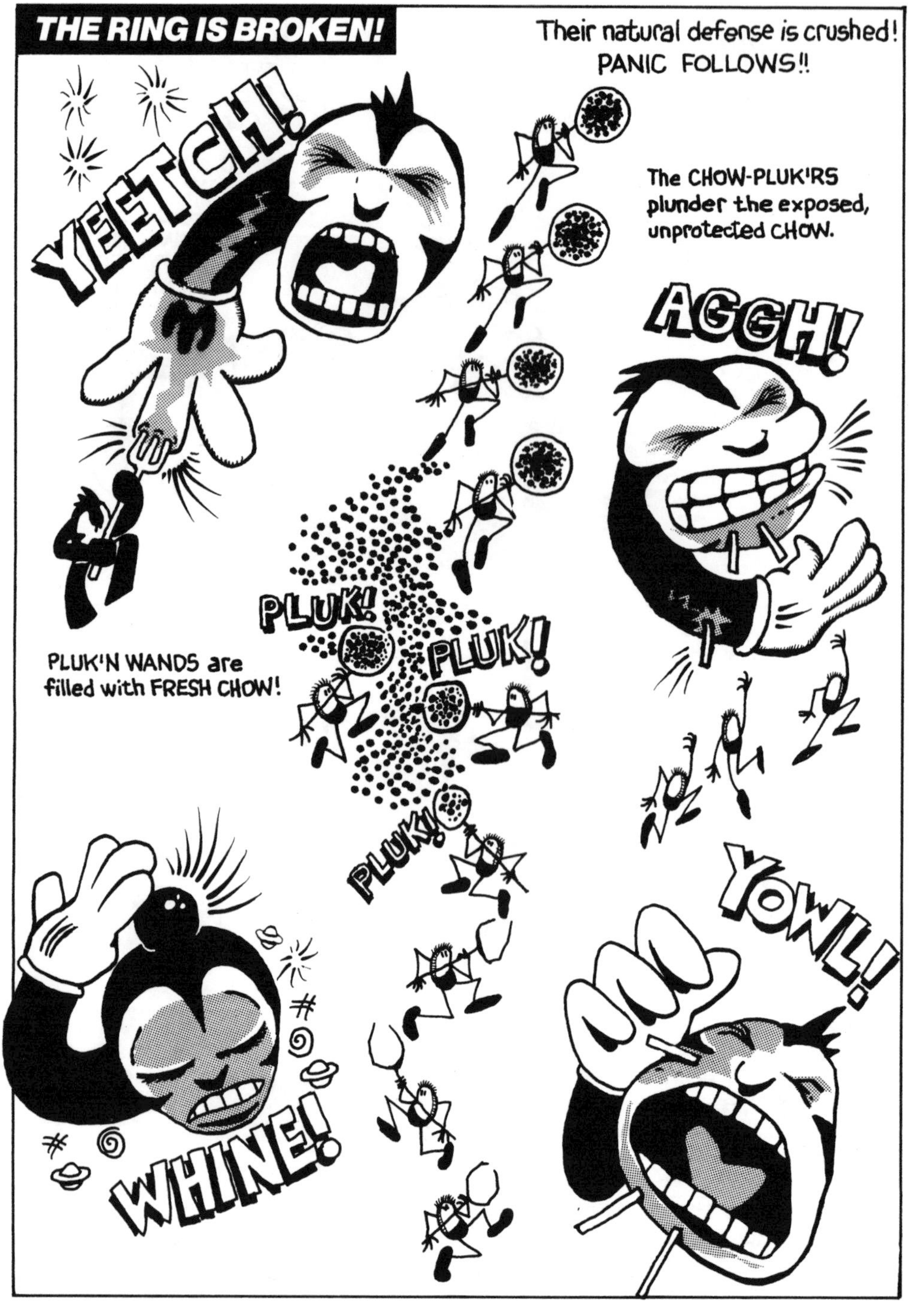
THE RING IS BROKEN!
Their natural defense is crushed!
PANIC FOLLOWS!!
YEETCH!
The CHOW-PLUK'RS plunder the exposed, unprotected CHOW.
AGGH!
PLUK!
PLUK!
PLUK'N WANDS are filled with FRESH CHOW!
PLUK!
YOWL!
WHINE!

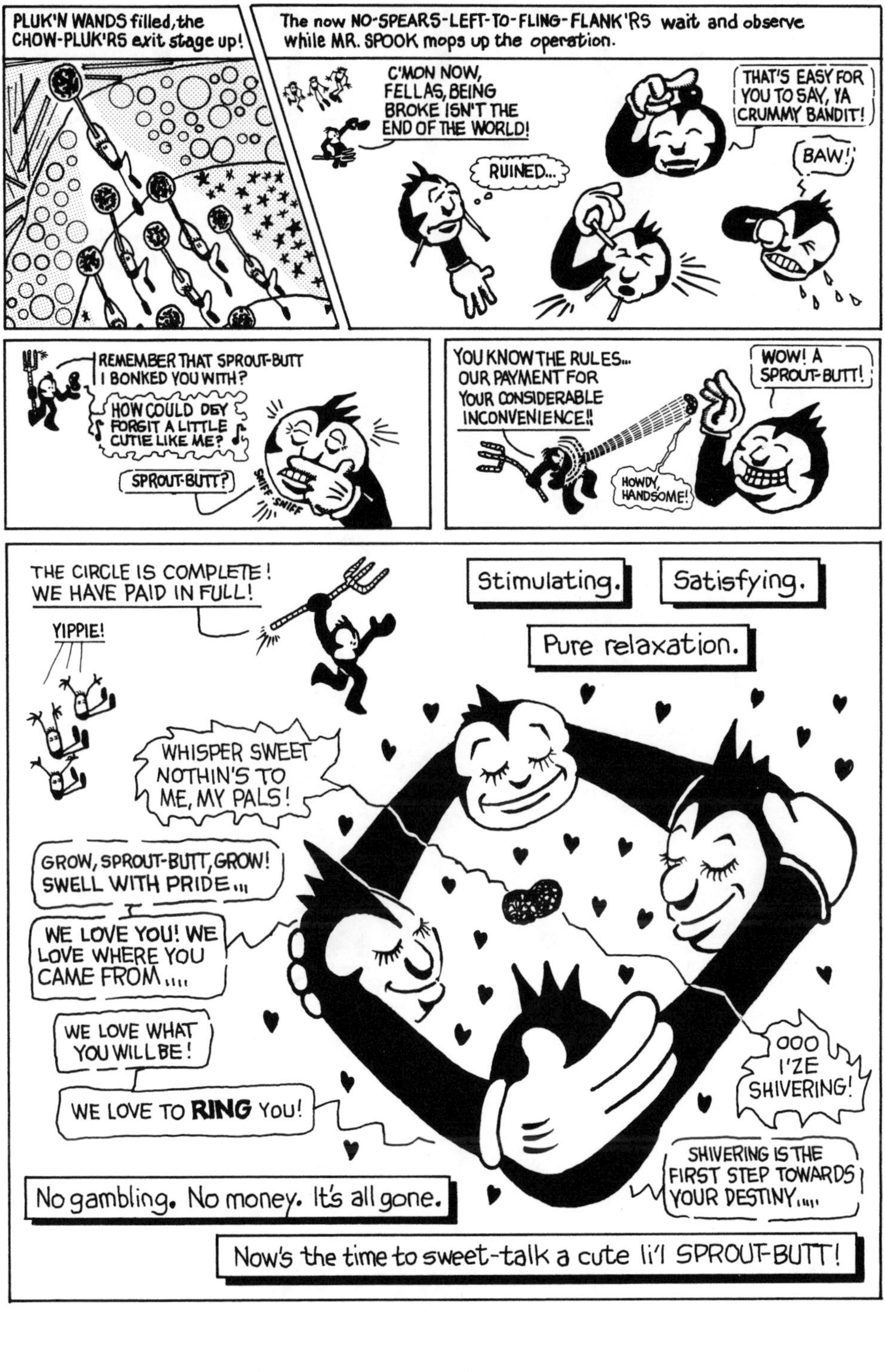
PLUK'N WANDS filled, the CHOW-PLUK'RS exit stage up!
The now NO-SPEARS-LEFT-TO-FLING-FLANK'RS wait and observe while MR. SPOOK mops up the operation.
C'MON NOW, FELLAS, BEING BROKE ISN'T THE END OF THE WORLD!
THAT'S EASY FOR YOU TO SAY, YA CRUMMY BANDIT!
RUINED...
BAW!
REMEMBER THAT SPROUT-BUTT I BONKED YOU WITH?
HOW COULD DEY FORGIT A LITTLE CUTIE LIKE ME?
SPROUT-BUTT?
SNIFF SNIFF
YOU KNOW THE RULES... OUR PAYMENT FOR YOUR CONSIDERABLE INCONVENIENCE!!
WOW! A SPROUT-BUTT!
HOWDY, HANDSOME!
THE CIRCLE IS COMPLETE! WE HAVE PAID IN FULL!
YIPPIE!
Stimulating.
Satisfying.
Pure relaxation.
WHISPER SWEET NOTHIN'S TO ME, MY PALS!
GROW, SPROUT-BUTT, GROW! SWELL WITH PRIDE...
WE LOVE YOU! WE LOVE WHERE YOU CAME FROM....
WE LOVE WHAT YOU WILL BE!
WE LOVE TO RING YOU!
OOO I'ZE SHIVERING!
SHIVERING IS THE FIRST STEP TOWARDS YOUR DESTINY....
No gambling. No money. It's all gone.
Now's the time to sweet-talk a cute li'l SPROUT-BUTT!

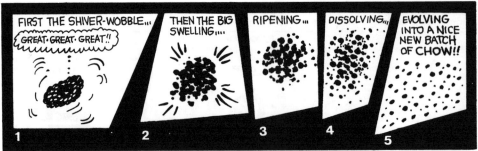

| | | | | |
|---|---|---|---|---|
| FIRST THE SHIVER-WOBBLE... GREAT·GREAT·GREAT!! | THEN THE BIG SWELLING.... | RIPENING... | DISSOLVING... | EVOLVING INTO A NICE NEW BATCH OF CHOW!! |
| 1 | 2 | 3 | 4 | 5 |

WE SPLIT THE CHOW-CROP UP AND GET BACK TO OUR F'LIT FING'R GAME WHERE WE LEFT OFF!!

WE WAIT UNTIL GRAN'MA'PA DROPS A SPROUT-BUTT BEFORE WE RAID.

WE ALWAYS LEAVE THE HOI-POLLOI A SPROUT-BUTT GIFT.

IT'S A WONDERFUL WAY TO MAKE A LIVING!!

HA·HA! SOMEDAY WE'LL RETURN AGAIN & STEAL ALL YOUR CHOW!

OF COURSE WE WILL LEAVE ANOTHER SPROUT-BUTT!

THE LIFE GRAN'-MA'PA PROVIDES IS PERFECT, AS LONG AS WE EACH FOLLOW OUR GIVEN JOBS!!

Mopping-up chores completed, the 4 CHOW SOL'JERS return to the surface world.

Point of entry: THE PROVERBIAL SANDY BEACH!

WE BETTER HURRY TO THE CHOWDOWN POOL!

RIGHT!

The CHOW SOL'JERS are HOME! A triumphant return: LOADS of CHOW & NO INJURIES!!

In the vanguard tramp the CHOW-PLUK'RS, hoisting their bulging PLUK'N WANDS!

They march along to the proud thumping CHOWDOWN tunes of the BOOM'R BAND!!

CHOW-PLUK'RS climb the stairs and encircle the CHOWDOWN POOL!

QUICK! QUICK! BROTHERS & SISTERS, WE'RE ALL HUNGRY TODAY!!

I KNOW, PROFESSOR GARBANZO. I CAN ALMOST TASTE THAT SCRUMPTIOUS SOUP NOW!!

MM-MM-GOOD!

PLUK'N WANDS wave over cool water. The CHOW falls into the pool.

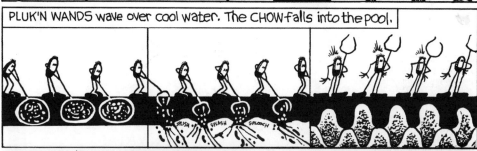

SPLISH    SPLASH    SPLOOCH

The water bubbles and rolls. Fresh CHOW in contact with water dissolves and crumbles into tiny chunks that emit heat and energy! A burbling pool of solvent CHOW means it's

# CHOWDOWN TIME!

EVERYONE INTO THE POOL!

The BEANS take a leisurely bathe in the life-giving soup. Each BEAN has the opportunity to soak up as much food as he or she desires.

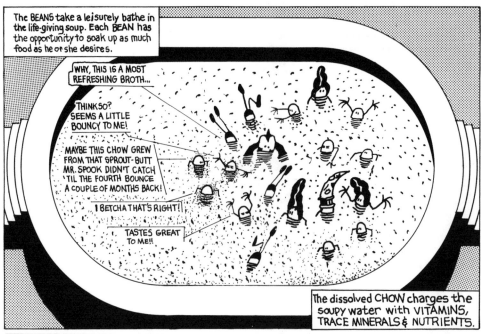

WHY, THIS IS A MOST REFRESHING BROTH...

THINK SO? SEEMS A LITTLE BOUNCY TO ME!

MAYBE THIS CHOW GREW FROM THAT SPROUT-BUTT MR. SPOOK DIDN'T CATCH 'TIL THE FOURTH BOUNCE A COUPLE OF MONTHS BACK!

I BETCHA THAT'S RIGHT!

TASTES GREAT TO ME!!

The dissolved CHOW charges the soupy water with VITAMINS, TRACE MINERALS & NUTRIENTS.

VITAMINS & NUTRIENTS are absorbed thru the head--TRACE MINERALS soak thru the feet!

As the sun sets, the sated BEANS withdraw from the CHOWDOWN POOL ---

---and settle down to snooze beneath the spreading arms of GRAN'MA'PA.

This is the way GRAN'MA'PA provides food for the BEANS of the BEANWORLD.

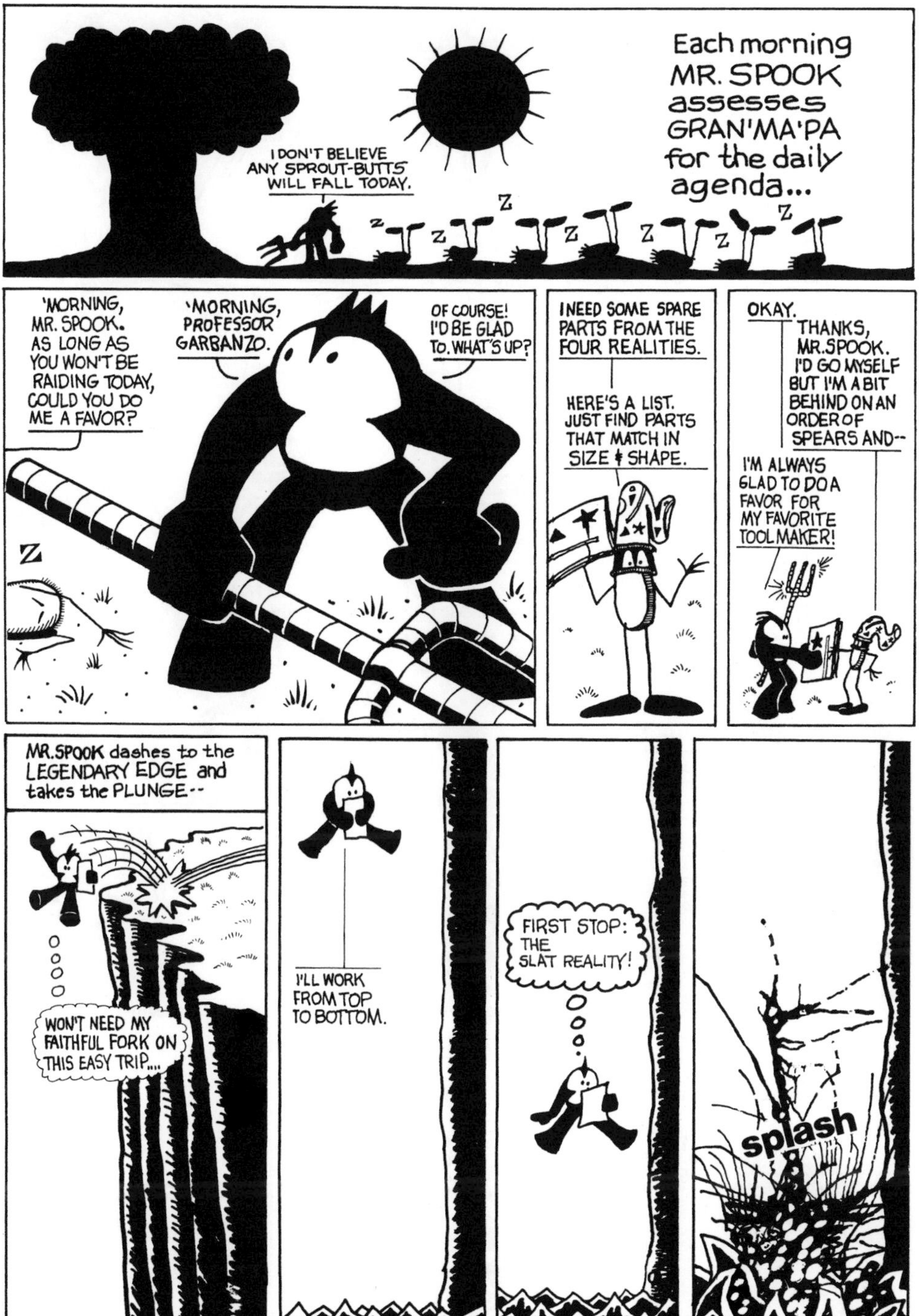
Each morning MR. SPOOK assesses GRAN'MA'PA for the daily agenda...
I DON'T BELIEVE ANY SPROUT-BUTTS WILL FALL TODAY.
Z
Z
Z
Z
Z
Z
'MORNING, MR. SPOOK. AS LONG AS YOU WON'T BE RAIDING TODAY, COULD YOU DO ME A FAVOR?
'MORNING, PROFESSOR GARBANZO.
OF COURSE! I'D BE GLAD TO. WHAT'S UP?
Z
I NEED SOME SPARE PARTS FROM THE FOUR REALITIES.
HERE'S A LIST. JUST FIND PARTS THAT MATCH IN SIZE & SHAPE.
OKAY.
THANKS, MR. SPOOK. I'D GO MYSELF BUT I'M A BIT BEHIND ON AN ORDER OF SPEARS AND--
I'M ALWAYS GLAD TO DO A FAVOR FOR MY FAVORITE TOOLMAKER!
MR. SPOOK dashes to the LEGENDARY EDGE and takes the PLUNGE--
WON'T NEED MY FAITHFUL FORK ON THIS EASY TRIP....
I'LL WORK FROM TOP TO BOTTOM.
FIRST STOP: THE SLAT REALITY!
splash

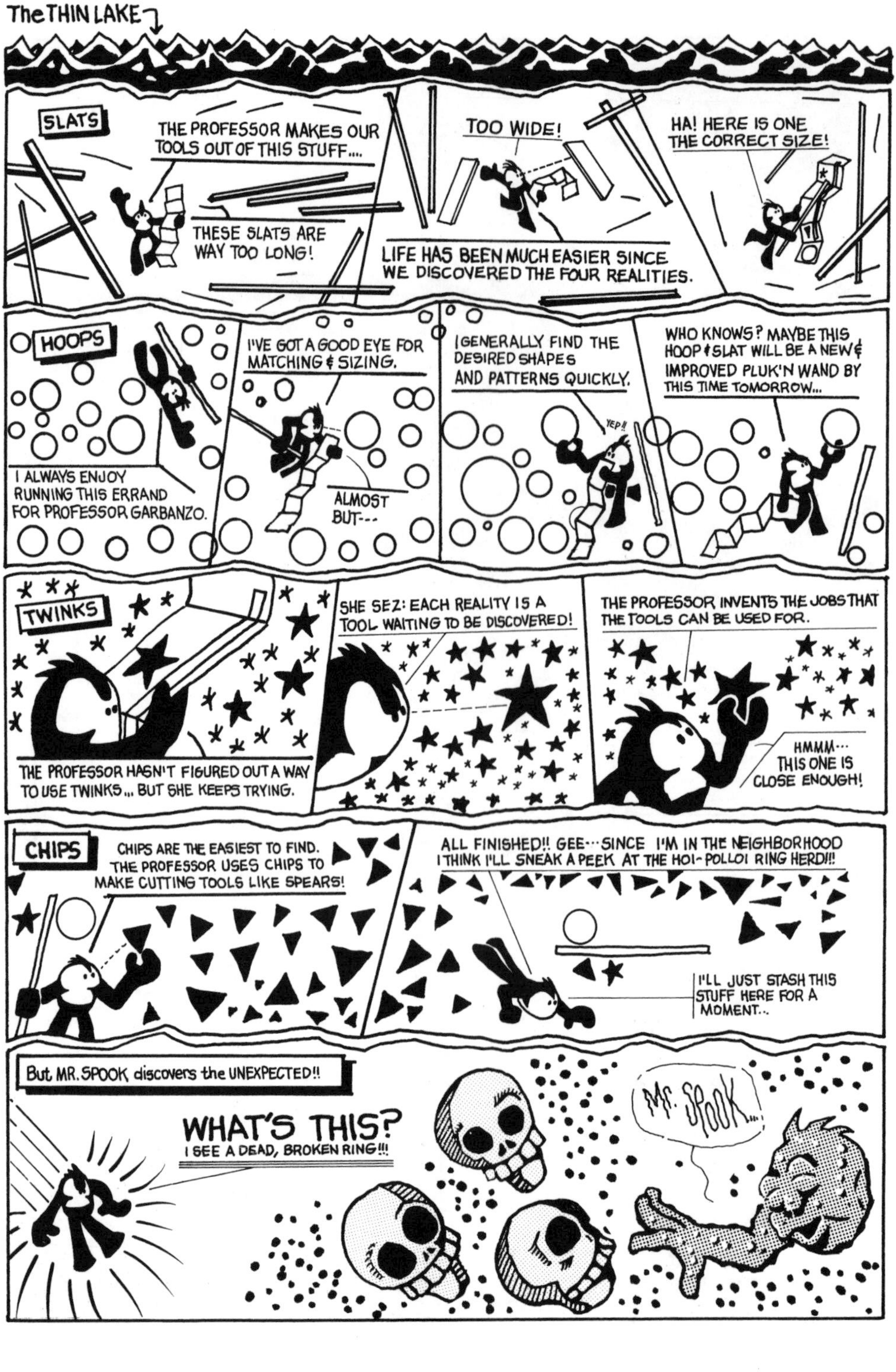
The THIN LAKE
SLATS
THE PROFESSOR MAKES OUR TOOLS OUT OF THIS STUFF....
THESE SLATS ARE WAY TOO LONG!
TOO WIDE!
LIFE HAS BEEN MUCH EASIER SINCE WE DISCOVERED THE FOUR REALITIES.
HA! HERE IS ONE THE CORRECT SIZE!
HOOPS
I ALWAYS ENJOY RUNNING THIS ERRAND FOR PROFESSOR GARBANZO.
I'VE GOT A GOOD EYE FOR MATCHING & SIZING.
ALMOST BUT---
I GENERALLY FIND THE DESIRED SHAPES AND PATTERNS QUICKLY.
YEP!!
WHO KNOWS? MAYBE THIS HOOP & SLAT WILL BE A NEW & IMPROVED PLUK'N WAND BY THIS TIME TOMORROW...
TWINKS
THE PROFESSOR HASN'T FIGURED OUT A WAY TO USE TWINKS... BUT SHE KEEPS TRYING.
SHE SEZ: EACH REALITY IS A TOOL WAITING TO BE DISCOVERED!
THE PROFESSOR INVENTS THE JOBS THAT THE TOOLS CAN BE USED FOR.
HMMM... THIS ONE IS CLOSE ENOUGH!
CHIPS
CHIPS ARE THE EASIEST TO FIND. THE PROFESSOR USES CHIPS TO MAKE CUTTING TOOLS LIKE SPEARS!
ALL FINISHED!! GEE... SINCE I'M IN THE NEIGHBORHOOD I THINK I'LL SNEAK A PEEK AT THE HOI-POLLOI RING HERD!!!
I'LL JUST STASH THIS STUFF HERE FOR A MOMENT...
But MR. SPOOK discovers the UNEXPECTED!!
WHAT'S THIS?
I SEE A DEAD, BROKEN RING!!!
MR. SPOOK...

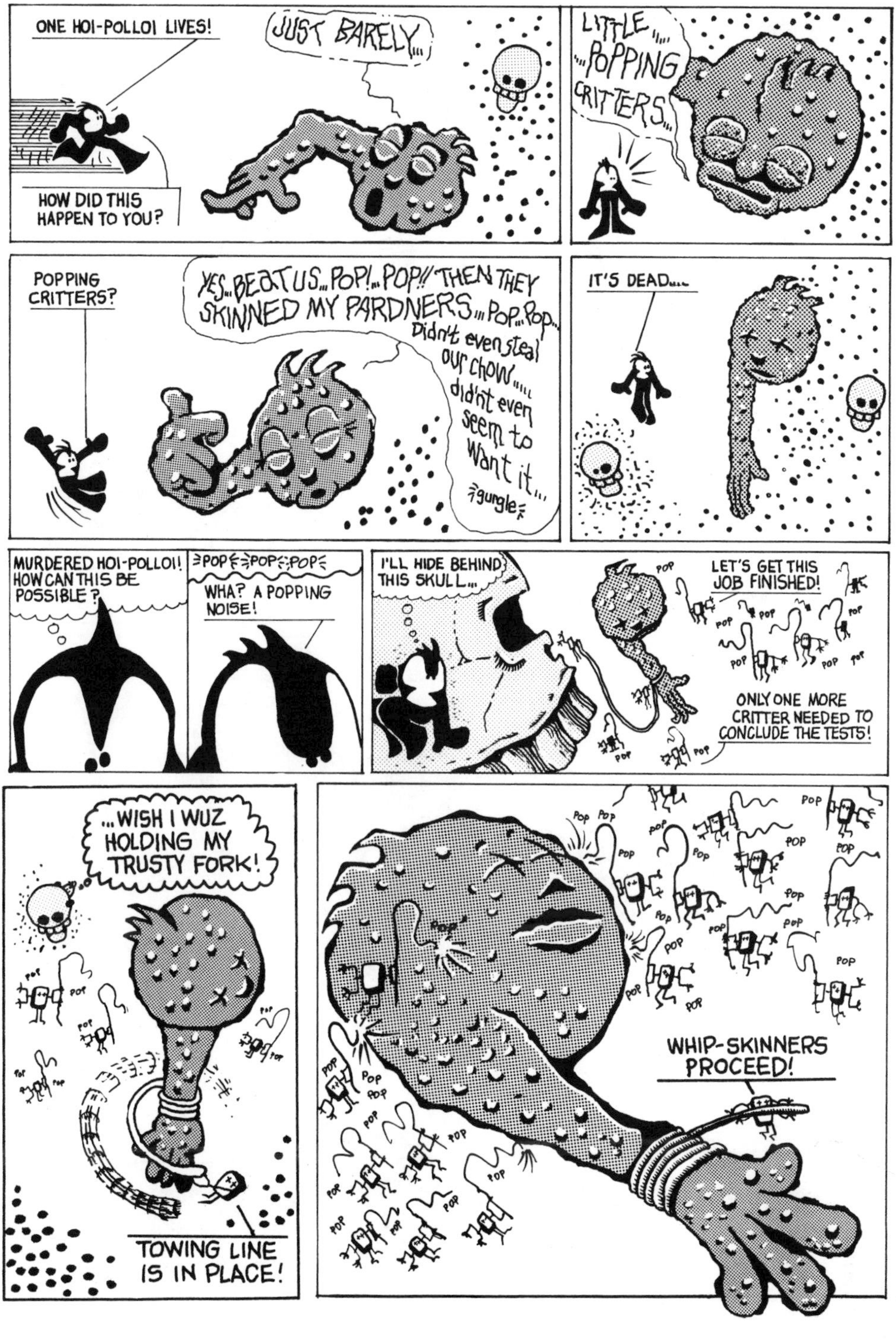
ONE HOI-POLLOI LIVES!
JUST BARELY...
HOW DID THIS HAPPEN TO YOU?
LITTLE... ...POPPING CRITTERS...
POPPING CRITTERS?
YES... BEAT US... POP!... POP!! THEN THEY SKINNED MY PARDNERS... POP... POP... Didn't even steal our chow...... didn't even seem to want it...
gurgle
IT'S DEAD...
MURDERED HOI-POLLOI! HOW CAN THIS BE POSSIBLE?
POP POP POP
WHA? A POPPING NOISE!
I'LL HIDE BEHIND THIS SKULL...
LET'S GET THIS JOB FINISHED!
ONLY ONE MORE CRITTER NEEDED TO CONCLUDE THE TESTS!
...WISH I WUZ HOLDING MY TRUSTY FORK!
TOWING LINE IS IN PLACE!
WHIP-SKINNERS PROCEED!

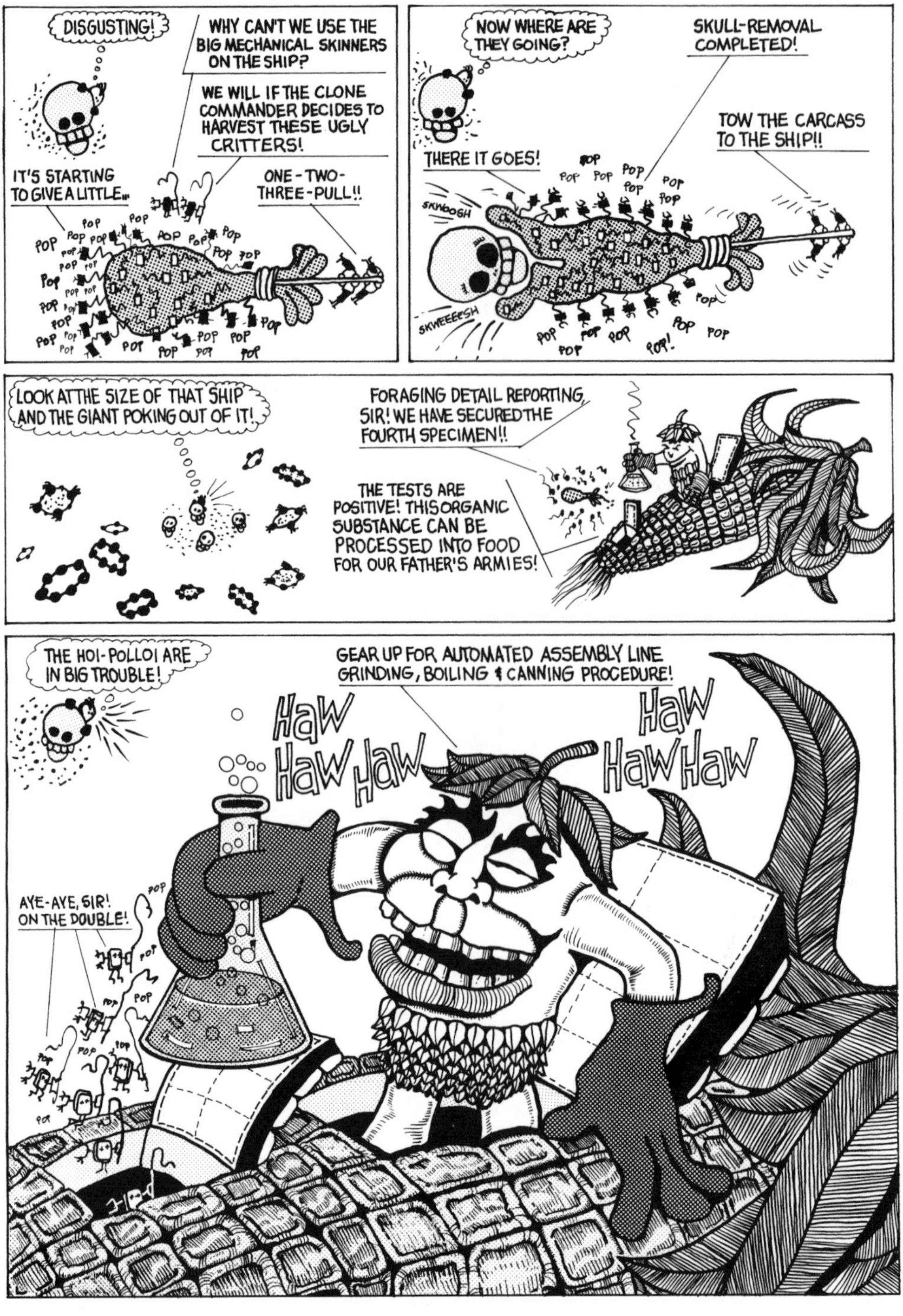

DISGUSTING!
WHY CAN'T WE USE THE BIG MECHANICAL SKINNERS ON THE SHIP?
WE WILL IF THE CLONE COMMANDER DECIDES TO HARVEST THESE UGLY CRITTERS!
IT'S STARTING TO GIVE A LITTLE...
ONE-TWO-THREE-PULL!!
NOW WHERE ARE THEY GOING?
SKULL-REMOVAL COMPLETED!
TOW THE CARCASS TO THE SHIP!!
THERE IT GOES!
SKWOOSH
SKWEEEESH
LOOK AT THE SIZE OF THAT SHIP AND THE GIANT POKING OUT OF IT!
FORAGING DETAIL REPORTING SIR! WE HAVE SECURED THE FOURTH SPECIMEN!!
THE TESTS ARE POSITIVE! THIS ORGANIC SUBSTANCE CAN BE PROCESSED INTO FOOD FOR OUR FATHER'S ARMIES!
THE HOI-POLLOI ARE IN BIG TROUBLE!
GEAR UP FOR AUTOMATED ASSEMBLY LINE GRINDING, BOILING & CANNING PROCEDURE!
HAW HAW HAW
HAW HAW HAW
AYE-AYE, SIR! ON THE DOUBLE!

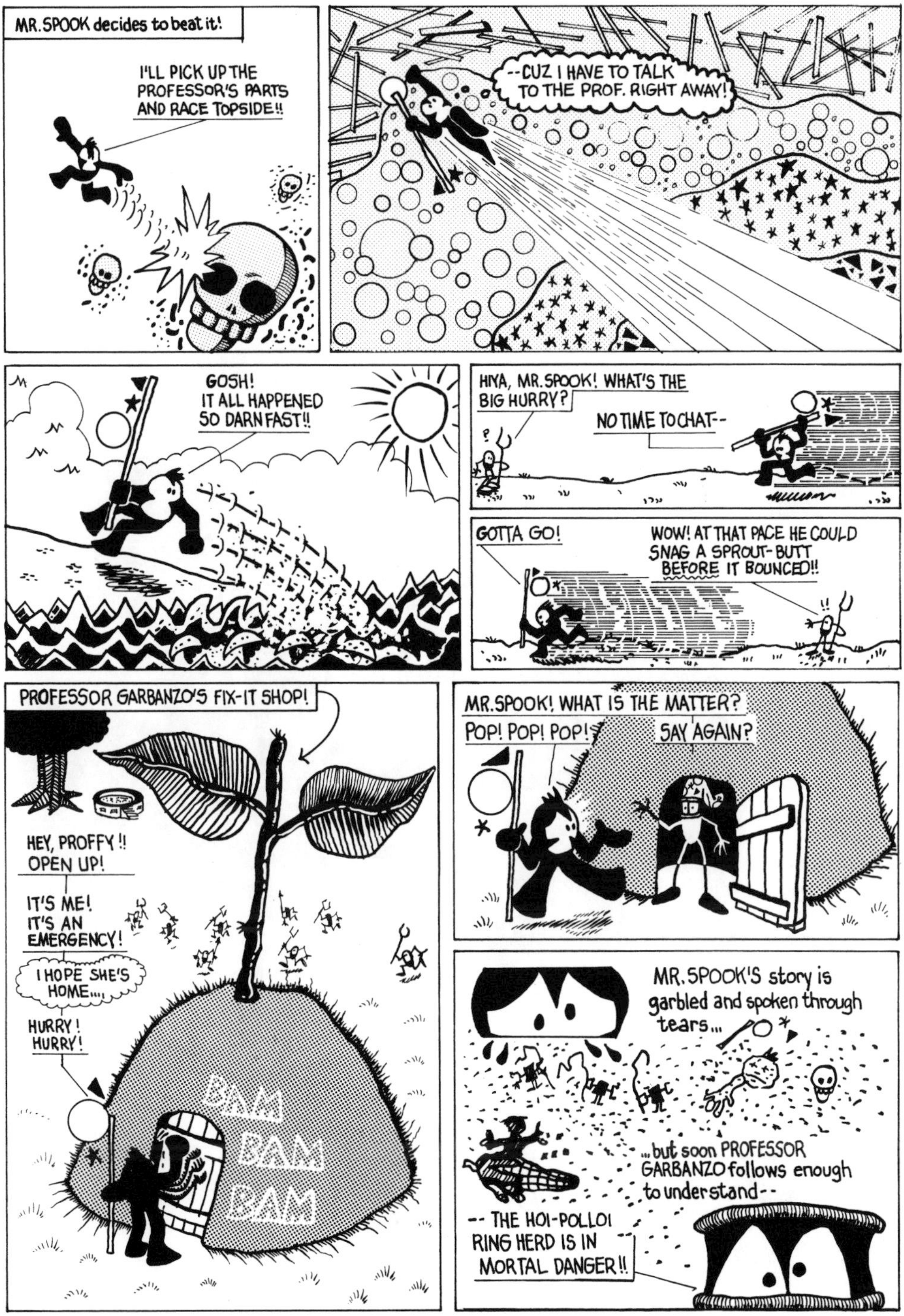
MR. SPOOK decides to beat it!
I'LL PICK UP THE PROFESSOR'S PARTS AND RACE TOPSIDE!!
--CUZ I HAVE TO TALK TO THE PROF. RIGHT AWAY!
GOSH! IT ALL HAPPENED SO DARN FAST!!
HIYA, MR. SPOOK! WHAT'S THE BIG HURRY?
NO TIME TO CHAT--
GOTTA GO!
WOW! AT THAT PACE HE COULD SNAG A SPROUT-BUTT BEFORE IT BOUNCED!!
PROFESSOR GARBANZO'S FIX-IT SHOP!
HEY, PROFFY!! OPEN UP!
IT'S ME! IT'S AN EMERGENCY!
I HOPE SHE'S HOME....
HURRY! HURRY!
BAM
BAM
BAM
MR. SPOOK! WHAT IS THE MATTER?
POP! POP! POP!
SAY AGAIN?
MR. SPOOK'S story is garbled and spoken through tears....
...but soon PROFESSOR GARBANZO follows enough to understand--
-- THE HOI-POLLOI RING HERD IS IN MORTAL DANGER!!

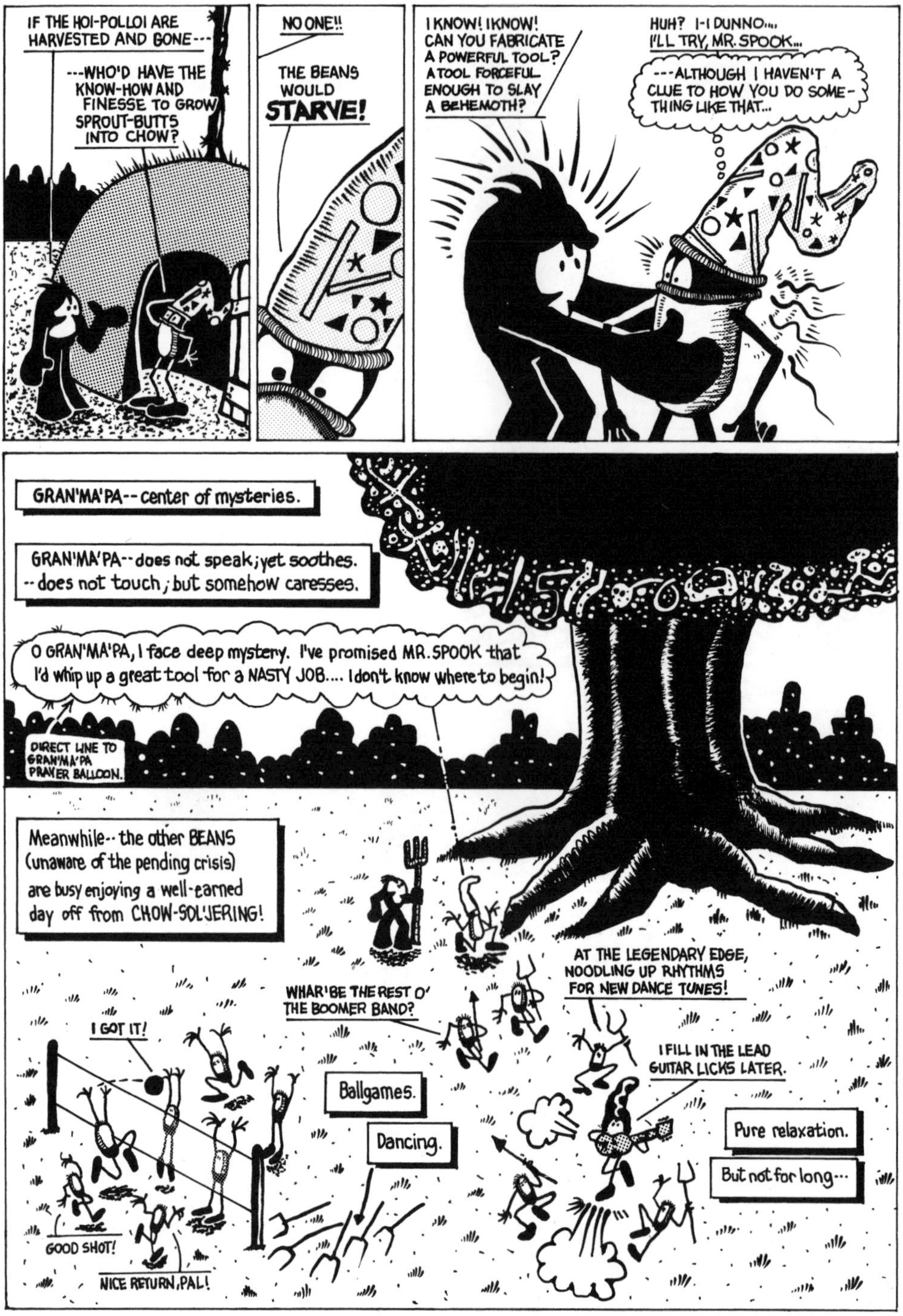
IF THE HOI-POLLOI ARE HARVESTED AND GONE---
---WHO'D HAVE THE KNOW-HOW AND FINESSE TO GROW SPROUT-BUTTS INTO CHOW?
NO ONE!!
THE BEANS WOULD STARVE!
I KNOW! I KNOW! CAN YOU FABRICATE A POWERFUL TOOL? A TOOL FORCEFUL ENOUGH TO SLAY A BEHEMOTH?
HUH? I-I DUNNO... I'LL TRY, MR. SPOOK...
---ALTHOUGH I HAVEN'T A CLUE TO HOW YOU DO SOMETHING LIKE THAT...
GRAN'MA'PA-- center of mysteries.
GRAN'MA'PA-- does not speak; yet soothes. --does not touch; but somehow caresses.
O GRAN'MA'PA, I face deep mystery. I've promised MR. SPOOK that I'd whip up a great tool for a NASTY JOB.... I don't know where to begin!
DIRECT LINE TO GRAN'MA'PA PRAYER BALLOON.
Meanwhile-- the other BEANS (unaware of the pending crisis) are busy enjoying a well-earned day off from CHOW-SOL'JERING!
AT THE LEGENDARY EDGE, NOODLING UP RHYTHMS FOR NEW DANCE TUNES!
WHAR'BE THE REST O' THE BOOMER BAND?
I GOT IT!
I FILL IN THE LEAD GUITAR LICKS LATER.
Ballgames.
Dancing.
Pure relaxation.
But not for long...
GOOD SHOT!
NICE RETURN, PAL!

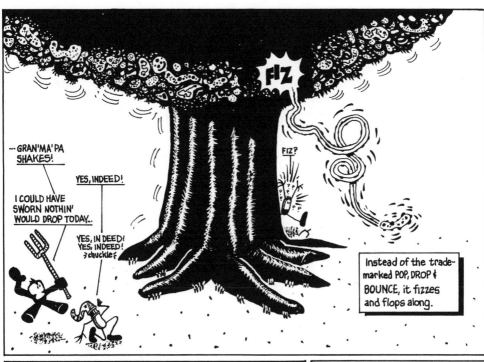

--GRAN'MA'PA SHAKES!

YES, INDEED!

I COULD HAVE SWORN NOTHIN' WOULD DROP TODAY...

YES, IN DEED! YES, INDEED! ≥chuckle≥

FIZ

FIZ?

Instead of the trade-marked POP, DROP & BOUNCE, it fizzes and flops along.

...IT FELL FROM GRAN'MA'PA!

GRAN'MA'PA SENDS US A REMARKABLE GIFT!

WHAT IS IT PROFESSOR?

THATS FOR US TO FIND OUT! IT'S NOT A SPROUT-BUTT, THAT'S FOR SURE!

IT PULSES!

I THOUGHT ONLY SPROUT-BUTTS FELL FROM GRAN'MA'PA!

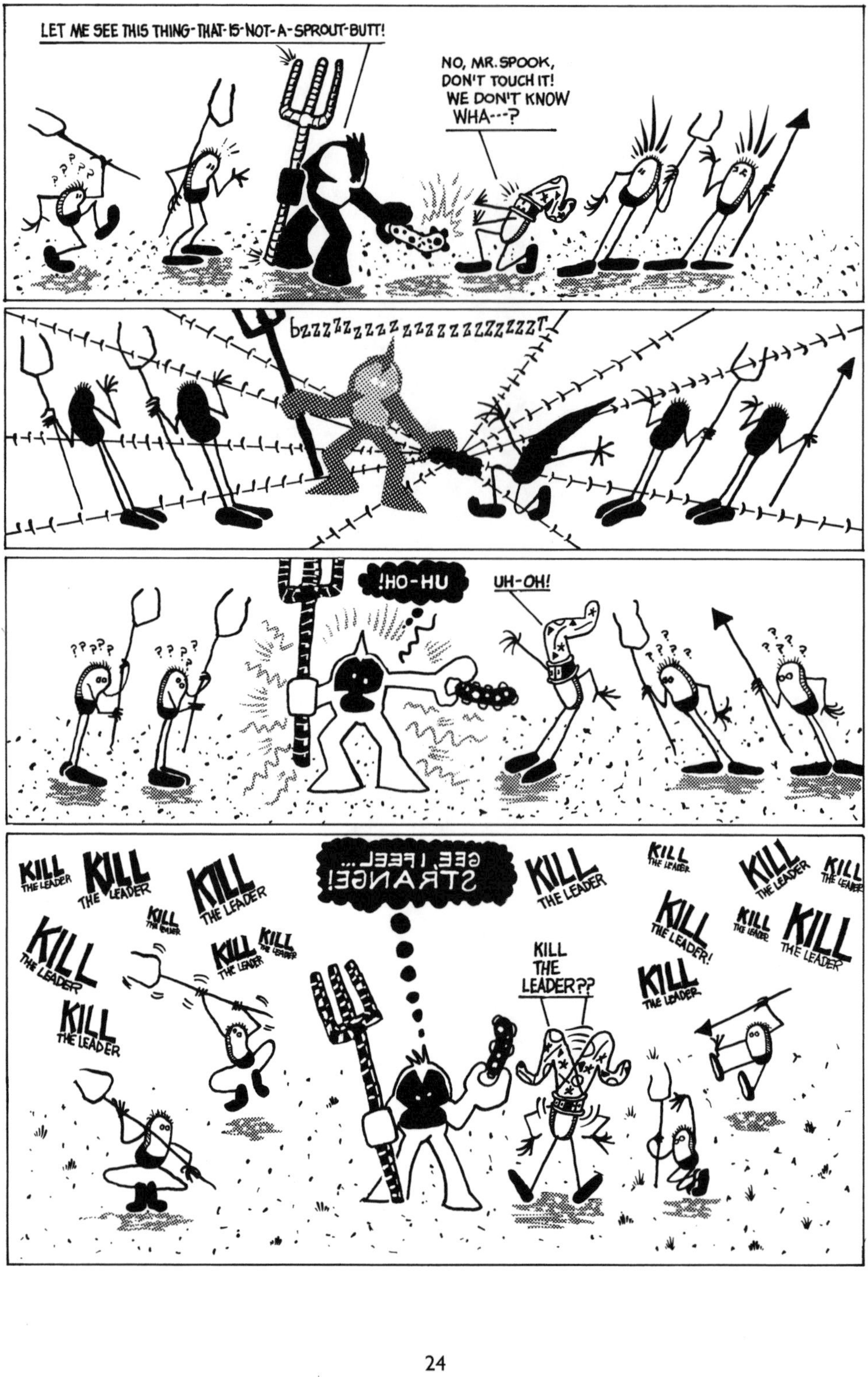
LET ME SEE THIS THING-THAT-IS-NOT-A-SPROUT-BUTT!
NO, MR. SPOOK, DON'T TOUCH IT! WE DON'T KNOW WHA---?
bzzzzzzzzzzzzzzzzzzzT
UH-OH!
UH-OH!
GEE, I FEEL... STRANGE!
KILL THE LEADER
KILL THE LEADER
KILL THE LEADER
KILL THE LEADER
KILL THE LEADER
KILL THE LEADER
KILL THE LEADER
KILL THE LEADER??
KILL THE LEADER
KILL THE LEADER
KILL THE LEADER
KILL THE LEADER
KILL THE LEADER!
KILL THE LEADER
KILL THE LEADER
KILL THE LEADER

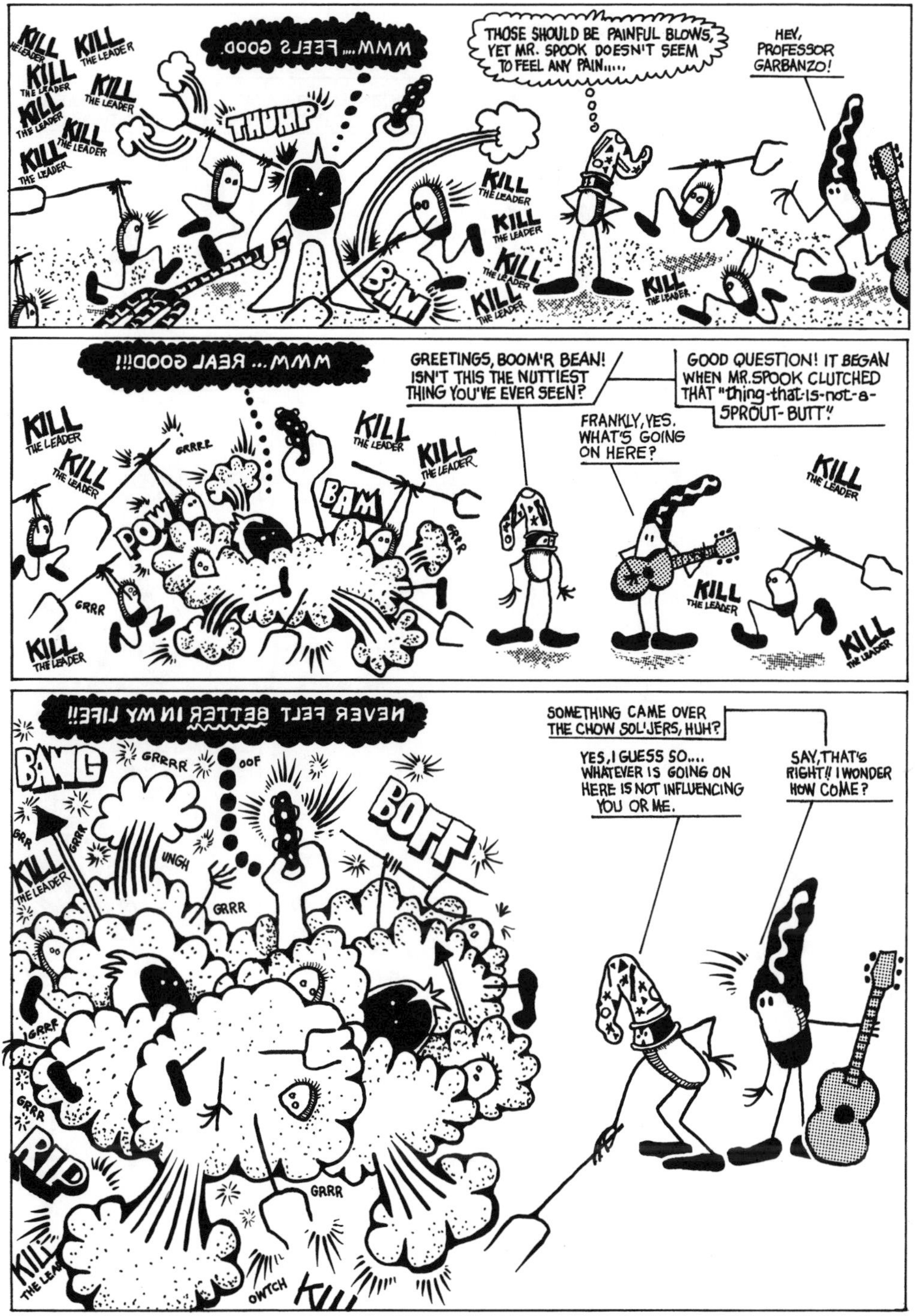
KILL THE LEADER
MMM... FEELS GOOD.
THUMP
BAM
THOSE SHOULD BE PAINFUL BLOWS, YET MR. SPOOK DOESN'T SEEM TO FEEL ANY PAIN....
HEY, PROFESSOR GARBANZO!
MMM... REAL GOOD!!!
GRRRR
POW
BAM
GRRR
GREETINGS, BOOM'R BEAN! ISN'T THIS THE NUTTIEST THING YOU'VE EVER SEEN?
FRANKLY, YES. WHAT'S GOING ON HERE?
GOOD QUESTION! IT BEGAN WHEN MR. SPOOK CLUTCHED THAT "thing-that-is-not-a-SPROUT-BUTT."
NEVER FELT BETTER IN MY LIFE!!
BANG
GRRRR
OOF
UNGH
BOFF
GRRR
RIP
OWTCH
SOMETHING CAME OVER THE CHOW SOL'JERS, HUH?
YES, I GUESS SO.... WHATEVER IS GOING ON HERE IS NOT INFLUENCING YOU OR ME.
SAY, THAT'S RIGHT!! I WONDER HOW COME?

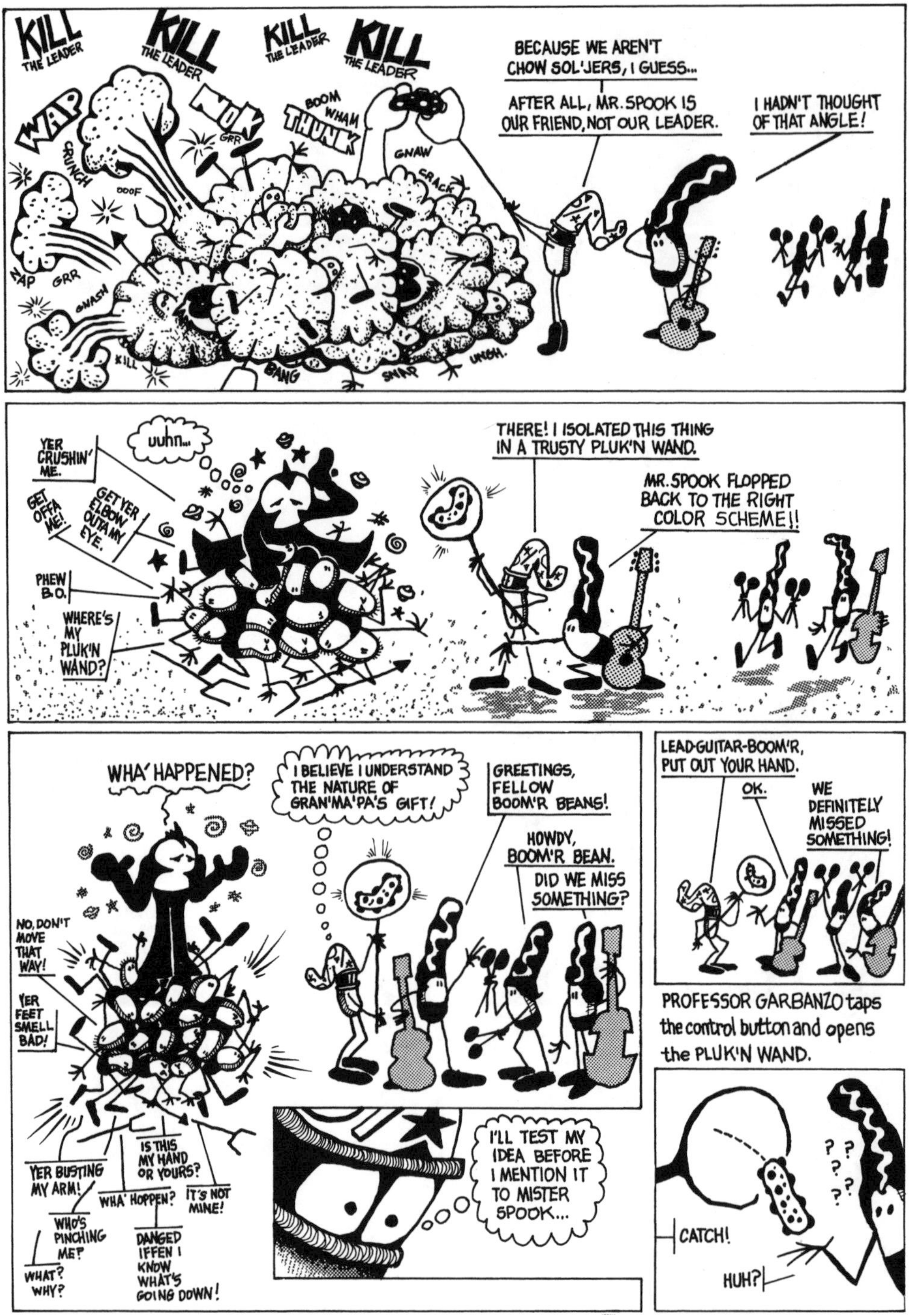
KILL THE LEADER
KILL THE LEADER
KILL THE LEADER
KILL THE LEADER
WAP
NOK
BOOM
WHAM
THUNK
CRUNCH
OOOF
GRR
GNAW
CRACK
GRR
GNASH
KILL
BANG
SNAP
UNGH.
BECAUSE WE AREN'T CHOW SOL'JERS, I GUESS...
AFTER ALL, MR. SPOOK IS OUR FRIEND, NOT OUR LEADER.
I HADN'T THOUGHT OF THAT ANGLE!
YER CRUSHIN' ME.
uuhn...
GET OFFA ME!
GET YER ELBOW OUTA MY EYE.
PHEW B.O.
WHERE'S MY PLUK'N WAND?
THERE! I ISOLATED THIS THING IN A TRUSTY PLUK'N WAND.
MR. SPOOK FLOPPED BACK TO THE RIGHT COLOR SCHEME!!
WHA' HAPPENED?
NO, DON'T MOVE THAT WAY!
YER FEET SMELL BAD!
YER BUSTING MY ARM!
IS THIS MY HAND OR YOURS?
WHA' HOPPEN?
IT'S NOT MINE!
WHO'S PINCHING ME?
DANGED IFFEN I KNOW WHAT'S GOING DOWN!
WHAT? WHY?
I BELIEVE I UNDERSTAND THE NATURE OF GRAN'MA'PA'S GIFT!
GREETINGS, FELLOW BOOM'R BEANS!
HOWDY, BOOM'R BEAN.
DID WE MISS SOMETHING?
I'LL TEST MY IDEA BEFORE I MENTION IT TO MISTER SPOOK...
LEAD-GUITAR-BOOM'R, PUT OUT YOUR HAND.
OK.
WE DEFINITELY MISSED SOMETHING!
PROFESSOR GARBANZO taps the control button and opens the PLUK'N WAND.
? ? ? ? ?
CATCH!
HUH?

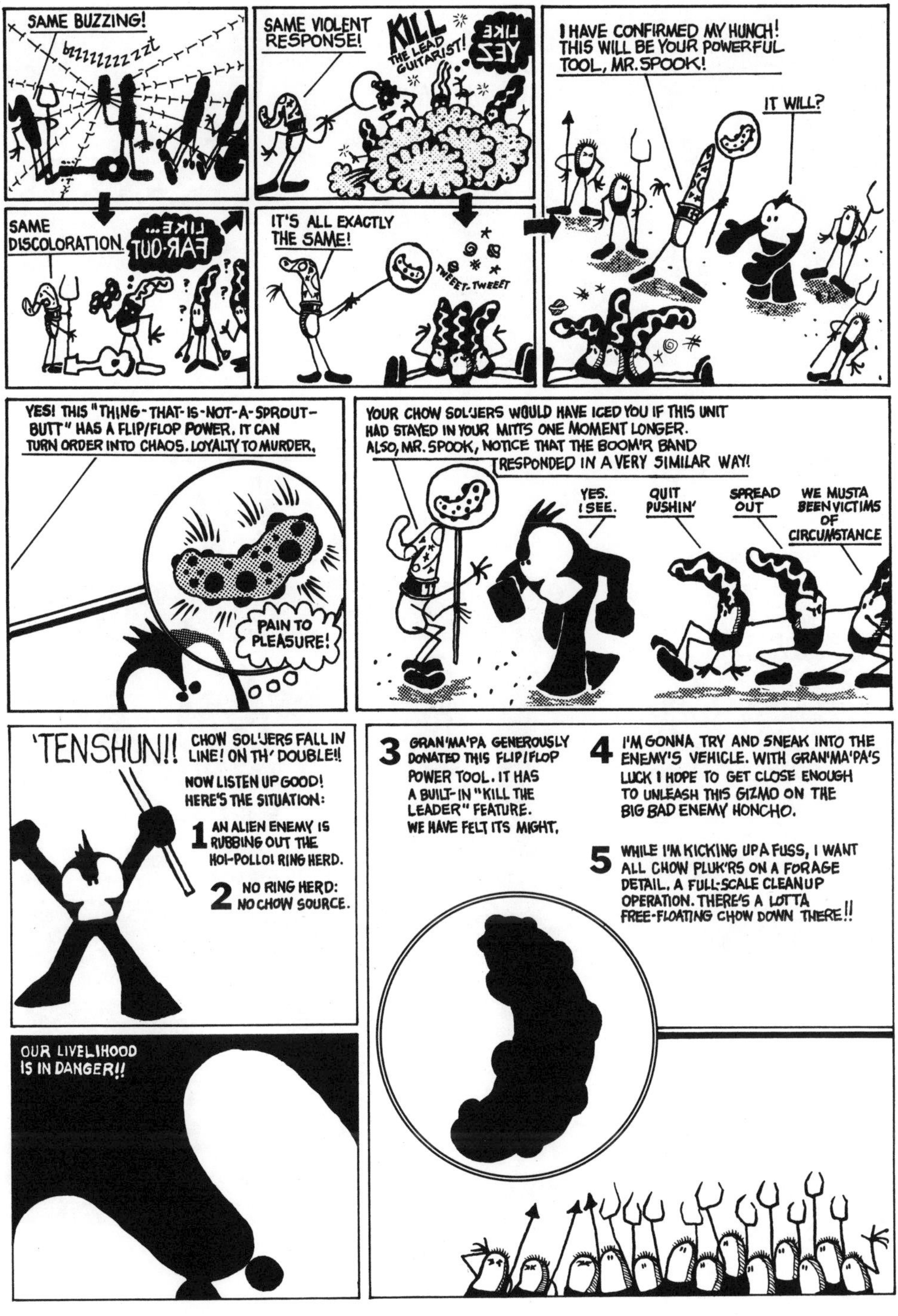
SAME BUZZING!
bzzzzzzzzzzt
SAME VIOLENT RESPONSE!
KILL THE LEAD GUITARIST!
LIKE YEZ
I HAVE CONFIRMED MY HUNCH! THIS WILL BE YOUR POWERFUL TOOL, MR. SPOOK!
IT WILL?
SAME DISCOLORATION.
LIKE... FAR-OUT
IT'S ALL EXACTLY THE SAME!
TWEEET-TWEEET
YES! THIS "THING-THAT-IS-NOT-A-SPROUT-BUTT" HAS A FLIP/FLOP POWER. IT CAN TURN ORDER INTO CHAOS. LOYALTY TO MURDER.
PAIN TO PLEASURE!
YOUR CHOW SOL'JERS WOULD HAVE ICED YOU IF THIS UNIT HAD STAYED IN YOUR MITTS ONE MOMENT LONGER. ALSO, MR. SPOOK, NOTICE THAT THE BOOM'R BAND RESPONDED IN A VERY SIMILAR WAY!
YES. I SEE.
QUIT PUSHIN'
SPREAD OUT
WE MUSTA BEEN VICTIMS OF CIRCUMSTANCE
'TENSHUN!!
CHOW SOL'JERS FALL IN LINE! ON TH' DOUBLE!!
NOW LISTEN UP GOOD! HERE'S THE SITUATION:
1 AN ALIEN ENEMY IS RUBBING OUT THE HOI-POLLOI RING HERD.
2 NO RING HERD: NO CHOW SOURCE.
OUR LIVELIHOOD IS IN DANGER!!
3 GRAN'MA'PA GENEROUSLY DONATED THIS FLIP/FLOP POWER TOOL. IT HAS A BUILT-IN "KILL THE LEADER" FEATURE. WE HAVE FELT ITS MIGHT.
4 I'M GONNA TRY AND SNEAK INTO THE ENEMY'S VEHICLE. WITH GRAN'MA'PA'S LUCK I HOPE TO GET CLOSE ENOUGH TO UNLEASH THIS GIZMO ON THE BIG BAD ENEMY HONCHO.
5 WHILE I'M KICKING UP A FUSS, I WANT ALL CHOW PLUK'RS ON A FORAGE DETAIL. A FULL-SCALE CLEANUP OPERATION. THERE'S A LOTTA FREE-FLOATING CHOW DOWN THERE!!

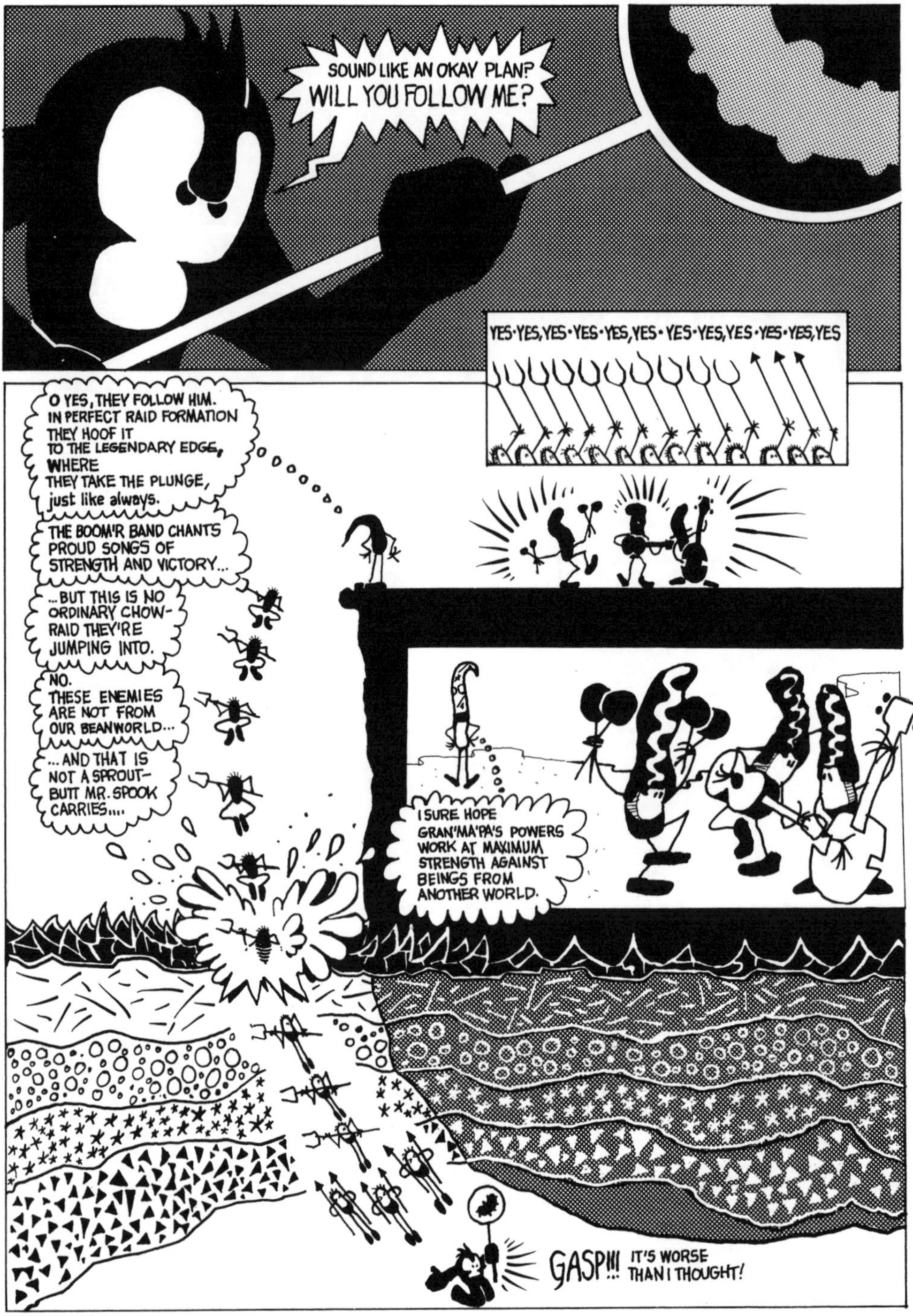
SOUND LIKE AN OKAY PLAN? WILL YOU FOLLOW ME?
YES·YES,YES·YES·YES,YES·YES·YES,YES·YES·YES,YES
O YES, THEY FOLLOW HIM. IN PERFECT RAID FORMATION THEY HOOF IT TO THE LEGENDARY EDGE, WHERE THEY TAKE THE PLUNGE, just like always.
THE BOOM'R BAND CHANTS PROUD SONGS OF STRENGTH AND VICTORY...
...BUT THIS IS NO ORDINARY CHOW-RAID THEY'RE JUMPING INTO.
NO. THESE ENEMIES ARE NOT FROM OUR BEANWORLD...
...AND THAT IS NOT A SPROUT-BUTT MR. SPOOK CARRIES....
I SURE HOPE GRAN'MA'PA'S POWERS WORK AT MAXIMUM STRENGTH AGAINST BEINGS FROM ANOTHER WORLD.
GASP!!! IT'S WORSE THAN I THOUGHT!

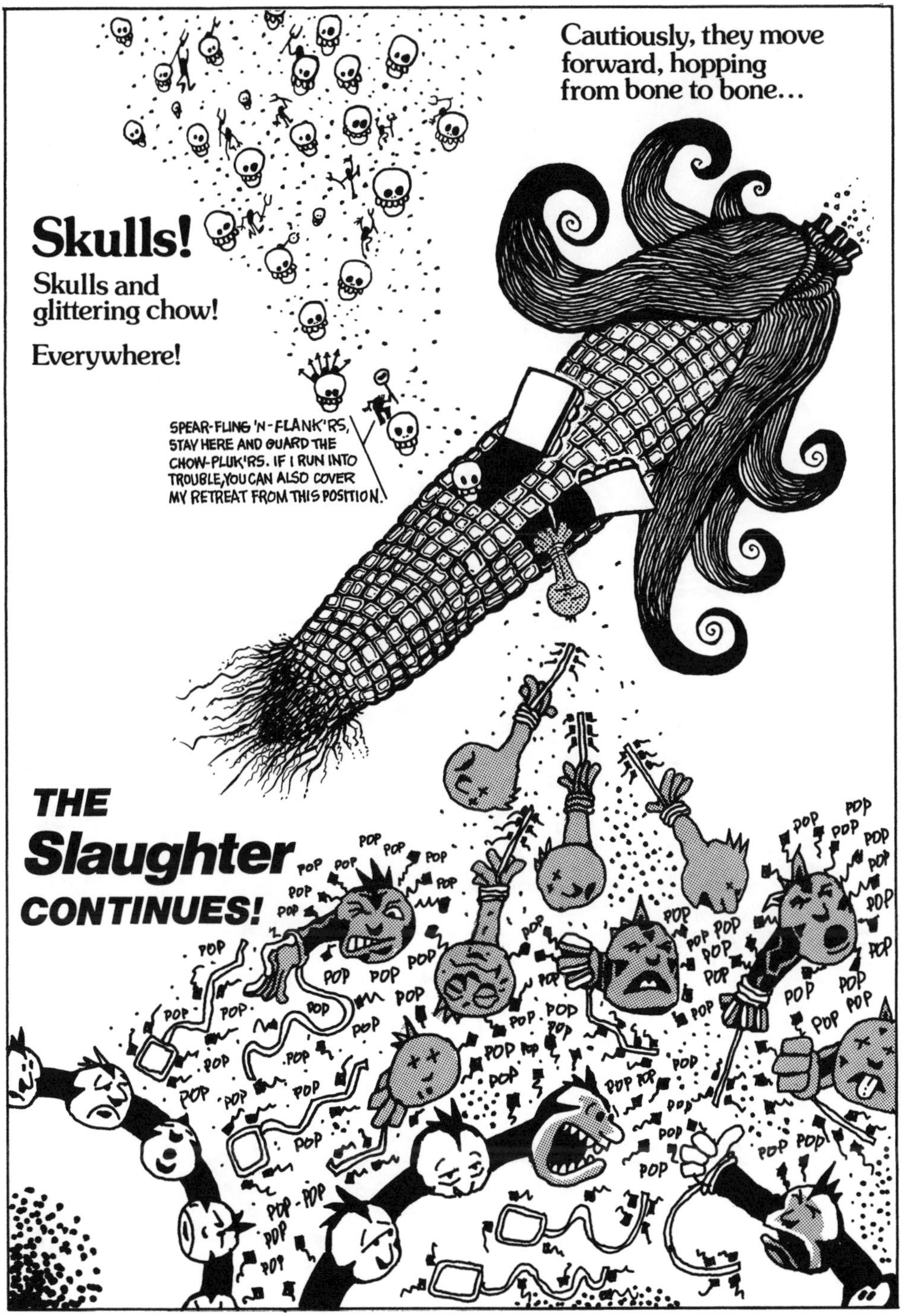

Cautiously, they move forward, hopping from bone to bone...
Skulls!
Skulls and glittering chow!
Everywhere!
SPEAR-FLING 'N-FLANK'RS, STAY HERE AND GUARD THE CHOW-PLUK'RS. IF I RUN INTO TROUBLE, YOU CAN ALSO COVER MY RETREAT FROM THIS POSITION.
THE Slaughter CONTINUES!
POP POP POP POP POP POP POP POP POP POP POP POP POP POP POP POP POP POP POP POP POP POP POP POP POP POP POP POP POP POP POP POP POP POP POP POP POP POP POP POP POP POP POP POP POP POP POP

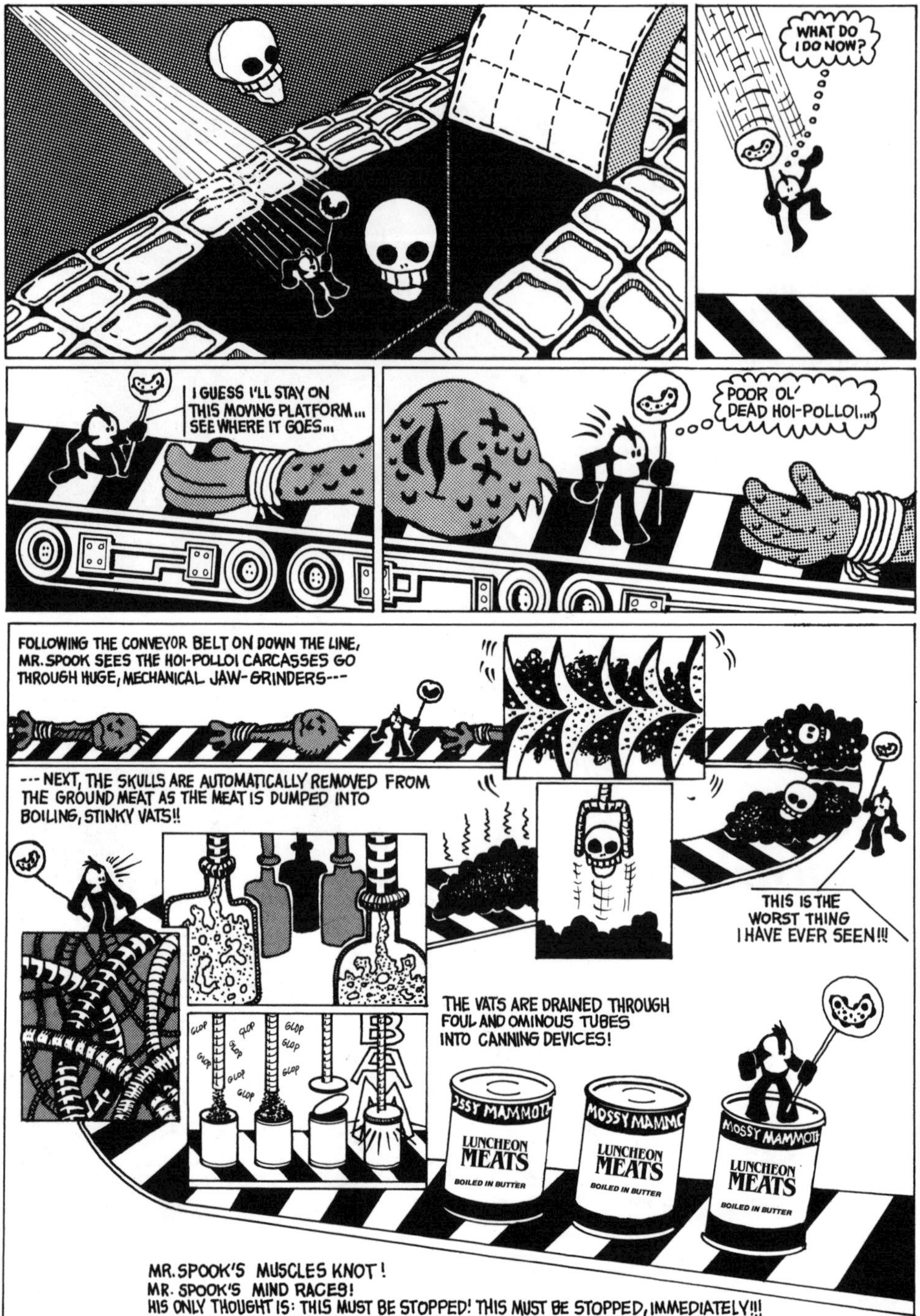
WHAT DO I DO NOW?
I GUESS I'LL STAY ON THIS MOVING PLATFORM... SEE WHERE IT GOES...
POOR OL' DEAD HOI-POLLOI...
FOLLOWING THE CONVEYOR BELT ON DOWN THE LINE, MR. SPOOK SEES THE HOI-POLLOI CARCASSES GO THROUGH HUGE, MECHANICAL JAW-GRINDERS---
--- NEXT, THE SKULLS ARE AUTOMATICALLY REMOVED FROM THE GROUND MEAT AS THE MEAT IS DUMPED INTO BOILING, STINKY VATS!!
THIS IS THE WORST THING I HAVE EVER SEEN!!!
THE VATS ARE DRAINED THROUGH FOUL AND OMINOUS TUBES INTO CANNING DEVICES!
GLOP GLOP GLOP GLOP GLOP GLOP GLOP GLOP GLOP
MOSSY MAMMOTH LUNCHEON MEATS BOILED IN BUTTER
MR. SPOOK'S MUSCLES KNOT!
MR. SPOOK'S MIND RACES!
HIS ONLY THOUGHT IS: THIS MUST BE STOPPED! THIS MUST BE STOPPED, IMMEDIATELY!!!

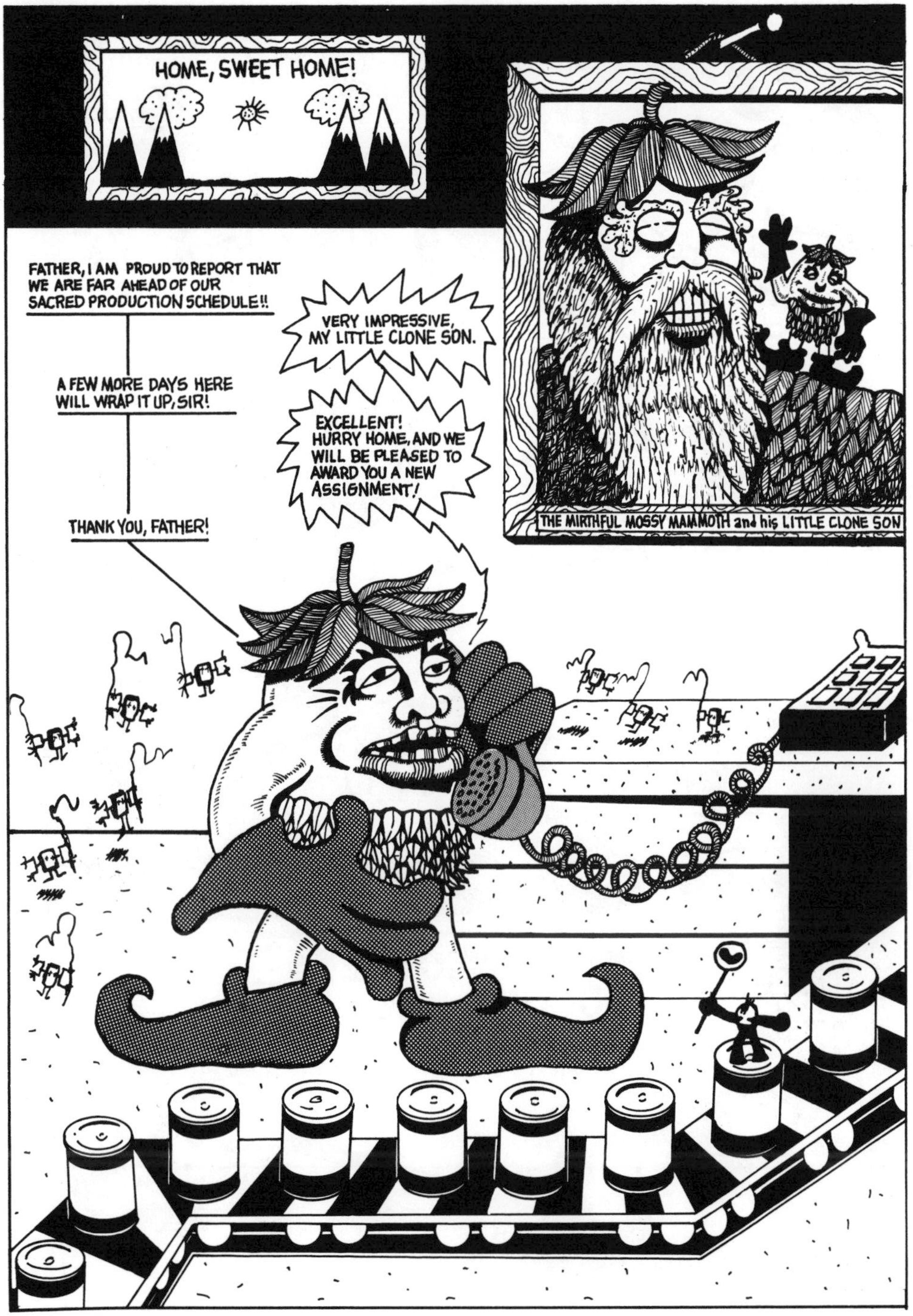
HOME, SWEET HOME!
FATHER, I AM PROUD TO REPORT THAT WE ARE FAR AHEAD OF OUR SACRED PRODUCTION SCHEDULE!!
VERY IMPRESSIVE, MY LITTLE CLONE SON.
A FEW MORE DAYS HERE WILL WRAP IT UP, SIR!
EXCELLENT! HURRY HOME, AND WE WILL BE PLEASED TO AWARD YOU A NEW ASSIGNMENT!
THANK YOU, FATHER!
THE MIRTHFUL MOSSY MAMMOTH and his LITTLE CLONE SON

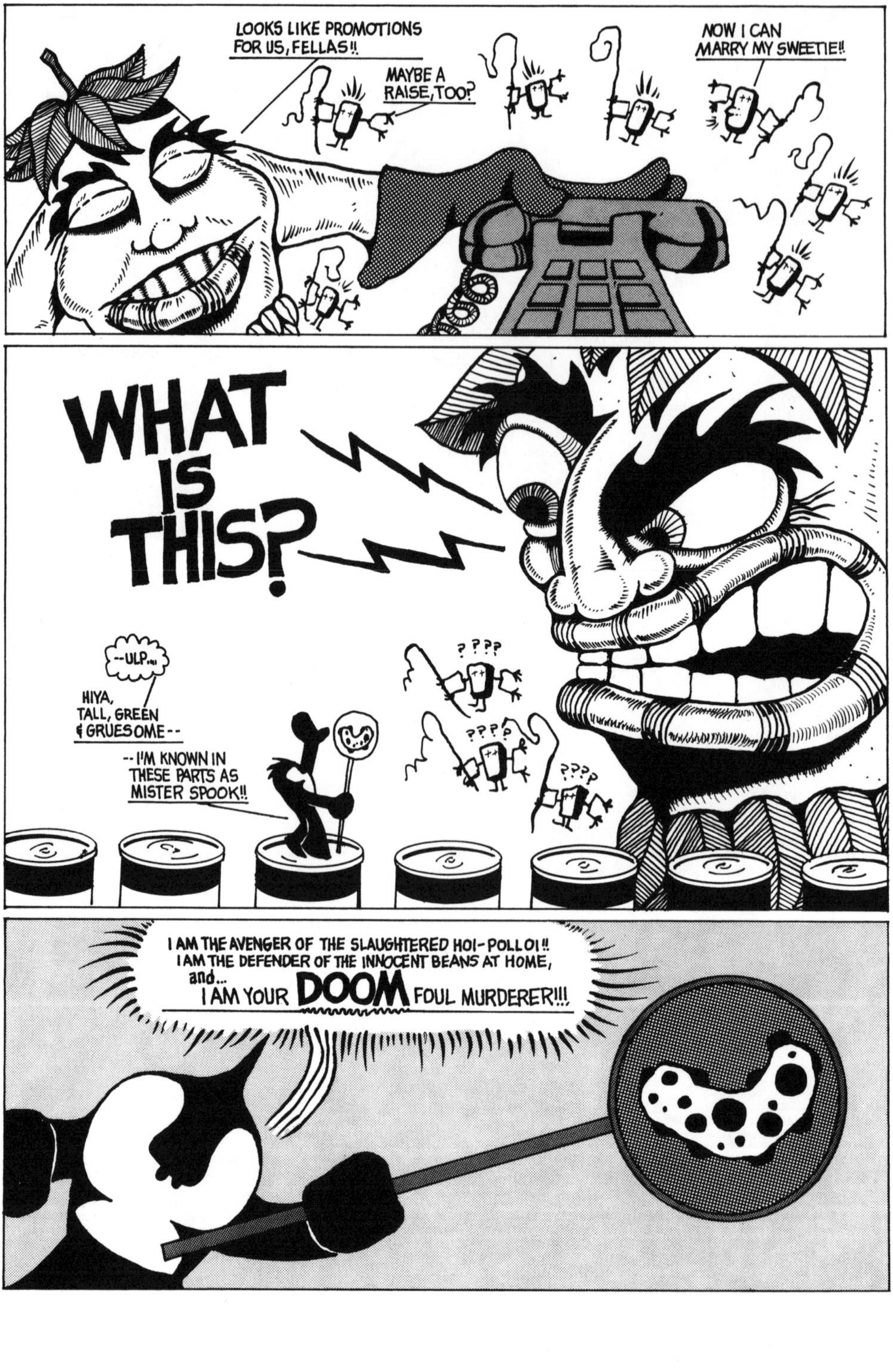
LOOKS LIKE PROMOTIONS FOR US, FELLAS!!
MAYBE A RAISE, TOO?
NOW I CAN MARRY MY SWEETIE!!
WHAT IS THIS?
--ULP...
HIYA, TALL, GREEN & GRUESOME--
--I'M KNOWN IN THESE PARTS AS MISTER SPOOK!!
????
????
????
I AM THE AVENGER OF THE SLAUGHTERED HOI-POLLOI!! I AM THE DEFENDER OF THE INNOCENT BEANS AT HOME, and... I AM YOUR DOOM FOUL MURDERER!!!

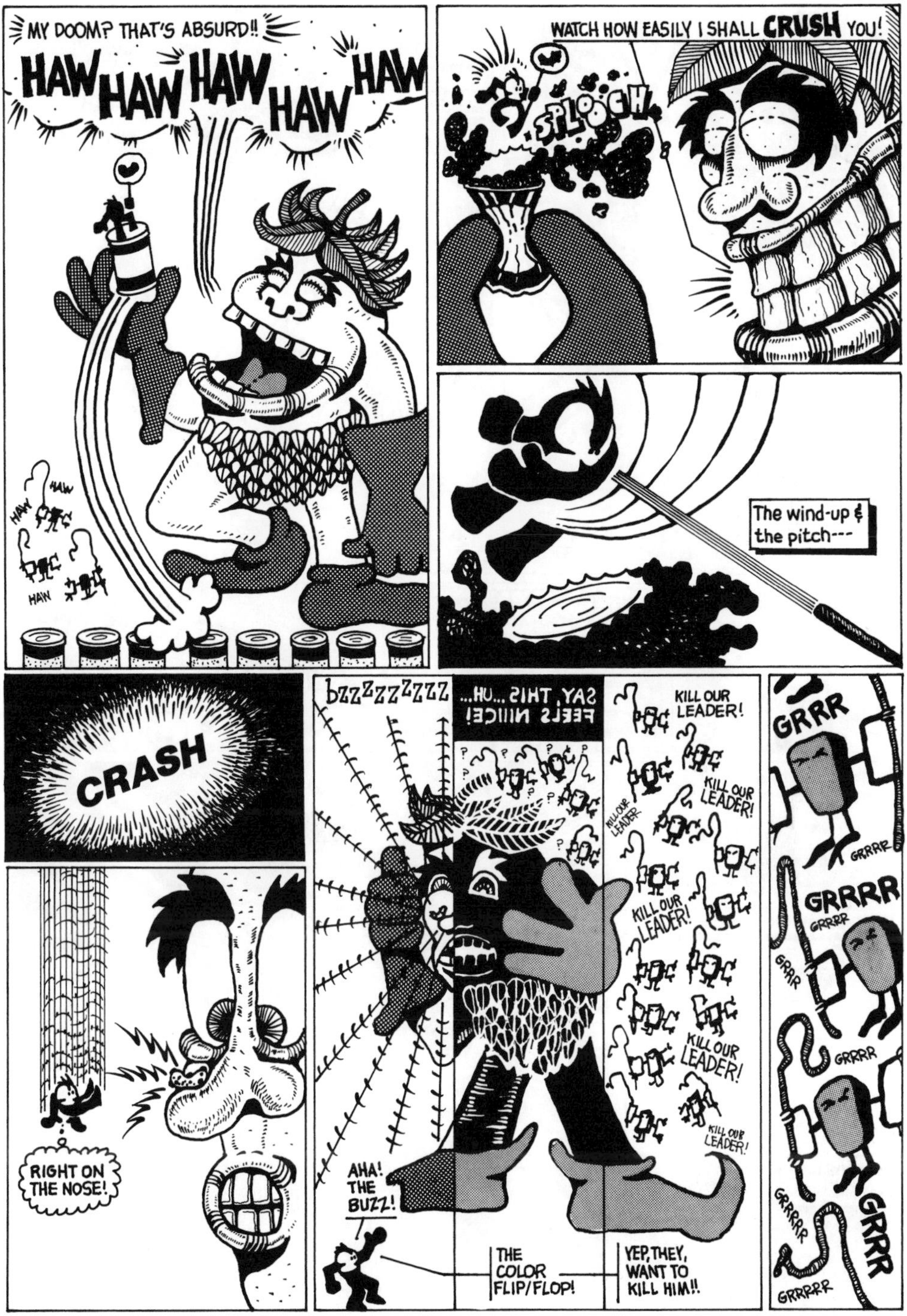
MY DOOM? THAT'S ABSURD!!
HAW HAW HAW HAW HAW
HAW HAW HAW
WATCH HOW EASILY I SHALL CRUSH YOU!
SPLOOCH
The wind-up & the pitch---
CRASH
RIGHT ON THE NOSE!
bzzzzzzzz
SAY, THIS ...UH... FEELS NIIICE!
AHA! THE BUZZ!
THE COLOR FLIP/FLOP!
KILL OUR LEADER!
KILL OUR LEADER!
KILL OUR LEADER!
KILL OUR LEADER!
KILL OUR LEADER!
KILL OUR LEADER!
YEP, THEY, WANT TO KILL HIM!!
GRRR
GRRRR
GRRRR
GRRRR
GRRR
GRRRR
GRRR
GRRRRR
GRRRRR

POP POP POP POP POP POP POP POP POP POP
WHEW! THEY'RE REALLY BUTCHERING THEIR BOSS!!
Pretty soon--
UH-OH, WE BLEW IT!!
WE ARE SHAMED!!
WE MUST ABORT THE MISSION--
THERE GO THE PROMOTIONS!
--AND OURSELVES!!
I'LL NEVER SEE MY SWEETIE AGAIN...sigh...
HEY! I SEE THE TOOL!!
THIS MIGHT COME IN HANDY AGAIN SOME DAY!
I BETTER SCRAM BEFORE THEY REMEMBER ME!!
I MADE IT OUT OF THE SHIP!
LOOK! MR. SPOOK! RETURNS!!
The ship begins to shake...
Thick, green husks curl down--
--enclosing the ship!
POP POP POP POP POP
It begins to pop and hiss...
BOOOM

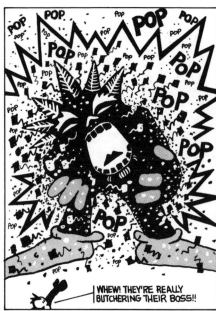

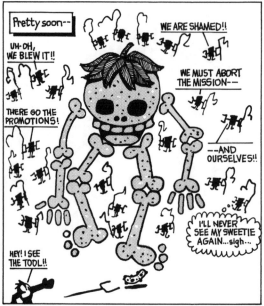

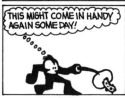

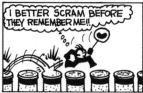

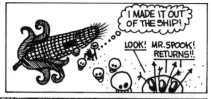

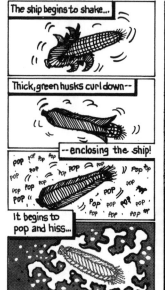

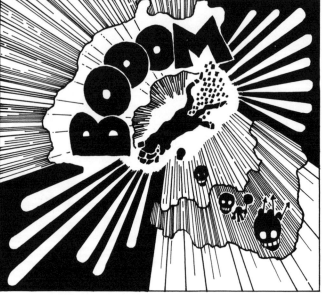

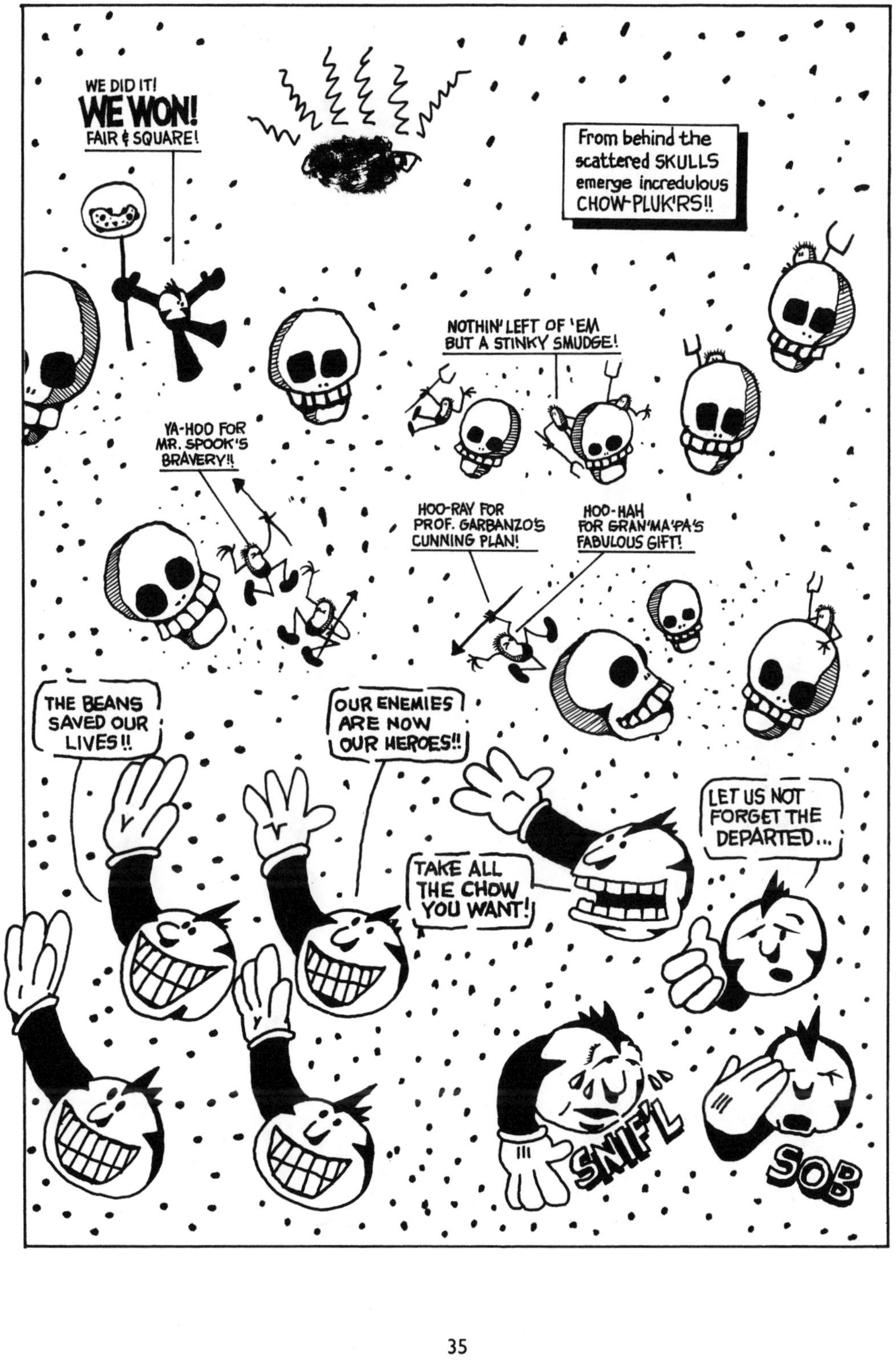
WE DID IT!
WE WON!
FAIR & SQUARE!
From behind the scattered SKULLS emerge incredulous CHOW-PLUK'RS!!
NOTHIN' LEFT OF 'EM BUT A STINKY SMUDGE!
YA-HOO FOR MR. SPOOK'S BRAVERY!!
HOO-RAY FOR PROF. GARBANZO'S CUNNING PLAN!
HOO-HAH FOR GRAN'MA'PA'S FABULOUS GIFT!
THE BEANS SAVED OUR LIVES!!
OUR ENEMIES ARE NOW OUR HEROES!!
TAKE ALL THE CHOW YOU WANT!
LET US NOT FORGET THE DEPARTED...
SNIF'L
SOB

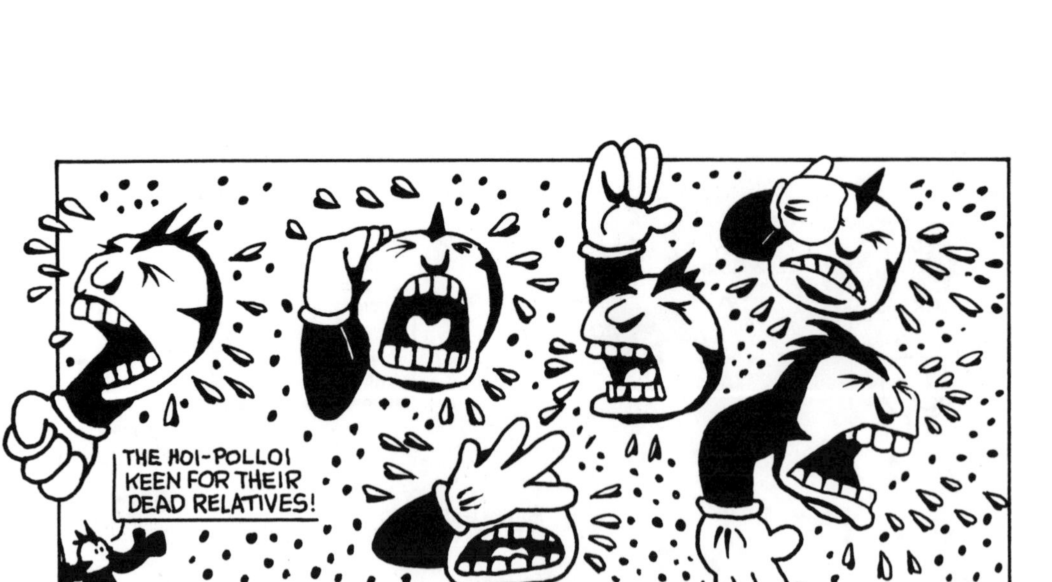
THE HOI-POLLOI KEEN FOR THEIR DEAD RELATIVES!

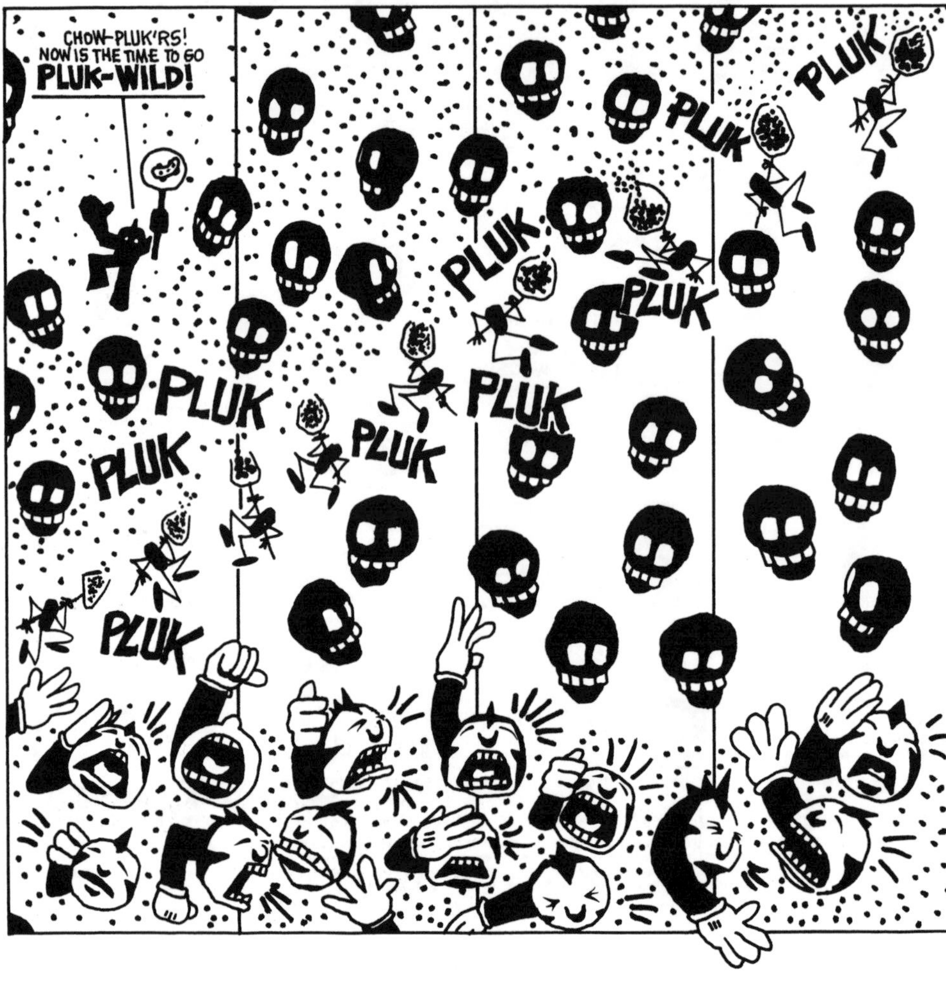
CHOW-PLUK'RS! NOW IS THE TIME TO GO PLUK-WILD!
PLUK
PLUK
PLUK
PLUK
PLUK
PLUK
PLUK
PLUK
PLUK

It is an eerie, silent march home through the SKULLS!

BECAUSE OF THESE SKULLS, WE'LL HAVE TO RAID FARTHER AWAY FROM NOW ON...

A MINOR INCONVENIENCE OUT OF WHAT COULD HAVE BEEN A MAJOR DISASTER!

THANK GRAN'MA'PA!

LAST TRIP!

THE PILE IS REALLY BIG!

THE CHOW SOL'JERS TELL ME YOU WENT ON QUITE A STRANGE RAID. THE TOOL WORKED, AT ANY RATE.

LIKE A CHARM!!

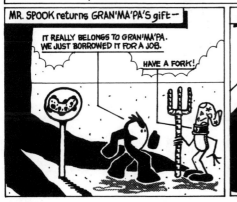

MR. SPOOK returns GRAN'MA'PA'S gift—

IT REALLY BELONGS TO GRAN'MA'PA. WE JUST BORROWED IT FOR A JOB.

HAVE A FORK!

A MOUNTAIN of CHOW!!

WE BETTER HURRY! THE PARTY HAS ALREADY STARTED!

HOOP-LA

WANG-DANG DOODLE

YIPPIE-EYE OH-KI-AYE

HOKA HEY

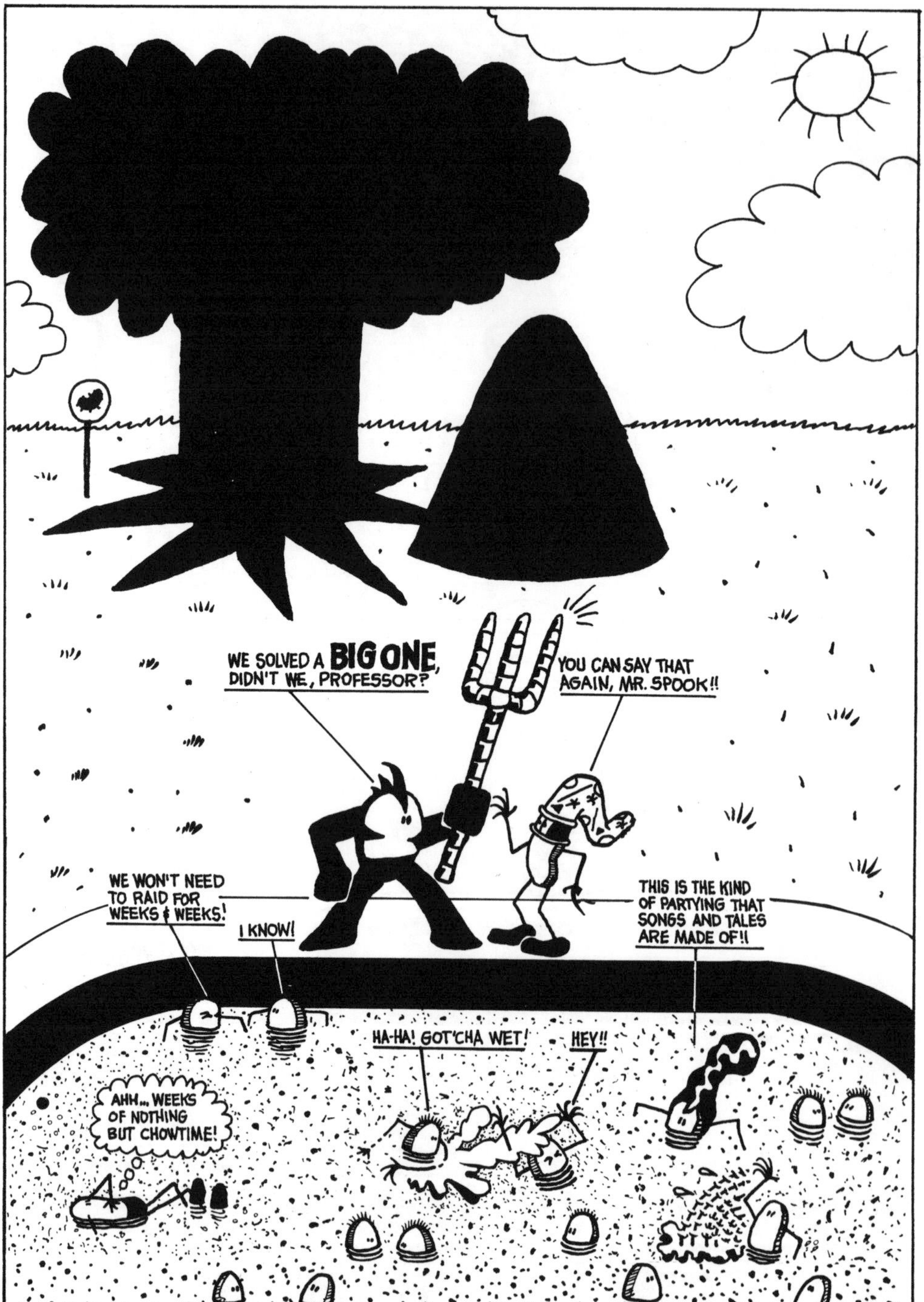
WE SOLVED A BIG ONE, DIDN'T WE, PROFESSOR?
YOU CAN SAY THAT AGAIN, MR. SPOOK!!
WE WON'T NEED TO RAID FOR WEEKS & WEEKS!
I KNOW!
THIS IS THE KIND OF PARTYING THAT SONGS AND TALES ARE MADE OF!!
HA-HA! GOT'CHA WET!
HEY!!
AHH... WEEKS OF NOTHING BUT CHOWTIME!

...END

# Too Much Chow!

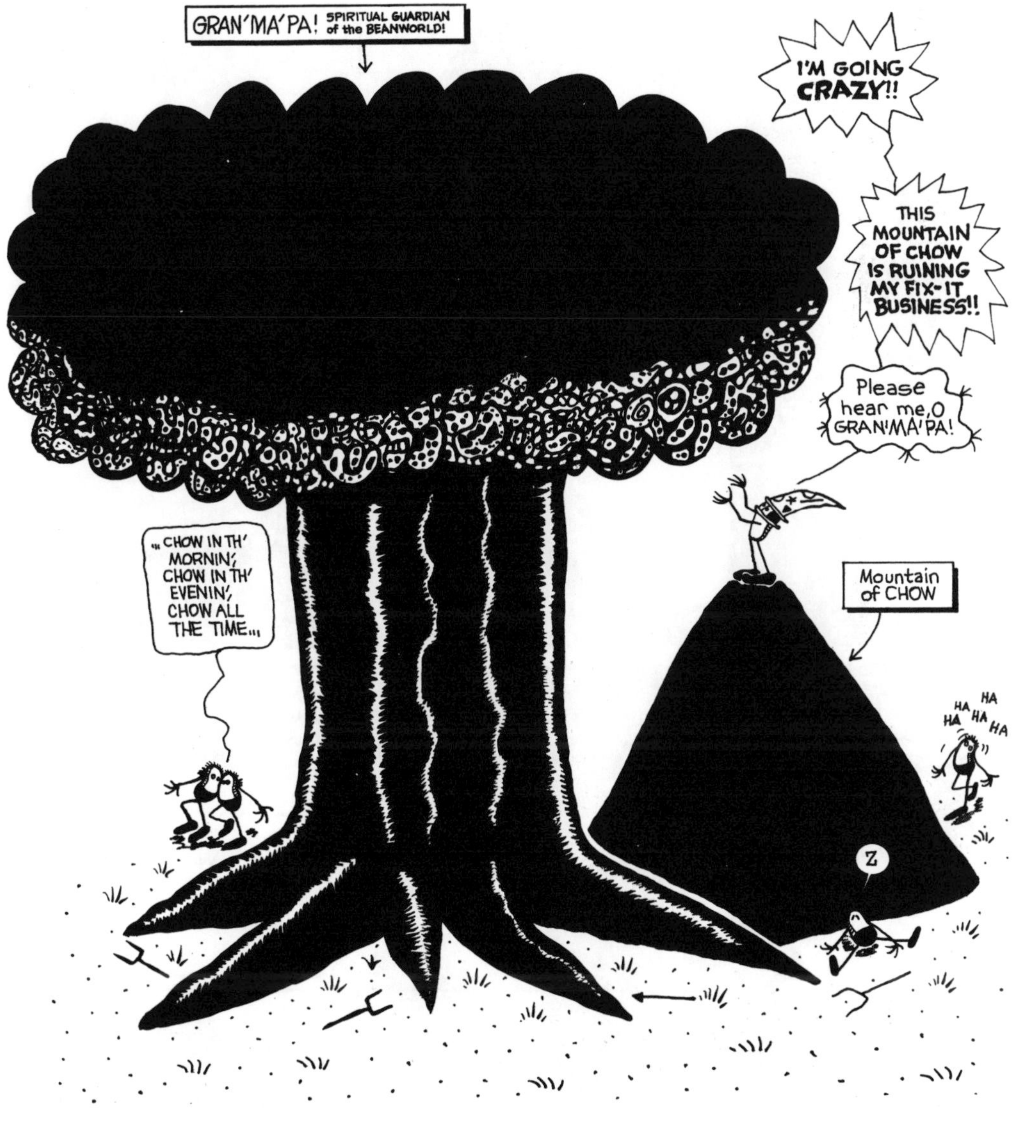
GRAN'MA'PA! SPIRITUAL GUARDIAN of the BEANWORLD!
I'M GOING CRAZY!!
THIS MOUNTAIN OF CHOW IS RUINING MY FIX-IT BUSINESS!!
Please hear me, O GRAN'MA'PA!
"CHOW IN TH' MORNIN', CHOW IN TH' EVENIN', CHOW ALL THE TIME..."
Mountain of CHOW
HA HA HA HA HA
Z

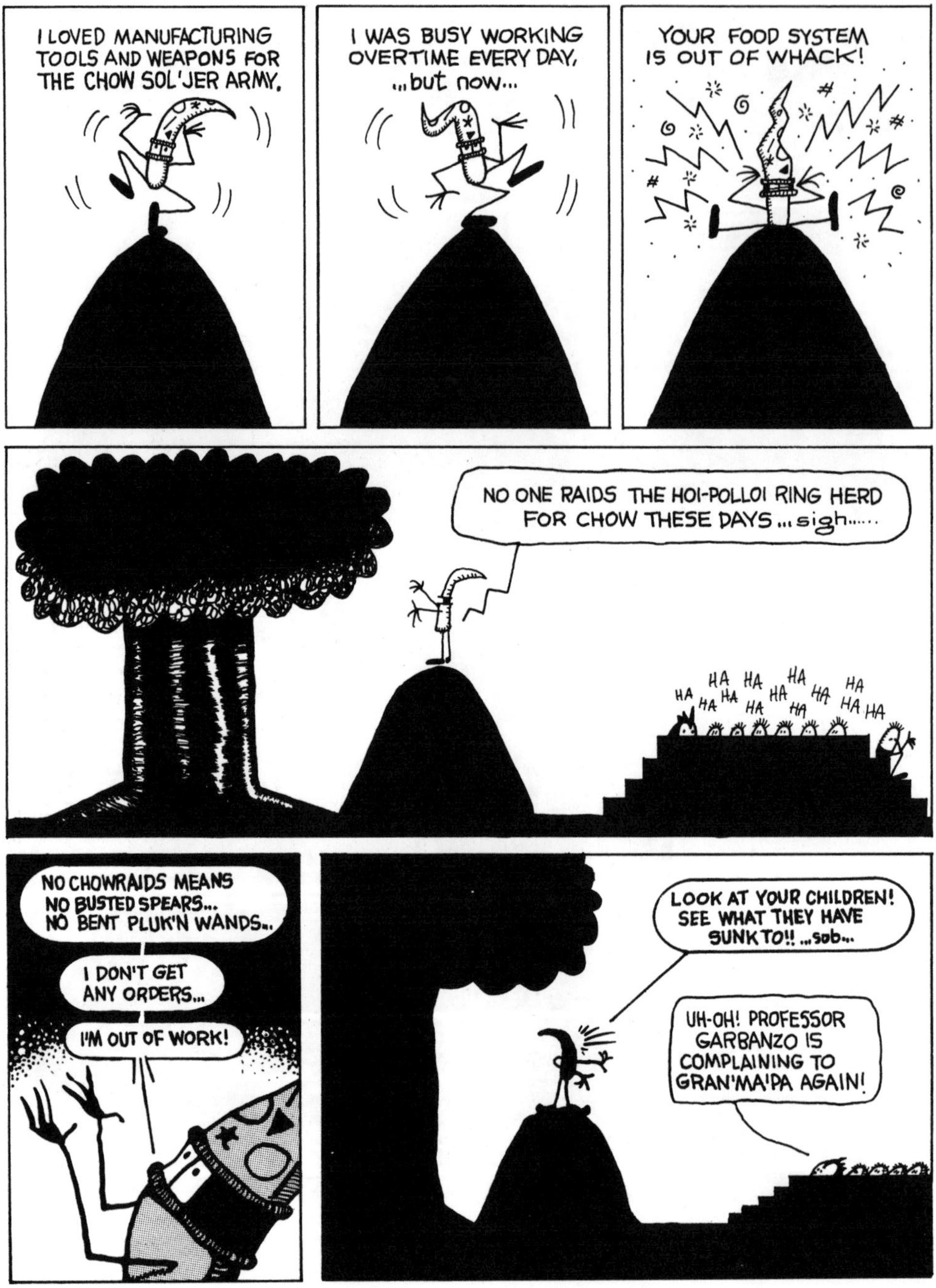
I LOVED MANUFACTURING TOOLS AND WEAPONS FOR THE CHOW SOL'JER ARMY.
I WAS BUSY WORKING OVERTIME EVERY DAY, ...but now...
YOUR FOOD SYSTEM IS OUT OF WHACK!
NO ONE RAIDS THE HOI-POLLOI RING HERD FOR CHOW THESE DAYS ... sigh......
HA HA HA HA HA HA HA HA HA HA HA HA HA HA HA
NO CHOWRAIDS MEANS NO BUSTED SPEARS... NO BENT PLUK'N WANDS...
I DON'T GET ANY ORDERS...
I'M OUT OF WORK!
LOOK AT YOUR CHILDREN! SEE WHAT THEY HAVE SUNK TO!! ...sob...
UH-OH! PROFESSOR GARBANZO IS COMPLAINING TO GRAN'MA'PA AGAIN!

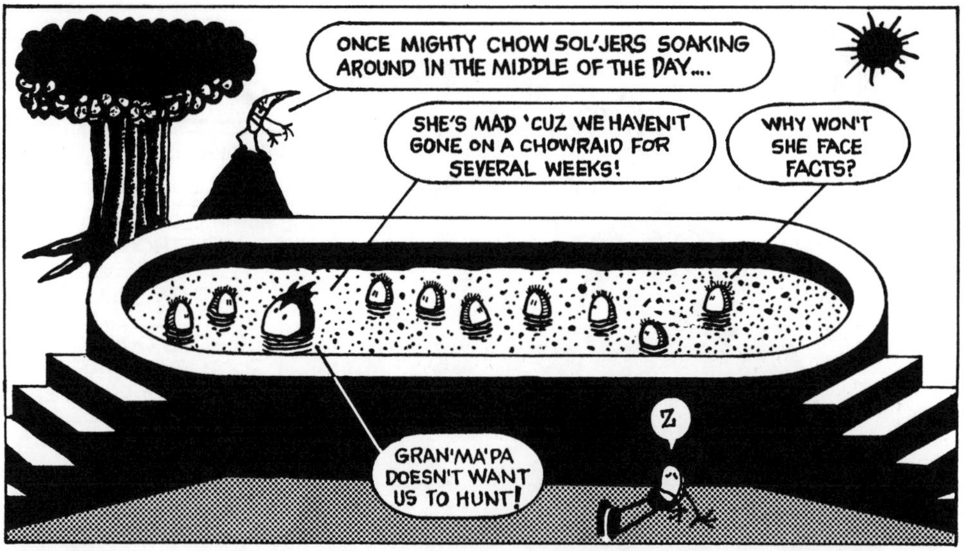
ONCE MIGHTY CHOW SOL'JERS SOAKING AROUND IN THE MIDDLE OF THE DAY....
SHE'S MAD 'CUZ WE HAVEN'T GONE ON A CHOWRAID FOR SEVERAL WEEKS!
WHY WON'T SHE FACE FACTS?
GRAN'MA'PA DOESN'T WANT US TO HUNT!
Z

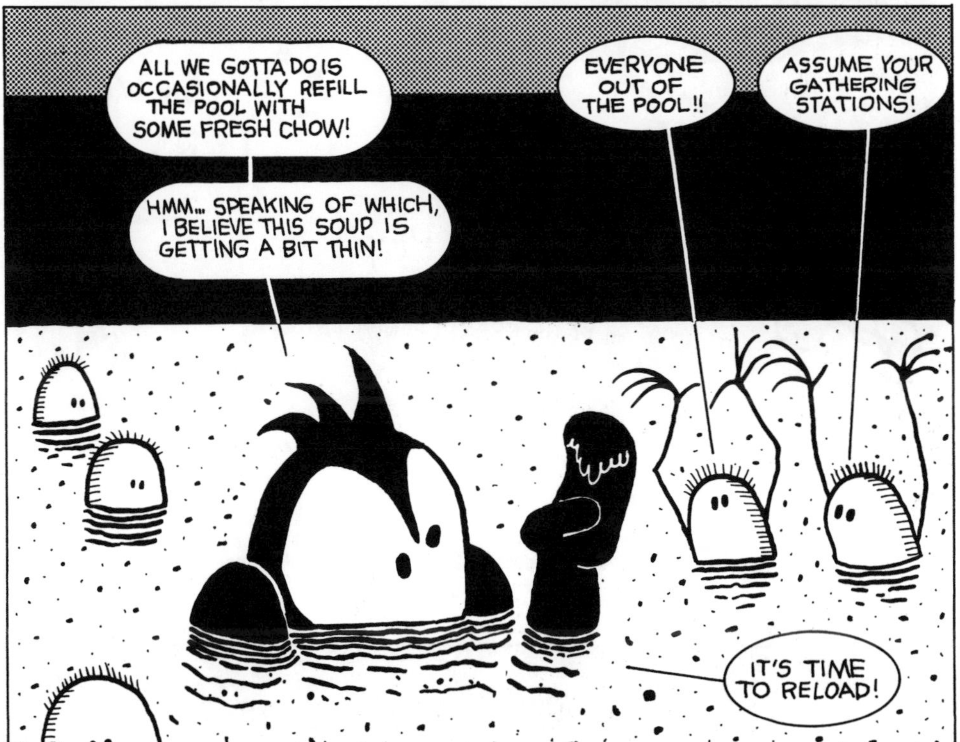
ALL WE GOTTA DO IS OCCASIONALLY REFILL THE POOL WITH SOME FRESH CHOW!
HMM... SPEAKING OF WHICH, I BELIEVE THIS SOUP IS GETTING A BIT THIN!
EVERYONE OUT OF THE POOL!!
ASSUME YOUR GATHERING STATIONS!
IT'S TIME TO RELOAD!

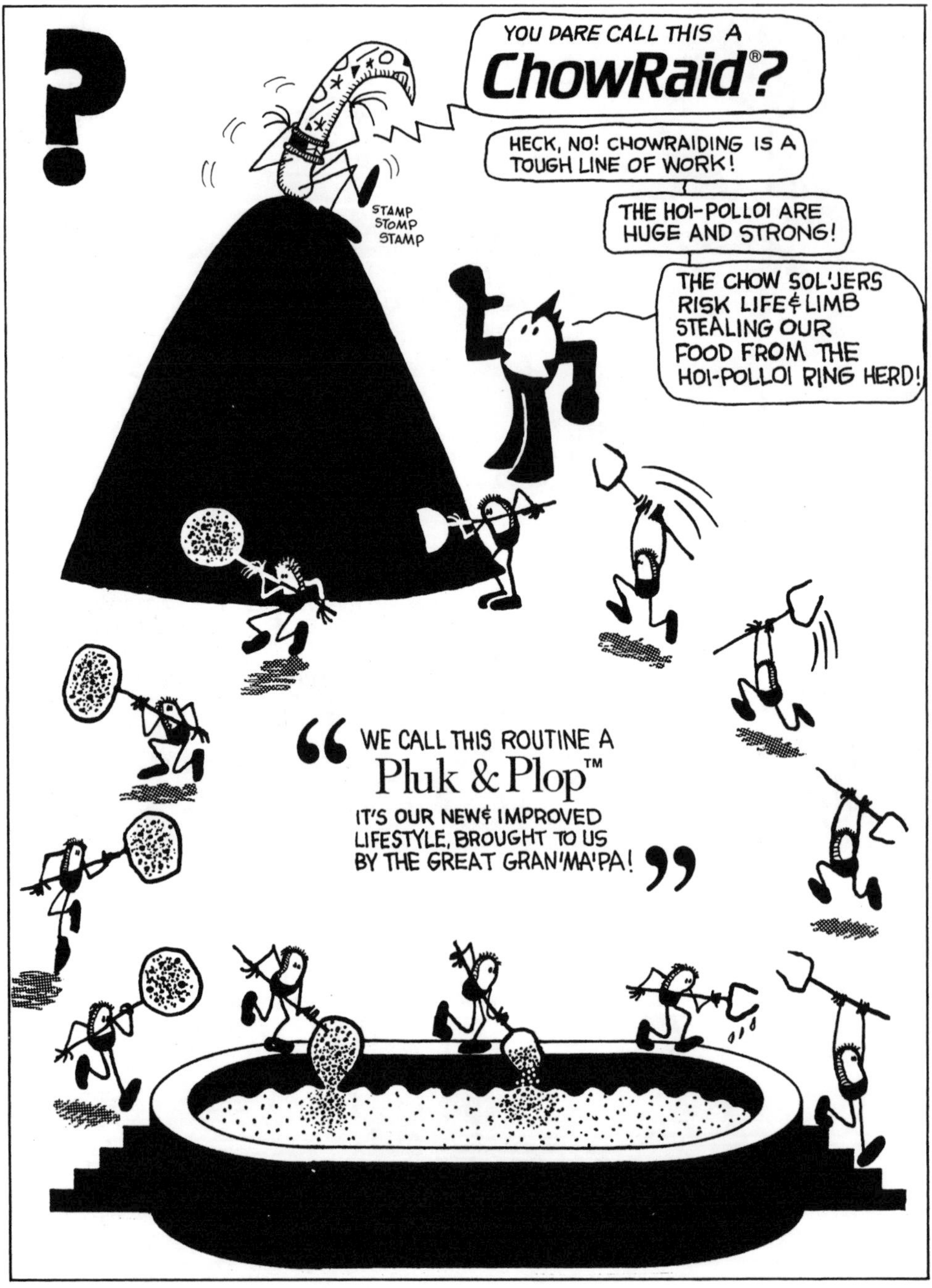
?
YOU DARE CALL THIS A ChowRaid®?
STAMP STOMP STAMP
HECK, NO! CHOWRAIDING IS A TOUGH LINE OF WORK!
THE HOI-POLLOI ARE HUGE AND STRONG!
THE CHOW SOL'JERS RISK LIFE & LIMB STEALING OUR FOOD FROM THE HOI-POLLOI RING HERD!
"WE CALL THIS ROUTINE A Pluk & Plop™ IT'S OUR NEW & IMPROVED LIFESTYLE, BROUGHT TO US BY THE GREAT GRAN'MA'PA!"

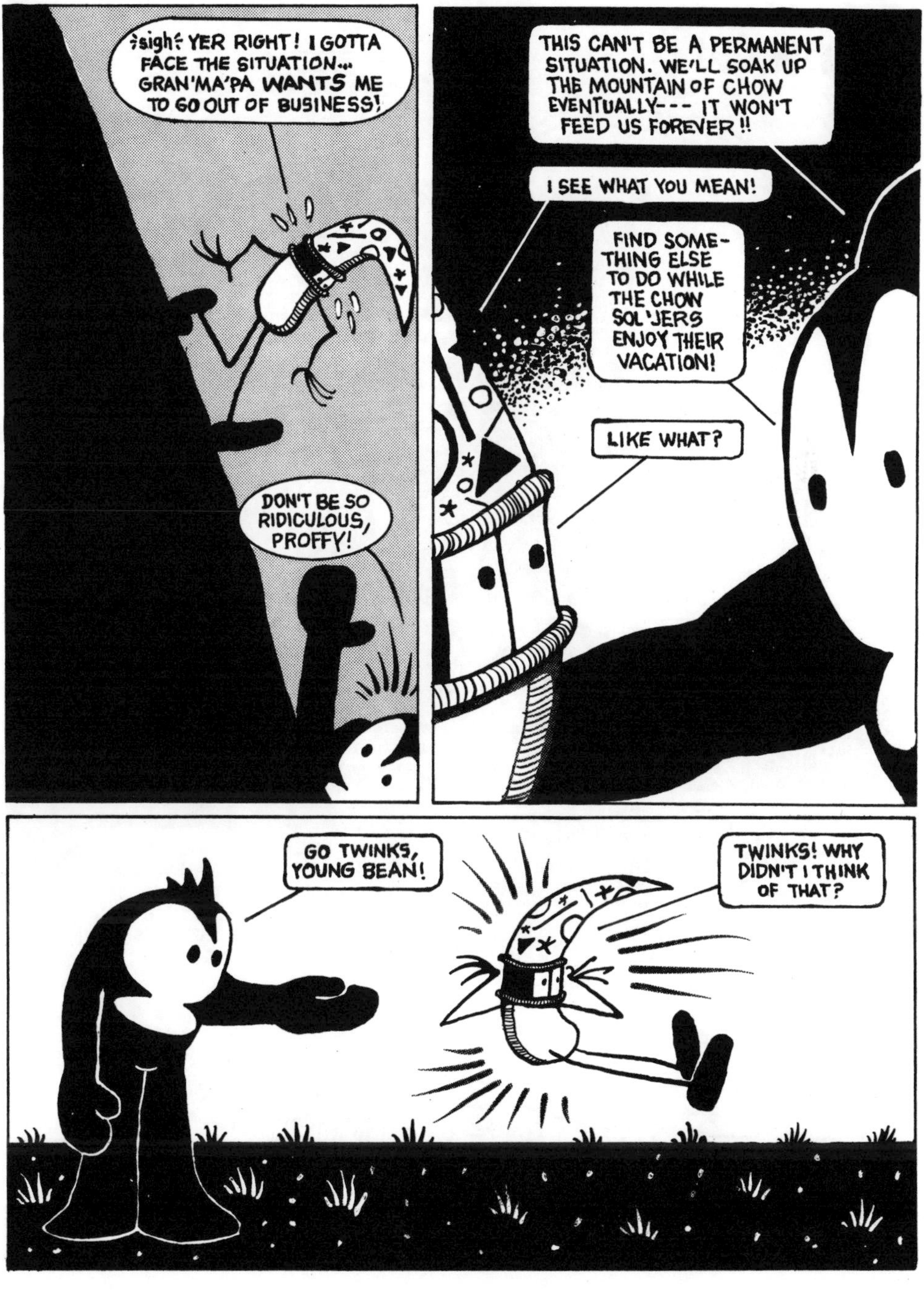

~sigh~ YER RIGHT! I GOTTA FACE THE SITUATION... GRAN'MA'PA WANTS ME TO GO OUT OF BUSINESS!
DON'T BE SO RIDICULOUS, PROFFY!
THIS CAN'T BE A PERMANENT SITUATION. WE'LL SOAK UP THE MOUNTAIN OF CHOW EVENTUALLY--- IT WON'T FEED US FOREVER!!
I SEE WHAT YOU MEAN!
FIND SOMETHING ELSE TO DO WHILE THE CHOW SOL'JERS ENJOY THEIR VACATION!
LIKE WHAT?
GO TWINKS, YOUNG BEAN!
TWINKS! WHY DIDN'T I THINK OF THAT?

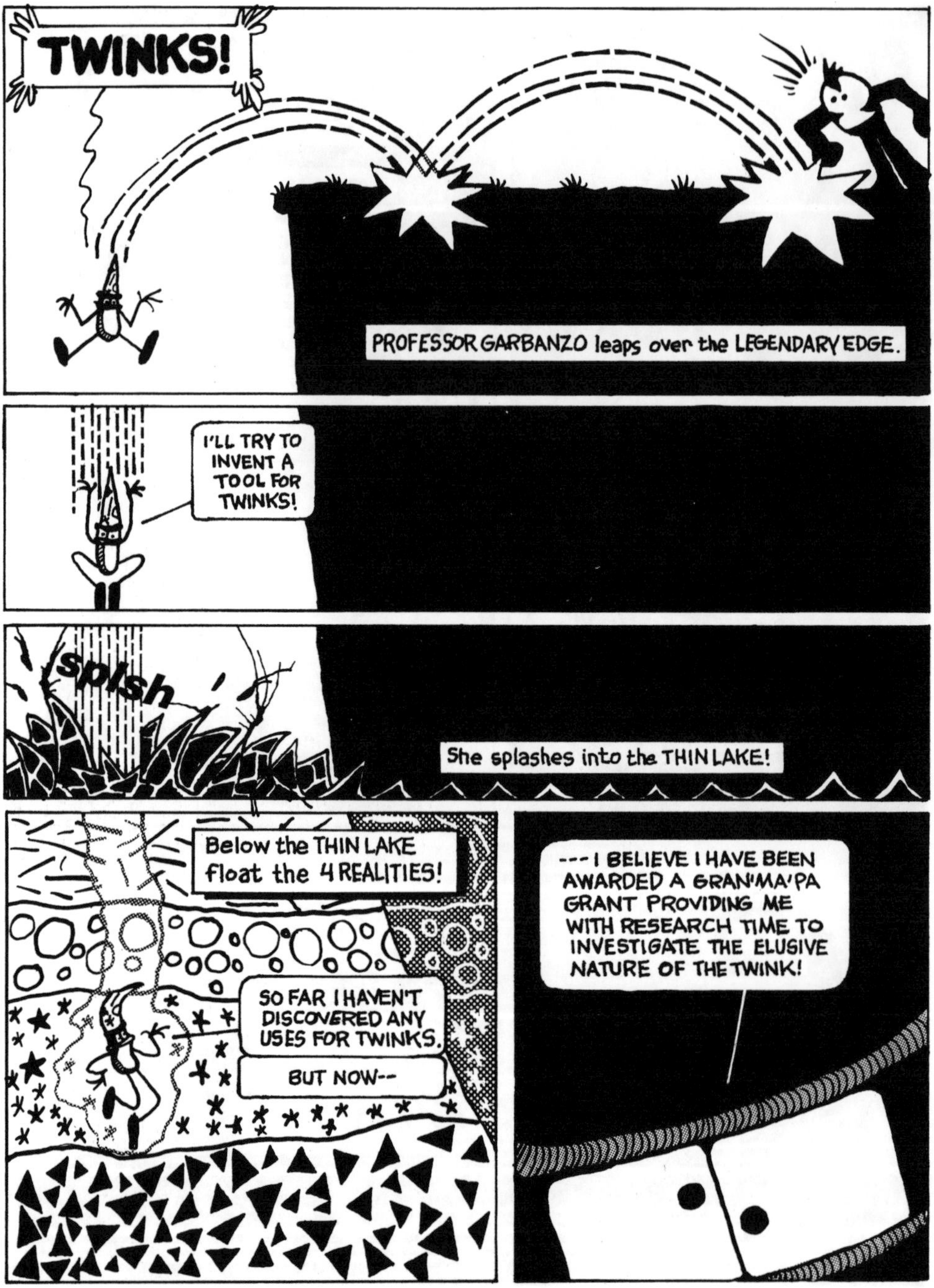
TWINKS!
PROFESSOR GARBANZO leaps over the LEGENDARY EDGE.
I'LL TRY TO INVENT A TOOL FOR TWINKS!
splsh
She splashes into the THIN LAKE!
Below the THIN LAKE float the 4 REALITIES!
SO FAR I HAVEN'T DISCOVERED ANY USES FOR TWINKS.
BUT NOW--
---I BELIEVE I HAVE BEEN AWARDED A GRAN'MA'PA GRANT PROVIDING ME WITH RESEARCH TIME TO INVESTIGATE THE ELUSIVE NATURE OF THE TWINK!

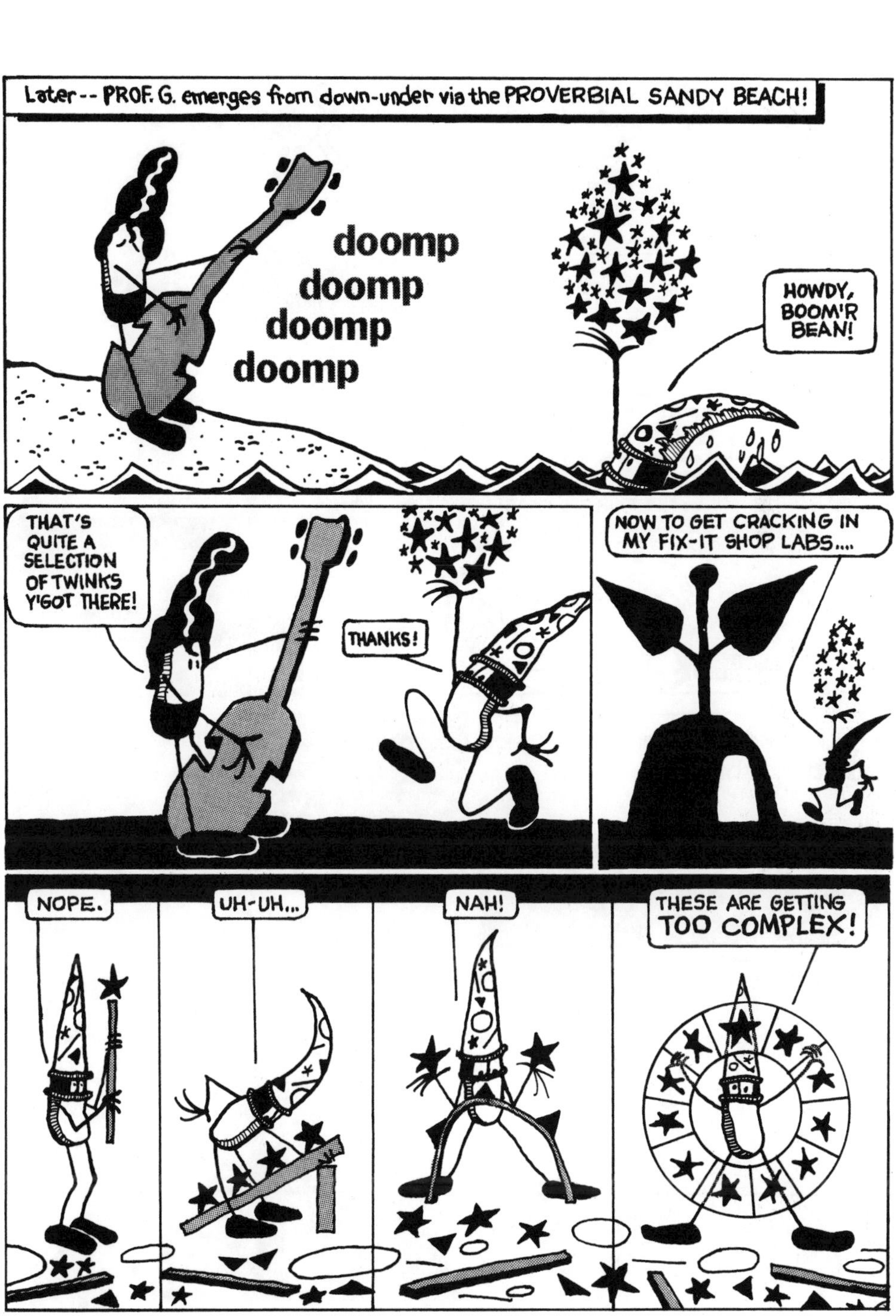

Later -- PROF. G. emerges from down-under via the PROVERBIAL SANDY BEACH!
doomp
doomp
doomp
doomp
HOWDY, BOOM'R BEAN!
THAT'S QUITE A SELECTION OF TWINKS Y'GOT THERE!
THANKS!
NOW TO GET CRACKING IN MY FIX-IT SHOP LABS....
NOPE.
UH-UH...
NAH!
THESE ARE GETTING TOO COMPLEX!

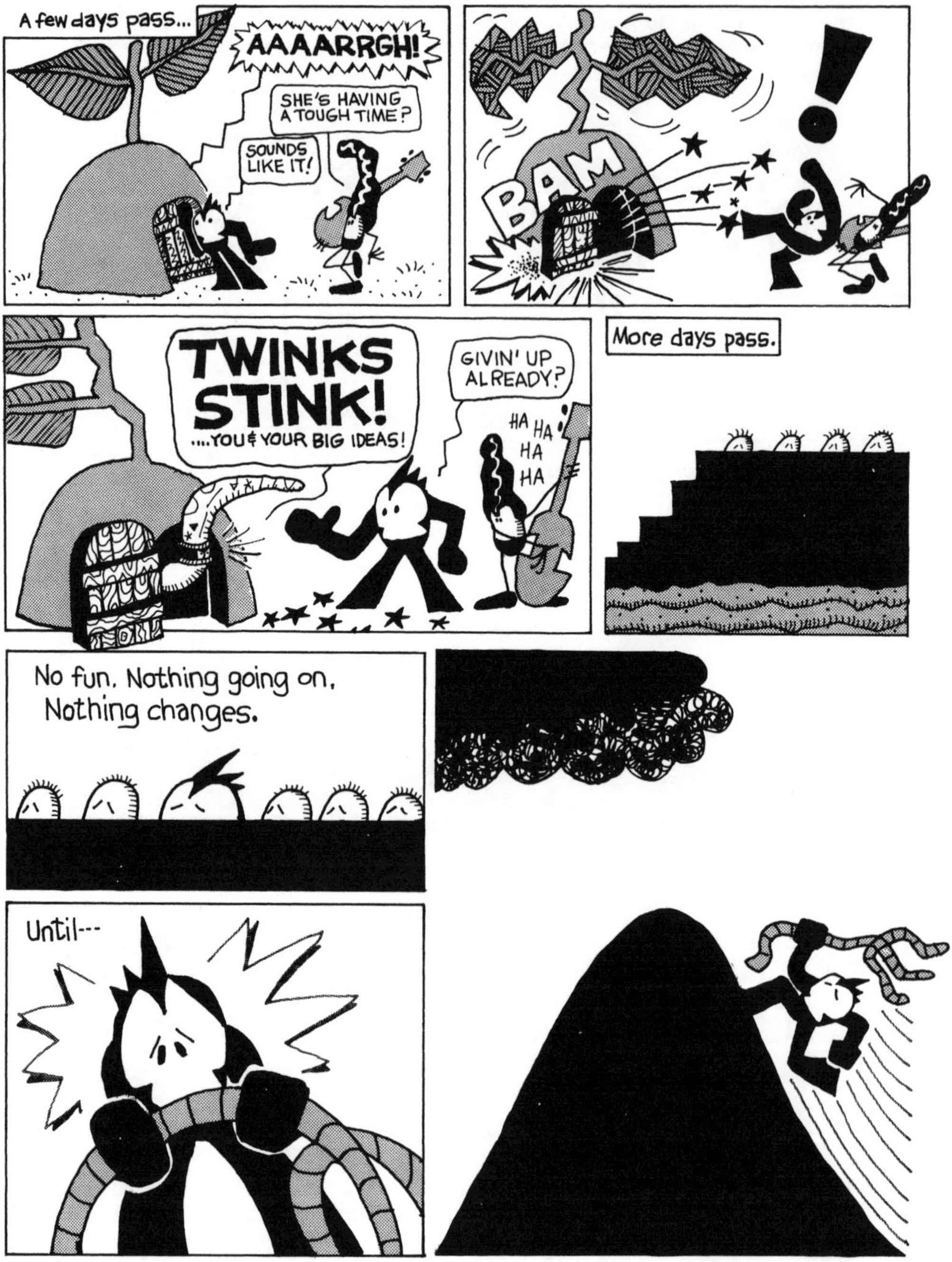
A few days pass...
AAAARRGH!
SHE'S HAVING A TOUGH TIME?
SOUNDS LIKE IT!
BAM
!
TWINKS STINK!
....YOU & YOUR BIG IDEAS!
GIVIN' UP ALREADY?
HA HA HA HA
More days pass.
No fun. Nothing going on. Nothing changes.
Until---

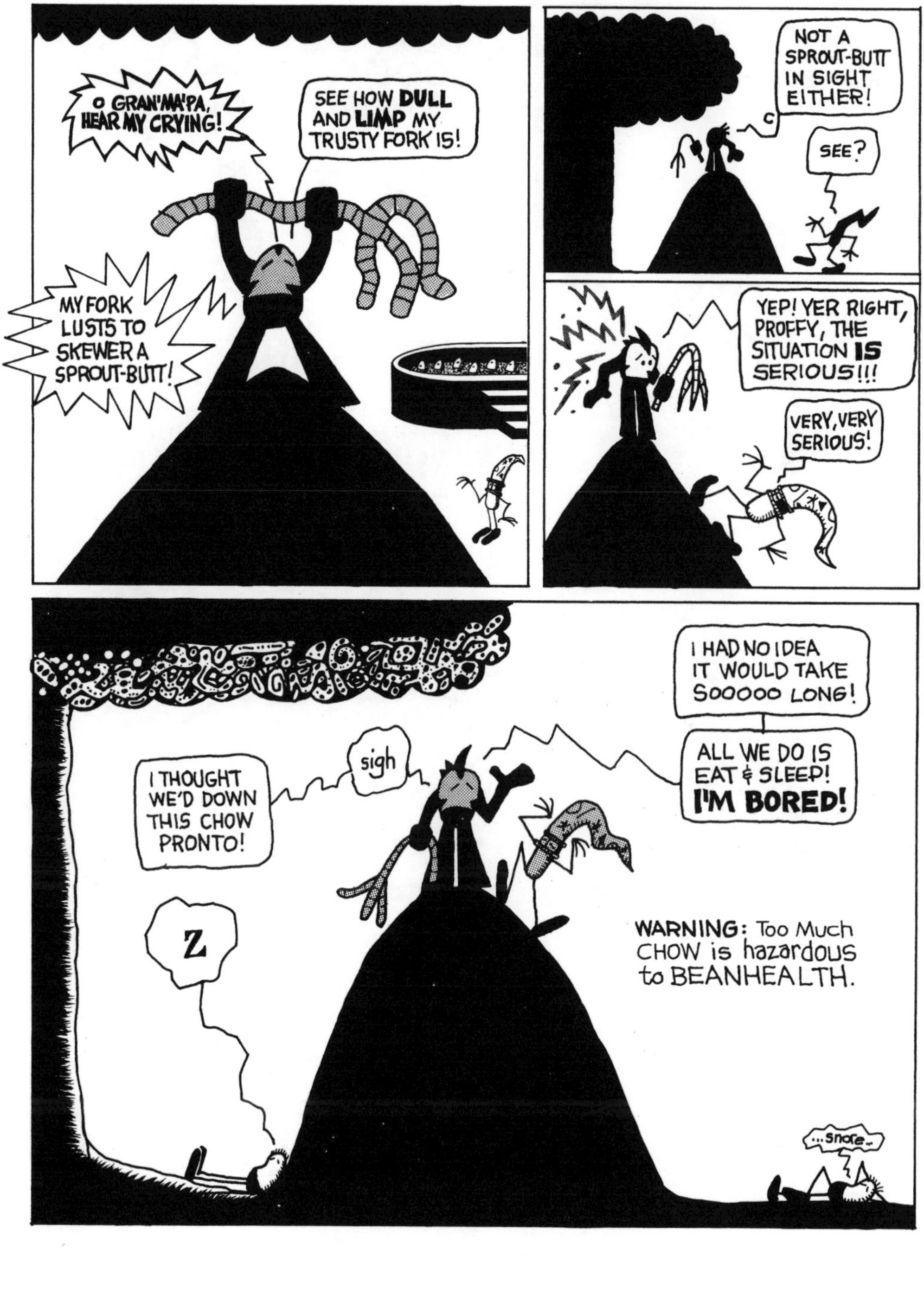
O GRAN'MA'PA, HEAR MY CRYING!
SEE HOW DULL AND LIMP MY TRUSTY FORK IS!
MY FORK LUSTS TO SKEWER A SPROUT-BUTT!
NOT A SPROUT-BUTT IN SIGHT EITHER!
SEE?
YEP! YER RIGHT, PROFFY, THE SITUATION IS SERIOUS!!!
VERY, VERY SERIOUS!
I HAD NO IDEA IT WOULD TAKE SOOOOO LONG!
ALL WE DO IS EAT & SLEEP! I'M BORED!
sigh
I THOUGHT WE'D DOWN THIS CHOW PRONTO!
Z
WARNING: Too Much CHOW is hazardous to BEANHEALTH.
...snore...

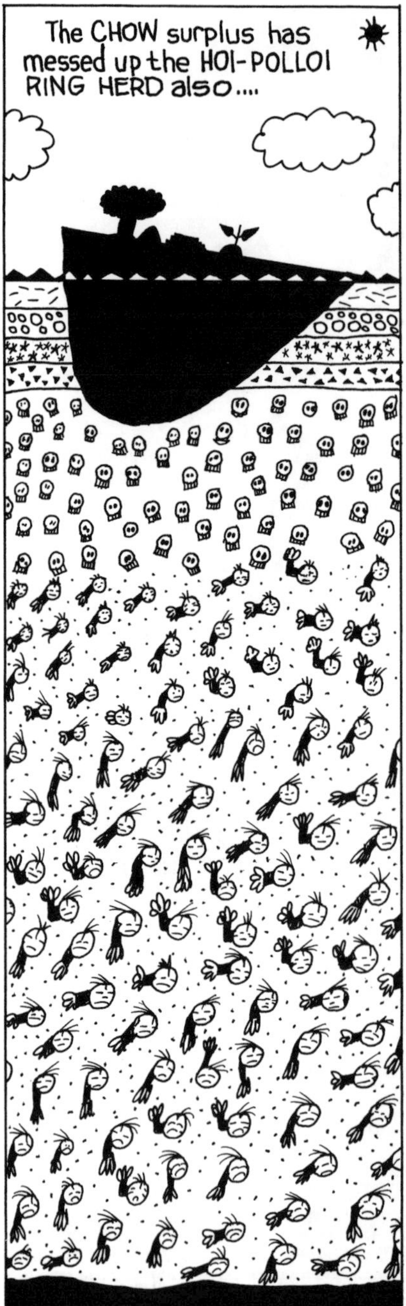
The CHOW surplus has messed up the HOI-POLLOI RING HERD also....

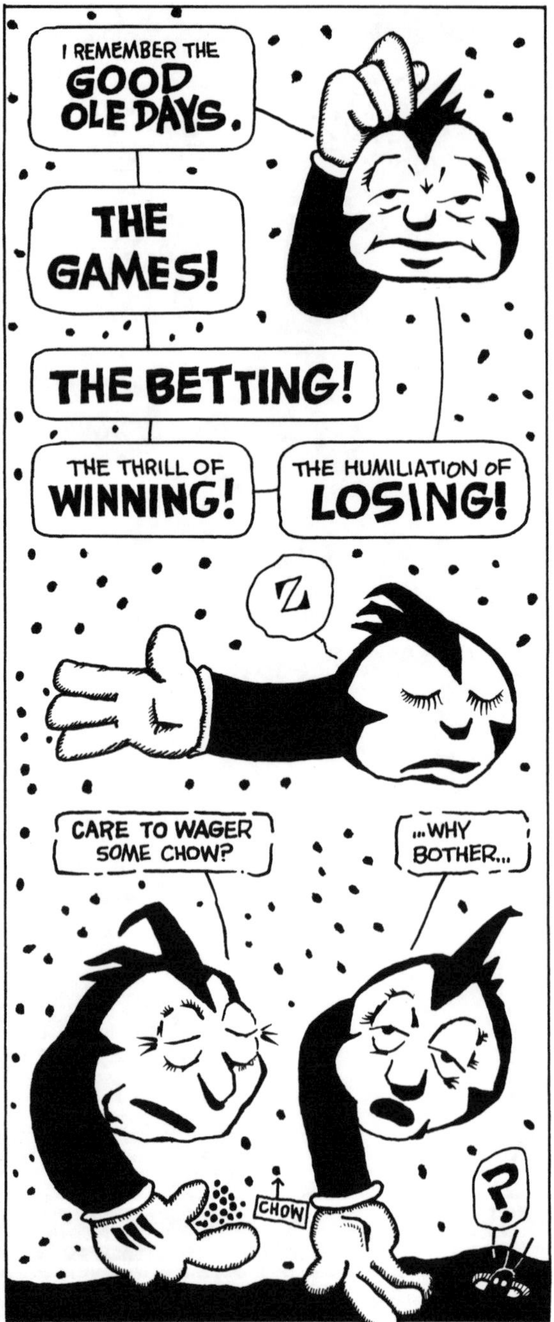
I REMEMBER THE GOOD OLE DAYS.
THE GAMES!
THE BETTING!
THE THRILL OF WINNING!
THE HUMILIATION OF LOSING!
Z
CARE TO WAGER SOME CHOW?
...WHY BOTHER...
CHOW
?

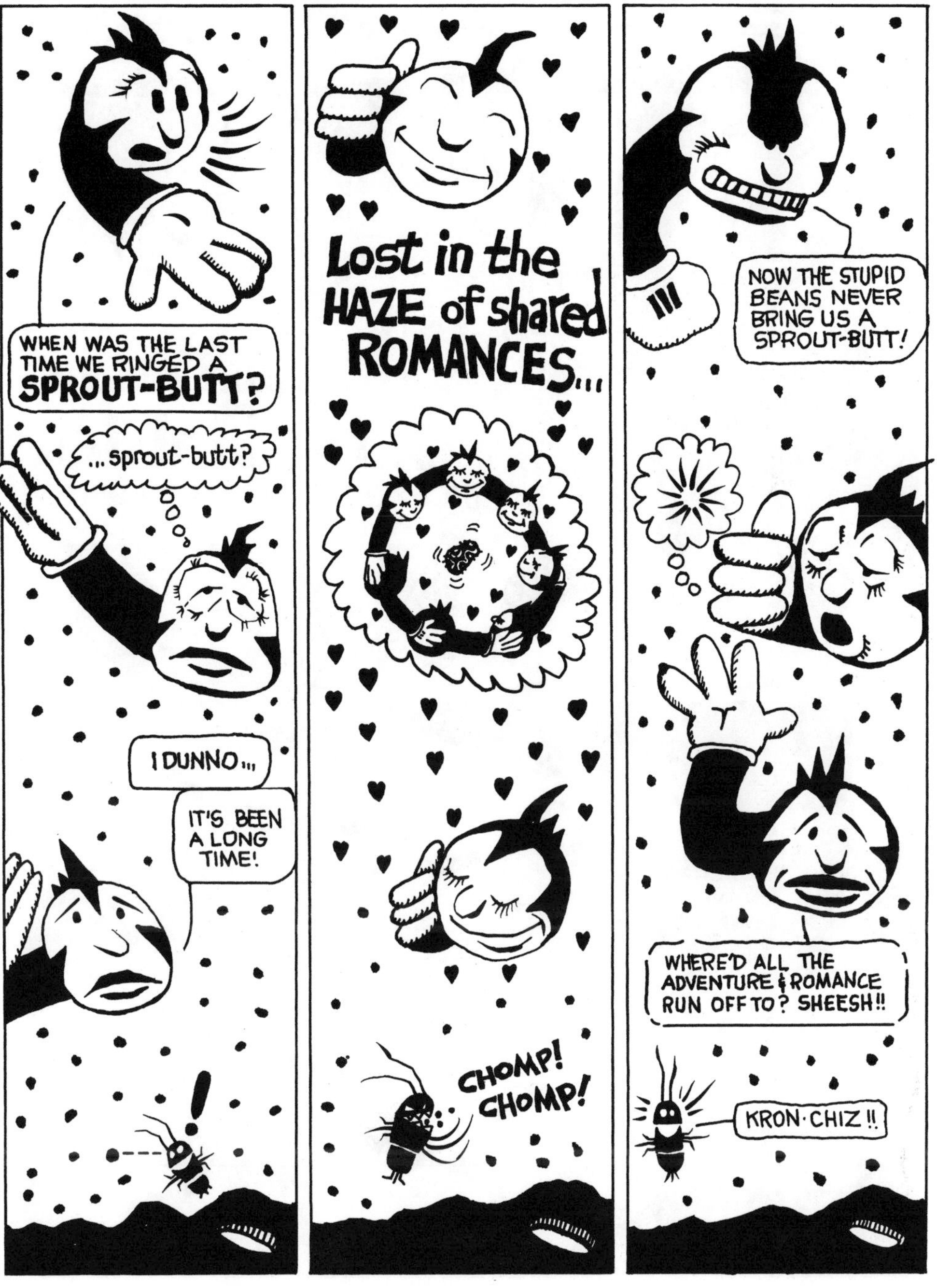
WHEN WAS THE LAST TIME WE RINGED A SPROUT-BUTT?
...sprout-butt?
I DUNNO...
IT'S BEEN A LONG TIME!
Lost in the HAZE of shared ROMANCES...
CHOMP! CHOMP!
NOW THE STUPID BEANS NEVER BRING US A SPROUT-BUTT!
WHERE'D ALL THE ADVENTURE & ROMANCE RUN OFF TO? SHEESH!!
KRON·CHIZ!!

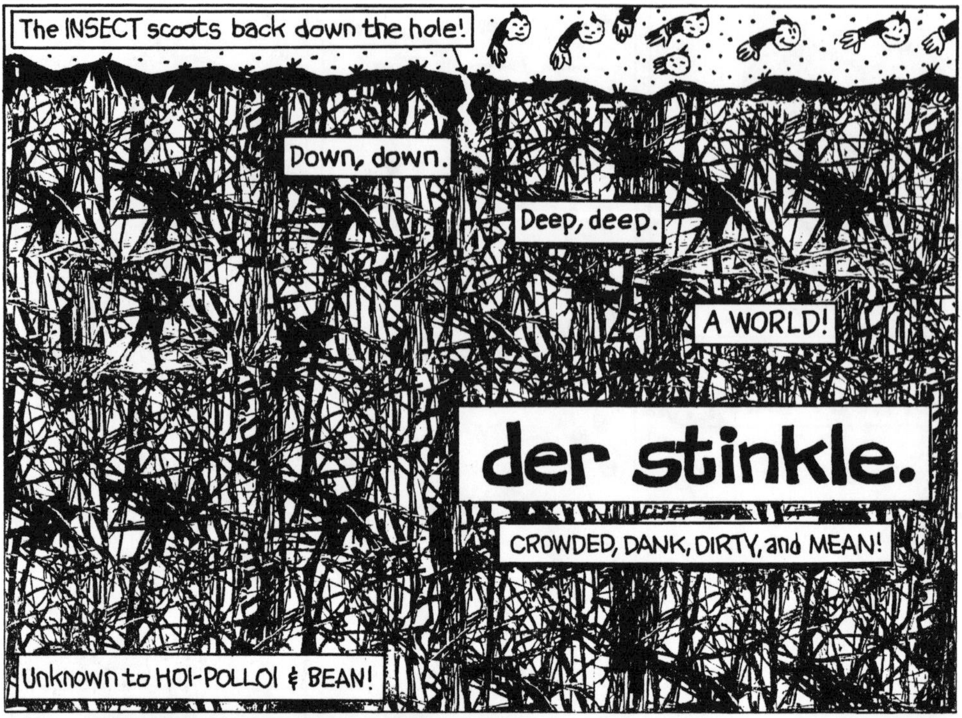
The INSECT scoots back down the hole!
Down, down.
Deep, deep.
A WORLD!
der stinkle.
CROWDED, DANK, DIRTY, and MEAN!
Unknown to HOI-POLLOI & BEAN!

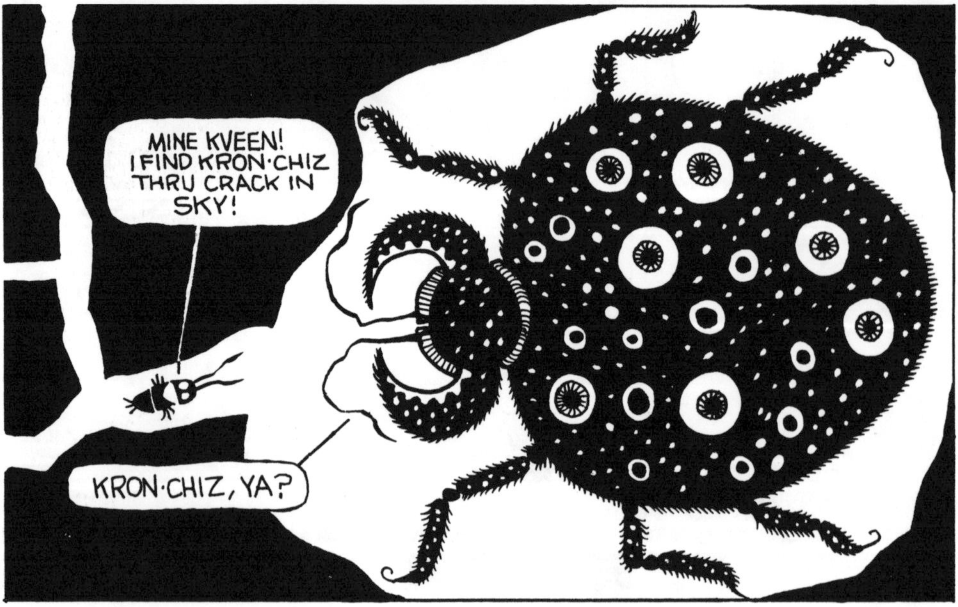
MINE KVEEN! I FIND KRON·CHIZ THRU CRACK IN SKY!
KRON·CHIZ, YA?

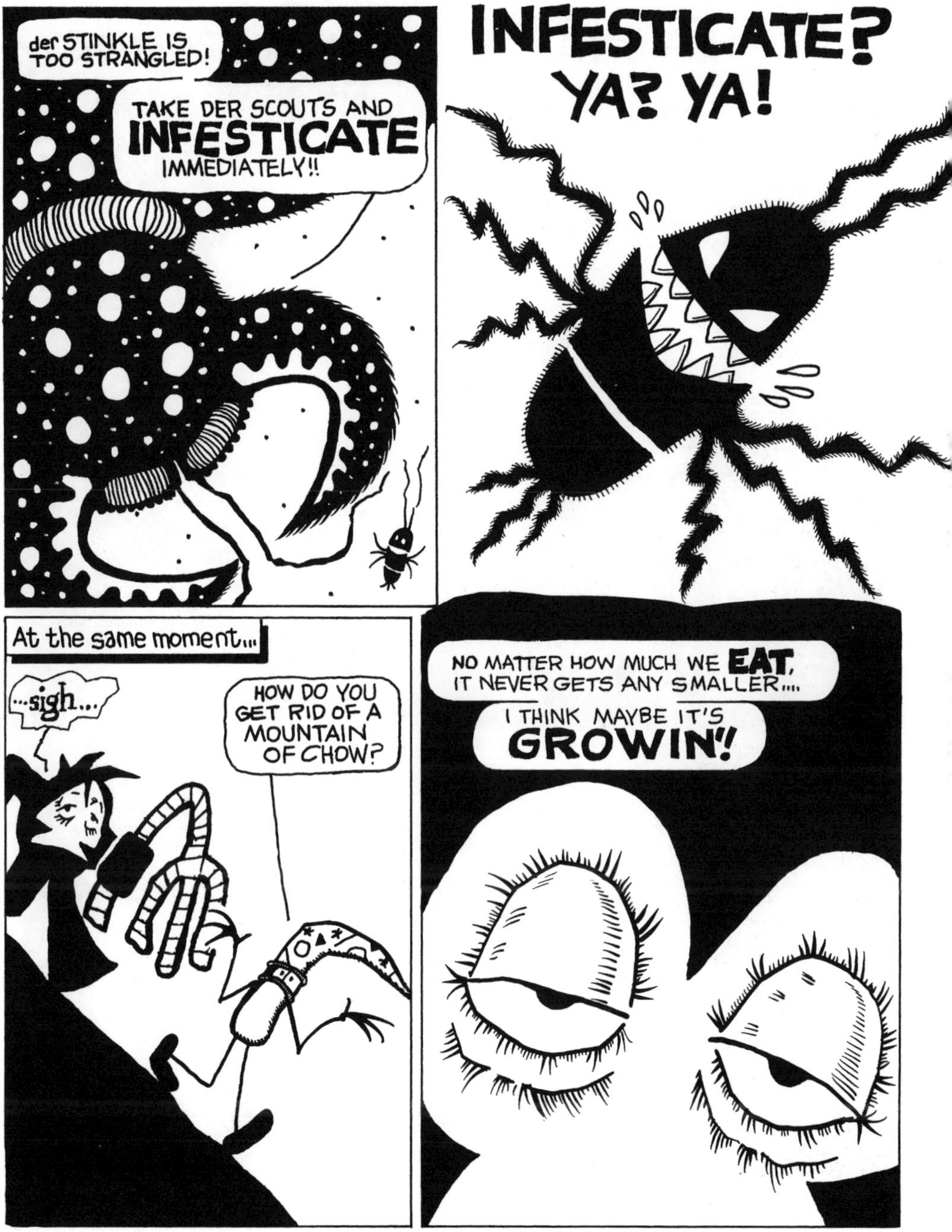
der STINKLE IS TOO STRANGLED!
TAKE DER SCOUTS AND INFESTICATE IMMEDIATELY!!
INFESTICATE? YA? YA!
At the same moment...
...sigh...
HOW DO YOU GET RID OF A MOUNTAIN OF CHOW?
NO MATTER HOW MUCH WE EAT, IT NEVER GETS ANY SMALLER....
I THINK MAYBE IT'S GROWIN'!

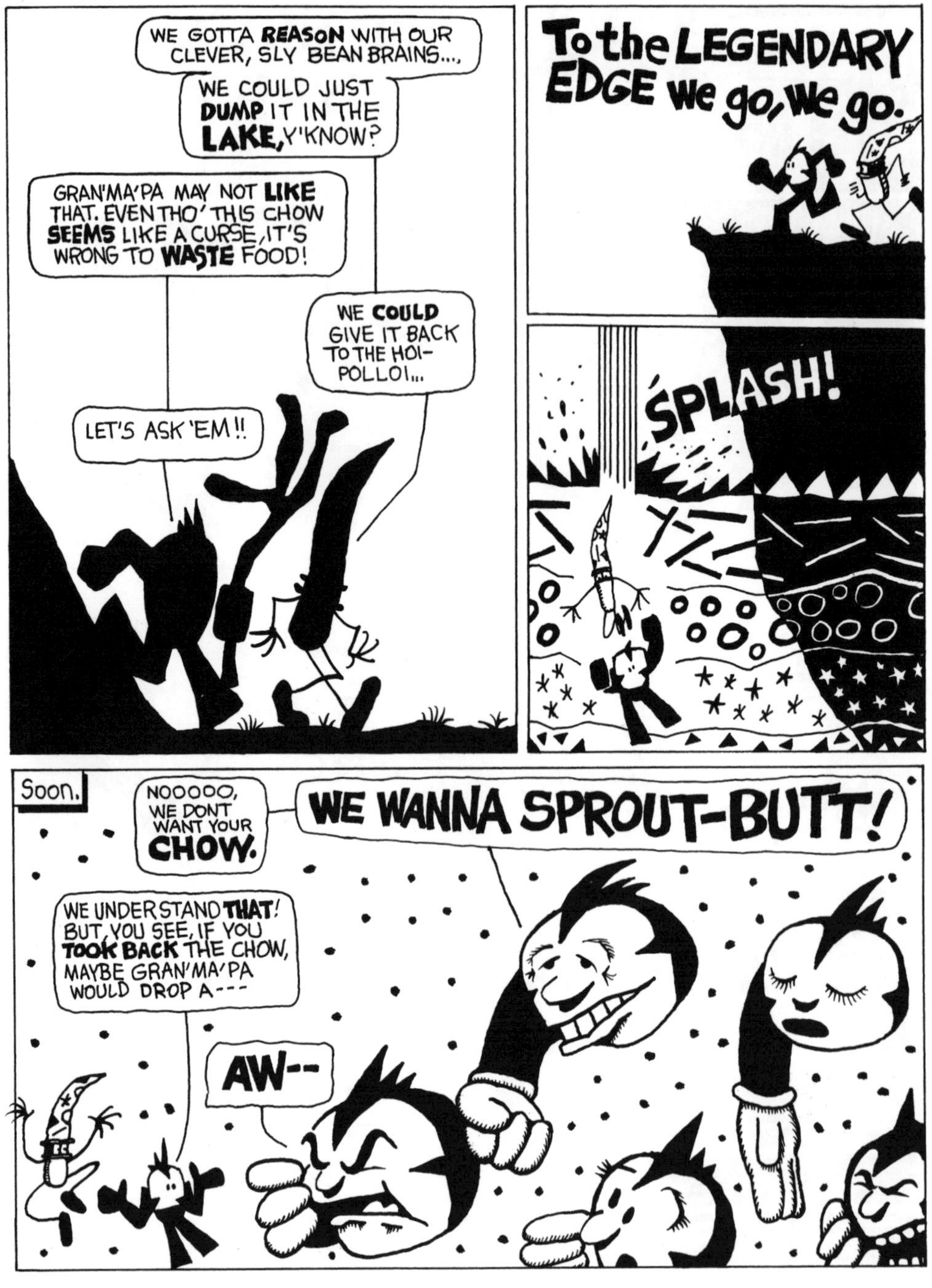
WE GOTTA REASON WITH OUR CLEVER, SLY BEAN BRAINS...,
WE COULD JUST DUMP IT IN THE LAKE, Y'KNOW?
GRAN'MA'PA MAY NOT LIKE THAT. EVEN THO' THIS CHOW SEEMS LIKE A CURSE, IT'S WRONG TO WASTE FOOD!
WE COULD GIVE IT BACK TO THE HOI-POLLOI...
LET'S ASK 'EM!!
To the LEGENDARY EDGE we go, we go.
SPLASH!
Soon.
NOOOOO, WE DONT WANT YOUR CHOW.
WE WANNA SPROUT-BUTT!
WE UNDERSTAND THAT! BUT, YOU SEE, IF YOU TOOK BACK THE CHOW, MAYBE GRAN'MA'PA WOULD DROP A---
AW--

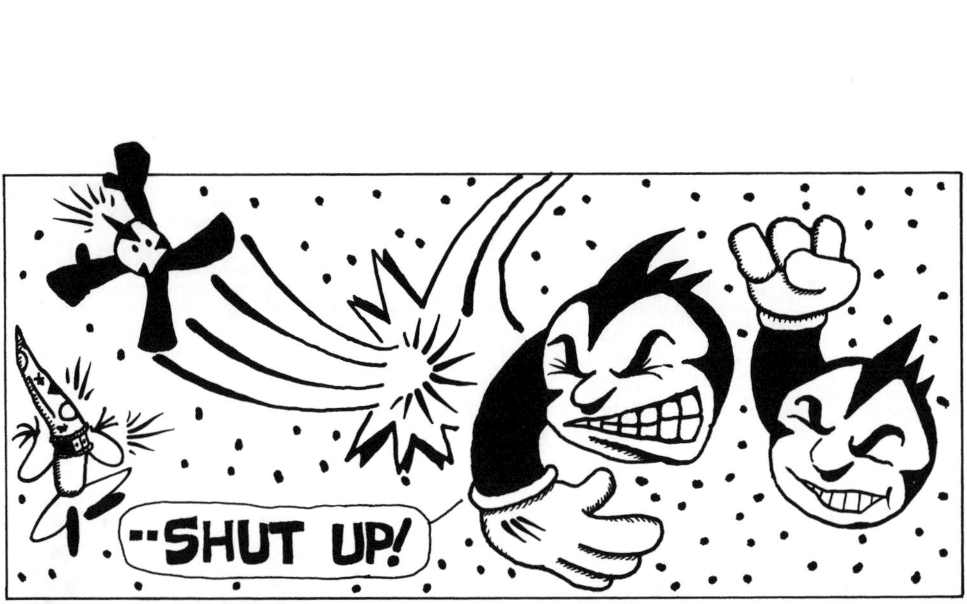
--SHUT UP!

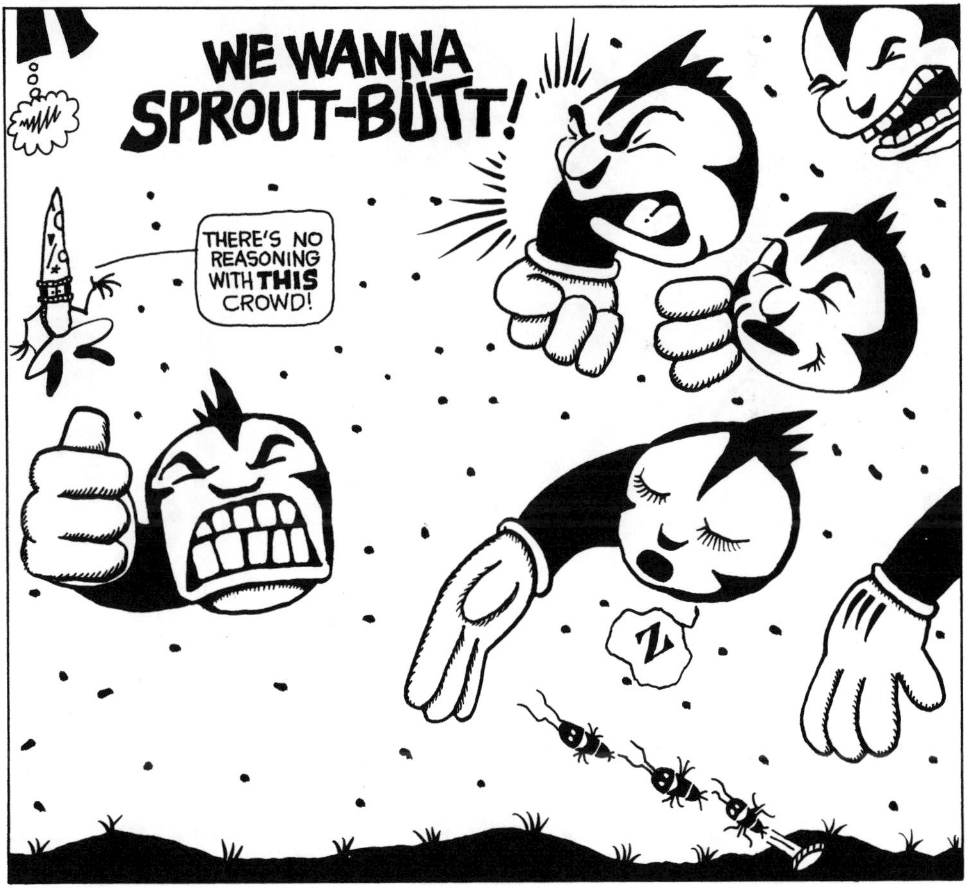
WE WANNA SPROUT-BUTT!
THERE'S NO REASONING WITH THIS CROWD!
Z

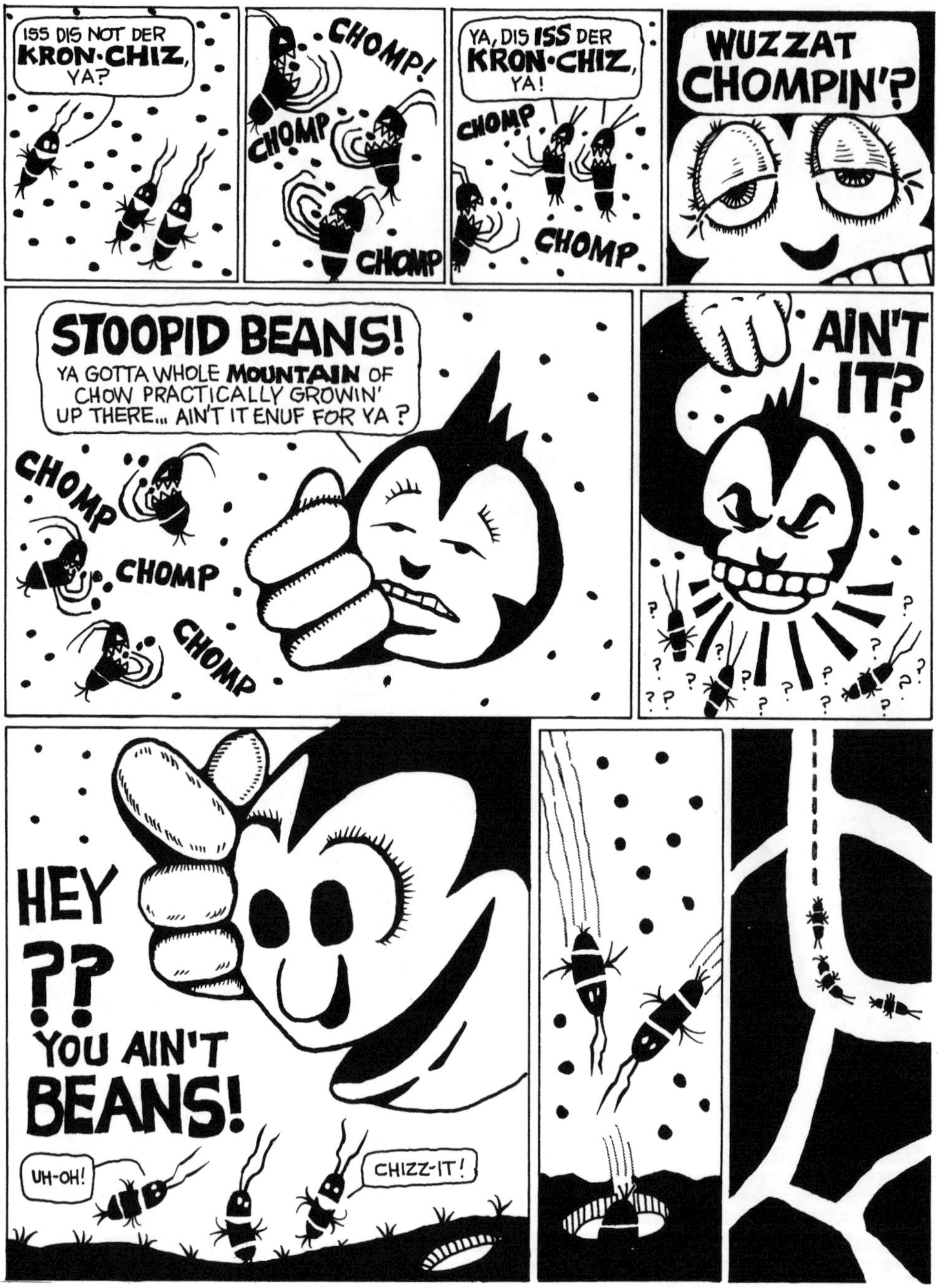
ISS DIS NOT DER KRON·CHIZ, YA?
CHOMP!
CHOMP
CHOMP
YA, DIS ISS DER KRON·CHIZ, YA!
CHOMP
CHOMP
WUZZAT CHOMPIN'?
STOOPID BEANS! YA GOTTA WHOLE MOUNTAIN OF CHOW PRACTICALLY GROWIN' UP THERE... AIN'T IT ENUF FOR YA?
CHOMP
CHOMP
CHOMP
AIN'T IT?
HEY ?? YOU AIN'T BEANS!
UH-OH!
CHIZZ-IT!

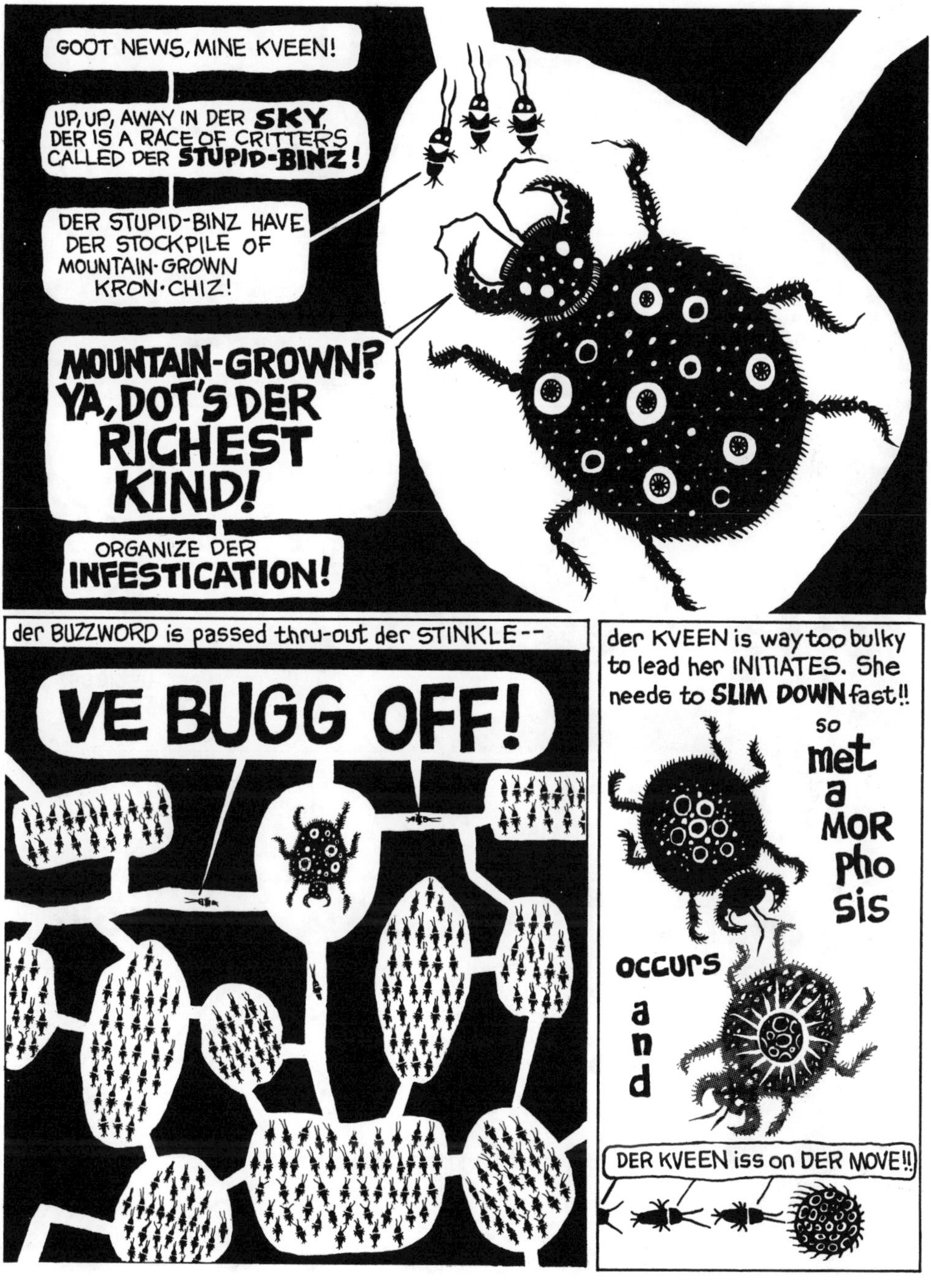
GOOT NEWS, MINE KVEEN!
UP, UP, AWAY IN DER SKY, DER IS A RACE OF CRITTERS CALLED DER STUPID-BINZ!
DER STUPID-BINZ HAVE DER STOCKPILE OF MOUNTAIN-GROWN KRON·CHIZ!
MOUNTAIN-GROWN? YA, DOT'S DER RICHEST KIND!
ORGANIZE DER INFESTICATION!
der BUZZWORD is passed thru-out der STINKLE--
VE BUGG OFF!
der KVEEN is way too bulky to lead her INITIATES. She needs to SLIM DOWN fast!!
so met a MOR pho sis
occurs
and
DER KVEEN iss on DER MOVE!!

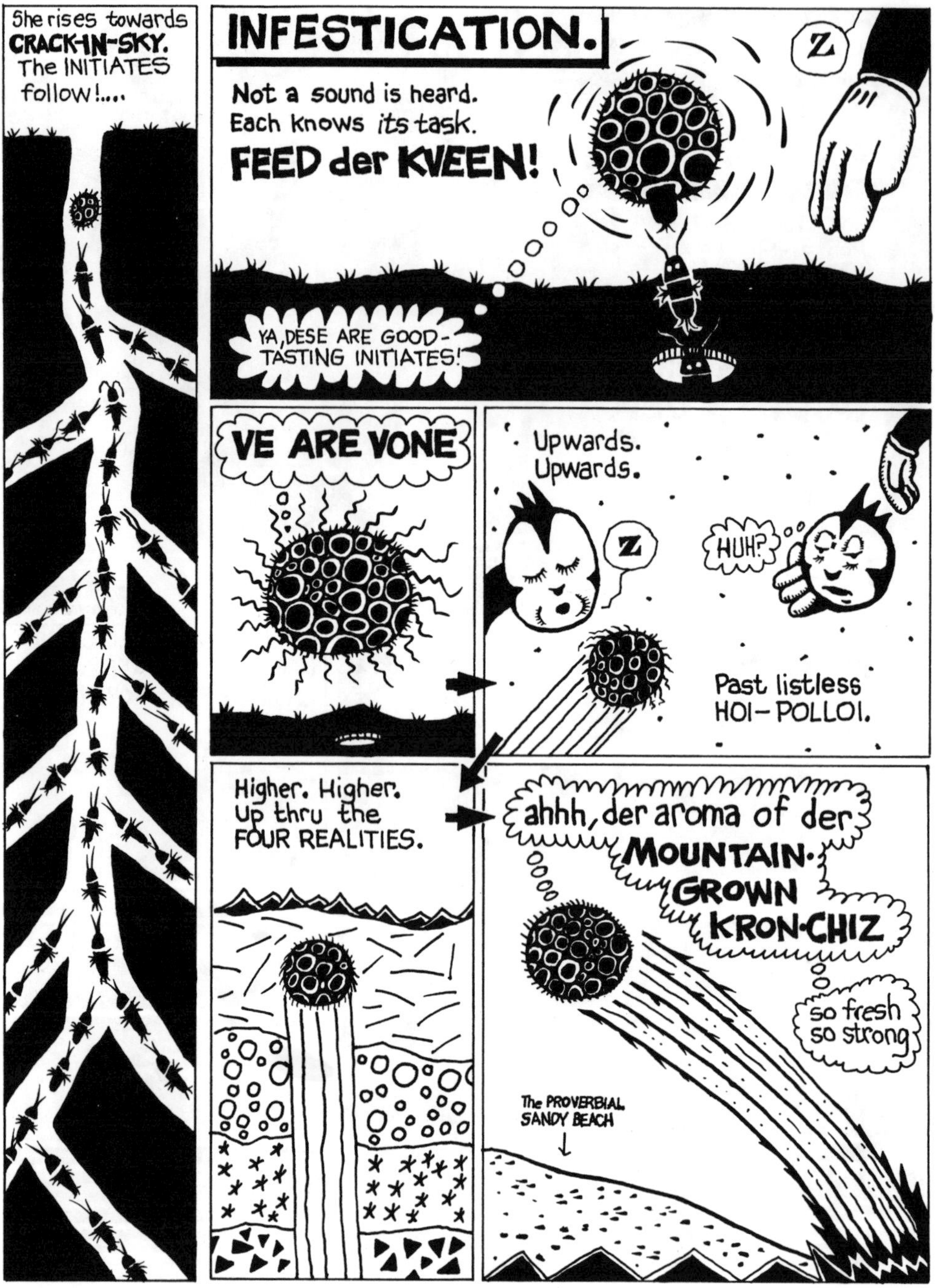
She rises towards CRACK-IN-SKY. The INITIATES follow!....
INFESTICATION.
Not a sound is heard. Each knows its task. FEED der KVEEN!
Z
YA, DESE ARE GOOD-TASTING INITIATES!
VE ARE VONE
Upwards. Upwards.
Z
HUH?
Past listless HOI-POLLOI.
Higher. Higher. Up thru the FOUR REALITIES.
ahhh, der aroma of der MOUNTAIN-GROWN KRON-CHIZ
so fresh so strong
The PROVERBIAL SANDY BEACH

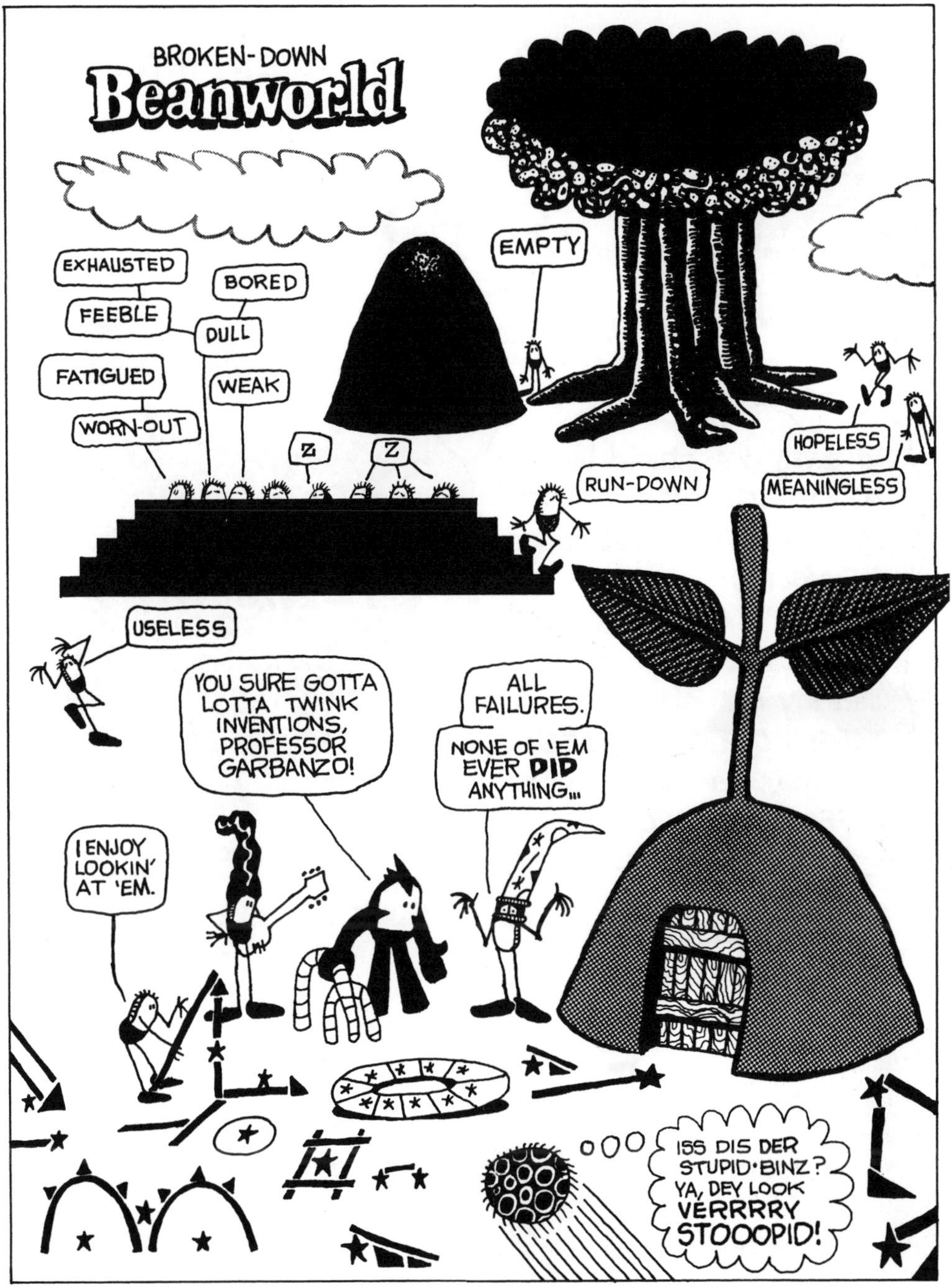
BROKEN-DOWN
Beanworld
EXHAUSTED
FEEBLE
BORED
DULL
FATIGUED
WEAK
WORN-OUT
Z
Z
EMPTY
RUN-DOWN
HOPELESS
MEANINGLESS
USELESS
YOU SURE GOTTA LOTTA TWINK INVENTIONS, PROFESSOR GARBANZO!
ALL FAILURES.
NONE OF 'EM EVER DID ANYTHING...
I ENJOY LOOKIN' AT 'EM.
ISS DIS DER STUPID·BINZ? YA, DEY LOOK VERRRRY STOOOPID!

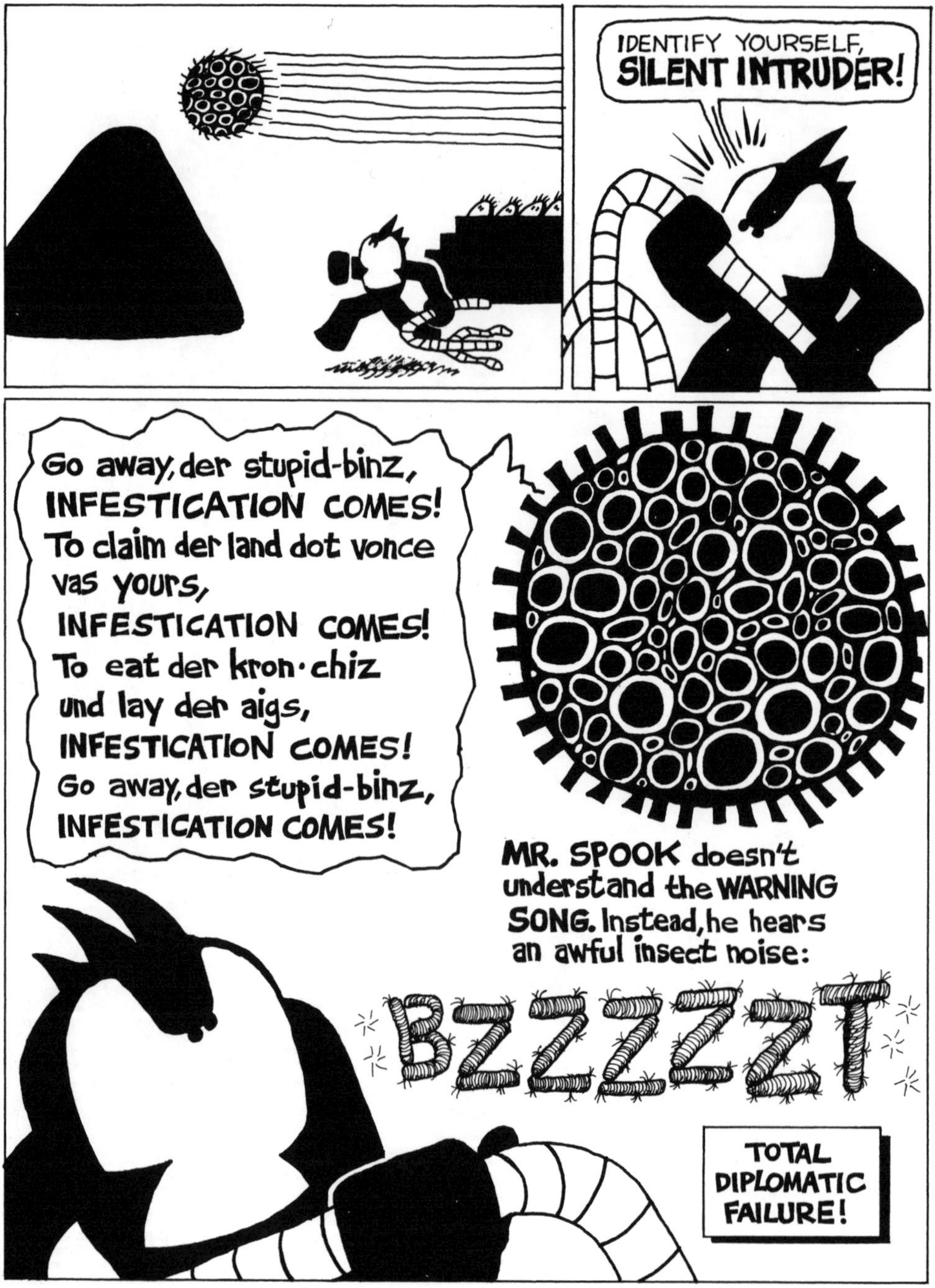
IDENTIFY YOURSELF, SILENT INTRUDER!
Go away, der stupid-binz, INFESTICATION COMES! To claim der land dot vonce vas yours, INFESTICATION COMES! To eat der kron·chiz und lay der aigs, INFESTICATION COMES! Go away, der stupid-binz, INFESTICATION COMES!
MR. SPOOK doesn't understand the WARNING SONG. Instead, he hears an awful insect noise:
BZZZZZT
TOTAL DIPLOMATIC FAILURE!

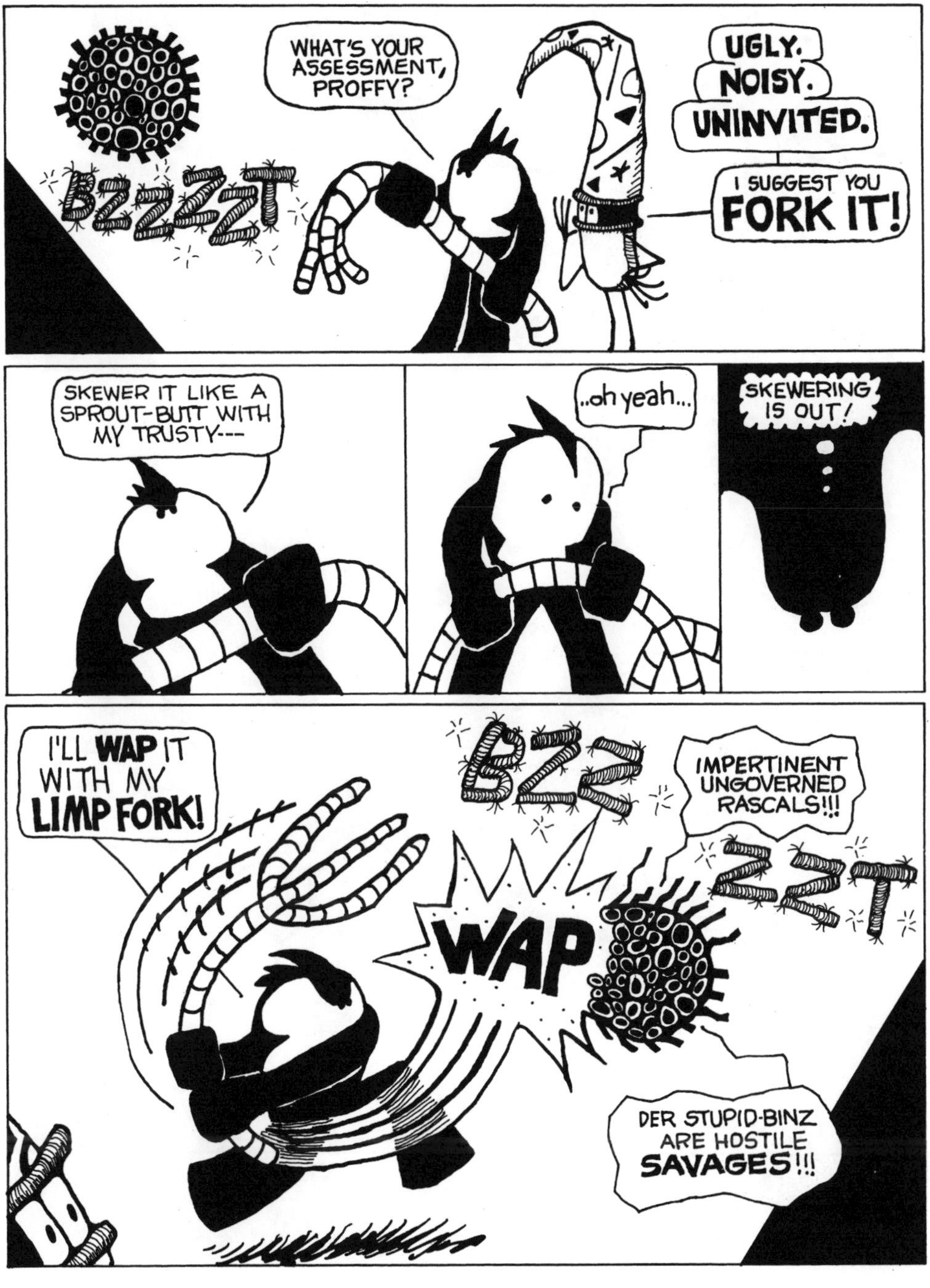

WHAT'S YOUR ASSESSMENT, PROFFY?
BZZZZT
UGLY.
NOISY.
UNINVITED.
I SUGGEST YOU FORK IT!
SKEWER IT LIKE A SPROUT-BUTT WITH MY TRUSTY---
..oh yeah...
SKEWERING IS OUT!
I'LL WAP IT WITH MY LIMP FORK!
BZZ
IMPERTINENT UNGOVERNED RASCALS!!!
ZZT
WAP
DER STUPID-BINZ ARE HOSTILE SAVAGES!!!

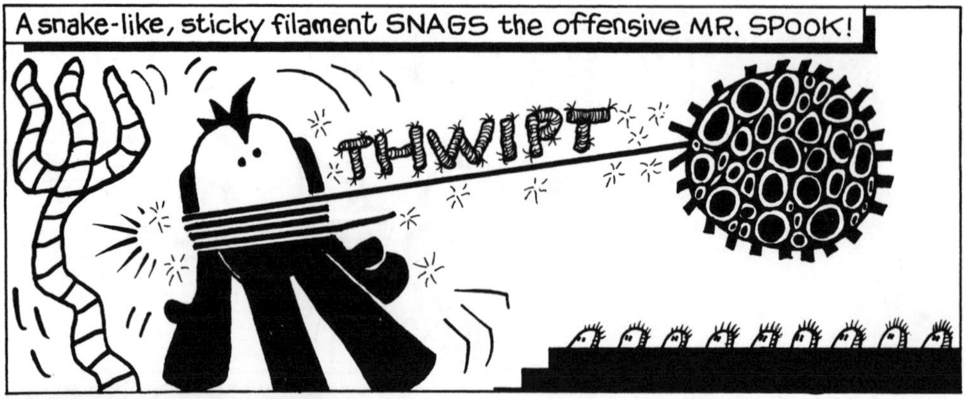
A snake-like, sticky filament SNAGS the offensive MR. SPOOK!
THWIPT

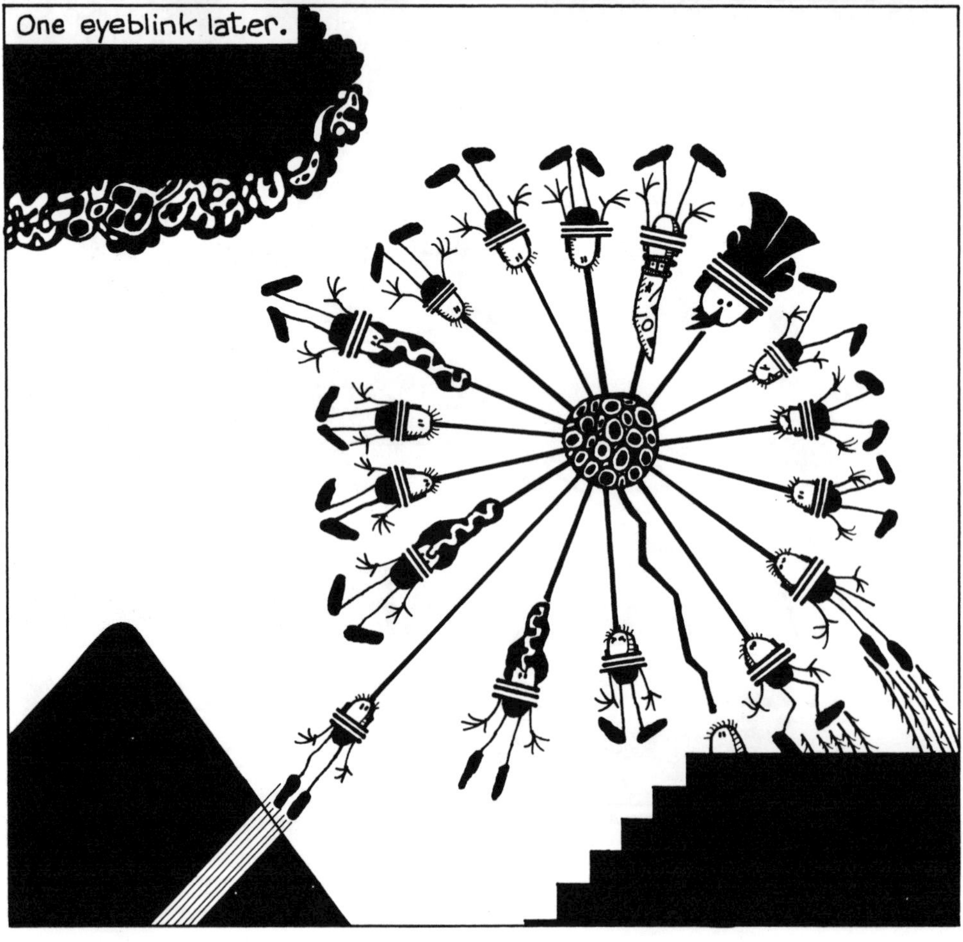
One eyeblink later.

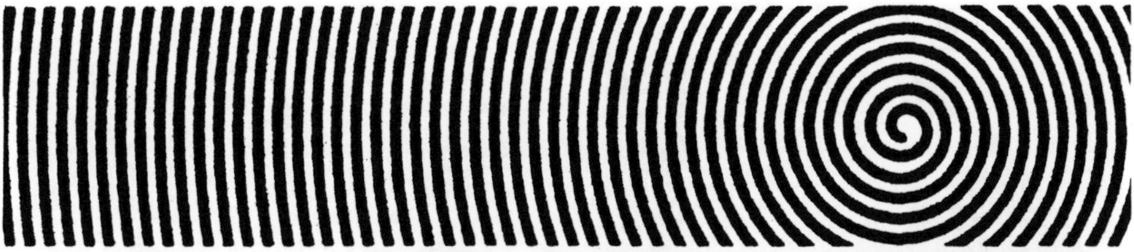

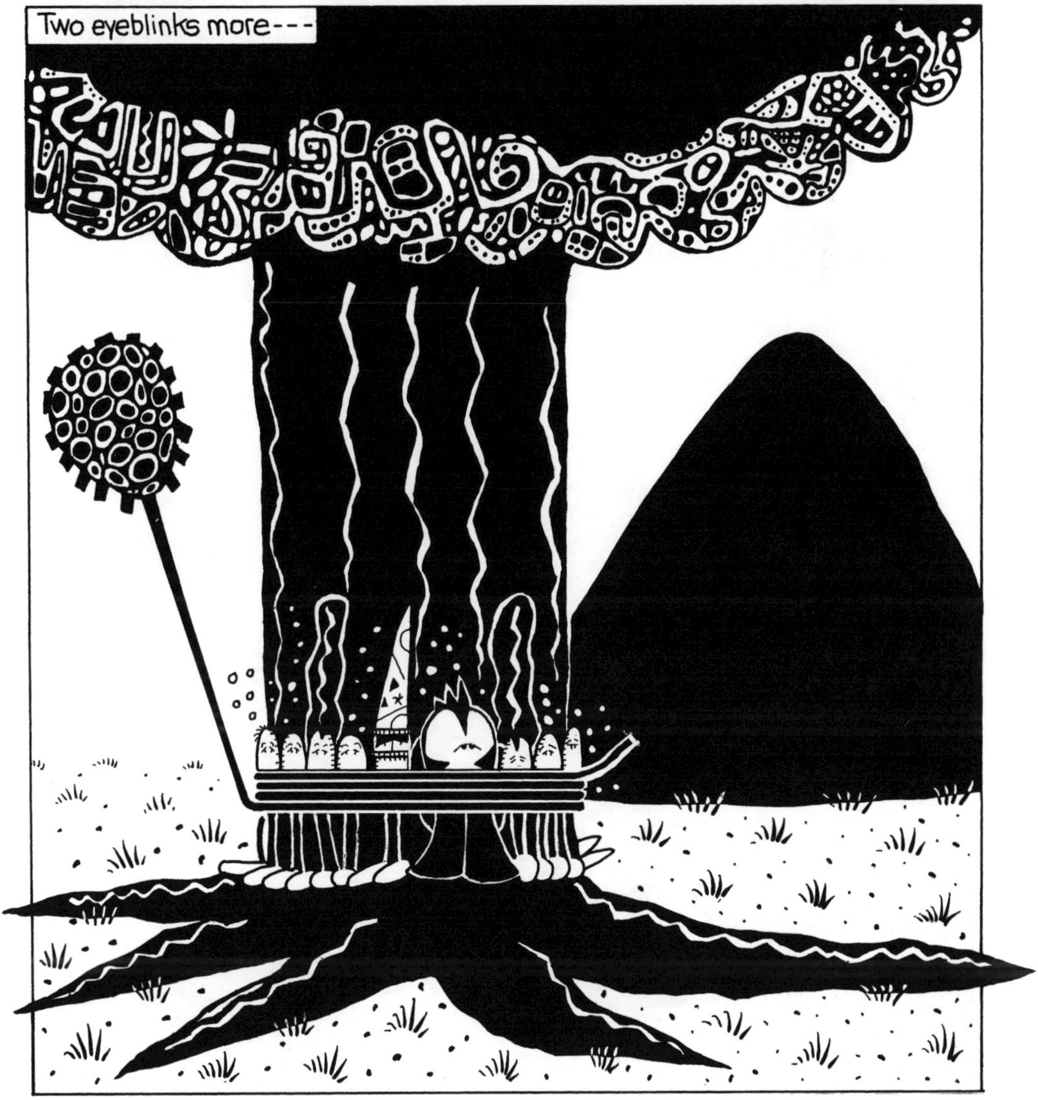
Two eyeblinks more---

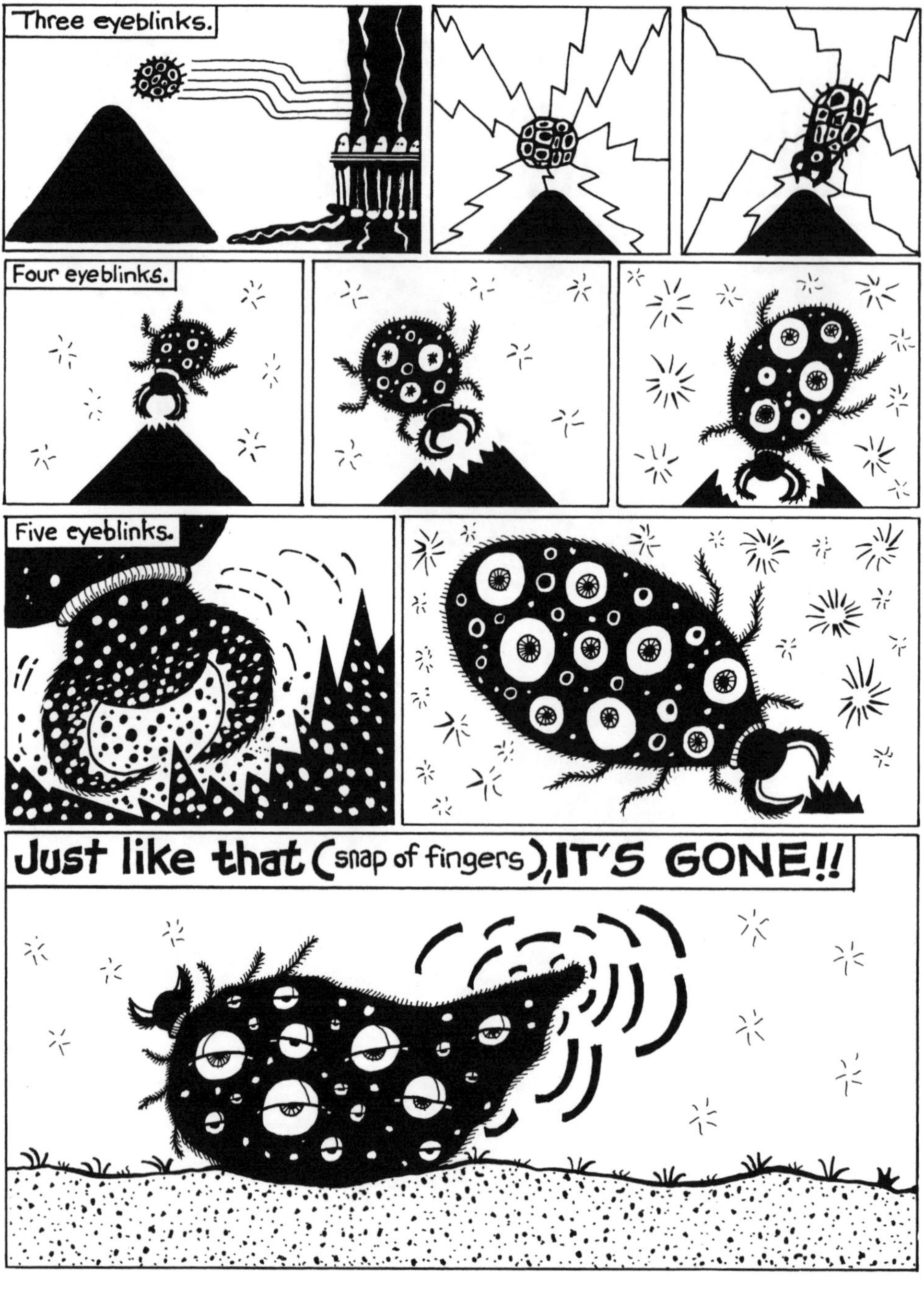
Three eyeblinks.
Four eyeblinks.
Five eyeblinks.
Just like that (snap of fingers), IT'S GONE!!

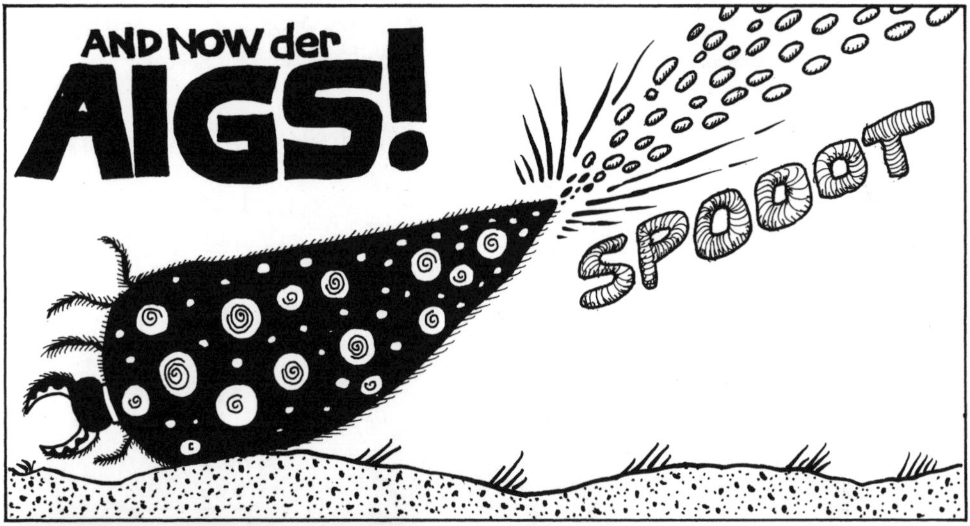
AND NOW der
AIGS!
SPOOOT

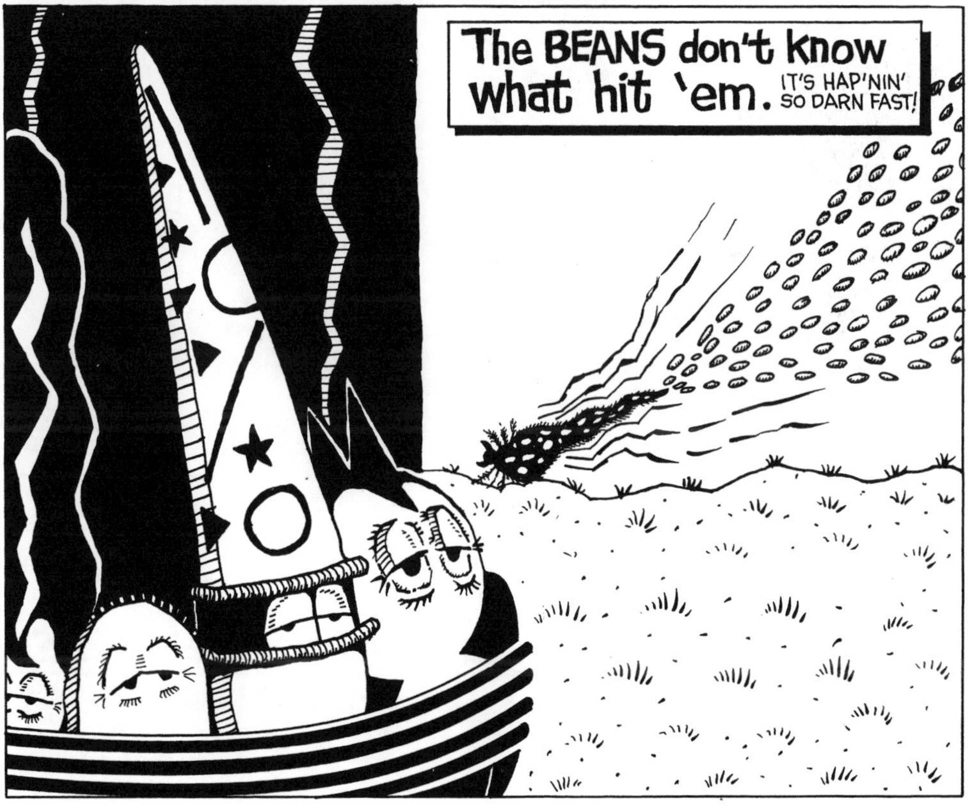
The BEANS don't know what hit 'em. IT'S HAP'NIN' SO DARN FAST!

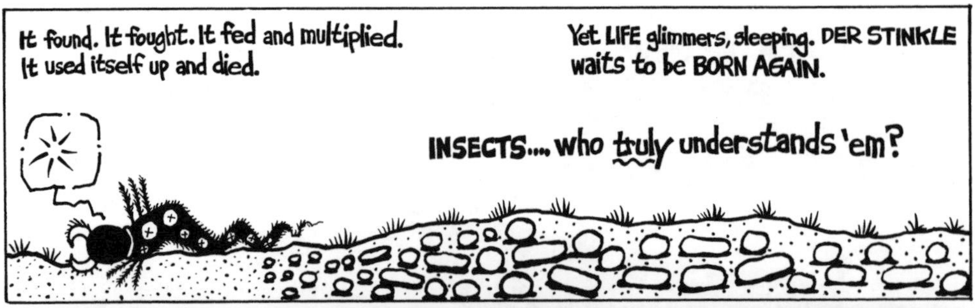
It found. It fought. It fed and multiplied. It used itself up and died.
Yet LIFE glimmers, sleeping. DER STINKLE waits to be BORN AGAIN.
INSECTS.... who truly understands 'em?

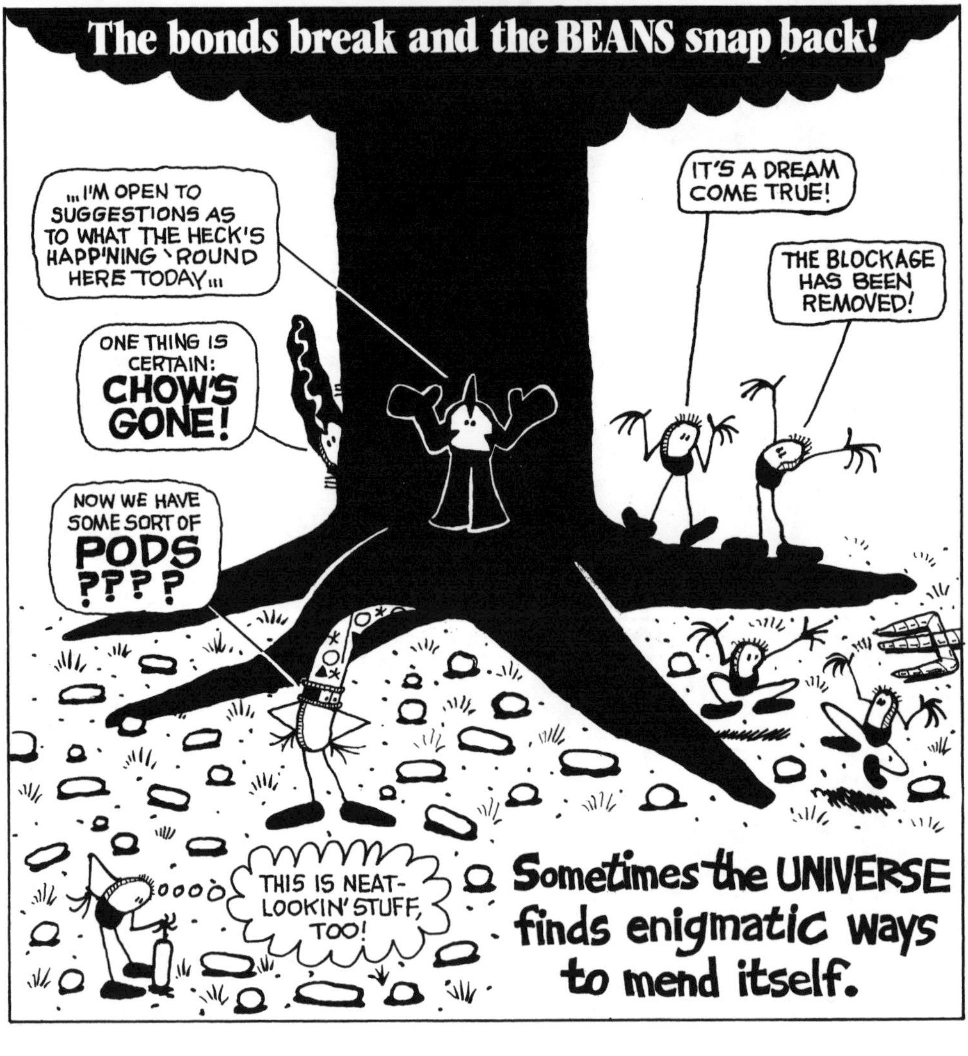
The bonds break and the BEANS snap back!
...I'M OPEN TO SUGGESTIONS AS TO WHAT THE HECK'S HAPP'NING 'ROUND HERE TODAY...
IT'S A DREAM COME TRUE!
THE BLOCKAGE HAS BEEN REMOVED!
ONE THING IS CERTAIN: CHOW'S GONE!
NOW WE HAVE SOME SORT OF PODS ????
THIS IS NEAT-LOOKIN' STUFF, TOO!
Sometimes the UNIVERSE finds enigmatic ways to mend itself.

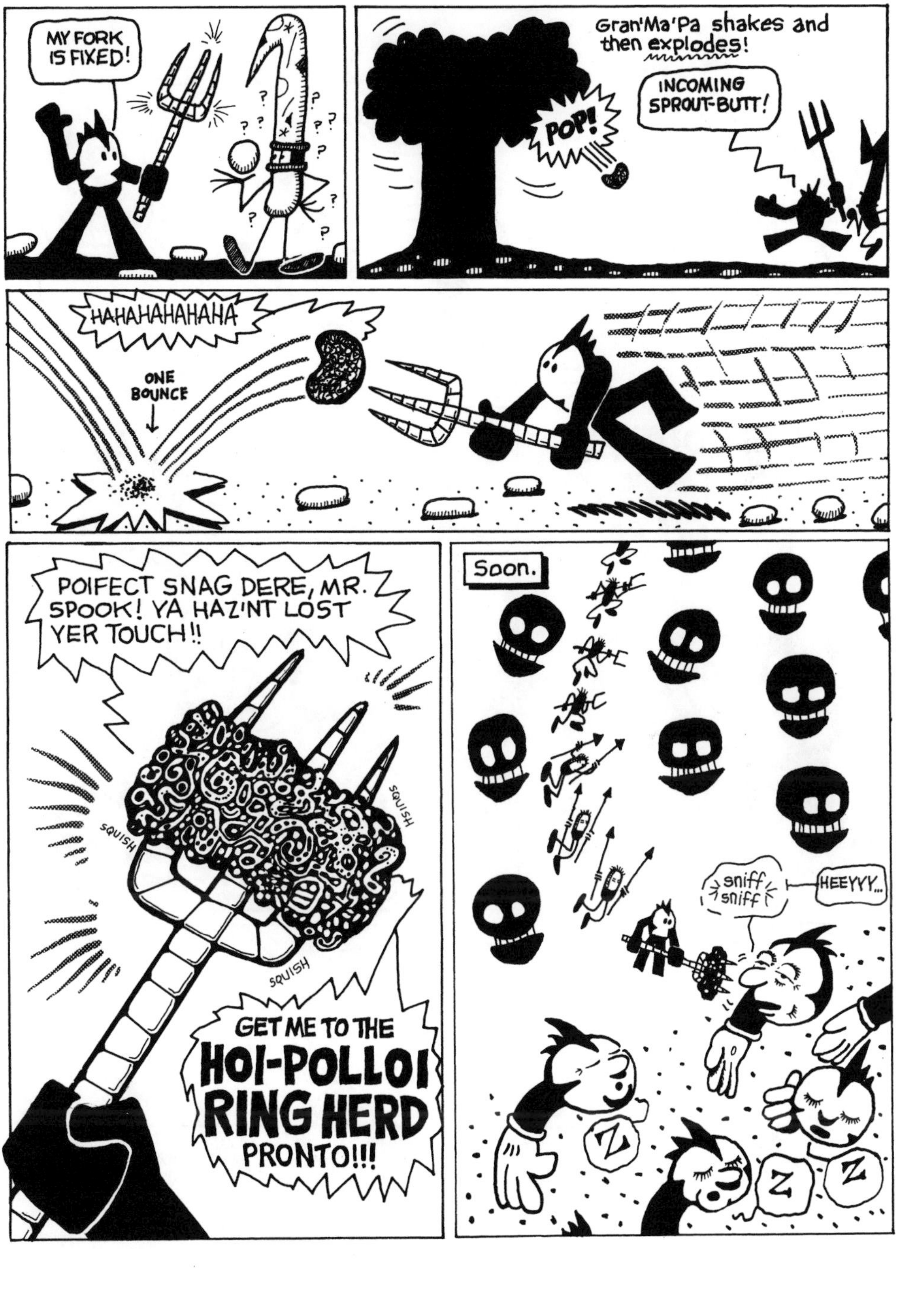

MY FORK IS FIXED!
Gran'Ma'Pa shakes and then explodes!
POP!
INCOMING SPROUT-BUTT!
HAHAHAHAHAHA
ONE BOUNCE
POIFECT SNAG DERE, MR. SPOOK! YA HAZ'NT LOST YER TOUCH!!
SQUISH
SQUISH
SQUISH
GET ME TO THE HOI-POLLOI RING HERD PRONTO!!!
Soon.
sniff sniff
HEEYYY...
Z
Z
Z

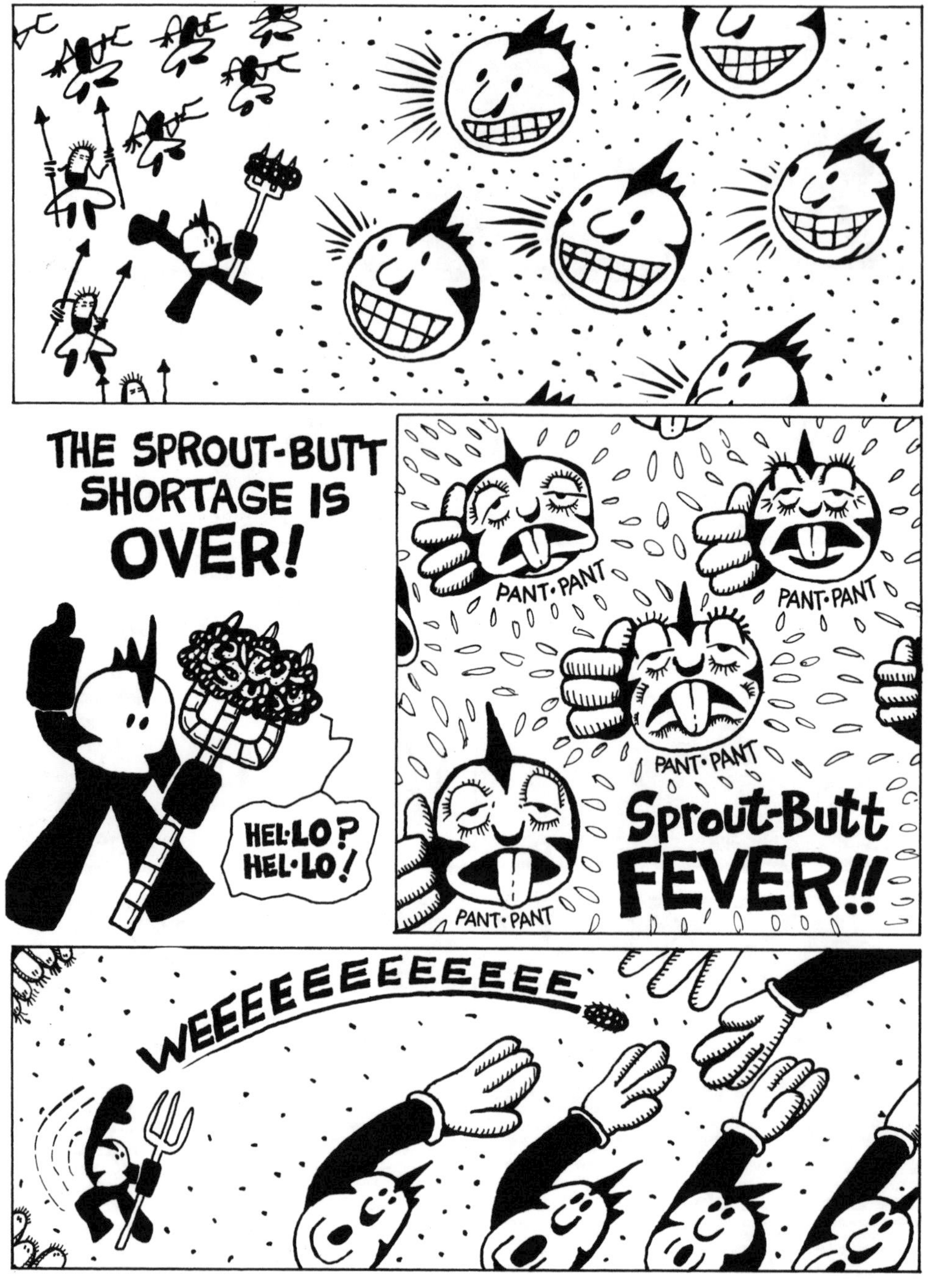
THE SPROUT-BUTT SHORTAGE IS OVER!
HEL·LO? HEL·LO!
PANT·PANT
PANT·PANT
PANT·PANT
PANT·PANT
Sprout-Butt FEVER!!
WEEEEEEEEEEEE

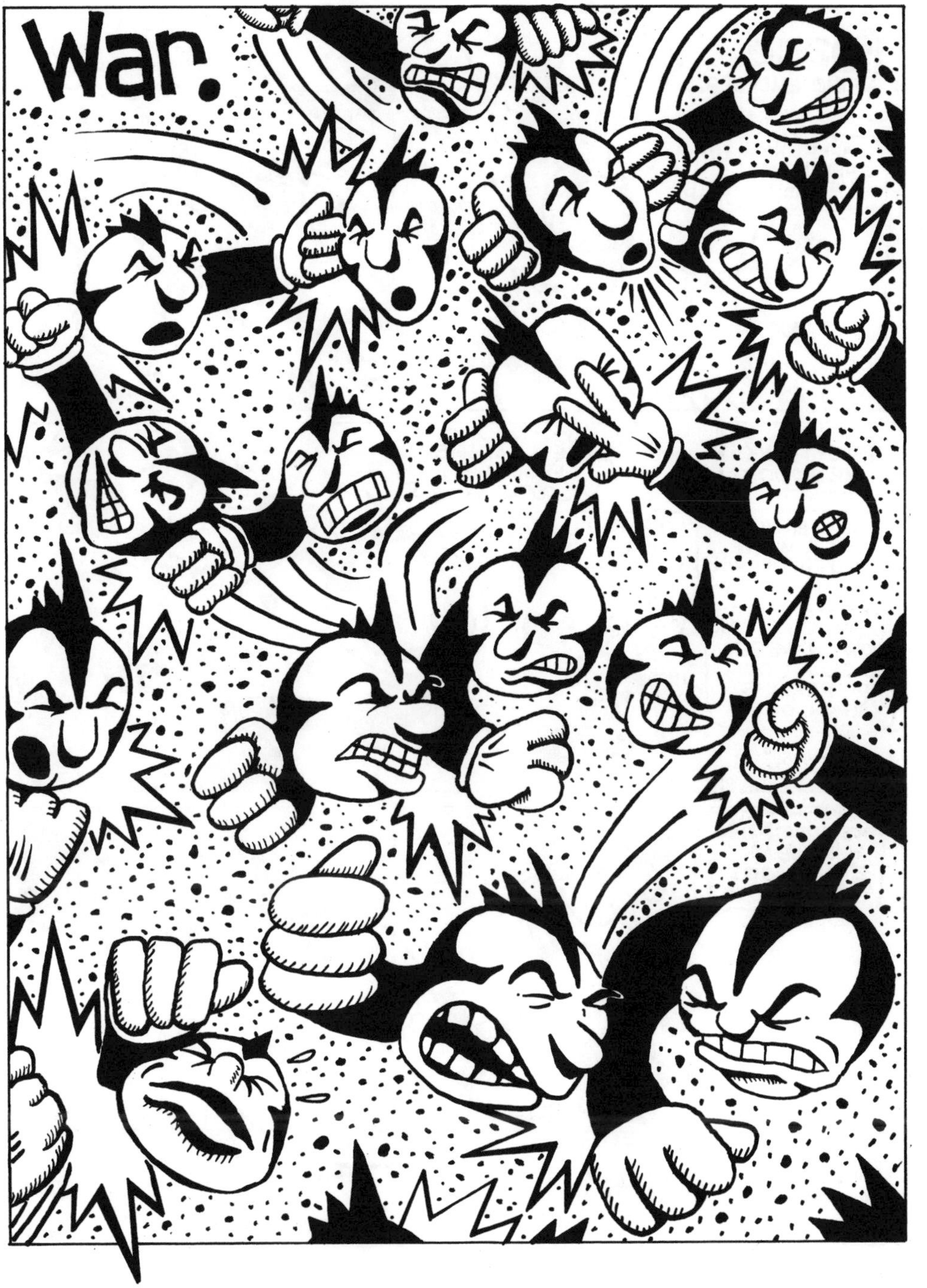
War.

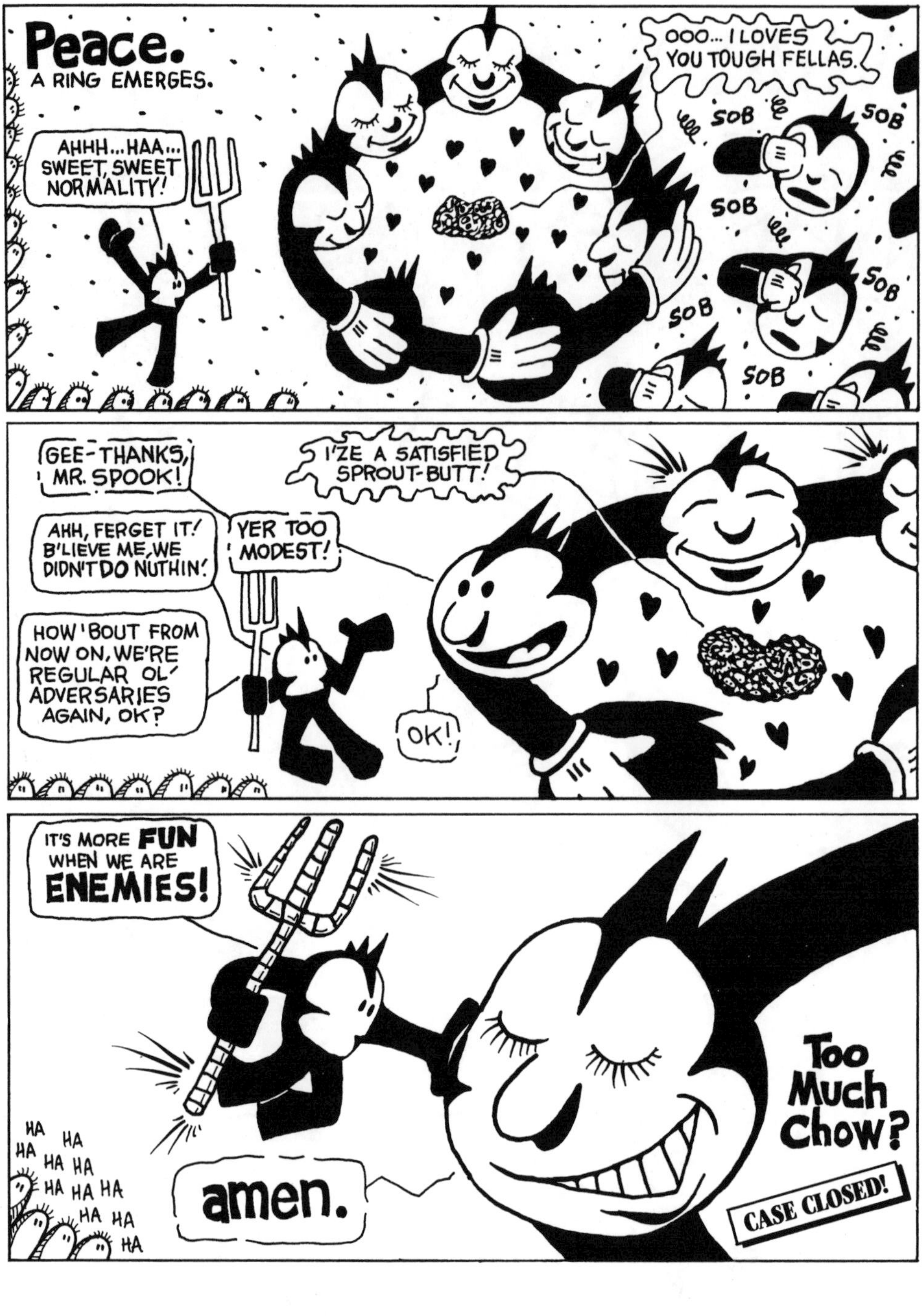
Peace.
A RING EMERGES.
AHHH...HAA... SWEET, SWEET NORMALITY!
OOO... I LOVES YOU TOUGH FELLAS.
SOB SOB SOB SOB SOB SOB
GEE-THANKS, MR. SPOOK!
I'ZE A SATISFIED SPROUT-BUTT!
AHH, FERGET IT! B'LIEVE ME, WE DIDN'T DO NUTHIN'.
YER TOO MODEST!
HOW 'BOUT FROM NOW ON, WE'RE REGULAR OL' ADVERSARIES AGAIN, OK?
OK!
IT'S MORE FUN WHEN WE ARE ENEMIES!
HA HA HA HA HA HA HA HA HA HA HA HA
amen.
Too Much Chow?
CASE CLOSED!

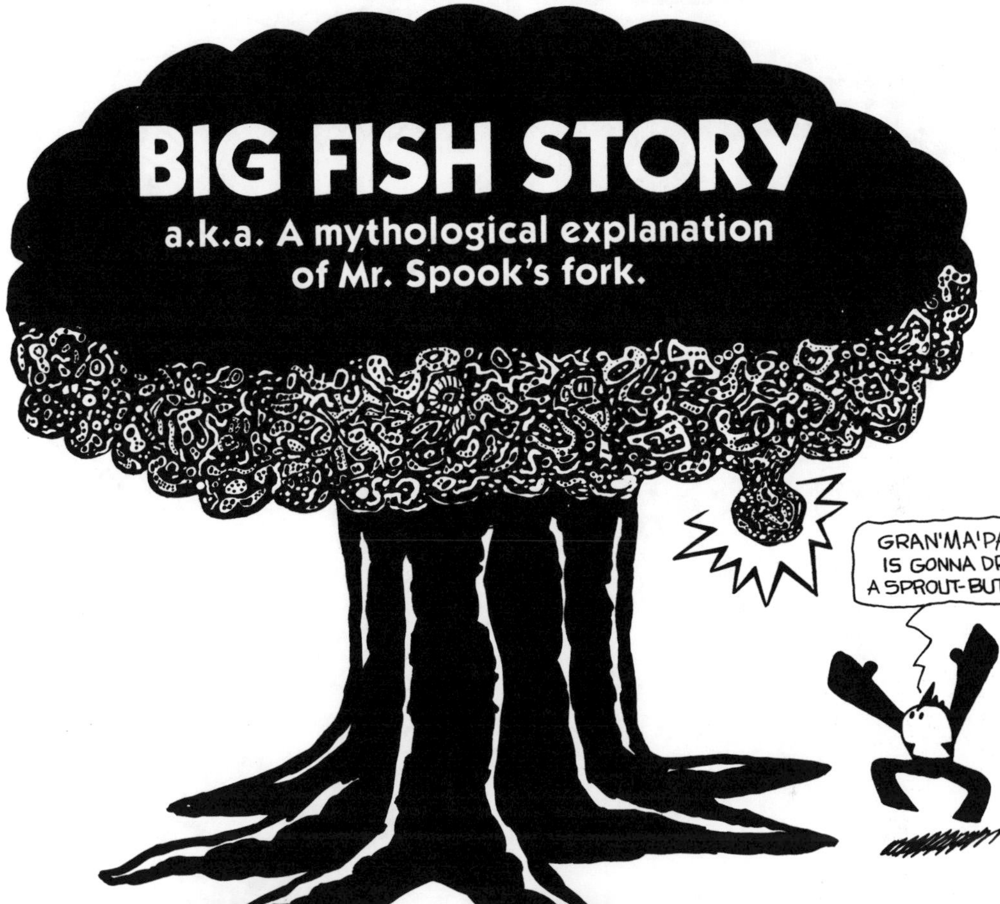
BIG FISH STORY
a.k.a. A mythological explanation of Mr. Spook's fork.
GRAN'MA'PA IS GONNA DROP A SPROUT-BUTT!

In the olden days, it was **hard** to catch a **SPROUT-BUTT**.

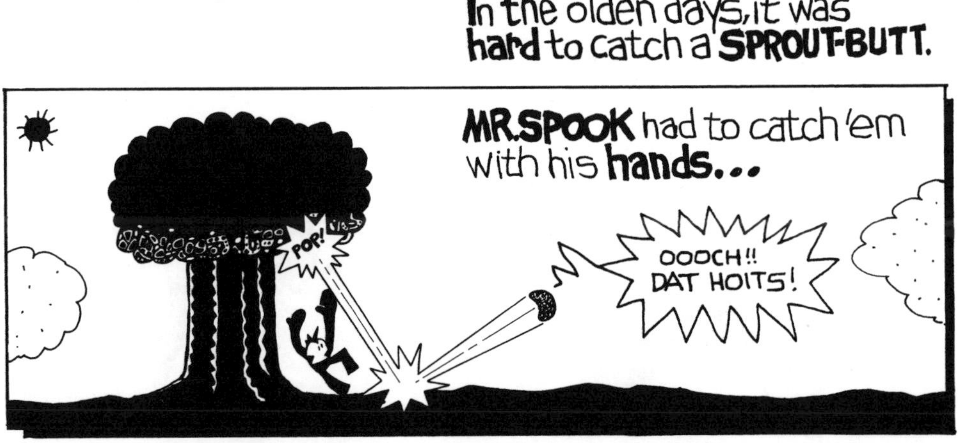
MR.SPOOK had to catch 'em with his hands...
POP!
OOOCH!! DAT HOITS!

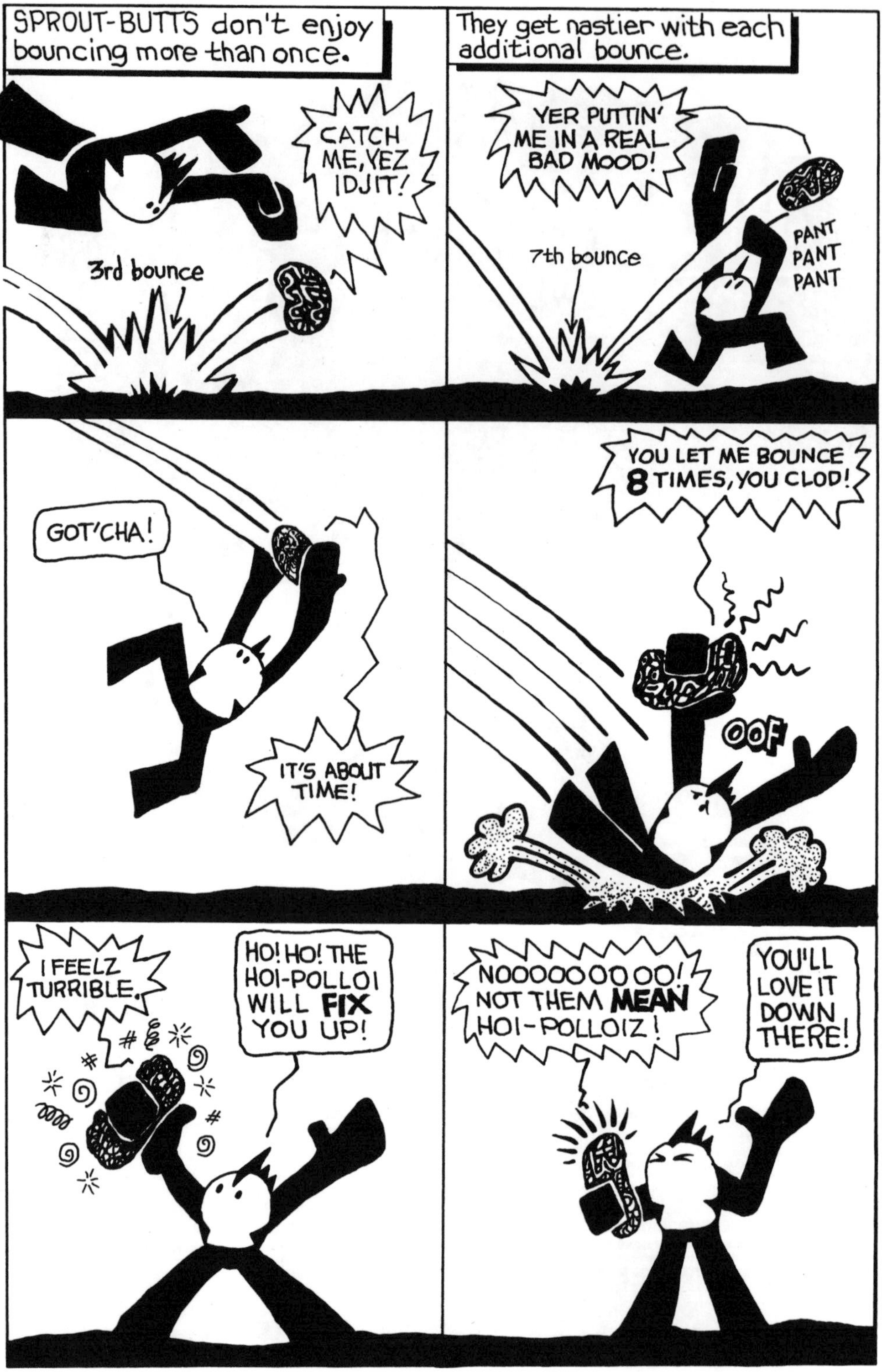
SPROUT-BUTTS don't enjoy bouncing more than once.
CATCH ME, YEZ IDJIT!
3rd bounce
They get nastier with each additional bounce.
YER PUTTIN' ME IN A REAL BAD MOOD!
7th bounce
PANT PANT PANT
GOT'CHA!
IT'S ABOUT TIME!
YOU LET ME BOUNCE 8 TIMES, YOU CLOD!
OOF
I FEELZ TURRIBLE.
HO! HO! THE HOI-POLLOI WILL FIX YOU UP!
NOOOOOOOOOO! NOT THEM MEAN HOI-POLLOIZ!
YOU'LL LOVE IT DOWN THERE!

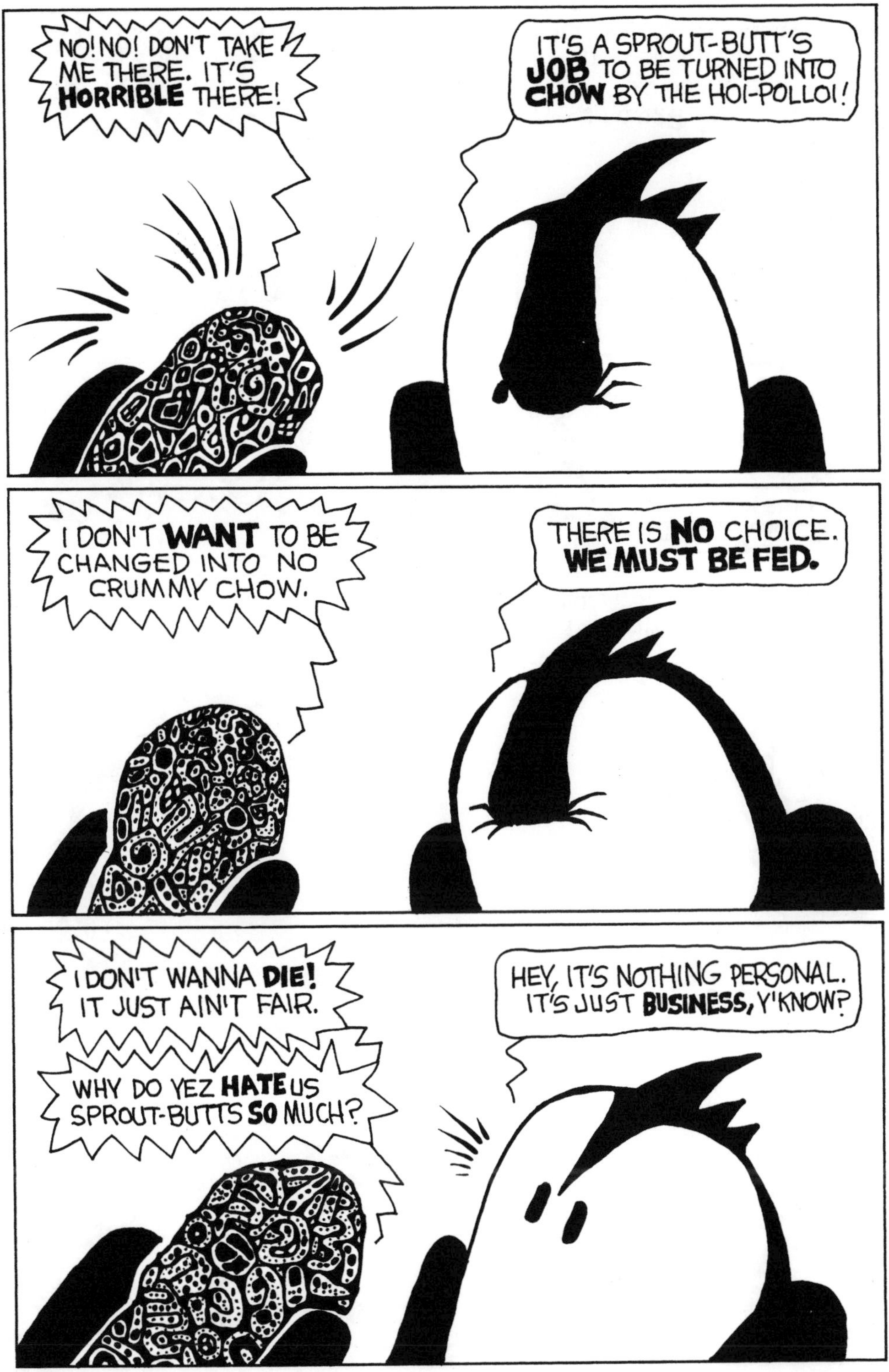
NO! NO! DON'T TAKE ME THERE. IT'S HORRIBLE THERE!
IT'S A SPROUT-BUTT'S JOB TO BE TURNED INTO CHOW BY THE HOI-POLLOI!
I DON'T WANT TO BE CHANGED INTO NO CRUMMY CHOW.
THERE IS NO CHOICE. WE MUST BE FED.
I DON'T WANNA DIE! IT JUST AIN'T FAIR.
WHY DO YEZ HATE US SPROUT-BUTTS SO MUCH?
HEY, IT'S NOTHING PERSONAL. IT'S JUST BUSINESS, Y'KNOW?

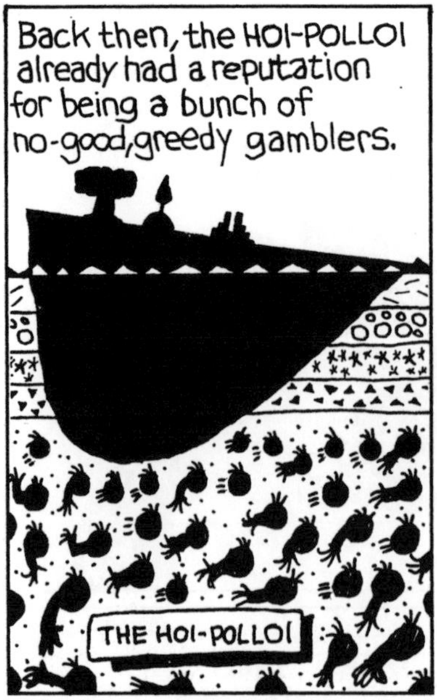
Back then, the HOI-POLLOI already had a reputation for being a bunch of no-good, greedy gamblers.
THE HOI-POLLOI

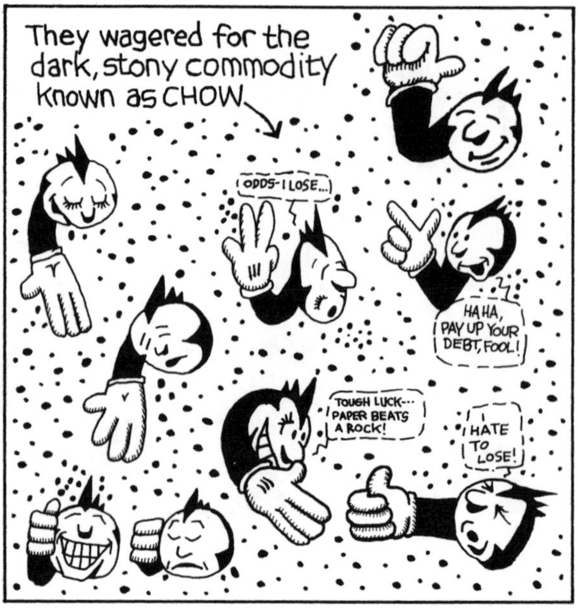
They wagered for the dark, stony commodity known as CHOW
ODDS-I LOSE...
HA HA, PAY UP YOUR DEBT, FOOL!
TOUGH LUCK--- PAPER BEATS A ROCK!
I HATE TO LOSE!

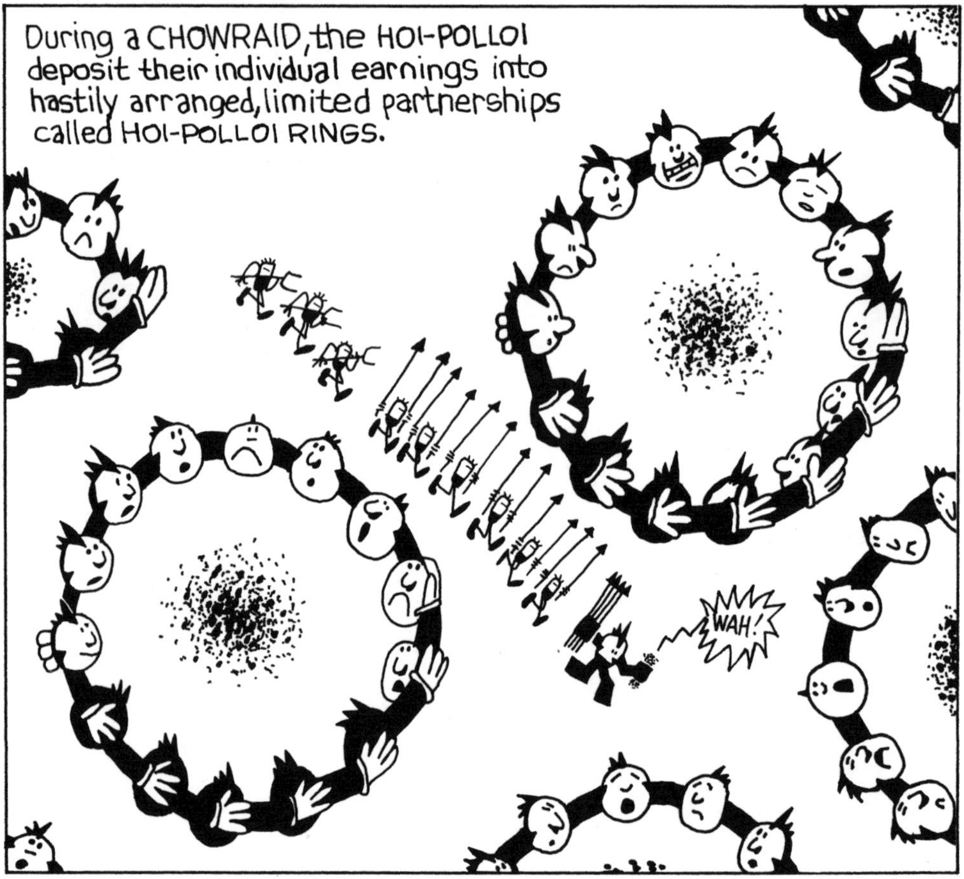
During a CHOWRAID, the HOI-POLLOI deposit their individual earnings into hastily arranged, limited partnerships called HOI-POLLOI RINGS.
WAH!

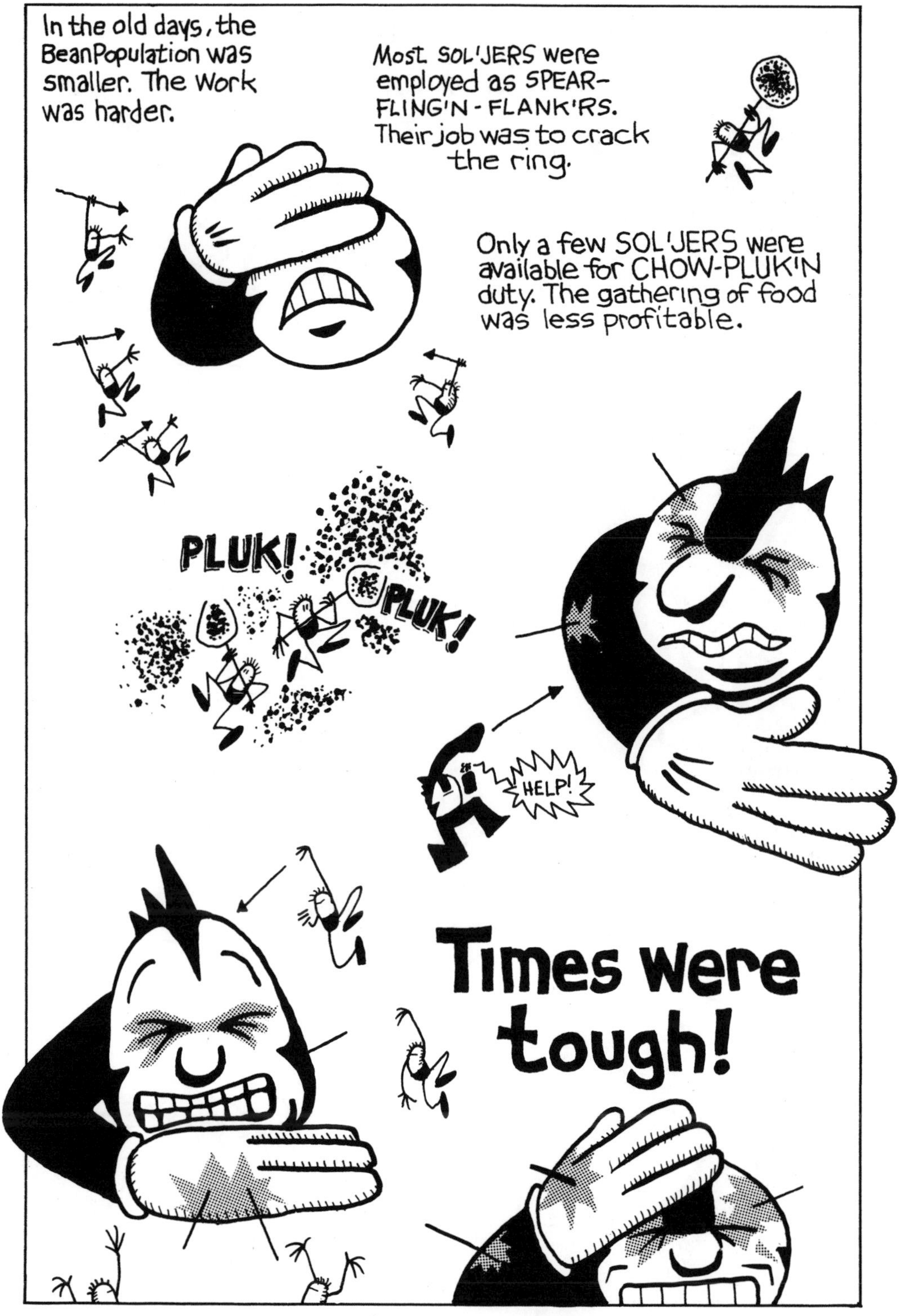
In the old days, the BeanPopulation was smaller. The Work was harder.
Most SOL'JERS were employed as SPEAR-FLING'N-FLANK'RS. Their job was to crack the ring.
Only a few SOL'JERS were available for CHOW-PLUK'N duty. The gathering of food was less profitable.
PLUK!
PLUK!
HELP!
Times were tough!

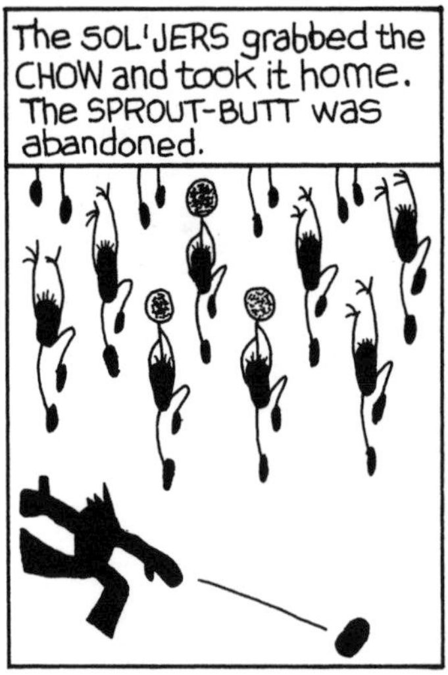
The SOL'JERS grabbed the CHOW and took it home. The SPROUT-BUTT was abandoned.

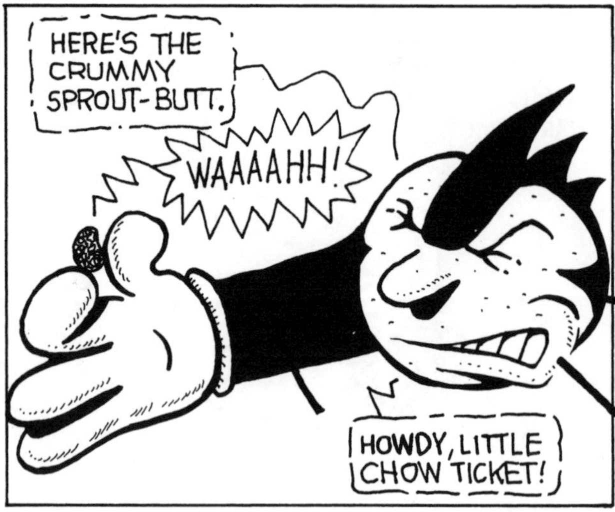
HERE'S THE CRUMMY SPROUT-BUTT.
WAAAAHH!
HOWDY, LITTLE CHOW TICKET!

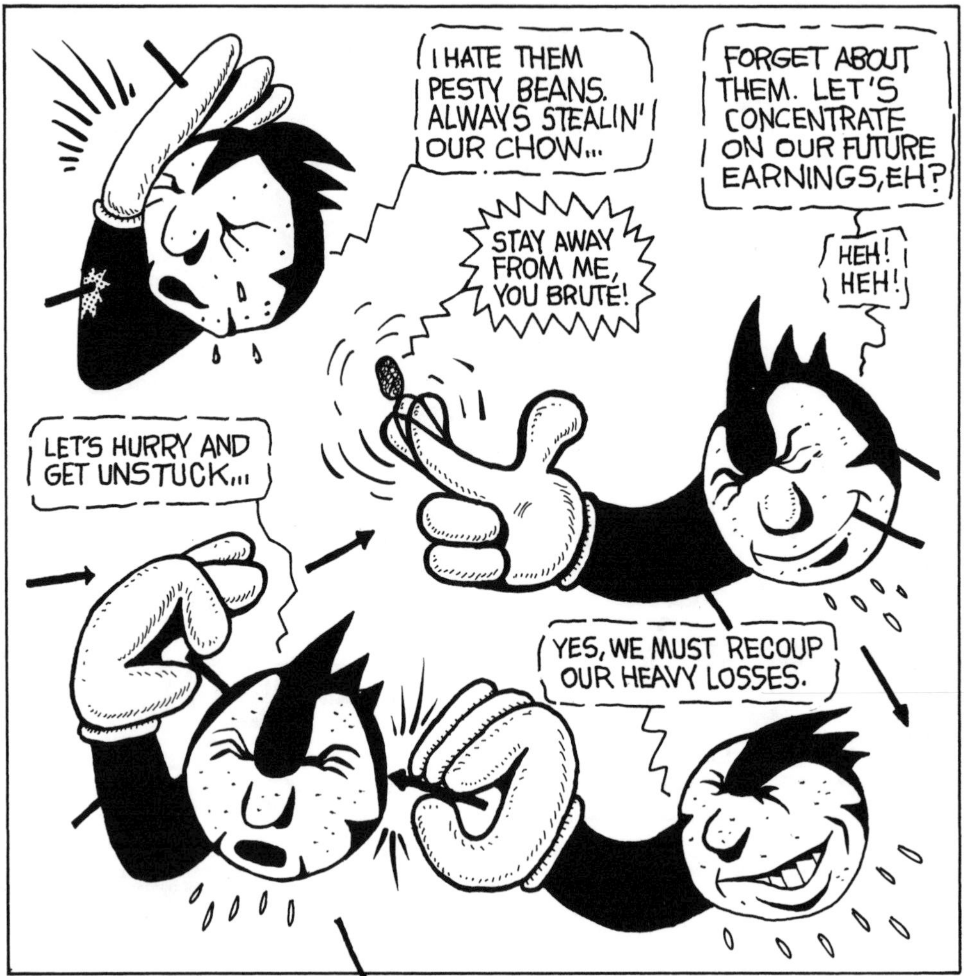
I HATE THEM PESTY BEANS. ALWAYS STEALIN' OUR CHOW...
FORGET ABOUT THEM. LET'S CONCENTRATE ON OUR FUTURE EARNINGS, EH?
STAY AWAY FROM ME, YOU BRUTE!
HEH! HEH!
LET'S HURRY AND GET UNSTUCK...
YES, WE MUST RECOUP OUR HEAVY LOSSES.

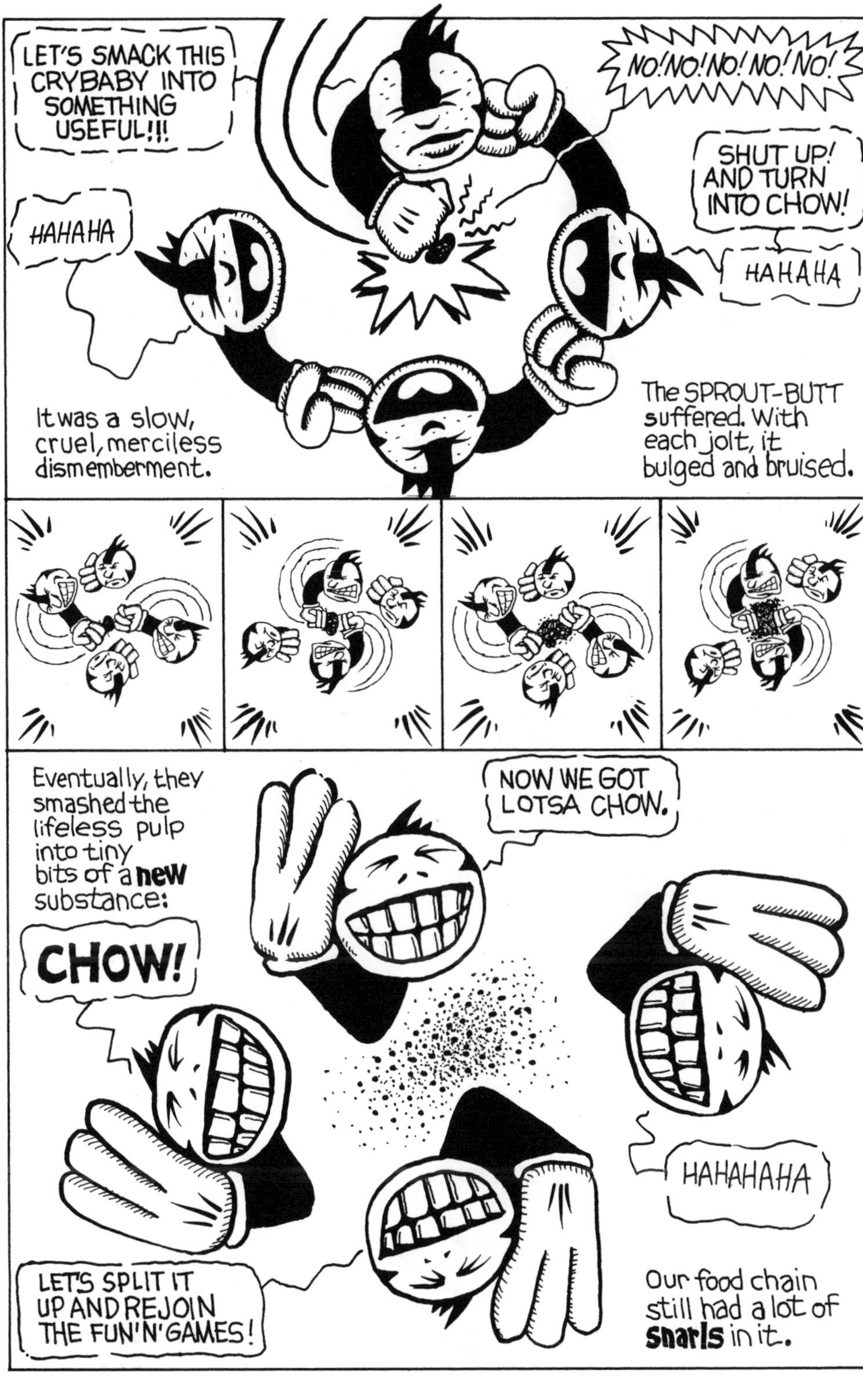
LET'S SMACK THIS CRYBABY INTO SOMETHING USEFUL!!!
NO! NO! NO! NO! NO!
SHUT UP! AND TURN INTO CHOW!
HAHAHA
HAHAHA
It was a slow, cruel, merciless dismemberment.
The SPROUT-BUTT suffered. With each jolt, it bulged and bruised.
Eventually, they smashed the lifeless pulp into tiny bits of a new substance:
CHOW!
NOW WE GOT LOTSA CHOW.
HAHAHAHA
LET'S SPLIT IT UP AND REJOIN THE FUN'N'GAMES!
Our food chain still had a lot of snarls in it.

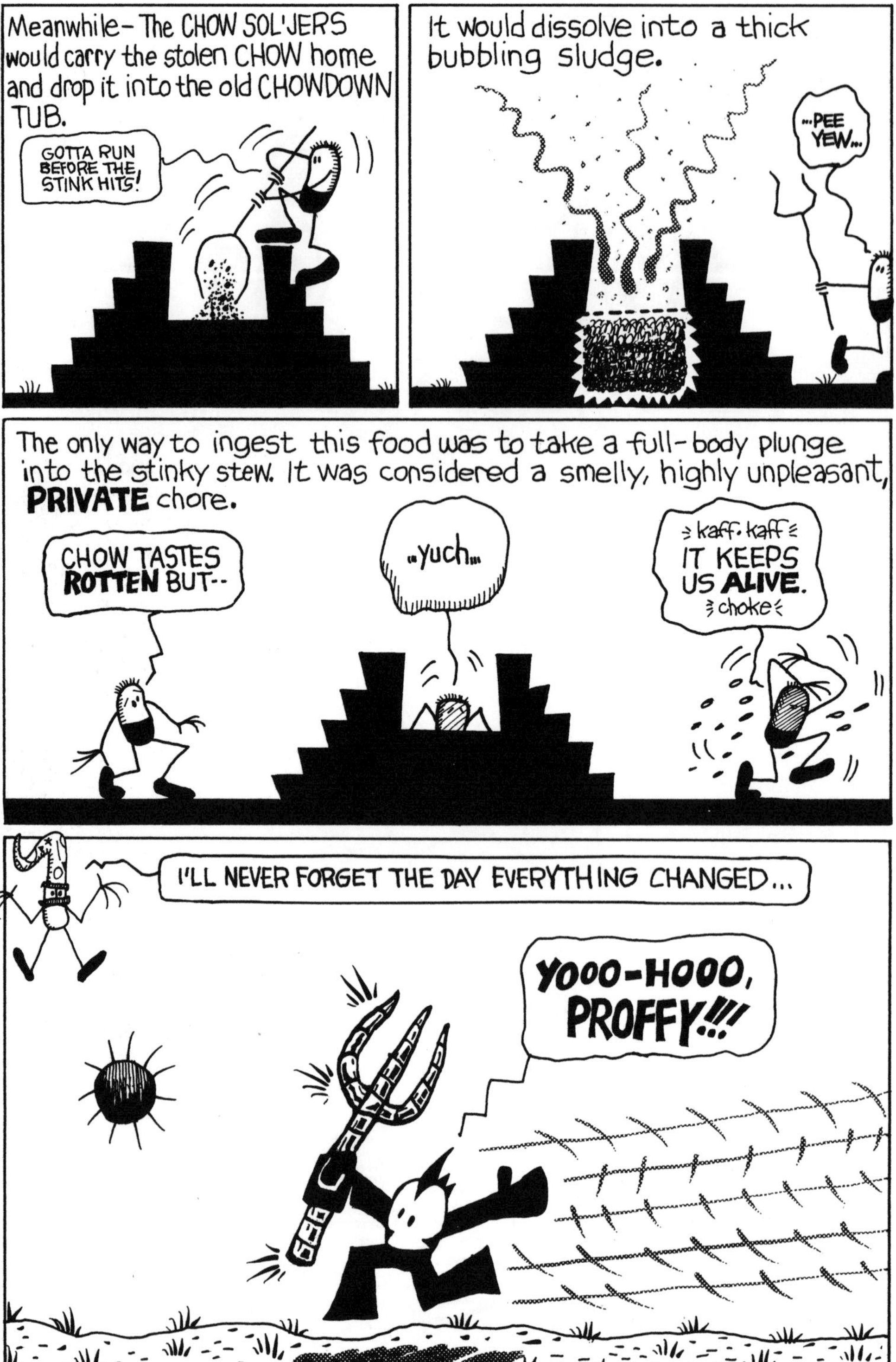
Meanwhile- The CHOW SOL'JERS would carry the stolen CHOW home and drop it into the old CHOWDOWN TUB.
GOTTA RUN BEFORE THE STINK HITS!
It would dissolve into a thick bubbling sludge.
...PEE YEW...
The only way to ingest this food was to take a full-body plunge into the stinky stew. It was considered a smelly, highly unpleasant, PRIVATE chore.
CHOW TASTES ROTTEN BUT--
...yuch...
kaff. kaff IT KEEPS US ALIVE. choke
I'LL NEVER FORGET THE DAY EVERYTHING CHANGED...
YOOO-HOOO, PROFFY!!!

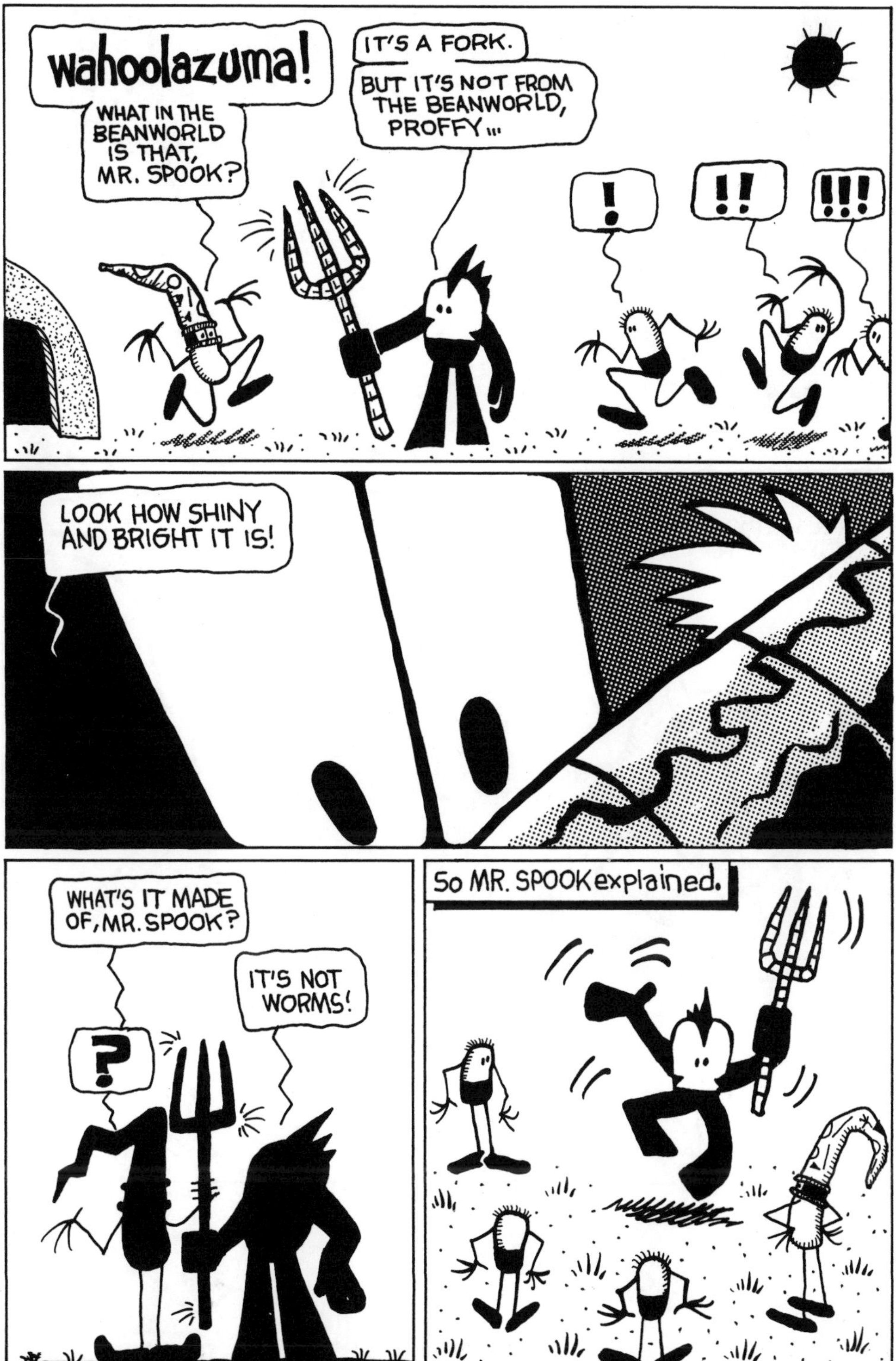
wahoolazuma!
WHAT IN THE BEANWORLD IS THAT, MR. SPOOK?
IT'S A FORK.
BUT IT'S NOT FROM THE BEANWORLD, PROFFY...
!
!!
!!!
LOOK HOW SHINY AND BRIGHT IT IS!
WHAT'S IT MADE OF, MR. SPOOK?
?
IT'S NOT WORMS!
So MR. SPOOK explained.

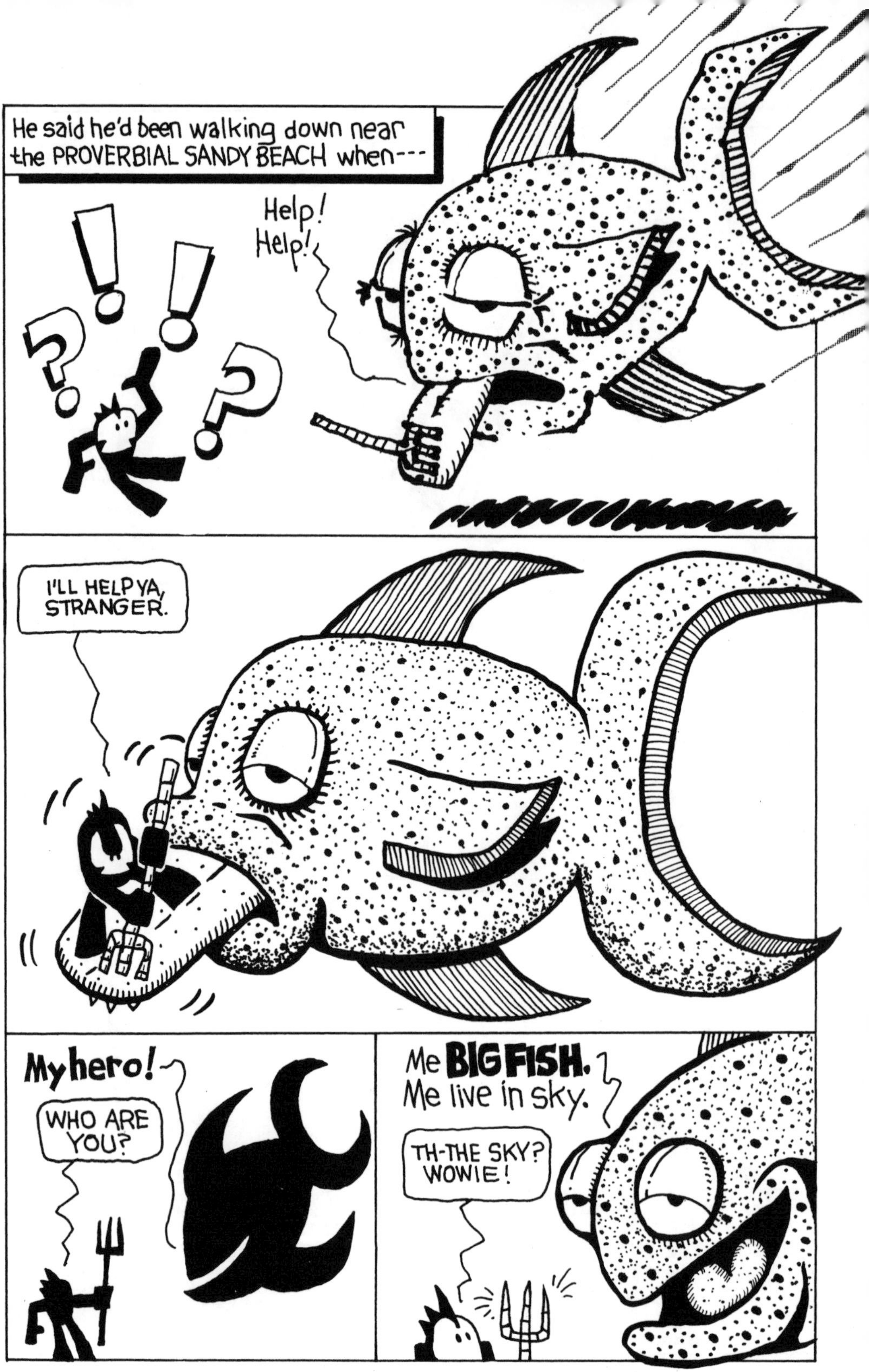
He said he'd been walking down near the PROVERBIAL SANDY BEACH when---
Help! Help!
I'LL HELP YA, STRANGER.
My hero!
WHO ARE YOU?
Me BIG FISH. Me live in sky.
TH-THE SKY? WOWIE!

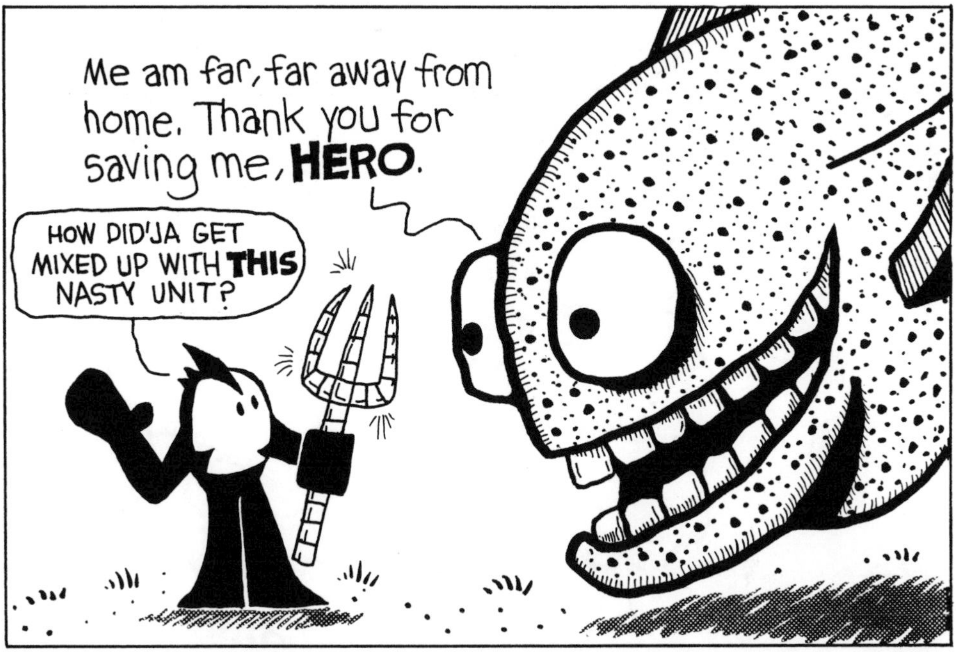
Me am far, far away from home. Thank you for saving me, **HERO**.
HOW DID'JA GET MIXED UP WITH **THIS** NASTY UNIT?

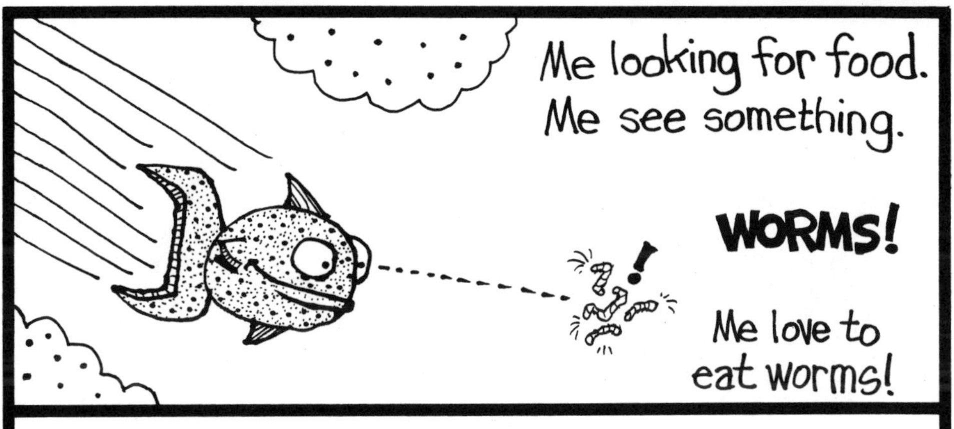
Me looking for food. Me see something.
**WORMS!**
Me love to eat worms!

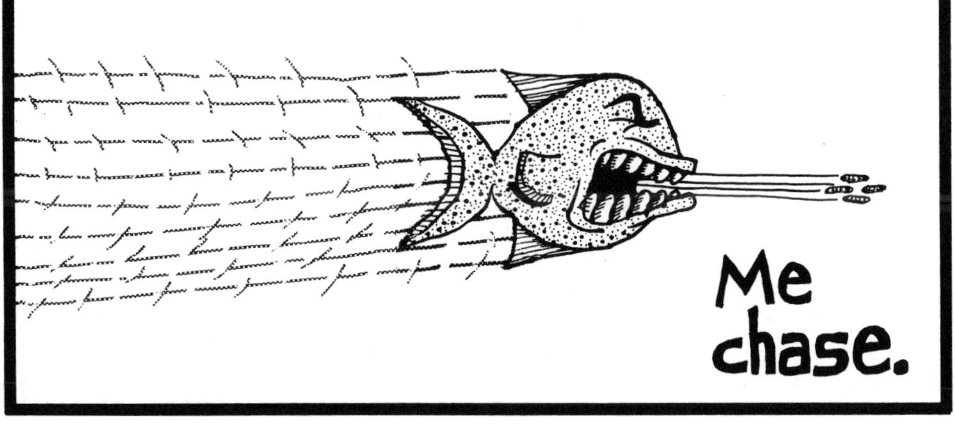
Me chase.

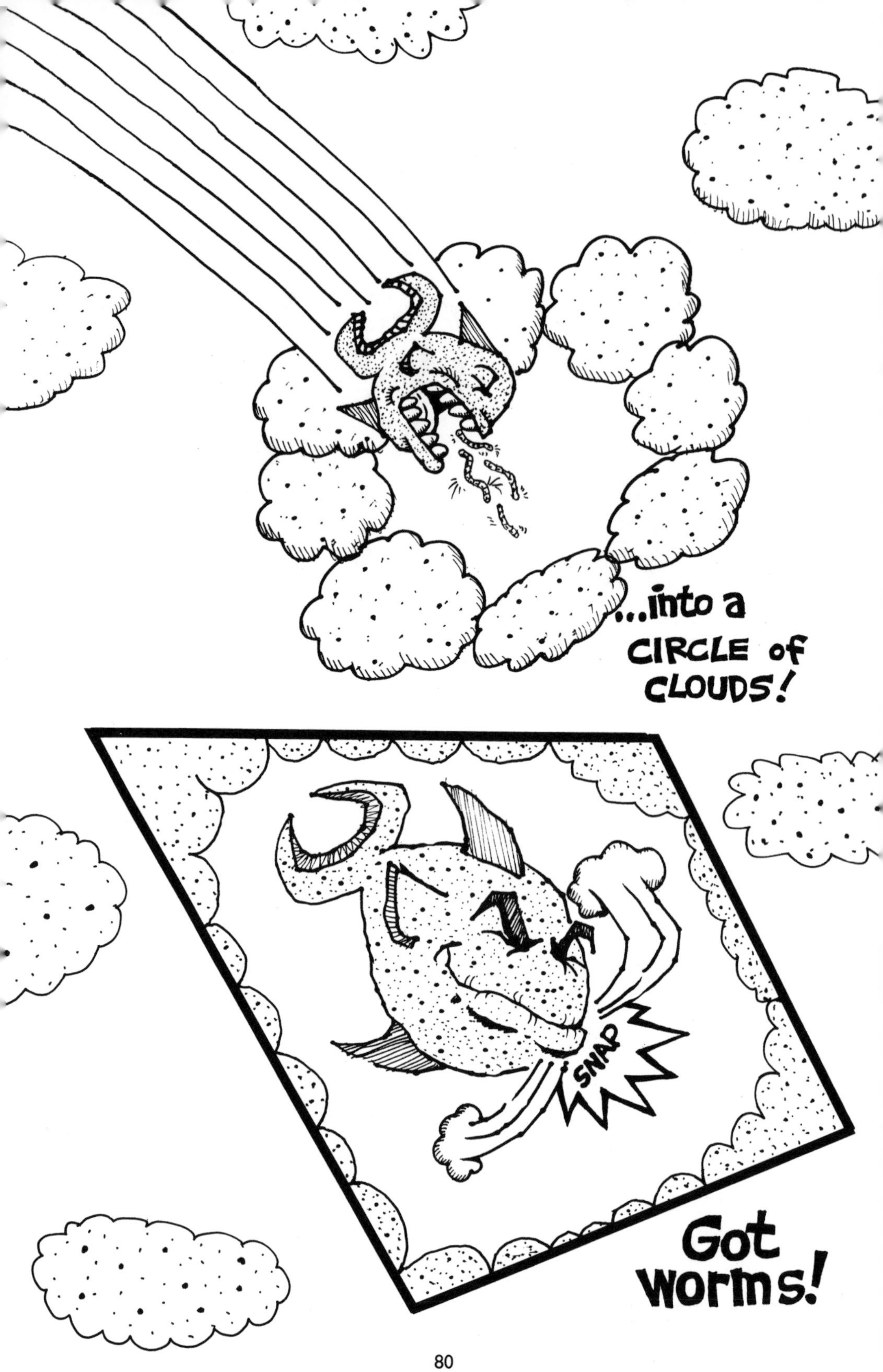
...into a CIRCLE of CLOUDS!
SNAP
Got worms!

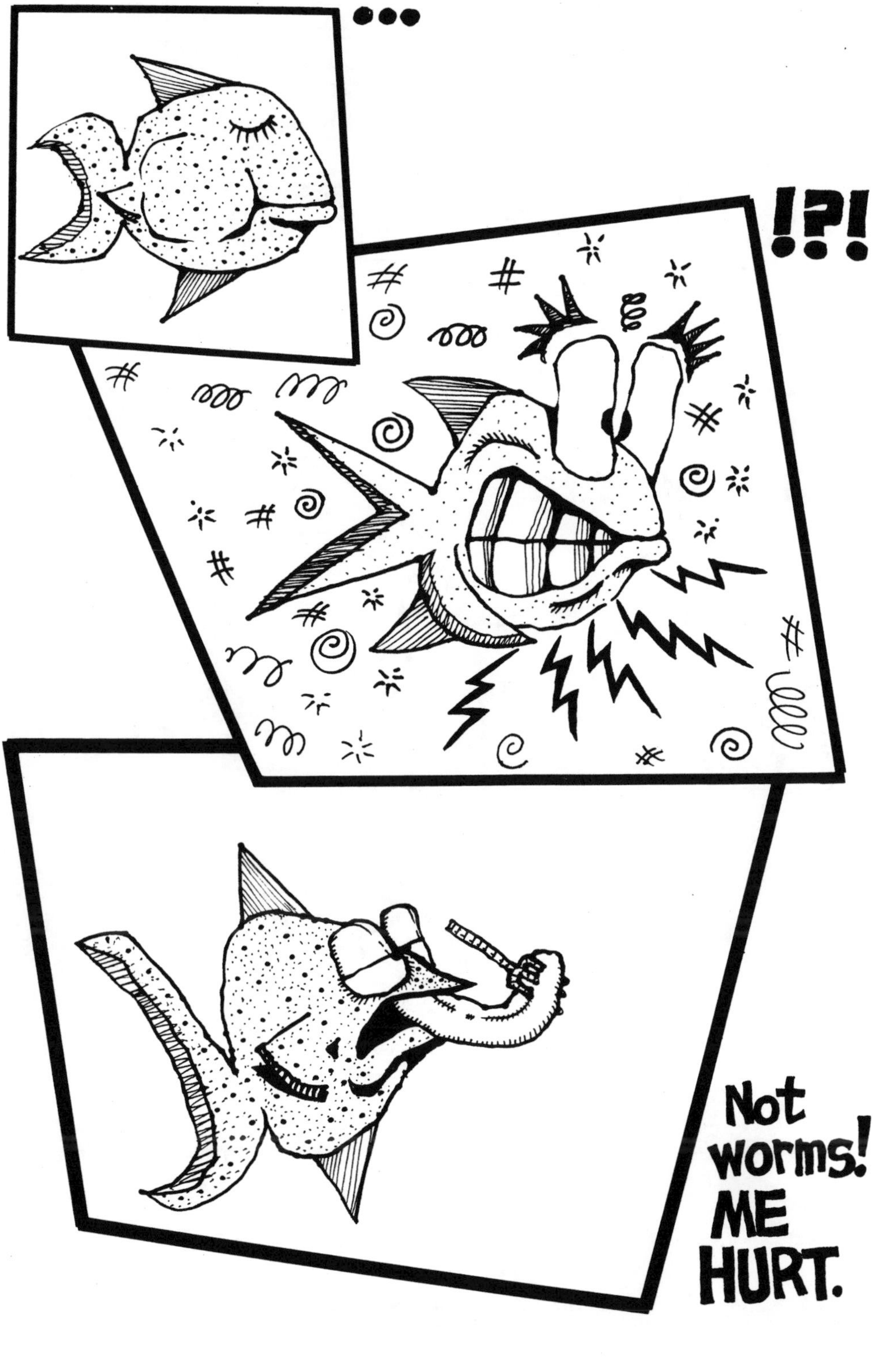
...
!?!
Not worms! ME HURT.

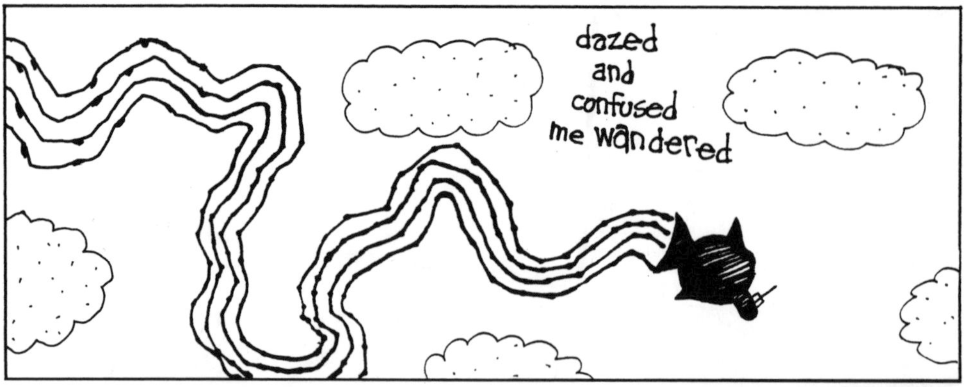
dazed
and
confused
me wandered

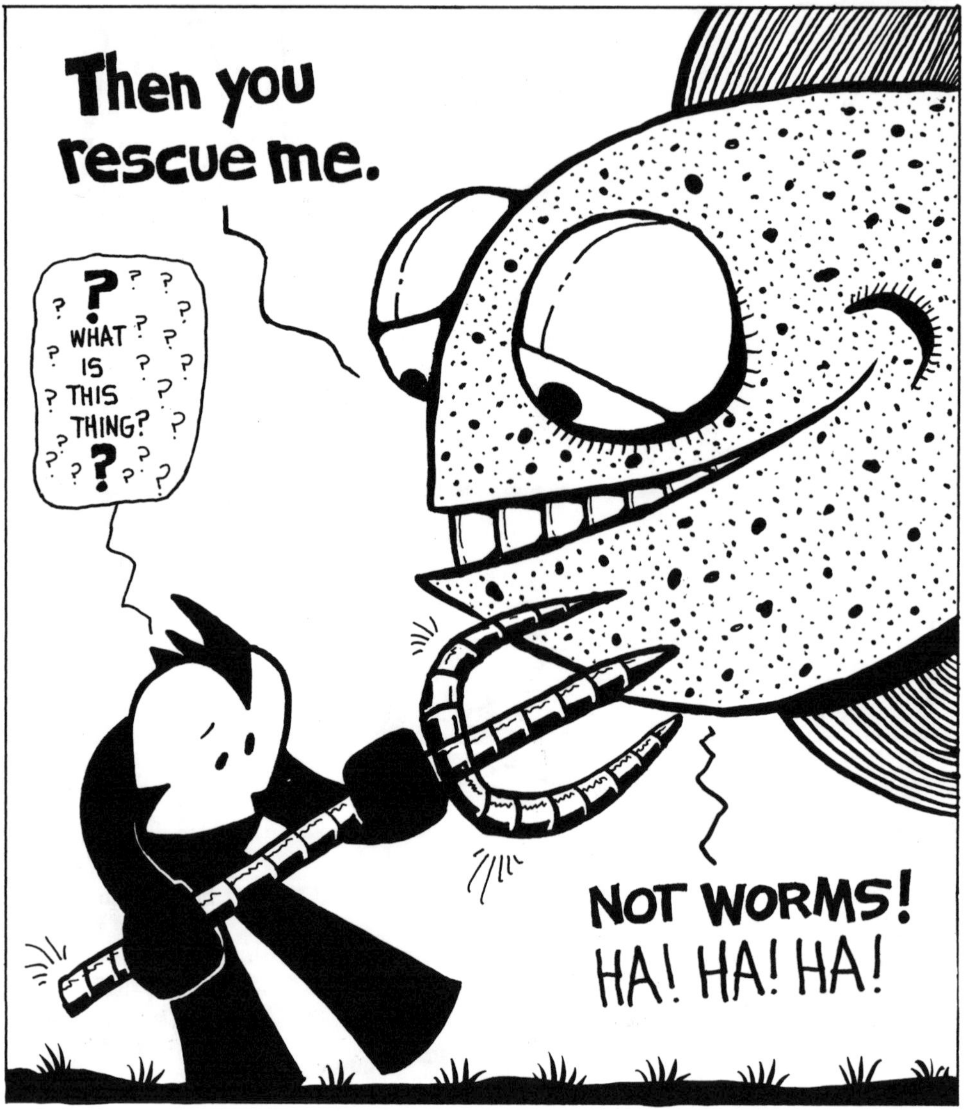
Then you rescue me.
? WHAT IS THIS THING? ?
NOT WORMS!
HA! HA! HA!

THIS ITEM IS DANGEROUS!

Me learn that all the time!!

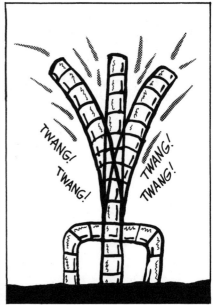

TWANG! TWANG! TWANG! TWANG!

THIS HAPPENS TO YOU OFTEN?

oh sure... Me get snagged quite frequently!

GEE...

Sometimes hook, sometimes arrow... always something...

But **you** always rescue me...

NOT **ME**, STRANGER. I NEVER SAW YOU BEFORE IN MY **LIFE**.

Ha, Ha, Ha!

Not **YOU**, you. You, **THE HERO**, you!

You rescue me, and I gift you something. Today is fork.

FORK?

OH, NO YA DON'T! I DON'T WANT NOTHING TO DO WITH THIS FORK!

HEH! HEH!

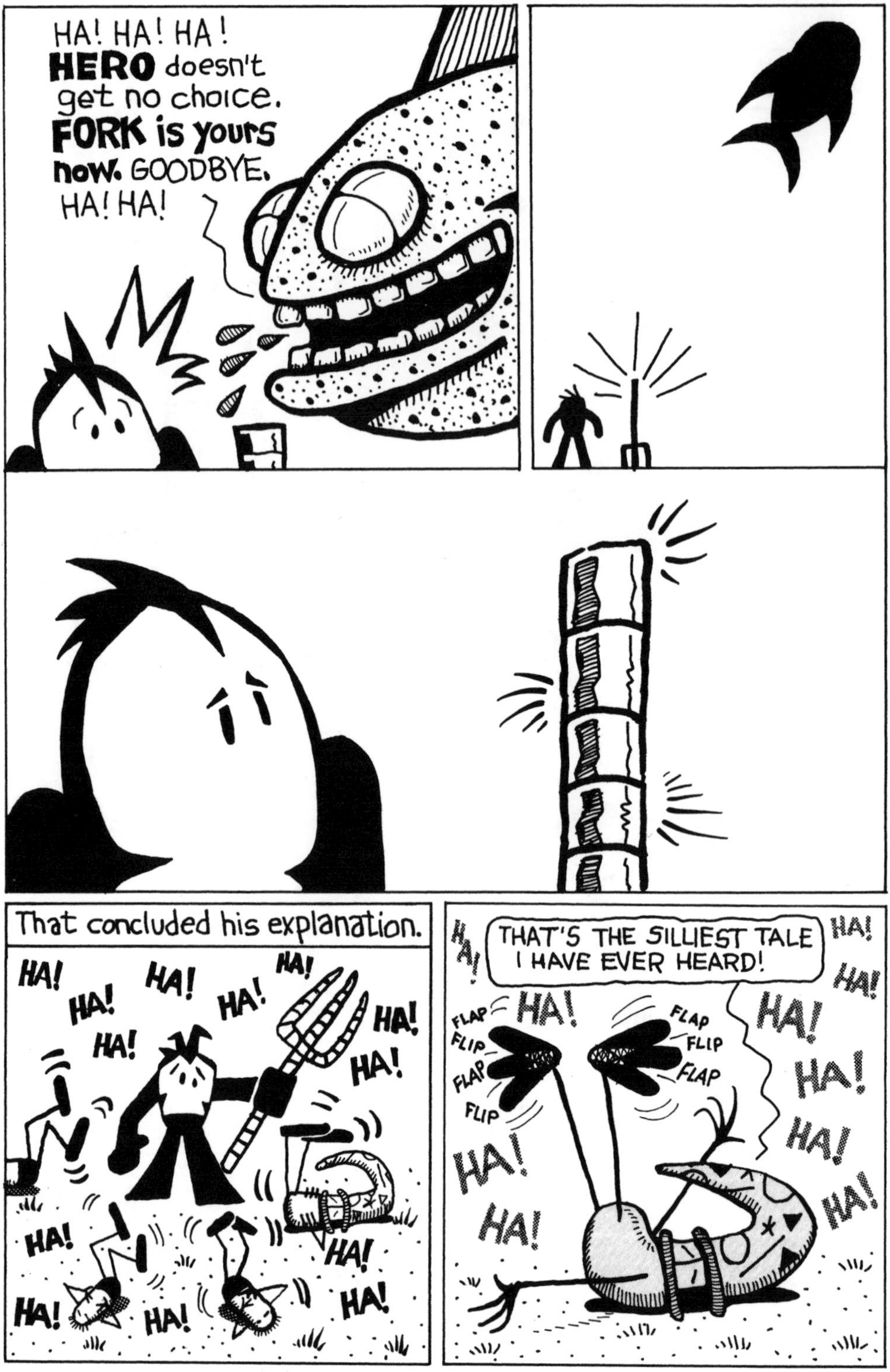
HA! HA! HA! HERO doesn't get no choice. FORK is yours now. GOODBYE. HA! HA!
That concluded his explanation.
HA! HA! HA! HA! HA! HA! HA! HA! HA! HA! HA! HA!
HA!
THAT'S THE SILLIEST TALE I HAVE EVER HEARD!
HA!
FLAP FLIP FLAP FLIP
HA!
FLAP FLIP FLAP
HA! HA! HA! HA! HA! HA! HA! HA!

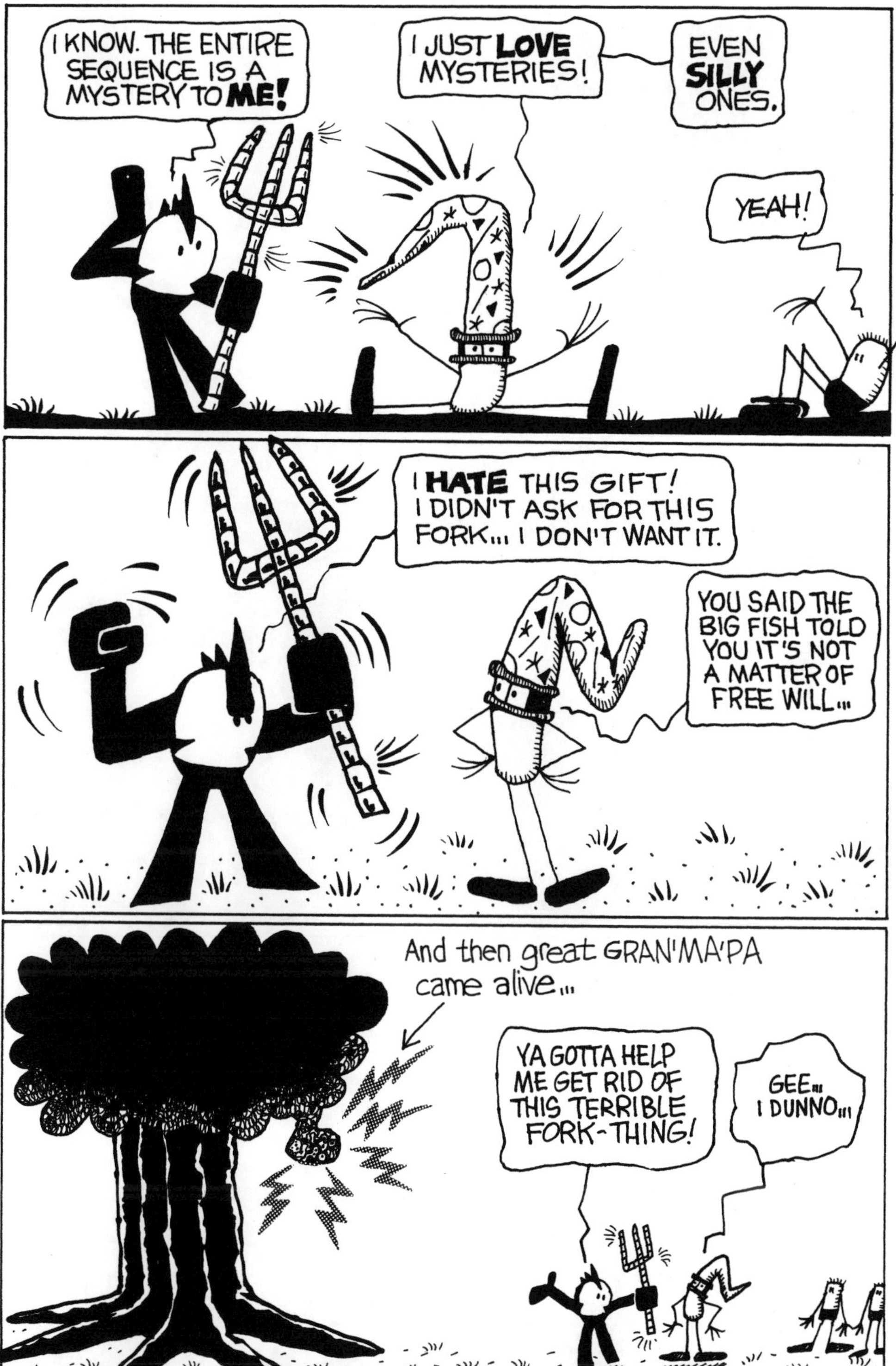
I KNOW. THE ENTIRE SEQUENCE IS A MYSTERY TO **ME!**
I JUST **LOVE** MYSTERIES!
EVEN **SILLY** ONES.
YEAH!
I **HATE** THIS GIFT! I DIDN'T ASK FOR THIS FORK... I DON'T WANT IT.
YOU SAID THE BIG FISH TOLD YOU IT'S NOT A MATTER OF FREE WILL...
And then great GRAN'MA'PA came alive...
YA GOTTA HELP ME GET RID OF THIS TERRIBLE FORK-THING!
GEE... I DUNNO...

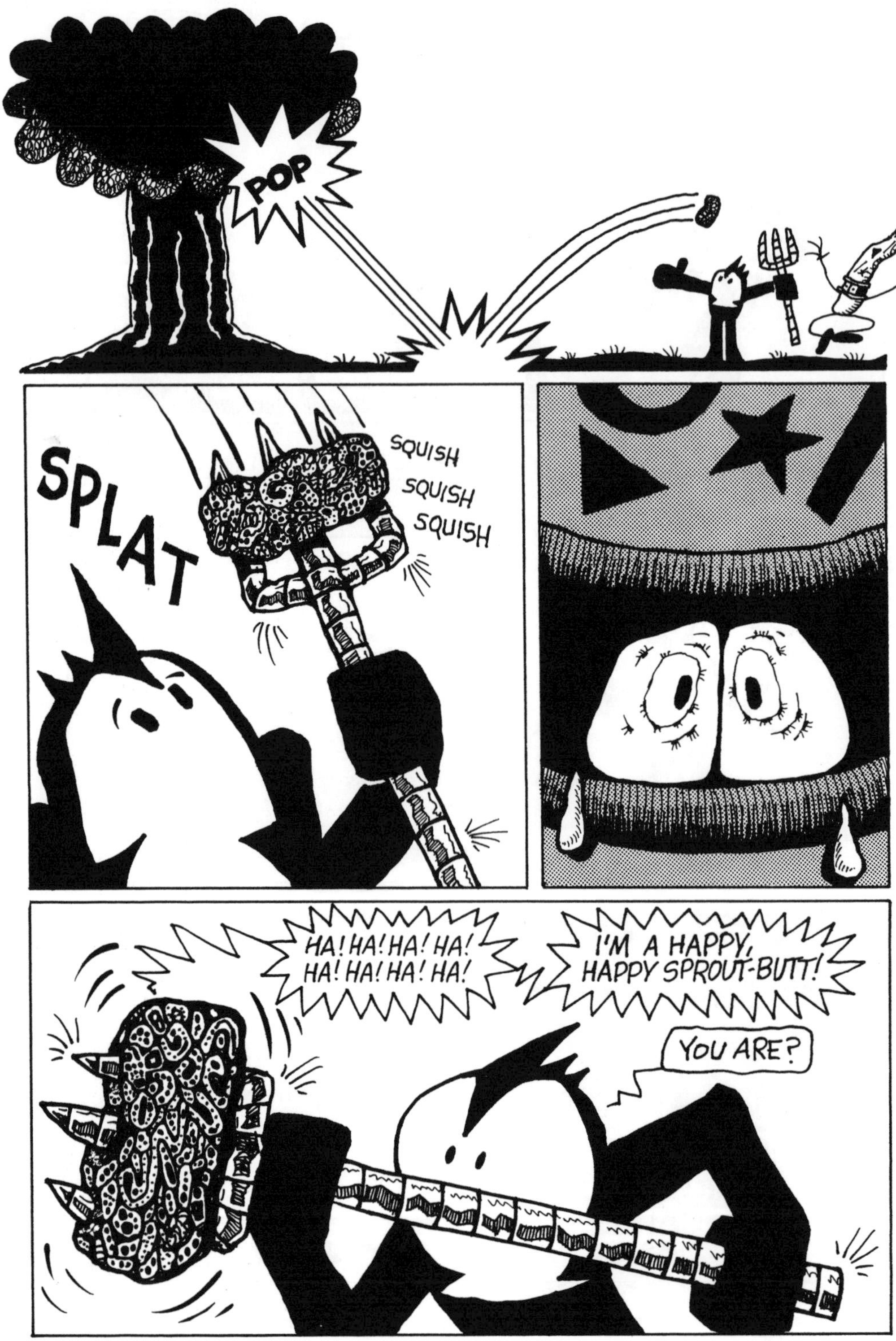
POP
SPLAT
SQUISH
SQUISH
SQUISH
HA! HA! HA! HA!
HA! HA! HA! HA!
I'M A HAPPY,
HAPPY SPROUT-BUTT!
YOU ARE?

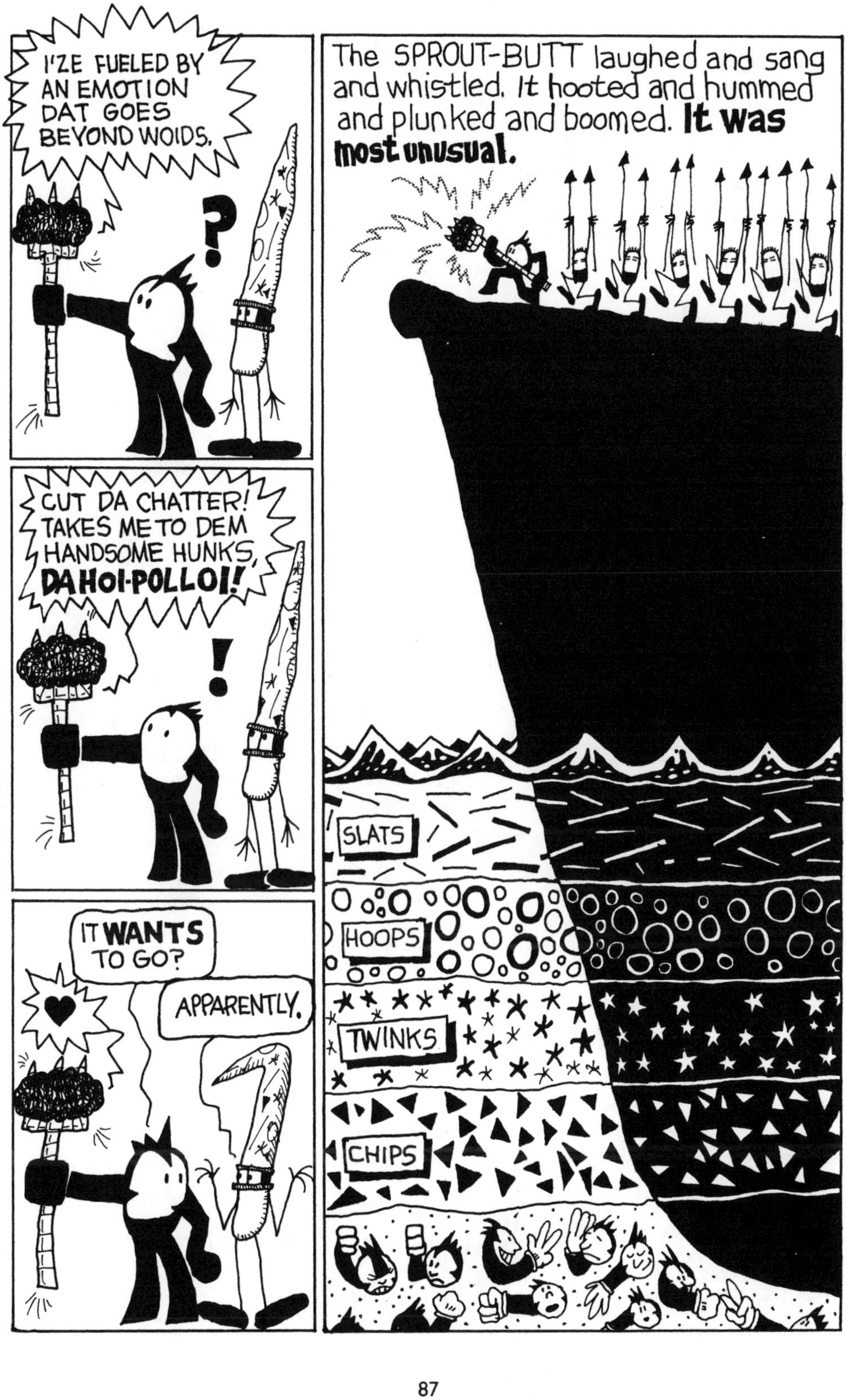
I'ZE FUELED BY AN EMOTION DAT GOES BEYOND WOIDS.
?
CUT DA CHATTER! TAKES ME TO DEM HANDSOME HUNKS, DA HOI-POLLOI!
!
IT WANTS TO GO?
APPARENTLY.
The SPROUT-BUTT laughed and sang and whistled. It hooted and hummed and plunked and boomed. It was most unusual.
SLATS
HOOPS
TWINKS
CHIPS

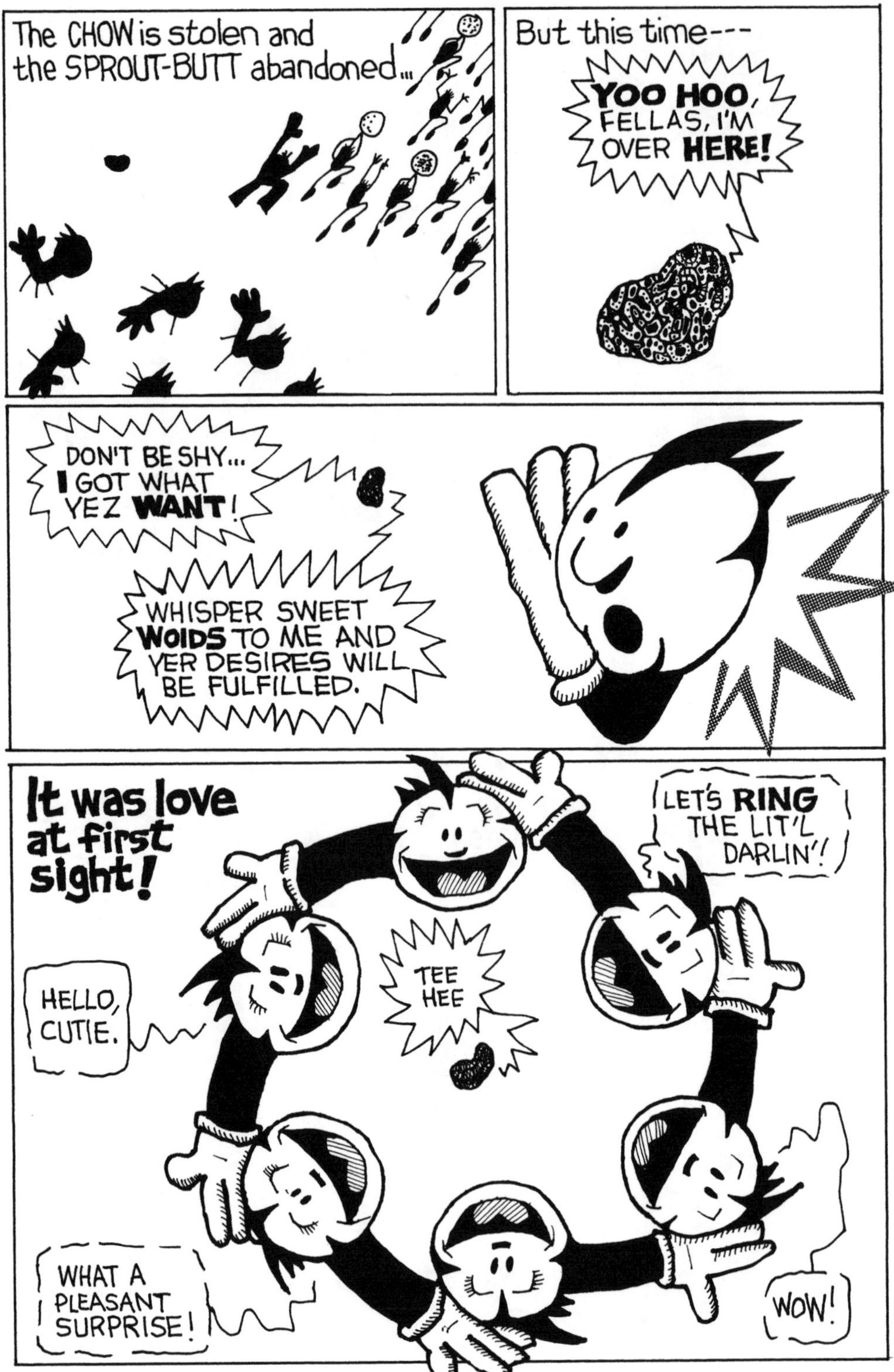
The CHOW is stolen and the SPROUT-BUTT abandoned...
But this time---
YOO HOO, FELLAS, I'M OVER HERE!
DON'T BE SHY... I GOT WHAT YEZ WANT!
WHISPER SWEET WOIDS TO ME AND YER DESIRES WILL BE FULFILLED.
It was love at first sight!
LET'S RING THE LIT'L DARLIN'!
HELLO, CUTIE.
TEE HEE
WHAT A PLEASANT SURPRISE!
WOW!

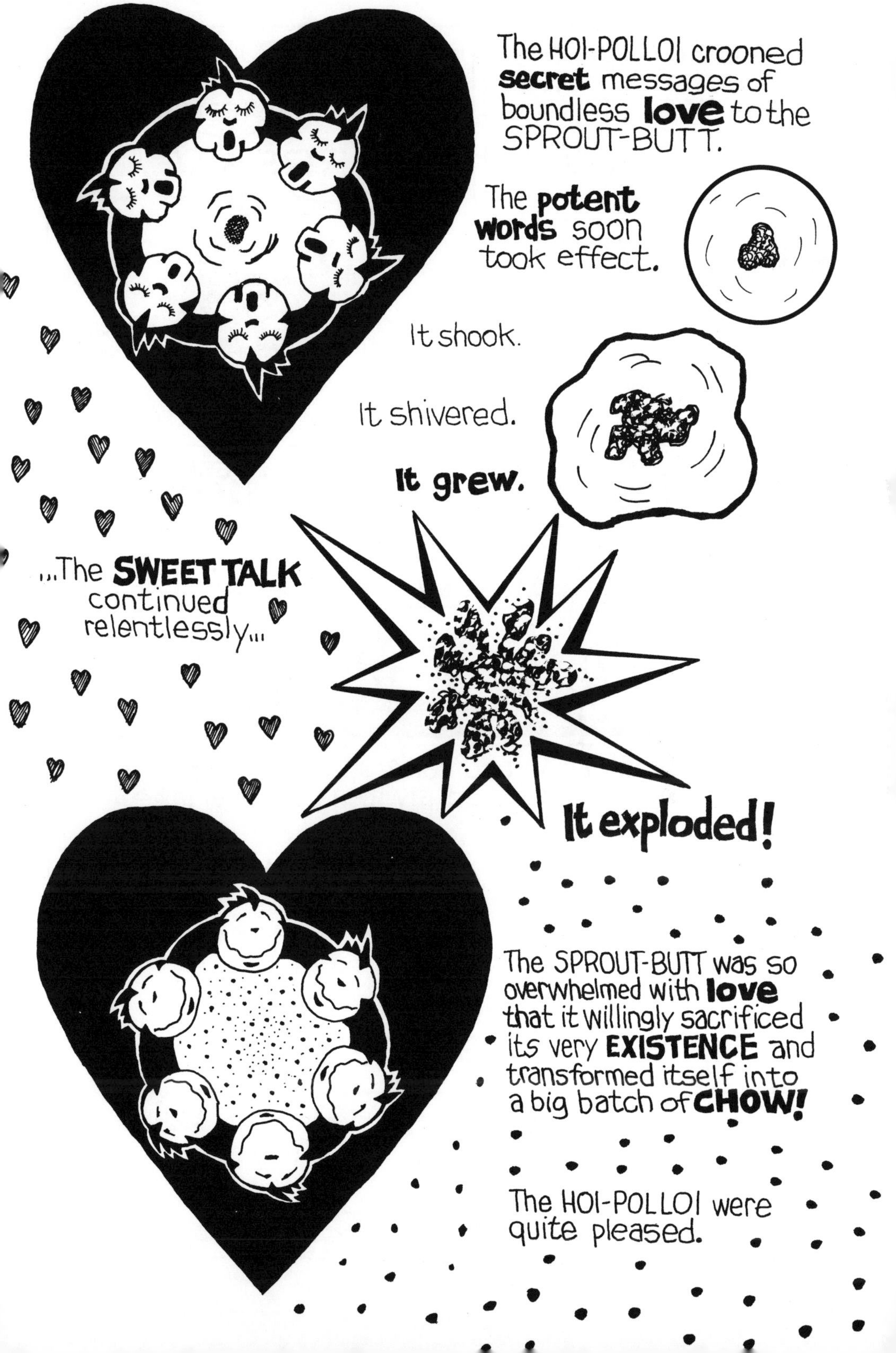

The HOI-POLLOI crooned **secret** messages of boundless **love** to the SPROUT-BUTT.
The **potent words** soon took effect.
It shook.
It shivered.
**It grew.**
...The **SWEET TALK** continued relentlessly...
**It exploded!**
The SPROUT-BUTT was so overwhelmed with **love** that it willingly sacrificed its very **EXISTENCE** and transformed itself into a big batch of **CHOW!**
The HOI-POLLOI were quite pleased.

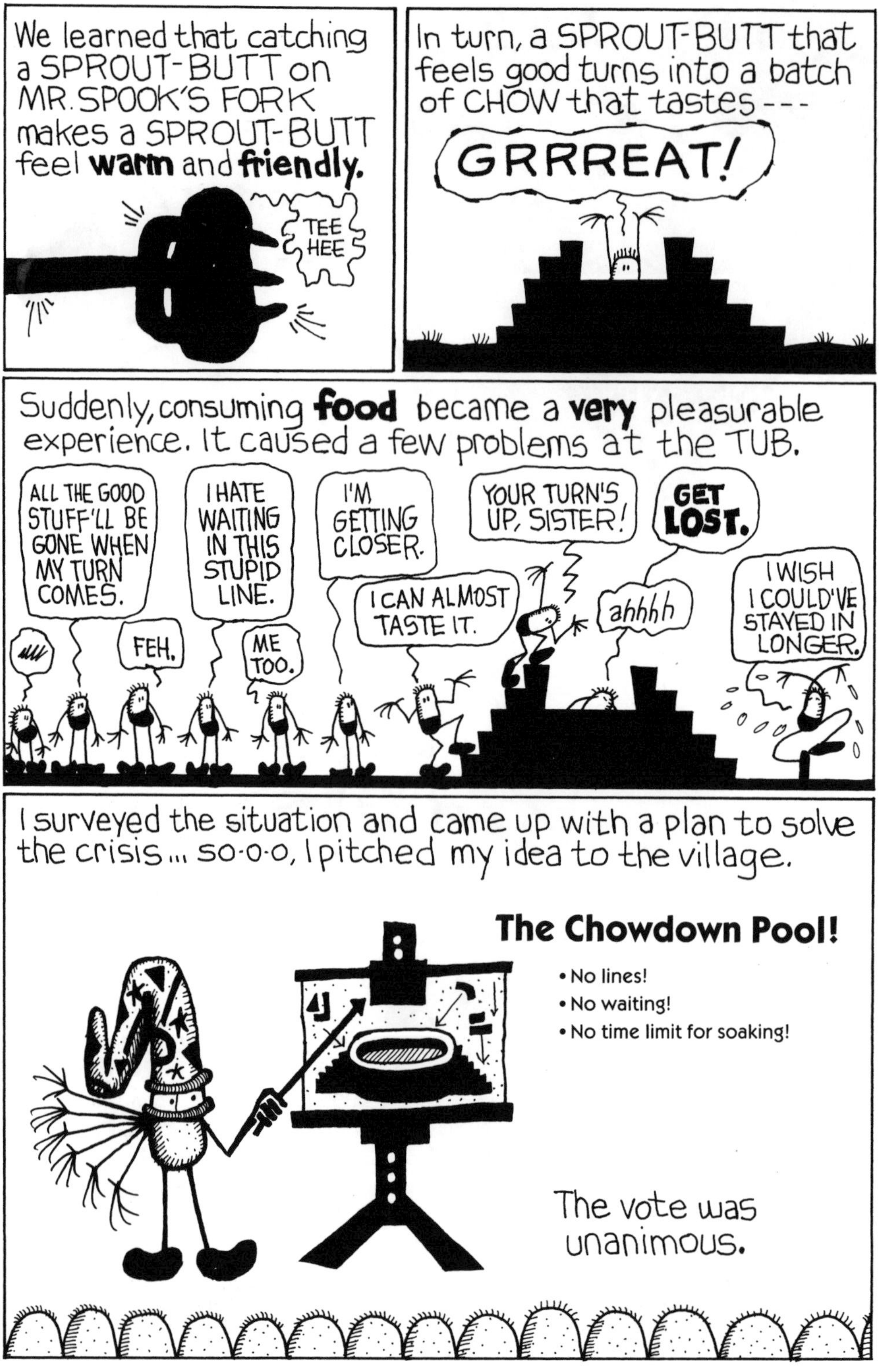
We learned that catching a SPROUT-BUTT on MR. SPOOK'S FORK makes a SPROUT-BUTT feel **warm** and **friendly.**
TEE HEE
In turn, a SPROUT-BUTT that feels good turns into a batch of CHOW that tastes ---
GRRREAT!
Suddenly, consuming **food** became a **very** pleasurable experience. It caused a few problems at the TUB.
ALL THE GOOD STUFF'LL BE GONE WHEN MY TURN COMES.
FEH.
I HATE WAITING IN THIS STUPID LINE.
ME TOO.
I'M GETTING CLOSER.
I CAN ALMOST TASTE IT.
YOUR TURN'S UP, SISTER!
GET LOST.
ahhhh
I WISH I COULD'VE STAYED IN LONGER.
I surveyed the situation and came up with a plan to solve the crisis... so-o-o, I pitched my idea to the village.
The Chowdown Pool!
• No lines!
• No waiting!
• No time limit for soaking!
The vote was unanimous.

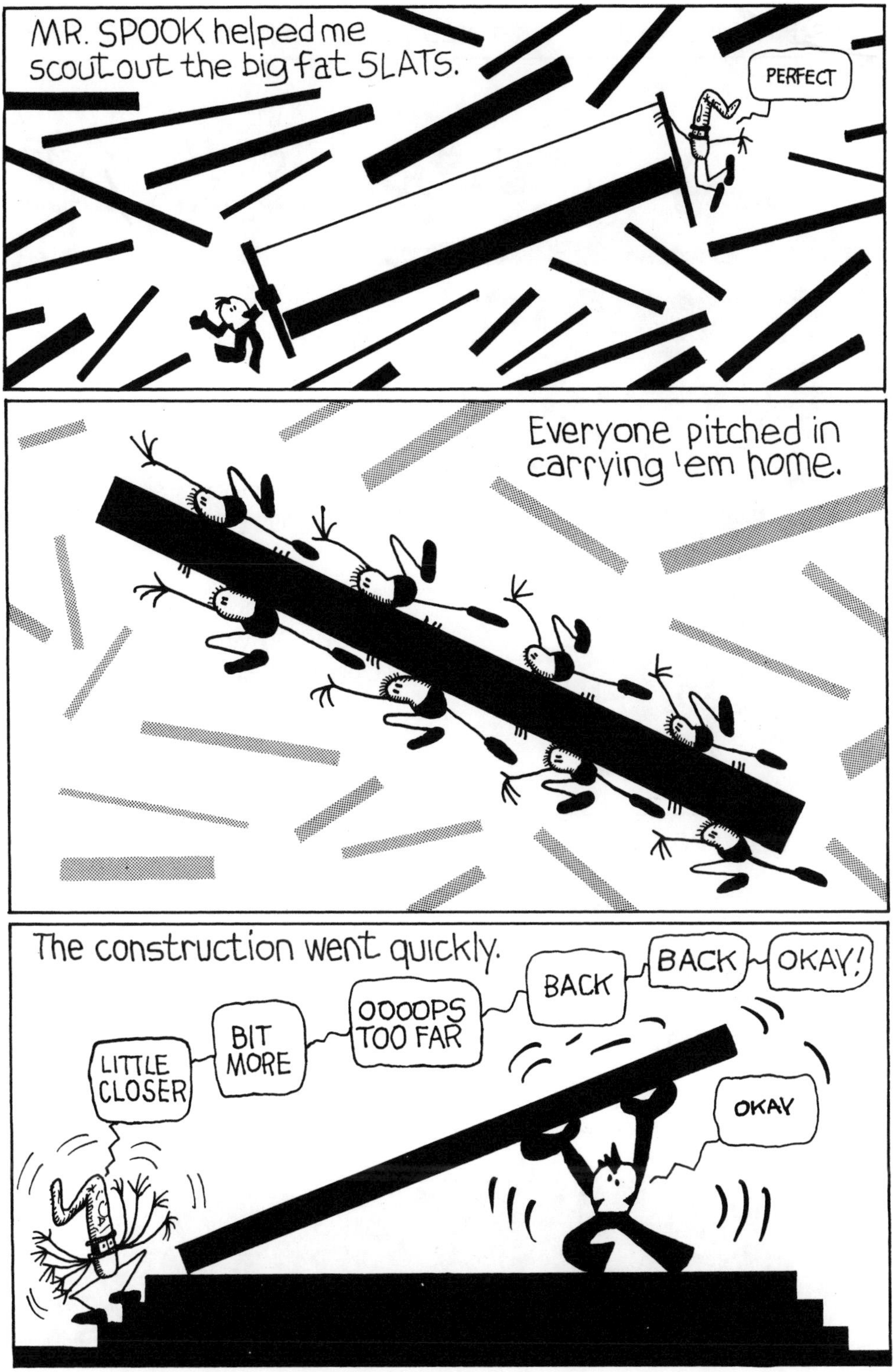
MR. SPOOK helped me scout out the big fat SLATS.
PERFECT
Everyone pitched in carrying 'em home.
The construction went quickly.
LITTLE CLOSER
BIT MORE
OOOOPS TOO FAR
BACK
BACK
OKAY!
OKAY

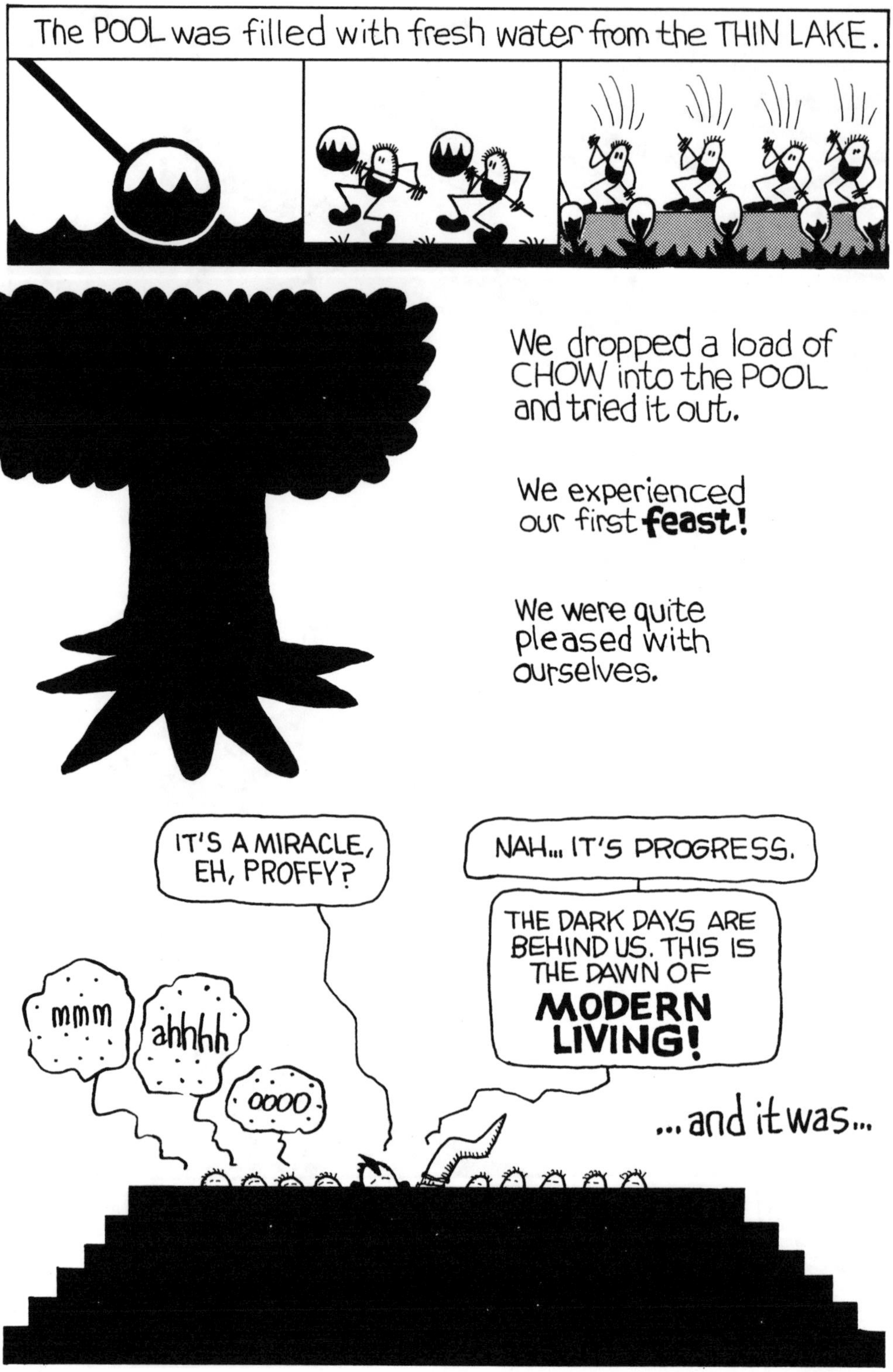
The POOL was filled with fresh water from the THIN LAKE.
We dropped a load of CHOW into the POOL and tried it out.
We experienced our first feast!
We were quite pleased with ourselves.
IT'S A MIRACLE, EH, PROFFY?
NAH... IT'S PROGRESS.
THE DARK DAYS ARE BEHIND US. THIS IS THE DAWN OF MODERN LIVING!
mmm
ahhhh
oooo
...and it was...

**The End**

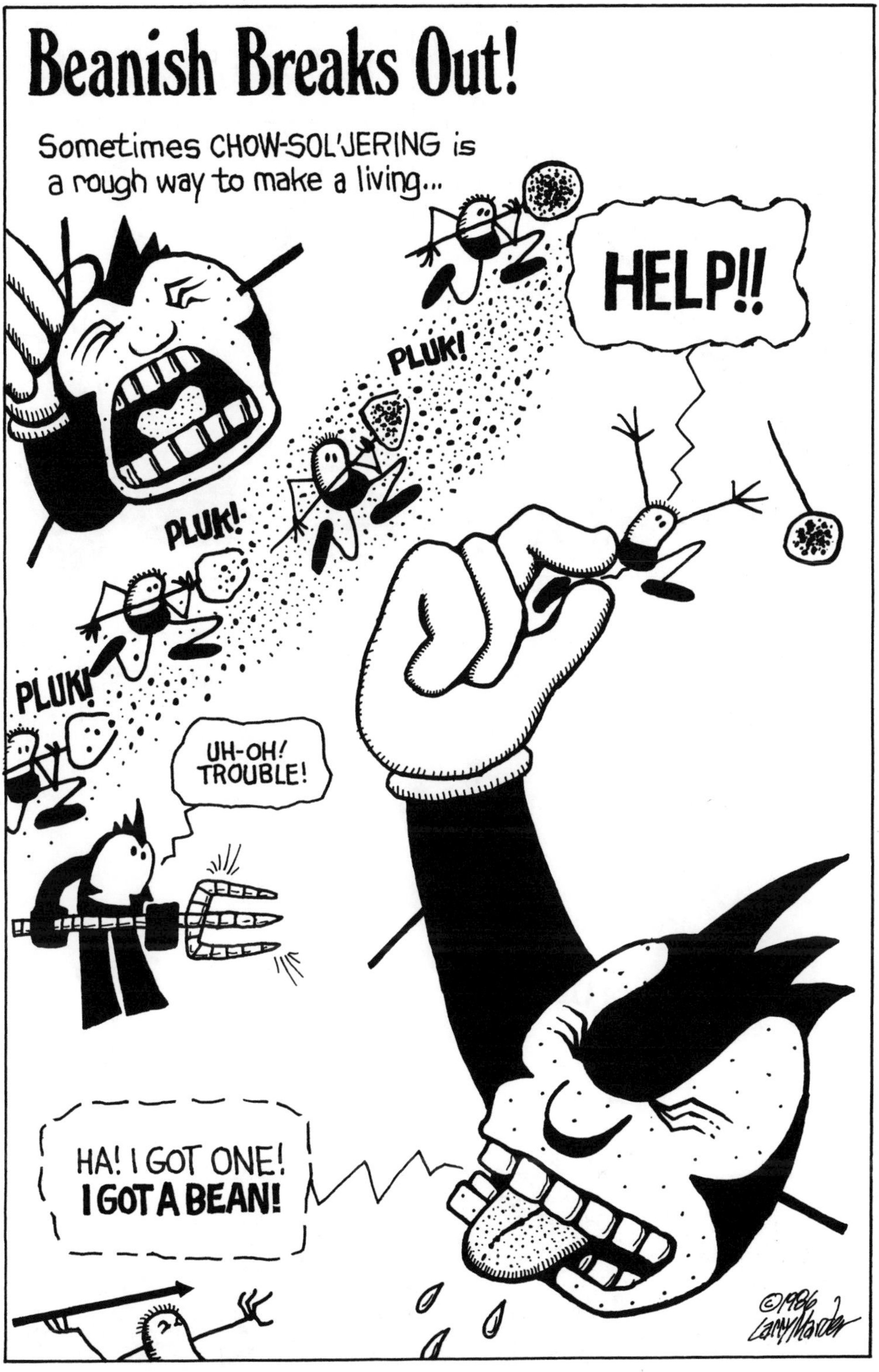
Beanish Breaks Out!
Sometimes CHOW-SOL'JERING is a rough way to make a living...
HELP!!
PLUK!
PLUK!
PLUK!
UH-OH! TROUBLE!
HA! I GOT ONE! I GOT A BEAN!
©1996 Larry Marder

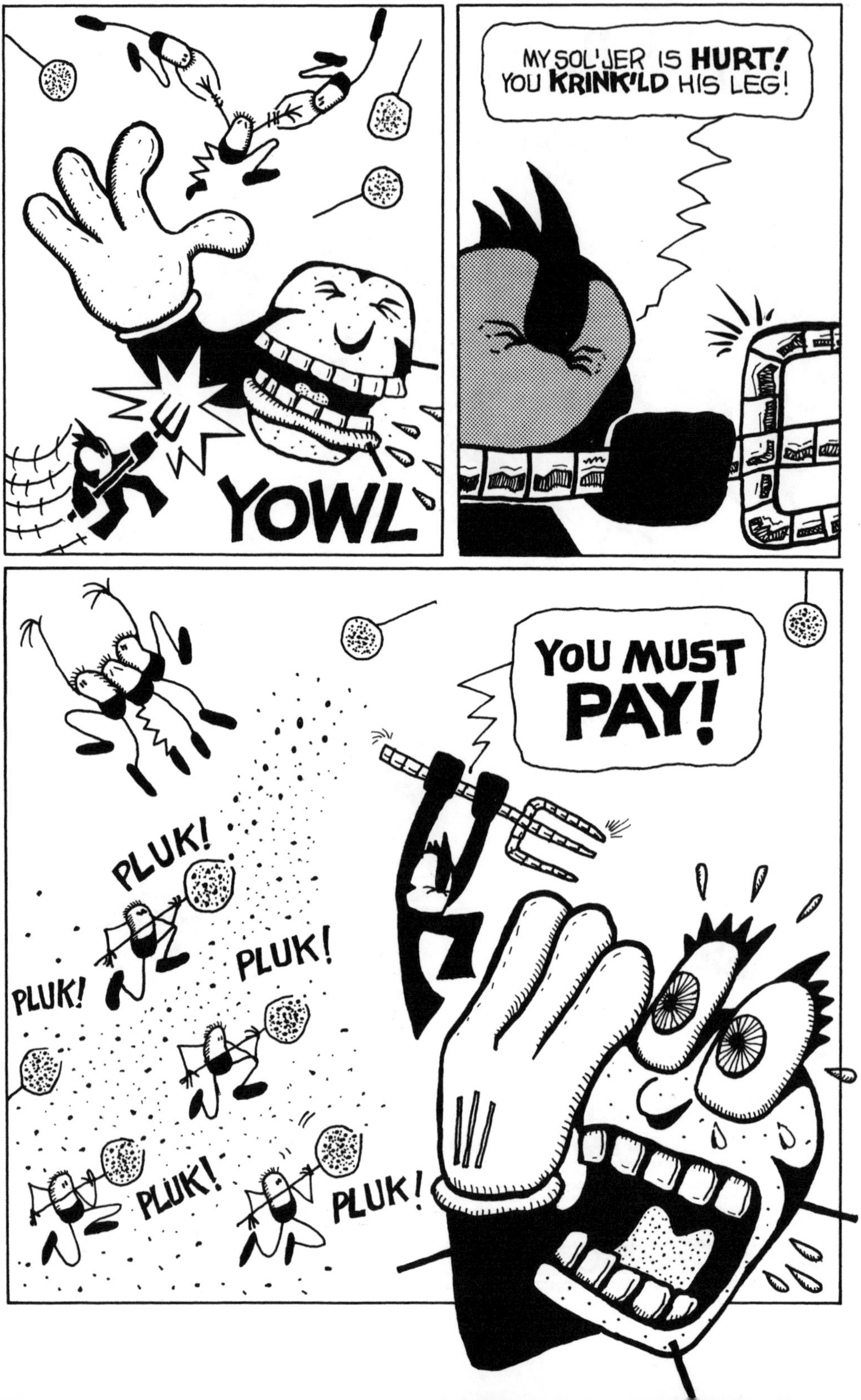
YOWL
MY SOL'JER IS HURT! YOU KRINK'LD HIS LEG!
YOU MUST PAY!
PLUK!
PLUK!
PLUK!
PLUK!
PLUK!

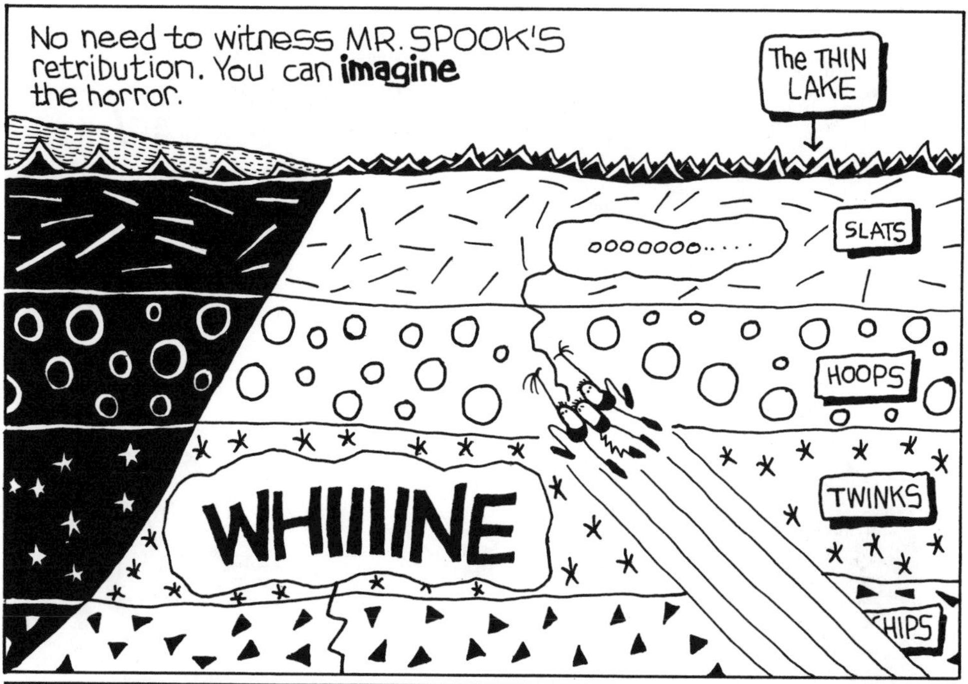
No need to witness MR. SPOOK'S retribution. You can **imagine** the horror.
The THIN LAKE
SLATS
oooooooo.....
HOOPS
TWINKS
WHIIIINE
CHIPS

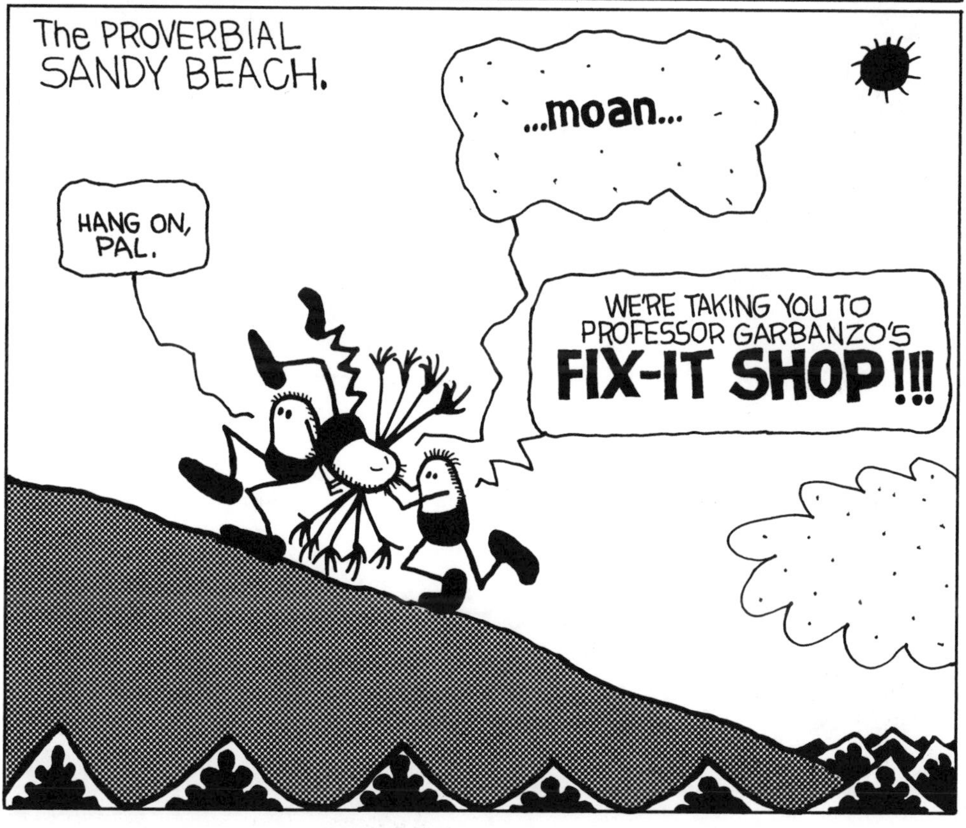
The PROVERBIAL SANDY BEACH.
...moan...
HANG ON, PAL.
WE'RE TAKING YOU TO PROFESSOR GARBANZO'S FIX-IT SHOP!!!

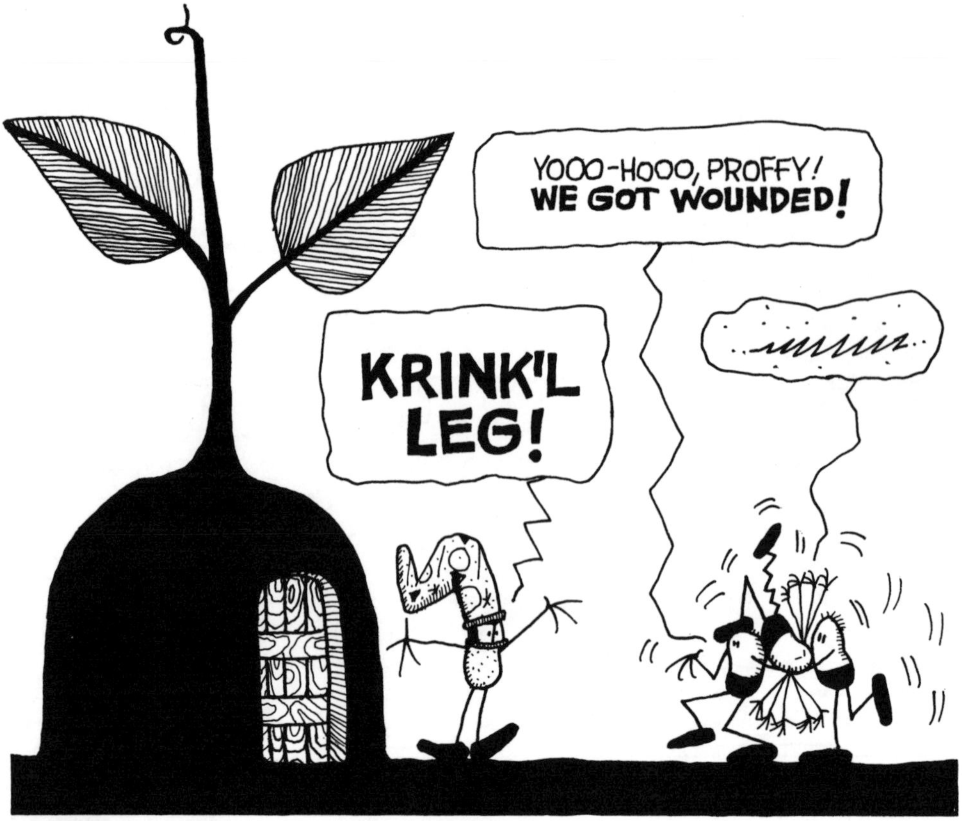
YOOO-HOOO, PROFFY!
**WE GOT WOUNDED!**
**KRINK'L LEG!**

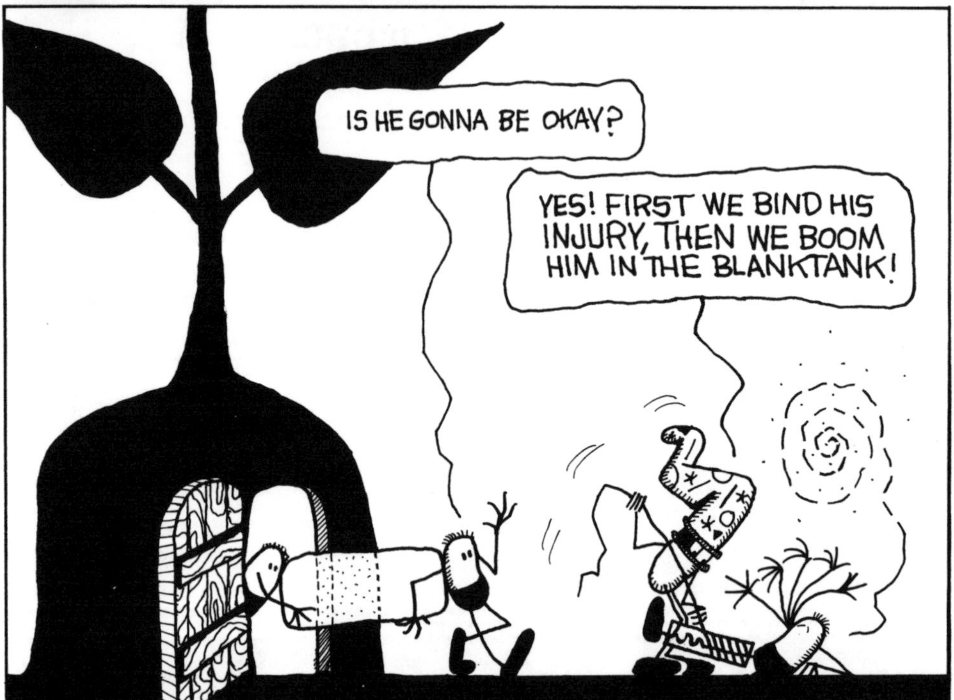
IS HE GONNA BE OKAY?
YES! FIRST WE BIND HIS INJURY, THEN WE BOOM HIM IN THE BLANKTANK!

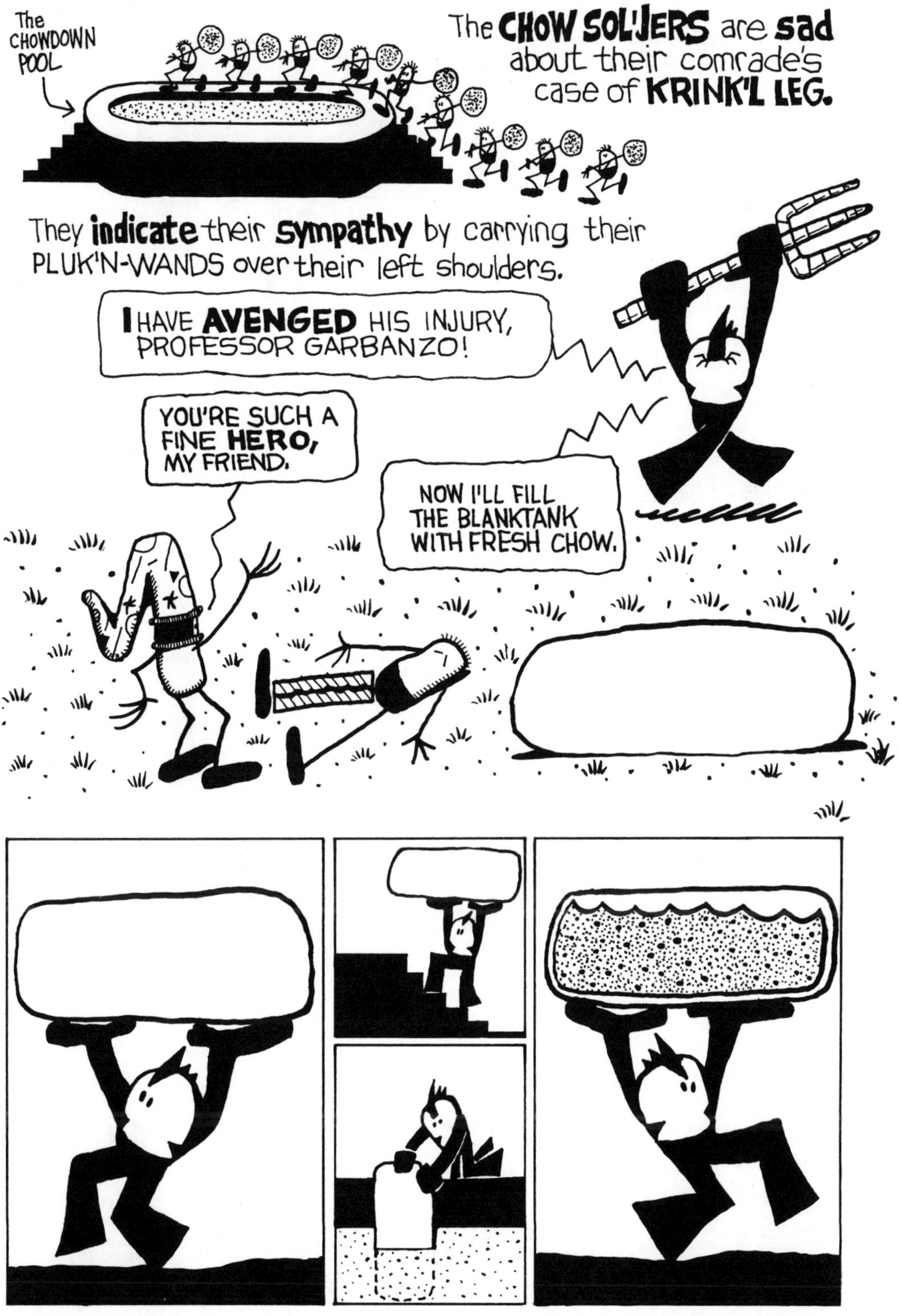

The CHOWDOWN POOL
The CHOW SOL'JERS are sad about their comrade's case of KRINK'L LEG.
They indicate their sympathy by carrying their PLUK'N-WANDS over their left shoulders.
I HAVE AVENGED HIS INJURY, PROFESSOR GARBANZO!
YOU'RE SUCH A FINE HERO, MY FRIEND.
NOW I'LL FILL THE BLANKTANK WITH FRESH CHOW.

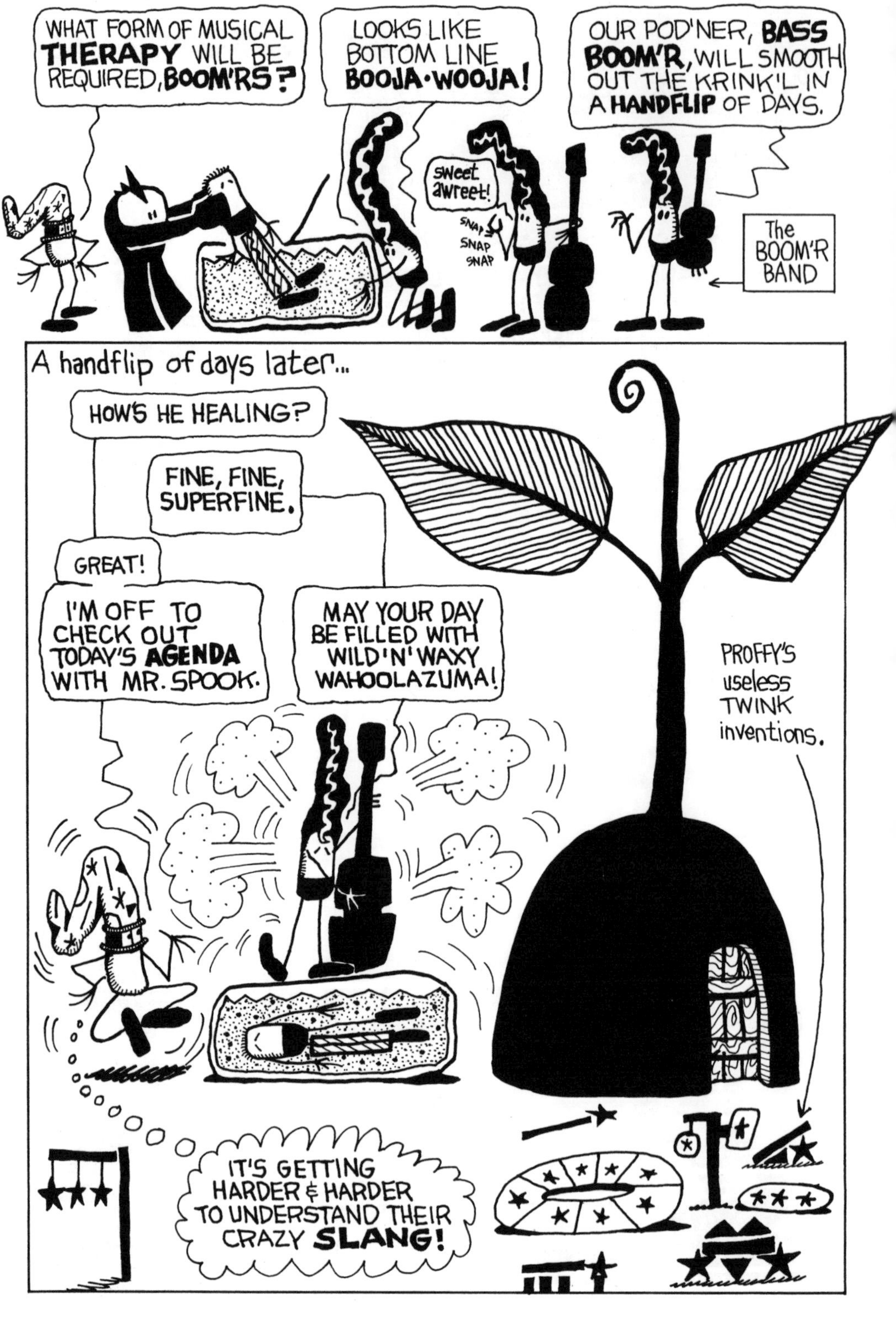
WHAT FORM OF MUSICAL THERAPY WILL BE REQUIRED, BOOM'RS?
LOOKS LIKE BOTTOM LINE BOOJA·WOOJA!
sweet awreet!
SNAP SNAP SNAP
OUR POD'NER, BASS BOOM'R, WILL SMOOTH OUT THE KRINK'L IN A HANDFLIP OF DAYS.
The BOOM'R BAND
A handflip of days later...
HOW'S HE HEALING?
FINE, FINE, SUPERFINE.
GREAT!
I'M OFF TO CHECK OUT TODAY'S AGENDA WITH MR. SPOOK.
MAY YOUR DAY BE FILLED WITH WILD'N' WAXY WAHOOLAZUMA!
PROFFY'S useless TWINK inventions.
IT'S GETTING HARDER & HARDER TO UNDERSTAND THEIR CRAZY SLANG!

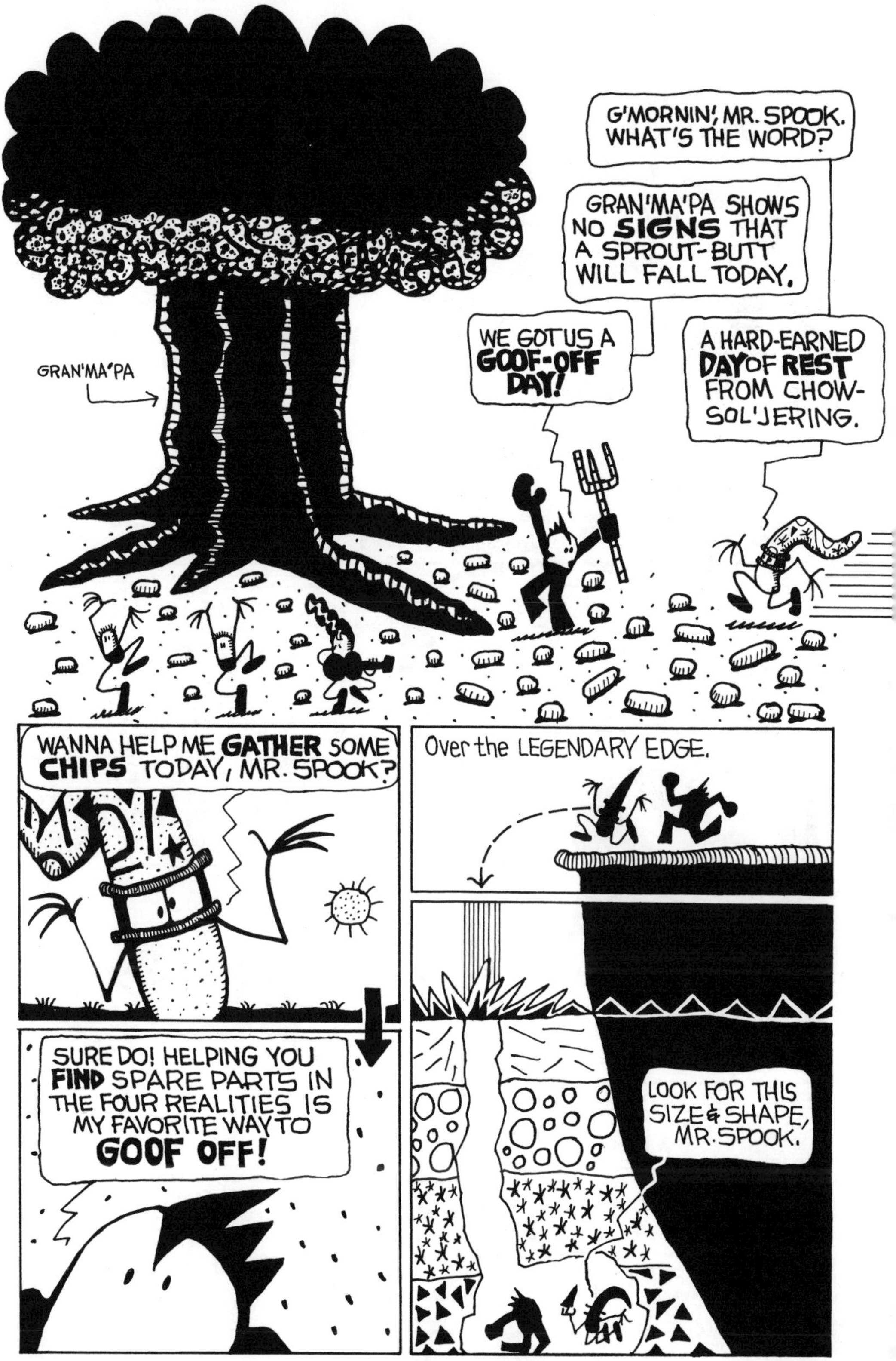
GRAN'MA'PA
G'MORNIN'! MR. SPOOK. WHAT'S THE WORD?
GRAN'MA'PA SHOWS NO **SIGNS** THAT A SPROUT-BUTT WILL FALL TODAY.
WE GOT US A **GOOF-OFF DAY!**
A HARD-EARNED **DAY** OF **REST** FROM CHOW-SOL'JERING.
WANNA HELP ME **GATHER** SOME **CHIPS** TODAY, MR. SPOOK?
Over the LEGENDARY EDGE.
SURE DO! HELPING YOU **FIND** SPARE PARTS IN THE FOUR REALITIES IS MY FAVORITE WAY TO **GOOF OFF!**
LOOK FOR THIS SIZE & SHAPE, MR. SPOOK.

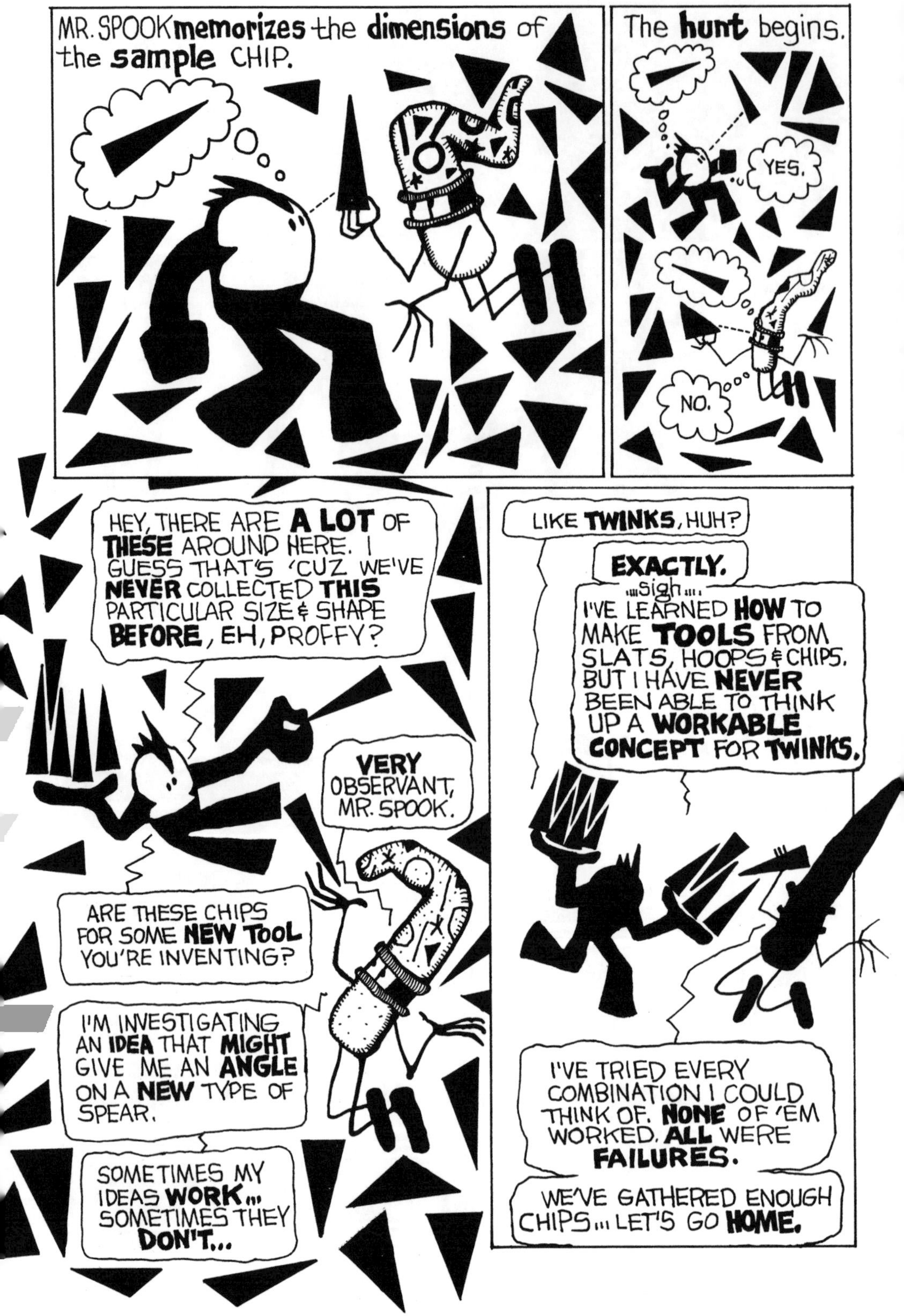

MR. SPOOK memorizes the dimensions of the sample CHIP.
The hunt begins.
YES.
NO.
HEY, THERE ARE A LOT OF THESE AROUND HERE. I GUESS THAT'S 'CUZ WE'VE NEVER COLLECTED THIS PARTICULAR SIZE & SHAPE BEFORE, EH, PROFFY?
VERY OBSERVANT, MR. SPOOK.
ARE THESE CHIPS FOR SOME NEW TOOL YOU'RE INVENTING?
I'M INVESTIGATING AN IDEA THAT MIGHT GIVE ME AN ANGLE ON A NEW TYPE OF SPEAR.
SOMETIMES MY IDEAS WORK... SOMETIMES THEY DON'T...
LIKE TWINKS, HUH?
EXACTLY.
...sigh...
I'VE LEARNED HOW TO MAKE TOOLS FROM SLATS, HOOPS & CHIPS. BUT I HAVE NEVER BEEN ABLE TO THINK UP A WORKABLE CONCEPT FOR TWINKS.
I'VE TRIED EVERY COMBINATION I COULD THINK OF. NONE OF 'EM WORKED. ALL WERE FAILURES.
WE'VE GATHERED ENOUGH CHIPS... LET'S GO HOME.

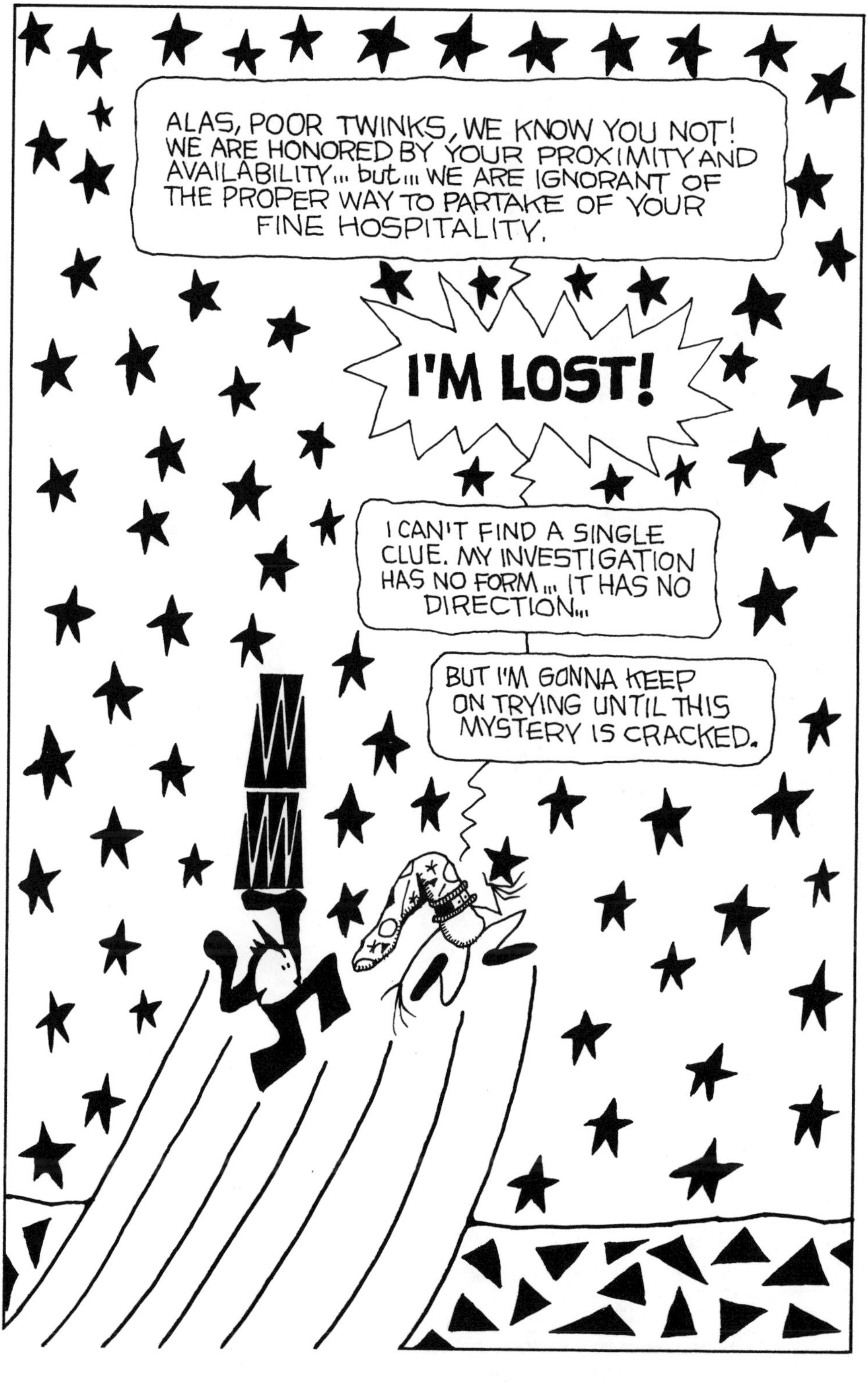
ALAS, POOR TWINKS, WE KNOW YOU NOT! WE ARE HONORED BY YOUR PROXIMITY AND AVAILABILITY... but... WE ARE IGNORANT OF THE PROPER WAY TO PARTAKE OF YOUR FINE HOSPITALITY.
I'M LOST!
I CAN'T FIND A SINGLE CLUE. MY INVESTIGATION HAS NO FORM... IT HAS NO DIRECTION...
BUT I'M GONNA KEEP ON TRYING UNTIL THIS MYSTERY IS CRACKED.

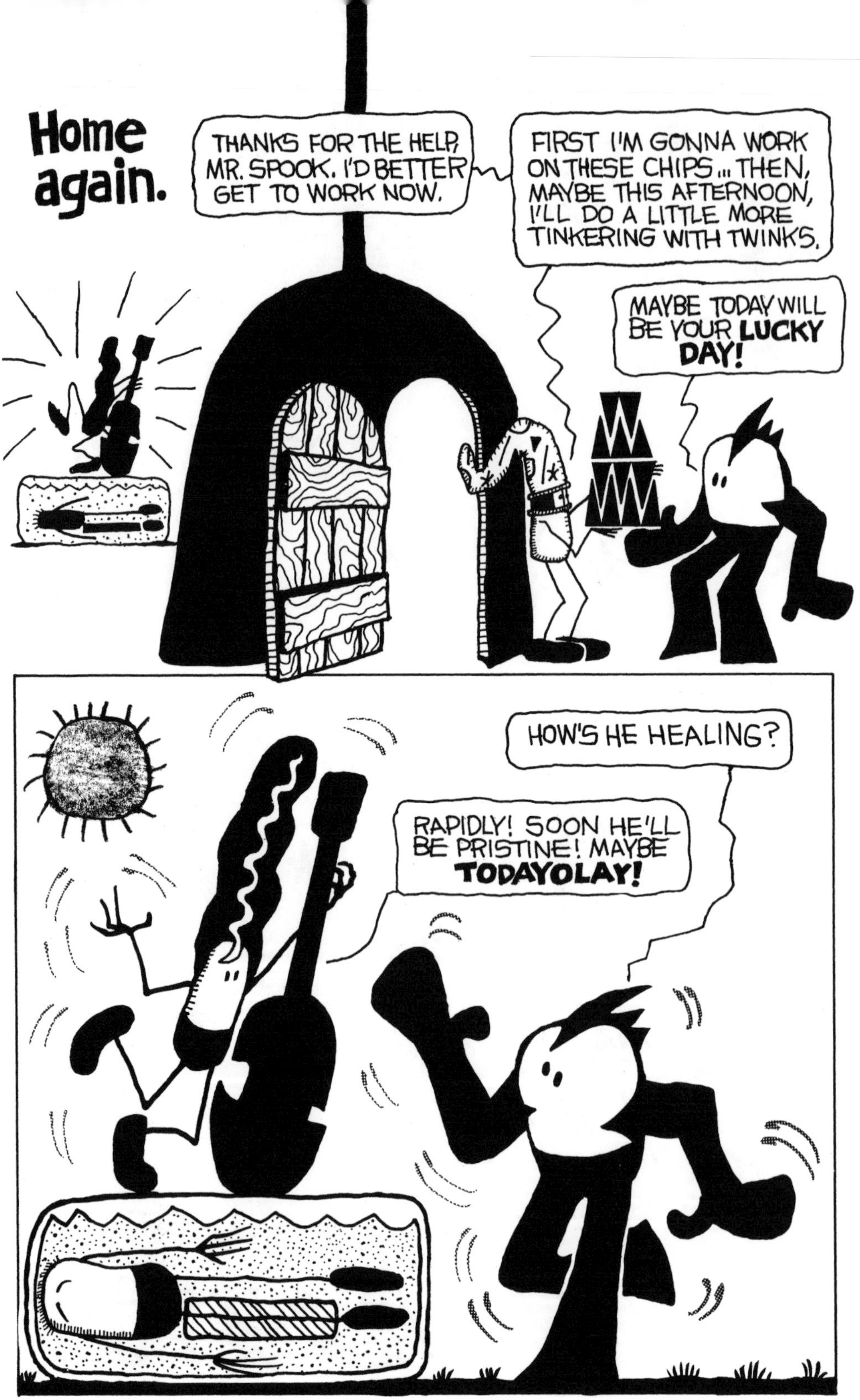
Home again.
THANKS FOR THE HELP, MR. SPOOK. I'D BETTER GET TO WORK NOW.
FIRST I'M GONNA WORK ON THESE CHIPS... THEN, MAYBE THIS AFTERNOON, I'LL DO A LITTLE MORE TINKERING WITH TWINKS.
MAYBE TODAY WILL BE YOUR **LUCKY DAY!**
HOW'S HE HEALING?
RAPIDLY! SOON HE'LL BE PRISTINE! MAYBE **TODAYOLAY!**

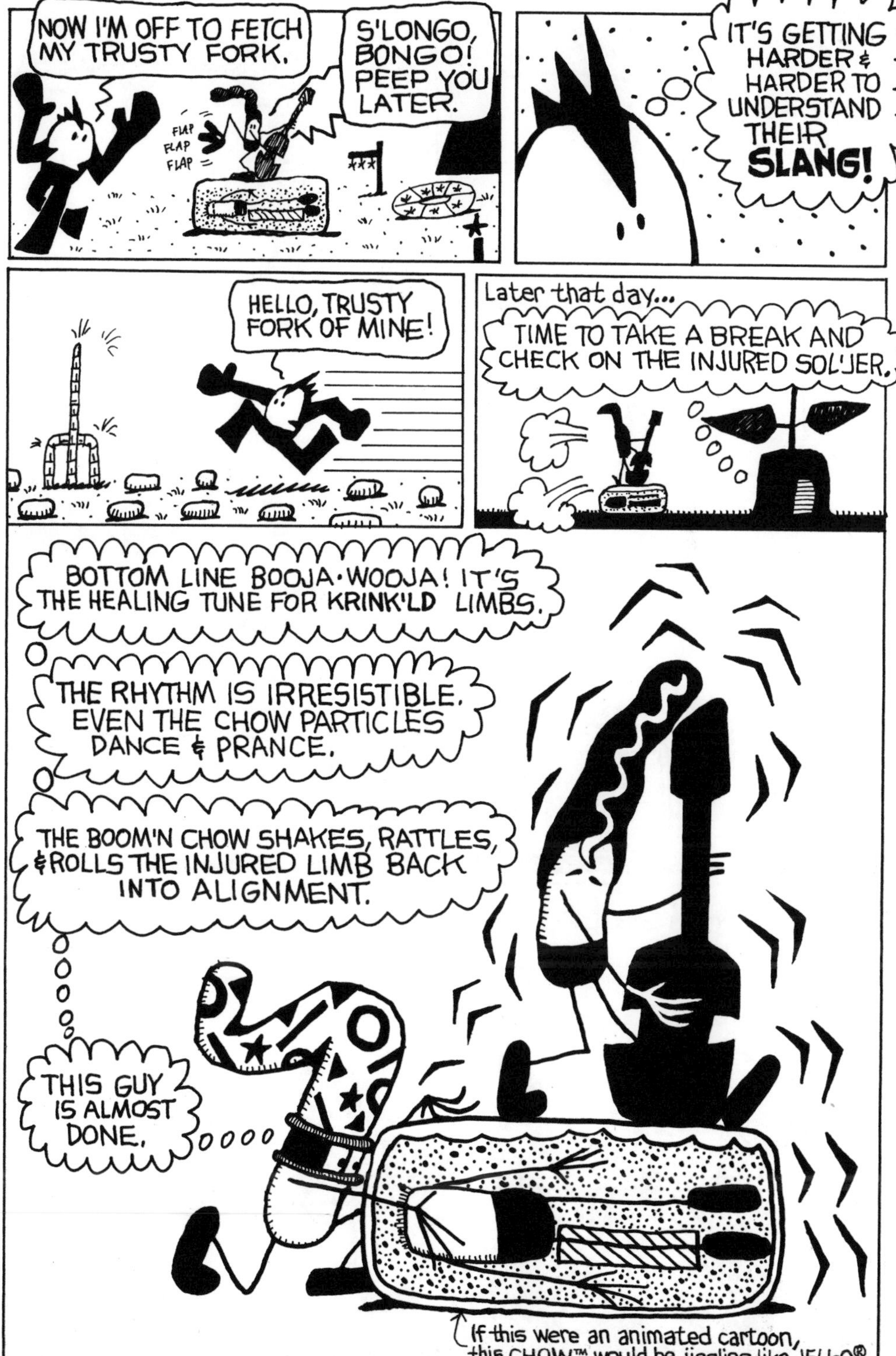
NOW I'M OFF TO FETCH MY TRUSTY FORK.
FLAP FLAP FLAP
S'LONGO, BONGO! PEEP YOU LATER.
IT'S GETTING HARDER & HARDER TO UNDERSTAND THEIR SLANG!
HELLO, TRUSTY FORK OF MINE!
Later that day...
TIME TO TAKE A BREAK AND CHECK ON THE INJURED SOL'JER.
BOTTOM LINE BOOJA·WOOJA! IT'S THE HEALING TUNE FOR KRINK'LD LIMBS.
THE RHYTHM IS IRRESISTIBLE. EVEN THE CHOW PARTICLES DANCE & PRANCE.
THE BOOM'N CHOW SHAKES, RATTLES, & ROLLS THE INJURED LIMB BACK INTO ALIGNMENT.
THIS GUY IS ALMOST DONE.
If this were an animated cartoon, this CHOW™ would be jiggling like JELL-O.®

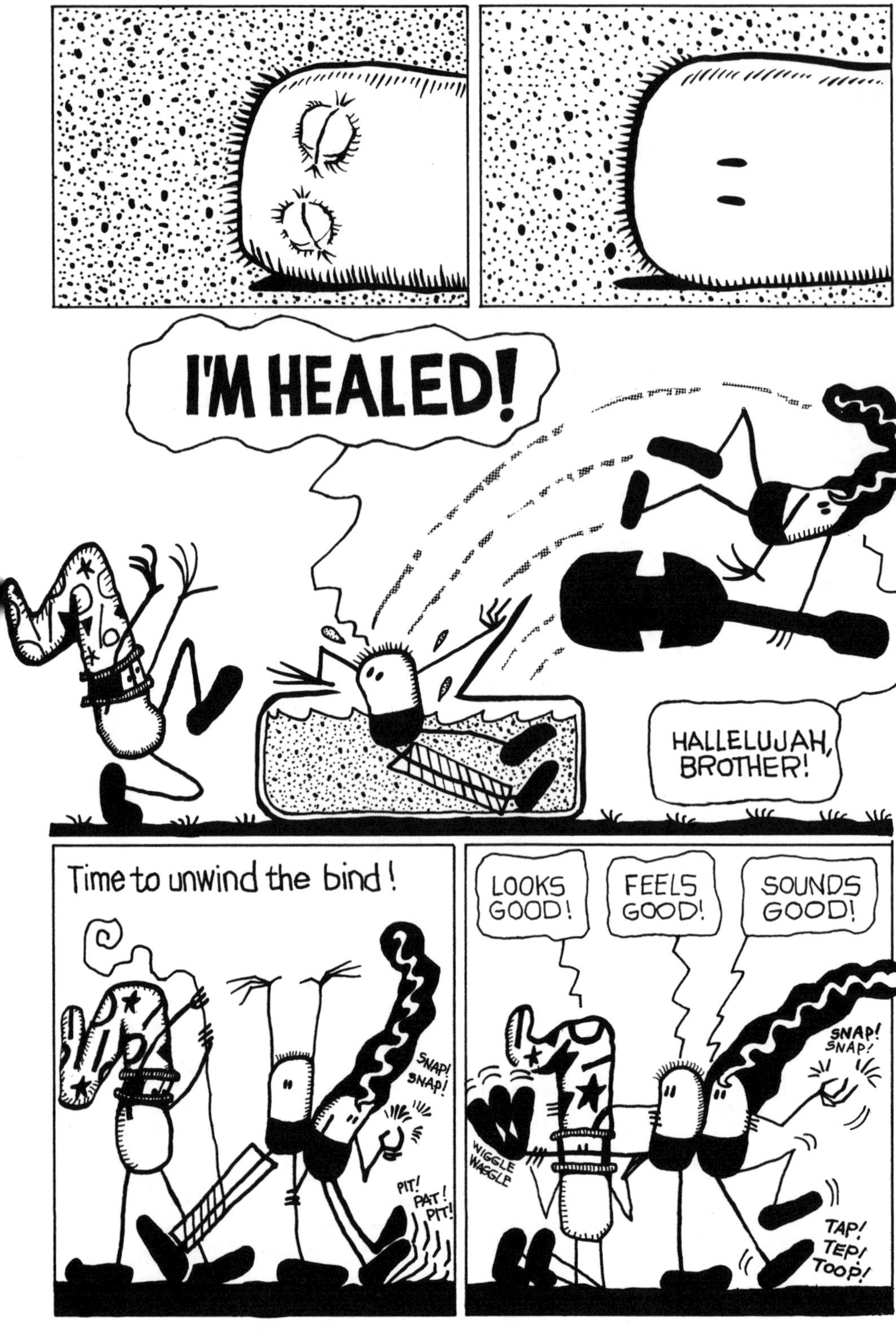
I'M HEALED!
HALLELUJAH, BROTHER!
Time to unwind the bind!
SNAP! SNAP!
PIT! PAT! PIT!
LOOKS GOOD!
FEELS GOOD!
SOUNDS GOOD!
SNAP! SNAP!
WIGGLE WAGGLE
TAP! TEP! TOOP!

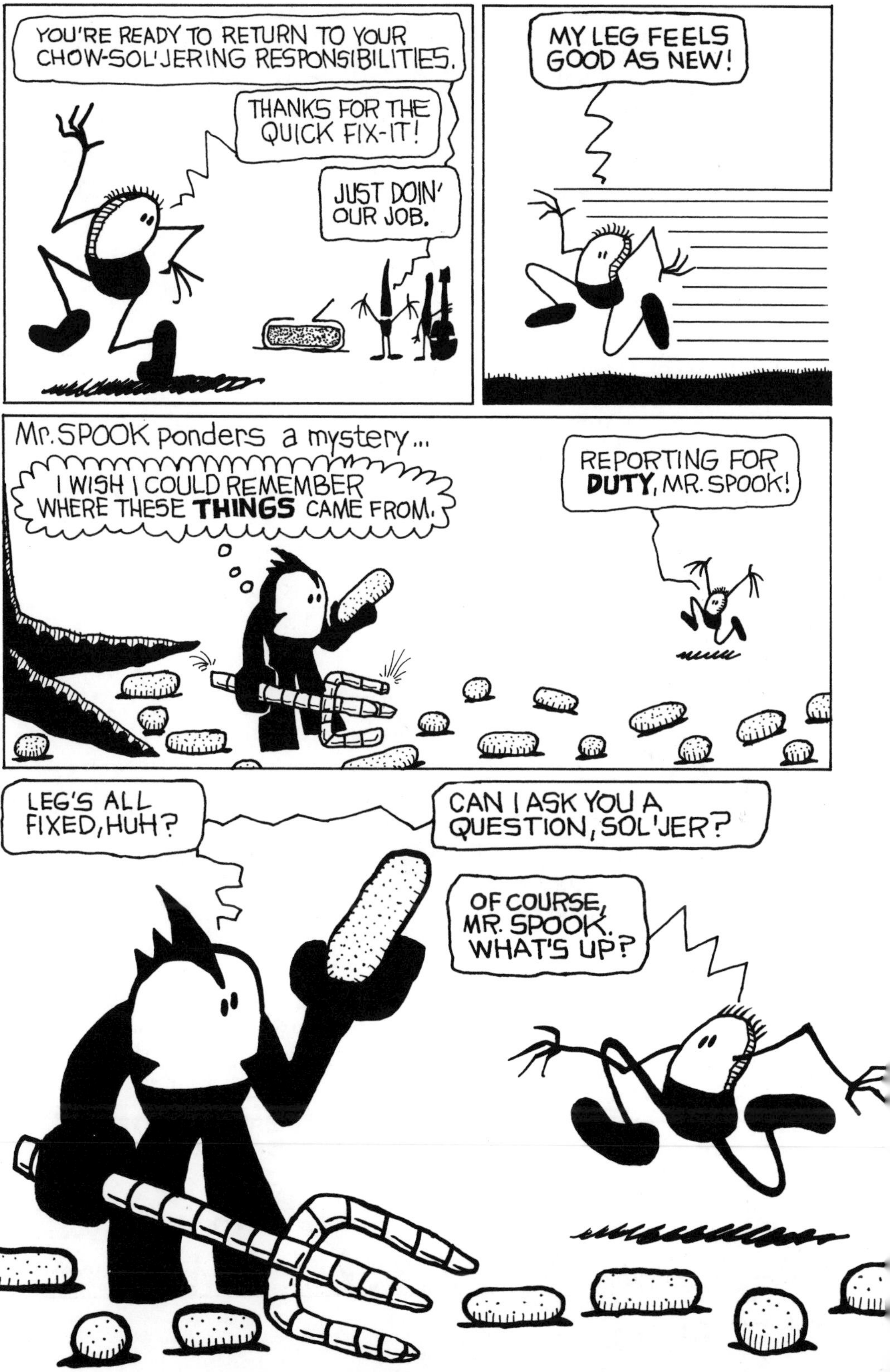
YOU'RE READY TO RETURN TO YOUR CHOW-SOL'JERING RESPONSIBILITIES.
THANKS FOR THE QUICK FIX-IT!
JUST DOIN' OUR JOB.
MY LEG FEELS GOOD AS NEW!
Mr. SPOOK ponders a mystery...
I WISH I COULD REMEMBER WHERE THESE **THINGS** CAME FROM.
REPORTING FOR **DUTY**, MR. SPOOK!
LEG'S ALL FIXED, HUH?
CAN I ASK YOU A QUESTION, SOL'JER?
OF COURSE, MR. SPOOK. WHAT'S UP?

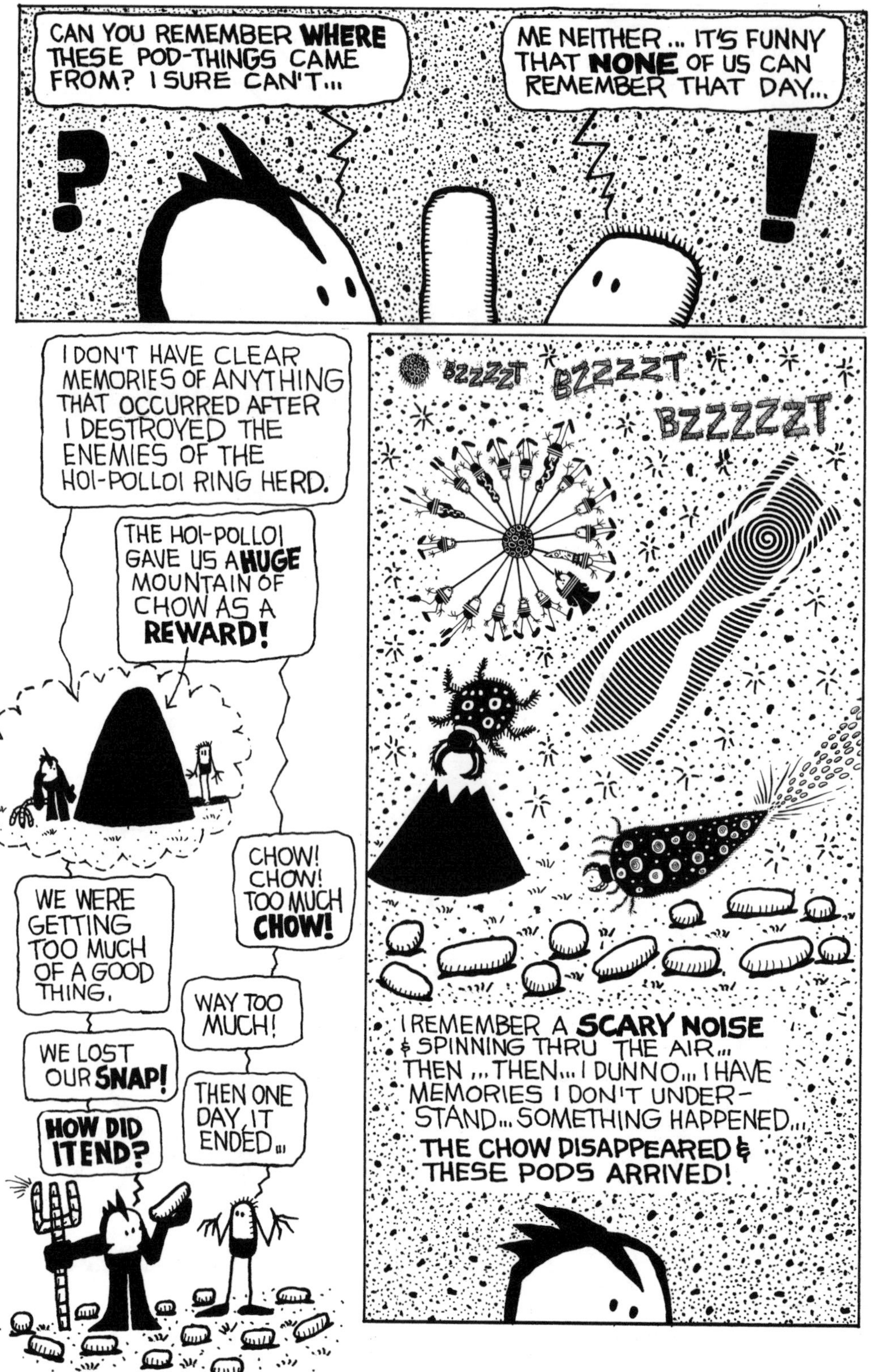
CAN YOU REMEMBER WHERE THESE POD-THINGS CAME FROM? I SURE CAN'T...
ME NEITHER... IT'S FUNNY THAT NONE OF US CAN REMEMBER THAT DAY...
I DON'T HAVE CLEAR MEMORIES OF ANYTHING THAT OCCURRED AFTER I DESTROYED THE ENEMIES OF THE HOI-POLLOI RING HERD.
THE HOI-POLLOI GAVE US A HUGE MOUNTAIN OF CHOW AS A REWARD!
WE WERE GETTING TOO MUCH OF A GOOD THING.
CHOW! CHOW! TOO MUCH CHOW!
WAY TOO MUCH!
WE LOST OUR SNAP!
THEN ONE DAY, IT ENDED...
HOW DID IT END?
BZZZZT BZZZZT BZZZZZT
I REMEMBER A SCARY NOISE & SPINNING THRU THE AIR... THEN ... THEN... I DUNNO... I HAVE MEMORIES I DON'T UNDER-STAND... SOMETHING HAPPENED...
THE CHOW DISAPPEARED & THESE PODS ARRIVED!

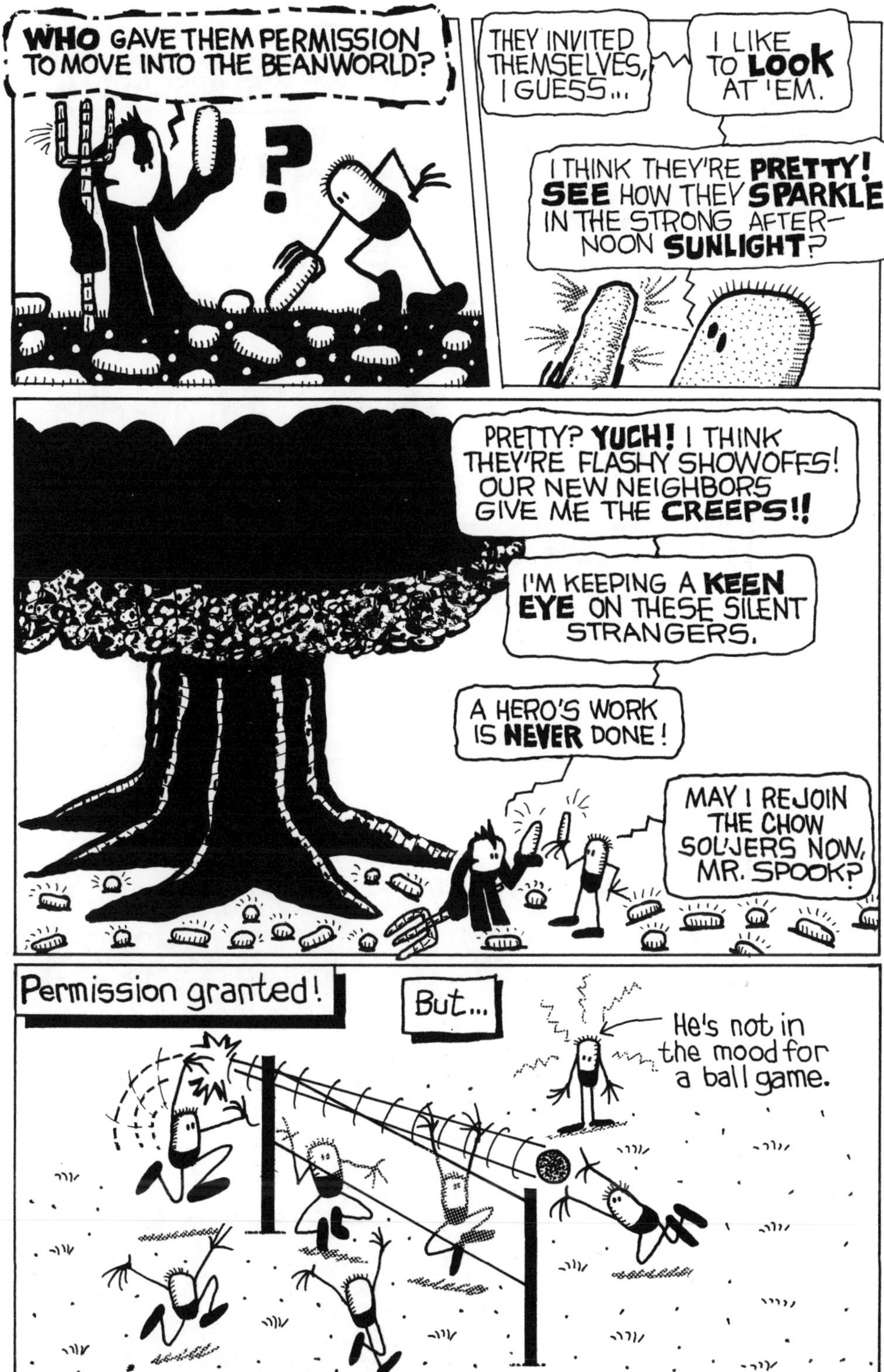

WHO GAVE THEM PERMISSION TO MOVE INTO THE BEANWORLD?
THEY INVITED THEMSELVES, I GUESS...
I LIKE TO LOOK AT 'EM.
I THINK THEY'RE PRETTY! SEE HOW THEY SPARKLE IN THE STRONG AFTER-NOON SUNLIGHT?
PRETTY? YUCH! I THINK THEY'RE FLASHY SHOWOFFS! OUR NEW NEIGHBORS GIVE ME THE CREEPS!!
I'M KEEPING A KEEN EYE ON THESE SILENT STRANGERS.
A HERO'S WORK IS NEVER DONE!
MAY I REJOIN THE CHOW SOL'JERS NOW, MR. SPOOK?
Permission granted!
But...
He's not in the mood for a ball game.

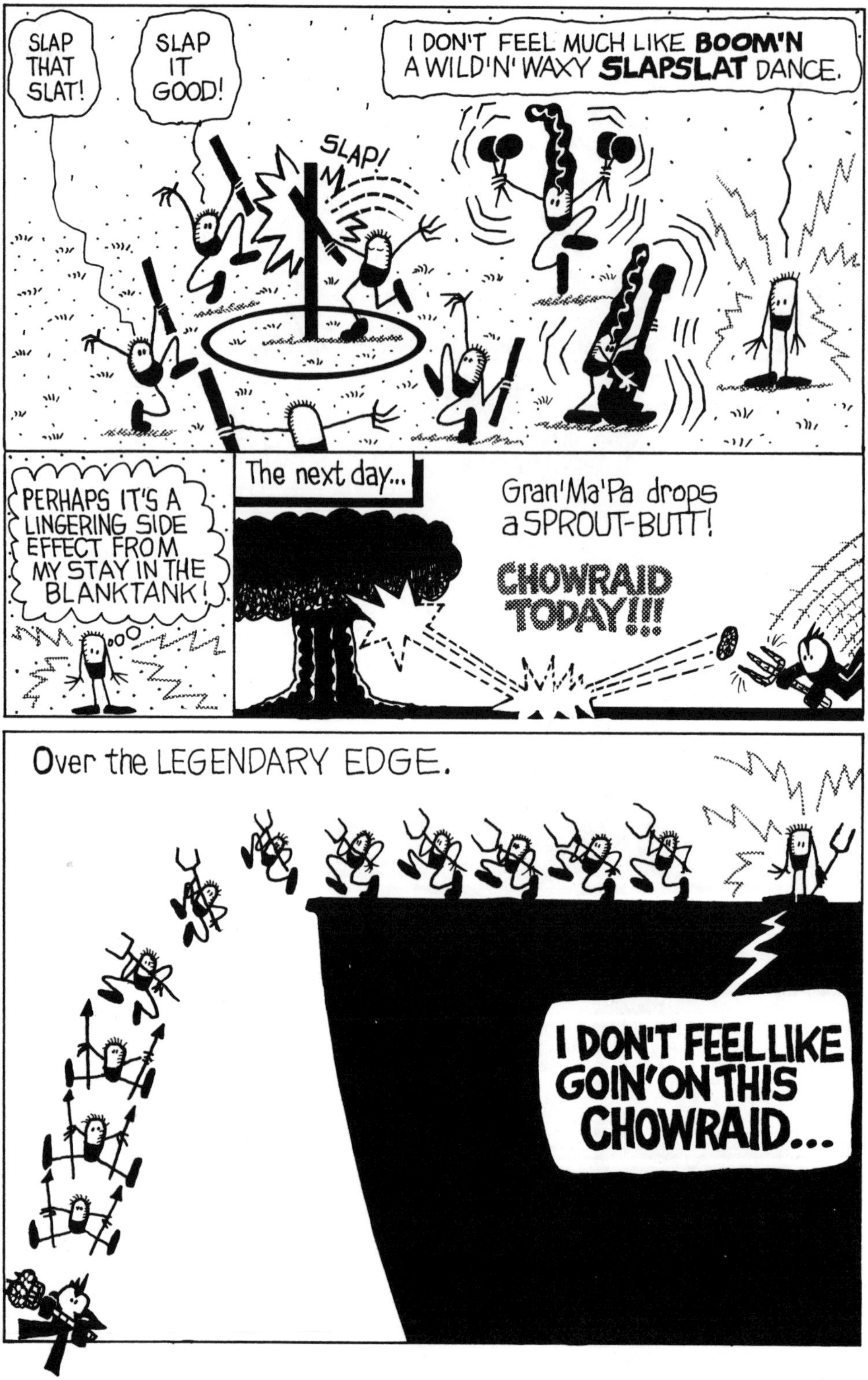
SLAP THAT SLAT!
SLAP IT GOOD!
I DON'T FEEL MUCH LIKE **BOOM'N** A WILD'N' WAXY **SLAPSLAT** DANCE.
SLAP!
PERHAPS IT'S A LINGERING SIDE EFFECT FROM MY STAY IN THE BLANKTANK!
The next day...
Gran'Ma'Pa drops a SPROUT-BUTT!
CHOWRAID TODAY!!!
Over the LEGENDARY EDGE.
I DON'T FEEL LIKE GOIN' ON THIS CHOWRAID...

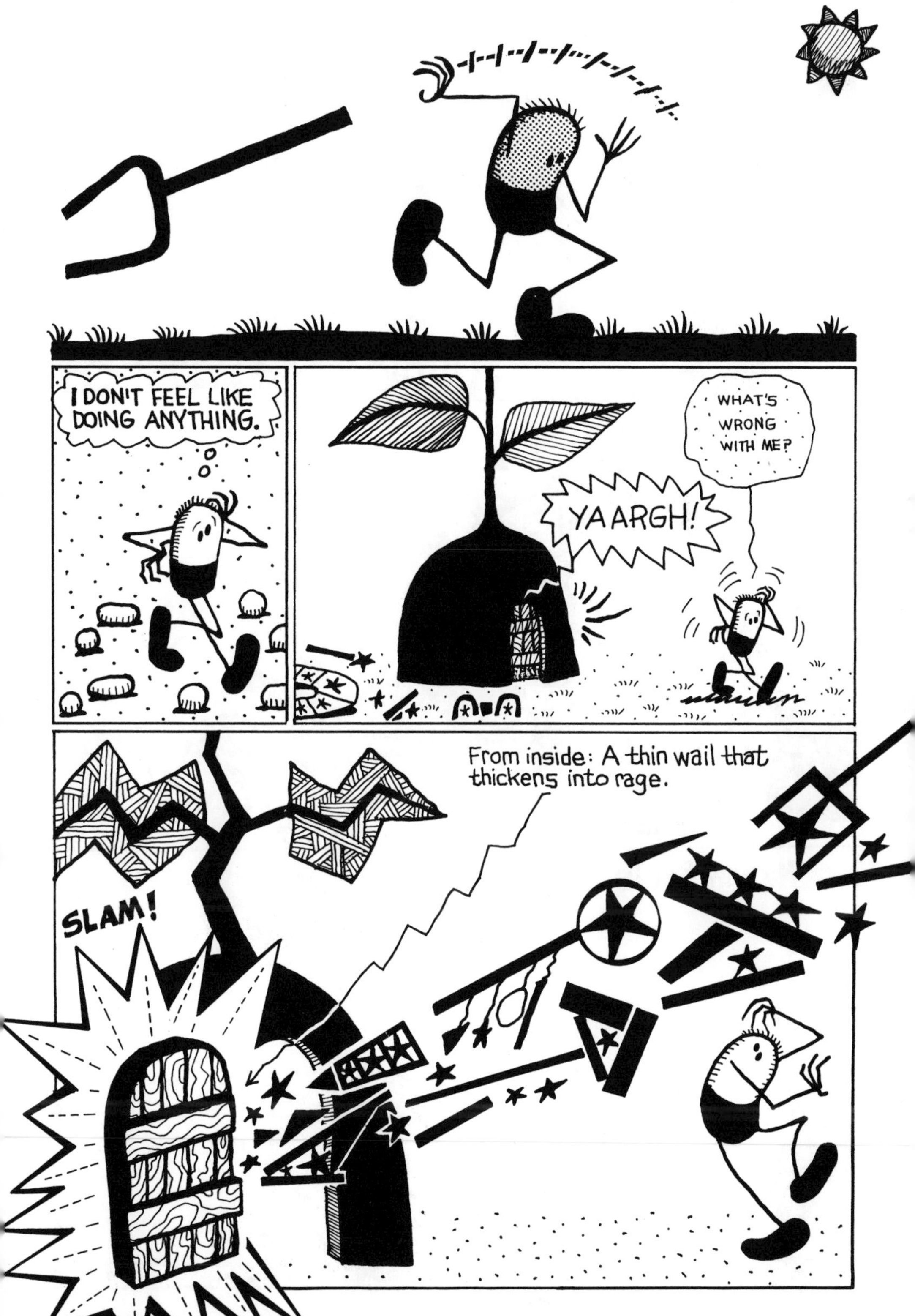
I DON'T FEEL LIKE DOING ANYTHING.
YAARGH!
WHAT'S WRONG WITH ME?
From inside: A thin wail that thickens into rage.
SLAM!

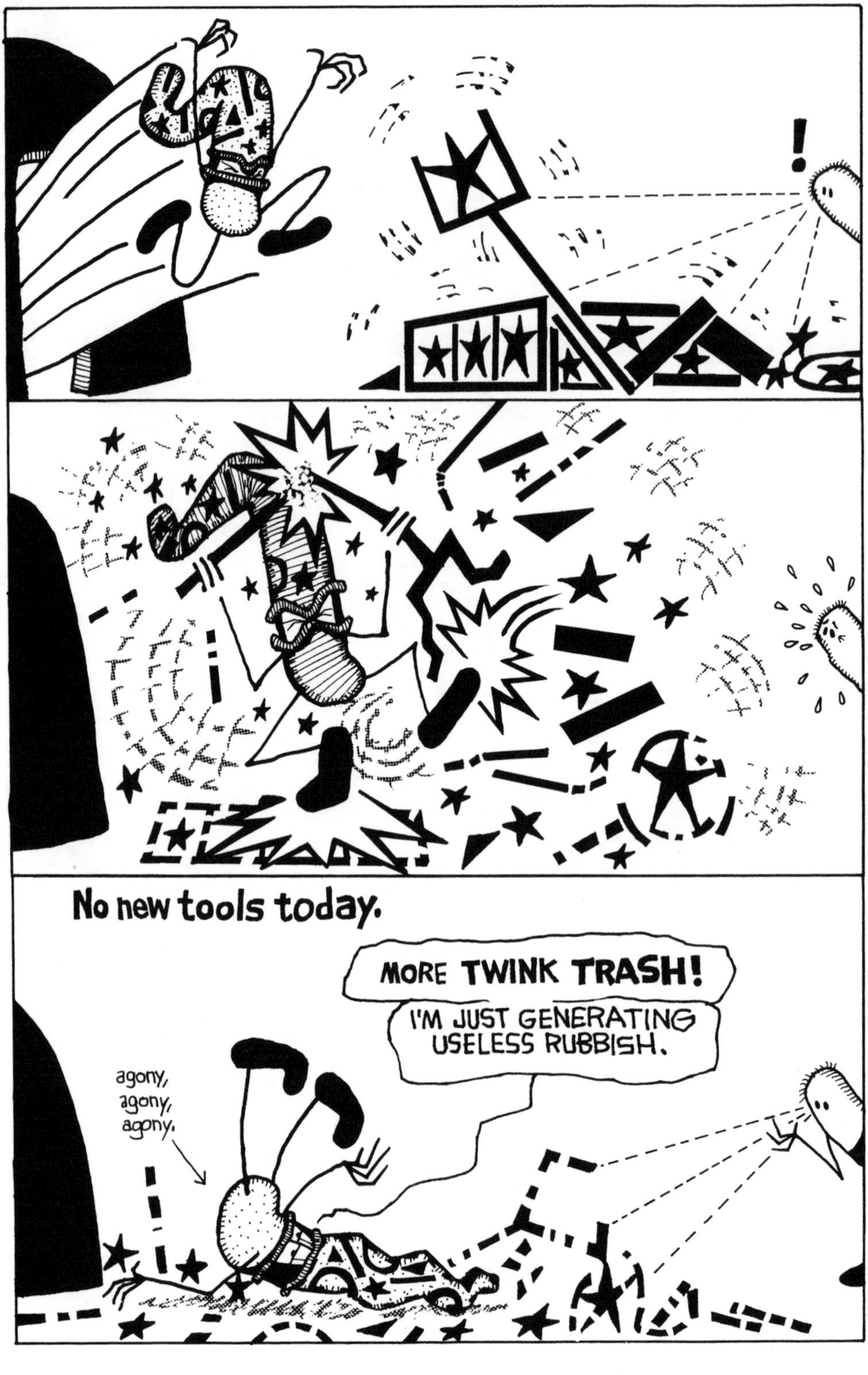
!
No new tools today.
MORE TWINK TRASH!
I'M JUST GENERATING USELESS RUBBISH.
agony, agony, agony.

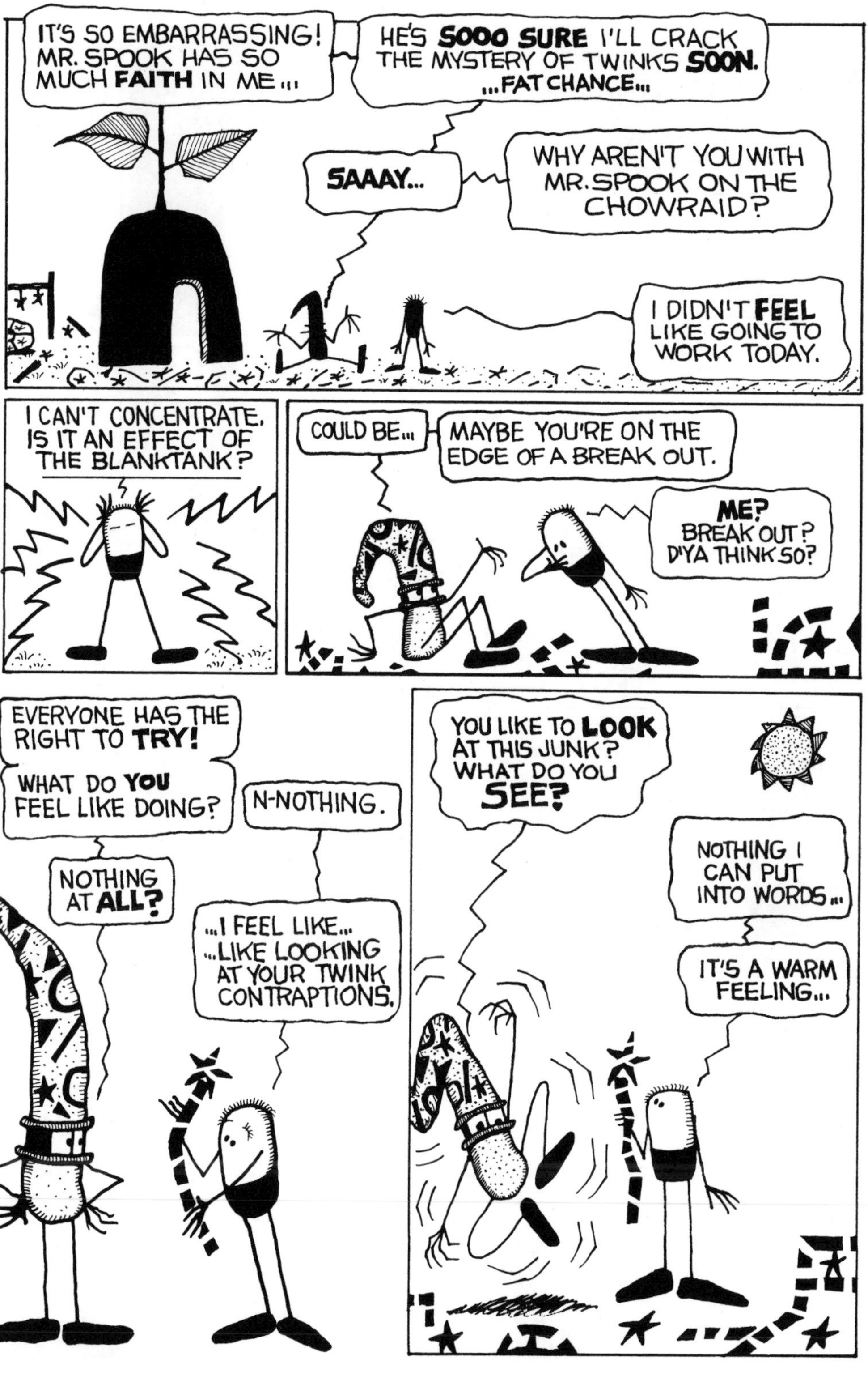
IT'S SO EMBARRASSING! MR. SPOOK HAS SO MUCH FAITH IN ME...
HE'S SOOO SURE I'LL CRACK THE MYSTERY OF TWINKS SOON. ...FAT CHANCE...
SAAAY...
WHY AREN'T YOU WITH MR. SPOOK ON THE CHOWRAID?
I DIDN'T FEEL LIKE GOING TO WORK TODAY.
I CAN'T CONCENTRATE. IS IT AN EFFECT OF THE BLANKTANK?
COULD BE...
MAYBE YOU'RE ON THE EDGE OF A BREAK OUT.
ME? BREAK OUT? D'YA THINK SO?
EVERYONE HAS THE RIGHT TO TRY!
WHAT DO YOU FEEL LIKE DOING?
N-NOTHING.
NOTHING AT ALL?
...I FEEL LIKE... ...LIKE LOOKING AT YOUR TWINK CONTRAPTIONS.
YOU LIKE TO LOOK AT THIS JUNK? WHAT DO YOU SEE?
NOTHING I CAN PUT INTO WORDS...
IT'S A WARM FEELING...

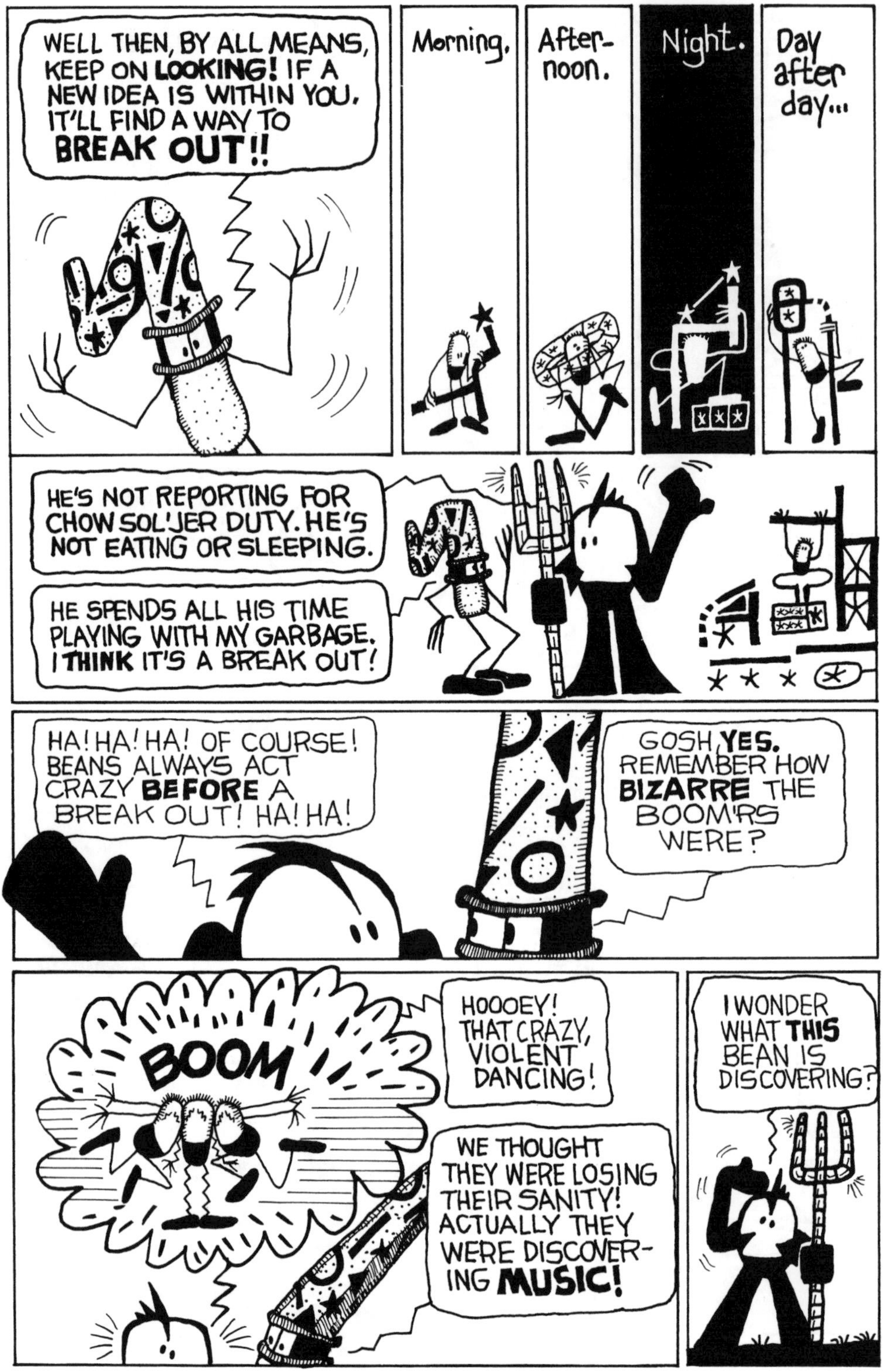
WELL THEN, BY ALL MEANS, KEEP ON LOOKING! IF A NEW IDEA IS WITHIN YOU, IT'LL FIND A WAY TO BREAK OUT!!
Morning.
After-noon.
Night.
Day after day...
HE'S NOT REPORTING FOR CHOW SOL'JER DUTY. HE'S NOT EATING OR SLEEPING.
HE SPENDS ALL HIS TIME PLAYING WITH MY GARBAGE. I THINK IT'S A BREAK OUT!
HA! HA! HA! OF COURSE! BEANS ALWAYS ACT CRAZY BEFORE A BREAK OUT! HA! HA!
GOSH YES. REMEMBER HOW BIZARRE THE BOOM'RS WERE?
BOOM
HOOOEY! THAT CRAZY, VIOLENT DANCING!
WE THOUGHT THEY WERE LOSING THEIR SANITY! ACTUALLY THEY WERE DISCOVER-ING MUSIC!
I WONDER WHAT THIS BEAN IS DISCOVERING?

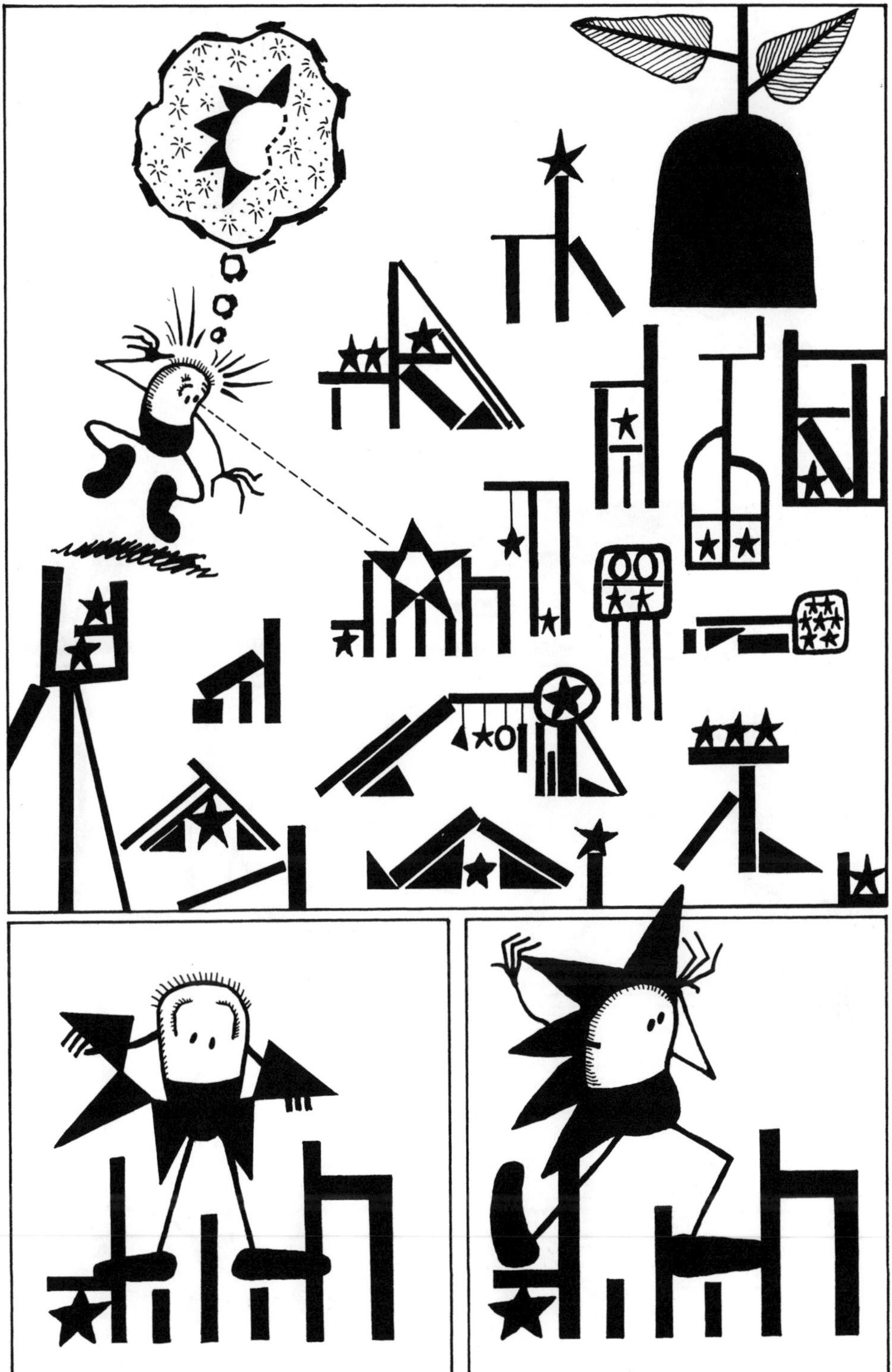

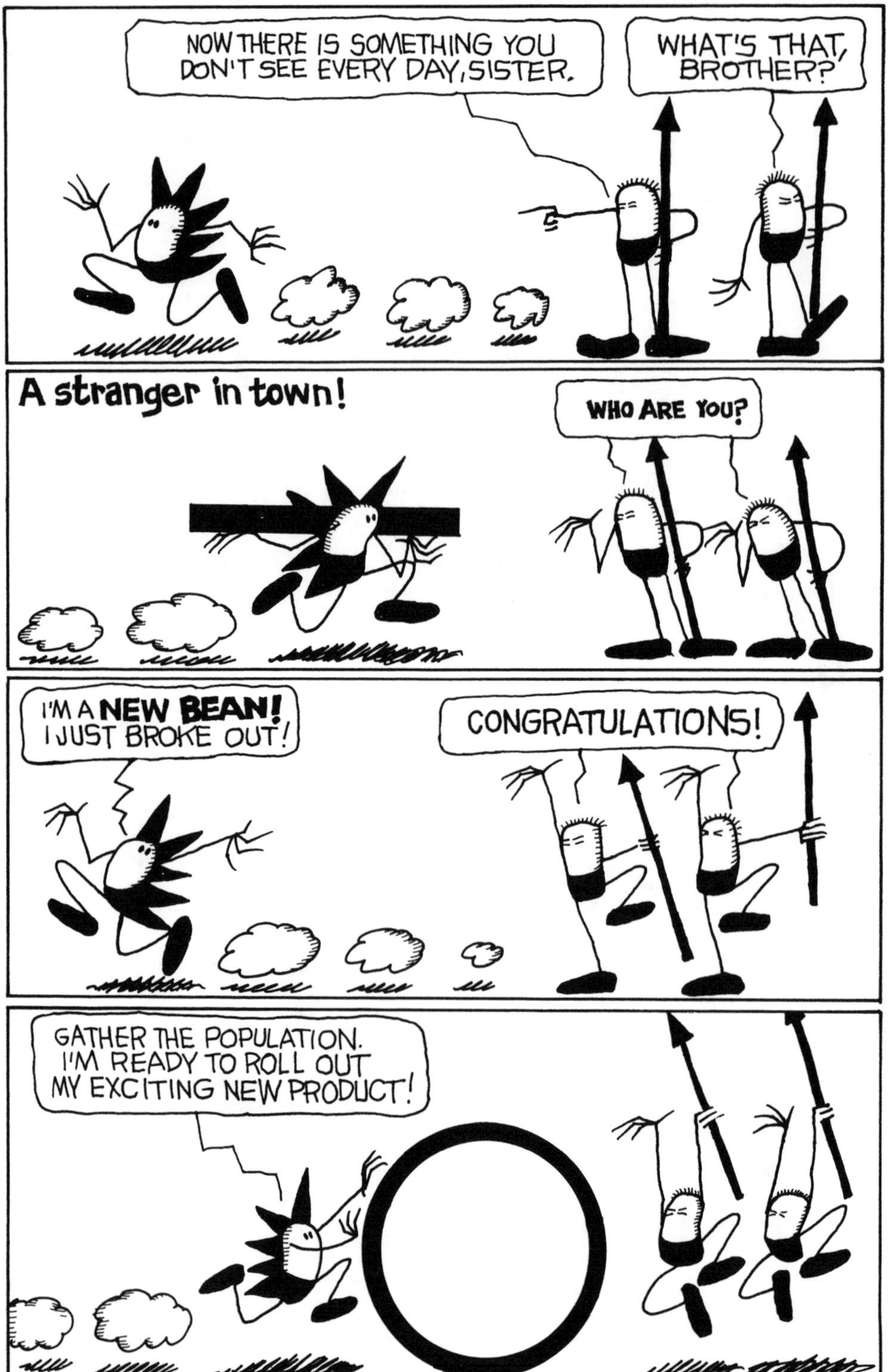
NOW THERE IS SOMETHING YOU DON'T SEE EVERY DAY, SISTER.
WHAT'S THAT, BROTHER?
A stranger in town!
WHO ARE YOU?
I'M A NEW BEAN! I JUST BROKE OUT!
CONGRATULATIONS!
GATHER THE POPULATION. I'M READY TO ROLL OUT MY EXCITING NEW PRODUCT!

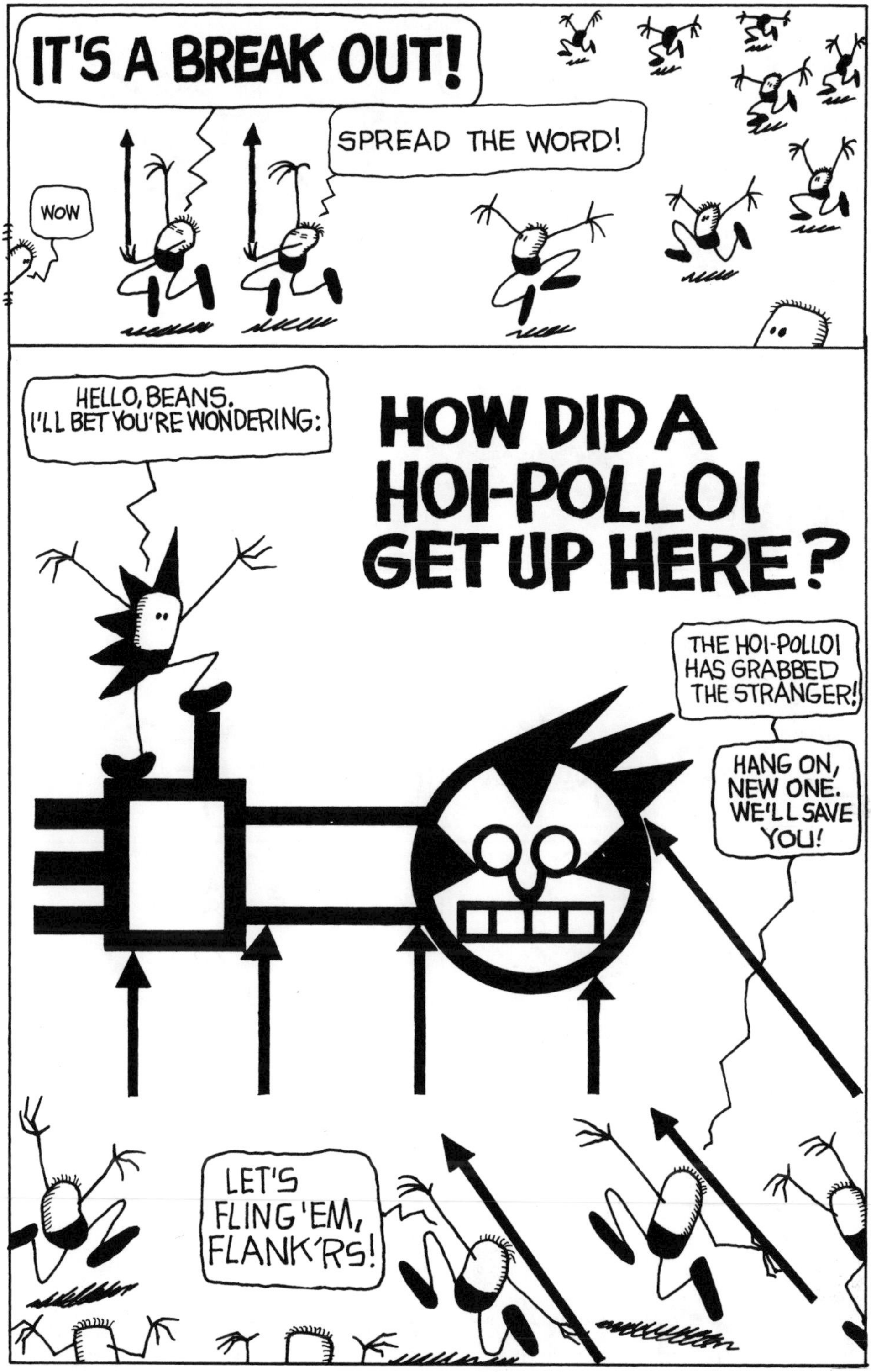
IT'S A BREAK OUT!
SPREAD THE WORD!
WOW
HELLO, BEANS. I'LL BET YOU'RE WONDERING:
HOW DID A HOI-POLLOI GET UP HERE?
THE HOI-POLLOI HAS GRABBED THE STRANGER!
HANG ON, NEW ONE. WE'LL SAVE YOU!
LET'S FLING 'EM, FLANK'RS!

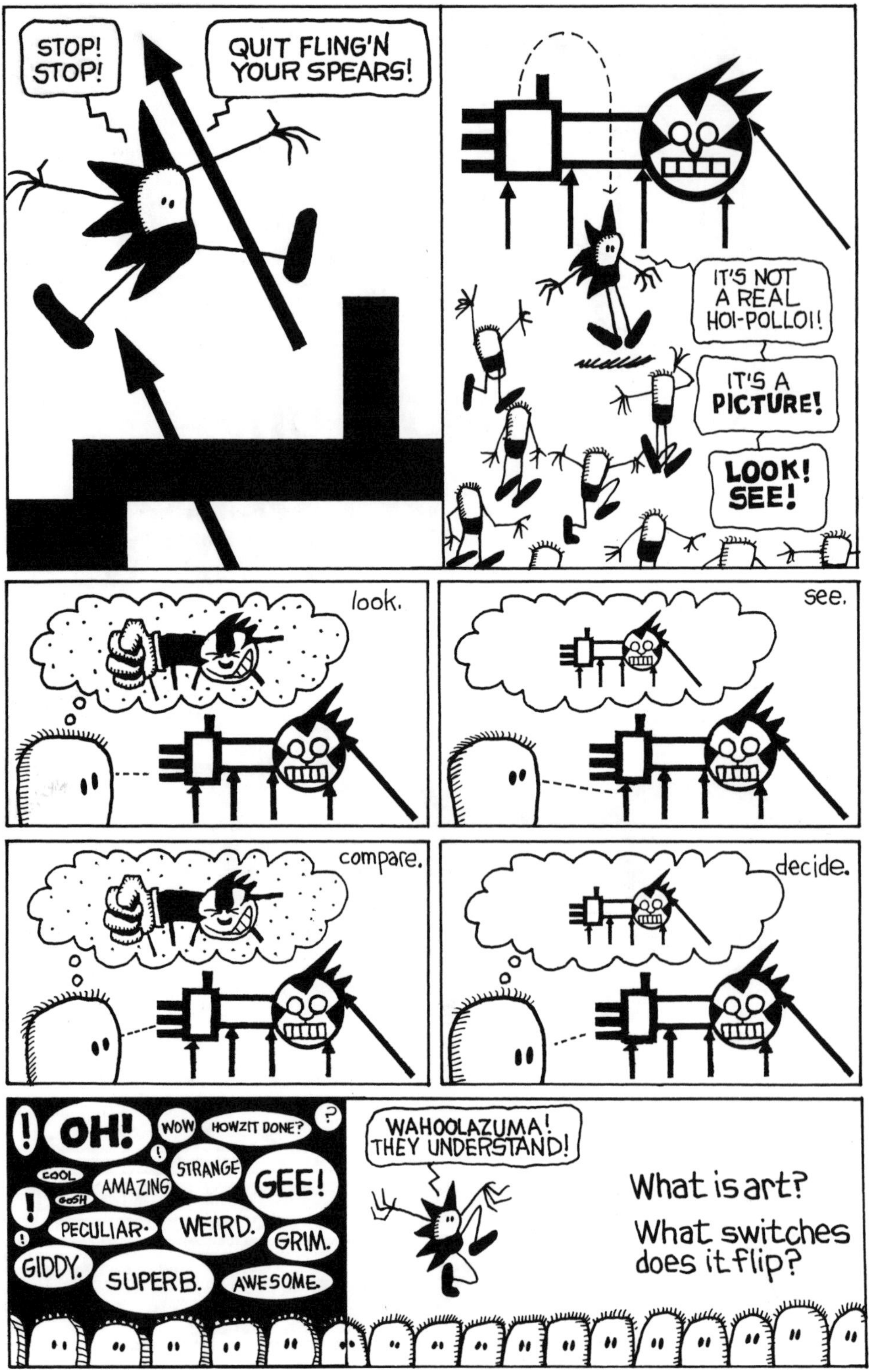
STOP! STOP!
QUIT FLING'N YOUR SPEARS!
IT'S NOT A REAL HOI-POLLOI!
IT'S A PICTURE!
LOOK! SEE!
look.
see.
compare.
decide.
OH!
WOW
HOWZIT DONE?
COOL
AMAZING
STRANGE
GEE!
GOSH
PECULIAR.
WEIRD.
GRIM.
GIDDY.
SUPERB.
AWESOME.
WAHOOLAZUMA! THEY UNDERSTAND!
What is art?
What switches does it flip?

What is this POWER that makes our minds race, our pulses pound?

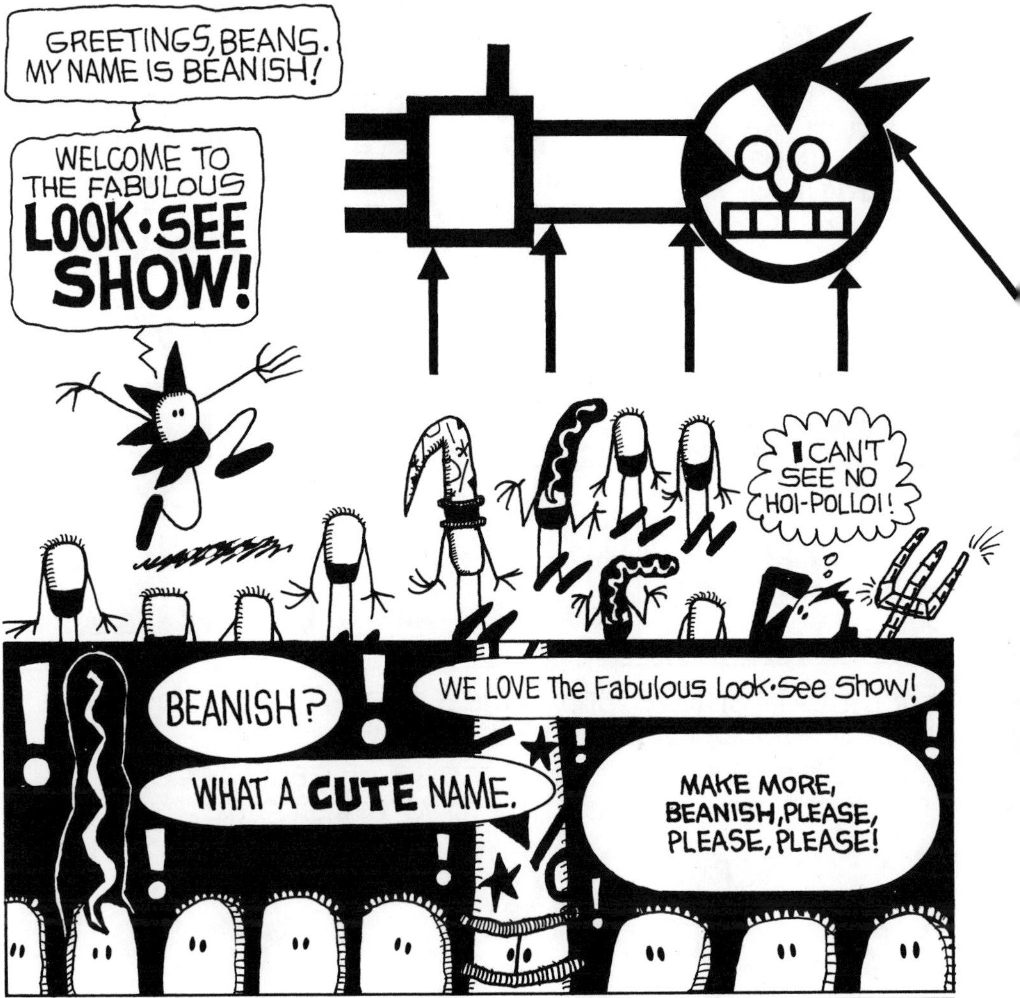
GREETINGS, BEANS. MY NAME IS BEANISH!
WELCOME TO THE FABULOUS LOOK·SEE SHOW!
I CAN'T SEE NO HOI-POLLOI!
BEANISH?
WE LOVE The Fabulous Look·See Show!
WHAT A CUTE NAME.
MAKE MORE, BEANISH, PLEASE, PLEASE, PLEASE!

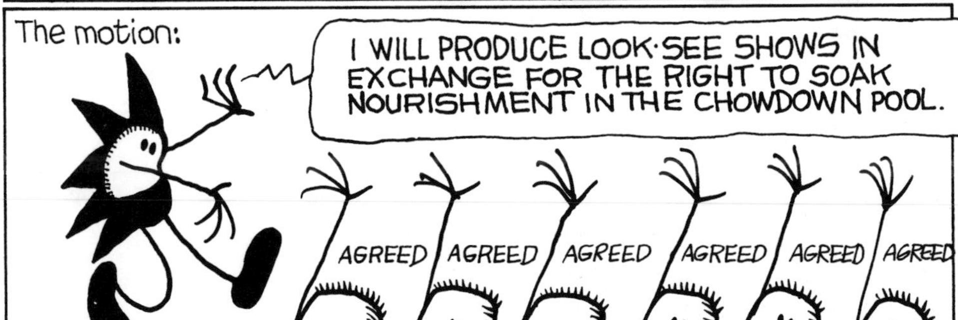
The motion:
I WILL PRODUCE LOOK·SEE SHOWS IN EXCHANGE FOR THE RIGHT TO SOAK NOURISHMENT IN THE CHOWDOWN POOL.
AGREED
AGREED
AGREED
AGREED
AGREED
AGREED

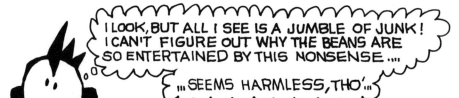

I LOOK, BUT ALL I SEE IS A JUMBLE OF JUNK! I CAN'T FIGURE OUT WHY THE BEANS ARE SO ENTERTAINED BY THIS NONSENSE ....

...SEEMS HARMLESS, THO'...

AWWW, I DON'T WANNA BE A PARTY POOP'R!

AGREED   AGREED   AGREED

BEANISH takes the BEANWORLD by **storm!** Here's the new routine: Every GOOF-OFF DAY, BEANISH produces a new version of the FABULOUS **LOOK·SEE SHOW!**

CHOW SOL'JER

Each BEAN enjoys and judges the FABULOUS LOOK·SEE SHOW in a personal way. BEANISH measures the success of each piece by the length of time the crowd remains at the SHOW.

I NEVER SEE NOTHING.

SELF-PORTRAIT

Soon, it's hard to remember what life was like before BEANISH broke out.

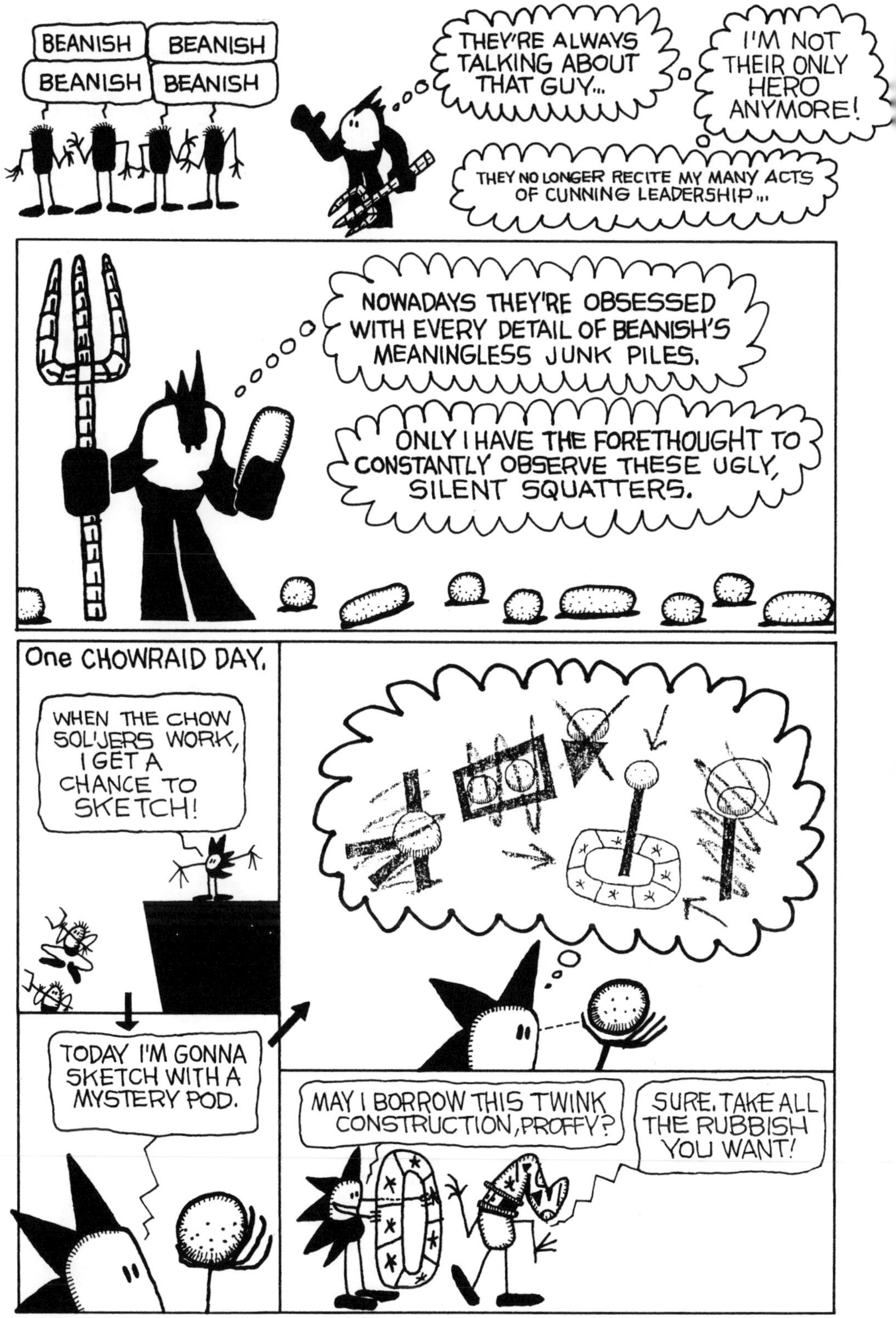
BEANISH
BEANISH
BEANISH
BEANISH
THEY'RE ALWAYS TALKING ABOUT THAT GUY...
I'M NOT THEIR ONLY HERO ANYMORE!
THEY NO LONGER RECITE MY MANY ACTS OF CUNNING LEADERSHIP...
NOWADAYS THEY'RE OBSESSED WITH EVERY DETAIL OF BEANISH'S MEANINGLESS JUNK PILES.
ONLY I HAVE THE FORETHOUGHT TO CONSTANTLY OBSERVE THESE UGLY, SILENT SQUATTERS.
One CHOWRAID DAY.
WHEN THE CHOW SOL'JERS WORK, I GET A CHANCE TO SKETCH!
TODAY I'M GONNA SKETCH WITH A MYSTERY POD.
MAY I BORROW THIS TWINK CONSTRUCTION, PROFFY?
SURE. TAKE ALL THE RUBBISH YOU WANT!

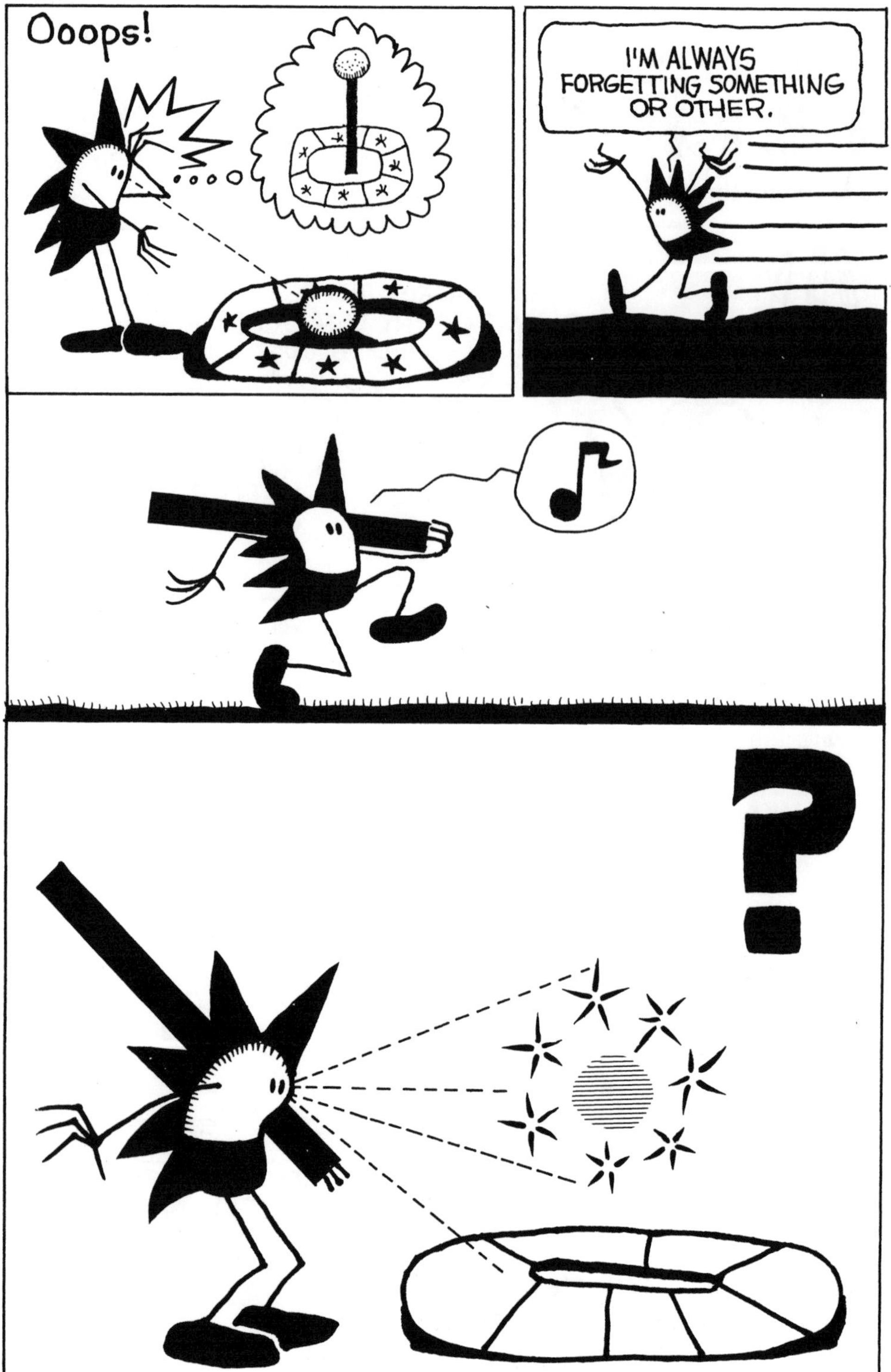
Ooops!
I'M ALWAYS FORGETTING SOMETHING OR OTHER.

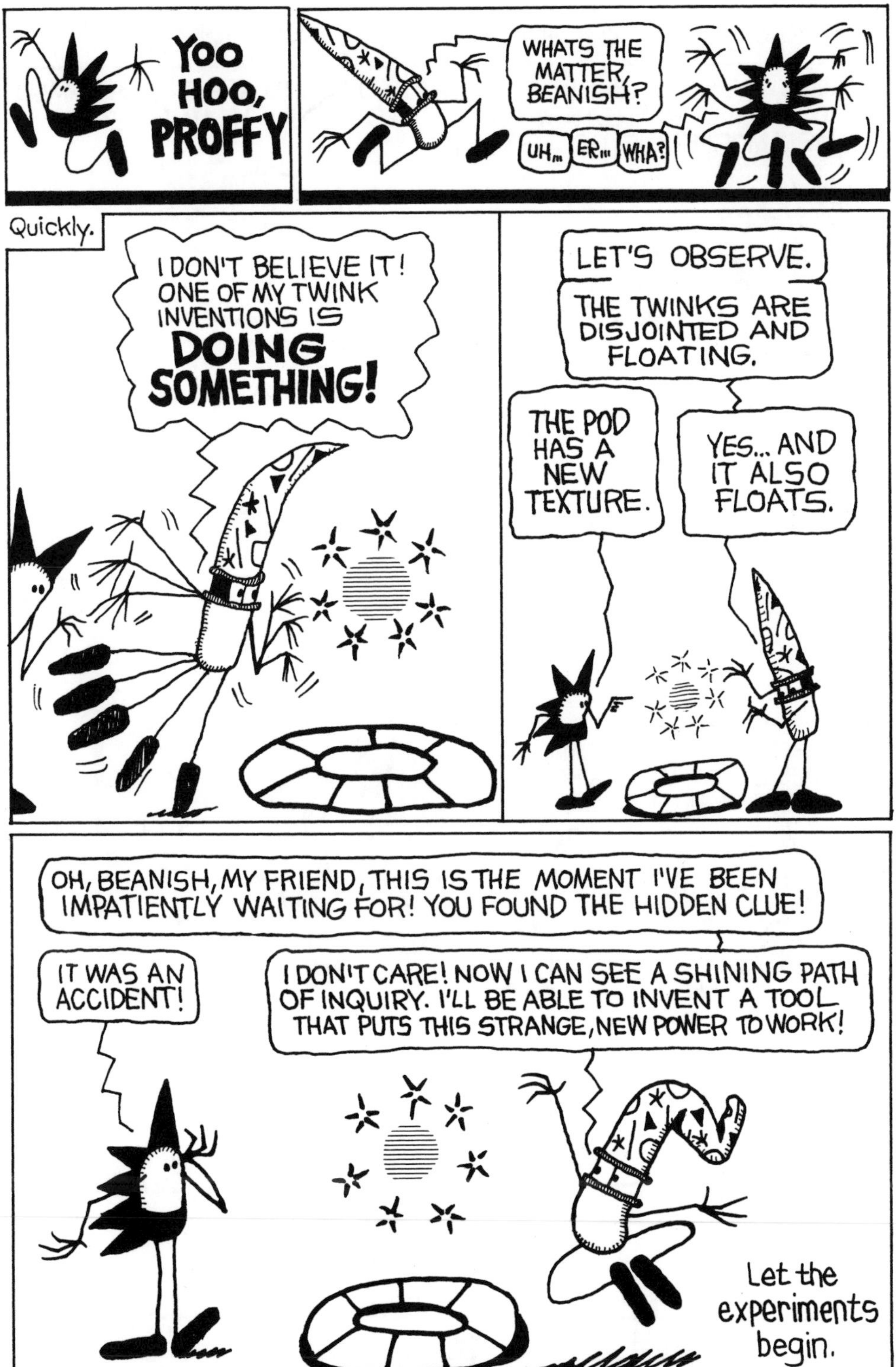
YOO HOO, PROFFY
WHATS THE MATTER, BEANISH?
UH... ER... WHA?
Quickly.
I DON'T BELIEVE IT! ONE OF MY TWINK INVENTIONS IS DOING SOMETHING!
LET'S OBSERVE.
THE TWINKS ARE DISJOINTED AND FLOATING.
THE POD HAS A NEW TEXTURE.
YES... AND IT ALSO FLOATS.
OH, BEANISH, MY FRIEND, THIS IS THE MOMENT I'VE BEEN IMPATIENTLY WAITING FOR! YOU FOUND THE HIDDEN CLUE!
IT WAS AN ACCIDENT!
I DON'T CARE! NOW I CAN SEE A SHINING PATH OF INQUIRY. I'LL BE ABLE TO INVENT A TOOL THAT PUTS THIS STRANGE, NEW POWER TO WORK!
Let the experiments begin.

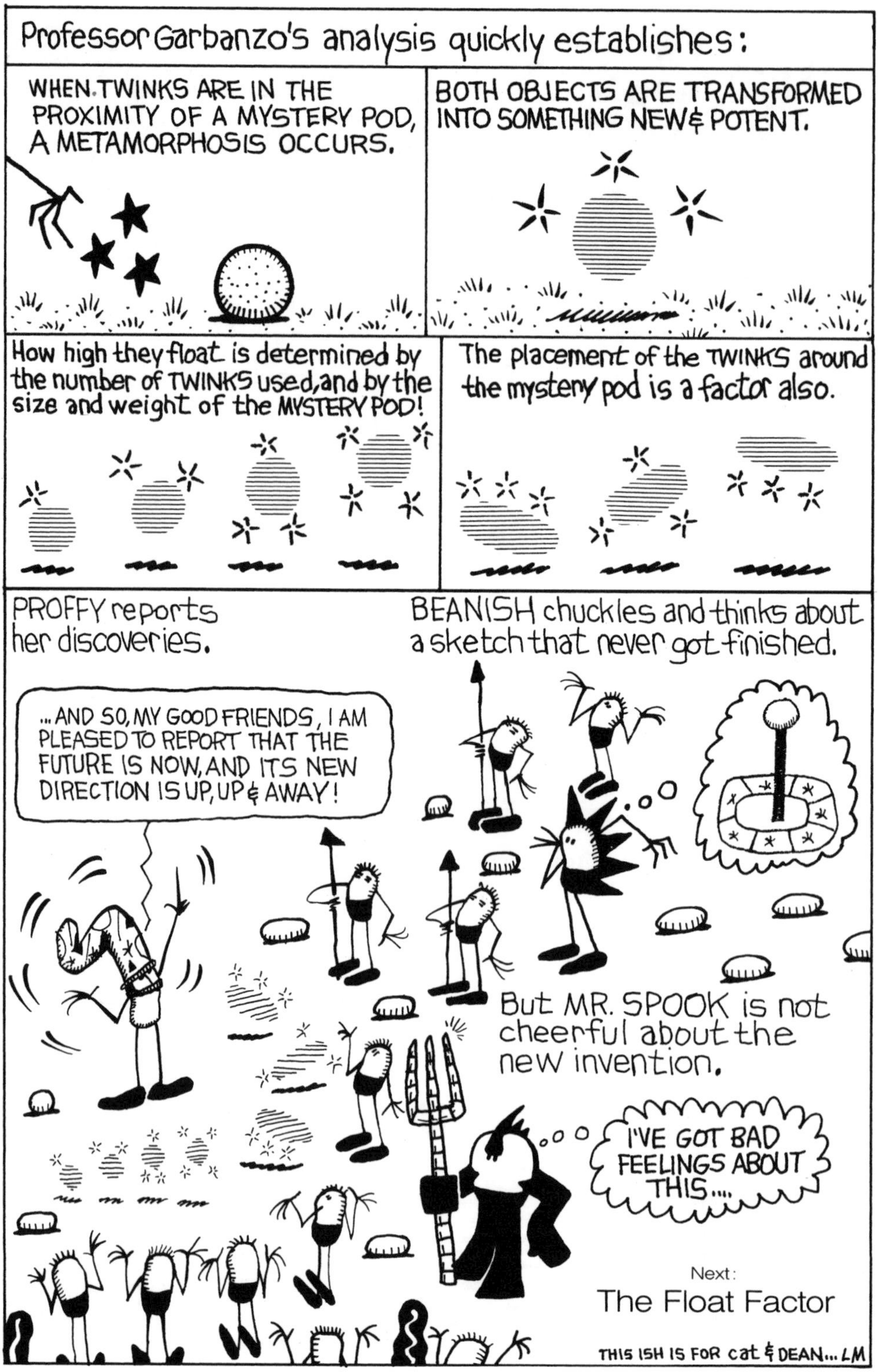
Professor Garbanzo's analysis quickly establishes:
WHEN TWINKS ARE IN THE PROXIMITY OF A MYSTERY POD, A METAMORPHOSIS OCCURS.
BOTH OBJECTS ARE TRANSFORMED INTO SOMETHING NEW & POTENT.
How high they float is determined by the number of TWINKS used, and by the size and weight of the MYSTERY POD!
The placement of the TWINKS around the mystery pod is a factor also.
PROFFY reports her discoveries.
...AND SO, MY GOOD FRIENDS, I AM PLEASED TO REPORT THAT THE FUTURE IS NOW, AND ITS NEW DIRECTION IS UP, UP & AWAY!
BEANISH chuckles and thinks about a sketch that never got finished.
But MR. SPOOK is not cheerful about the new invention.
I'VE GOT BAD FEELINGS ABOUT THIS....
Next:
The Float Factor
THIS ISH IS FOR cat & DEAN... LM

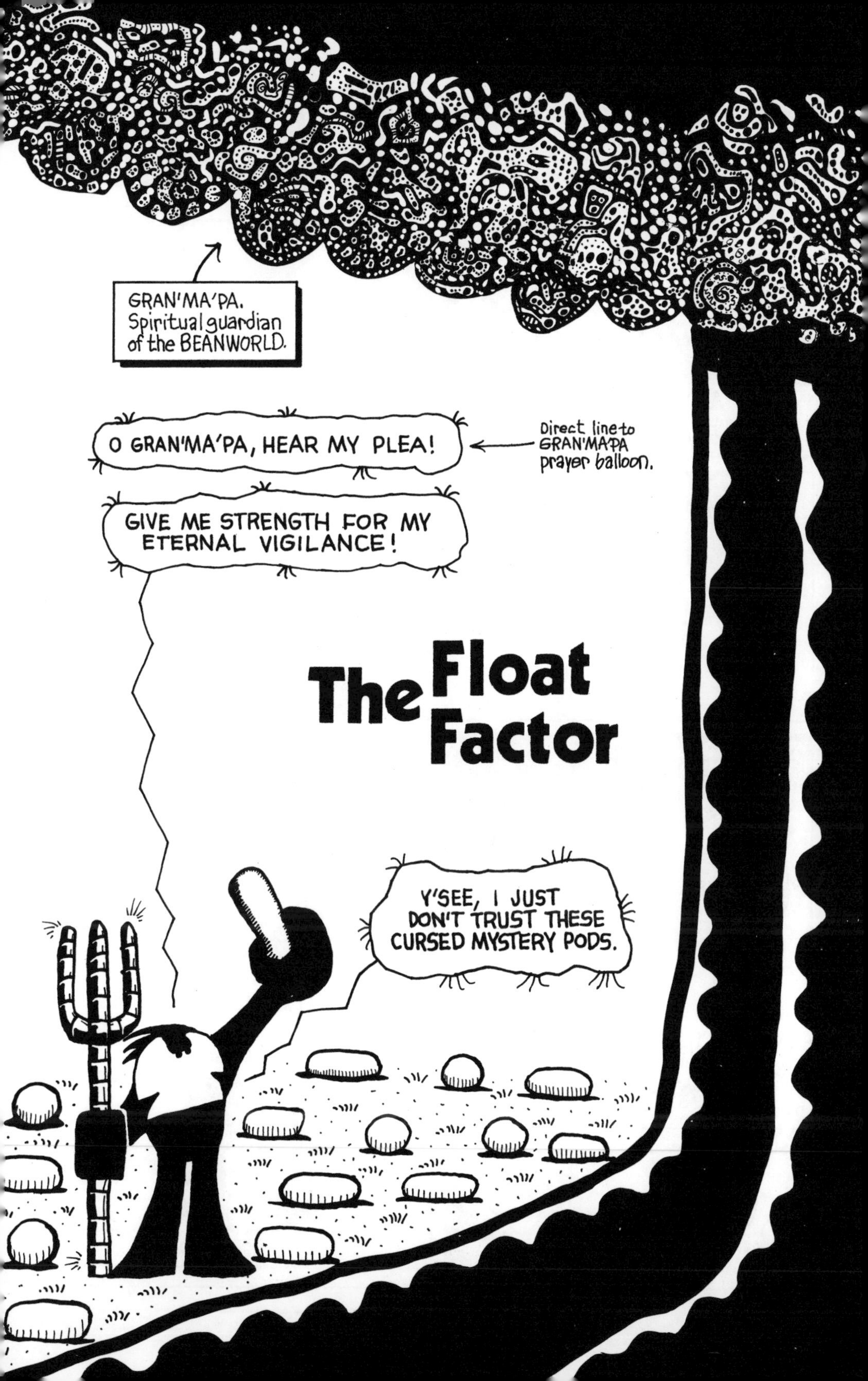
GRAN'MA'PA. Spiritual guardian of the BEANWORLD.
O GRAN'MA'PA, HEAR MY PLEA!
Direct line to GRAN'MA'PA prayer balloon.
GIVE ME STRENGTH FOR MY ETERNAL VIGILANCE!
The Float Factor
Y'SEE, I JUST DON'T TRUST THESE CURSED MYSTERY PODS.

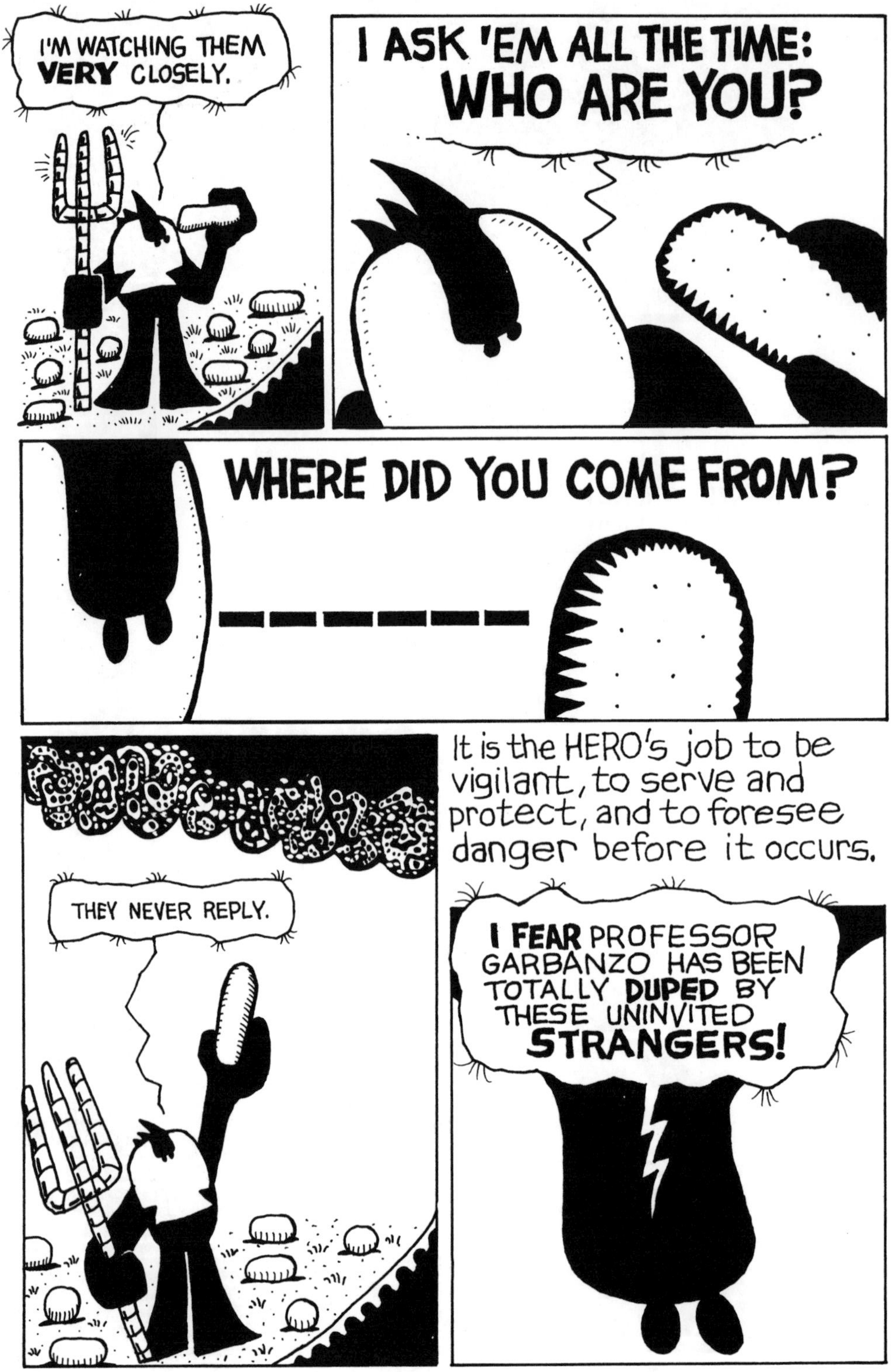
I'M WATCHING THEM **VERY** CLOSELY.
I ASK 'EM ALL THE TIME: WHO ARE YOU?
WHERE DID YOU COME FROM?
THEY NEVER REPLY.
It is the HERO's job to be vigilant, to serve and protect, and to foresee danger before it occurs.
**I FEAR** PROFESSOR GARBANZO HAS BEEN TOTALLY **DUPED** BY THESE UNINVITED **STRANGERS!**

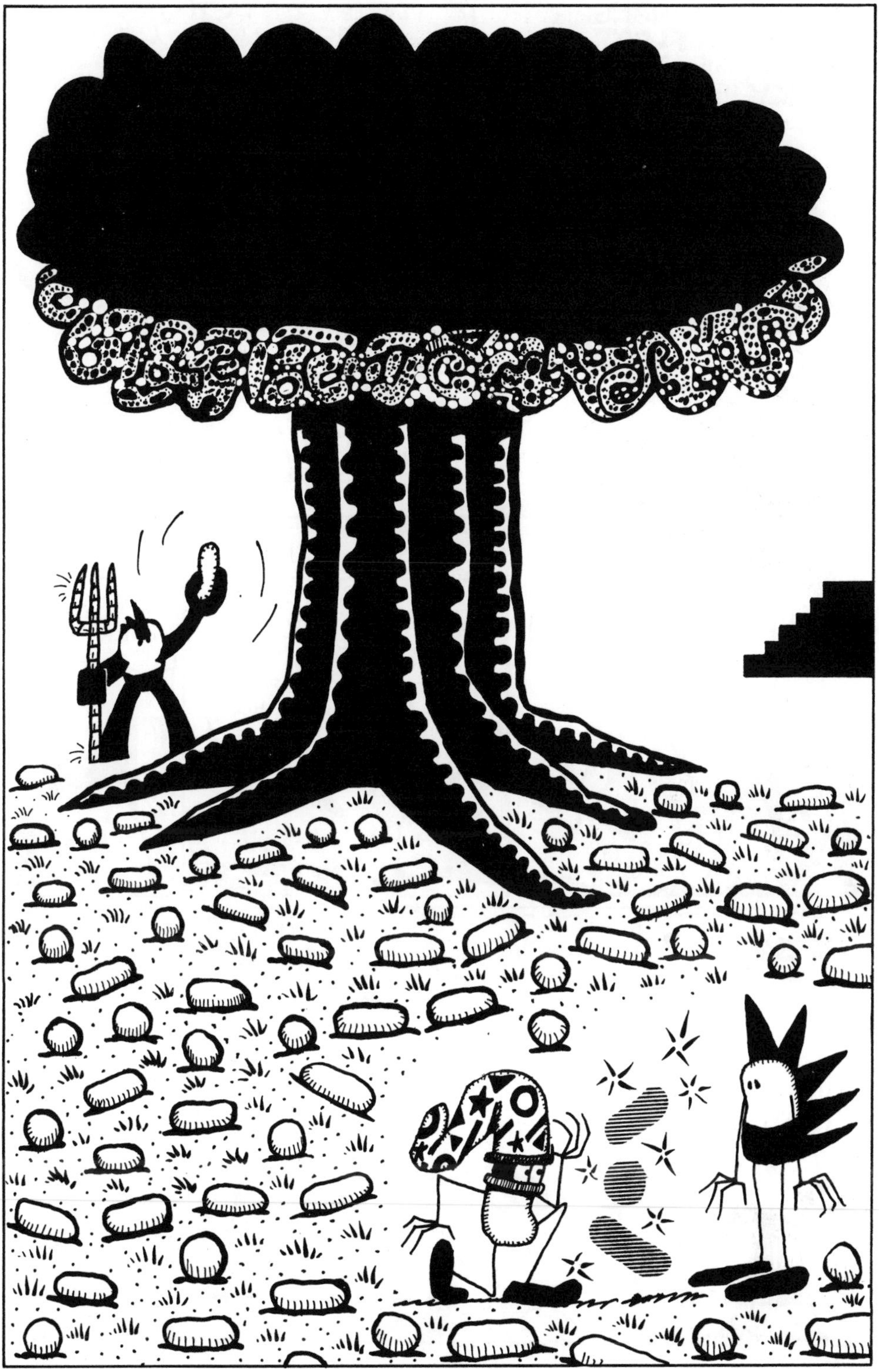

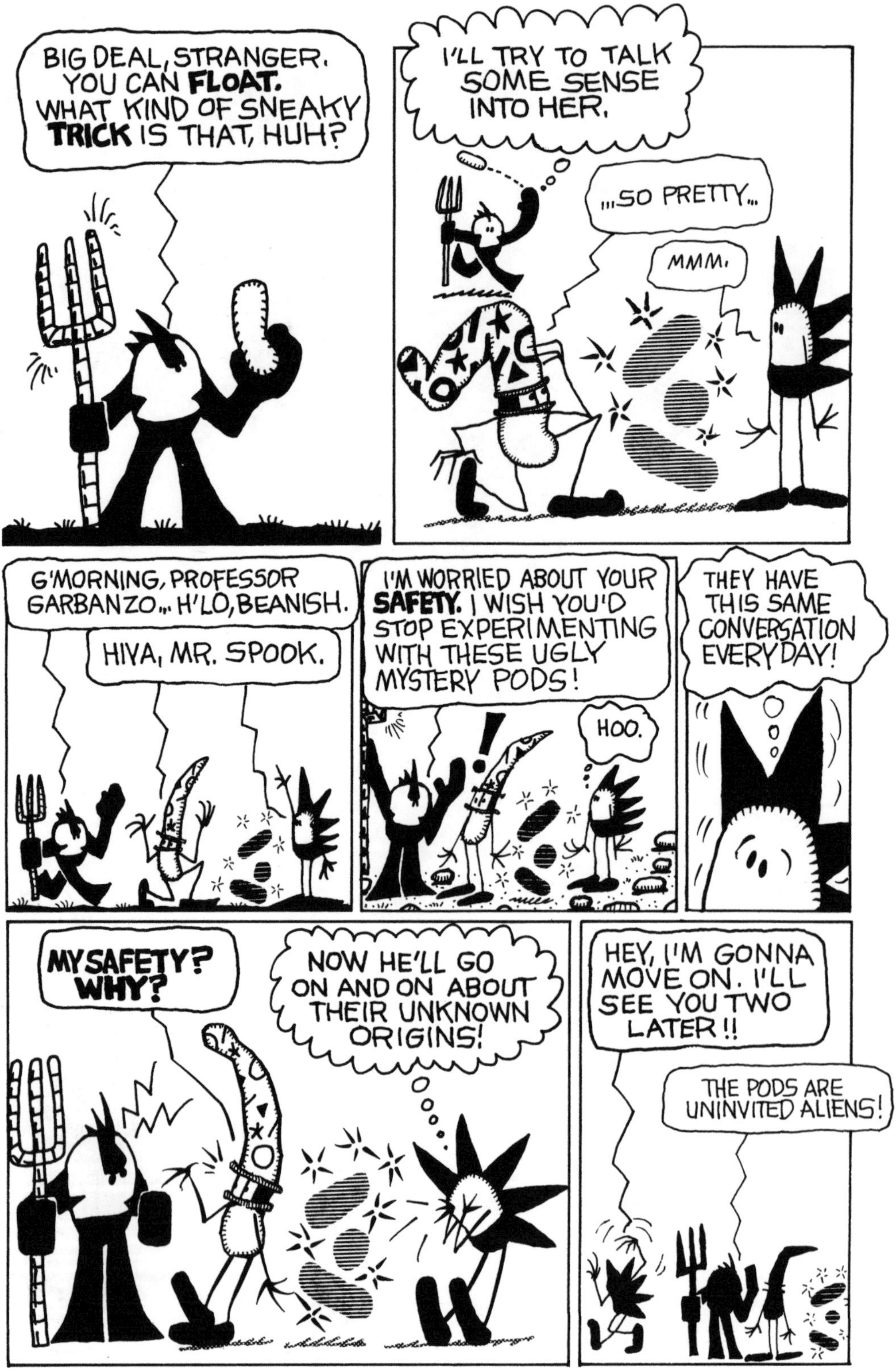
BIG DEAL, STRANGER. YOU CAN **FLOAT.** WHAT KIND OF SNEAKY **TRICK** IS THAT, HUH?
I'LL TRY TO TALK SOME SENSE INTO HER.
...SO PRETTY...
MMM.
G'MORNING, PROFESSOR GARBANZO... H'LO, BEANISH.
HIYA, MR. SPOOK.
I'M WORRIED ABOUT YOUR **SAFETY.** I WISH YOU'D STOP EXPERIMENTING WITH THESE UGLY MYSTERY PODS!
HOO.
THEY HAVE THIS SAME CONVERSATION EVERYDAY!
**MY SAFETY? WHY?**
NOW HE'LL GO ON AND ON ABOUT THEIR UNKNOWN ORIGINS!
HEY, I'M GONNA MOVE ON. I'LL SEE YOU TWO LATER!!
THE PODS ARE UNINVITED ALIENS!

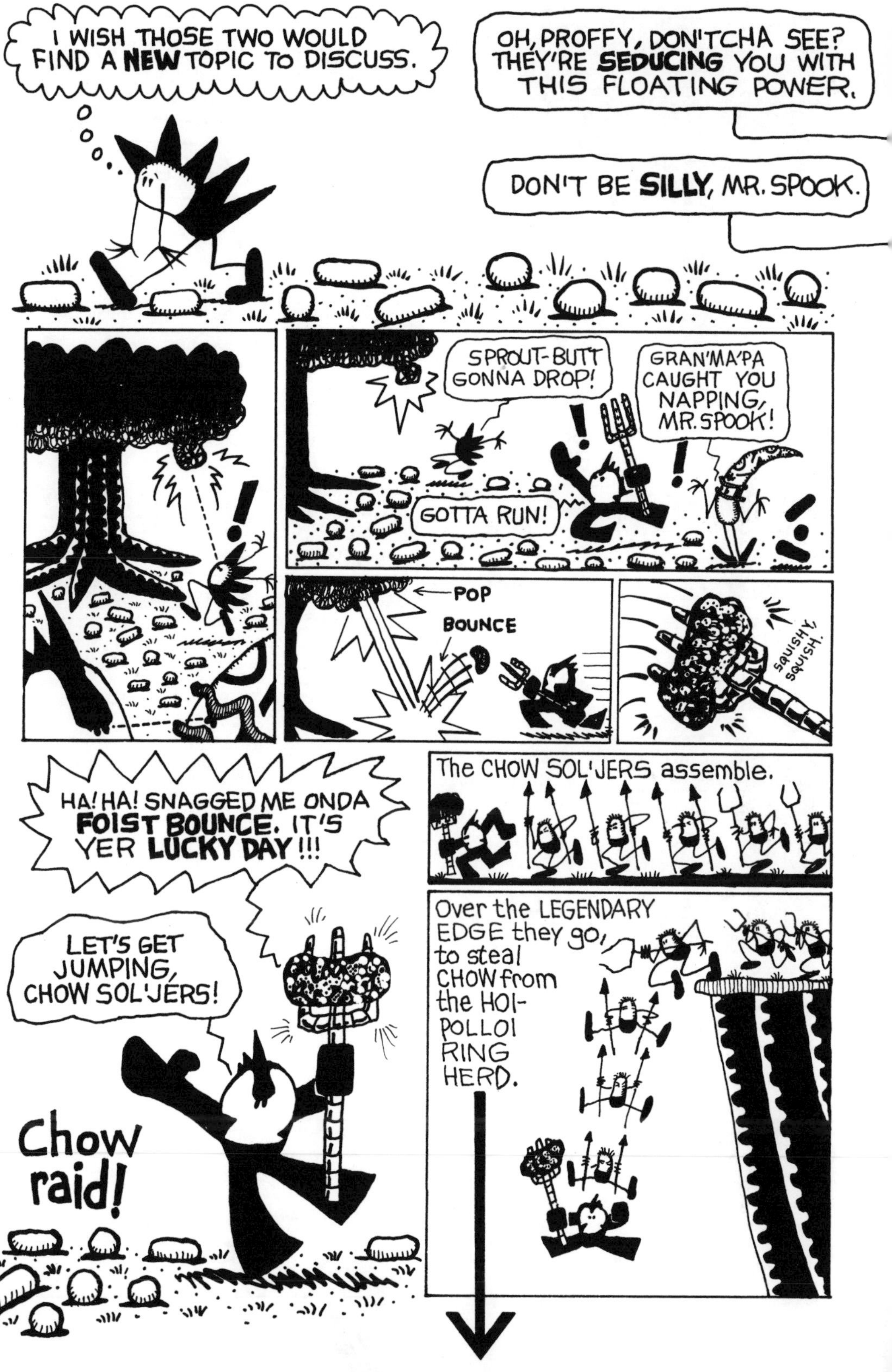
I WISH THOSE TWO WOULD FIND A NEW TOPIC TO DISCUSS.
OH, PROFFY, DON'TCHA SEE? THEY'RE SEDUCING YOU WITH THIS FLOATING POWER.
DON'T BE SILLY, MR. SPOOK.
SPROUT-BUTT GONNA DROP!
GOTTA RUN!
GRAN'MA'PA CAUGHT YOU NAPPING, MR. SPOOK!
POP
BOUNCE
SQUISHY, SQUISH.
HA! HA! SNAGGED ME ONDA FOIST BOUNCE. IT'S YER LUCKY DAY!!!
The CHOW SOL'JERS assemble.
LET'S GET JUMPING, CHOW SOL'JERS!
Chow raid!
Over the LEGENDARY EDGE they go, to steal CHOW from the HOI-POLLOI RING HERD.

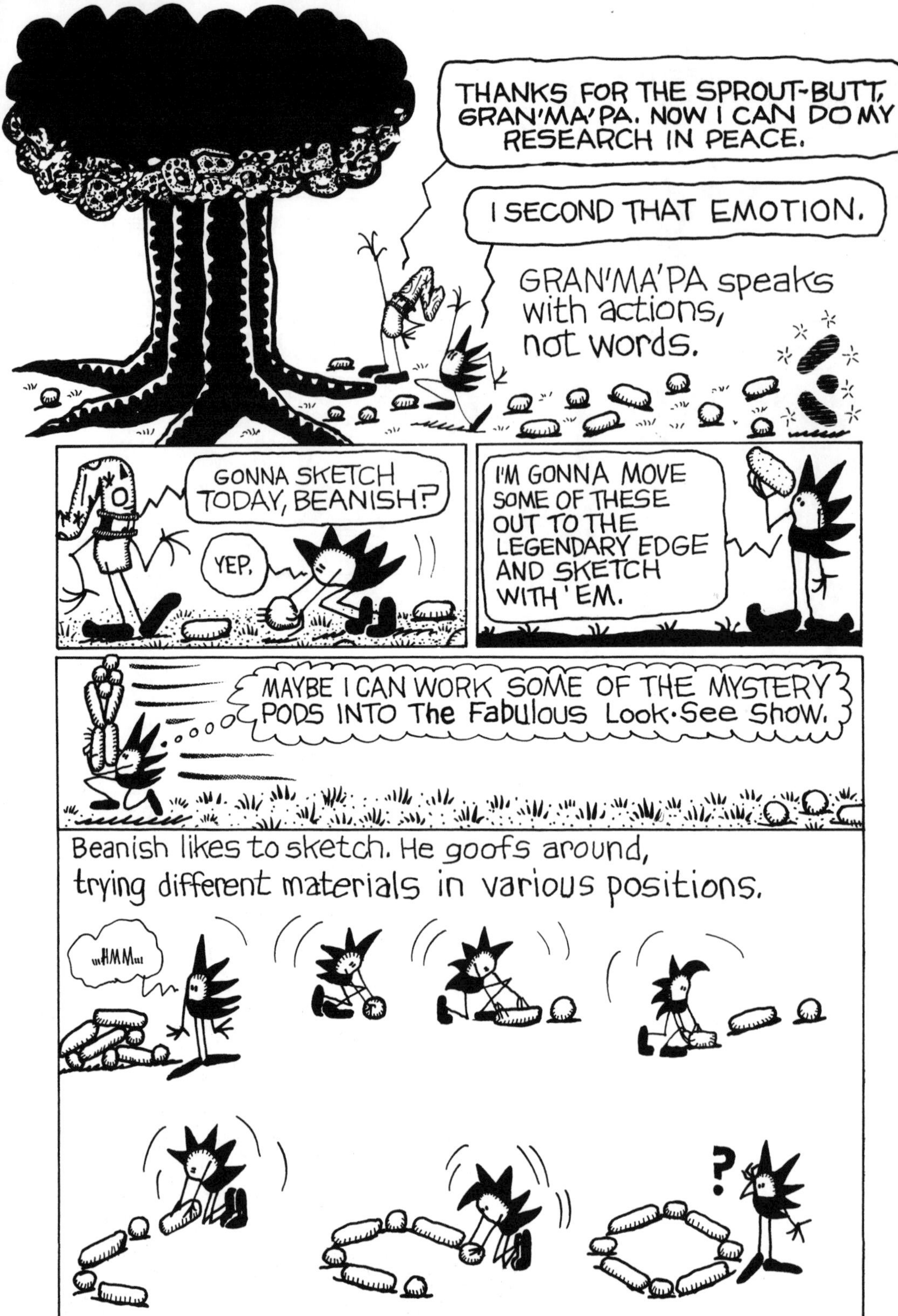
THANKS FOR THE SPROUT-BUTT, GRAN'MA'PA. NOW I CAN DO MY RESEARCH IN PEACE.
I SECOND THAT EMOTION.
GRAN'MA'PA speaks with actions, not words.
GONNA SKETCH TODAY, BEANISH?
YEP.
I'M GONNA MOVE SOME OF THESE OUT TO THE LEGENDARY EDGE AND SKETCH WITH 'EM.
MAYBE I CAN WORK SOME OF THE MYSTERY PODS INTO The Fabulous Look·See Show.
Beanish likes to sketch. He goofs around, trying different materials in various positions.
...HMM...
?

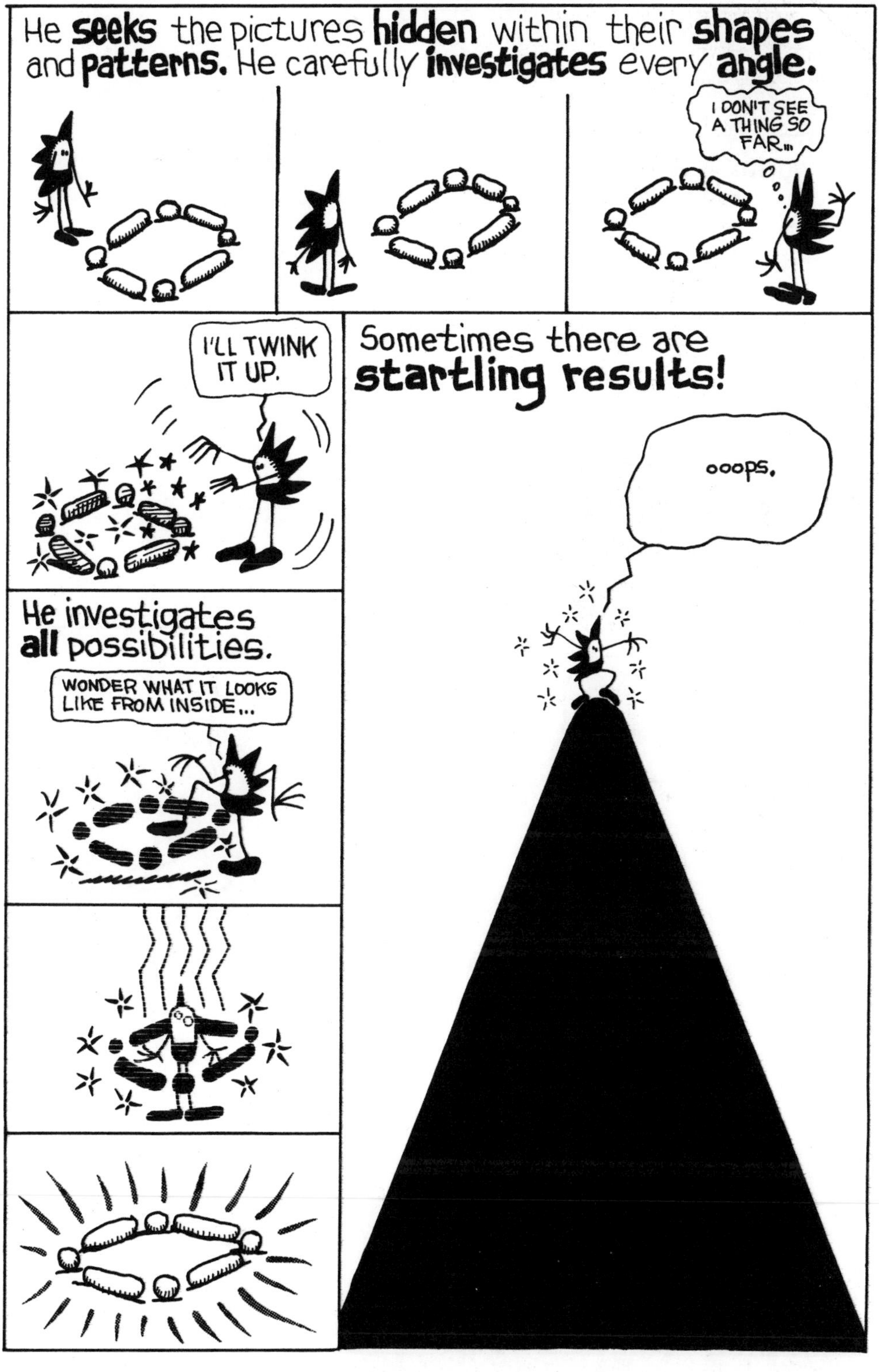
He seeks the pictures hidden within their shapes and patterns. He carefully investigates every angle.
I DON'T SEE A THING SO FAR...
I'LL TWINK IT UP.
He investigates all possibilities.
WONDER WHAT IT LOOKS LIKE FROM INSIDE...
Sometimes there are startling results!
ooops.

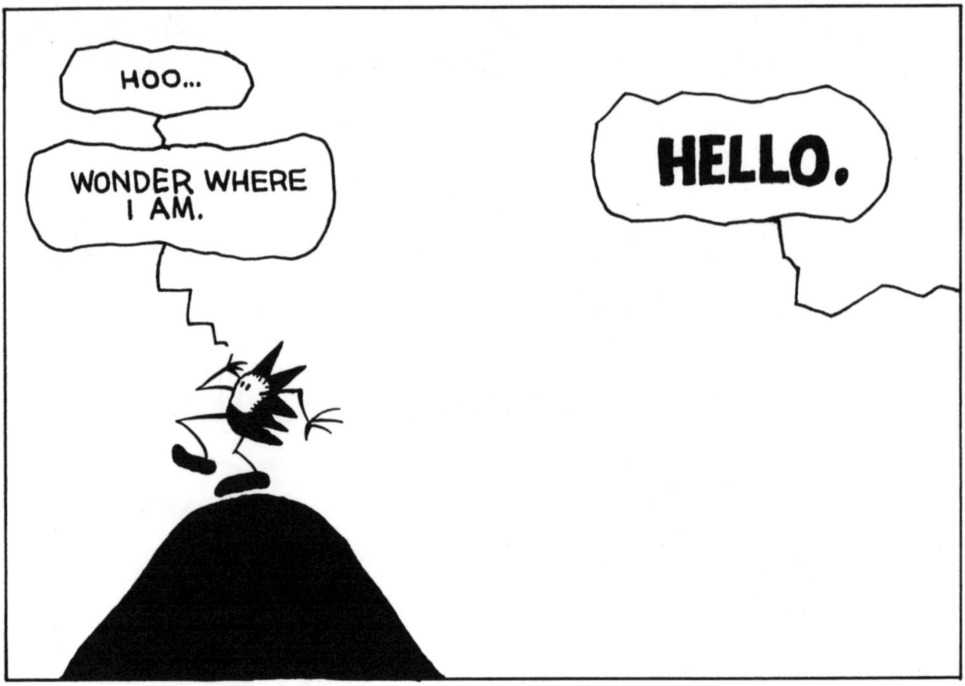
HOO...
WONDER WHERE I AM.
HELLO.
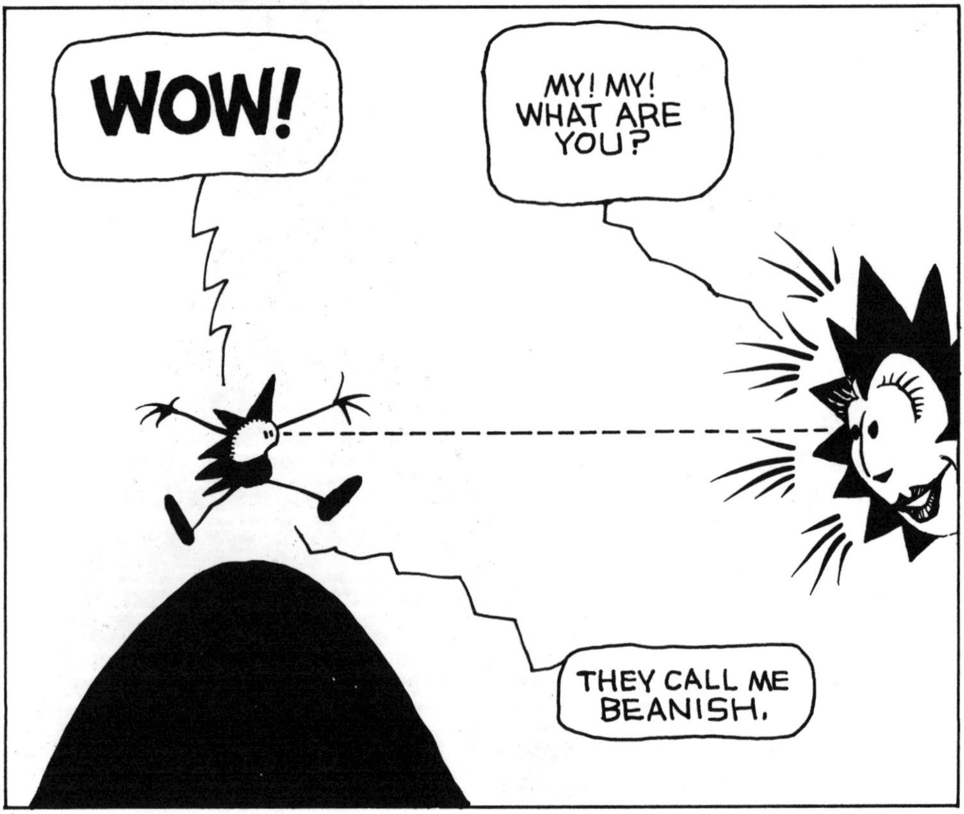
WOW!
MY! MY! WHAT ARE YOU?
THEY CALL ME BEANISH.

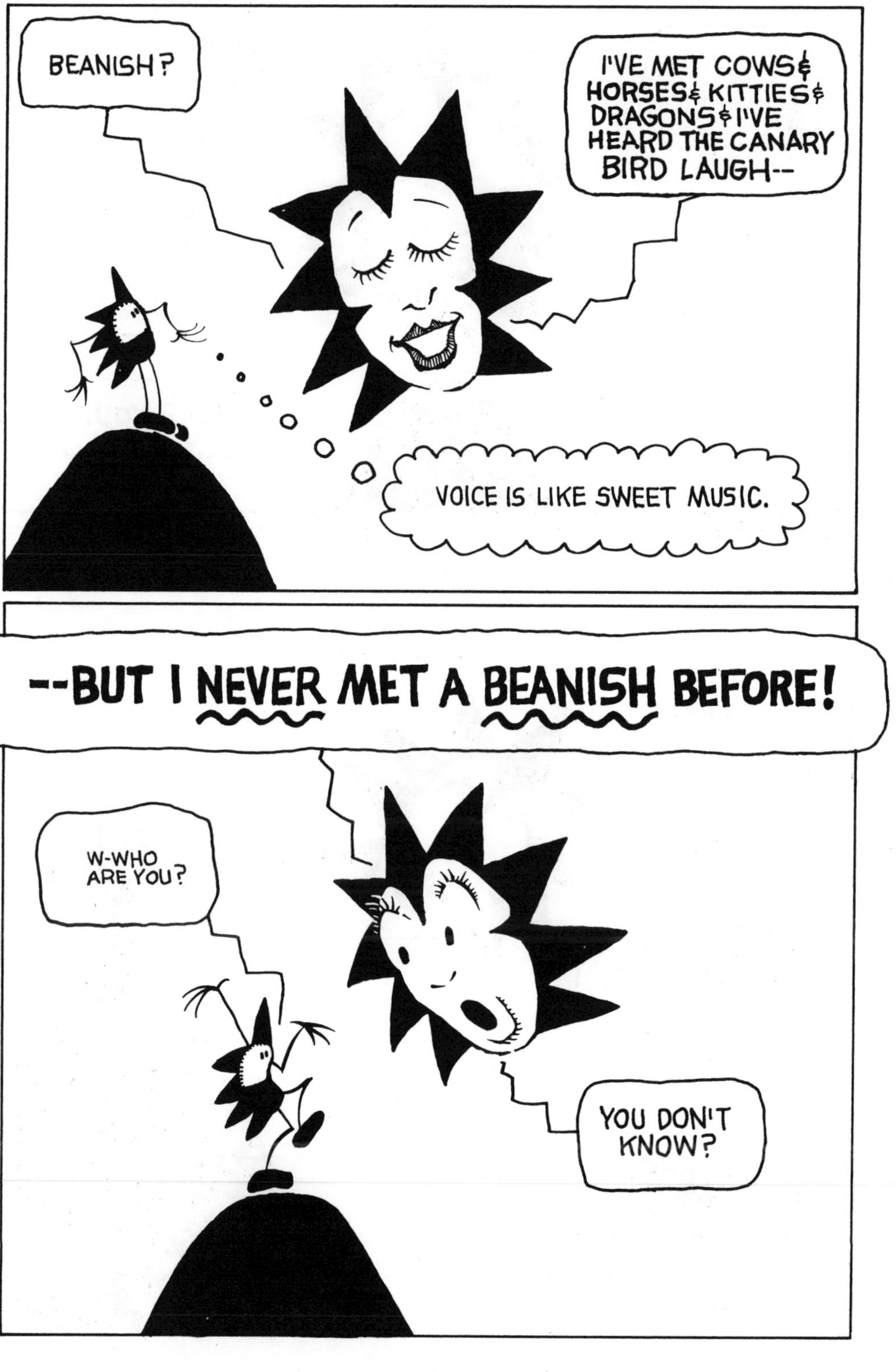
BEANISH?
I'VE MET COWS & HORSES & KITTIES & DRAGONS & I'VE HEARD THE CANARY BIRD LAUGH--
VOICE IS LIKE SWEET MUSIC.
--BUT I NEVER MET A BEANISH BEFORE!
W-WHO ARE YOU?
YOU DON'T KNOW?

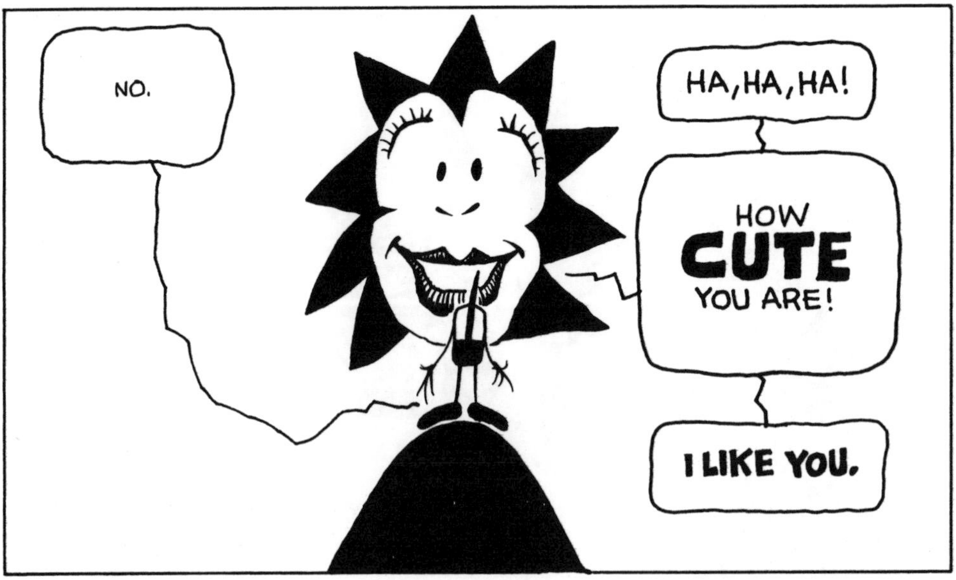
NO.
HA,HA,HA!
HOW CUTE YOU ARE!
I LIKE YOU.

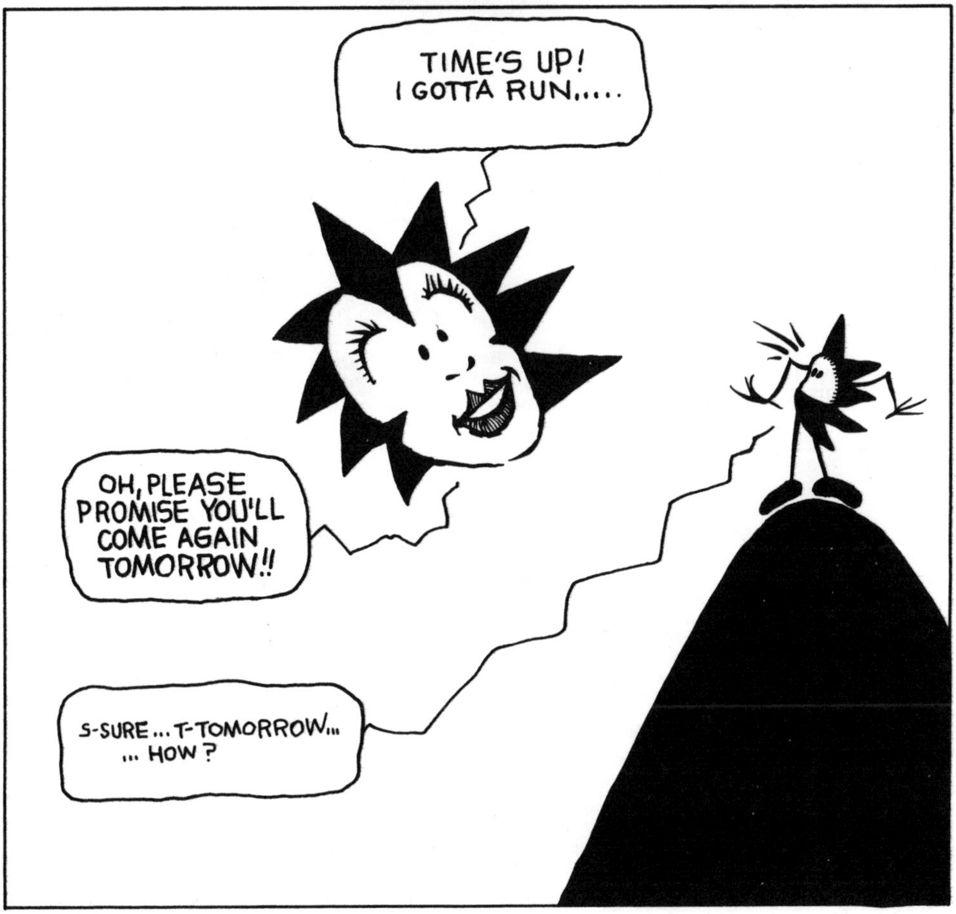
TIME'S UP! I GOTTA RUN.....
OH, PLEASE PROMISE YOU'LL COME AGAIN TOMORROW!!
S-SURE... T-TOMORROW... ... HOW?

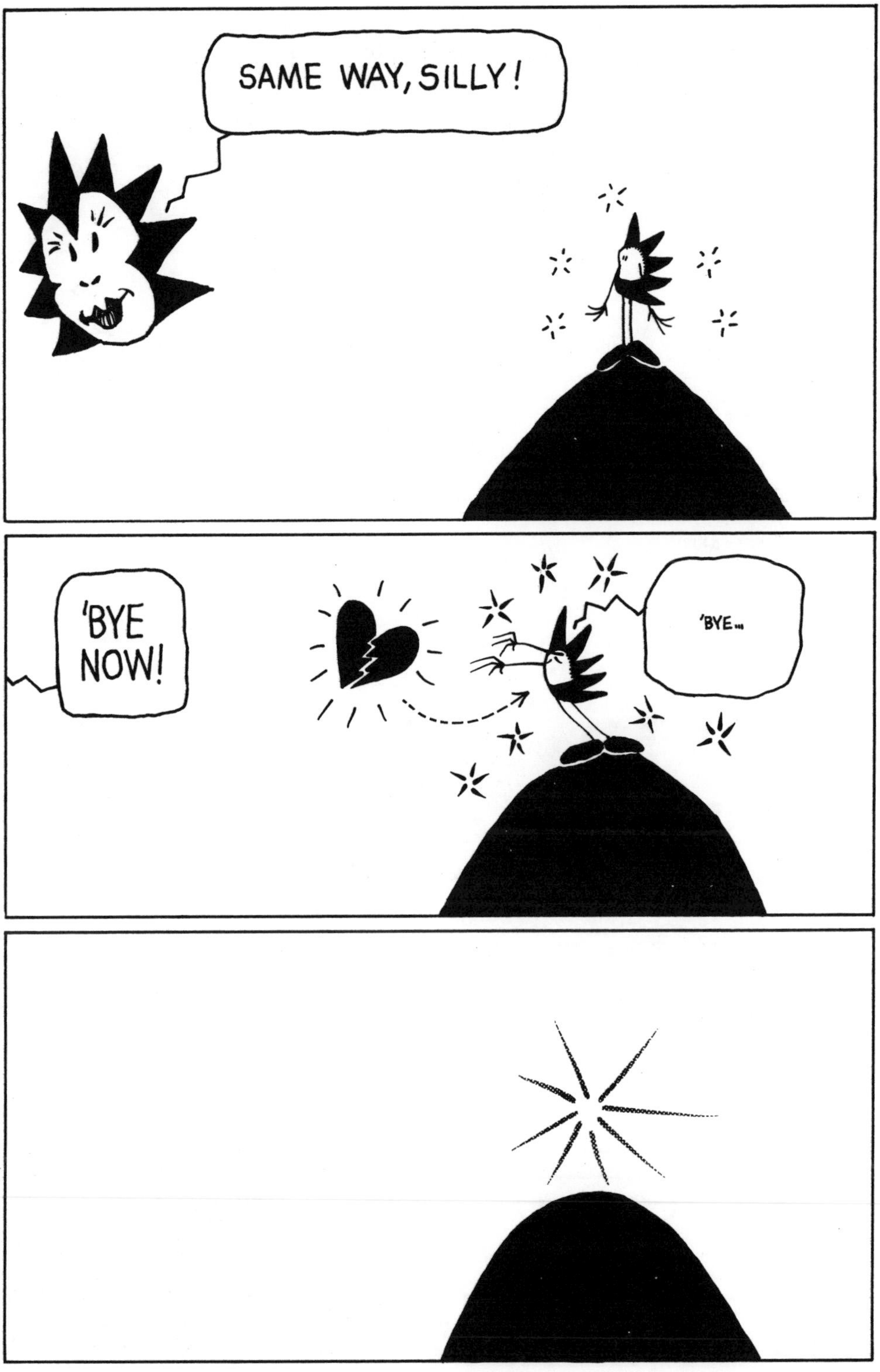
SAME WAY, SILLY!
'BYE NOW!
'BYE...

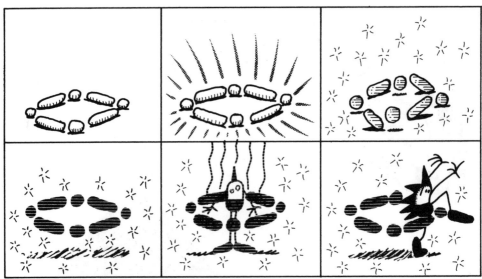

RADIANT SHINE

OOOH ... THAT WAS **BEAUTIFUL!!**

daMMMMM Lille

COME AGAIN.

TOMORROW. SAME WAY.

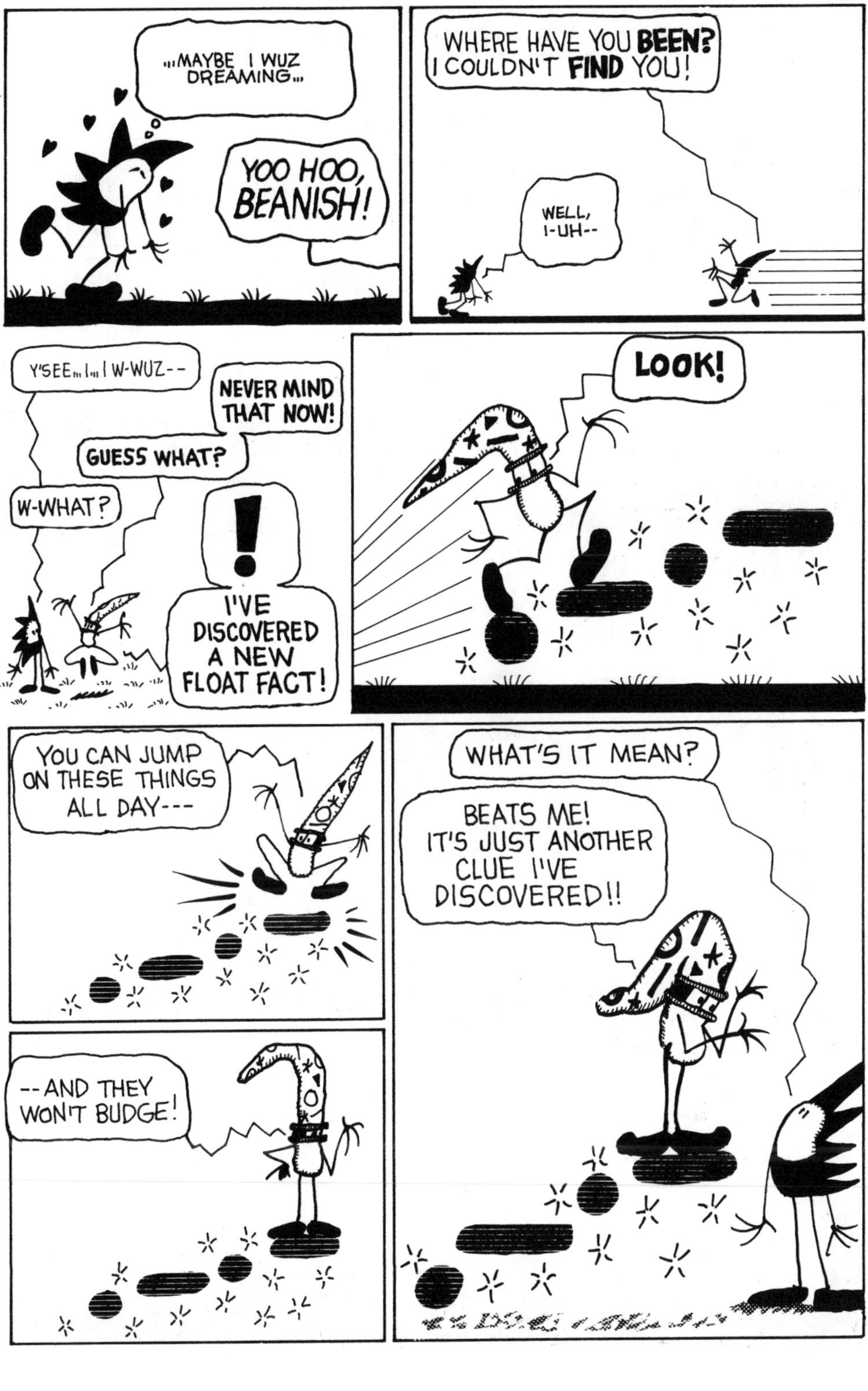
...MAYBE I WUZ DREAMING...
YOO HOO, BEANISH!
WHERE HAVE YOU BEEN? I COULDN'T FIND YOU!
WELL, I-UH--
Y'SEE... I... I W-WUZ--
NEVER MIND THAT NOW!
GUESS WHAT?
W-WHAT?
!
I'VE DISCOVERED A NEW FLOAT FACT!
LOOK!
YOU CAN JUMP ON THESE THINGS ALL DAY---
--AND THEY WON'T BUDGE!
WHAT'S IT MEAN?
BEATS ME! IT'S JUST ANOTHER CLUE I'VE DISCOVERED!!

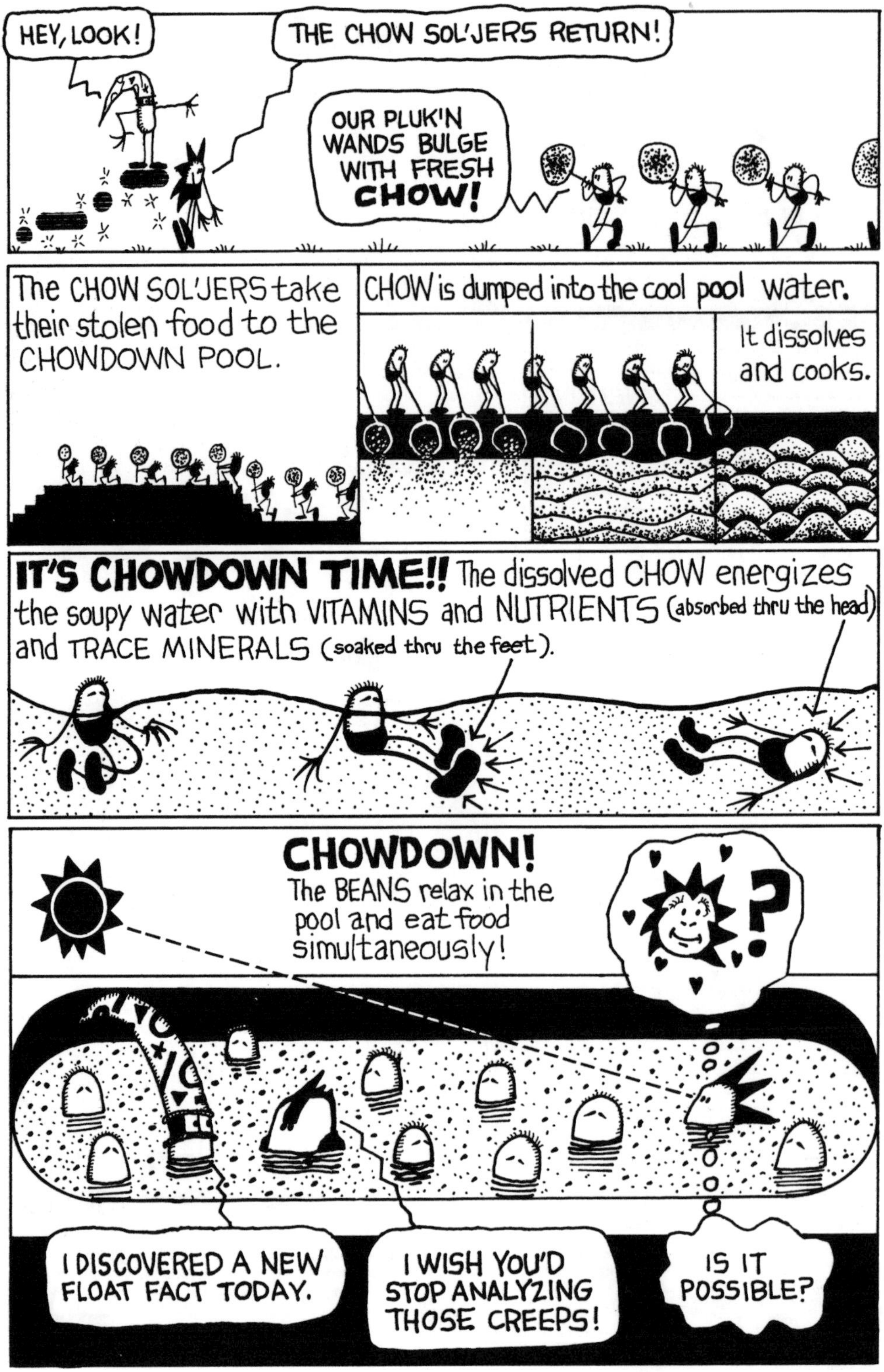

HEY, LOOK!
THE CHOW SOL'JERS RETURN!
OUR PLUK'N WANDS BULGE WITH FRESH CHOW!
The CHOW SOL'JERS take their stolen food to the CHOWDOWN POOL.
CHOW is dumped into the cool pool water.
It dissolves and cooks.
IT'S CHOWDOWN TIME!! The dissolved CHOW energizes the soupy water with VITAMINS and NUTRIENTS (absorbed thru the head) and TRACE MINERALS (soaked thru the feet).
CHOWDOWN!
The BEANS relax in the pool and eat food simultaneously!
I DISCOVERED A NEW FLOAT FACT TODAY.
I WISH YOU'D STOP ANALYZING THOSE CREEPS!
IS IT POSSIBLE?

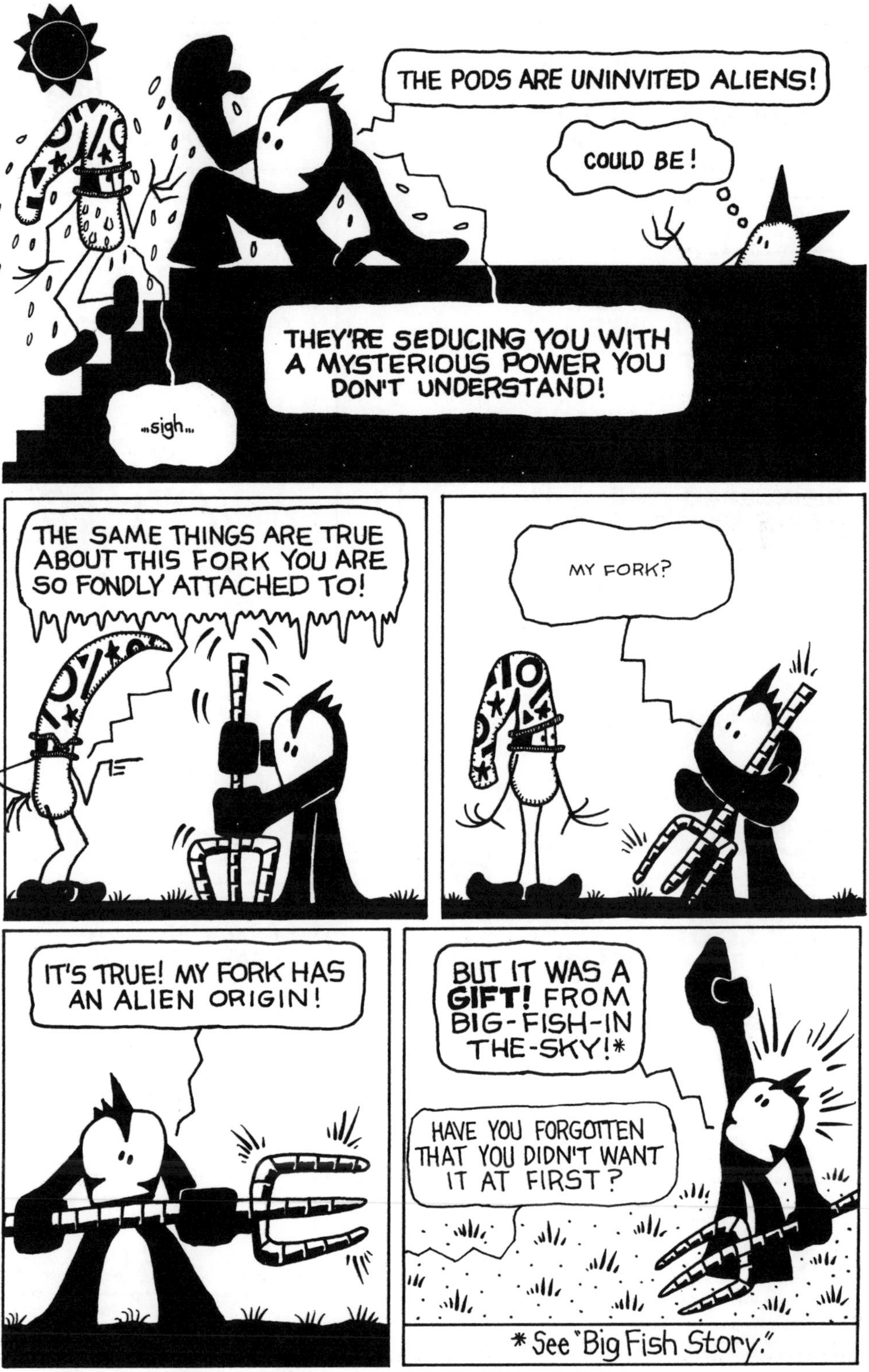
THE PODS ARE UNINVITED ALIENS!
COULD BE!
THEY'RE SEDUCING YOU WITH A MYSTERIOUS POWER YOU DON'T UNDERSTAND!
...sigh...
THE SAME THINGS ARE TRUE ABOUT THIS FORK YOU ARE SO FONDLY ATTACHED TO!
MY FORK?
IT'S TRUE! MY FORK HAS AN ALIEN ORIGIN!
BUT IT WAS A GIFT! FROM BIG-FISH-IN THE-SKY!*
HAVE YOU FORGOTTEN THAT YOU DIDN'T WANT IT AT FIRST?
* See "Big Fish Story."

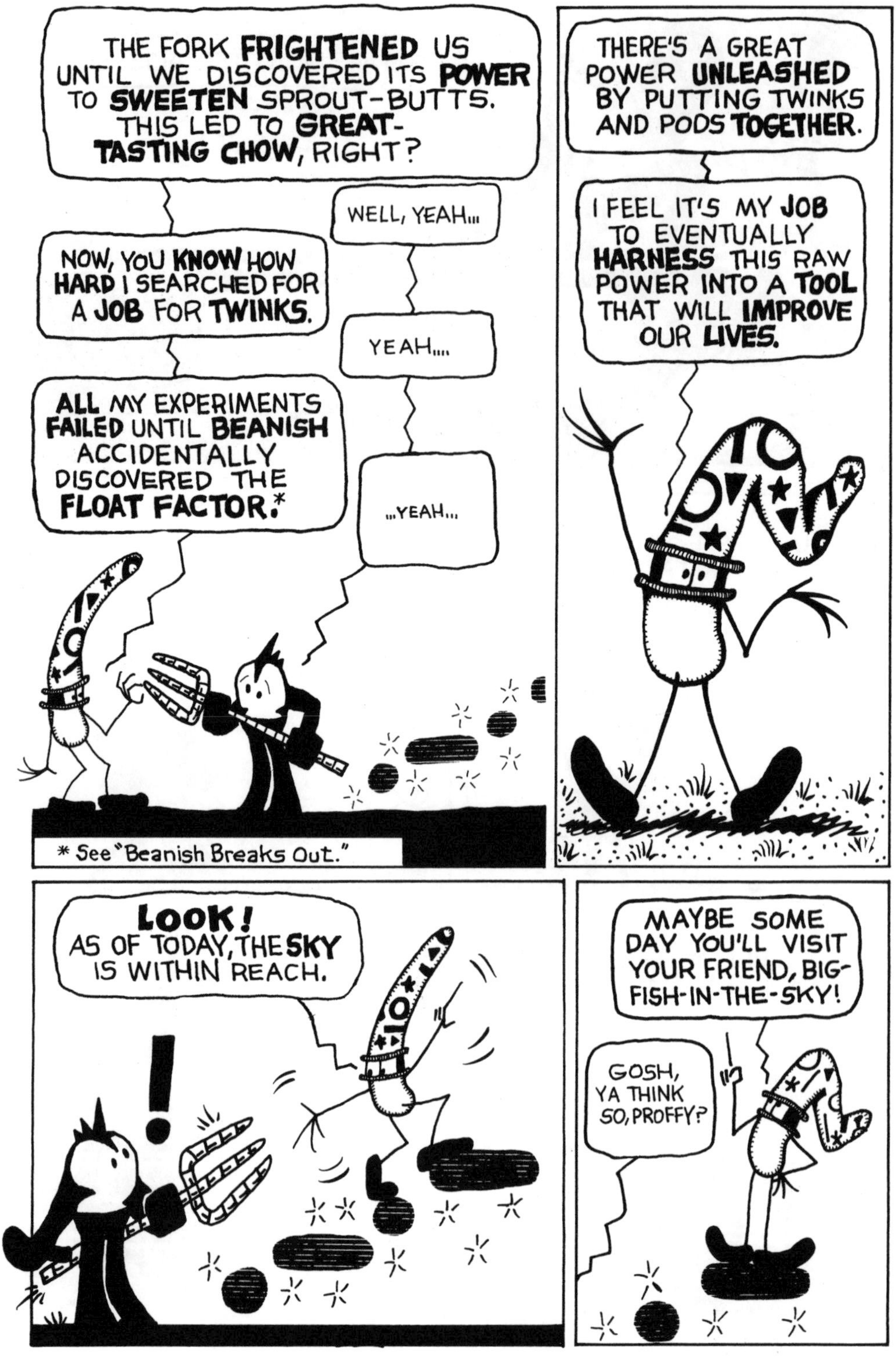
THE FORK FRIGHTENED US UNTIL WE DISCOVERED ITS POWER TO SWEETEN SPROUT-BUTTS. THIS LED TO GREAT-TASTING CHOW, RIGHT?
WELL, YEAH...
NOW, YOU KNOW HOW HARD I SEARCHED FOR A JOB FOR TWINKS.
YEAH....
ALL MY EXPERIMENTS FAILED UNTIL BEANISH ACCIDENTALLY DISCOVERED THE FLOAT FACTOR.*
...YEAH...
* See "Beanish Breaks Out."
THERE'S A GREAT POWER UNLEASHED BY PUTTING TWINKS AND PODS TOGETHER.
I FEEL IT'S MY JOB TO EVENTUALLY HARNESS THIS RAW POWER INTO A TOOL THAT WILL IMPROVE OUR LIVES.
LOOK! AS OF TODAY, THE SKY IS WITHIN REACH.
!
MAYBE SOME DAY YOU'LL VISIT YOUR FRIEND, BIG-FISH-IN-THE-SKY!
GOSH, YA THINK SO, PROFFY?

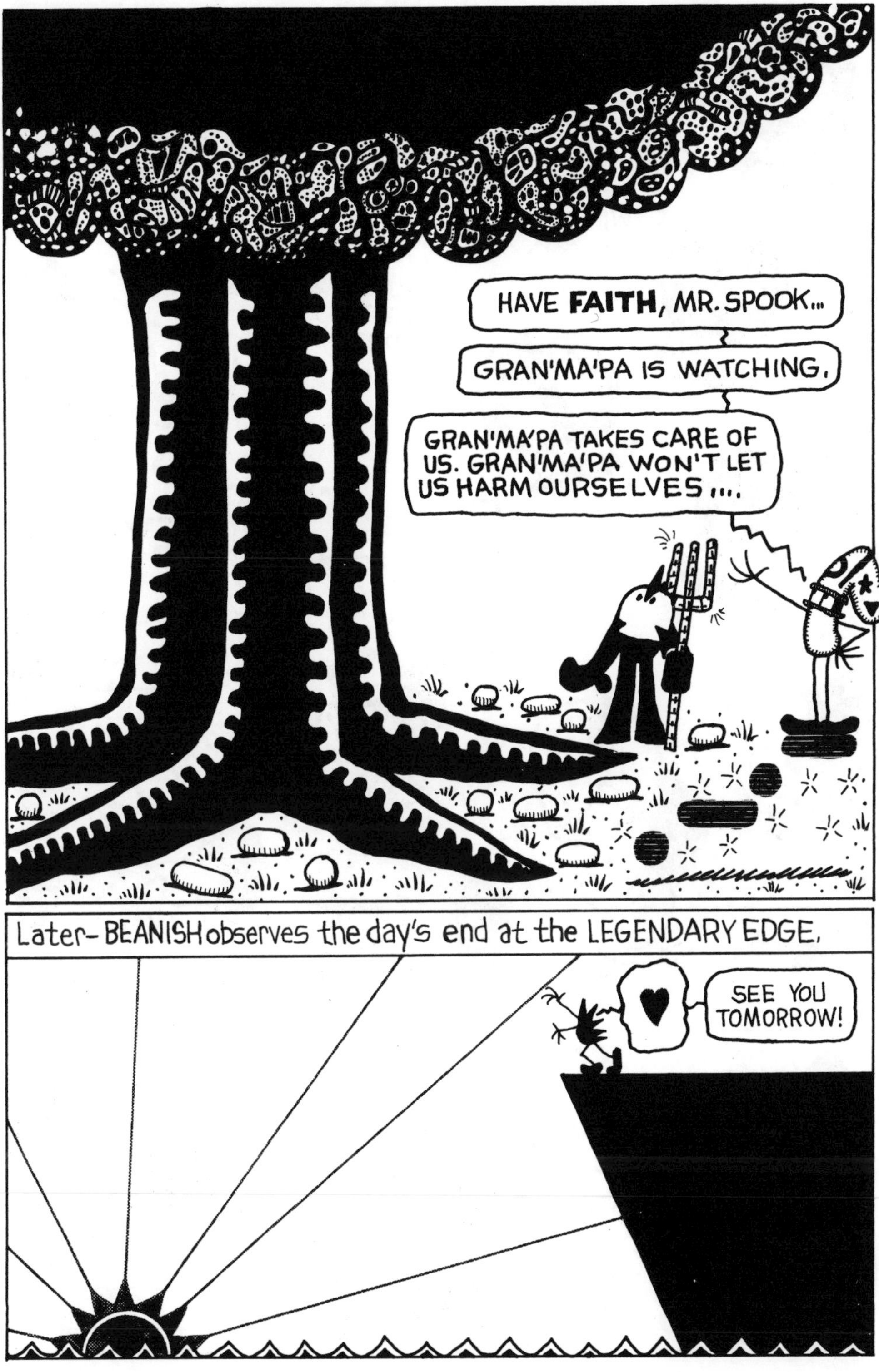
HAVE FAITH, MR. SPOOK...
GRAN'MA'PA IS WATCHING.
GRAN'MA'PA TAKES CARE OF US. GRAN'MA'PA WON'T LET US HARM OURSELVES....
Later- BEANISH observes the day's end at the LEGENDARY EDGE.
SEE YOU TOMORROW!

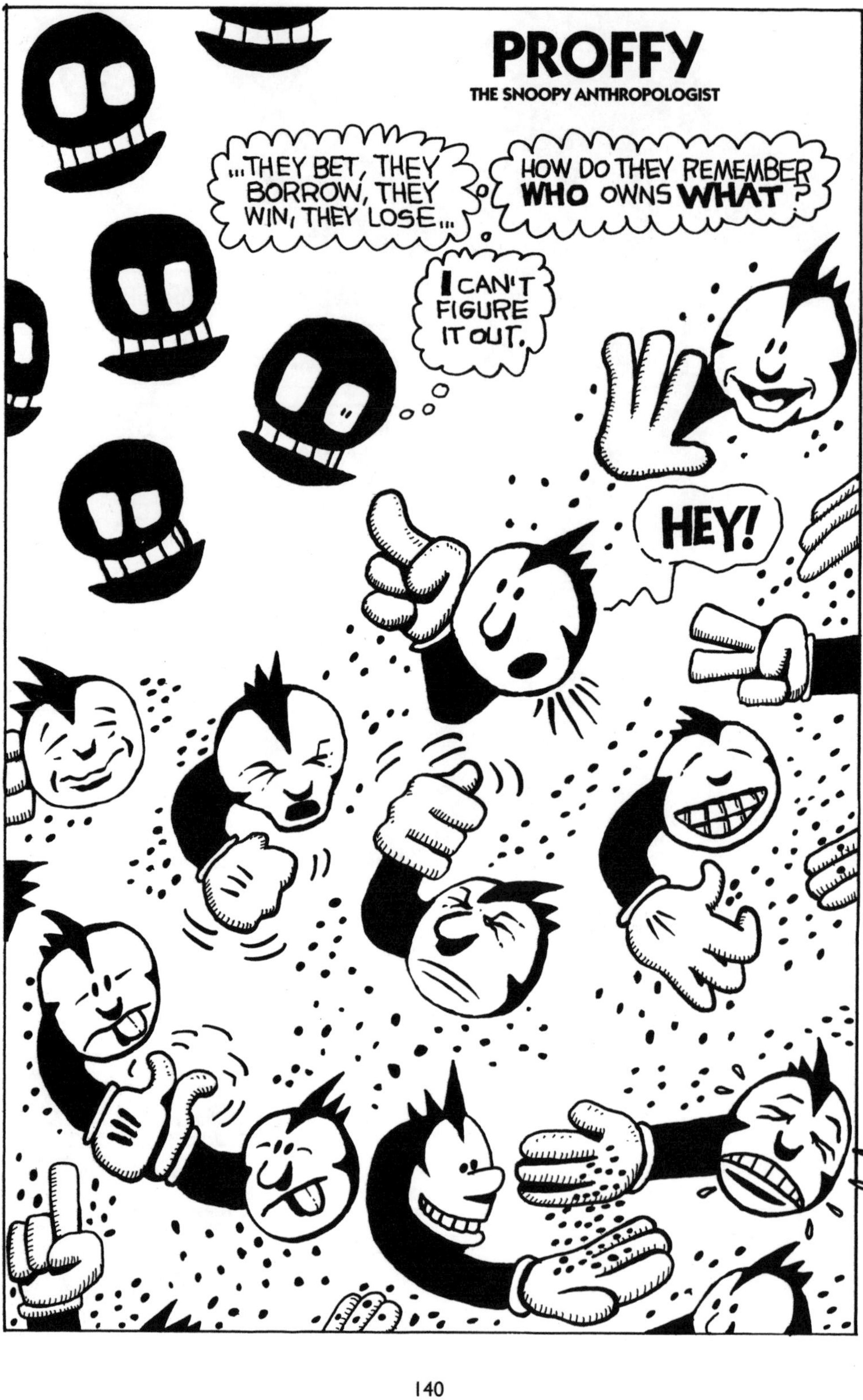
PROFFY
THE SNOOPY ANTHROPOLOGIST
...THEY BET, THEY BORROW, THEY WIN, THEY LOSE...
HOW DO THEY REMEMBER WHO OWNS WHAT?
I CAN'T FIGURE IT OUT.
HEY!

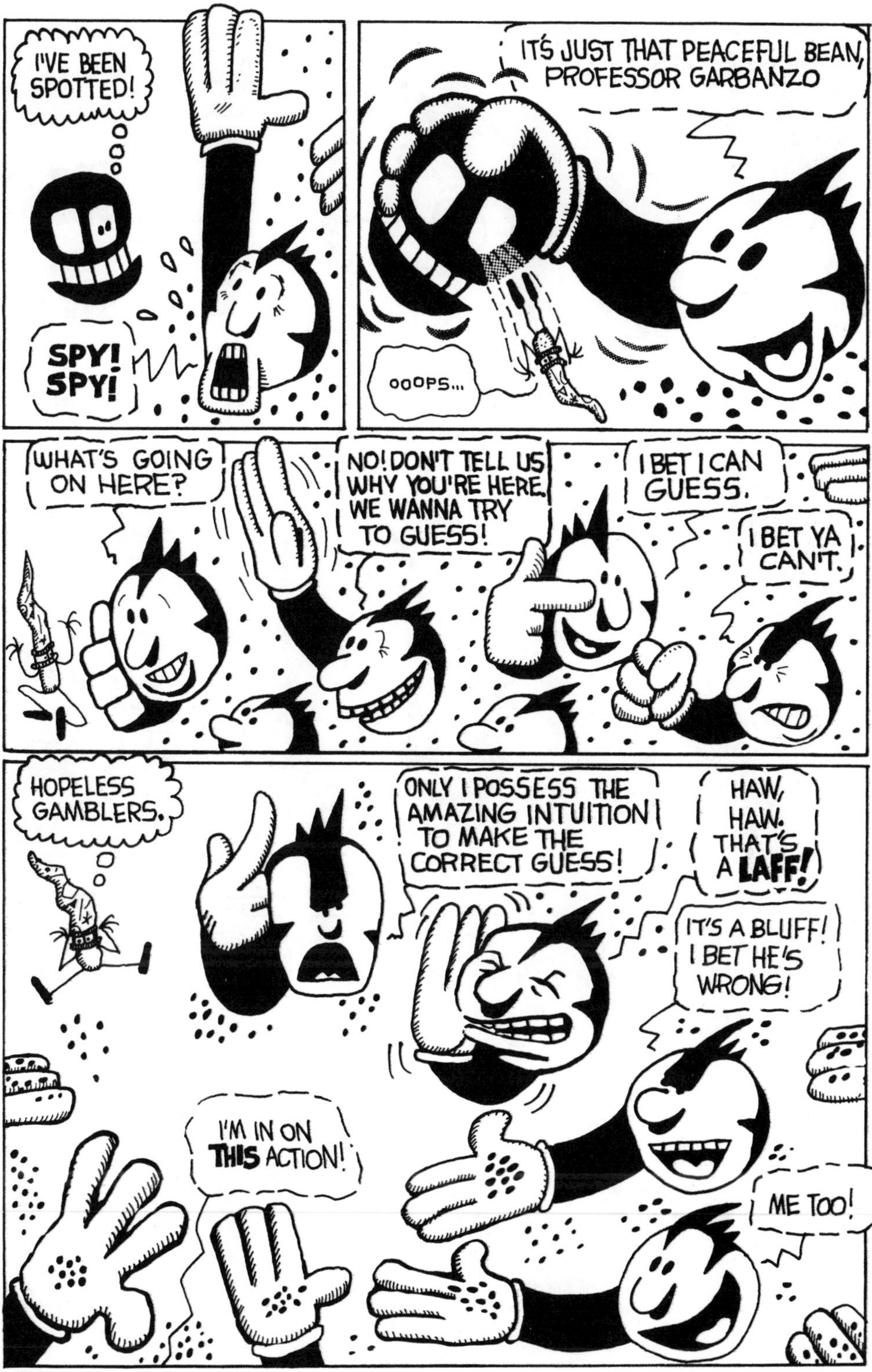
I'VE BEEN SPOTTED!
SPY! SPY!
IT'S JUST THAT PEACEFUL BEAN, PROFESSOR GARBANZO
OOOPS...
WHAT'S GOING ON HERE?
NO! DON'T TELL US WHY YOU'RE HERE. WE WANNA TRY TO GUESS!
I BET I CAN GUESS.
I BET YA CAN'T.
HOPELESS GAMBLERS.
ONLY I POSSESS THE AMAZING INTUITION TO MAKE THE CORRECT GUESS!
HAW, HAW. THAT'S A LAFF!
IT'S A BLUFF! I BET HE'S WRONG!
I'M IN ON THIS ACTION!
ME TOO!

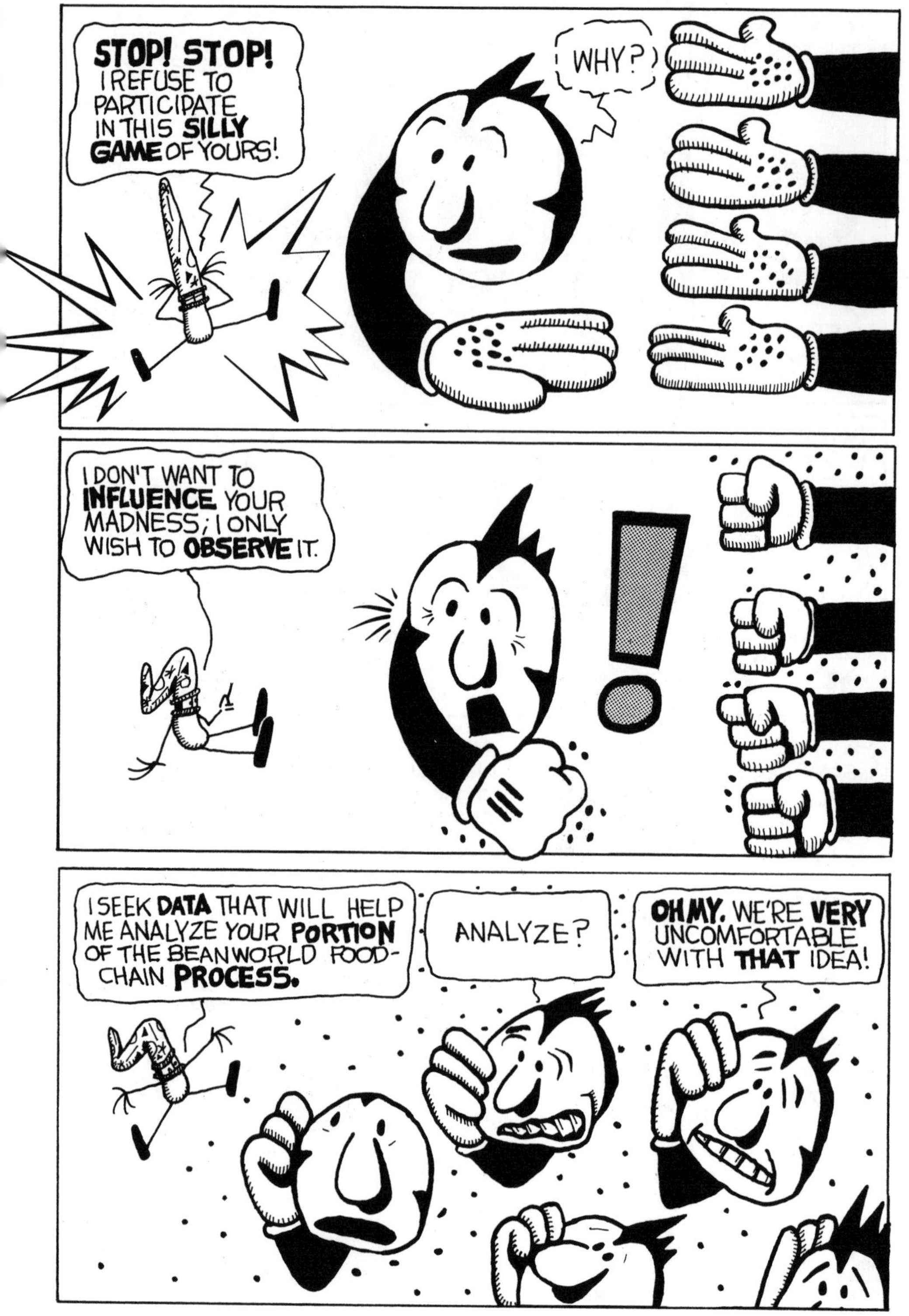
STOP! STOP! I REFUSE TO PARTICIPATE IN THIS SILLY GAME OF YOURS!
WHY?
I DON'T WANT TO INFLUENCE YOUR MADNESS; I ONLY WISH TO OBSERVE IT.
!
I SEEK DATA THAT WILL HELP ME ANALYZE YOUR PORTION OF THE BEANWORLD FOOD-CHAIN PROCESS.
ANALYZE?
OH MY. WE'RE VERY UNCOMFORTABLE WITH THAT IDEA!

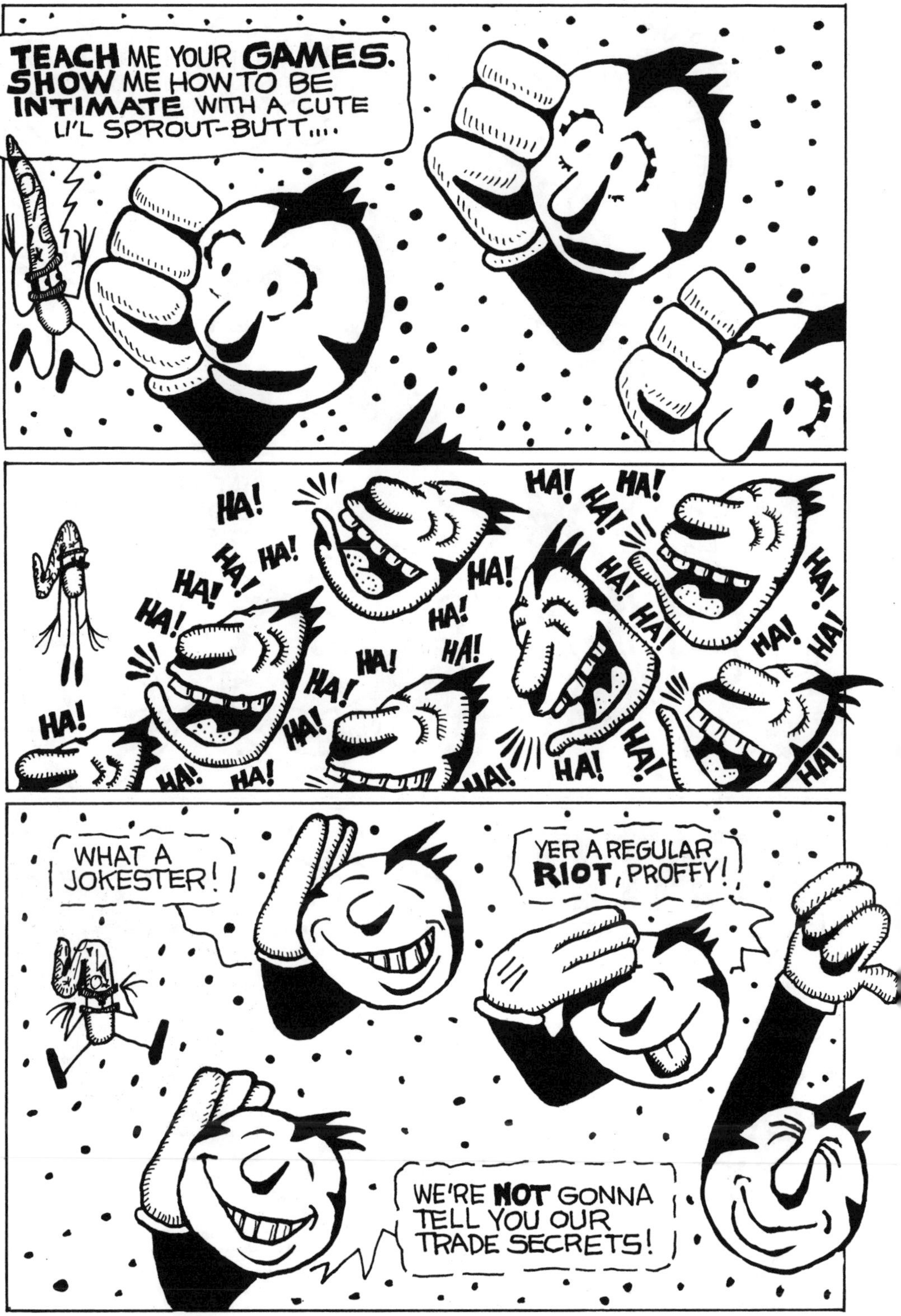
TEACH ME YOUR GAMES. SHOW ME HOW TO BE INTIMATE WITH A CUTE LI'L SPROUT-BUTT....
HA! HA! HA! HA! HA! HA! HA! HA! HA! HA! HA! HA! HA! HA! HA! HA! HA! HA! HA! HA! HA! HA! HA! HA! HA!
WHAT A JOKESTER!
YER A REGULAR RIOT, PROFFY!
WE'RE NOT GONNA TELL YOU OUR TRADE SECRETS!

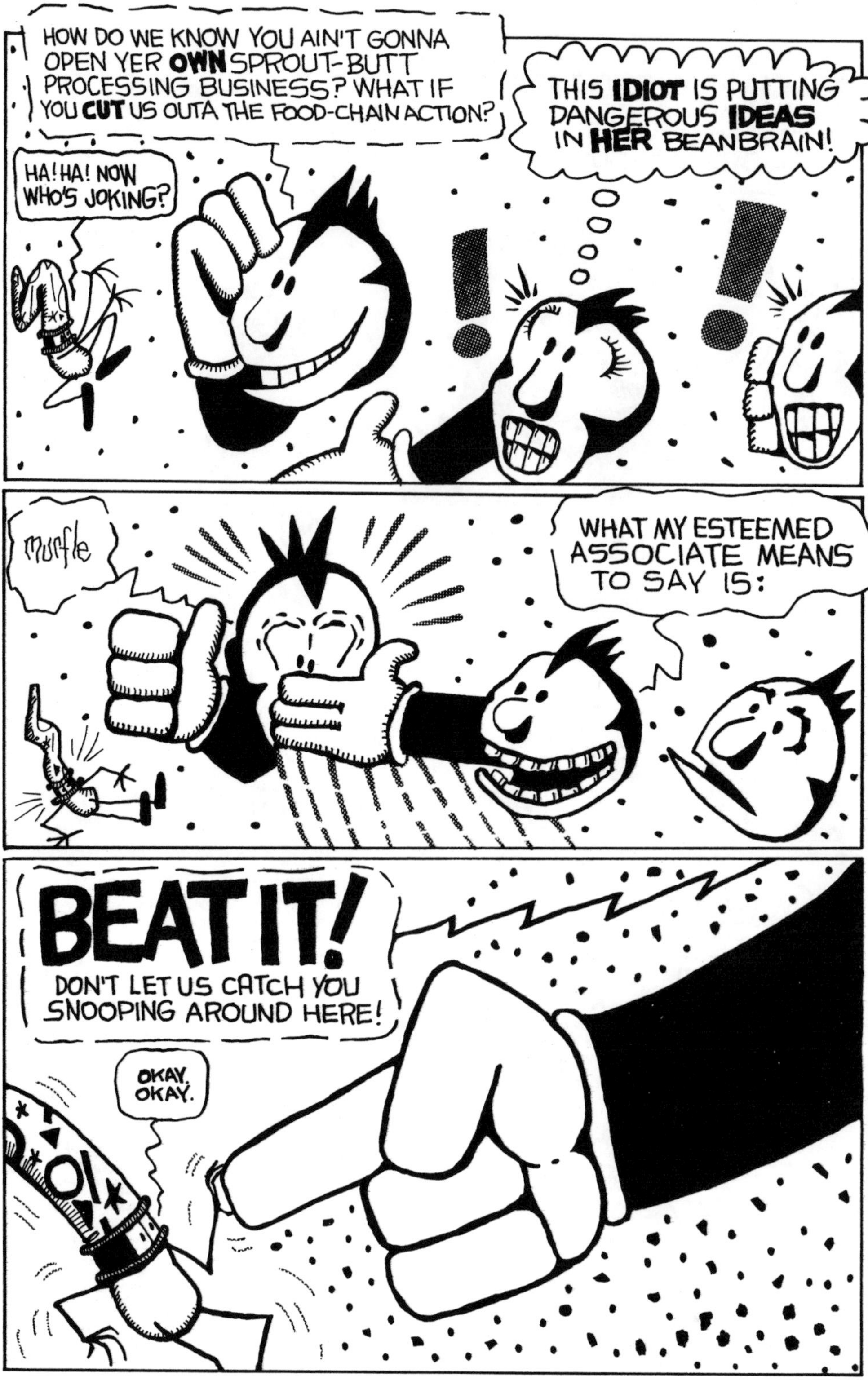
HOW DO WE KNOW YOU AIN'T GONNA OPEN YER **OWN** SPROUT-BUTT PROCESSING BUSINESS? WHAT IF YOU **CUT** US OUTA THE FOOD-CHAIN ACTION?
THIS **IDIOT** IS PUTTING DANGEROUS **IDEAS** IN **HER** BEANBRAIN!
HA! HA! NOW WHO'S JOKING?
murfle
WHAT MY ESTEEMED ASSOCIATE MEANS TO SAY IS:
BEAT IT!
DON'T LET US CATCH YOU SNOOPING AROUND HERE!
OKAY. OKAY.

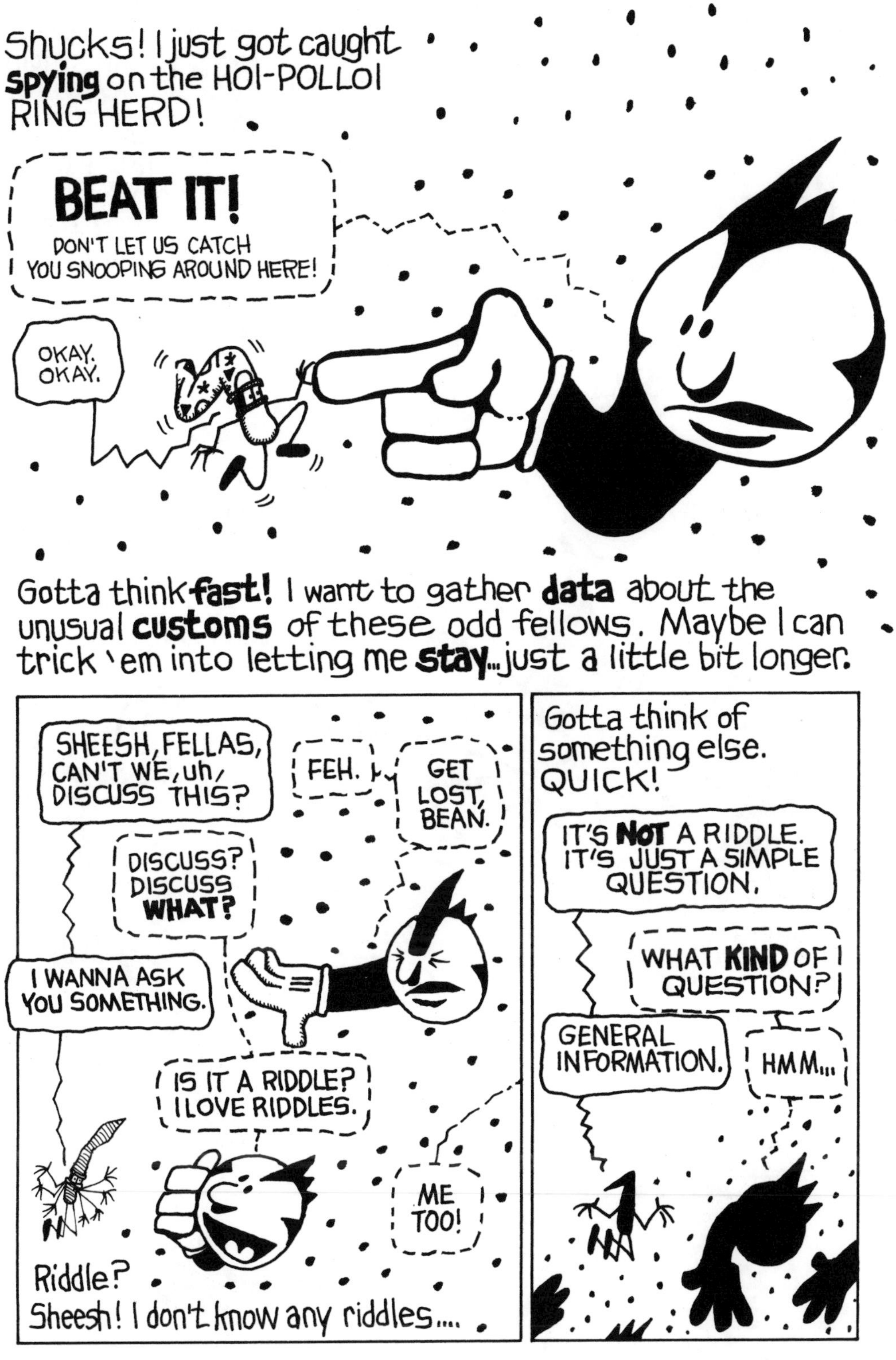
Shucks! I just got caught spying on the HOI-POLLOI RING HERD!
BEAT IT!
DON'T LET US CATCH YOU SNOOPING AROUND HERE!
OKAY. OKAY.
Gotta think fast! I want to gather data about the unusual customs of these odd fellows. Maybe I can trick 'em into letting me stay...just a little bit longer.
SHEESH, FELLAS, CAN'T WE, uh, DISCUSS THIS?
FEH.
GET LOST, BEAN.
DISCUSS? DISCUSS WHAT?
I WANNA ASK YOU SOMETHING.
IS IT A RIDDLE? I LOVE RIDDLES.
ME TOO!
Riddle? Sheesh! I don't know any riddles....
Gotta think of something else. QUICK!
IT'S NOT A RIDDLE. IT'S JUST A SIMPLE QUESTION.
WHAT KIND OF QUESTION?
GENERAL INFORMATION.
HMM...

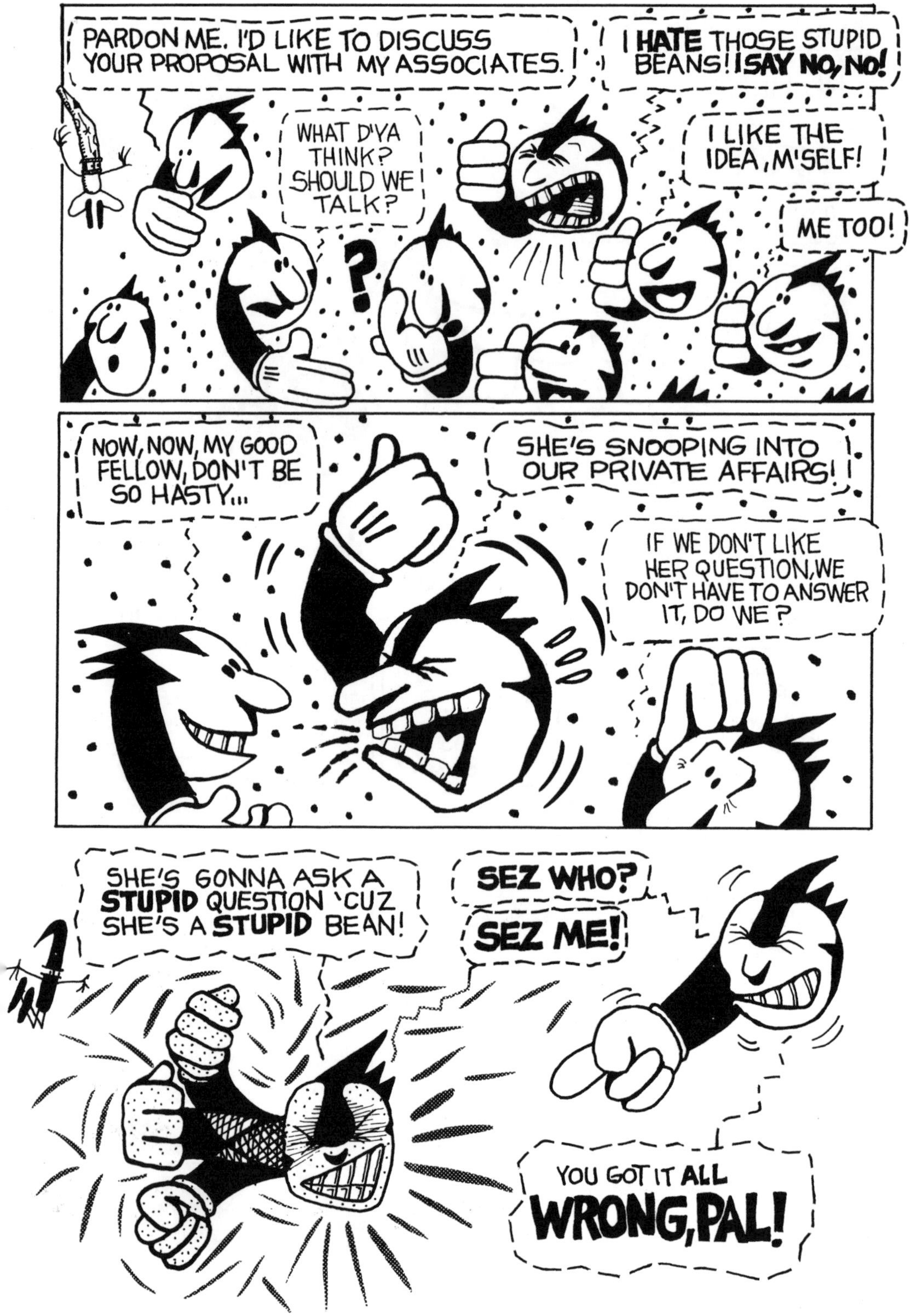

PARDON ME. I'D LIKE TO DISCUSS YOUR PROPOSAL WITH MY ASSOCIATES.
I HATE THOSE STUPID BEANS! I SAY NO, NO!
WHAT D'YA THINK? SHOULD WE TALK?
I LIKE THE IDEA, M'SELF!
ME TOO!
?
NOW, NOW, MY GOOD FELLOW, DON'T BE SO HASTY...
SHE'S SNOOPING INTO OUR PRIVATE AFFAIRS!
IF WE DON'T LIKE HER QUESTION, WE DON'T HAVE TO ANSWER IT, DO WE?
SHE'S GONNA ASK A STUPID QUESTION 'CUZ SHE'S A STUPID BEAN!
SEZ WHO?
SEZ ME!
YOU GOT IT ALL WRONG, PAL!

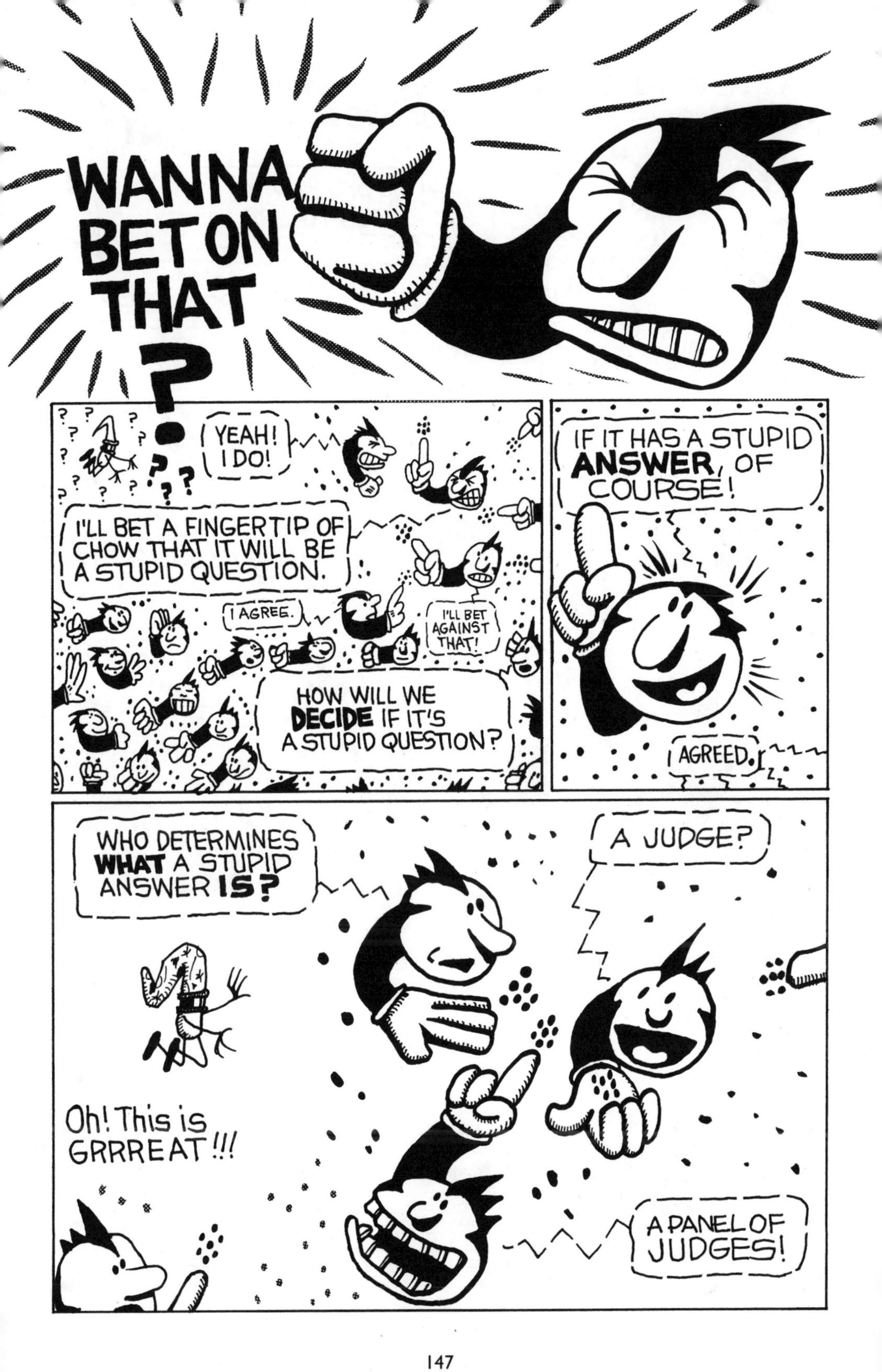
WANNA BET ON THAT ?
YEAH! I DO!
I'LL BET A FINGERTIP OF CHOW THAT IT WILL BE A STUPID QUESTION.
I AGREE.
I'LL BET AGAINST THAT!
HOW WILL WE DECIDE IF IT'S A STUPID QUESTION?
IF IT HAS A STUPID ANSWER, OF COURSE!
AGREED.
WHO DETERMINES WHAT A STUPID ANSWER IS?
A JUDGE?
Oh! This is GRRREAT!!!
A PANEL OF JUDGES!

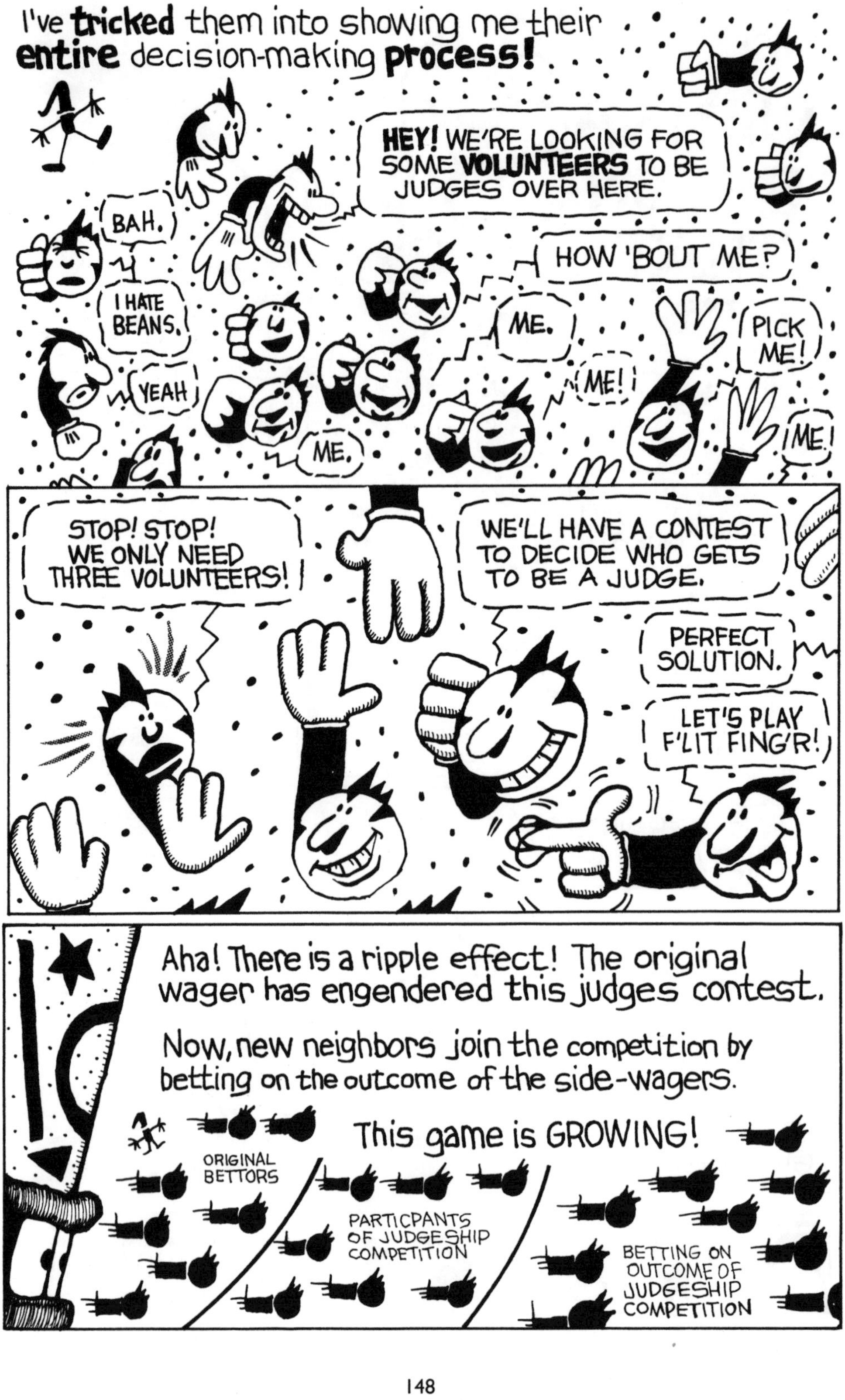

I've **tricked** them into showing me their **entire** decision-making **process!**
HEY! WE'RE LOOKING FOR SOME VOLUNTEERS TO BE JUDGES OVER HERE.
BAH.
I HATE BEANS.
YEAH
HOW 'BOUT ME?
ME.
PICK ME!
ME!
ME.
ME!
STOP! STOP! WE ONLY NEED THREE VOLUNTEERS!
WE'LL HAVE A CONTEST TO DECIDE WHO GETS TO BE A JUDGE.
PERFECT SOLUTION.
LET'S PLAY F'LIT FING'R!
Aha! There is a ripple effect! The original wager has engendered this judges contest.
Now, new neighbors join the competition by betting on the outcome of the side-wagers.
This game is GROWING!
ORIGINAL BETTORS
PARTICPANTS OF JUDGESHIP COMPETITION
BETTING ON OUTCOME OF JUDGESHIP COMPETITION

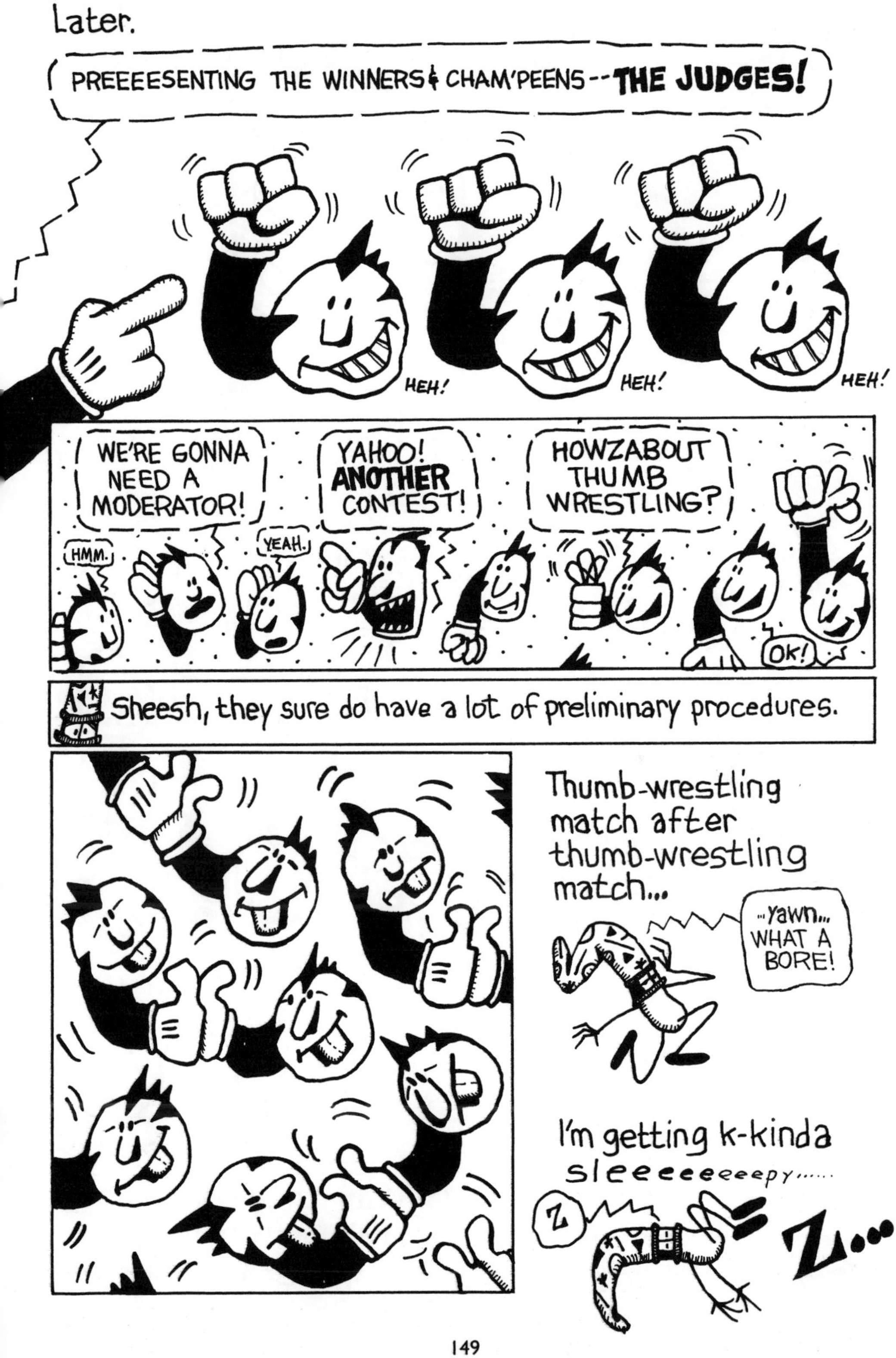
Later.
PREEEESENTING THE WINNERS & CHAM'PEENS--THE JUDGES!
HEH!
HEH!
HEH!
WE'RE GONNA NEED A MODERATOR!
HMM.
YEAH.
YAHOO! ANOTHER CONTEST!
HOWZABOUT THUMB WRESTLING?
OK!
Sheesh, they sure do have a lot of preliminary procedures.
Thumb-wrestling match after thumb-wrestling match...
...yawn... WHAT A BORE!
I'm getting k-kinda sleeeeeeeeepy......
Z
Z...

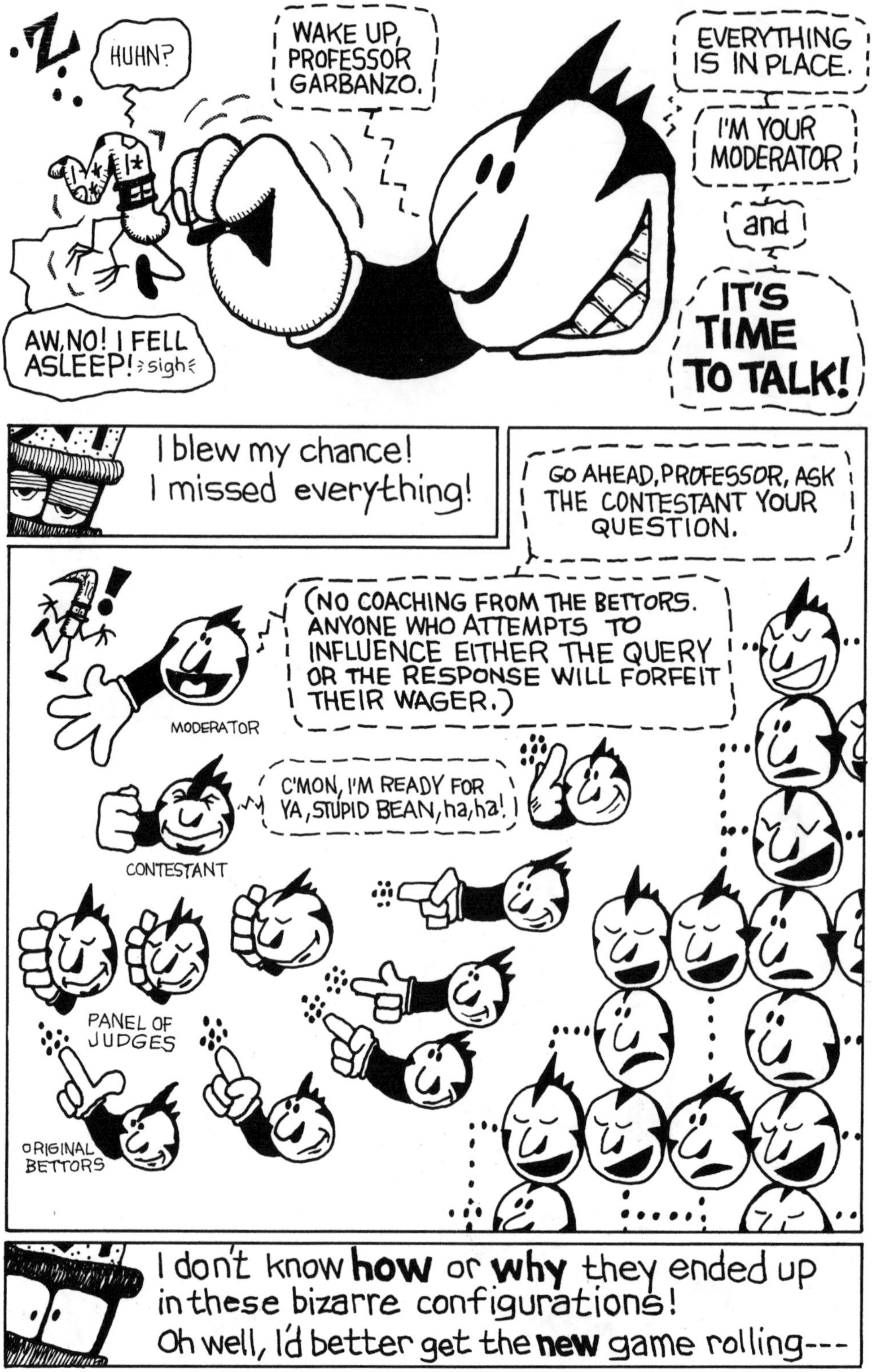

Z
HUHN?
WAKE UP, PROFESSOR GARBANZO.
EVERYTHING IS IN PLACE.
I'M YOUR MODERATOR
and
IT'S TIME TO TALK!
AW, NO! I FELL ASLEEP! sigh
I blew my chance! I missed everything!
GO AHEAD, PROFESSOR, ASK THE CONTESTANT YOUR QUESTION.
(NO COACHING FROM THE BETTORS. ANYONE WHO ATTEMPTS TO INFLUENCE EITHER THE QUERY OR THE RESPONSE WILL FORFEIT THEIR WAGER.)
MODERATOR
C'MON, I'M READY FOR YA, STUPID BEAN, ha, ha!
CONTESTANT
PANEL OF JUDGES
ORIGINAL BETTORS
I don't know **how** or **why** they ended up in these bizarre configurations!
Oh well, I'd better get the **new** game rolling---

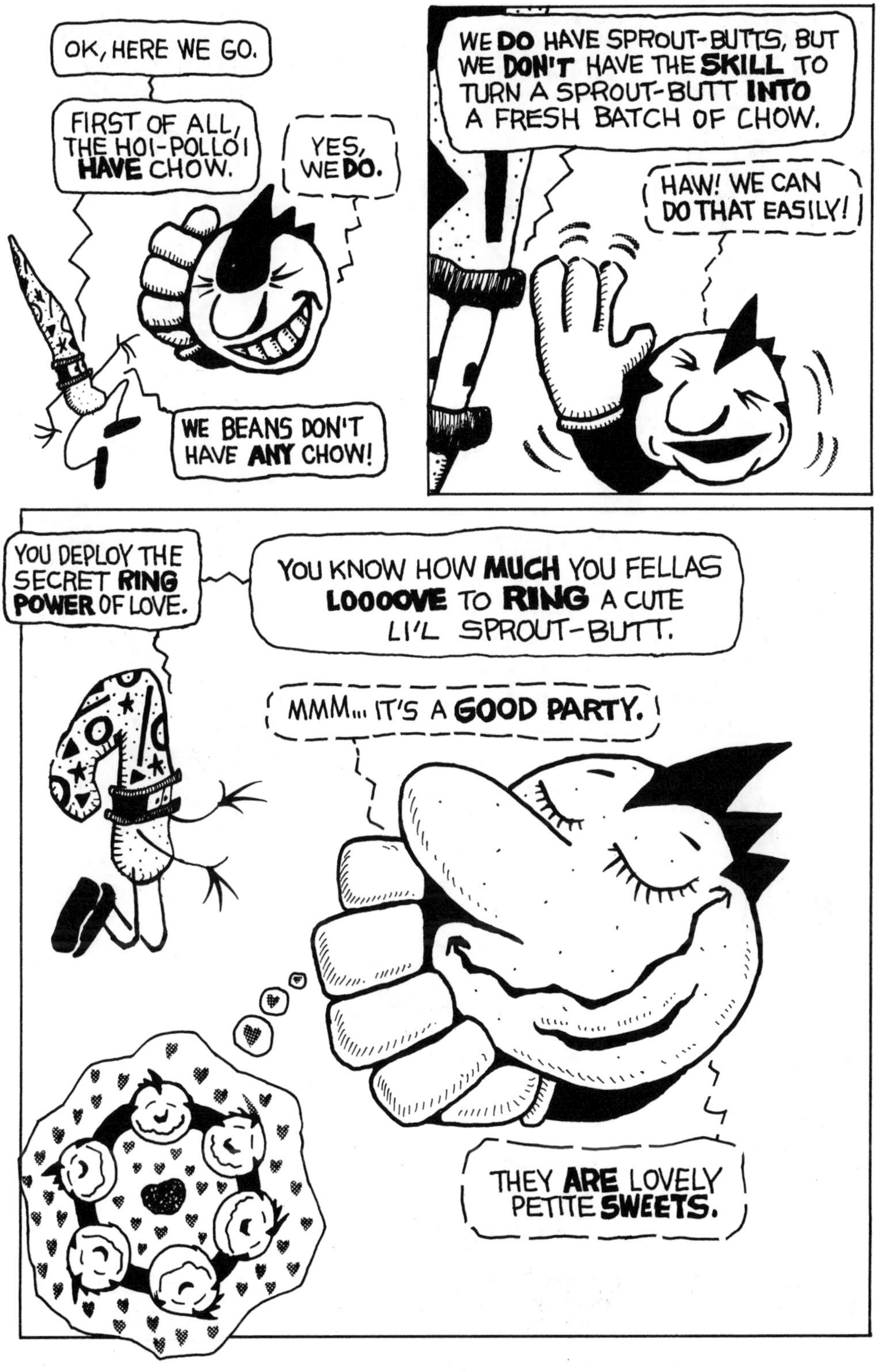

OK, HERE WE GO.
FIRST OF ALL, THE HOI-POLLOI HAVE CHOW.
YES, WE DO.
WE BEANS DON'T HAVE ANY CHOW!
WE DO HAVE SPROUT-BUTTS, BUT WE DON'T HAVE THE SKILL TO TURN A SPROUT-BUTT INTO A FRESH BATCH OF CHOW.
HAW! WE CAN DO THAT EASILY!
YOU DEPLOY THE SECRET RING POWER OF LOVE.
YOU KNOW HOW MUCH YOU FELLAS LOOOOVE TO RING A CUTE LI'L SPROUT-BUTT.
MMM... IT'S A GOOD PARTY.
THEY ARE LOVELY PETITE SWEETS.

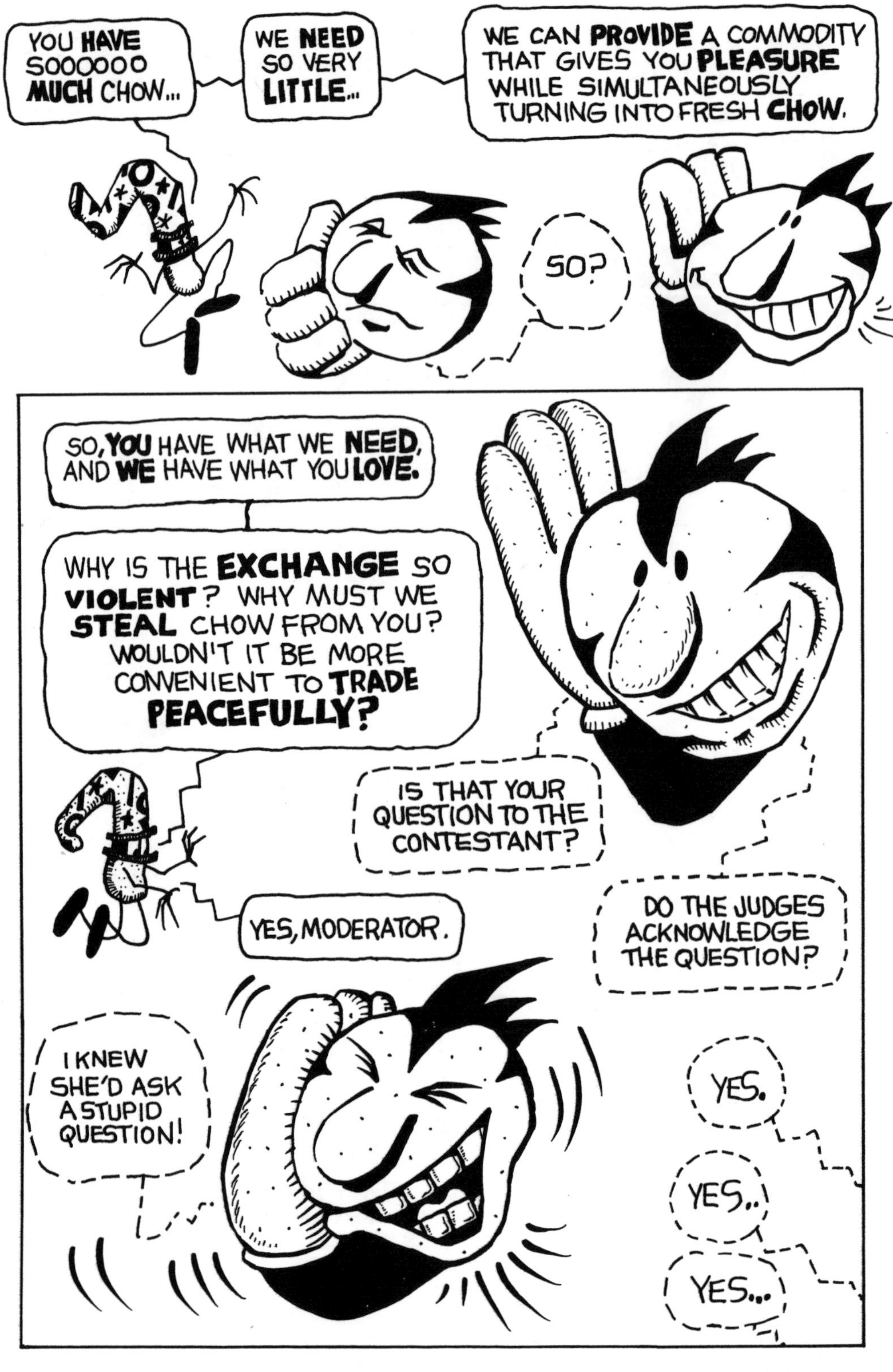

YOU HAVE SOOOOOO MUCH CHOW...
WE NEED SO VERY LITTLE...
WE CAN PROVIDE A COMMODITY THAT GIVES YOU PLEASURE WHILE SIMULTANEOUSLY TURNING INTO FRESH CHOW.
SO?
SO, YOU HAVE WHAT WE NEED, AND WE HAVE WHAT YOU LOVE.
WHY IS THE EXCHANGE SO VIOLENT? WHY MUST WE STEAL CHOW FROM YOU? WOULDN'T IT BE MORE CONVENIENT TO TRADE PEACEFULLY?
IS THAT YOUR QUESTION TO THE CONTESTANT?
YES, MODERATOR.
DO THE JUDGES ACKNOWLEDGE THE QUESTION?
I KNEW SHE'D ASK A STUPID QUESTION!
YES.
YES..
YES...

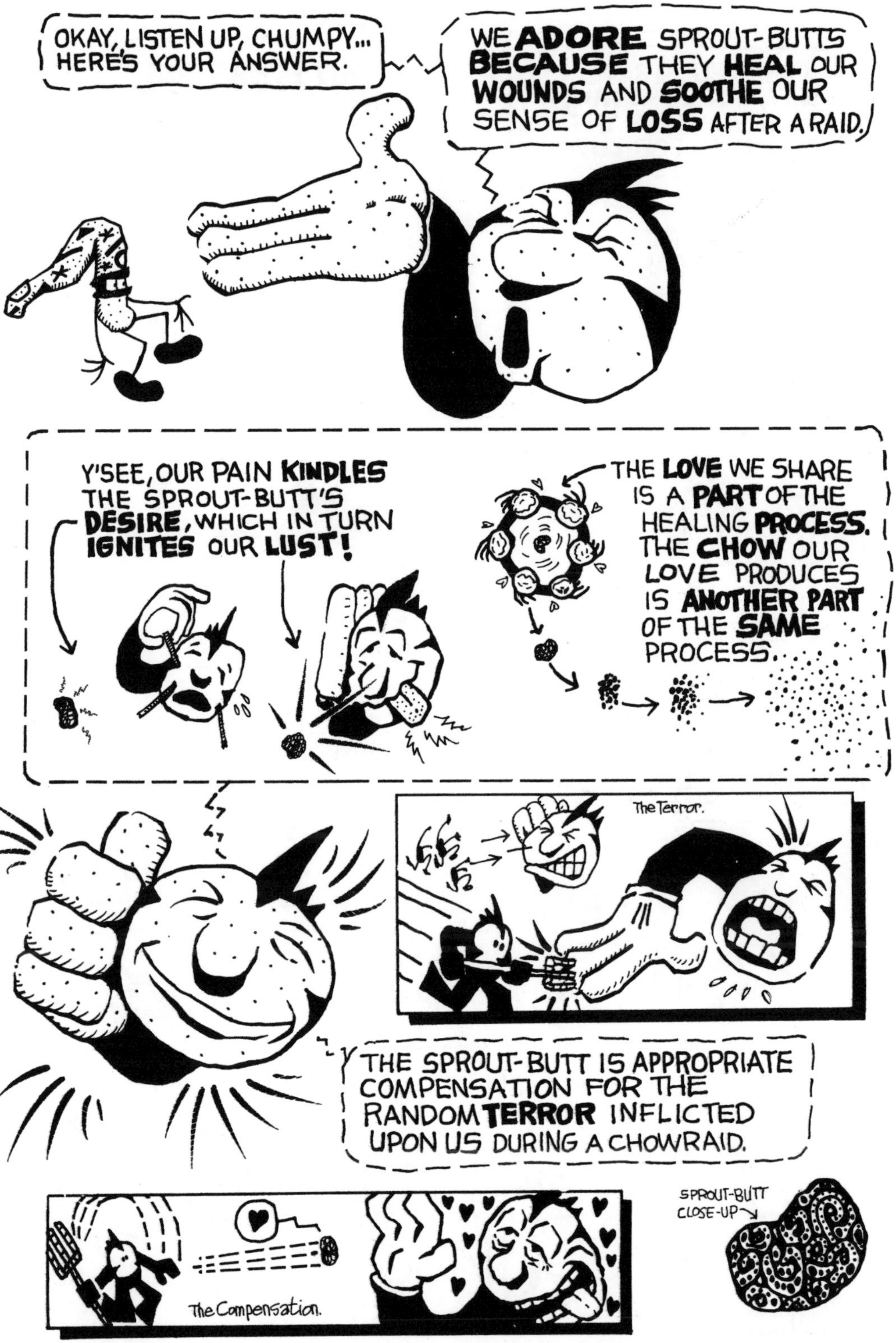
OKAY, LISTEN UP, CHUMPY... HERE'S YOUR ANSWER.
WE ADORE SPROUT-BUTTS BECAUSE THEY HEAL OUR WOUNDS AND SOOTHE OUR SENSE OF LOSS AFTER A RAID.
Y'SEE, OUR PAIN KINDLES THE SPROUT-BUTT'S DESIRE, WHICH IN TURN IGNITES OUR LUST!
THE LOVE WE SHARE IS A PART OF THE HEALING PROCESS. THE CHOW OUR LOVE PRODUCES IS ANOTHER PART OF THE SAME PROCESS.
The Terror.
THE SPROUT-BUTT IS APPROPRIATE COMPENSATION FOR THE RANDOM TERROR INFLICTED UPON US DURING A CHOWRAID.
The Compensation.
SPROUT-BUTT CLOSE-UP

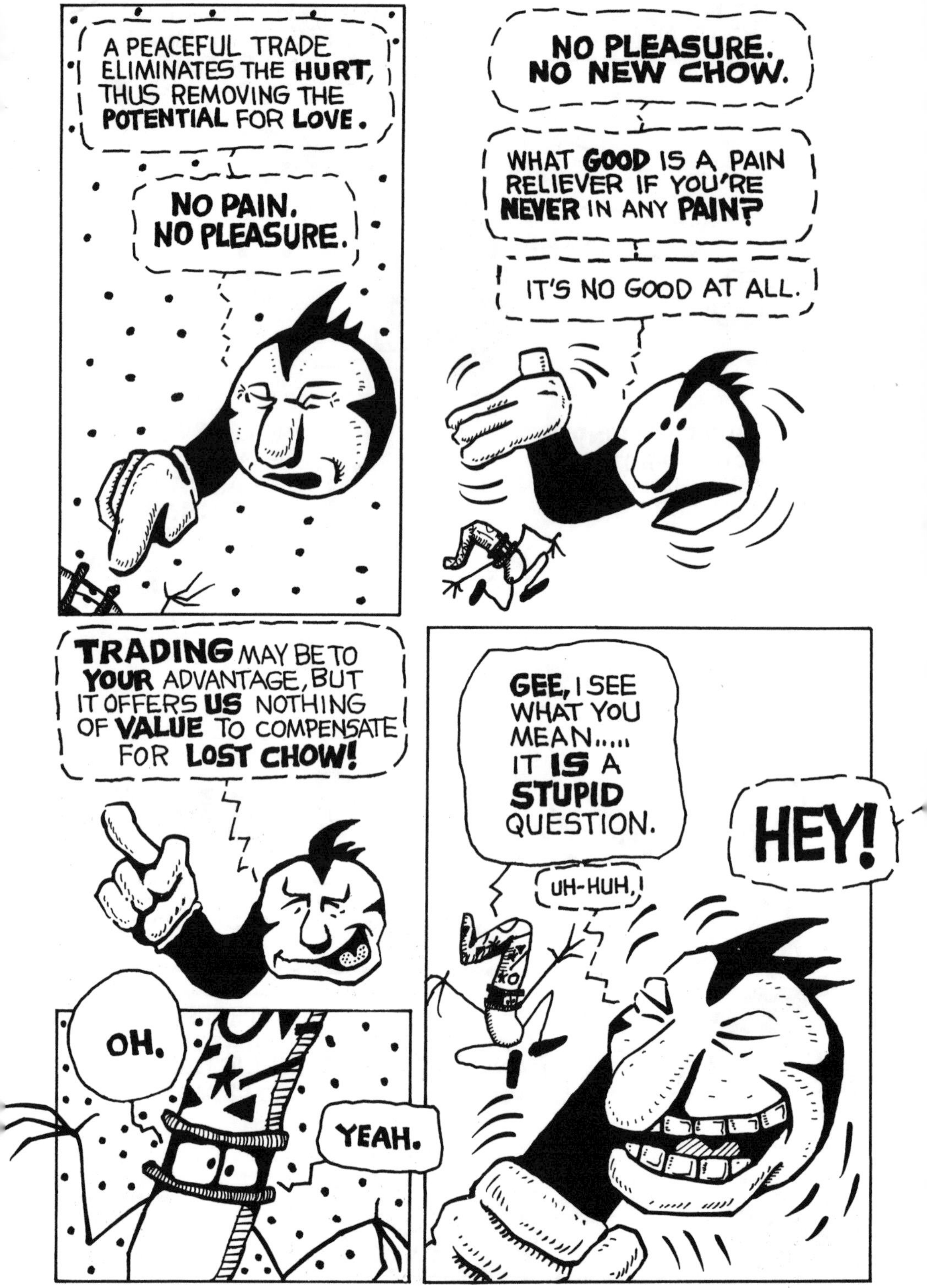
A PEACEFUL TRADE ELIMINATES THE HURT, THUS REMOVING THE POTENTIAL FOR LOVE.
NO PAIN. NO PLEASURE.
NO PLEASURE. NO NEW CHOW.
WHAT GOOD IS A PAIN RELIEVER IF YOU'RE NEVER IN ANY PAIN?
IT'S NO GOOD AT ALL.
TRADING MAY BE TO YOUR ADVANTAGE, BUT IT OFFERS US NOTHING OF VALUE TO COMPENSATE FOR LOST CHOW!
OH.
YEAH.
GEE, I SEE WHAT YOU MEAN..... IT IS A STUPID QUESTION.
UH-HUH,
HEY!

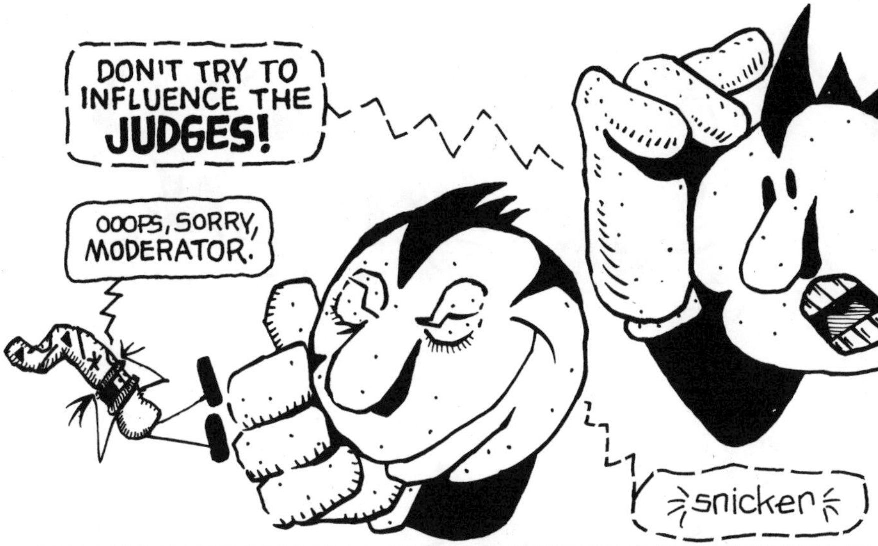
DON'T TRY TO INFLUENCE THE JUDGES!
OOOPS, SORRY, MODERATOR.
snicker

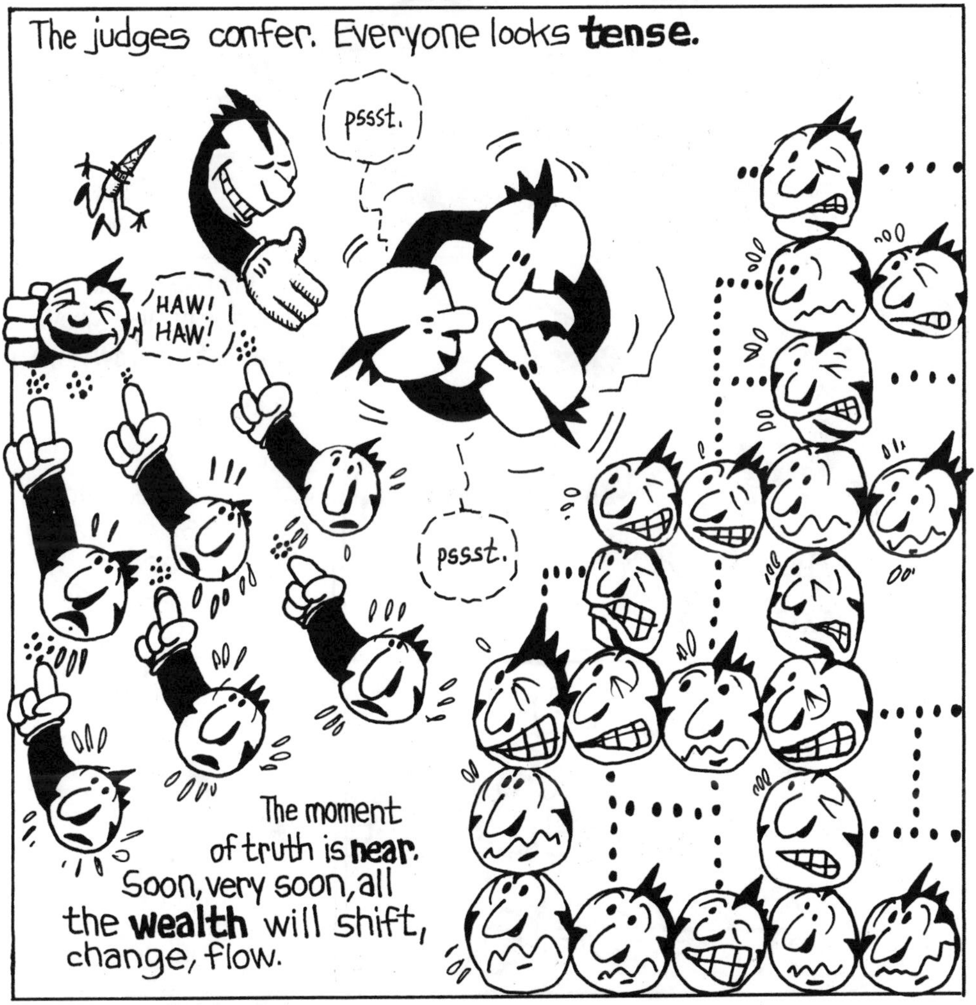
The judges confer. Everyone looks **tense.**
pssst.
HAW! HAW!
pssst.
The moment of truth is **near.** Soon, very soon, all the **wealth** will shift, change, flow.

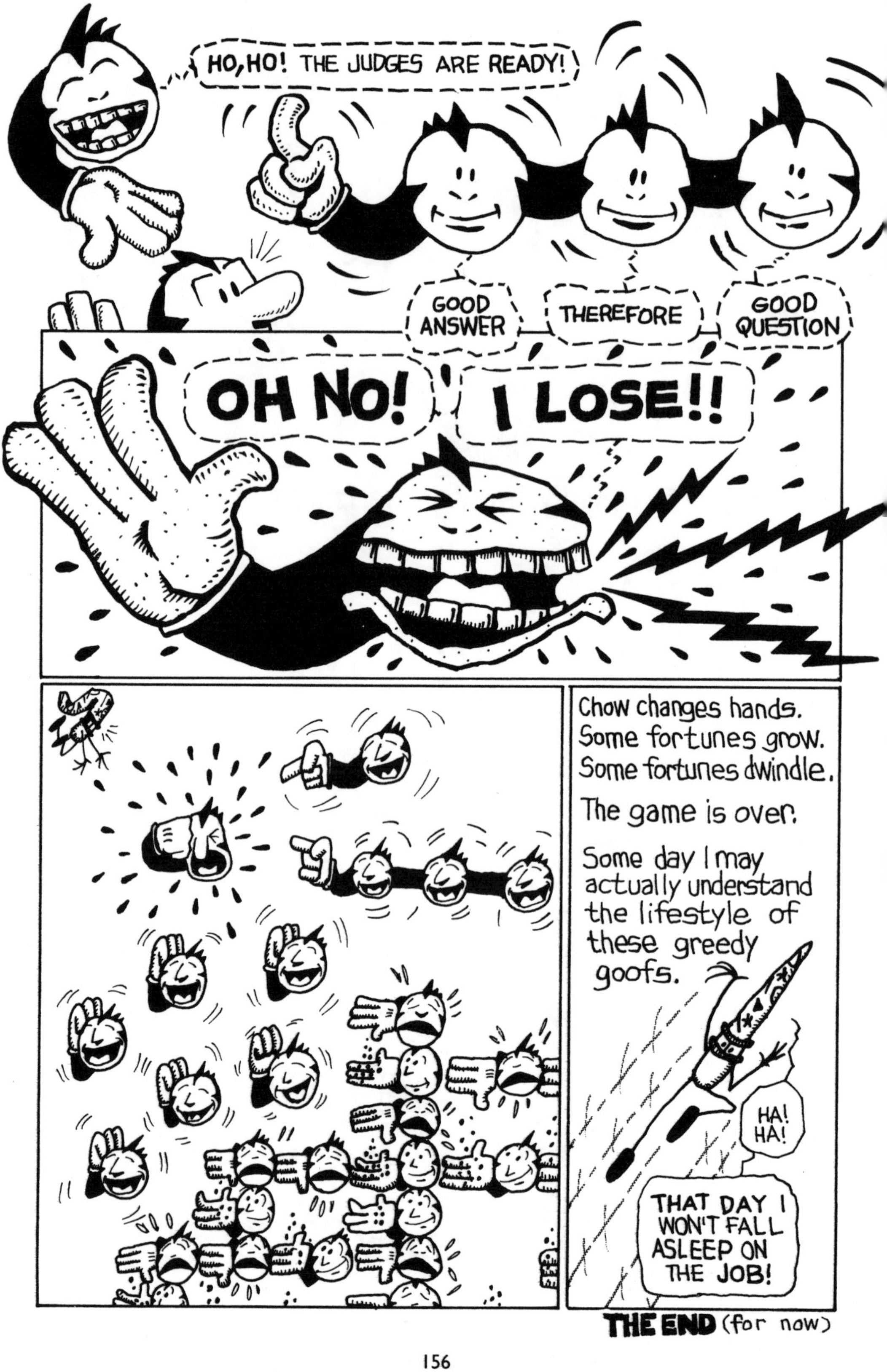
HO, HO! THE JUDGES ARE READY!
GOOD ANSWER
THEREFORE
GOOD QUESTION
OH NO!
I LOSE!!
Chow changes hands. Some fortunes grow. Some fortunes dwindle.
The game is over.
Some day I may actually understand the lifestyle of these greedy goofs.
HA! HA!
THAT DAY I WON'T FALL ASLEEP ON THE JOB!

**THE END** (for now)

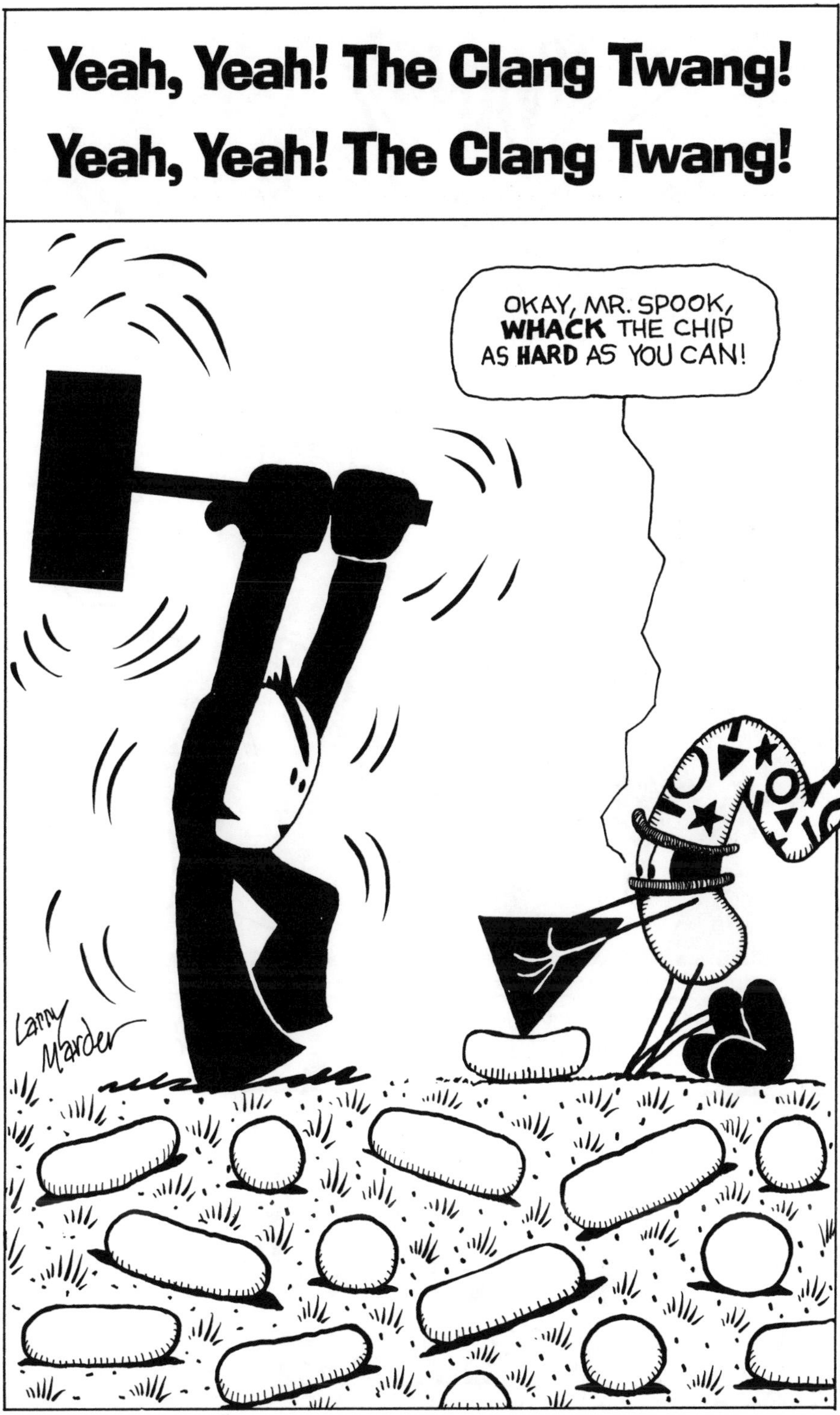
Yeah, Yeah! The Clang Twang!
Yeah, Yeah! The Clang Twang!
OKAY, MR. SPOOK, WHACK THE CHIP AS HARD AS YOU CAN!
Larry Marder

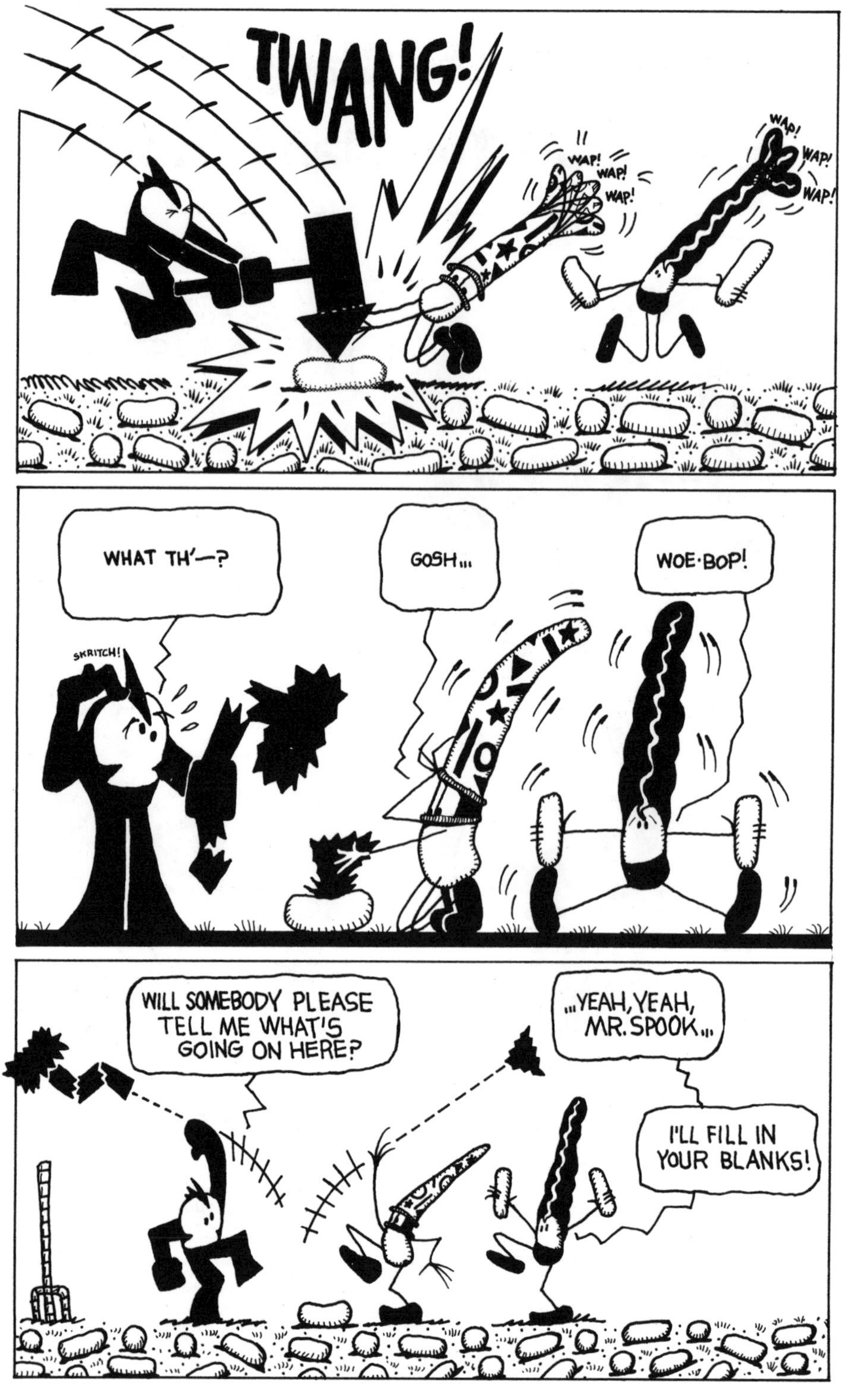
TWANG!
WAP!
WAP!
WAP!
WAP!
WAP!
WAP!
SKRITCH!
WHAT TH'—?
GOSH...
WOE·BOP!
WILL SOMEBODY PLEASE TELL ME WHAT'S GOING ON HERE?
...YEAH, YEAH, MR. SPOOK...
I'LL FILL IN YOUR BLANKS!

UH-OH! I CAN NEVER QUITE UNDERSTAND THE CRAZY LINGO THE BOOM'R BAND SPEAKS.

IT WUZ EARLY INTO A HOT BOOM'R BAND REHEARSAL-JAM; WE WUZ GETTING WILD 'N' WAXY ON A FINE NEW TUNE...

WE SOUND WAHOOLAZUMA TODAY, EH?

TOTALLY YOHO-CHIMPO!

I GOT SO BOOM'D-UP I DROPPED ONE OF MY RATTLES...

I RETRIEVED THE WRONG ITEM.

YOU AIN'T NO RATTLE!

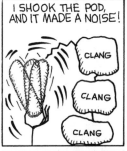

I SHOOK THE POD, AND IT MADE A NOISE!

CLANG

CLANG

CLANG

IT SPOKE TO YOU? A MYSTERY POD SPOKE TO YOU?

NO, I DIDN'T SAY THAT. I SAID IT MADE A SOUND: THIS SOUND!

CLANG

CLANG

CLAN

I BROUGHT THE POD TO PROFFY'S ATTENTION.

CLANG CLANG

CLANG

SHE GOT WISE!

LET'S SEE HOW MANY PODS MAKE NOISES.

WE LOOKED AND LISTENED...

SILENT

HERE'S ANOTHER ONE, PROFFY!

SILENT

SILENT

CLANG

CLANG

CLANG

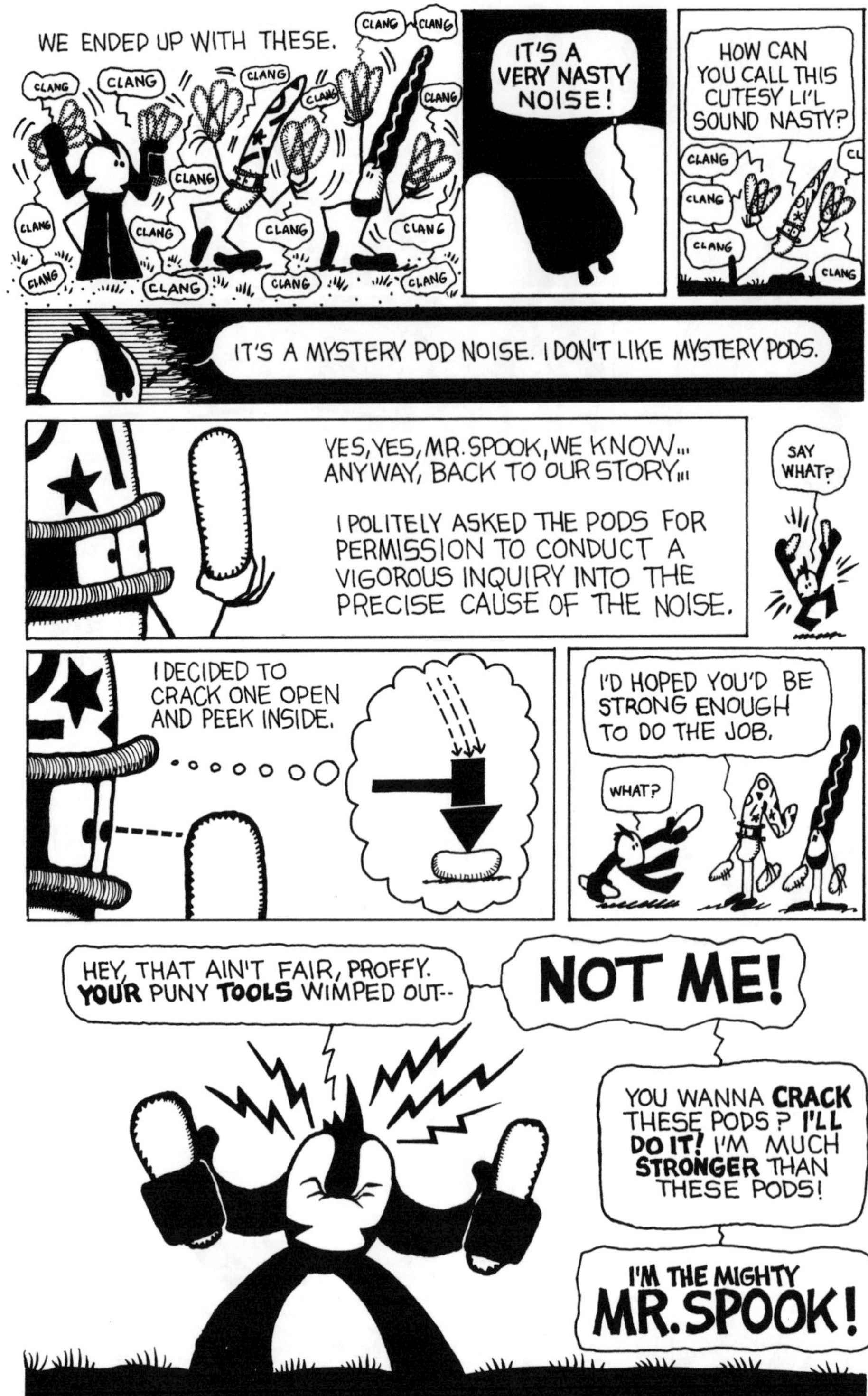
WE ENDED UP WITH THESE.
CLANG
IT'S A VERY NASTY NOISE!
HOW CAN YOU CALL THIS CUTESY LI'L SOUND NASTY?
IT'S A MYSTERY POD NOISE. I DON'T LIKE MYSTERY PODS.
YES, YES, MR. SPOOK, WE KNOW... ANYWAY, BACK TO OUR STORY...
I POLITELY ASKED THE PODS FOR PERMISSION TO CONDUCT A VIGOROUS INQUIRY INTO THE PRECISE CAUSE OF THE NOISE.
SAY WHAT?
I DECIDED TO CRACK ONE OPEN AND PEEK INSIDE.
I'D HOPED YOU'D BE STRONG ENOUGH TO DO THE JOB.
WHAT?
HEY, THAT AIN'T FAIR, PROFFY. YOUR PUNY TOOLS WIMPED OUT--
NOT ME!
YOU WANNA CRACK THESE PODS? I'LL DO IT! I'M MUCH STRONGER THAN THESE PODS!
I'M THE MIGHTY MR. SPOOK!

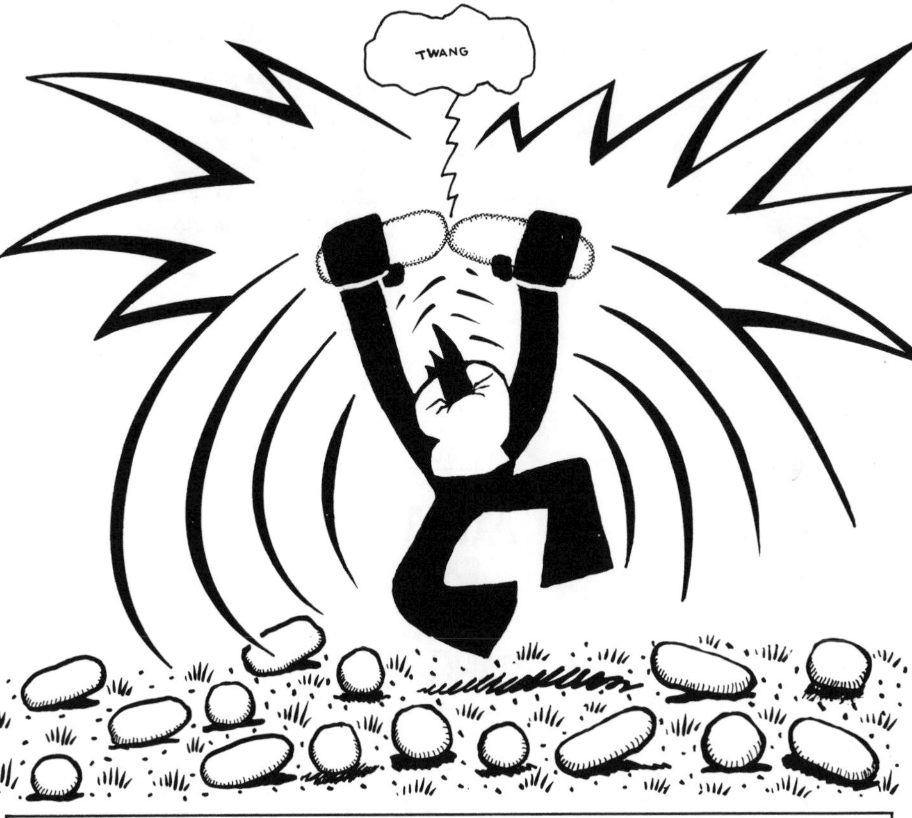
TWANG

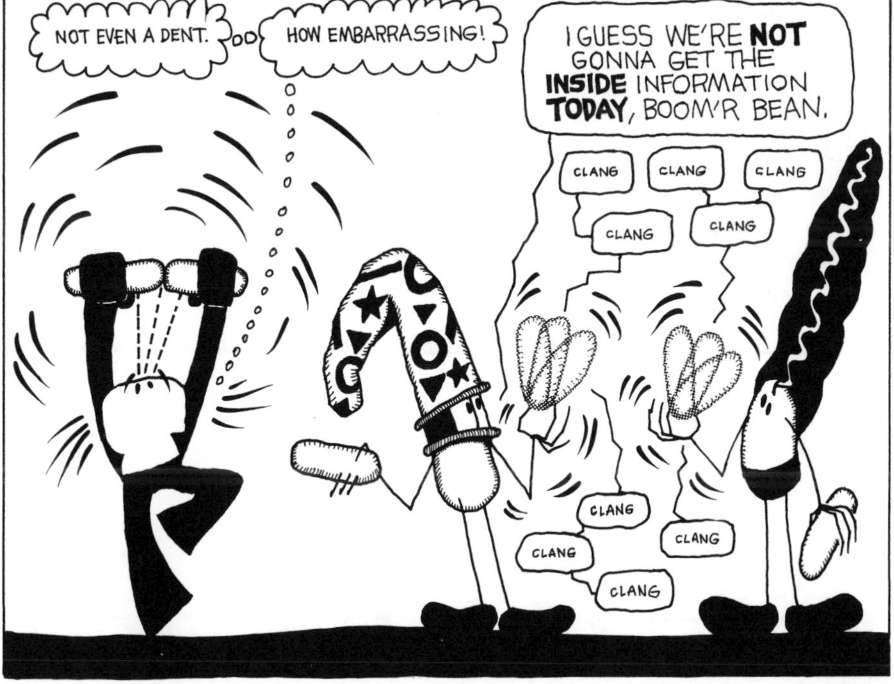
NOT EVEN A DENT.
HOW EMBARRASSING!
I GUESS WE'RE **NOT** GONNA GET THE **INSIDE** INFORMATION **TODAY**, BOOM'R BEAN.
CLANG
CLANG
CLANG
CLANG
CLANG
CLANG
CLANG
CLANG
CLANG

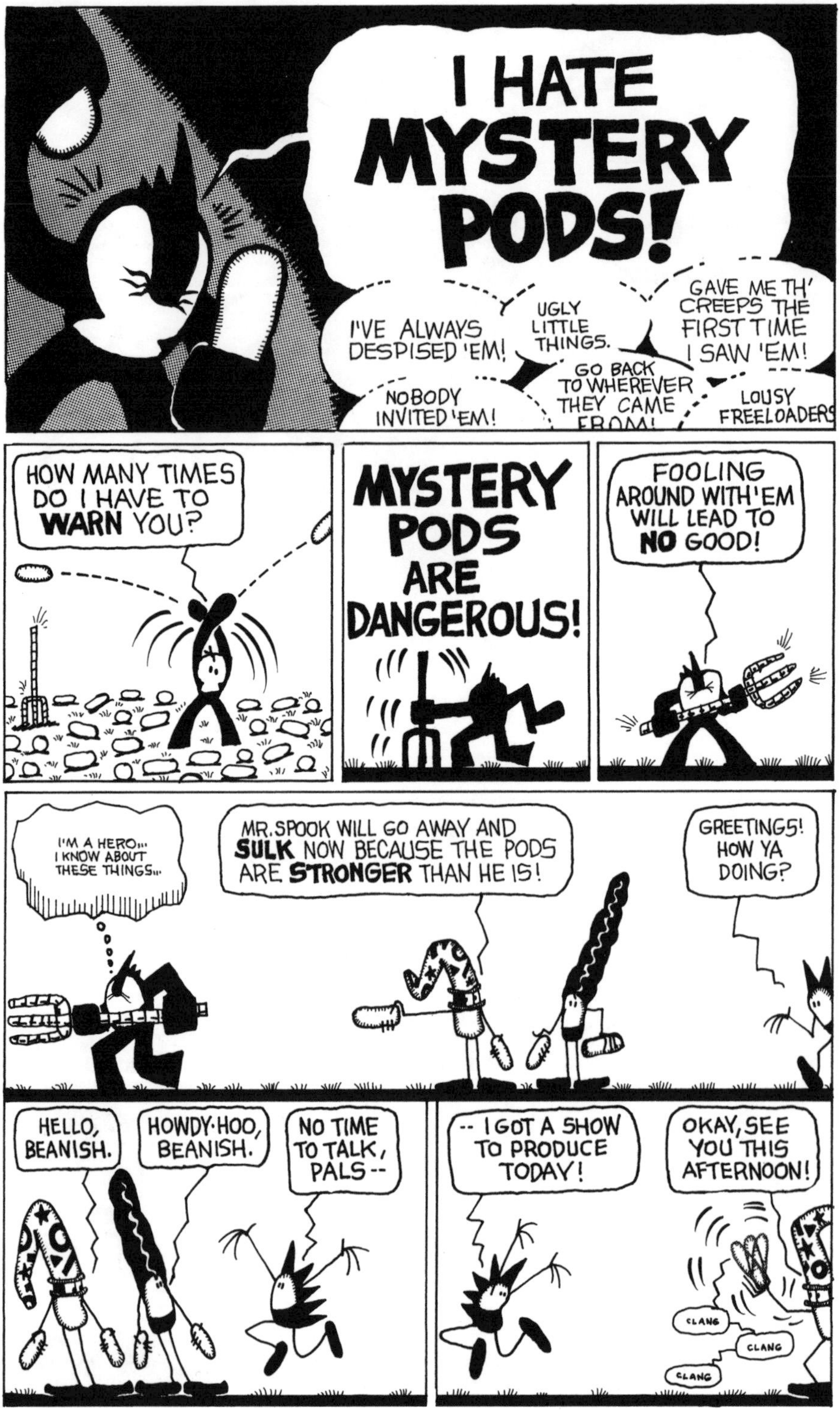
I HATE MYSTERY PODS!
I'VE ALWAYS DESPISED 'EM!
UGLY LITTLE THINGS.
GAVE ME TH' CREEPS THE FIRST TIME I SAW 'EM!
NOBODY INVITED 'EM!
GO BACK TO WHEREVER THEY CAME FROM!
LOUSY FREELOADERS
HOW MANY TIMES DO I HAVE TO WARN YOU?
MYSTERY PODS ARE DANGEROUS!
FOOLING AROUND WITH 'EM WILL LEAD TO NO GOOD!
I'M A HERO... I KNOW ABOUT THESE THINGS...
MR. SPOOK WILL GO AWAY AND SULK NOW BECAUSE THE PODS ARE STRONGER THAN HE IS!
GREETINGS! HOW YA DOING?
HELLO, BEANISH.
HOWDY-HOO, BEANISH.
NO TIME TO TALK, PALS --
-- I GOT A SHOW TO PRODUCE TODAY!
OKAY, SEE YOU THIS AFTERNOON!
CLANG
CLANG
CLANG

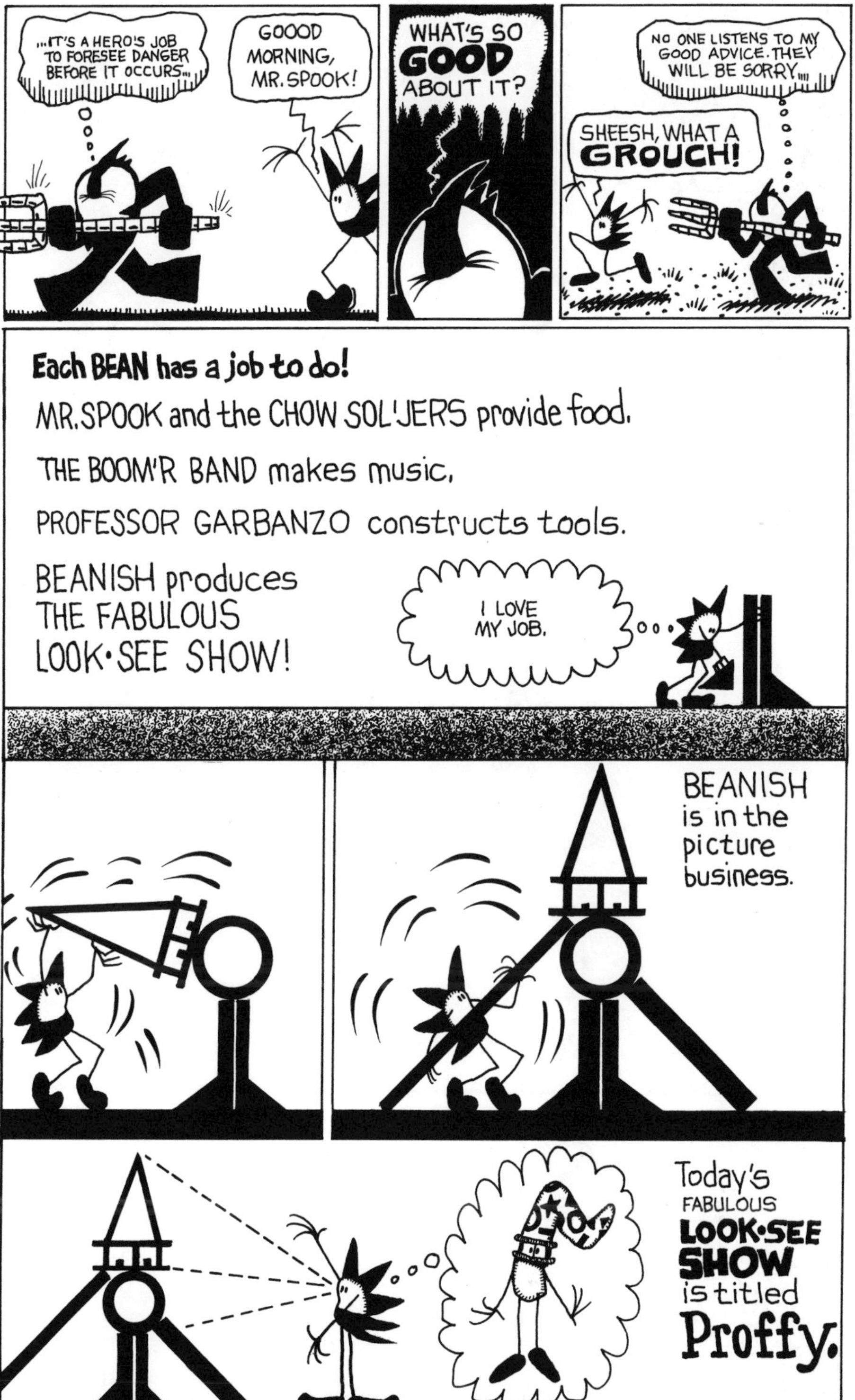
...IT'S A HERO'S JOB TO FORESEE DANGER BEFORE IT OCCURS...
GOOOD MORNING, MR. SPOOK!
WHAT'S SO GOOD ABOUT IT?
NO ONE LISTENS TO MY GOOD ADVICE. THEY WILL BE SORRY...
SHEESH, WHAT A GROUCH!
Each BEAN has a job to do!
MR. SPOOK and the CHOW SOL'JERS provide food.
THE BOOM'R BAND makes music.
PROFESSOR GARBANZO constructs tools.
BEANISH produces THE FABULOUS LOOK•SEE SHOW!
I LOVE MY JOB.
BEANISH is in the picture business.
Today's FABULOUS LOOK•SEE SHOW is titled Proffy.

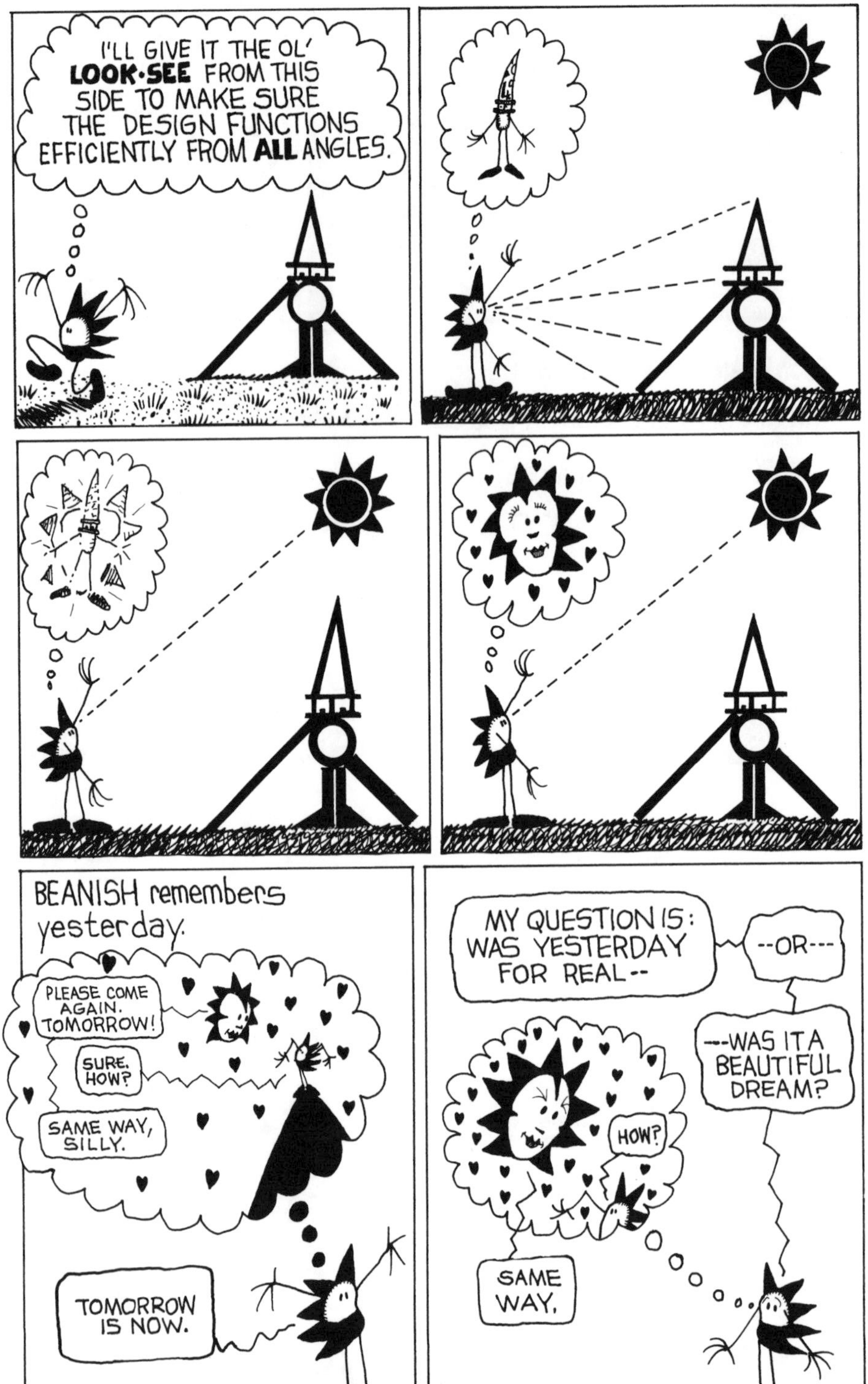

I'LL GIVE IT THE OL' **LOOK·SEE** FROM THIS SIDE TO MAKE SURE THE DESIGN FUNCTIONS EFFICIENTLY FROM **ALL** ANGLES.
BEANISH remembers yesterday.
PLEASE COME AGAIN. TOMORROW!
SURE. HOW?
SAME WAY, SILLY.
TOMORROW IS NOW.
MY QUESTION IS: WAS YESTERDAY FOR REAL--
--OR---
---WAS IT A BEAUTIFUL DREAM?
HOW?
SAME WAY.

I'LL REPEAT MY ACTIONS PREVIOUS TO THE ALLEGED EXPERIENCE.

I WILL RETURN TO THE SKETCH AND STEP INSIDE OF IT.

IF NOTHING OCCURS--IT WAS A DREAM.

IF SOMETHING HAPPENS--IT WAS GENUINE.

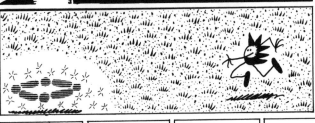

YBOING

NOTHING...

THEN IT WAS ONLY A SWEET DREAM...

UNLESS...

PERHAPS I OVERLOOKED A DETAIL IN MY DUPLICATION OF YESTERDAY'S EVENTS.

I MUST BE AS CLEVER AS PROFFY. I MUST EXAMINE THE MYSTERY FROM EVERY ANGLE.

yesterday.

AHA!

IT'S NOT THE SAME TIME OF DAY!

GOTTA WAIT AND SEE WHAT HAPPENS AT MIDDAY.

I HATE LONG WAITS.

TAP TAP TAP

IT WON'T BE LONG NOW...

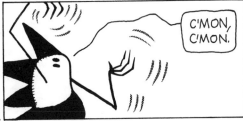

C'MON, C'MON.

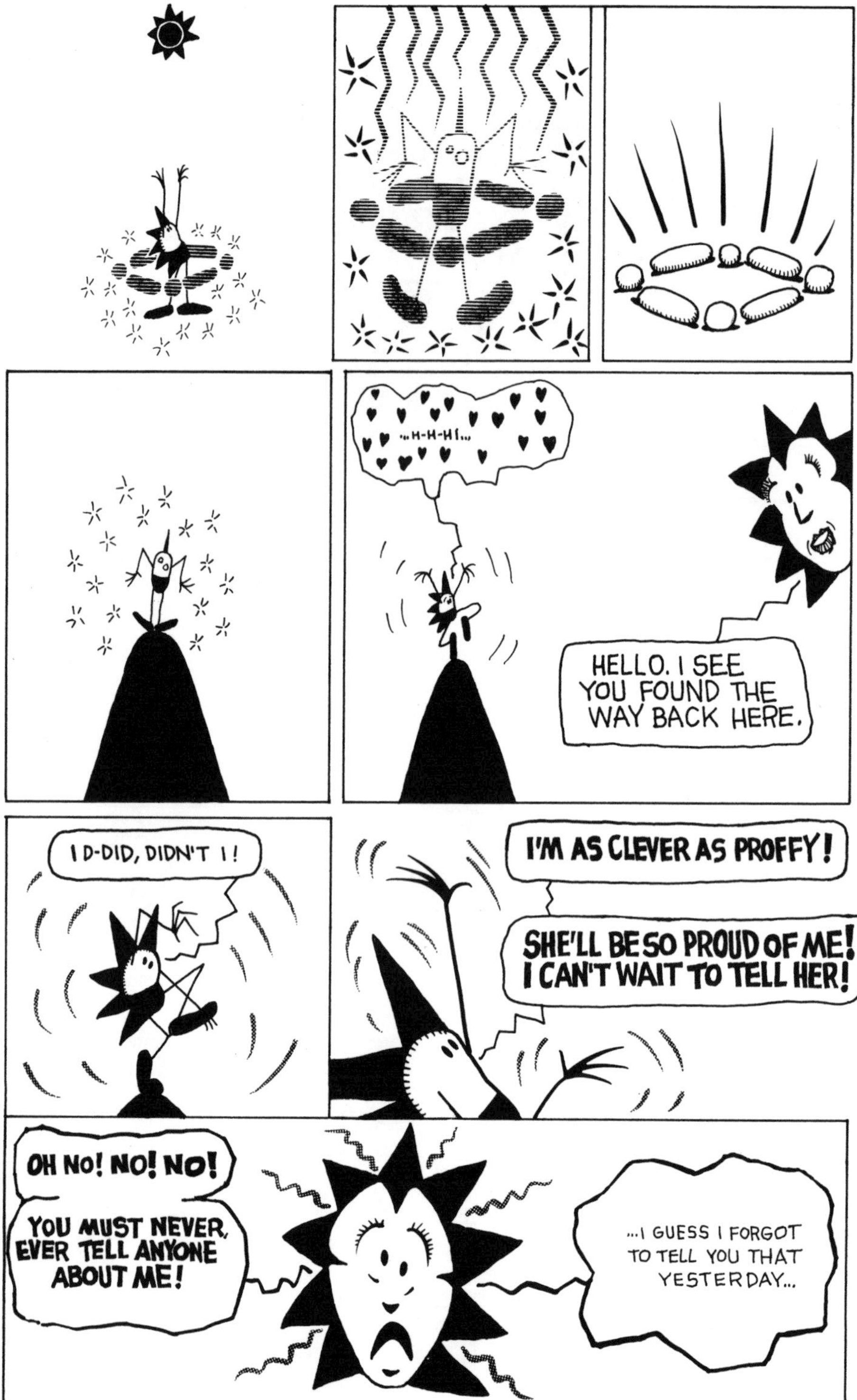
...H-H-HI...
HELLO. I SEE YOU FOUND THE WAY BACK HERE.
I D-DID, DIDN'T I!
I'M AS CLEVER AS PROFFY!
SHE'LL BE SO PROUD OF ME! I CAN'T WAIT TO TELL HER!
OH NO! NO! NO!
YOU MUST NEVER, EVER TELL ANYONE ABOUT ME!
...I GUESS I FORGOT TO TELL YOU THAT YESTERDAY...

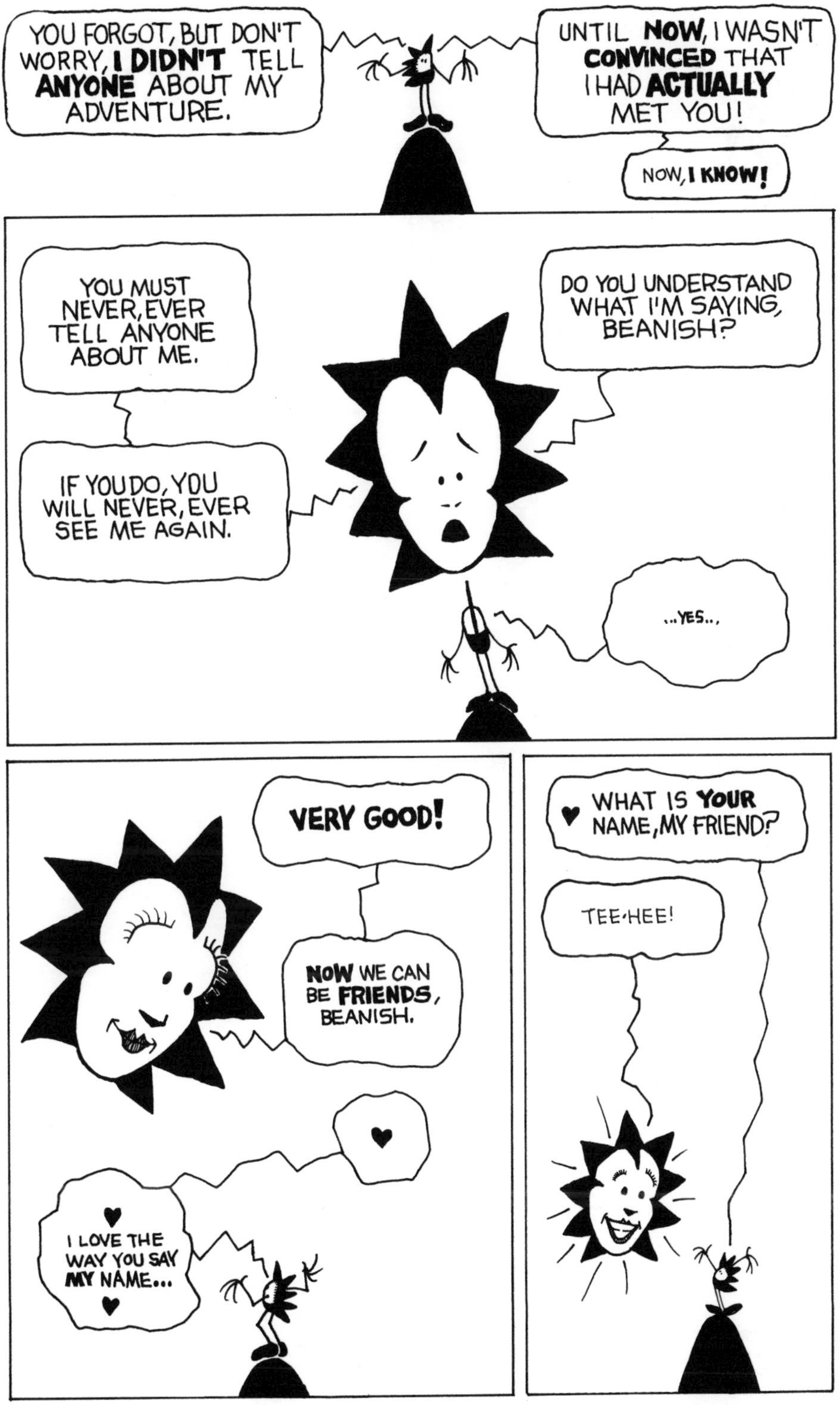
YOU FORGOT, BUT DON'T WORRY, I DIDN'T TELL ANYONE ABOUT MY ADVENTURE.
UNTIL NOW, I WASN'T CONVINCED THAT I HAD ACTUALLY MET YOU!
NOW, I KNOW!
YOU MUST NEVER, EVER TELL ANYONE ABOUT ME.
IF YOU DO, YOU WILL NEVER, EVER SEE ME AGAIN.
DO YOU UNDERSTAND WHAT I'M SAYING, BEANISH?
...YES...
VERY GOOD!
NOW WE CAN BE FRIENDS, BEANISH.
I LOVE THE WAY YOU SAY MY NAME...
WHAT IS YOUR NAME, MY FRIEND?
TEE-HEE!

I HAVE MANY, MANY NAMES, BEANISH!

COME BACK TOMORROW AND I **MIGHT** TELL YOU **ONE**.

T-TOMORROW?

SAME WAY!

...sigh...

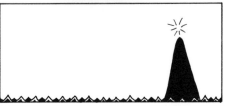

...MIDDAY, TOMORROW. MIDDAY, TOMORROW. MIDDAY, TOMORROW

Also occurring at midday, **today.**

SO FAR WE HAVE IDENTIFIED **TWO** SOUNDS.

CLANG
CLANG
CLANG
CLANG
CLANG
CLANG

TWANG

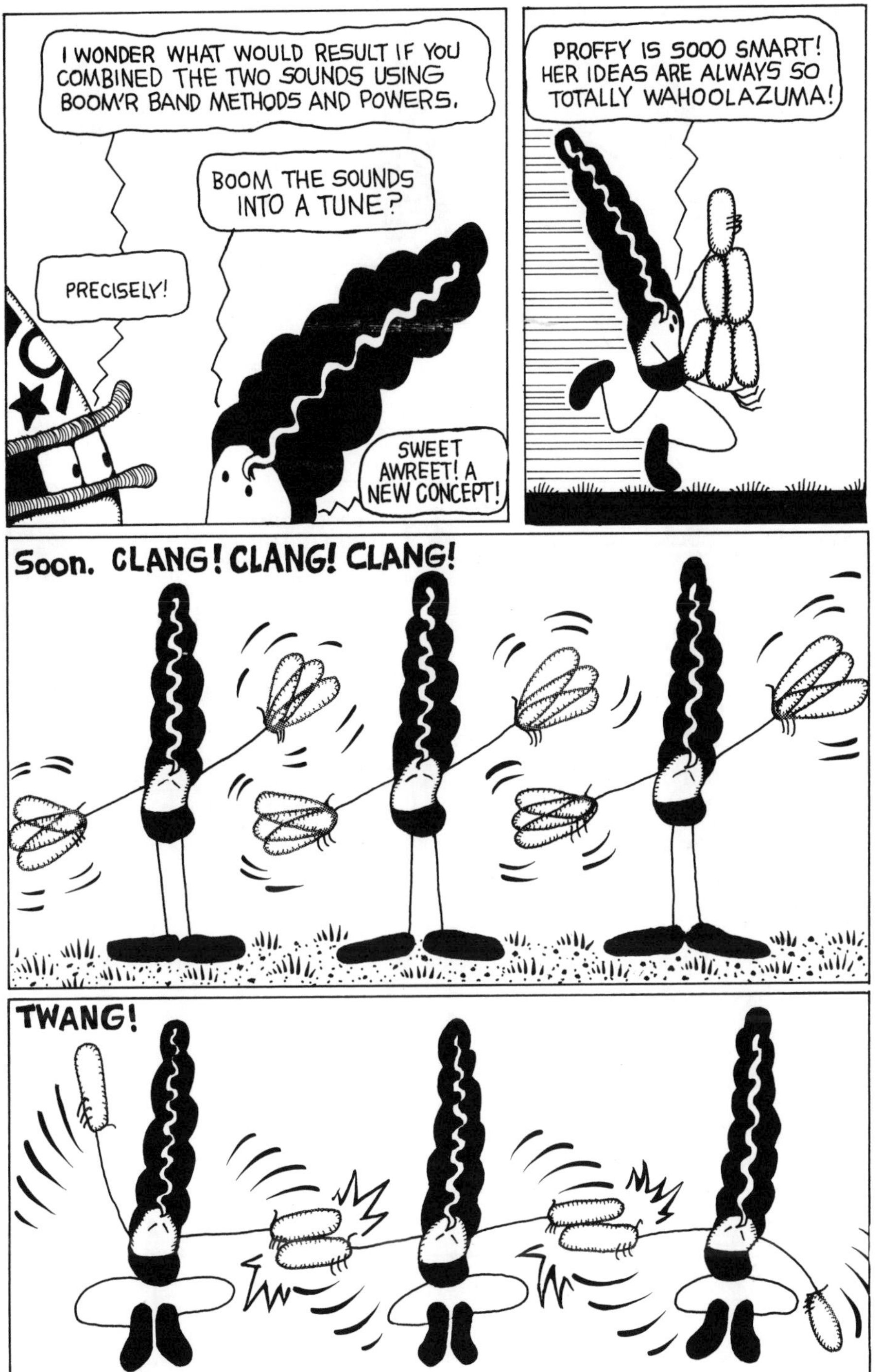
I WONDER WHAT WOULD RESULT IF YOU COMBINED THE TWO SOUNDS USING BOOM'R BAND METHODS AND POWERS.
BOOM THE SOUNDS INTO A TUNE?
PRECISELY!
SWEET AWREET! A NEW CONCEPT!
PROFFY IS SOOO SMART! HER IDEAS ARE ALWAYS SO TOTALLY WAHOOLAZUMA!
Soon. CLANG! CLANG! CLANG!
TWANG!

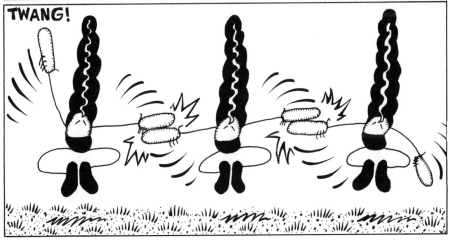

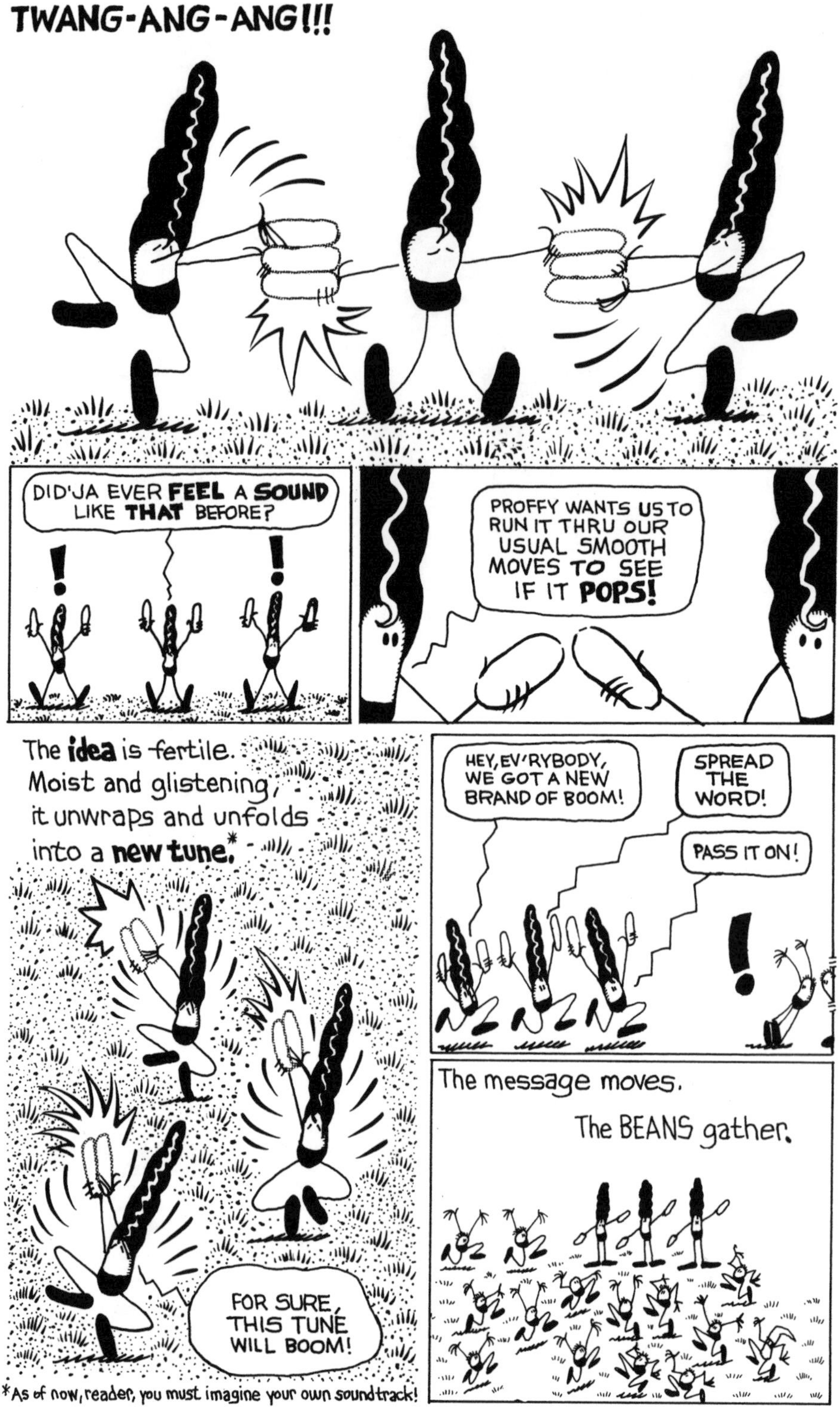
TWANG-ANG-ANG!!!
DID'JA EVER FEEL A SOUND LIKE THAT BEFORE?
PROFFY WANTS US TO RUN IT THRU OUR USUAL SMOOTH MOVES TO SEE IF IT POPS!
The idea is fertile. Moist and glistening, it unwraps and unfolds into a new tune.*
FOR SURE, THIS TUNE WILL BOOM!
HEY, EV'RYBODY, WE GOT A NEW BRAND OF BOOM!
SPREAD THE WORD!
PASS IT ON!
The message moves.
The BEANS gather.
*As of now, reader, you must imagine your own soundtrack!

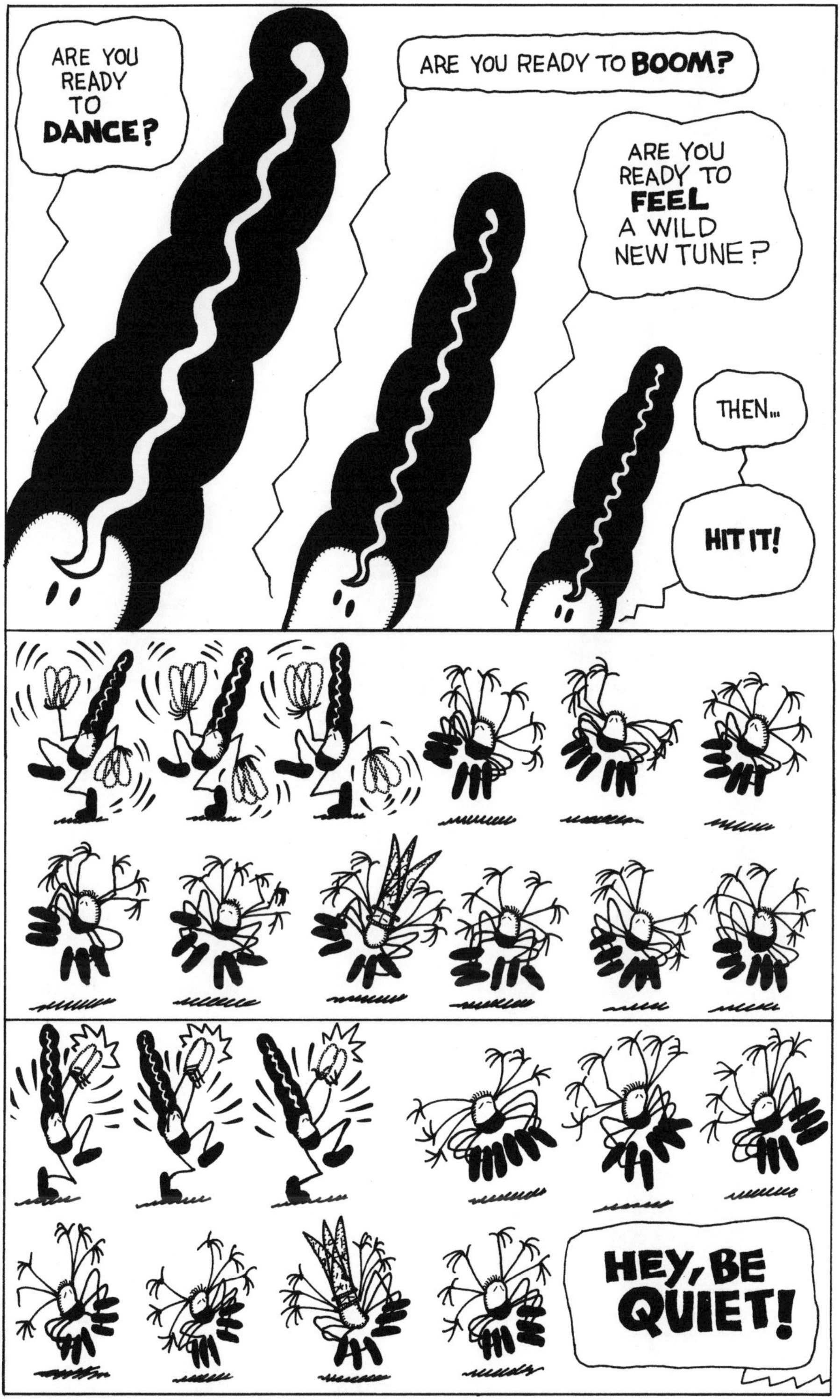
ARE YOU READY TO DANCE?
ARE YOU READY TO BOOM?
ARE YOU READY TO FEEL A WILD NEW TUNE?
THEN...
HIT IT!
HEY, BE QUIET!

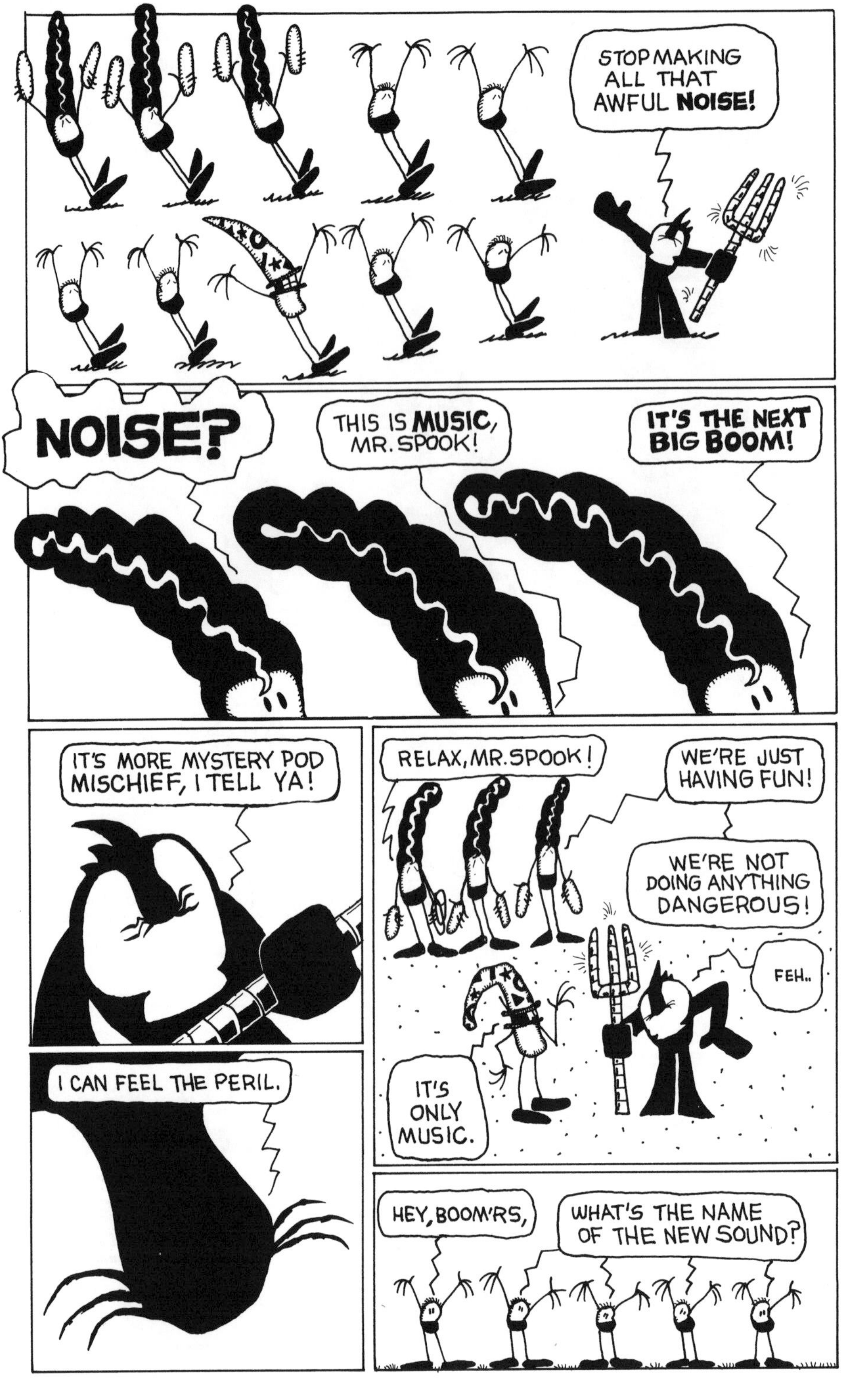
STOP MAKING ALL THAT AWFUL NOISE!
NOISE?
THIS IS MUSIC, MR. SPOOK!
IT'S THE NEXT BIG BOOM!
IT'S MORE MYSTERY POD MISCHIEF, I TELL YA!
I CAN FEEL THE PERIL.
RELAX, MR. SPOOK!
WE'RE JUST HAVING FUN!
WE'RE NOT DOING ANYTHING DANGEROUS!
FEH..
IT'S ONLY MUSIC.
HEY, BOOM'RS,
WHAT'S THE NAME OF THE NEW SOUND?

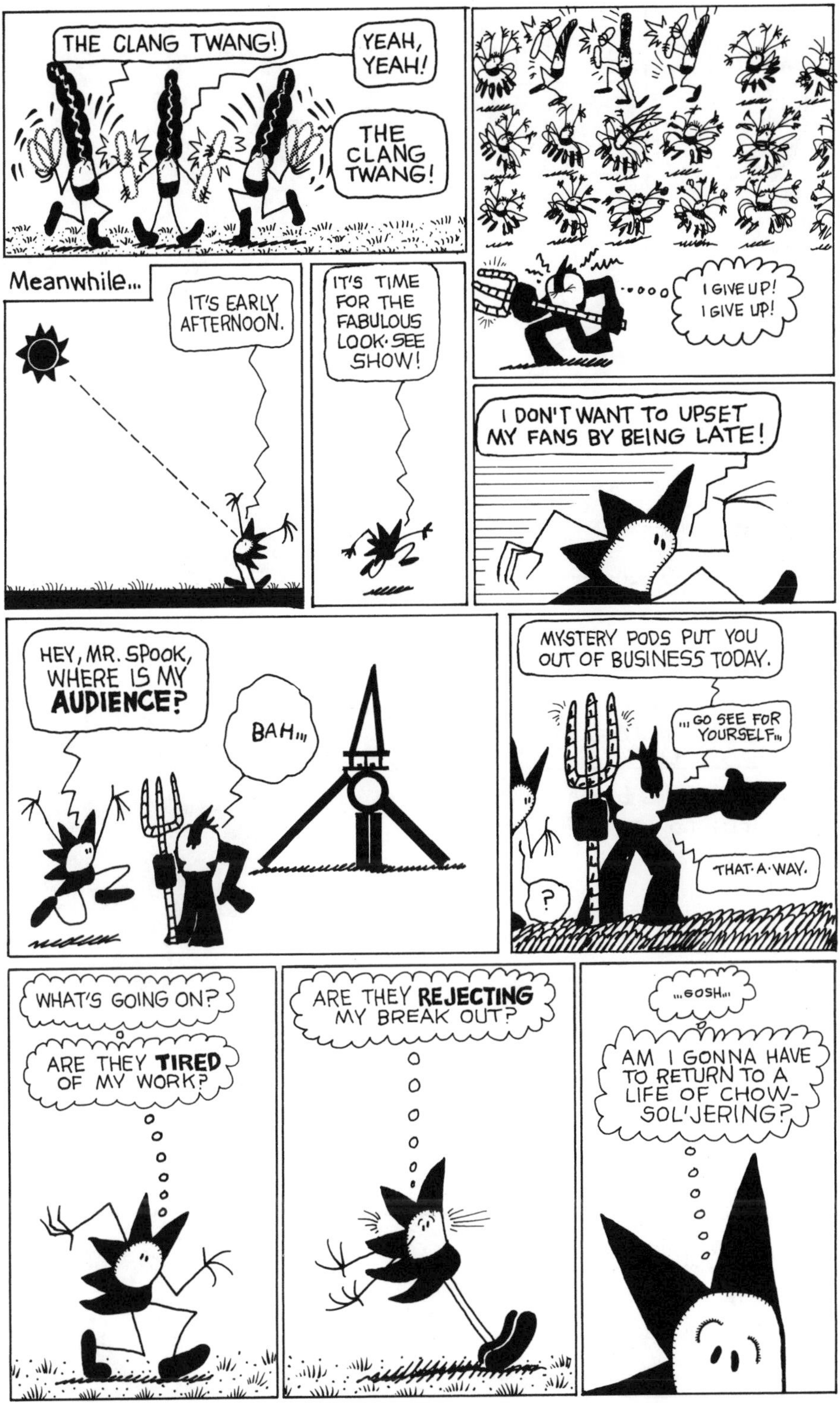
THE CLANG TWANG!
YEAH, YEAH!
THE CLANG TWANG!
I GIVE UP! I GIVE UP!
Meanwhile...
IT'S EARLY AFTERNOON.
IT'S TIME FOR THE FABULOUS LOOK-SEE SHOW!
I DON'T WANT TO UPSET MY FANS BY BEING LATE!
HEY, MR. SPOOK, WHERE IS MY AUDIENCE?
BAH...
MYSTERY PODS PUT YOU OUT OF BUSINESS TODAY.
...GO SEE FOR YOURSELF...
THAT-A-WAY.
?
WHAT'S GOING ON?
ARE THEY TIRED OF MY WORK?
ARE THEY REJECTING MY BREAK OUT?
...GOSH...
AM I GONNA HAVE TO RETURN TO A LIFE OF CHOW-SOL'JERING?

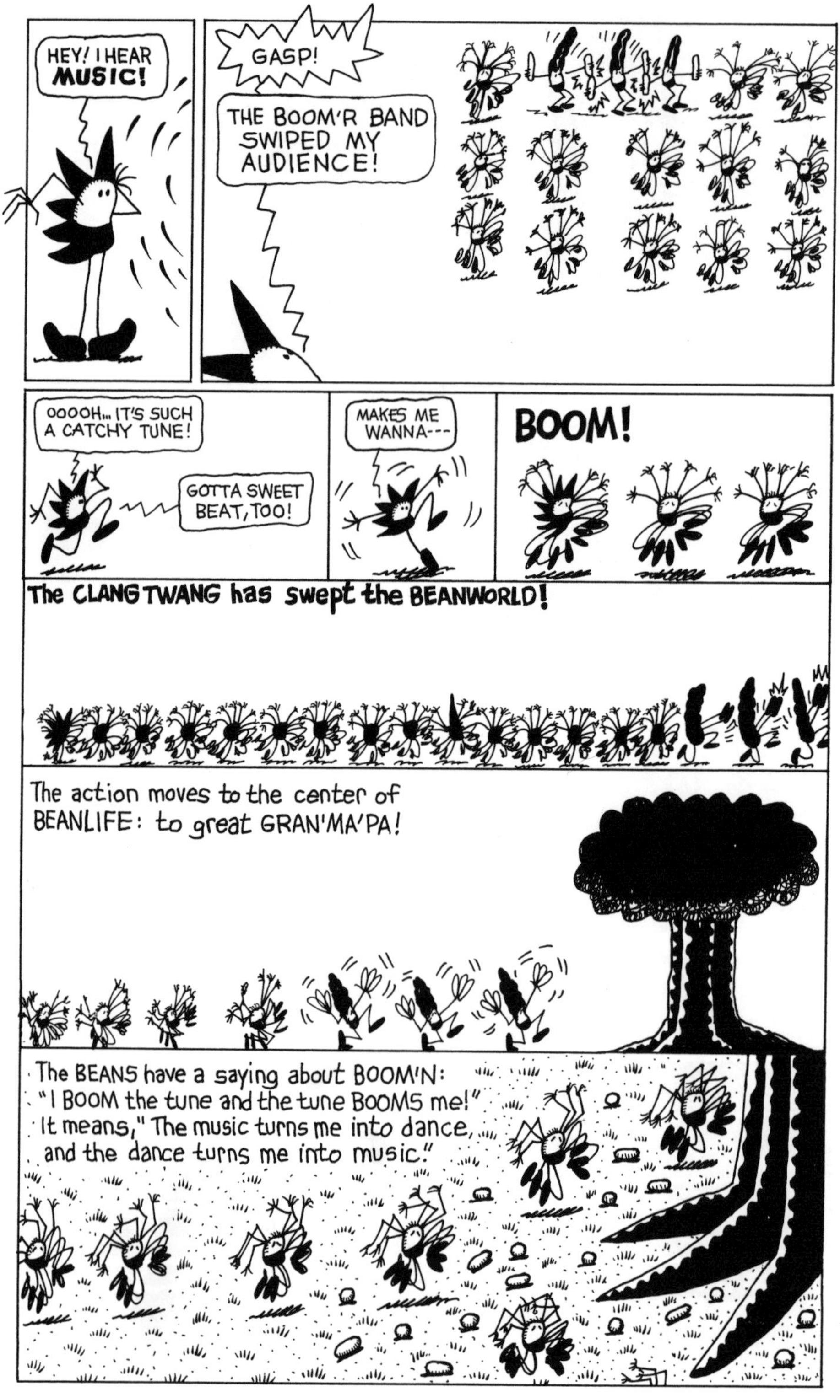
HEY! I HEAR MUSIC!
GASP!
THE BOOM'R BAND SWIPED MY AUDIENCE!
OOOOH... IT'S SUCH A CATCHY TUNE!
GOTTA SWEET BEAT, TOO!
MAKES ME WANNA---
BOOM!
The CLANGTWANG has swept the BEANWORLD!
The action moves to the center of BEANLIFE: to great GRAN'MA'PA!
The BEANS have a saying about BOOM'N: "I BOOM the tune and the tune BOOMS me!" It means, "The music turns me into dance, and the dance turns me into music."

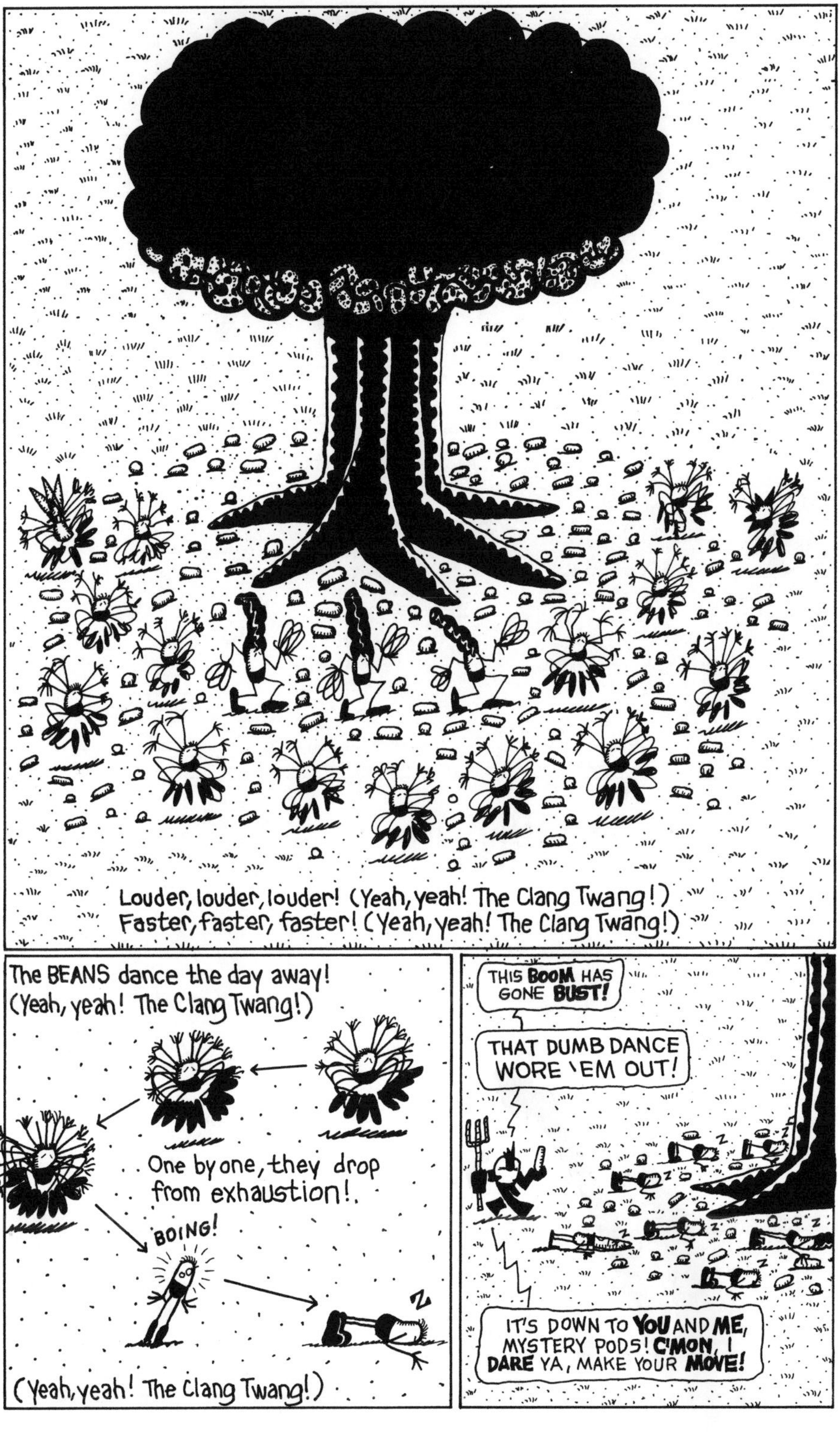
Louder, louder, louder! (Yeah, yeah! The Clang Twang!)
Faster, faster, faster! (Yeah, yeah! The Clang Twang!)
The BEANS dance the day away!
(Yeah, yeah! The Clang Twang!)
One by one, they drop from exhaustion!
BOING!
Z
(Yeah, yeah! The Clang Twang!)
THIS BOOM HAS GONE BUST!
THAT DUMB DANCE WORE 'EM OUT!
IT'S DOWN TO YOU AND ME, MYSTERY PODS! C'MON, I DARE YA, MAKE YOUR MOVE!

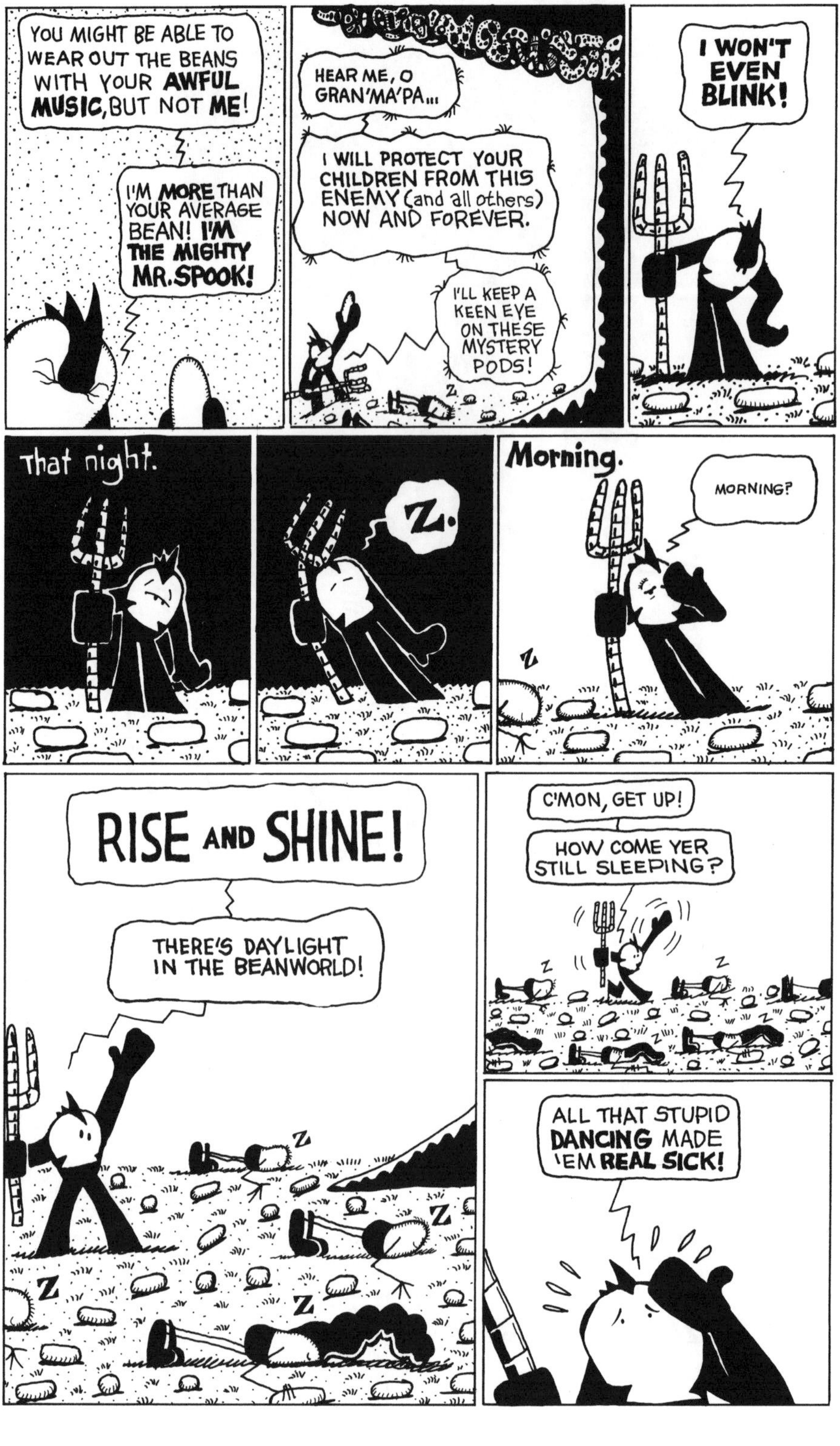
YOU MIGHT BE ABLE TO WEAR OUT THE BEANS WITH YOUR AWFUL MUSIC, BUT NOT ME!
I'M MORE THAN YOUR AVERAGE BEAN! I'M THE MIGHTY MR. SPOOK!
HEAR ME, O GRAN'MA'PA...
I WILL PROTECT YOUR CHILDREN FROM THIS ENEMY (and all others) NOW AND FOREVER.
I'LL KEEP A KEEN EYE ON THESE MYSTERY PODS!
Z
I WON'T EVEN BLINK!
That night.
Z.
Morning.
MORNING?
Z
RISE AND SHINE!
THERE'S DAYLIGHT IN THE BEANWORLD!
Z
Z
Z
Z
C'MON, GET UP!
HOW COME YER STILL SLEEPING?
Z
Z
Z
Z
ALL THAT STUPID DANCING MADE 'EM REAL SICK!

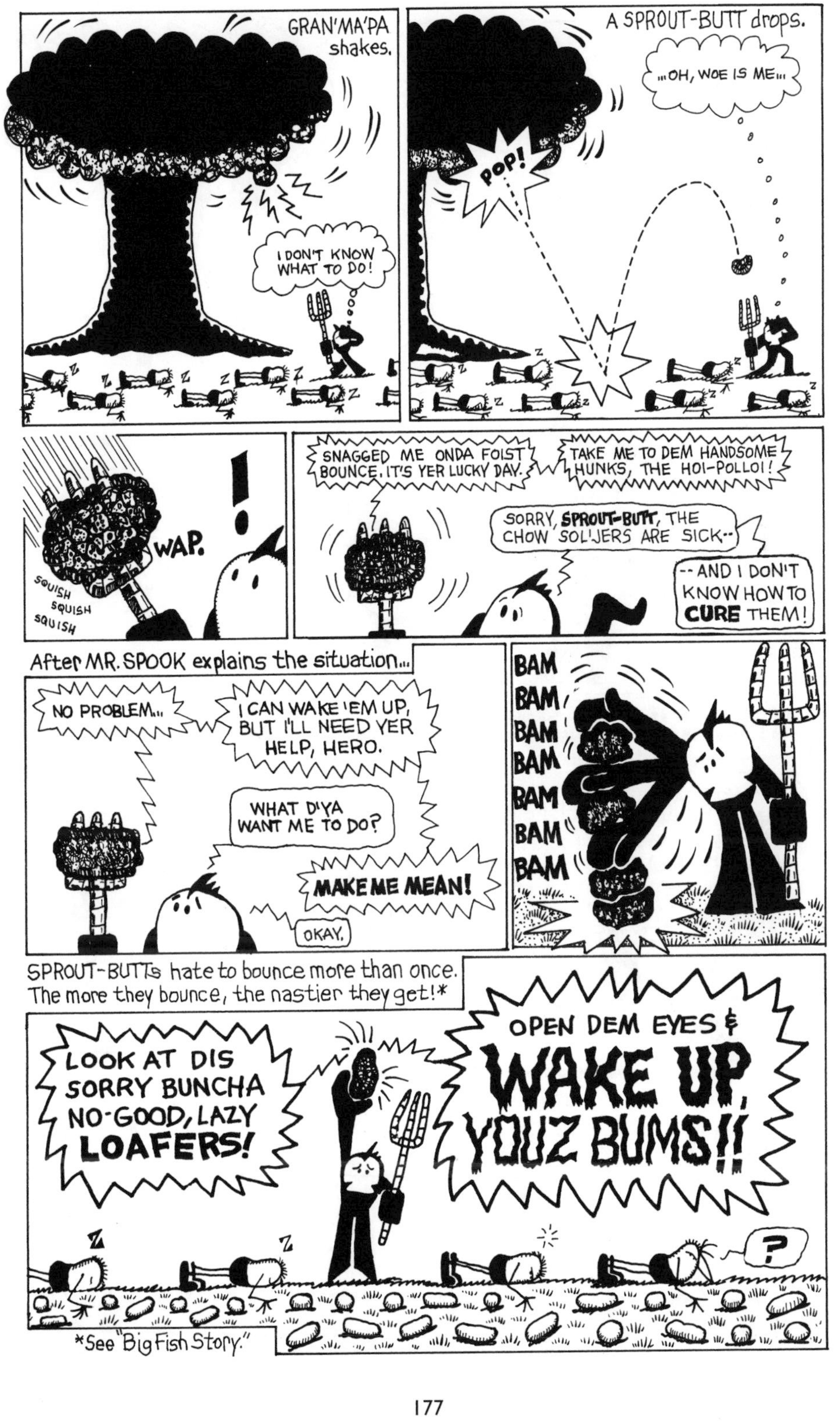
GRAN'MA'PA shakes.
I DON'T KNOW WHAT TO DO!
A SPROUT-BUTT drops.
...OH, WOE IS ME...
POP!
WAP.
SQUISH SQUISH SQUISH
!
SNAGGED ME ONDA FOIST BOUNCE. IT'S YER LUCKY DAY.
TAKE ME TO DEM HANDSOME HUNKS, THE HOI-POLLOI!
SORRY, SPROUT-BUTT, THE CHOW SOL'JERS ARE SICK--
--AND I DON'T KNOW HOW TO CURE THEM!
After MR. SPOOK explains the situation...
NO PROBLEM...
I CAN WAKE 'EM UP, BUT I'LL NEED YER HELP, HERO.
WHAT D'YA WANT ME TO DO?
MAKE ME MEAN!
OKAY.
BAM BAM BAM BAM BAM BAM BAM
SPROUT-BUTTs hate to bounce more than once. The more they bounce, the nastier they get!*
LOOK AT DIS SORRY BUNCHA NO-GOOD, LAZY LOAFERS!
OPEN DEM EYES & WAKE UP, YOUZ BUMS!!
?
*See "Big Fish Story."

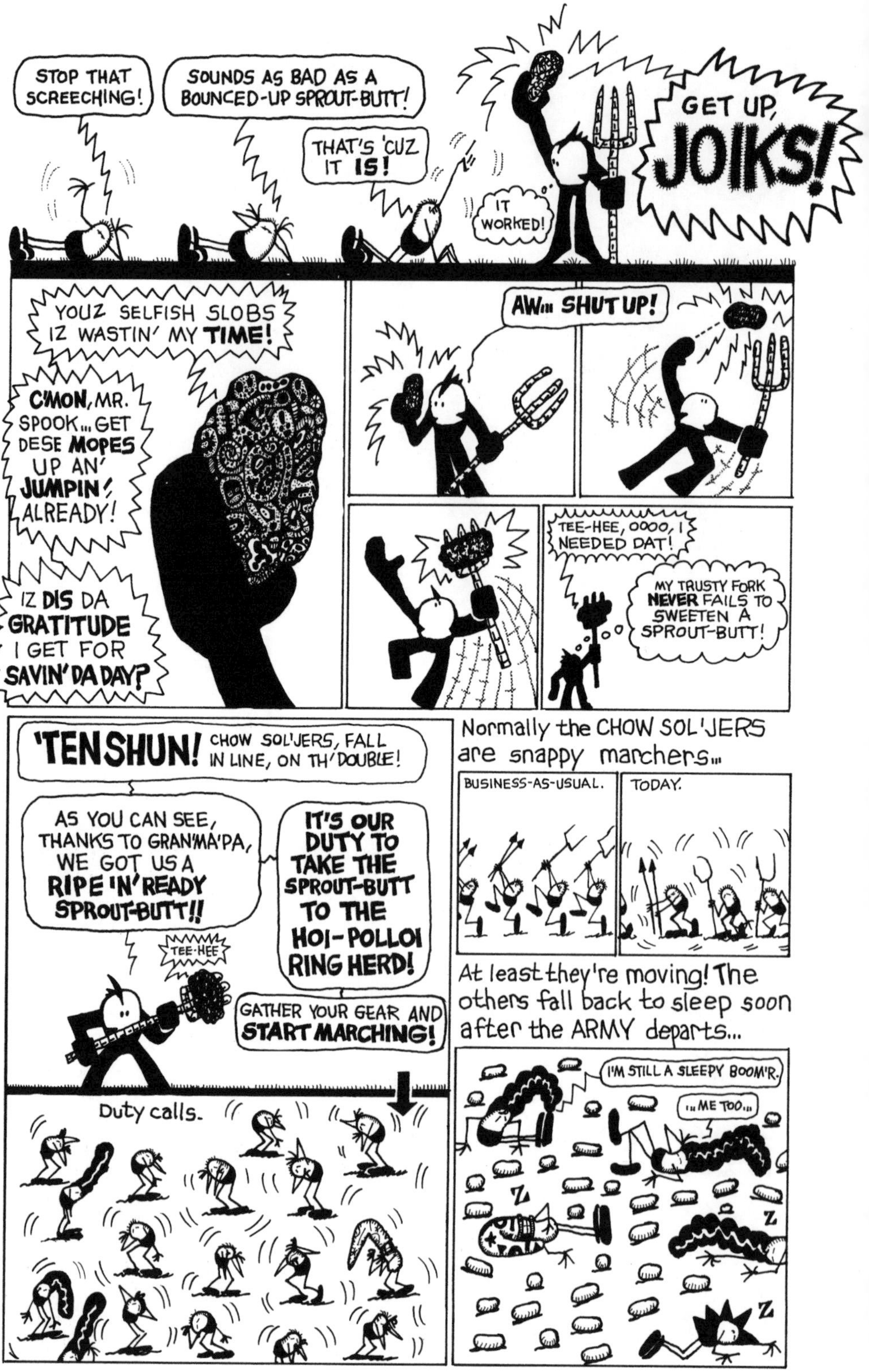
STOP THAT SCREECHING!
SOUNDS AS BAD AS A BOUNCED-UP SPROUT-BUTT!
THAT'S 'CUZ IT IS!
IT WORKED!
GET UP, JOIKS!
YOUZ SELFISH SLOBS IZ WASTIN' MY TIME!
C'MON, MR. SPOOK... GET DESE MOPES UP AN' JUMPIN', ALREADY!
IZ DIS DA GRATITUDE I GET FOR SAVIN' DA DAY?
AW... SHUT UP!
TEE-HEE, OOOO, I NEEDED DAT!
MY TRUSTY FORK NEVER FAILS TO SWEETEN A SPROUT-BUTT!
'TENSHUN! CHOW SOL'JERS, FALL IN LINE, ON TH' DOUBLE!
AS YOU CAN SEE, THANKS TO GRAN'MA'PA, WE GOT US A RIPE 'N' READY SPROUT-BUTT!!
IT'S OUR DUTY TO TAKE THE SPROUT-BUTT TO THE HOI-POLLOI RING HERD!
TEE-HEE
GATHER YOUR GEAR AND START MARCHING!
Normally the CHOW SOL'JERS are snappy marchers...
BUSINESS-AS-USUAL.
TODAY.
At least they're moving! The others fall back to sleep soon after the ARMY departs...
Duty calls.
I'M STILL A SLEEPY BOOM'R.
...ME TOO...
Z
Z
Z

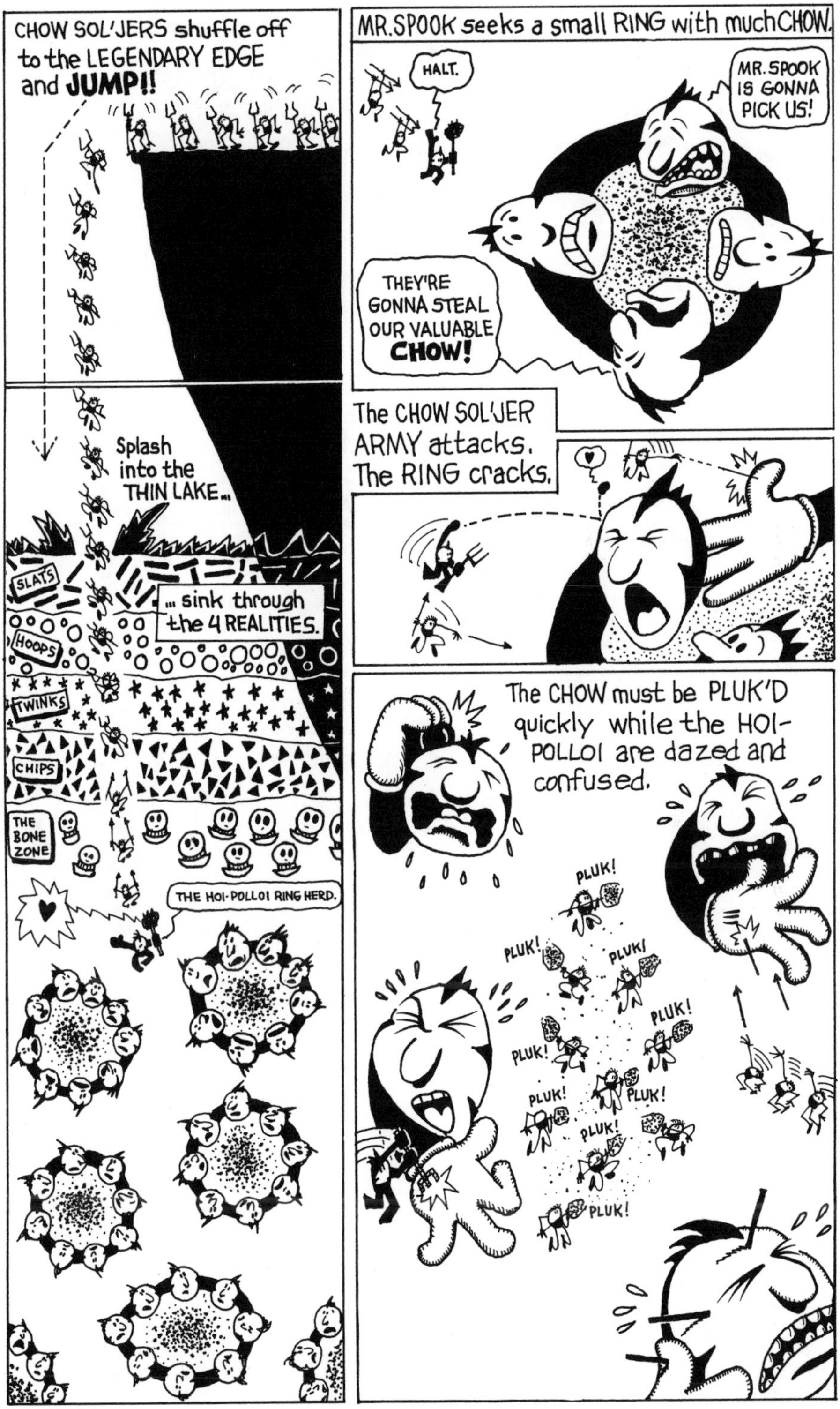
CHOW SOL'JERS shuffle off to the LEGENDARY EDGE and JUMP!!
Splash into the THIN LAKE...
... sink through the 4 REALITIES.
SLATS
HOOPS
TWINKS
CHIPS
THE BONE ZONE
THE HOI-POLLOI RING HERD.
MR.SPOOK seeks a small RING with much CHOW.
HALT.
MR.SPOOK IS GONNA PICK US!
THEY'RE GONNA STEAL OUR VALUABLE CHOW!
The CHOW SOL'JER ARMY attacks. The RING cracks.
The CHOW must be PLUK'D quickly while the HOI-POLLOI are dazed and confused.
PLUK!
PLUK!
PLUK!
PLUK!
PLUK!
PLUK!
PLUK!
PLUK!
PLUK!

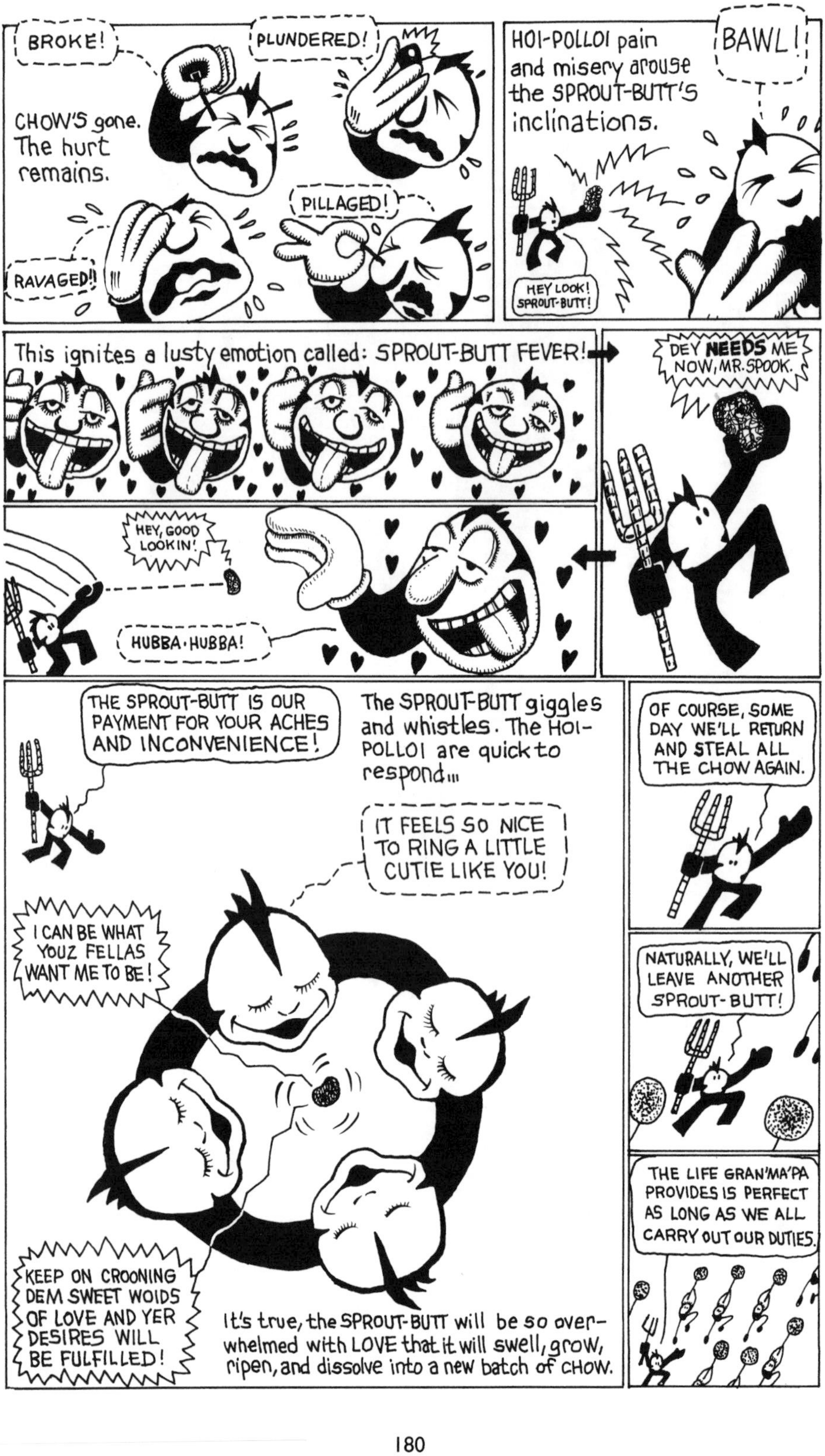
BROKE!
PLUNDERED!
CHOW'S gone. The hurt remains.
RAVAGED!!
PILLAGED!
HOI-POLLOI pain and misery arouse the SPROUT-BUTT'S inclinations.
BAWL!!
HEY LOOK! SPROUT-BUTT!
This ignites a lusty emotion called: SPROUT-BUTT FEVER!
DEY NEEDS ME NOW, MR. SPOOK.
HEY, GOOD LOOKIN'!
HUBBA-HUBBA!
THE SPROUT-BUTT IS OUR PAYMENT FOR YOUR ACHES AND INCONVENIENCE!
The SPROUT-BUTT giggles and whistles. The HOI-POLLOI are quick to respond...
IT FEELS SO NICE TO RING A LITTLE CUTIE LIKE YOU!
I CAN BE WHAT YOUZ FELLAS WANT ME TO BE!
KEEP ON CROONING DEM SWEET WOIDS OF LOVE AND YER DESIRES WILL BE FULFILLED!
It's true, the SPROUT-BUTT will be so overwhelmed with LOVE that it will swell, grow, ripen, and dissolve into a new batch of CHOW.
OF COURSE, SOME DAY WE'LL RETURN AND STEAL ALL THE CHOW AGAIN.
NATURALLY, WE'LL LEAVE ANOTHER SPROUT-BUTT!
THE LIFE GRAN'MA'PA PROVIDES IS PERFECT AS LONG AS WE ALL CARRY OUT OUR DUTIES.

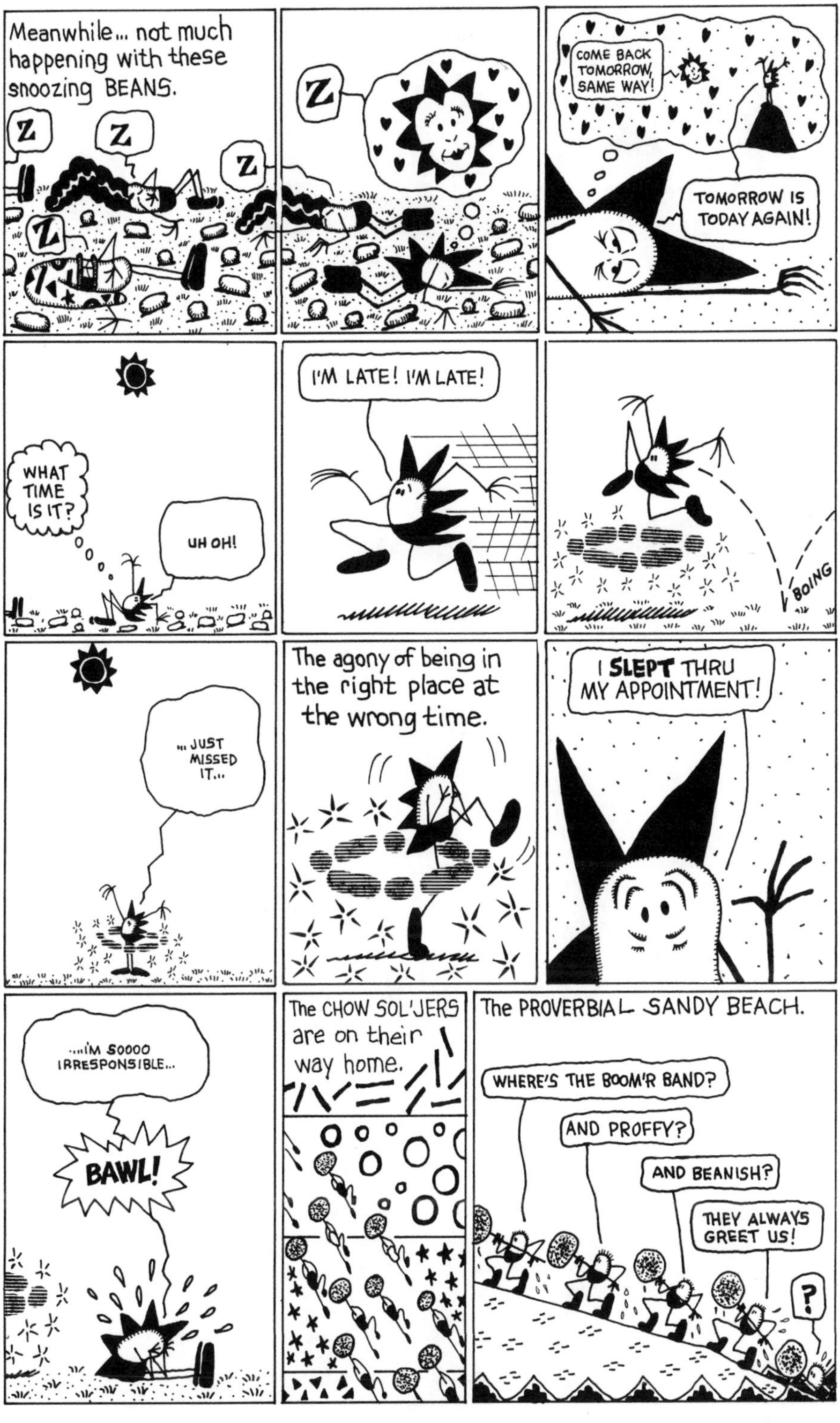
Meanwhile... not much happening with these snoozing BEANS.
Z
Z
Z
Z
Z
COME BACK TOMORROW, SAME WAY!
TOMORROW IS TODAY AGAIN!
WHAT TIME IS IT?
UH OH!
I'M LATE! I'M LATE!
BOING
...JUST MISSED IT...
The agony of being in the right place at the wrong time.
I SLEPT THRU MY APPOINTMENT!
...I'M SOOOO IRRESPONSIBLE...
BAWL!
The CHOW SOL'JERS are on their way home.
The PROVERBIAL SANDY BEACH.
WHERE'S THE BOOM'R BAND?
AND PROFFY?
AND BEANISH?
THEY ALWAYS GREET US!
?

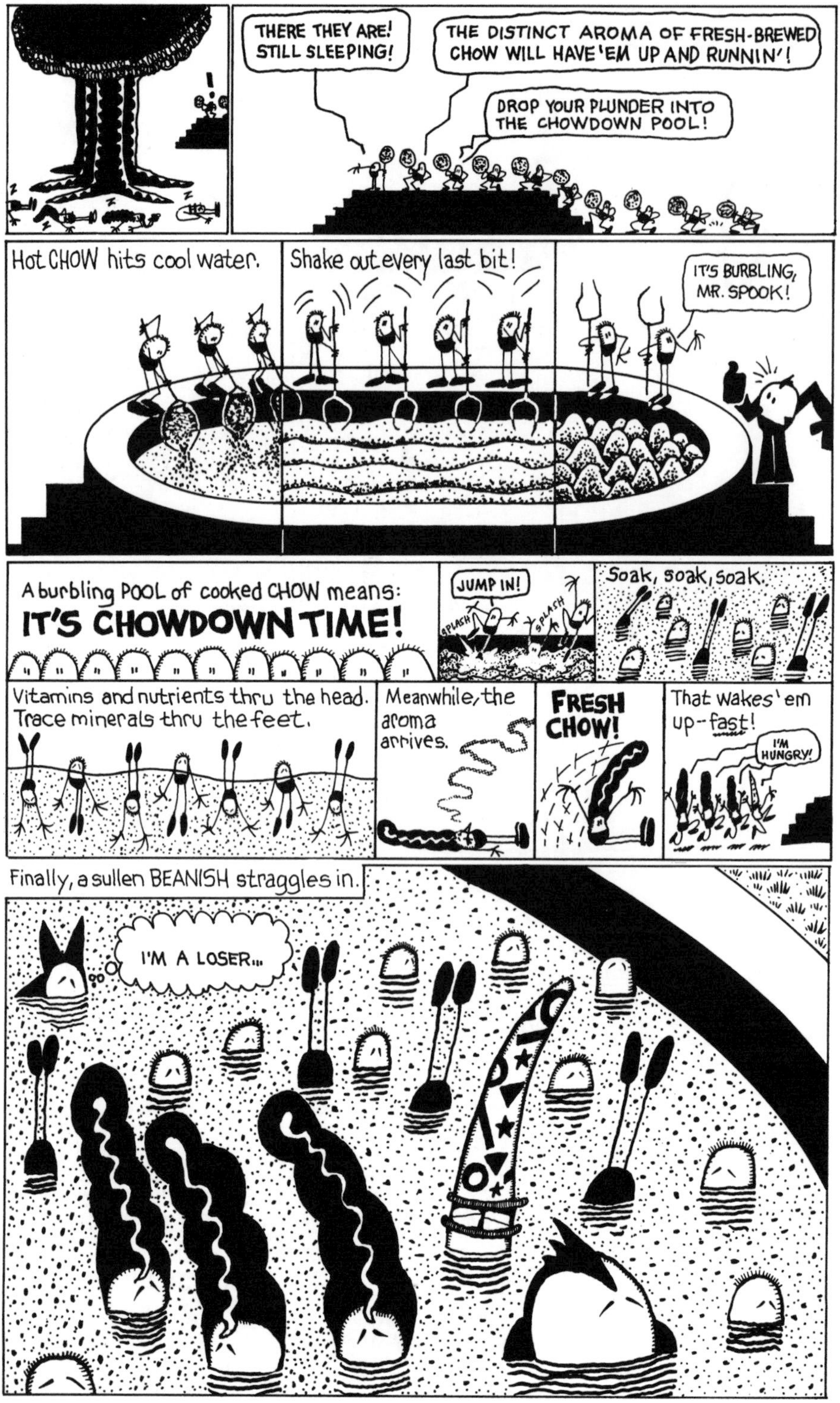

THERE THEY ARE! STILL SLEEPING!
THE DISTINCT AROMA OF FRESH-BREWED CHOW WILL HAVE 'EM UP AND RUNNIN'!
DROP YOUR PLUNDER INTO THE CHOWDOWN POOL!
Hot CHOW hits cool water.
Shake out every last bit!
IT'S BURBLING, MR. SPOOK!
A burbling POOL of cooked CHOW means:
IT'S CHOWDOWN TIME!
JUMP IN!
SPLASH
SPLASH
Soak, soak, soak.
Vitamins and nutrients thru the head. Trace minerals thru the feet.
Meanwhile, the aroma arrives.
FRESH CHOW!
That wakes 'em up—fast!
I'M HUNGRY!
Finally, a sullen BEANISH straggles in.
I'M A LOSER...

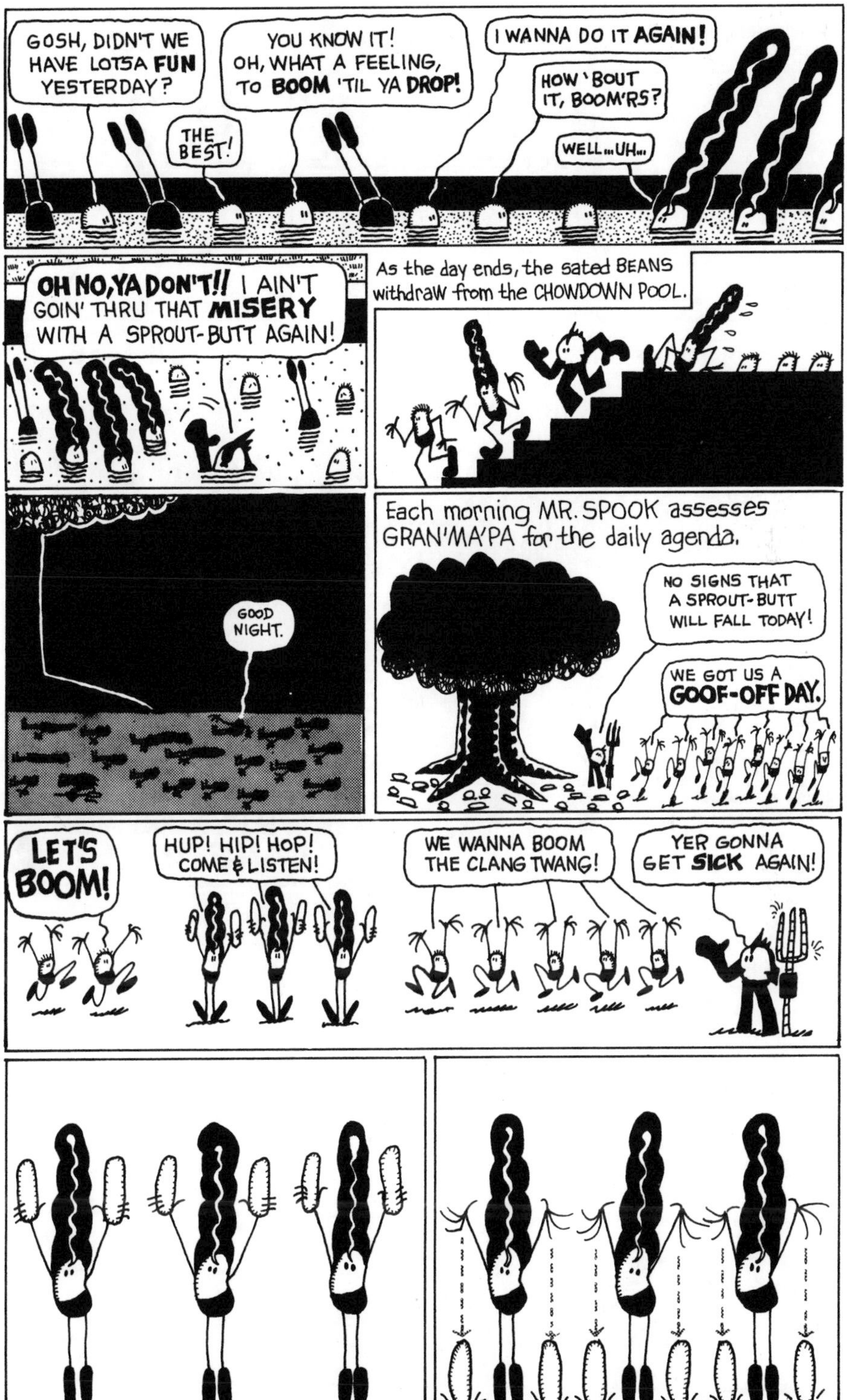
GOSH, DIDN'T WE HAVE LOTSA FUN YESTERDAY?
THE BEST!
YOU KNOW IT! OH, WHAT A FEELING, TO BOOM 'TIL YA DROP!
I WANNA DO IT AGAIN!
HOW 'BOUT IT, BOOM'RS?
WELL...UH...
OH NO, YA DON'T!! I AIN'T GOIN' THRU THAT MISERY WITH A SPROUT-BUTT AGAIN!
As the day ends, the sated BEANS withdraw from the CHOWDOWN POOL.
GOOD NIGHT.
Each morning MR. SPOOK assesses GRAN'MA'PA for the daily agenda.
NO SIGNS THAT A SPROUT-BUTT WILL FALL TODAY!
WE GOT US A GOOF-OFF DAY.
LET'S BOOM!
HUP! HIP! HOP! COME & LISTEN!
WE WANNA BOOM THE CLANG TWANG!
YER GONNA GET SICK AGAIN!

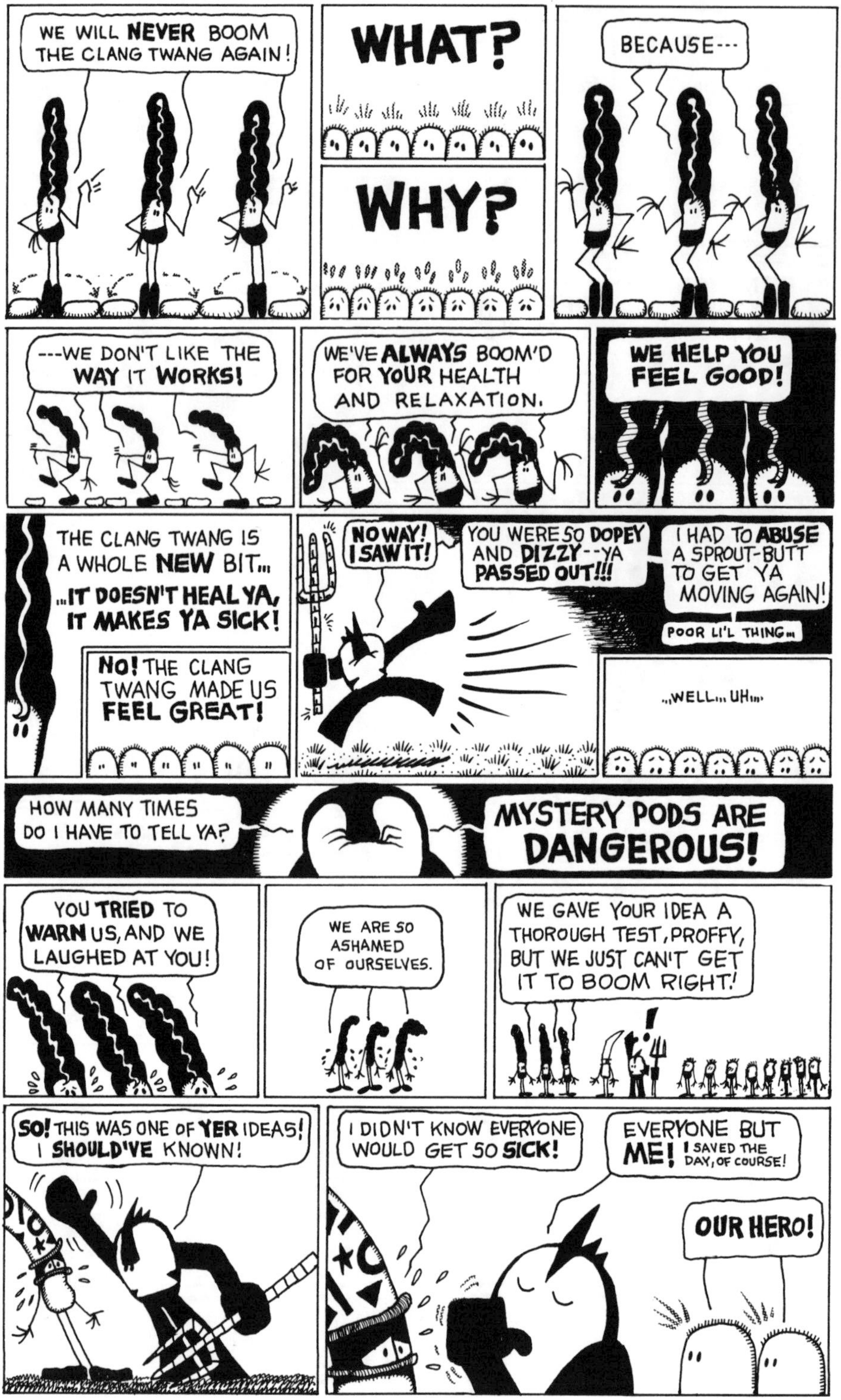
WE WILL NEVER BOOM THE CLANG TWANG AGAIN!
WHAT?
WHY?
BECAUSE---
---WE DON'T LIKE THE WAY IT WORKS!
WE'VE ALWAYS BOOM'D FOR YOUR HEALTH AND RELAXATION.
WE HELP YOU FEEL GOOD!
THE CLANG TWANG IS A WHOLE NEW BIT... ...IT DOESN'T HEAL YA, IT MAKES YA SICK!
NO! THE CLANG TWANG MADE US FEEL GREAT!
NO WAY! I SAW IT!
YOU WERE SO DOPEY AND DIZZY--YA PASSED OUT!!!
I HAD TO ABUSE A SPROUT-BUTT TO GET YA MOVING AGAIN!
POOR LI'L THING...
...WELL... UH...
HOW MANY TIMES DO I HAVE TO TELL YA?
MYSTERY PODS ARE DANGEROUS!
YOU TRIED TO WARN US, AND WE LAUGHED AT YOU!
WE ARE SO ASHAMED OF OURSELVES.
WE GAVE YOUR IDEA A THOROUGH TEST, PROFFY, BUT WE JUST CAN'T GET IT TO BOOM RIGHT!
SO! THIS WAS ONE OF YER IDEAS! I SHOULD'VE KNOWN!
I DIDN'T KNOW EVERYONE WOULD GET SO SICK!
EVERYONE BUT ME! I SAVED THE DAY, OF COURSE!
OUR HERO!

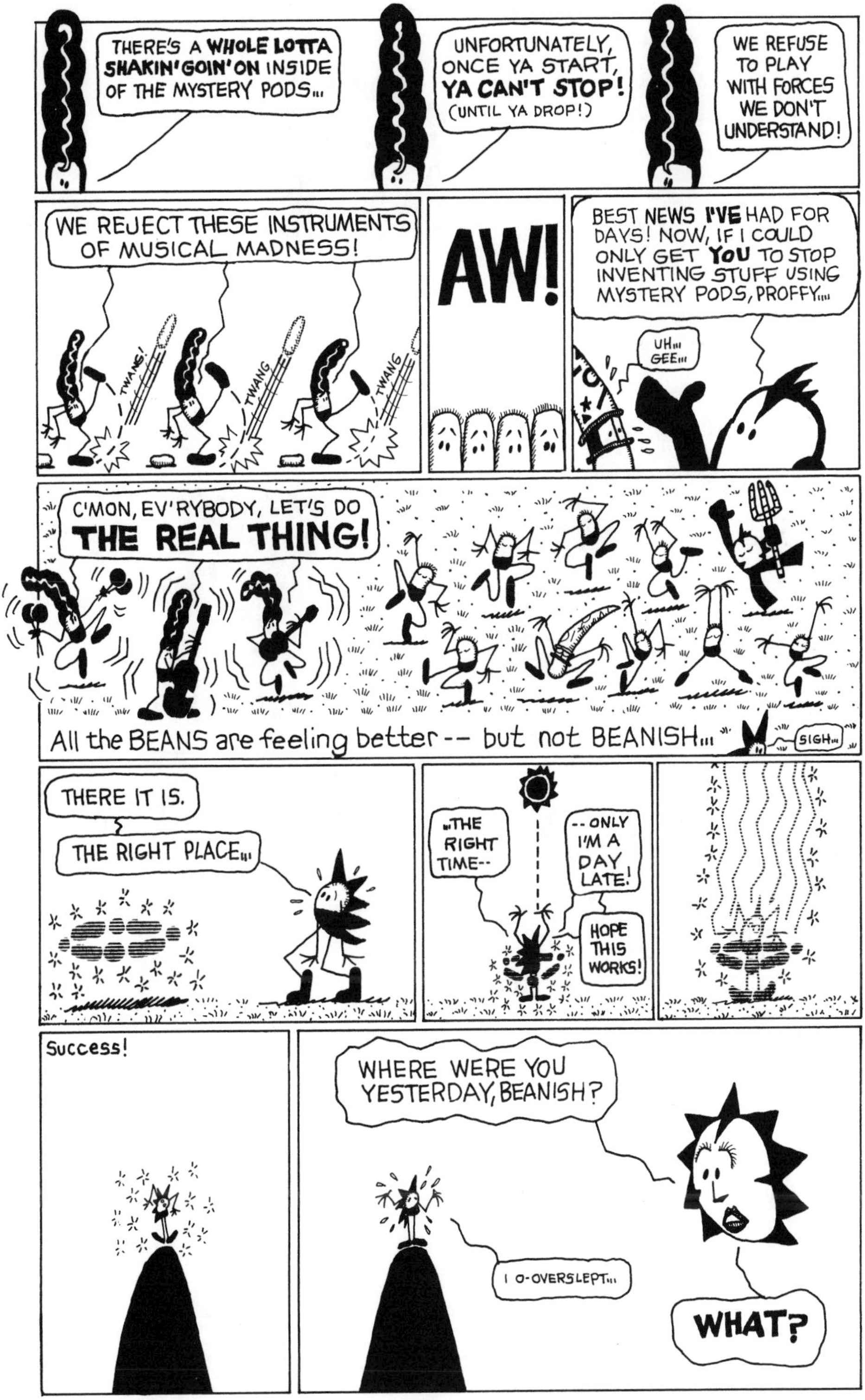
THERE'S A WHOLE LOTTA SHAKIN' GOIN' ON INSIDE OF THE MYSTERY PODS...
UNFORTUNATELY, ONCE YA START, YA CAN'T STOP! (UNTIL YA DROP!)
WE REFUSE TO PLAY WITH FORCES WE DON'T UNDERSTAND!
WE REJECT THESE INSTRUMENTS OF MUSICAL MADNESS!
TWANG!
TWANG
TWANG
AW!
BEST NEWS I'VE HAD FOR DAYS! NOW, IF I COULD ONLY GET YOU TO STOP INVENTING STUFF USING MYSTERY PODS, PROFFY...
UH... GEE...
C'MON, EV'RYBODY, LET'S DO THE REAL THING!
All the BEANS are feeling better -- but not BEANISH...
SIGH...
THERE IT IS.
THE RIGHT PLACE...
...THE RIGHT TIME--
--ONLY I'M A DAY LATE!
HOPE THIS WORKS!
Success!
WHERE WERE YOU YESTERDAY, BEANISH?
I O-OVERSLEPT...
WHAT?

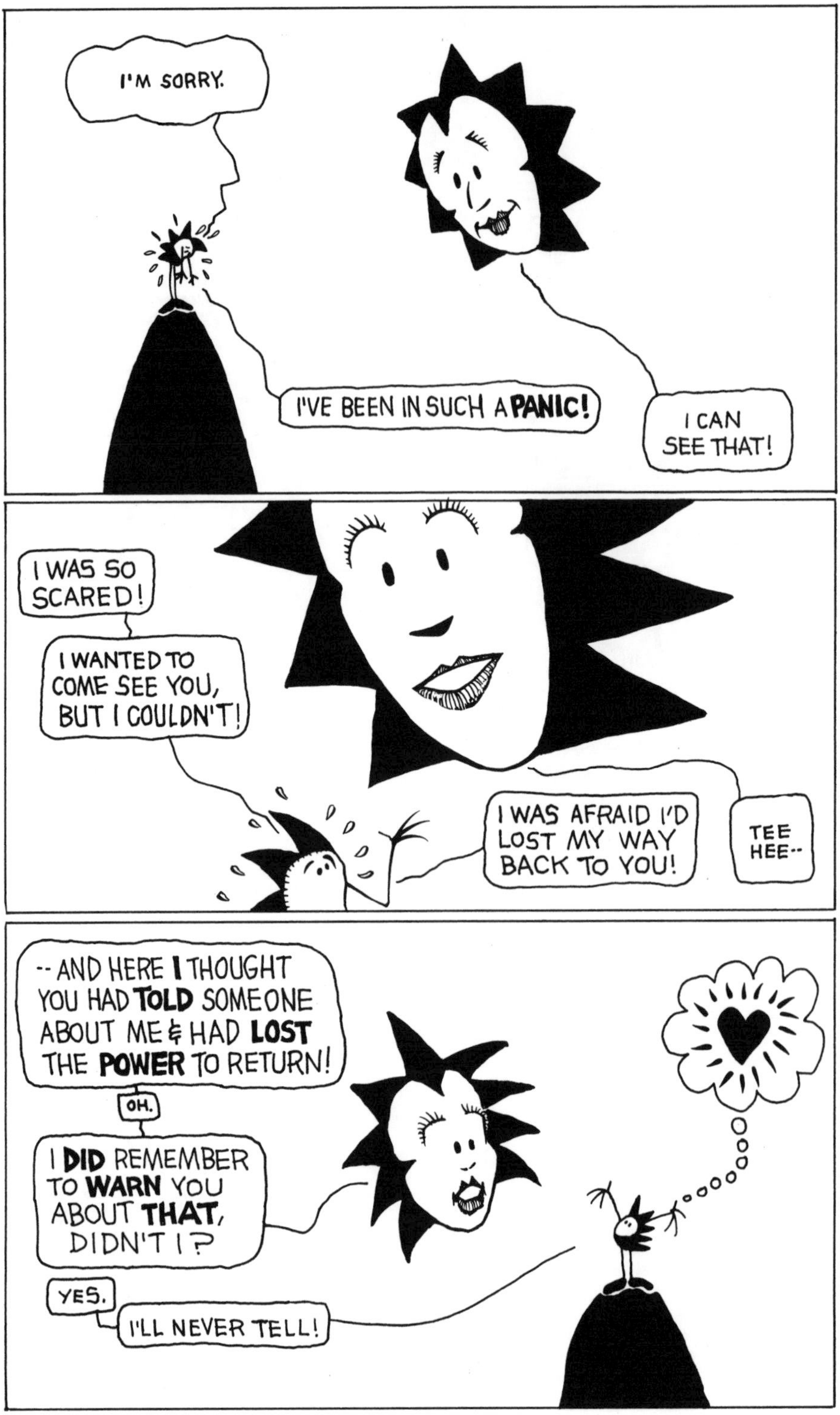
I'M SORRY.
I'VE BEEN IN SUCH A **PANIC!**
I CAN SEE THAT!
I WAS SO SCARED!
I WANTED TO COME SEE YOU, BUT I COULDN'T!
I WAS AFRAID I'D LOST MY WAY BACK TO YOU!
TEE HEE--
--AND HERE **I** THOUGHT YOU HAD **TOLD** SOMEONE ABOUT ME & HAD **LOST** THE **POWER** TO RETURN!
OH.
I **DID** REMEMBER TO **WARN** YOU ABOUT **THAT**, DIDN'T I?
YES.
I'LL NEVER TELL!

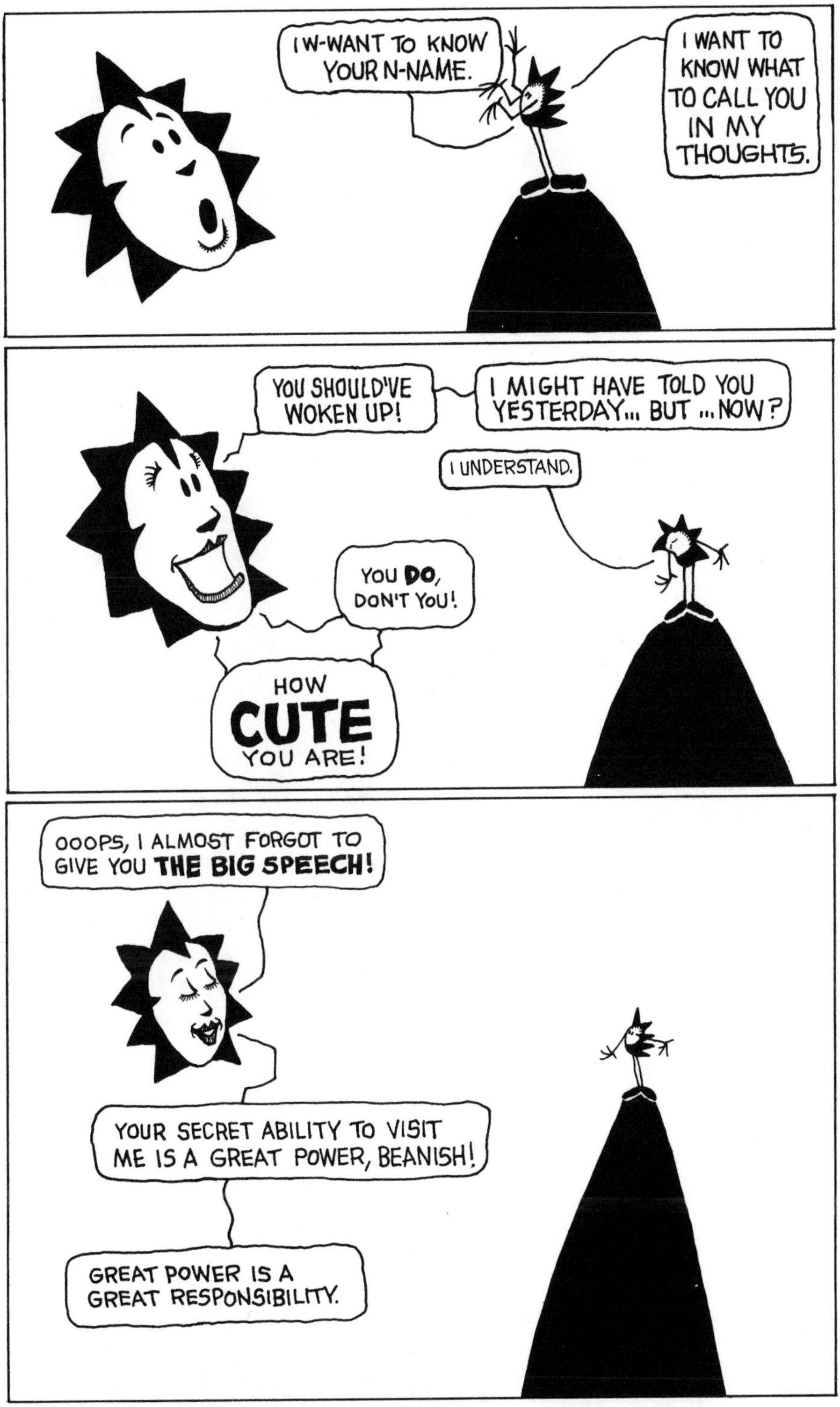
I W-WANT TO KNOW YOUR N-NAME.
I WANT TO KNOW WHAT TO CALL YOU IN MY THOUGHTS.
YOU SHOULD'VE WOKEN UP!
I MIGHT HAVE TOLD YOU YESTERDAY... BUT ...NOW?
I UNDERSTAND.
YOU DO, DON'T YOU!
HOW CUTE YOU ARE!
OOOPS, I ALMOST FORGOT TO GIVE YOU THE BIG SPEECH!
YOUR SECRET ABILITY TO VISIT ME IS A GREAT POWER, BEANISH!
GREAT POWER IS A GREAT RESPONSIBILITY.

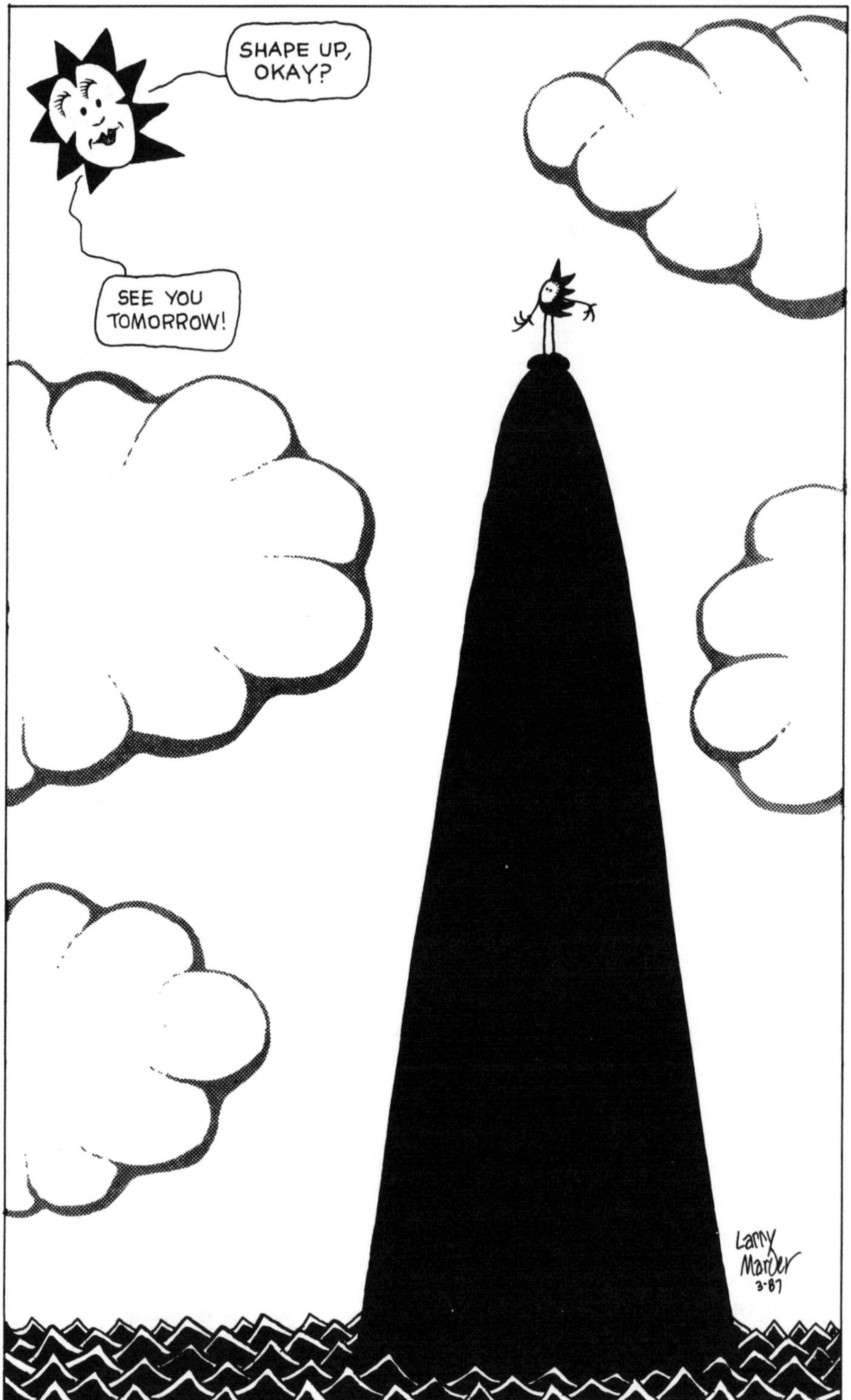
SHAPE UP, OKAY?
SEE YOU TOMORROW!
Larry Marder 3-87

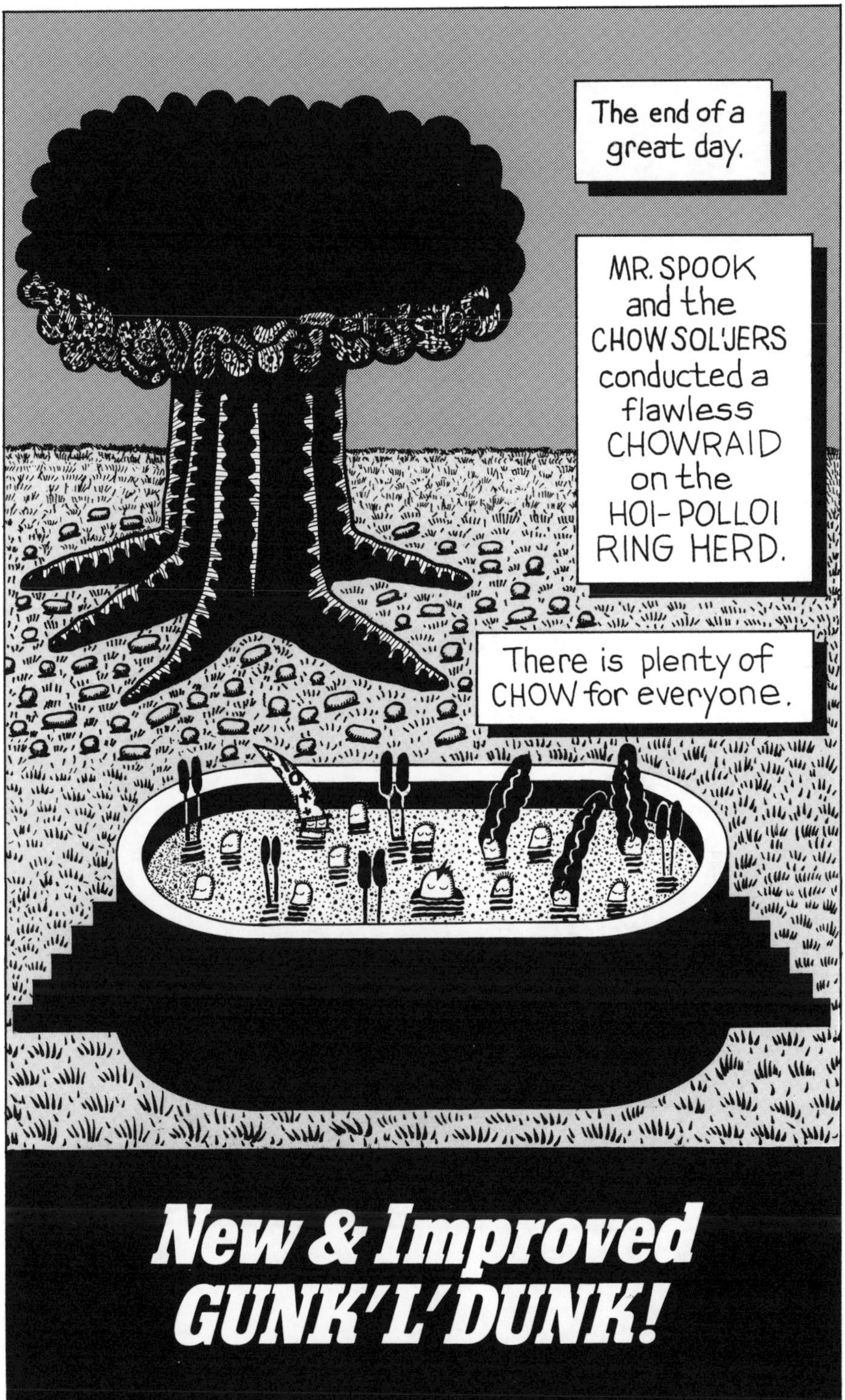
The end of a great day.
MR. SPOOK and the CHOW SOL'JERS conducted a flawless CHOWRAID on the HOI-POLLOI RING HERD.
There is plenty of CHOW for everyone.
New & Improved GUNK'L'DUNK!

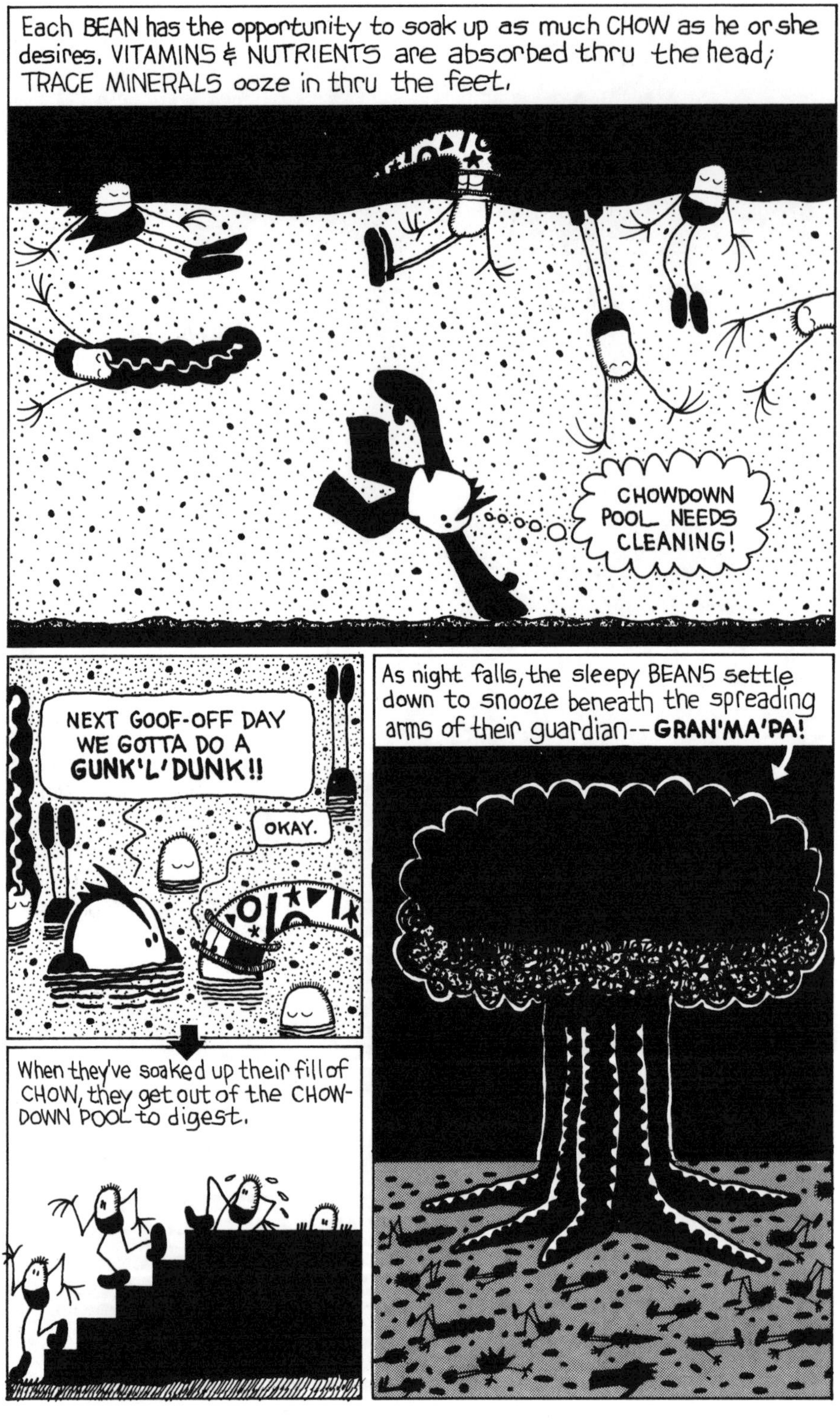
Each BEAN has the opportunity to soak up as much CHOW as he or she desires. VITAMINS & NUTRIENTS are absorbed thru the head; TRACE MINERALS ooze in thru the feet.
CHOWDOWN POOL NEEDS CLEANING!
NEXT GOOF-OFF DAY WE GOTTA DO A GUNK'L'DUNK!!
OKAY.
When they've soaked up their fill of CHOW, they get out of the CHOW-DOWN POOL to digest.
As night falls, the sleepy BEANS settle down to snooze beneath the spreading arms of their guardian--GRAN'MA'PA!

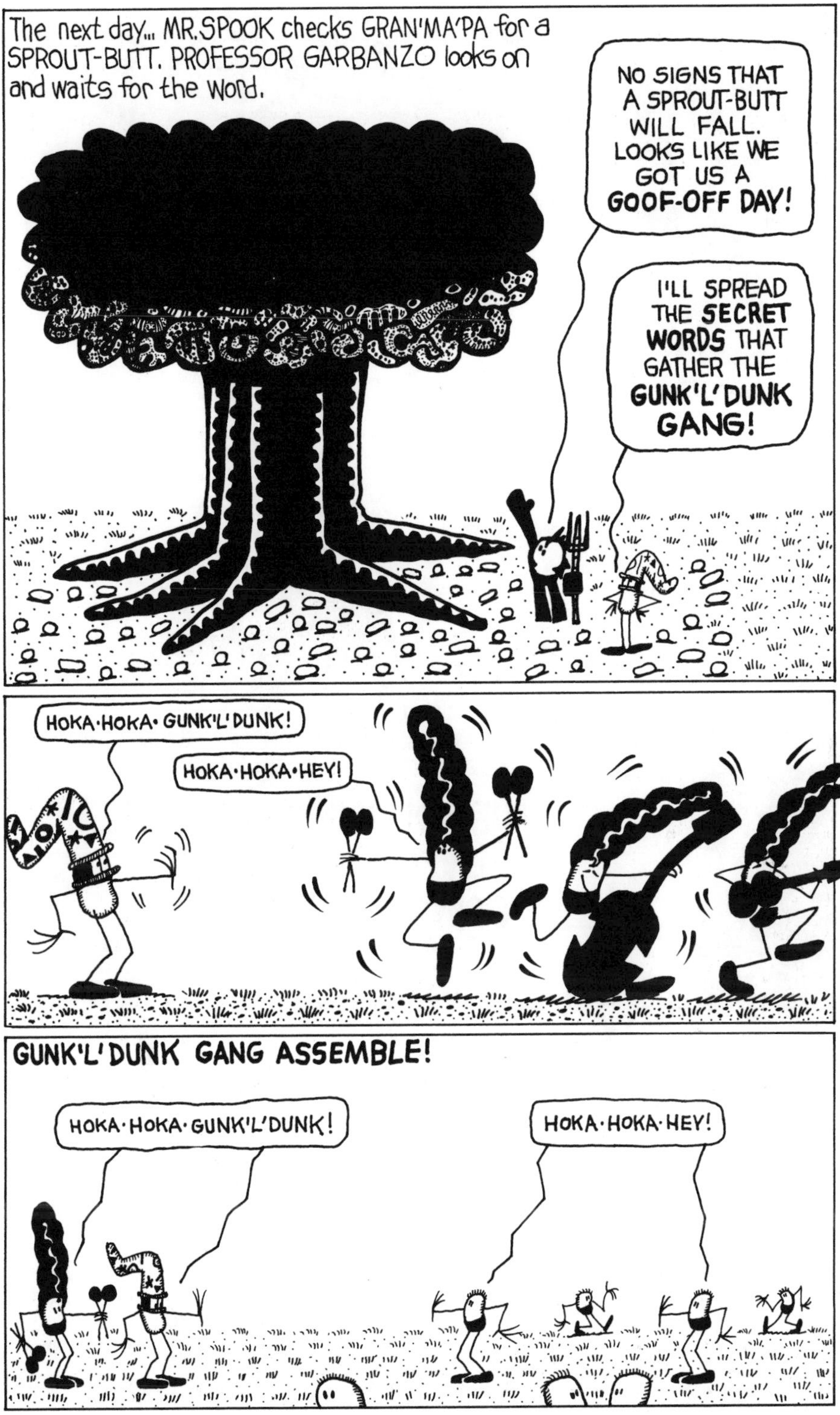
The next day... MR. SPOOK checks GRAN'MA'PA for a SPROUT-BUTT. PROFESSOR GARBANZO looks on and waits for the word.
NO SIGNS THAT A SPROUT-BUTT WILL FALL. LOOKS LIKE WE GOT US A GOOF-OFF DAY!
I'LL SPREAD THE SECRET WORDS THAT GATHER THE GUNK'L'DUNK GANG!
HOKA·HOKA· GUNK'L'DUNK!
HOKA·HOKA·HEY!
GUNK'L'DUNK GANG ASSEMBLE!
HOKA·HOKA·GUNK'L'DUNK!
HOKA·HOKA·HEY!

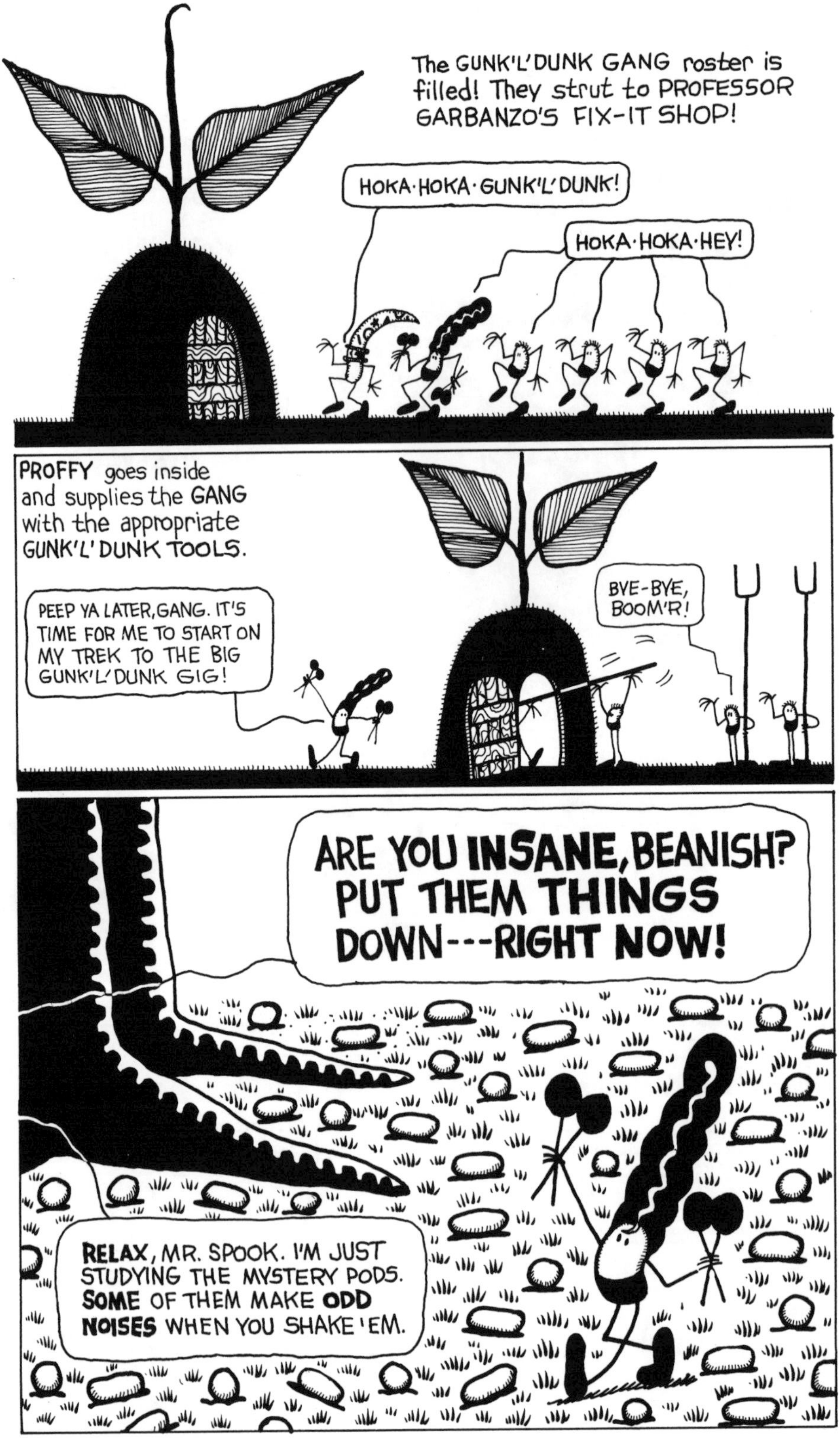
The GUNK'L'DUNK GANG roster is filled! They strut to PROFESSOR GARBANZO'S FIX-IT SHOP!
HOKA·HOKA·GUNK'L'DUNK!
HOKA·HOKA·HEY!
PROFFY goes inside and supplies the GANG with the appropriate GUNK'L'DUNK TOOLS.
PEEP YA LATER, GANG. IT'S TIME FOR ME TO START ON MY TREK TO THE BIG GUNK'L'DUNK GIG!
BYE-BYE, BOOM'R!
ARE YOU INSANE, BEANISH? PUT THEM THINGS DOWN---RIGHT NOW!
RELAX, MR. SPOOK. I'M JUST STUDYING THE MYSTERY PODS. SOME OF THEM MAKE ODD NOISES WHEN YOU SHAKE 'EM.

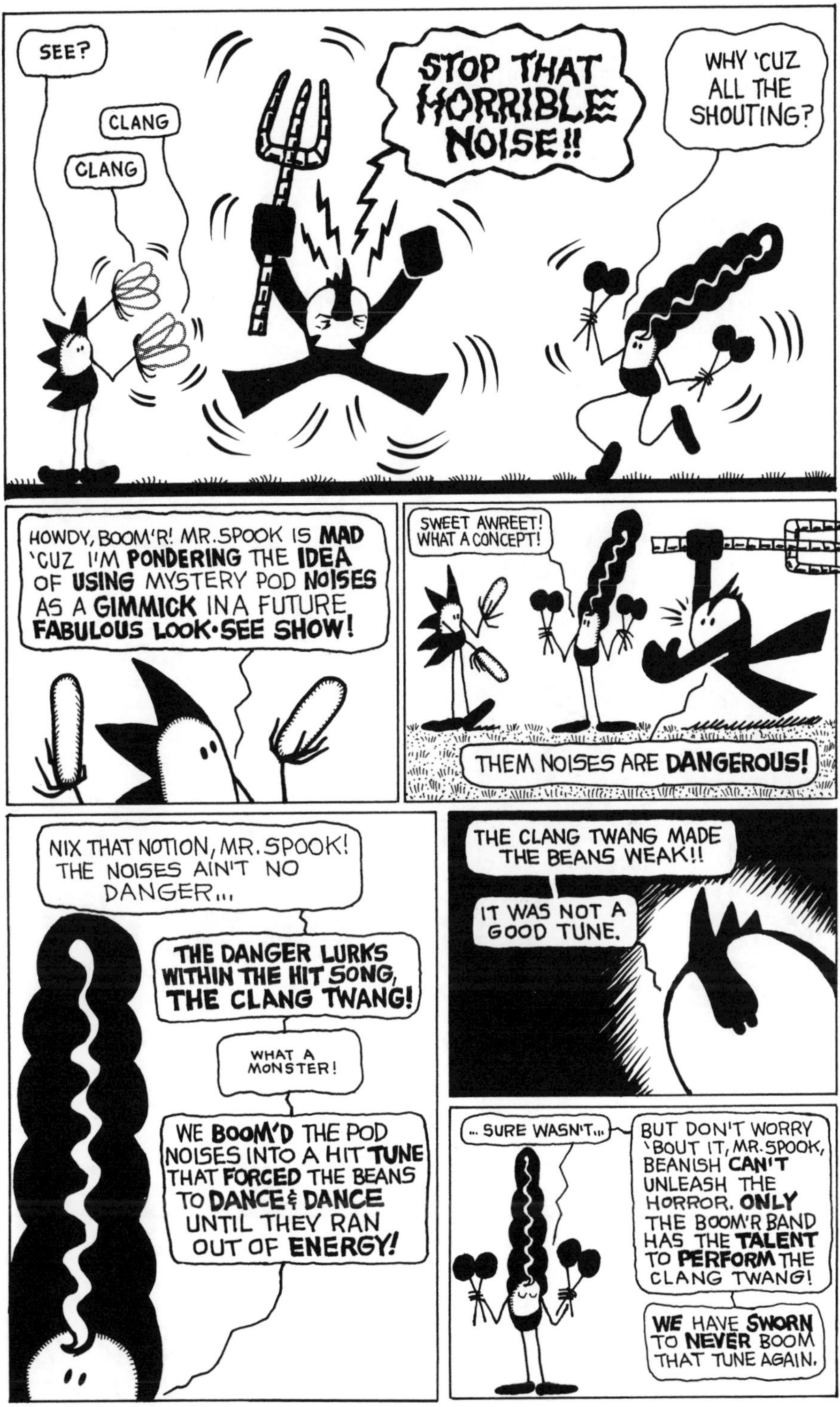
SEE?
CLANG
CLANG
STOP THAT HORRIBLE NOISE!!
WHY 'CUZ ALL THE SHOUTING?
HOWDY, BOOM'R! MR. SPOOK IS MAD 'CUZ I'M PONDERING THE IDEA OF USING MYSTERY POD NOISES AS A GIMMICK IN A FUTURE FABULOUS LOOK·SEE SHOW!
SWEET AWREET! WHAT A CONCEPT!
THEM NOISES ARE DANGEROUS!
NIX THAT NOTION, MR. SPOOK! THE NOISES AIN'T NO DANGER...
THE DANGER LURKS WITHIN THE HIT SONG, THE CLANG TWANG!
WHAT A MONSTER!
WE BOOM'D THE POD NOISES INTO A HIT TUNE THAT FORCED THE BEANS TO DANCE & DANCE UNTIL THEY RAN OUT OF ENERGY!
THE CLANG TWANG MADE THE BEANS WEAK!!
IT WAS NOT A GOOD TUNE.
...SURE WASN'T...
BUT DON'T WORRY 'BOUT IT, MR. SPOOK, BEANISH CAN'T UNLEASH THE HORROR. ONLY THE BOOM'R BAND HAS THE TALENT TO PERFORM THE CLANG TWANG!
WE HAVE SWORN TO NEVER BOOM THAT TUNE AGAIN.

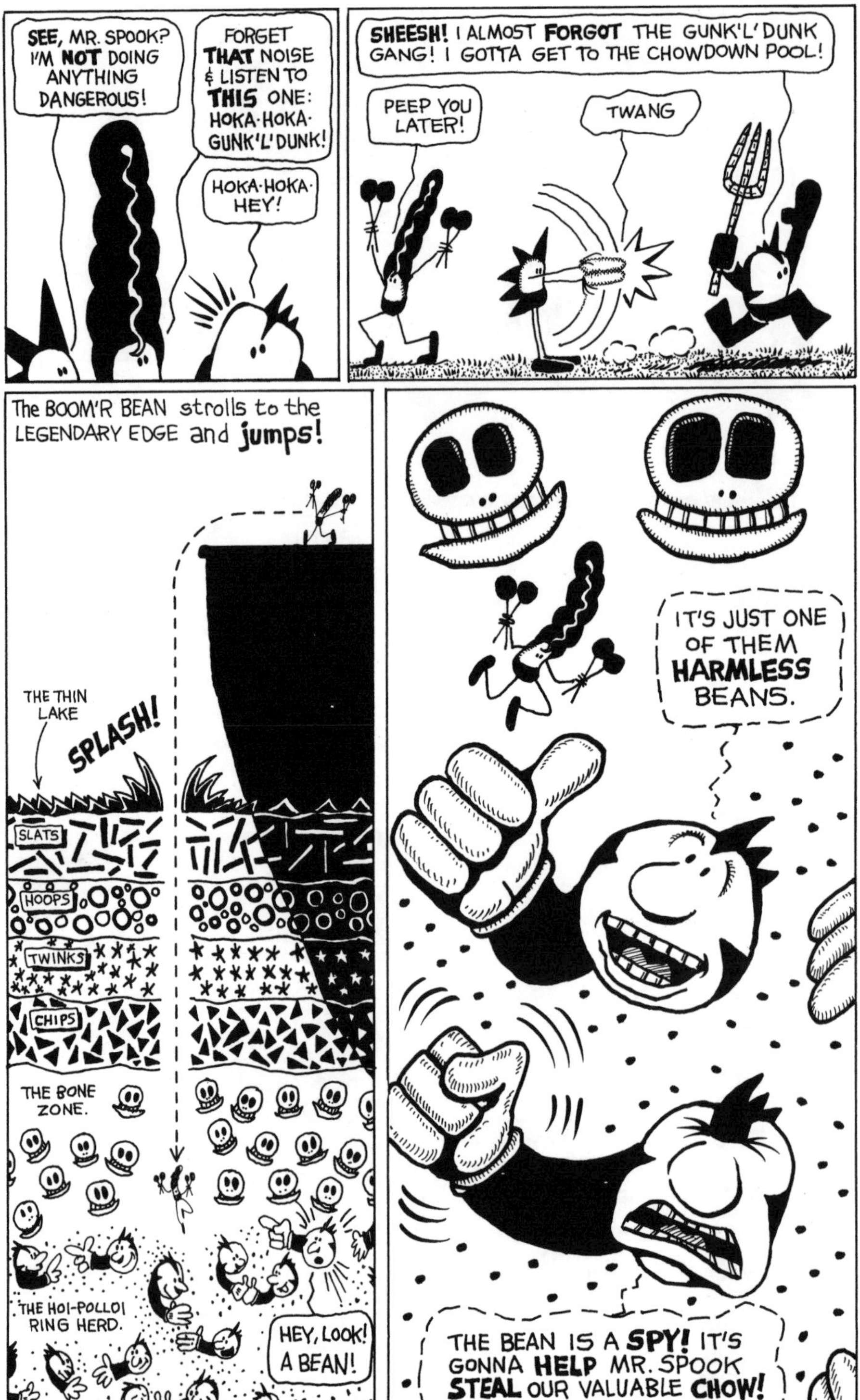
SEE, MR. SPOOK? I'M NOT DOING ANYTHING DANGEROUS!
FORGET THAT NOISE & LISTEN TO THIS ONE: HOKA-HOKA-GUNK'L'DUNK!
HOKA-HOKA-HEY!
SHEESH! I ALMOST FORGOT THE GUNK'L'DUNK GANG! I GOTTA GET TO THE CHOWDOWN POOL!
PEEP YOU LATER!
TWANG
The BOOM'R BEAN strolls to the LEGENDARY EDGE and jumps!
THE THIN LAKE
SPLASH!
SLATS
HOOPS
TWINKS
CHIPS
THE BONE ZONE.
THE HOI-POLLOI RING HERD.
HEY, LOOK! A BEAN!
IT'S JUST ONE OF THEM HARMLESS BEANS.
THE BEAN IS A SPY! IT'S GONNA HELP MR. SPOOK STEAL OUR VALUABLE CHOW!

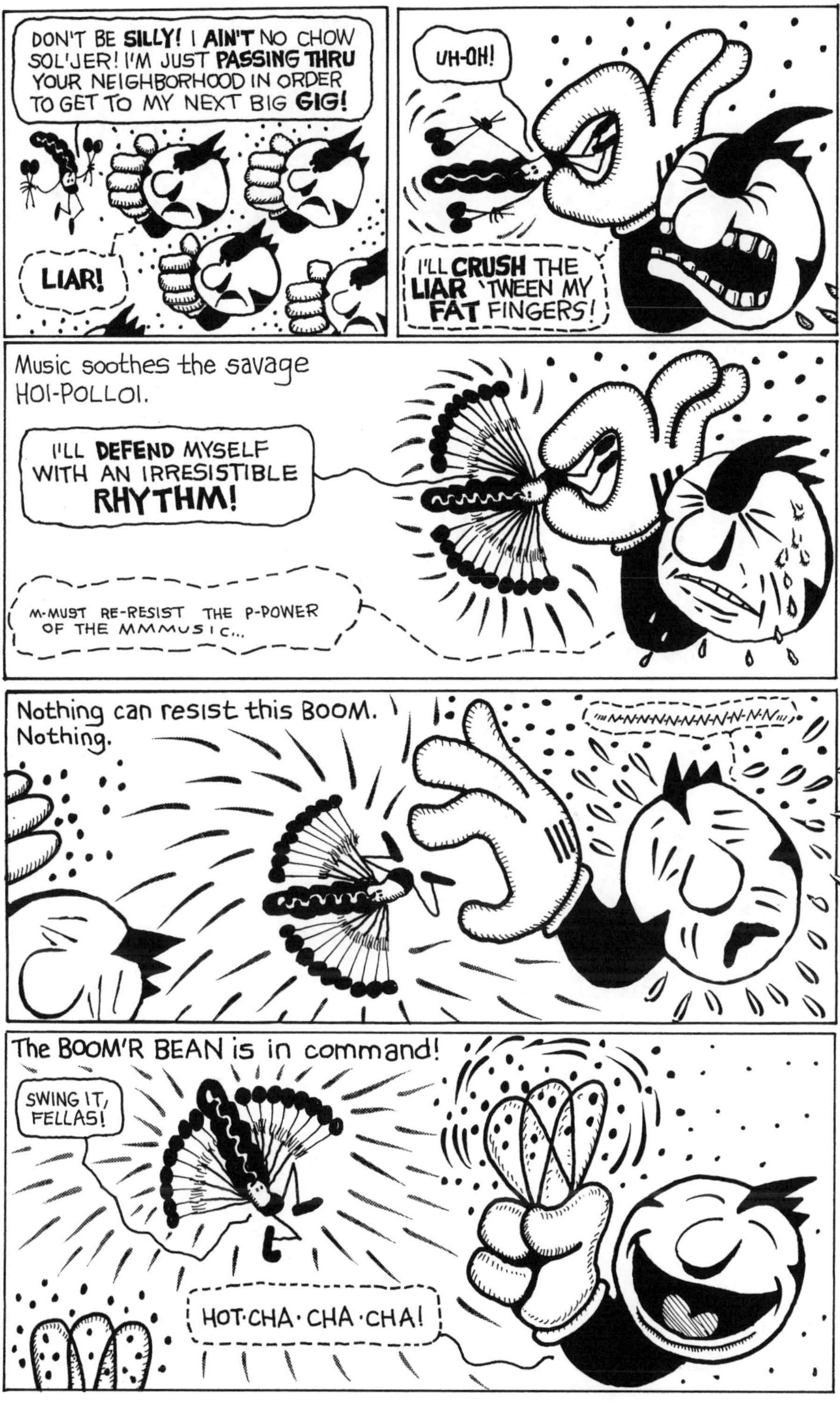
DON'T BE SILLY! I AIN'T NO CHOW SOL'JER! I'M JUST PASSING THRU YOUR NEIGHBORHOOD IN ORDER TO GET TO MY NEXT BIG GIG!
LIAR!
UH-OH!
I'LL CRUSH THE LIAR 'TWEEN MY FAT FINGERS!
Music soothes the savage HOI-POLLOI.
I'LL DEFEND MYSELF WITH AN IRRESISTIBLE RHYTHM!
M-MUST RE-RESIST THE P-POWER OF THE MMMUSIC...
Nothing can resist this BOOM. Nothing.
N-N-N-N-N-N-N-N-N-N-N-N
The BOOM'R BEAN is in command!
SWING IT, FELLAS!
HOT·CHA·CHA·CHA!

**INVOLUNTARY RESPONSE!** Fingers rattling in clusters of dark, stony CHOW echo the pursuasive rhythms created by the BOOM'R.

THIS IS AN EXCELLENT WARMUP ROUTINE FOR THE GUNK'L'DUNK GIG!

The music surrounds the BOOM'R BEAN like a protective shield...

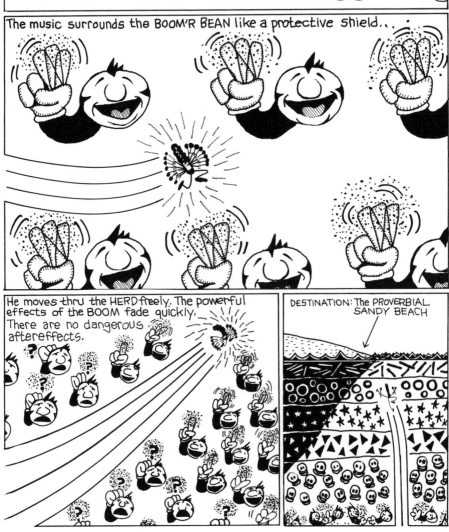

He moves thru the HERD freely. The powerful effects of the BOOM fade quickly. There are no dangerous aftereffects.

DESTINATION: The PROVERBIAL SANDY BEACH

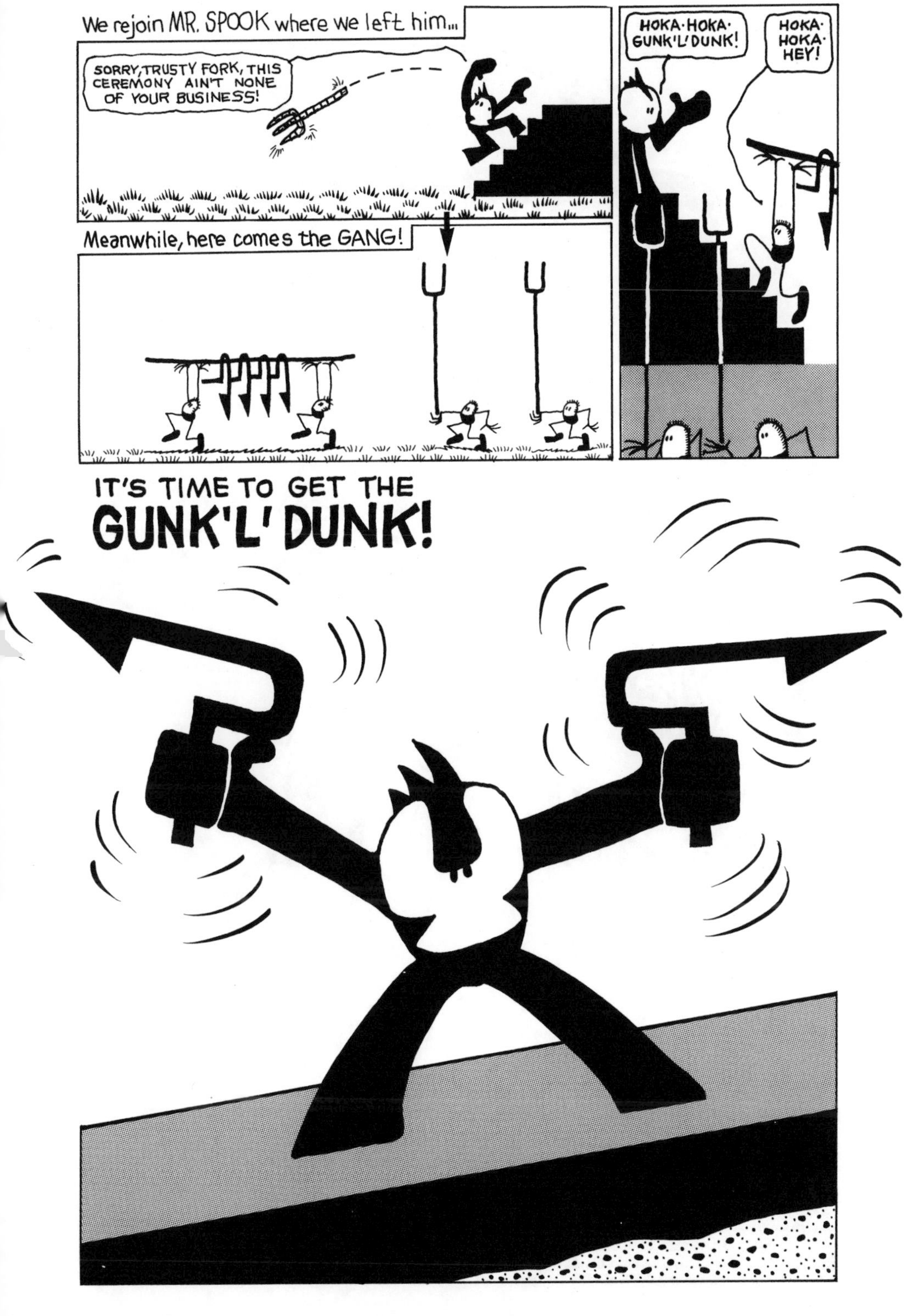

We rejoin MR. SPOOK where we left him...
SORRY, TRUSTY FORK, THIS CEREMONY AIN'T NONE OF YOUR BUSINESS!
HOKA·HOKA· GUNK'L'DUNK!
HOKA· HOKA· HEY!
Meanwhile, here comes the GANG!
IT'S TIME TO GET THE GUNK'L' DUNK!

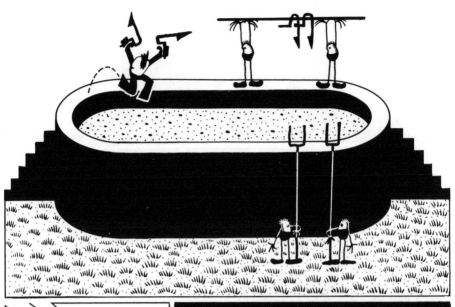

GUNK'L'DUNK: A gelatinous residue of uneaten CHOW that accumulates on the floor of the CHOWDOWN POOL.

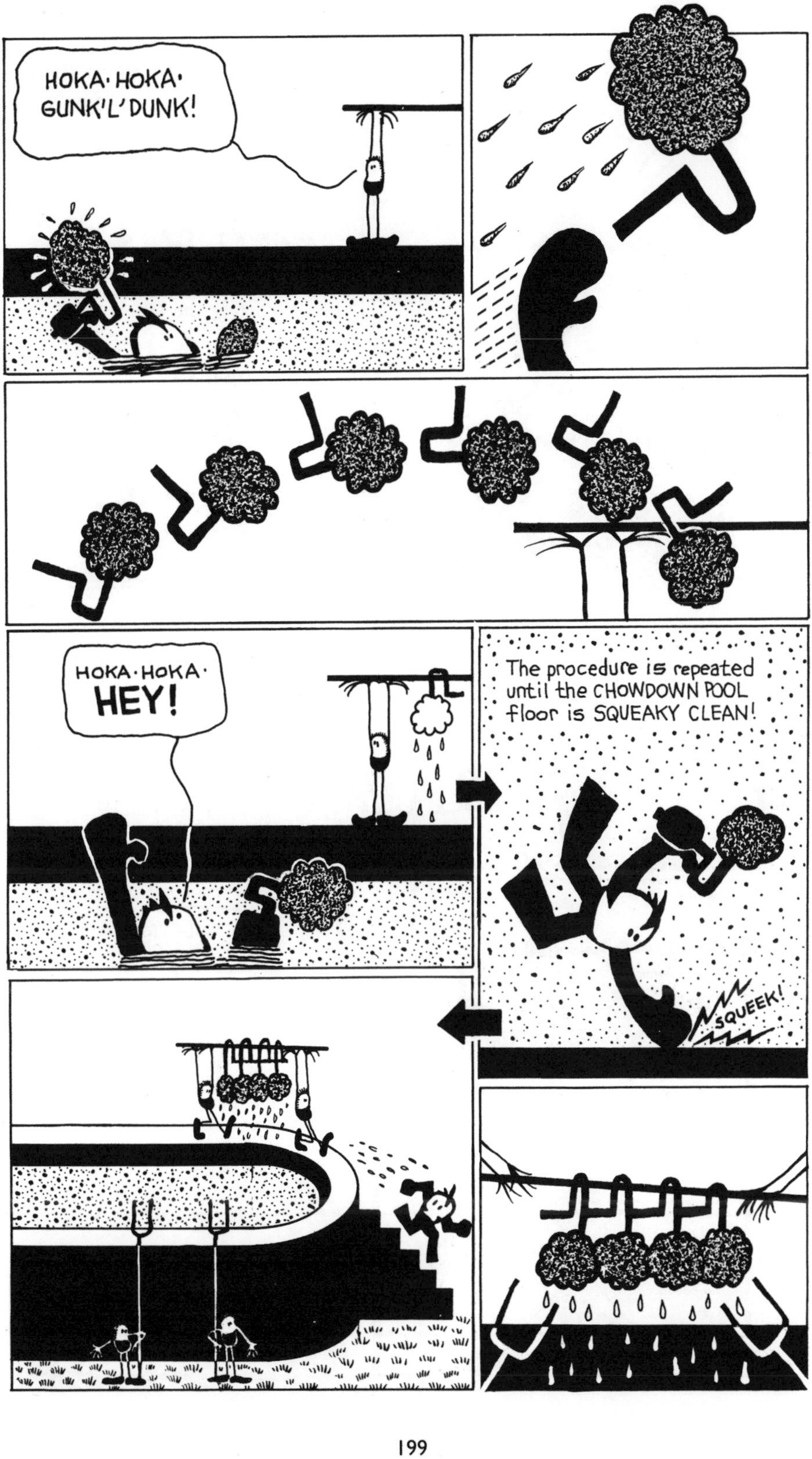
HOKA·HOKA·
GUNK'L'DUNK!
HOKA·HOKA·
HEY!
The procedure is repeated until the CHOWDOWN POOL floor is SQUEAKY CLEAN!
SQUEEK!

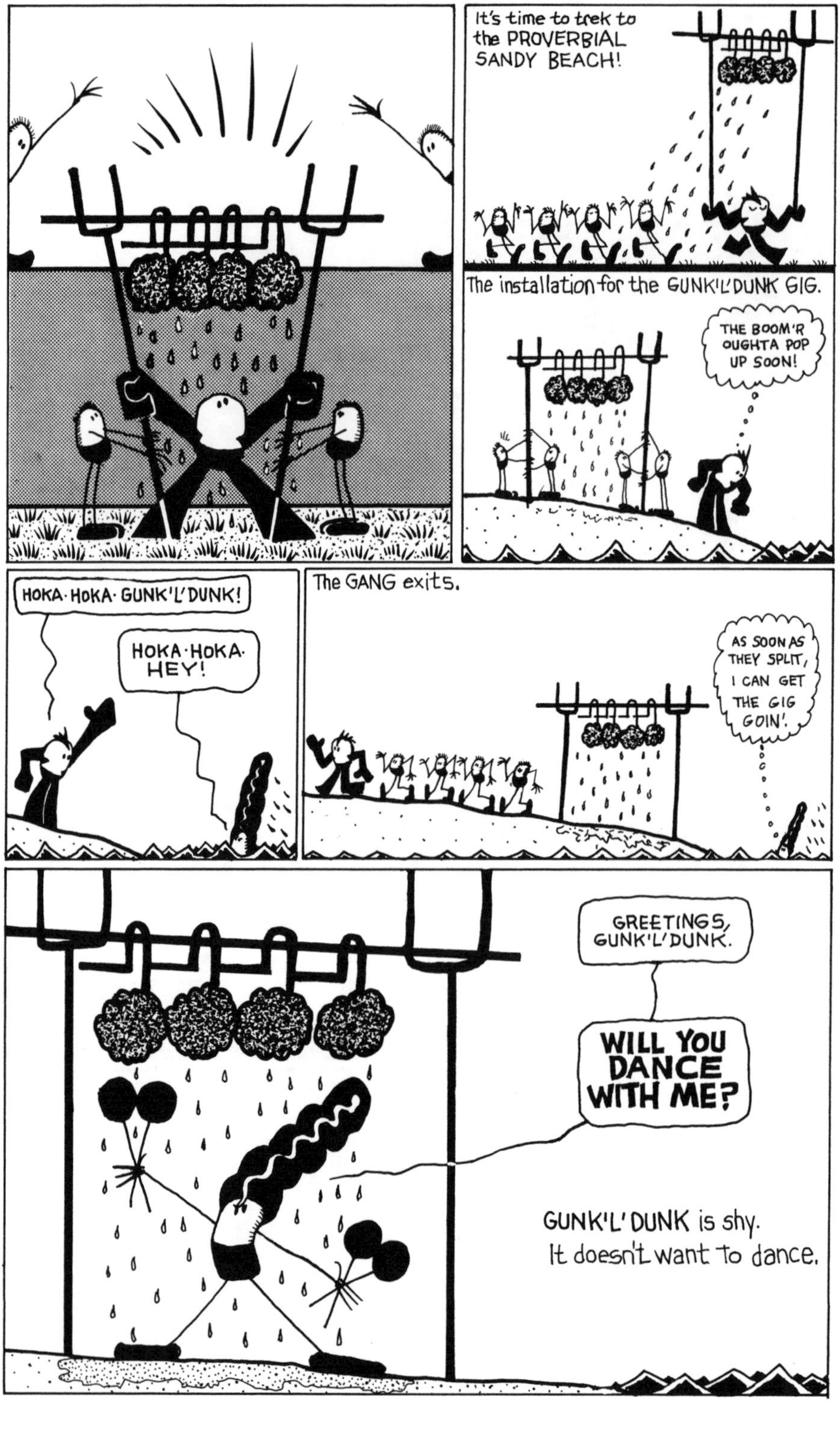

It's time to trek to the PROVERBIAL SANDY BEACH!
The installation for the GUNK'L'DUNK GIG.
THE BOOM'R OUGHTA POP UP SOON!
HOKA·HOKA·GUNK'L'DUNK!
HOKA·HOKA· HEY!
The GANG exits.
AS SOON AS THEY SPLIT, I CAN GET THE GIG GOIN'.
GREETINGS, GUNK'L'DUNK.
WILL YOU DANCE WITH ME?
GUNK'L'DUNK is shy.
It doesn't want to dance.

GUNK'L'DUNK resists the rhythm. The BOOM'R persuades with his power & talent.

Nothing can resist this BOOM. Nothing.

The BOOM'R BEAN is in command! GUNK'L'DUNK bounces; moisture flies. This is one tough GIG!

Eventually, he whacks out all the wetness. GUNK'L'DUNK has been properly pickled.

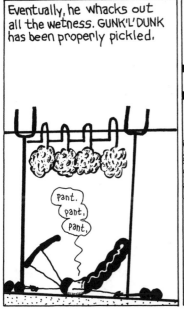

pant.
pant,
pant,

PERFECT!

PHEW... I'M BEAT...

HOKA·HOKA·GUNK'L'DUNK!
HOKA·HOKA·HEY!

THINK I'LL GO TAKE A NAP.

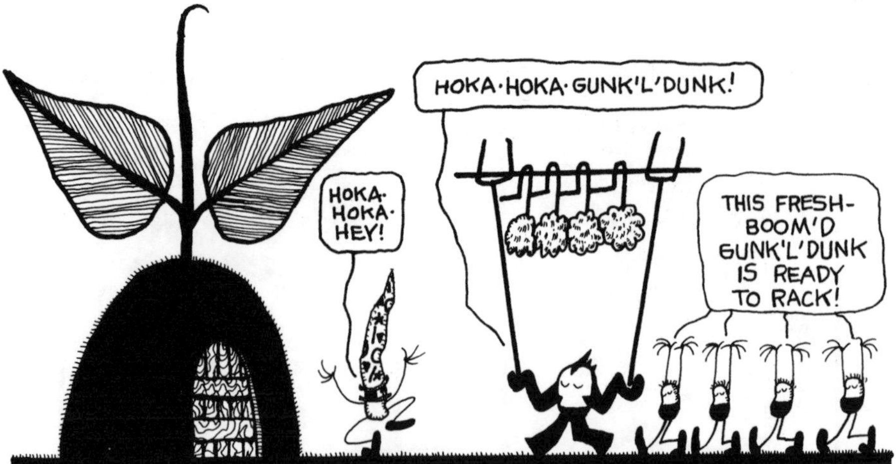
HOKA·HOKA·GUNK'L'DUNK!
HOKA-HOKA-HEY!
THIS FRESH-BOOM'D GUNK'L'DUNK IS READY TO RACK!

They store the GUNK'L'DUNK deep inside PROFFY'S FIX-IT SHOP. **What is this GUNK'L'DUNK junk??** It's an **adhesive**, and this is how it operates:

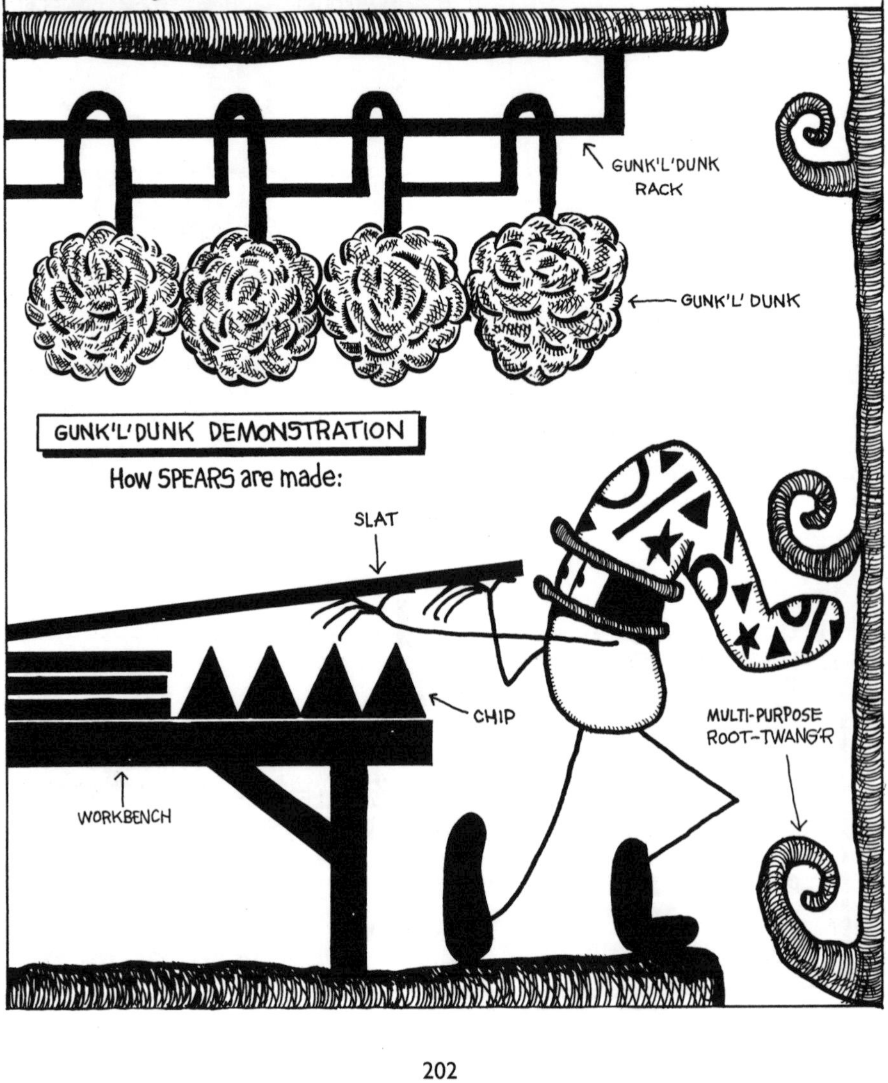
GUNK'L'DUNK RACK
GUNK'L' DUNK
GUNK'L'DUNK DEMONSTRATION
How SPEARS are made:
SLAT
CHIP
WORKBENCH
MULTI-PURPOSE ROOT-TWANG'R

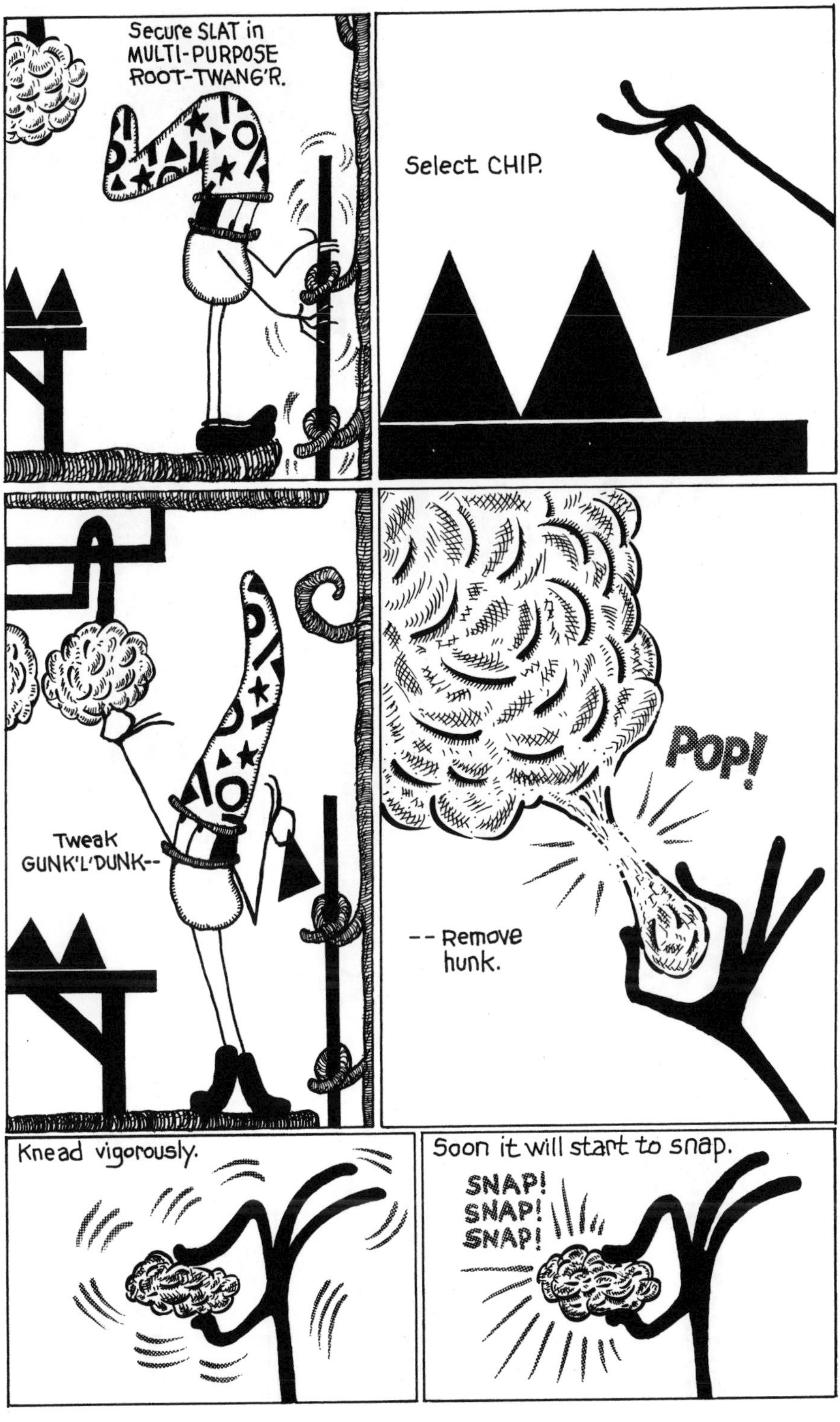
Secure SLAT in MULTI-PURPOSE ROOT-TWANG'R.
Select CHIP.
Tweak GUNK'L'DUNK--
POP!
--Remove hunk.
Knead vigorously.
Soon it will start to snap.
SNAP!
SNAP!
SNAP!

Move quickly!

SNAP! SNAP! SNAP! SNAP! SNAP! SNAP! SNAP! SNAP!

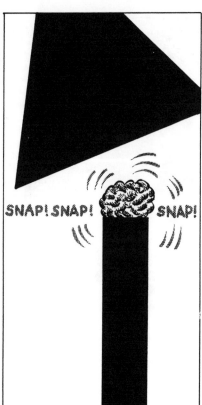

SNAP! SNAP! SNAP!

SNAP! SNAP!     SNAP! SNAP!

All pieces must be in place before the KRAK'L occurs.

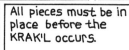

SNAP! SNAP!     KRAK'L!

The KRAK'L indicates a heavy-duty, extra-strong bond has taken place.

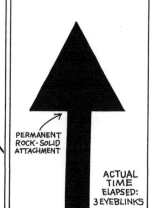

PERMANENT ROCK-SOLID ATTACHMENT

ACTUAL TIME ELAPSED: 3 EYEBLINKS

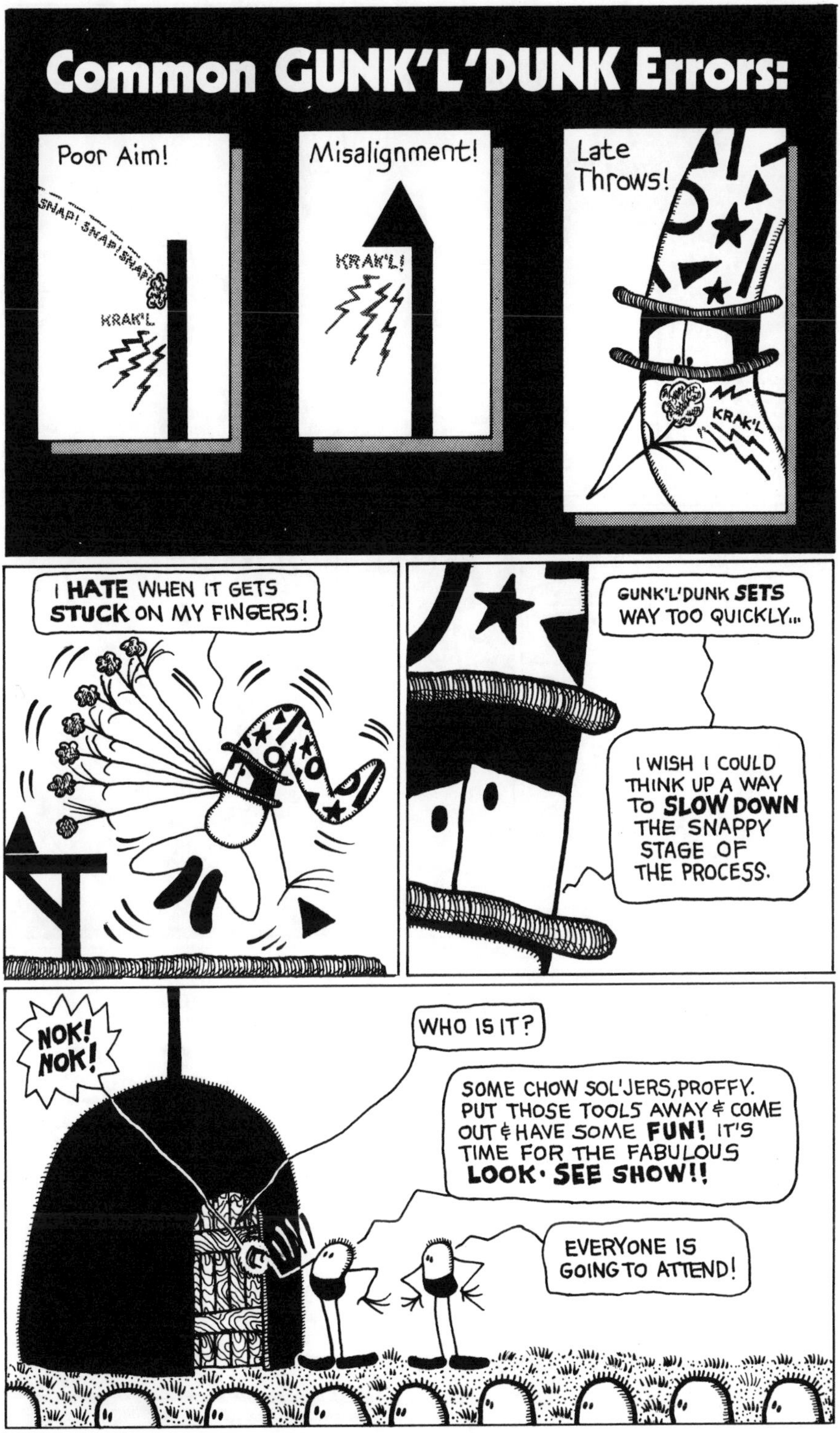
Common GUNK'L'DUNK Errors:
Poor Aim!
SNAP! SNAP! SNAP!
KRAK'L
Misalignment!
KRAK'L!
Late Throws!
KRAK'L
I HATE WHEN IT GETS STUCK ON MY FINGERS!
GUNK'L'DUNK SETS WAY TOO QUICKLY...
I WISH I COULD THINK UP A WAY TO SLOW DOWN THE SNAPPY STAGE OF THE PROCESS.
NOK! NOK!
WHO IS IT?
SOME CHOW SOL'JERS, PROFFY. PUT THOSE TOOLS AWAY & COME OUT & HAVE SOME FUN! IT'S TIME FOR THE FABULOUS LOOK·SEE SHOW!!
EVERYONE IS GOING TO ATTEND!

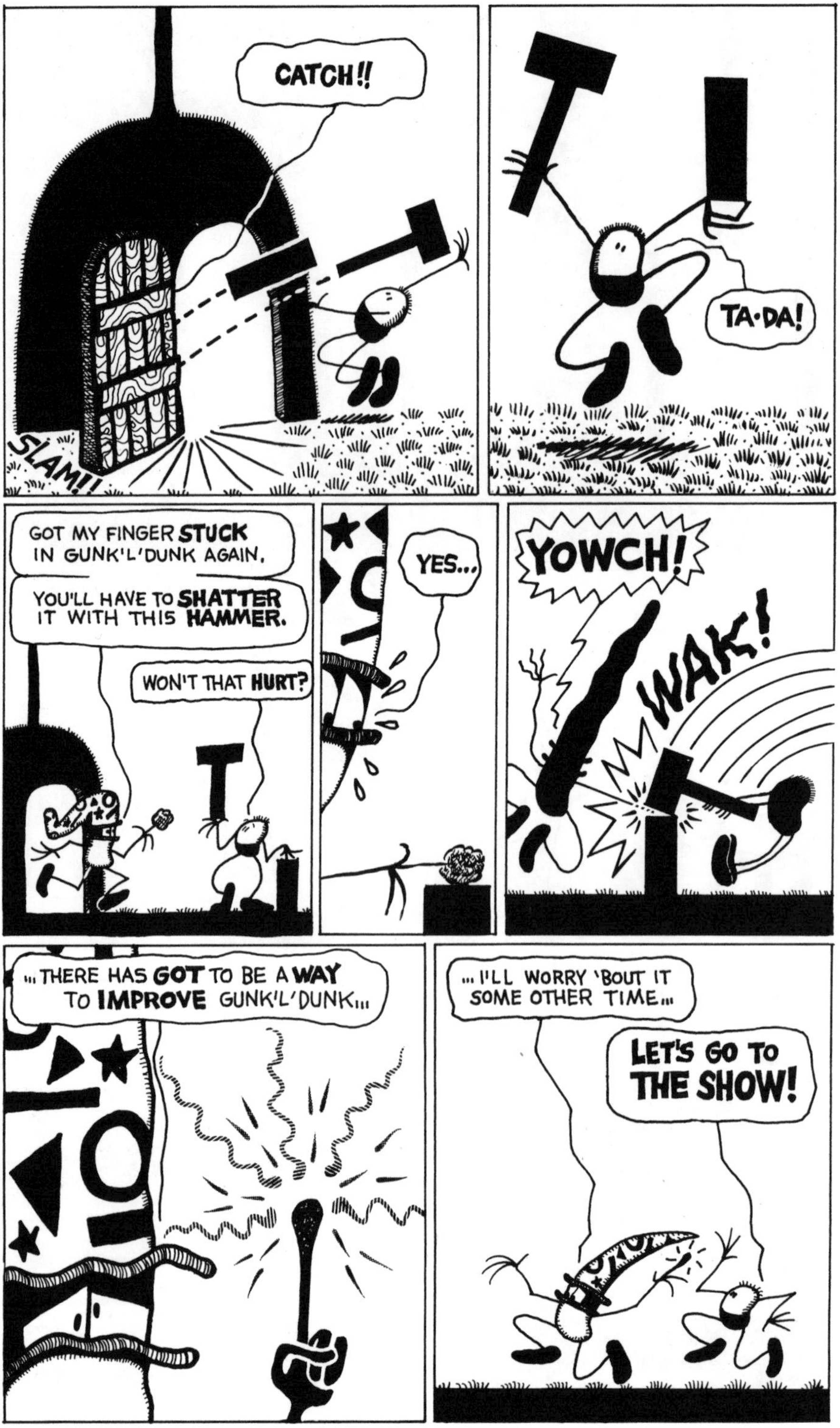
CATCH!!
SLAM!!
TA·DA!
GOT MY FINGER STUCK IN GUNK'L'DUNK AGAIN.
YOU'LL HAVE TO SHATTER IT WITH THIS HAMMER.
WON'T THAT HURT?
YES...
YOWCH!
WAK!
...THERE HAS GOT TO BE A WAY TO IMPROVE GUNK'L'DUNK...
...I'LL WORRY 'BOUT IT SOME OTHER TIME...
LET'S GO TO THE SHOW!

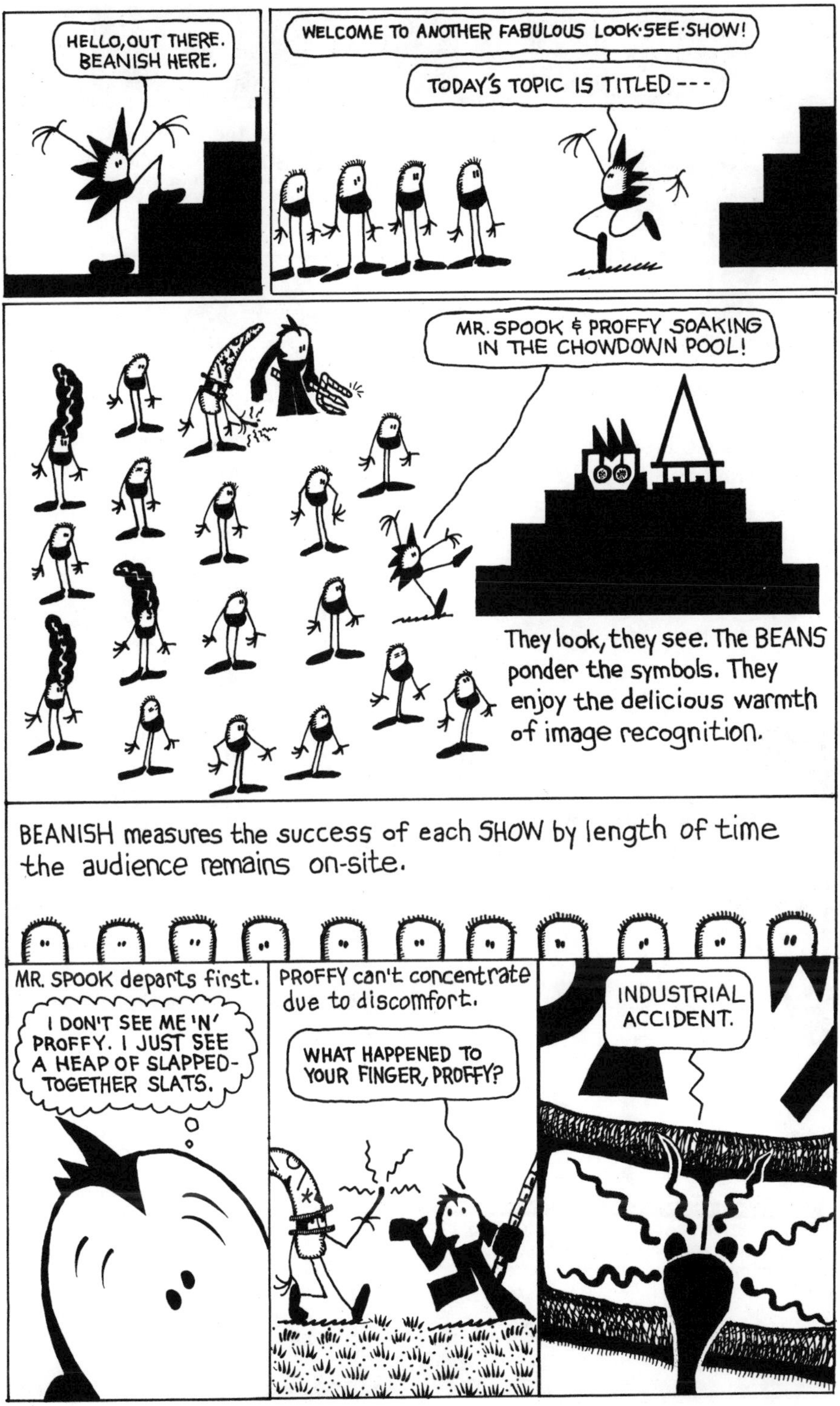
HELLO, OUT THERE. BEANISH HERE.
WELCOME TO ANOTHER FABULOUS LOOK·SEE·SHOW!
TODAY'S TOPIC IS TITLED ---
MR. SPOOK & PROFFY SOAKING IN THE CHOWDOWN POOL!
They look, they see. The BEANS ponder the symbols. They enjoy the delicious warmth of image recognition.
BEANISH measures the success of each SHOW by length of time the audience remains on-site.
MR. SPOOK departs first.
I DON'T SEE ME 'N' PROFFY. I JUST SEE A HEAP OF SLAPPED-TOGETHER SLATS.
PROFFY can't concentrate due to discomfort.
WHAT HAPPENED TO YOUR FINGER, PROFFY?
INDUSTRIAL ACCIDENT.

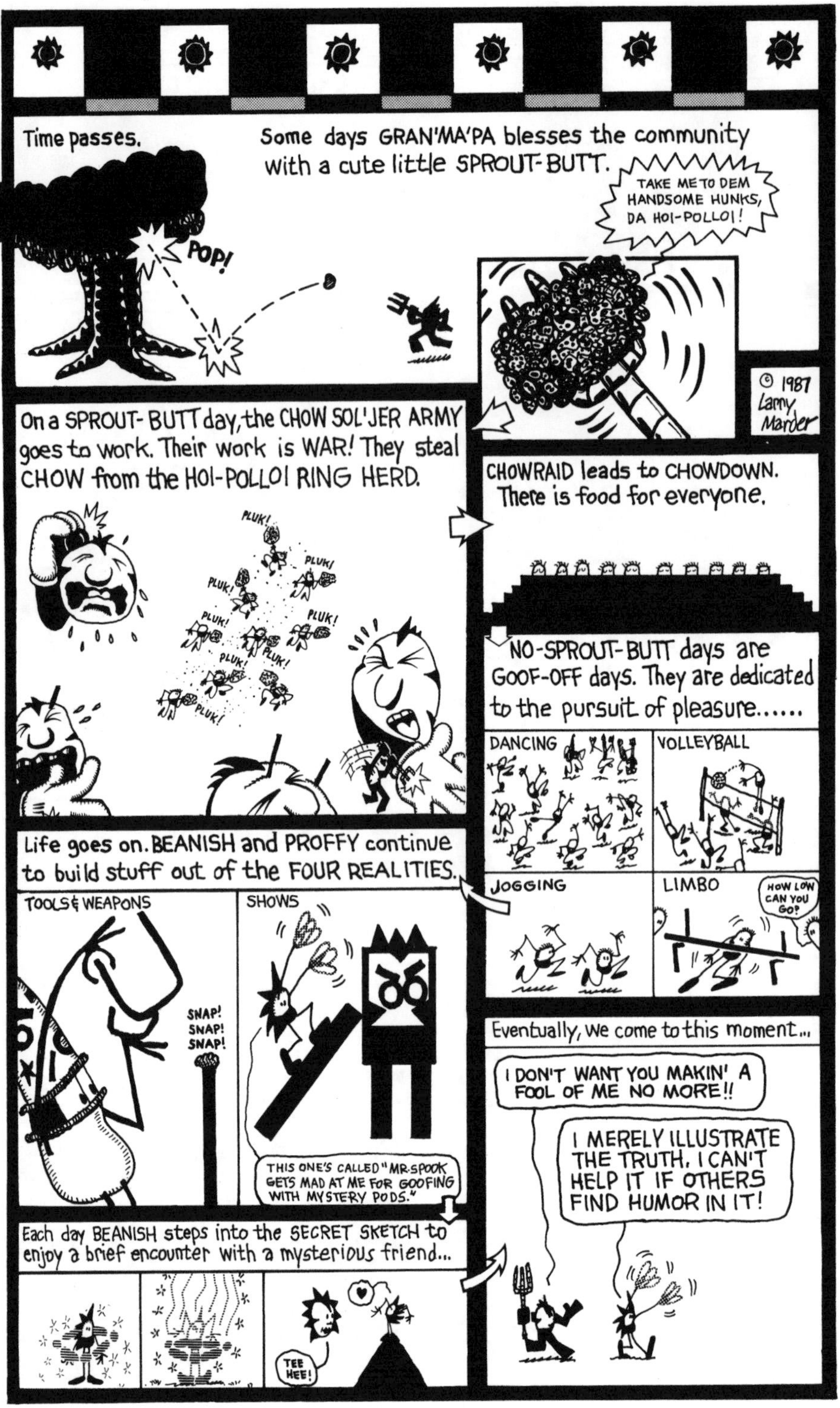

Time passes.
Some days GRAN'MA'PA blesses the community with a cute little SPROUT-BUTT.
POP!
TAKE ME TO DEM HANDSOME HUNKS, DA HOI-POLLOI!
© 1987 Larry Marder
On a SPROUT-BUTT day, the CHOW SOL'JER ARMY goes to work. Their work is WAR! They steal CHOW from the HOI-POLLOI RING HERD.
PLUK!
PLUK!
PLUK!
PLUK!
PLUK!
PLUK!
PLUK!
PLUK!
PLUK!
CHOWRAID leads to CHOWDOWN. There is food for everyone.
NO-SPROUT-BUTT days are GOOF-OFF days. They are dedicated to the pursuit of pleasure......
DANCING
VOLLEYBALL
JOGGING
LIMBO
HOW LOW CAN YOU GO?
Life goes on. BEANISH and PROFFY continue to build stuff out of the FOUR REALITIES.
TOOLS & WEAPONS
SNAP! SNAP! SNAP!
SHOWS
THIS ONE'S CALLED "MR. SPOOK GETS MAD AT ME FOR GOOFING WITH MYSTERY PODS."
Each day BEANISH steps into the SECRET SKETCH to enjoy a brief encounter with a mysterious friend...
TEE HEE!
Eventually, we come to this moment...
I DON'T WANT YOU MAKIN' A FOOL OF ME NO MORE!!
I MERELY ILLUSTRATE THE TRUTH. I CAN'T HELP IT IF OTHERS FIND HUMOR IN IT!

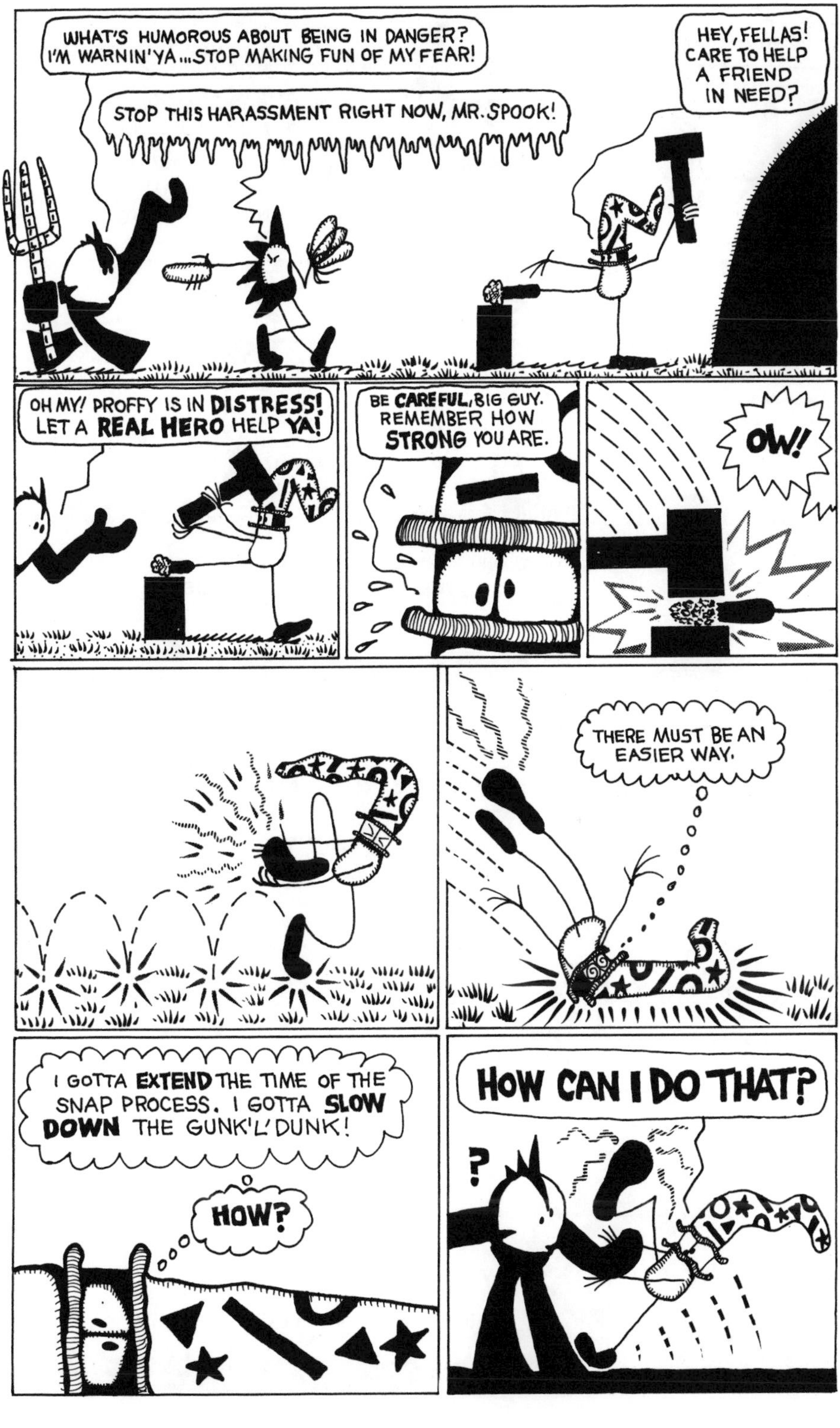
WHAT'S HUMOROUS ABOUT BEING IN DANGER? I'M WARNIN'YA...STOP MAKING FUN OF MY FEAR!
STOP THIS HARASSMENT RIGHT NOW, MR. SPOOK!
HEY, FELLAS! CARE TO HELP A FRIEND IN NEED?
OH MY! PROFFY IS IN DISTRESS! LET A REAL HERO HELP YA!
BE CAREFUL, BIG GUY. REMEMBER HOW STRONG YOU ARE.
OW!
THERE MUST BE AN EASIER WAY.
I GOTTA EXTEND THE TIME OF THE SNAP PROCESS. I GOTTA SLOW DOWN THE GUNK'L'DUNK!
HOW?
?
HOW CAN I DO THAT?

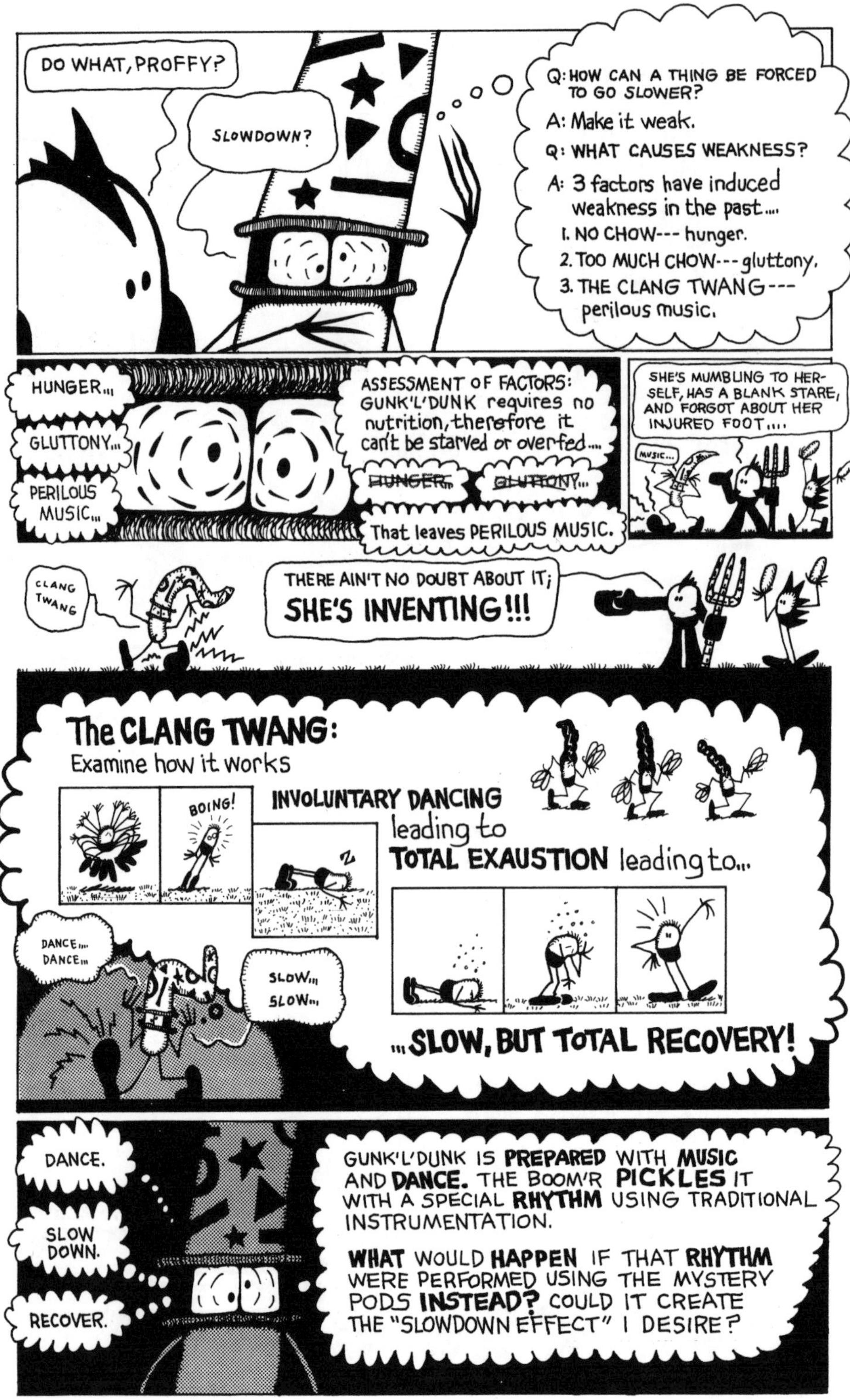
DO WHAT, PROFFY?
SLOWDOWN?
Q: HOW CAN A THING BE FORCED TO GO SLOWER?
A: Make it weak.
Q: WHAT CAUSES WEAKNESS?
A: 3 factors have induced weakness in the past....
1. NO CHOW--- hunger.
2. TOO MUCH CHOW--- gluttony.
3. THE CLANG TWANG--- perilous music.
HUNGER...
GLUTTONY...
PERILOUS MUSIC...
ASSESSMENT OF FACTORS: GUNK'L'DUNK requires no nutrition, therefore it can't be starved or overfed....
HUNGER...
GLUTTONY...
That leaves PERILOUS MUSIC.
SHE'S MUMBLING TO HERSELF, HAS A BLANK STARE, AND FORGOT ABOUT HER INJURED FOOT....
MUSIC...
CLANG TWANG
THERE AIN'T NO DOUBT ABOUT IT; SHE'S INVENTING!!!
The CLANG TWANG:
Examine how it works
BOING!
INVOLUNTARY DANCING leading to
TOTAL EXAUSTION leading to...
Z
DANCE... DANCE...
SLOW... SLOW...
...SLOW, BUT TOTAL RECOVERY!
DANCE.
SLOW DOWN.
RECOVER.
GUNK'L'DUNK IS PREPARED WITH MUSIC AND DANCE. THE BOOM'R PICKLES IT WITH A SPECIAL RHYTHM USING TRADITIONAL INSTRUMENTATION.
WHAT WOULD HAPPEN IF THAT RHYTHM WERE PERFORMED USING THE MYSTERY PODS INSTEAD? COULD IT CREATE THE "SLOWDOWN EFFECT" I DESIRE?

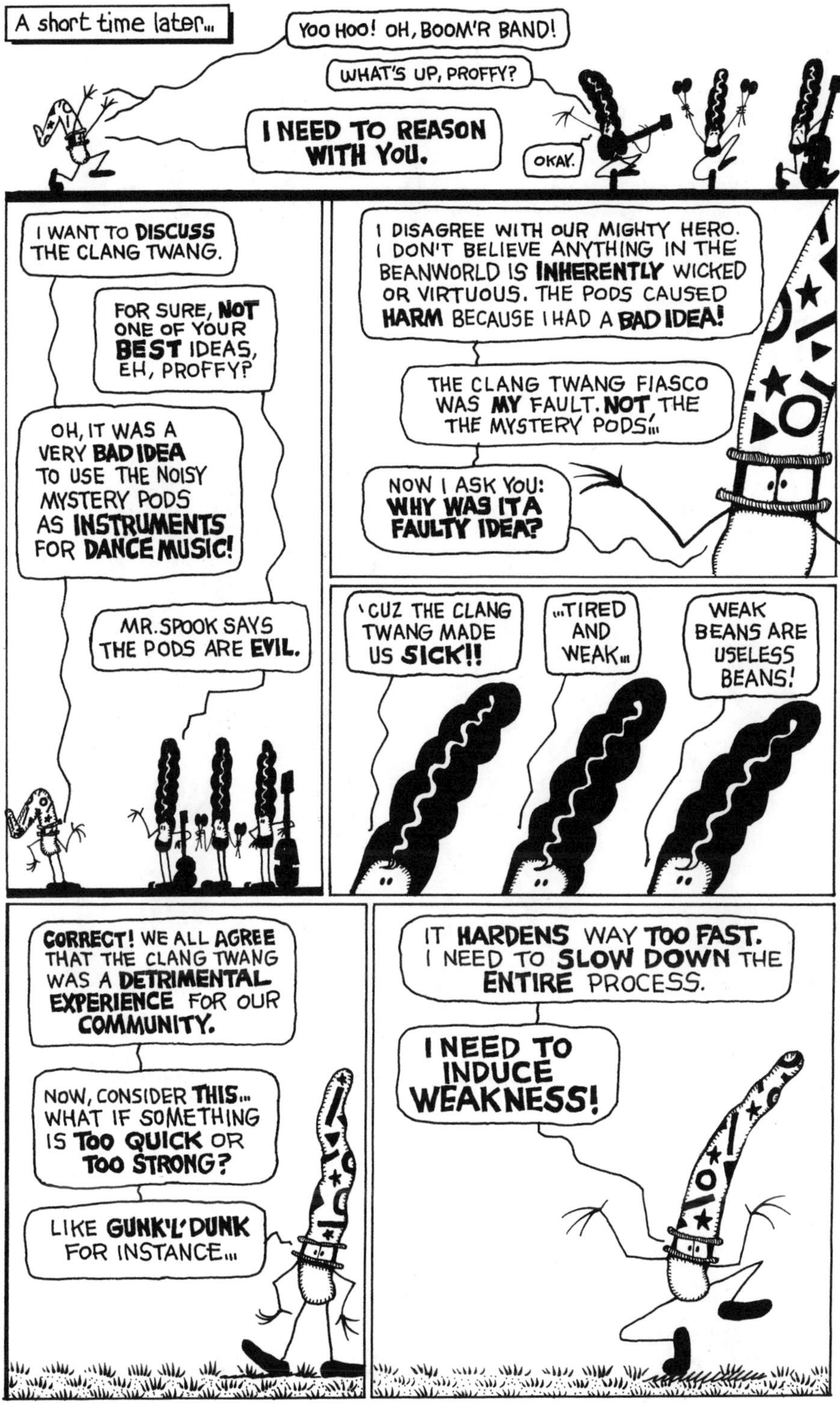
A short time later...
YOO HOO! OH, BOOM'R BAND!
WHAT'S UP, PROFFY?
I NEED TO REASON WITH YOU.
OKAY.
I WANT TO DISCUSS THE CLANG TWANG.
FOR SURE, NOT ONE OF YOUR BEST IDEAS, EH, PROFFY?
OH, IT WAS A VERY BAD IDEA TO USE THE NOISY MYSTERY PODS AS INSTRUMENTS FOR DANCE MUSIC!
MR. SPOOK SAYS THE PODS ARE EVIL.
I DISAGREE WITH OUR MIGHTY HERO. I DON'T BELIEVE ANYTHING IN THE BEANWORLD IS INHERENTLY WICKED OR VIRTUOUS. THE PODS CAUSED HARM BECAUSE I HAD A BAD IDEA!
THE CLANG TWANG FIASCO WAS MY FAULT. NOT THE THE MYSTERY PODS!...
NOW I ASK YOU: WHY WAS IT A FAULTY IDEA?
'CUZ THE CLANG TWANG MADE US SICK!!
...TIRED AND WEAK...
WEAK BEANS ARE USELESS BEANS!
CORRECT! WE ALL AGREE THAT THE CLANG TWANG WAS A DETRIMENTAL EXPERIENCE FOR OUR COMMUNITY.
NOW, CONSIDER THIS... WHAT IF SOMETHING IS TOO QUICK OR TOO STRONG?
LIKE GUNK'L'DUNK FOR INSTANCE...
IT HARDENS WAY TOO FAST. I NEED TO SLOW DOWN THE ENTIRE PROCESS.
I NEED TO INDUCE WEAKNESS!

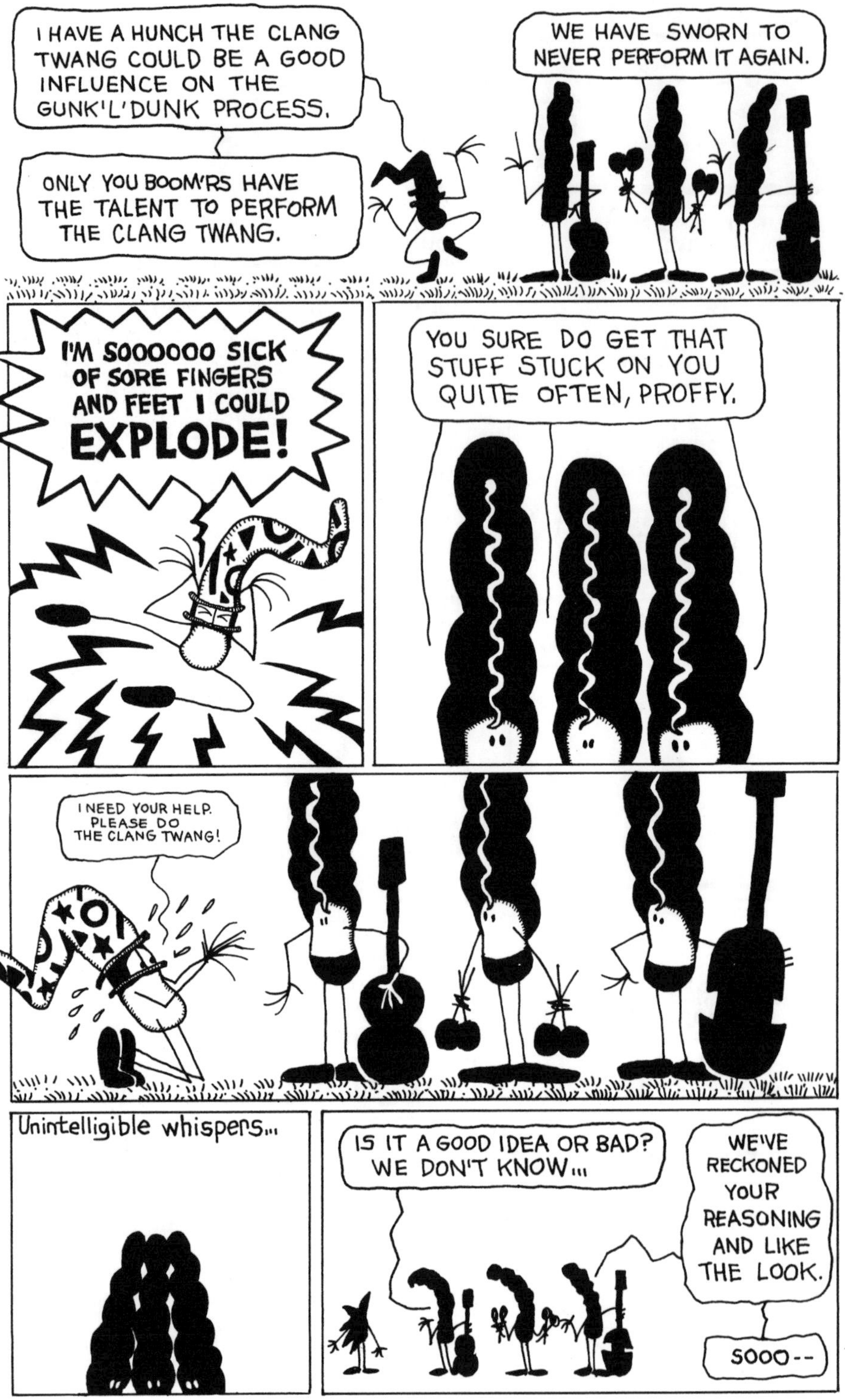
I HAVE A HUNCH THE CLANG TWANG COULD BE A GOOD INFLUENCE ON THE GUNK'L'DUNK PROCESS.
ONLY YOU BOOM'RS HAVE THE TALENT TO PERFORM THE CLANG TWANG.
WE HAVE SWORN TO NEVER PERFORM IT AGAIN.
I'M SOOOOOO SICK OF SORE FINGERS AND FEET I COULD EXPLODE!
YOU SURE DO GET THAT STUFF STUCK ON YOU QUITE OFTEN, PROFFY.
I NEED YOUR HELP. PLEASE DO THE CLANG TWANG!
Unintelligible whispers...
IS IT A GOOD IDEA OR BAD? WE DON'T KNOW...
WE'VE RECKONED YOUR REASONING AND LIKE THE LOOK.
SOOO--

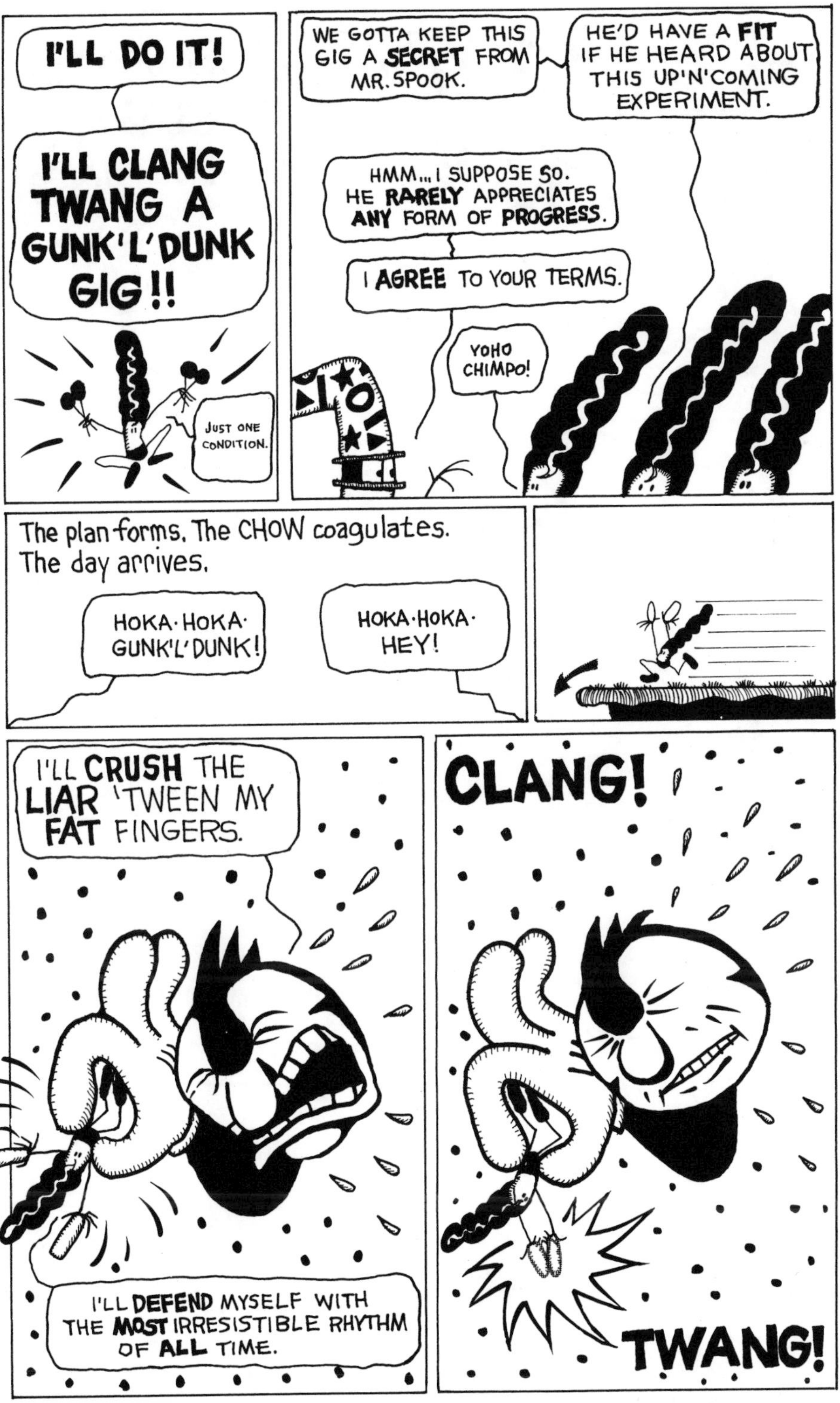
I'LL DO IT!
I'LL CLANG TWANG A GUNK'L'DUNK GIG!!
JUST ONE CONDITION.
WE GOTTA KEEP THIS GIG A SECRET FROM MR. SPOOK.
HE'D HAVE A FIT IF HE HEARD ABOUT THIS UP'N'COMING EXPERIMENT.
HMM... I SUPPOSE SO. HE RARELY APPRECIATES ANY FORM OF PROGRESS.
I AGREE TO YOUR TERMS.
YOHO CHIMPO!
The plan forms. The CHOW coagulates. The day arrives.
HOKA·HOKA· GUNK'L'DUNK!
HOKA·HOKA· HEY!
I'LL CRUSH THE LIAR 'TWEEN MY FAT FINGERS.
I'LL DEFEND MYSELF WITH THE MOST IRRESISTIBLE RHYTHM OF ALL TIME.
CLANG!
TWANG!

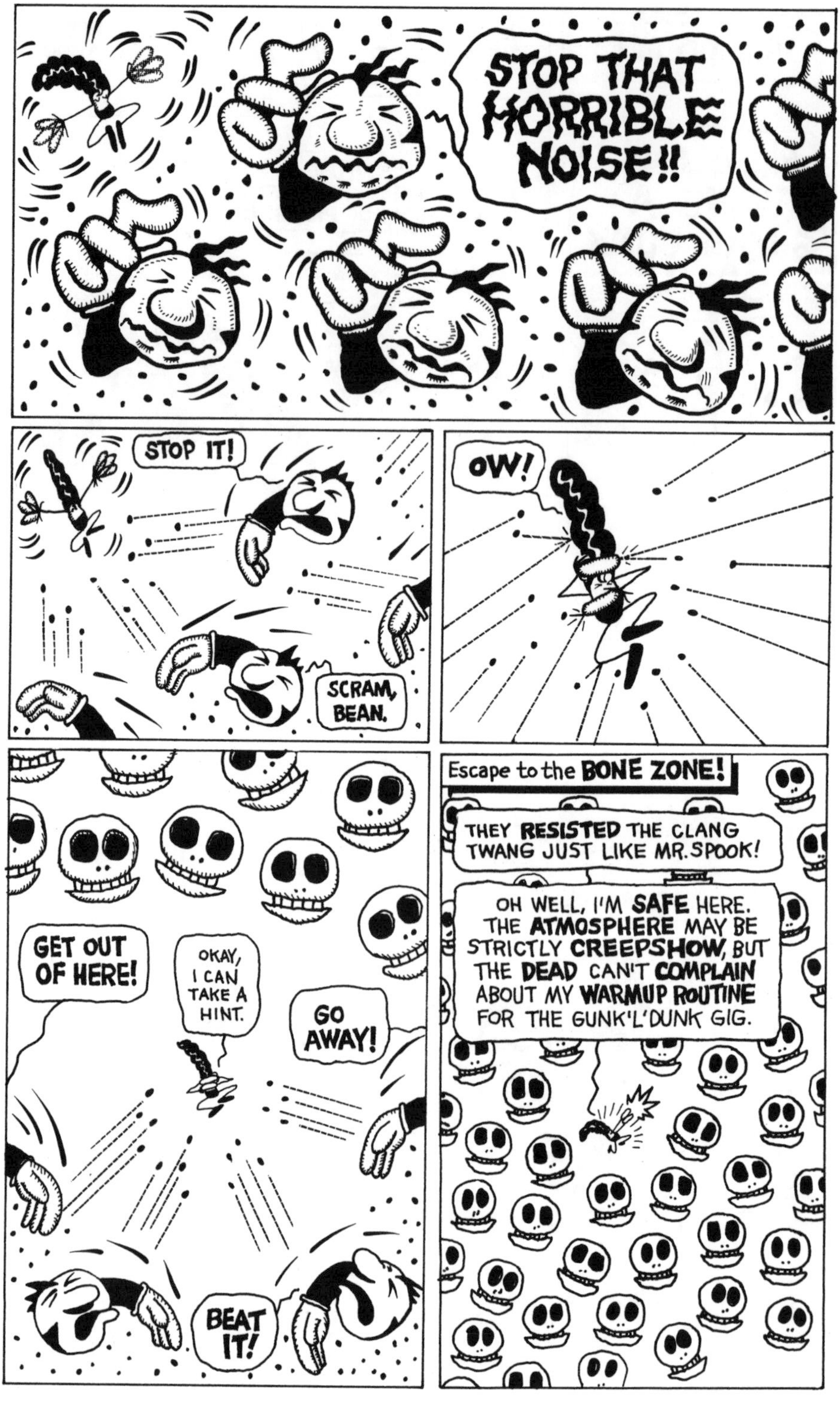
STOP THAT HORRIBLE NOISE!!
STOP IT!
SCRAM, BEAN.
OW!
GET OUT OF HERE!
OKAY, I CAN TAKE A HINT.
GO AWAY!
BEAT IT!
Escape to the BONE ZONE!
THEY RESISTED THE CLANG TWANG JUST LIKE MR. SPOOK!
OH WELL, I'M SAFE HERE. THE ATMOSPHERE MAY BE STRICTLY CREEPSHOW, BUT THE DEAD CAN'T COMPLAIN ABOUT MY WARMUP ROUTINE FOR THE GUNK'L'DUNK GIG.

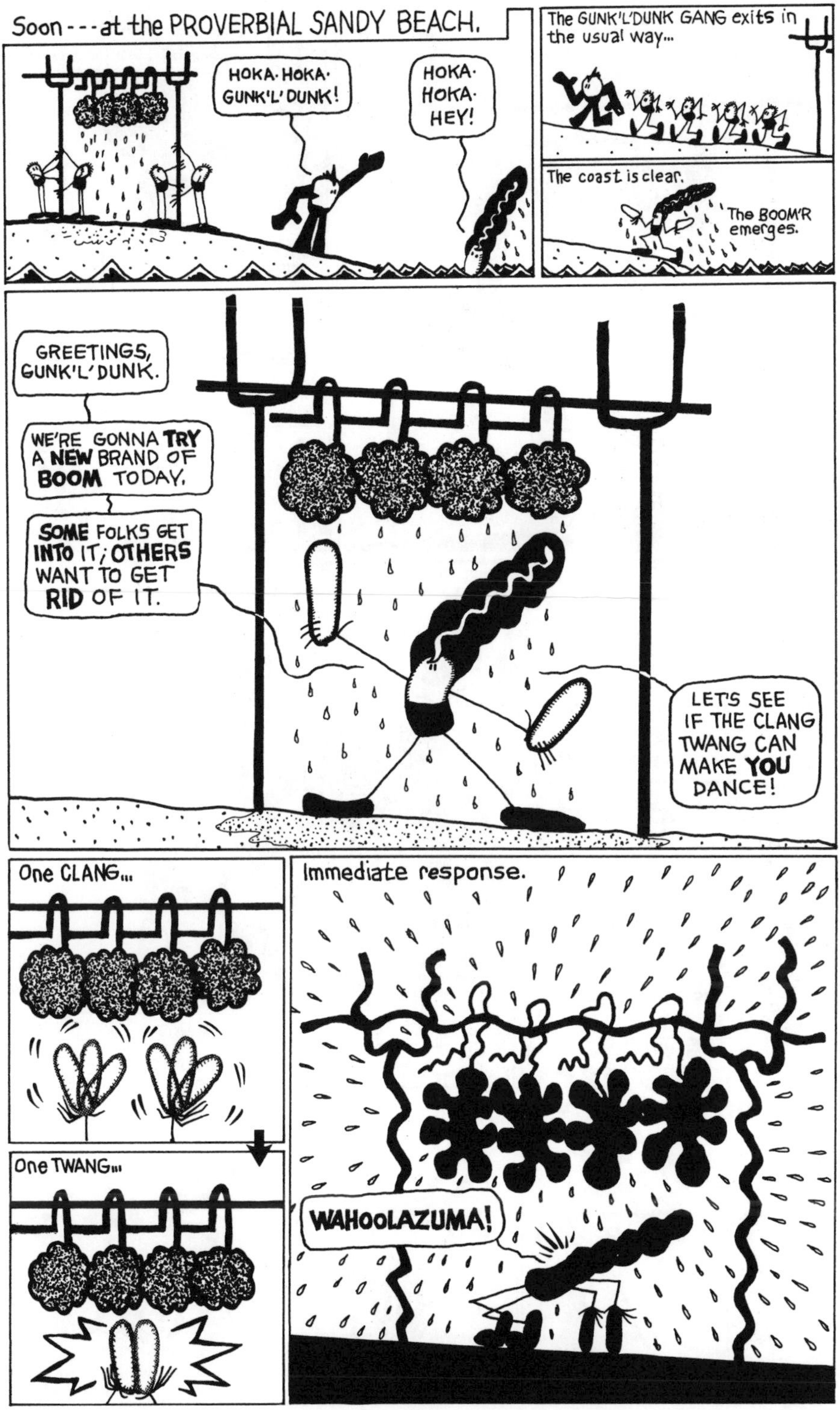
Soon---at the PROVERBIAL SANDY BEACH.
HOKA·HOKA· GUNK'L'DUNK!
HOKA· HOKA· HEY!
The GUNK'L'DUNK GANG exits in the usual way...
The coast is clear.
The BOOM'R emerges.
GREETINGS, GUNK'L'DUNK.
WE'RE GONNA TRY A NEW BRAND OF BOOM TODAY.
SOME FOLKS GET INTO IT; OTHERS WANT TO GET RID OF IT.
LET'S SEE IF THE CLANG TWANG CAN MAKE YOU DANCE!
One CLANG...
One TWANG...
Immediate response.
WAHOOLAZUMA!

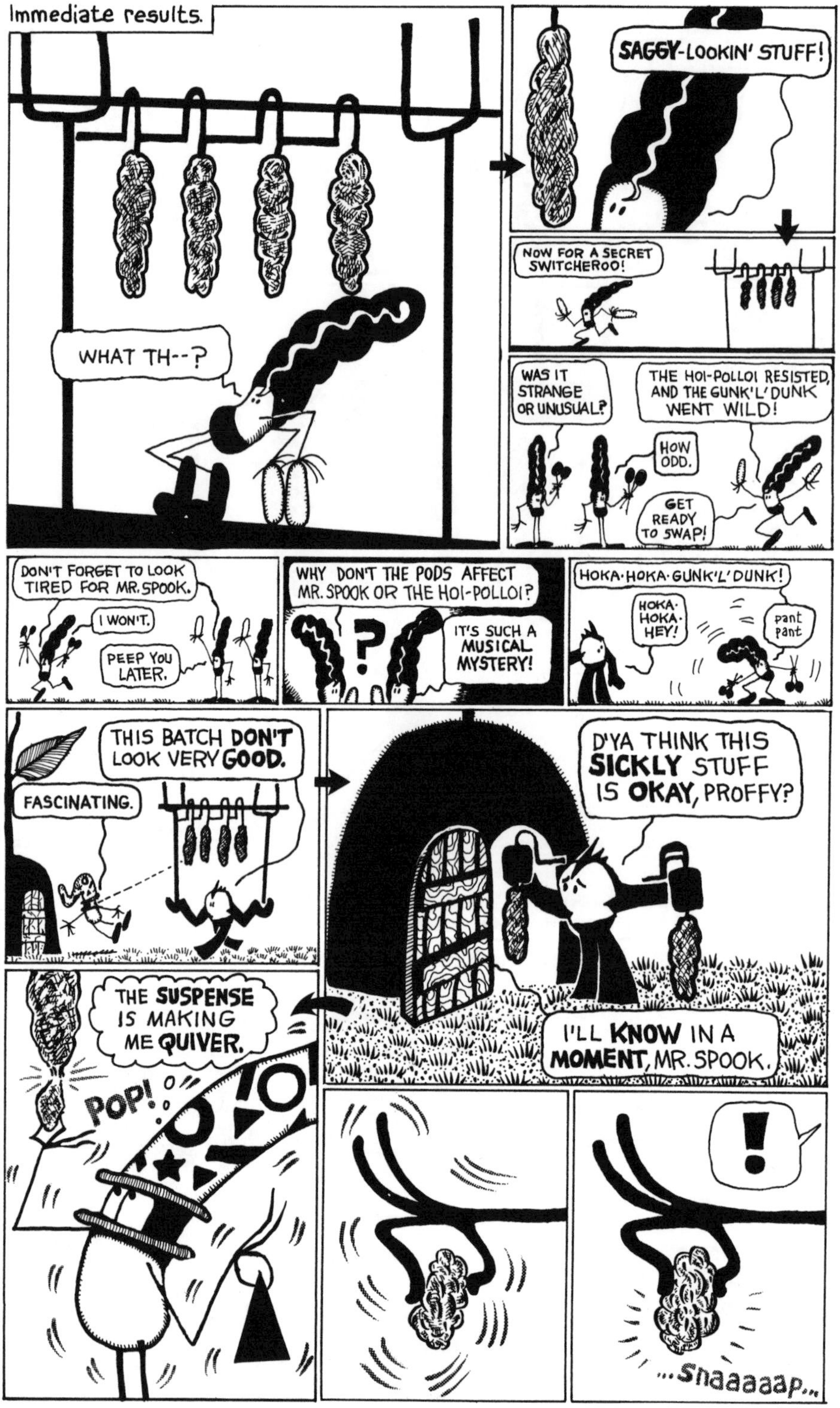
Immediate results.
WHAT TH--?
SAGGY-LOOKIN' STUFF!
NOW FOR A SECRET SWITCHEROO!
WAS IT STRANGE OR UNUSUAL?
THE HOI-POLLOI RESISTED, AND THE GUNK'L'DUNK WENT WILD!
HOW ODD.
GET READY TO SWAP!
DON'T FORGET TO LOOK TIRED FOR MR. SPOOK.
I WON'T.
PEEP YOU LATER.
WHY DON'T THE PODS AFFECT MR. SPOOK OR THE HOI-POLLOI?
?
IT'S SUCH A MUSICAL MYSTERY!
HOKA·HOKA·GUNK'L'DUNK!
HOKA· HOKA· HEY!
pant pant
THIS BATCH DON'T LOOK VERY GOOD.
FASCINATING.
D'YA THINK THIS SICKLY STUFF IS OKAY, PROFFY?
I'LL KNOW IN A MOMENT, MR. SPOOK.
THE SUSPENSE IS MAKING ME QUIVER.
POP!
!
...snaaaaap...

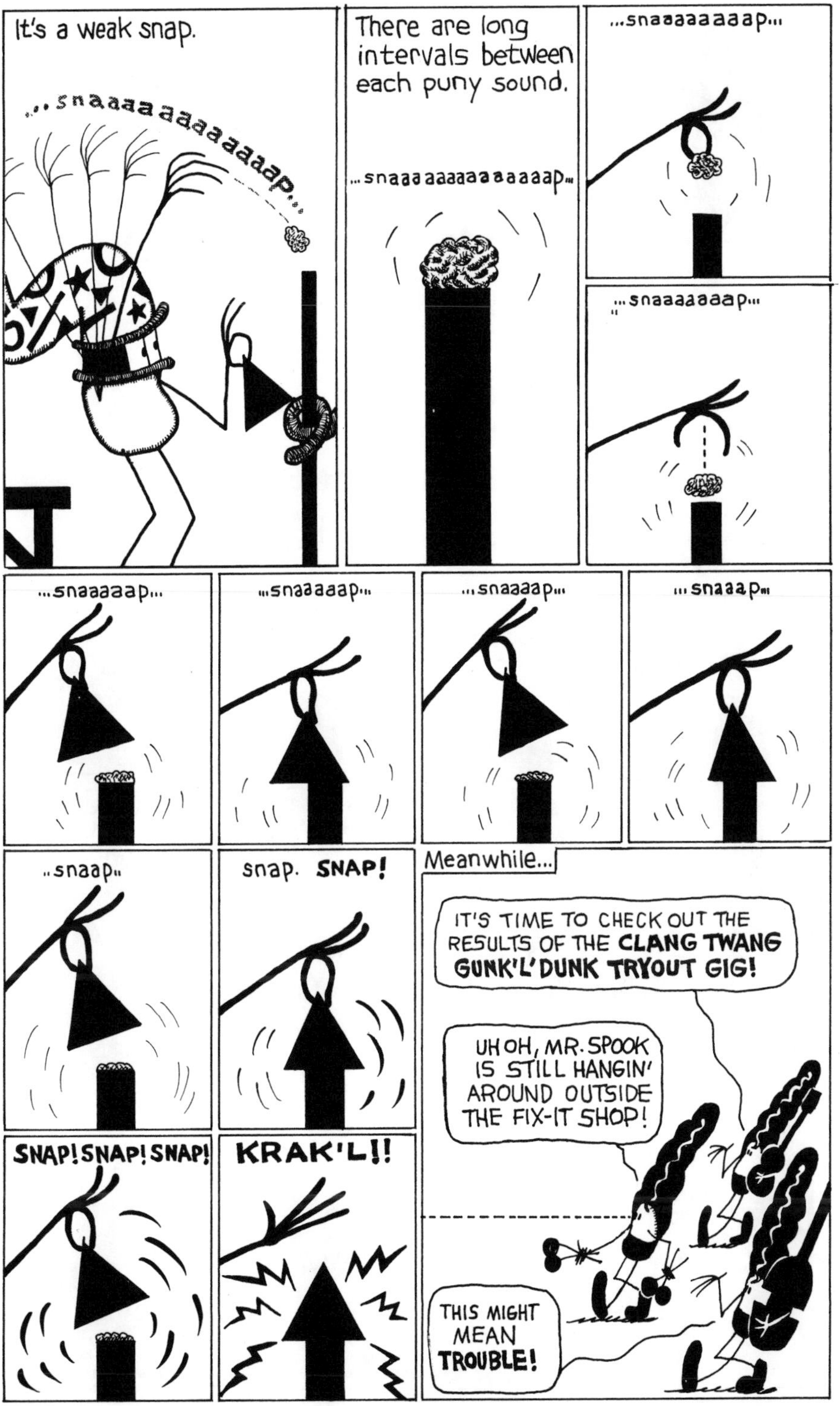

It's a weak snap.
...snaaaaaaaaaaaaap...
There are long intervals between each puny sound.
...snaaaaaaaaaaaaap...
...snaaaaaaaap...
...snaaaaaaap...
...snaaaaap...
...snaaaap...
...snaaaap...
...snaaap...
..snaap..
snap. SNAP!
SNAP! SNAP! SNAP!
KRAK'L!!
Meanwhile...
IT'S TIME TO CHECK OUT THE RESULTS OF THE CLANG TWANG GUNK'L'DUNK TRYOUT GIG!
UH OH, MR. SPOOK IS STILL HANGIN' AROUND OUTSIDE THE FIX-IT SHOP!
THIS MIGHT MEAN TROUBLE!

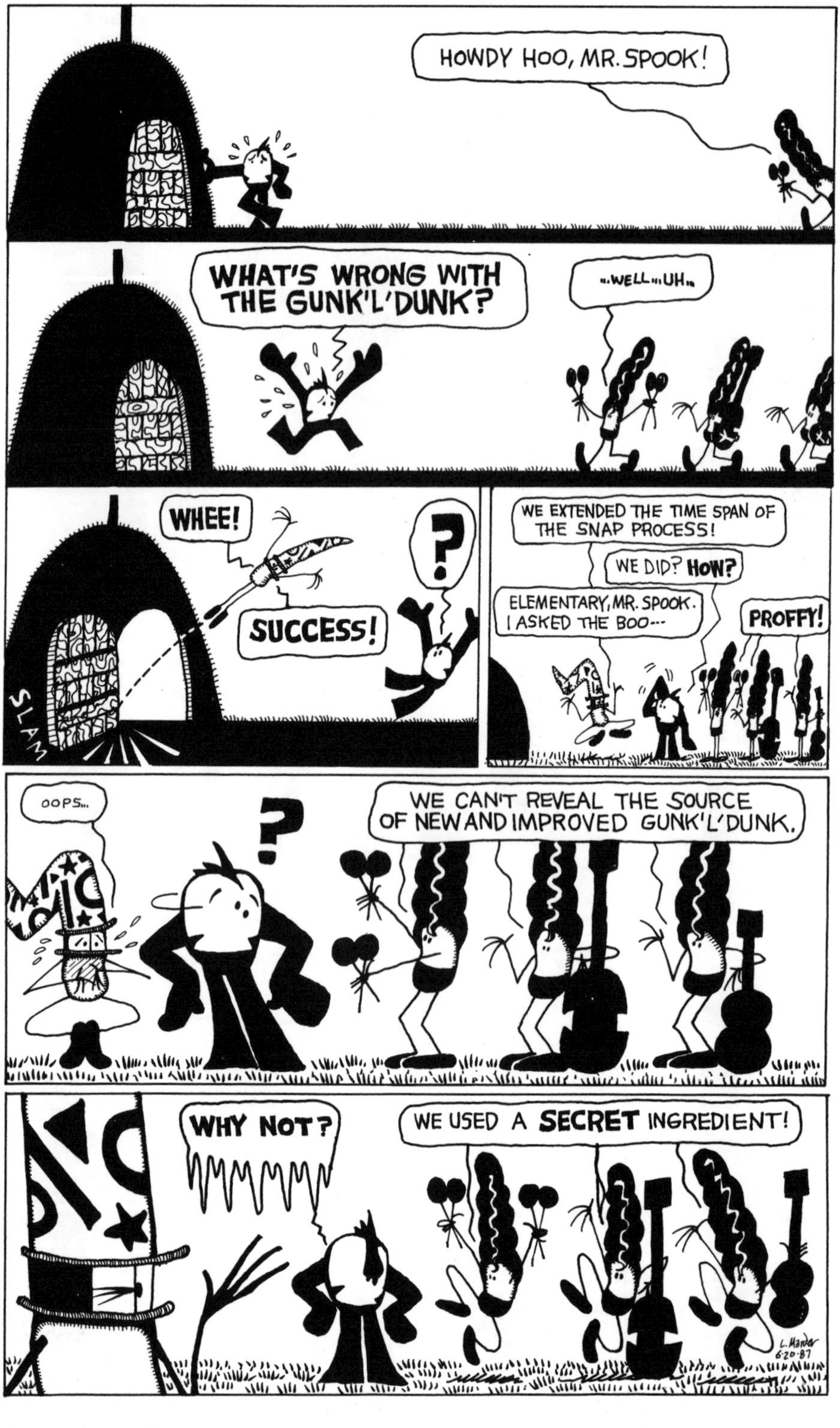
HOWDY HOO, MR. SPOOK!
WHAT'S WRONG WITH THE GUNK'L'DUNK?
..WELL...UH..
WHEE!
SUCCESS!
?
SLAM
WE EXTENDED THE TIME SPAN OF THE SNAP PROCESS!
WE DID? HOW?
ELEMENTARY, MR. SPOOK. I ASKED THE BOO---
PROFFY!
OOPS...
?
WE CAN'T REVEAL THE SOURCE OF NEW AND IMPROVED GUNK'L'DUNK.
WHY NOT?
WE USED A SECRET INGREDIENT!
L. Marder 6·20·87

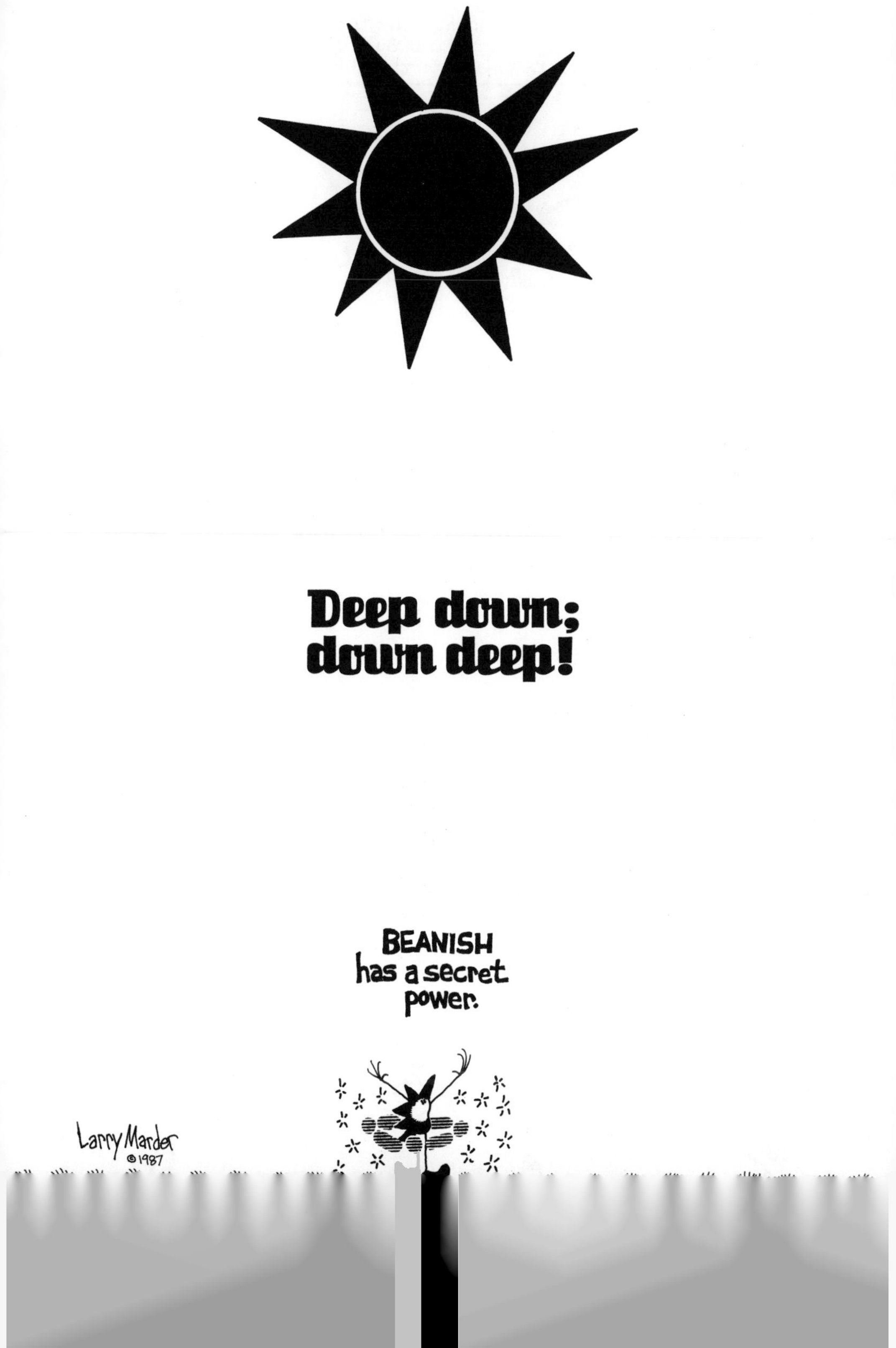
Deep down; down deep!
BEANISH has a secret power.
Larry Marder ©1987

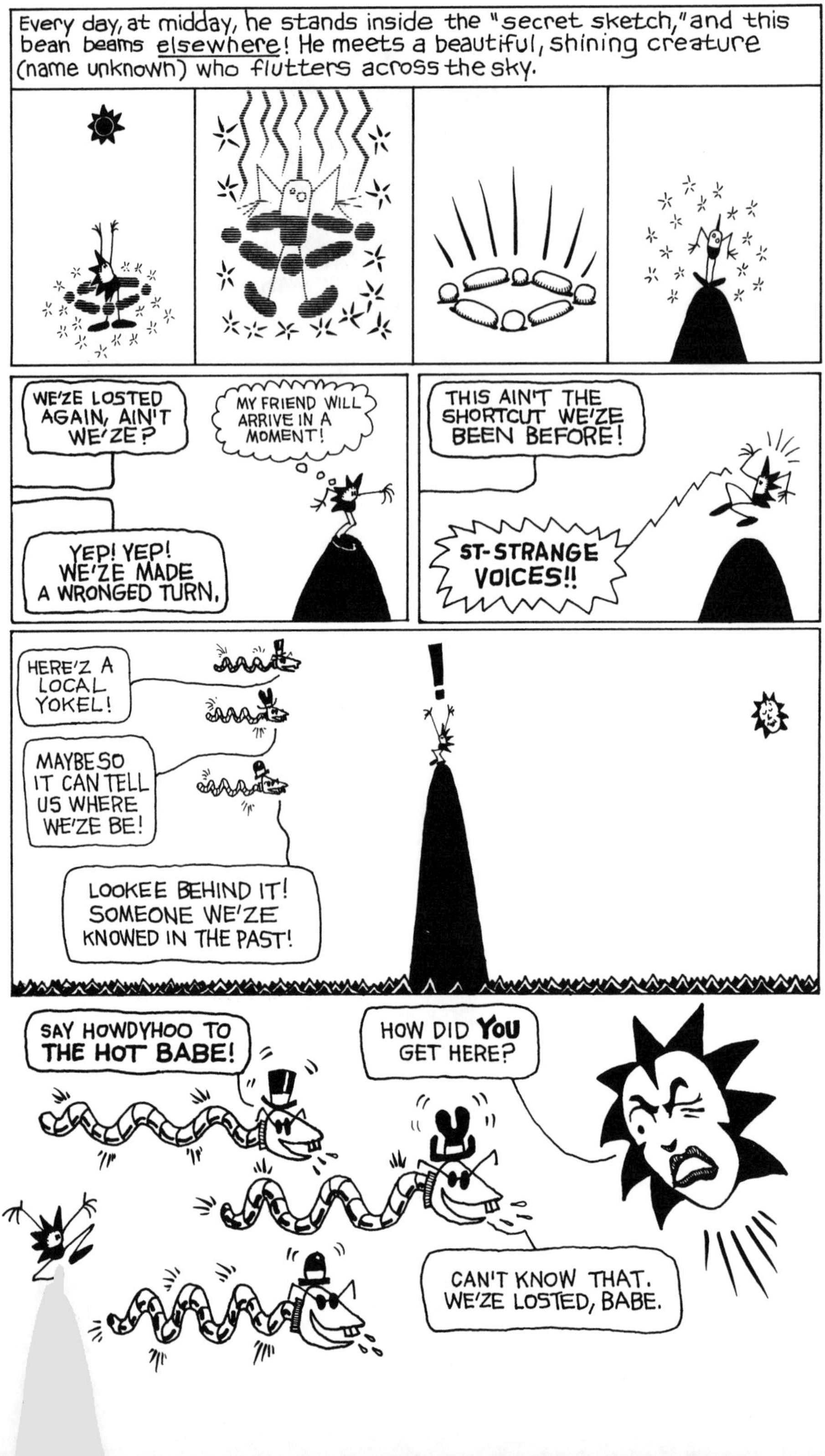
Every day, at midday, he stands inside the "secret sketch," and this bean beams elsewhere! He meets a beautiful, shining creature (name unknown) who flutters across the sky.
WE'ZE LOSTED AGAIN, AIN'T WE'ZE?
MY FRIEND WILL ARRIVE IN A MOMENT!
YEP! YEP! WE'ZE MADE A WRONGED TURN.
THIS AIN'T THE SHORTCUT WE'ZE BEEN BEFORE!
ST-STRANGE VOICES!!
HERE'Z A LOCAL YOKEL!
MAYBESO IT CAN TELL US WHERE WE'ZE BE!
LOOKEE BEHIND IT! SOMEONE WE'ZE KNOWED IN THE PAST!
!
SAY HOWDYHOO TO THE HOT BABE!
HOW DID YOU GET HERE?
CAN'T KNOW THAT. WE'ZE LOSTED, BABE.

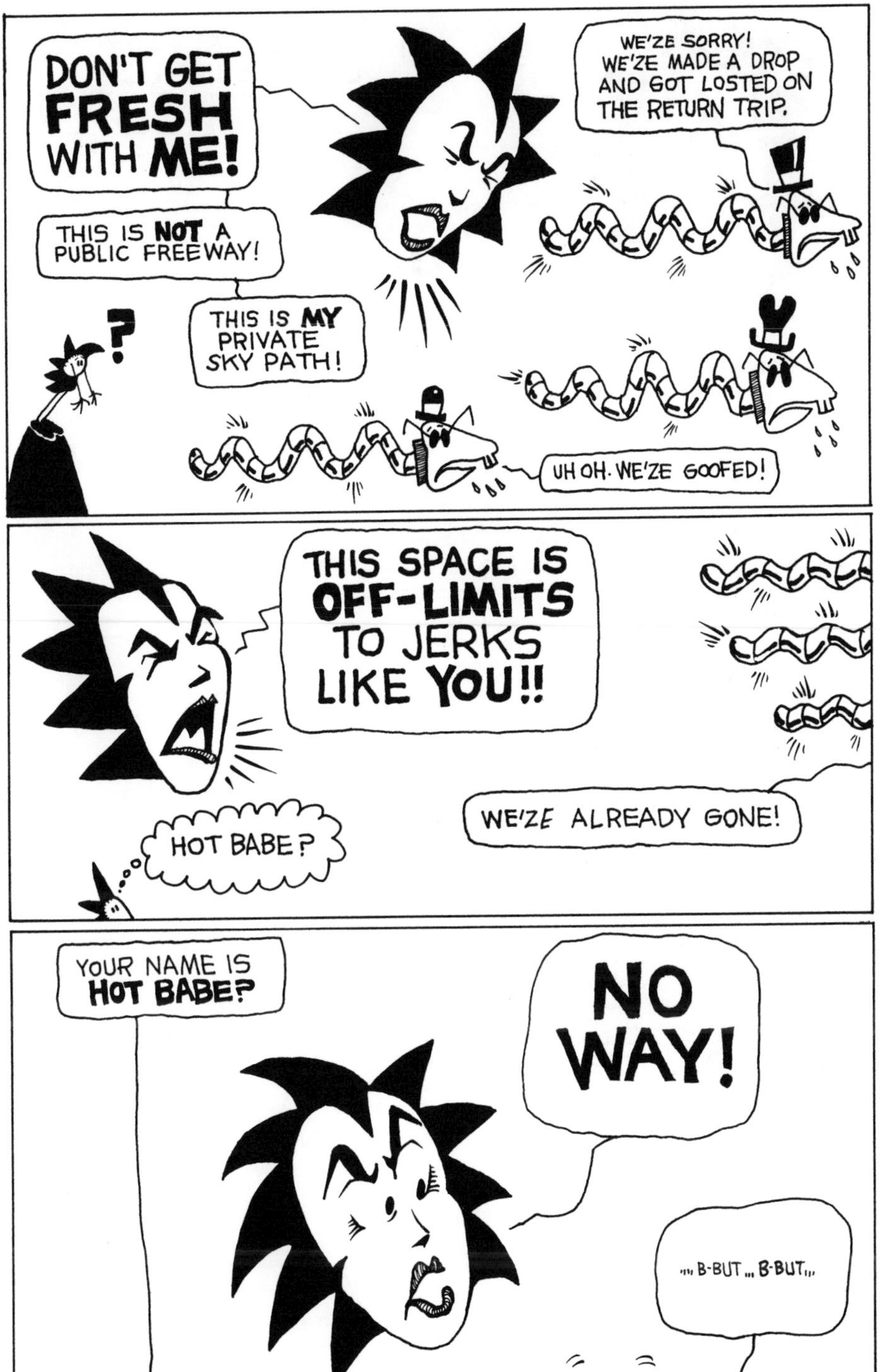
DON'T GET FRESH WITH ME!
THIS IS NOT A PUBLIC FREEWAY!
THIS IS MY PRIVATE SKY PATH!
WE'ZE SORRY! WE'ZE MADE A DROP AND GOT LOSTED ON THE RETURN TRIP.
?
UH OH. WE'ZE GOOFED!
THIS SPACE IS OFF-LIMITS TO JERKS LIKE YOU!!
WE'ZE ALREADY GONE!
HOT BABE?
YOUR NAME IS HOT BABE?
NO WAY!
... B-BUT ... B-BUT ...

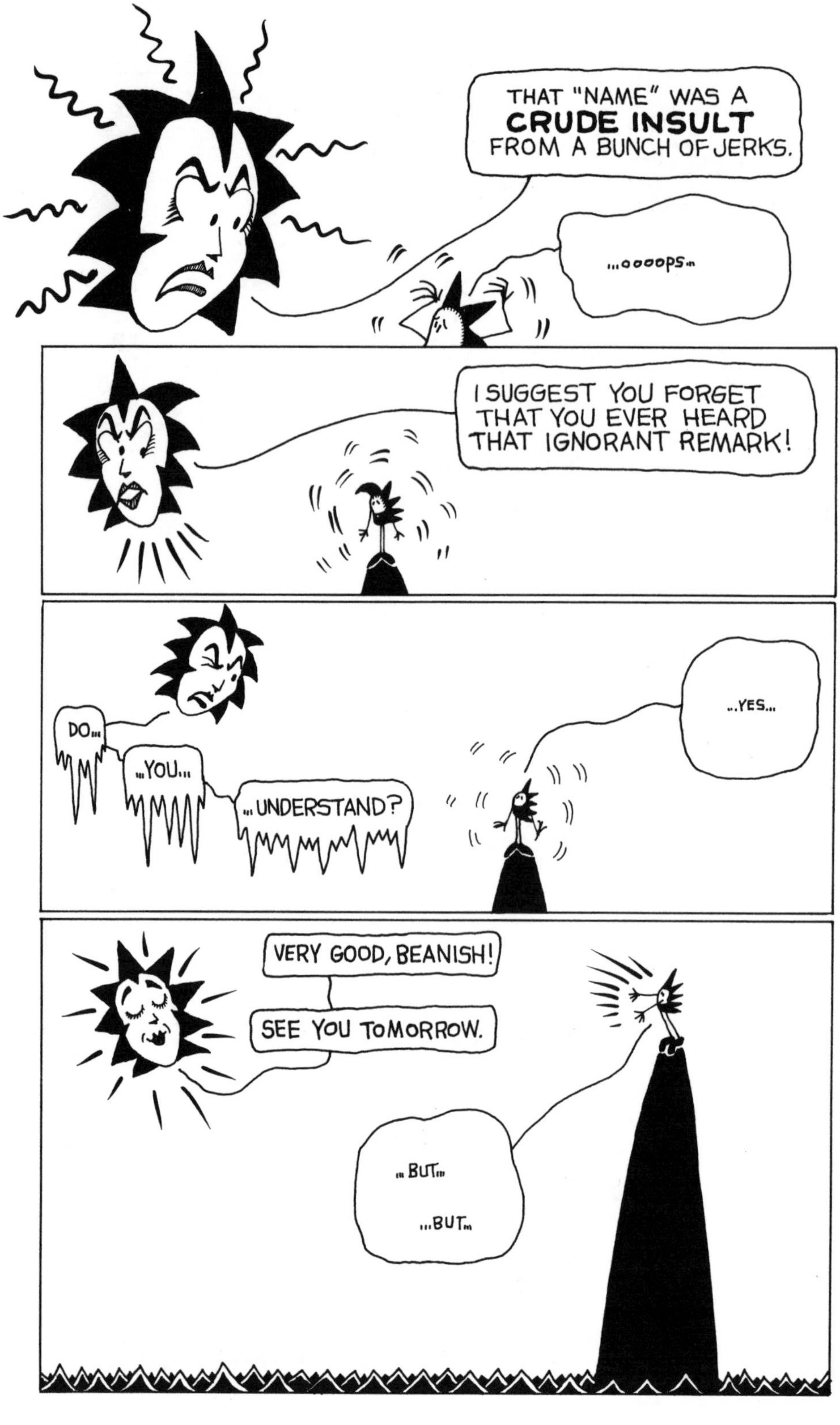
THAT "NAME" WAS A **CRUDE INSULT** FROM A BUNCH OF JERKS.
...OOOOPS...
I SUGGEST YOU FORGET THAT YOU EVER HEARD THAT IGNORANT REMARK!
DO...
...YOU...
...UNDERSTAND?
...YES...
VERY GOOD, BEANISH!
SEE YOU TOMORROW.
...BUT...
...BUT...

WHAT WAS **THAT** ALL ABOUT?

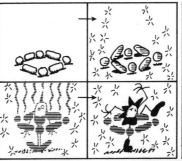

WOW! I JUST REALIZED HOW MUCH THOSE "JERKS" LOOK LIKE MR. SPOOK'S **TRUSTY FORK!**

I WONDER WHAT THAT MEANS?

I'D BETTER GO ASK PROFESSOR GARBANZO!

WHAT AM I THINKING? **I CAN'T CONSULT PROFFY!**

THAT WOULD BE A **CONTRACT VIOLATION:**

YOUR SECRET ABILITY TO VISIT ME IS A GREAT POWER, BEANISH!

**BUT** YOU MUST NEVER, EVER TELL ANYONE ABOUT ME.

DO YOU UNDERSTAND WHAT I'M SAYING, BEANISH?

IF YOU DO, YOU WILL NEVER, EVER SEE ME AGAIN.

yes....

AAGH!!

MY SECRET POWER IS SOOOOOO **FRUSTRATING** SOMETIMES.

It takes tremendous self-control not to speak of such amazing adventures. Fortunately, the <u>intensity</u> of the experience fades quickly upon return to the <u>real world</u>, the BEANWORLD.

I'M HUNGRY....

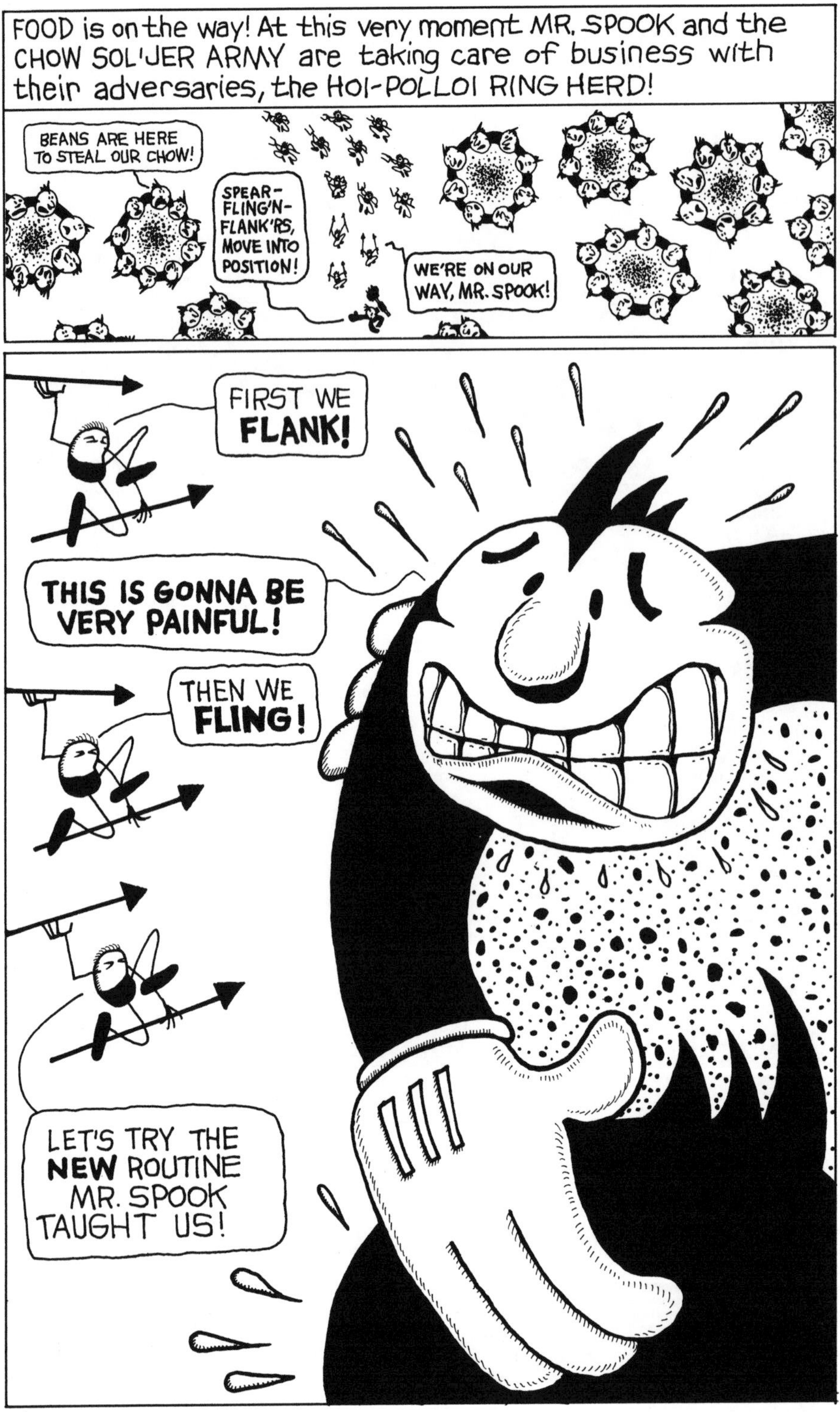
FOOD is on the way! At this very moment MR. SPOOK and the CHOW SOL'JER ARMY are taking care of business with their adversaries, the HOI-POLLOI RING HERD!
BEANS ARE HERE TO STEAL OUR CHOW!
SPEAR-FLING'N-FLANK'RS, MOVE INTO POSITION!
WE'RE ON OUR WAY, MR. SPOOK!
FIRST WE **FLANK!**
**THIS IS GONNA BE VERY PAINFUL!**
THEN WE **FLING!**
LET'S TRY THE **NEW** ROUTINE MR. SPOOK TAUGHT US!

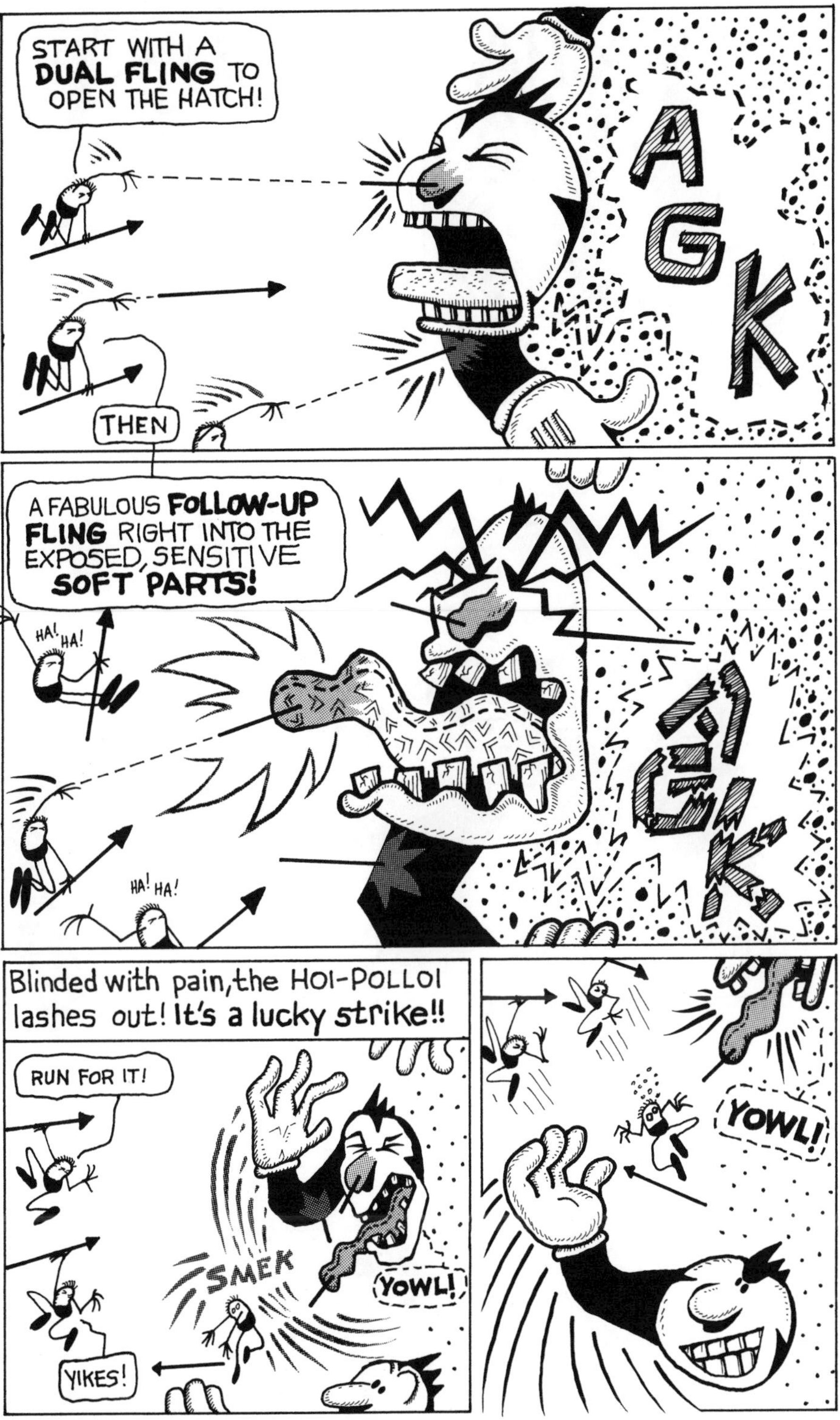

START WITH A DUAL FLING TO OPEN THE HATCH!
AGK
THEN
A FABULOUS FOLLOW-UP FLING RIGHT INTO THE EXPOSED, SENSITIVE SOFT PARTS!
HA! HA!
AGK
HA! HA!
Blinded with pain, the HOI-POLLOI lashes out! It's a lucky strike!!
RUN FOR IT!
SMEK
YOWL!
YIKES!
YOWL!

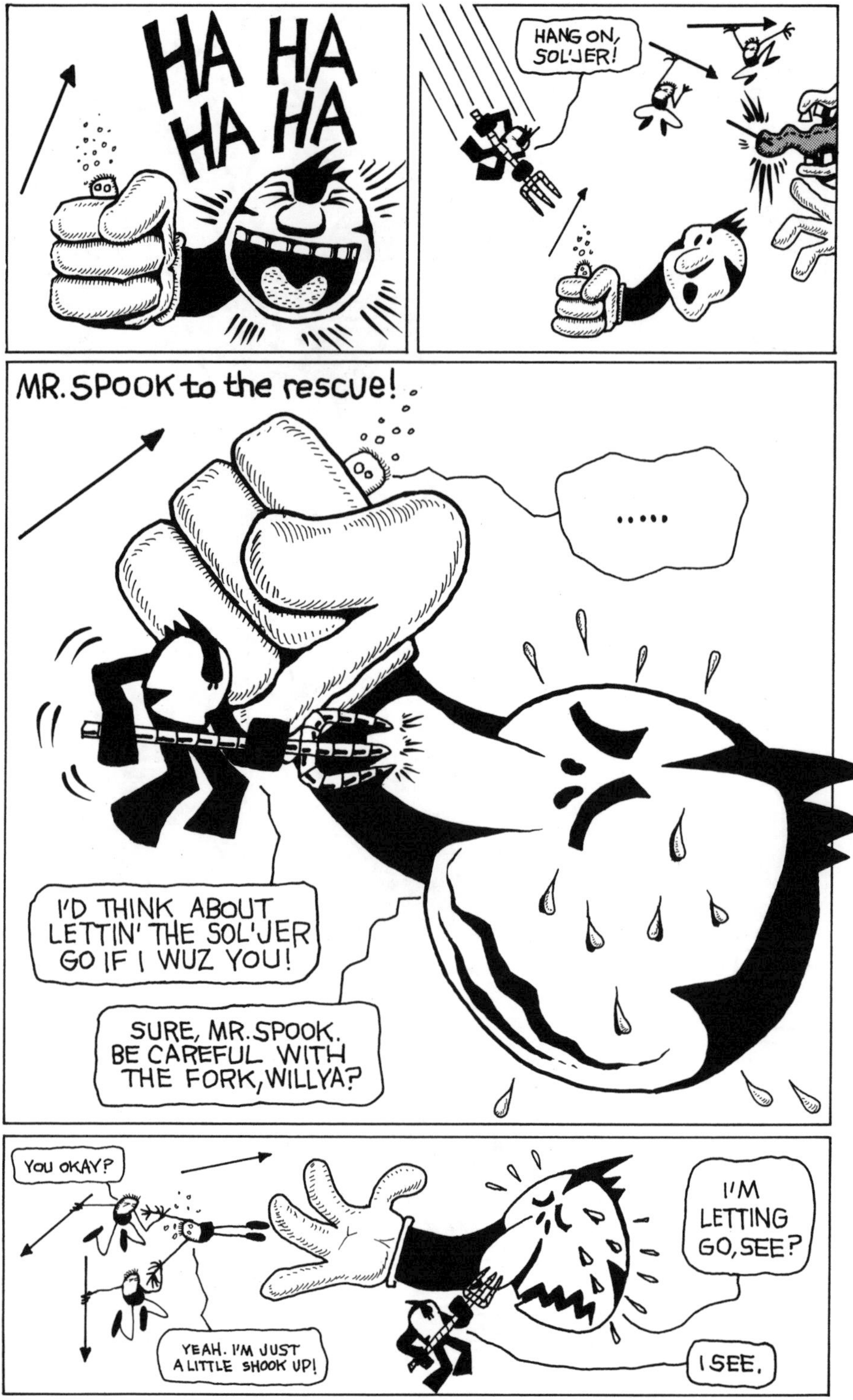
HA HA
HA HA
HANG ON, SOL'JER!
MR. SPOOK to the rescue!
.....
I'D THINK ABOUT LETTIN' THE SOL'JER GO IF I WUZ YOU!
SURE, MR. SPOOK. BE CAREFUL WITH THE FORK, WILLYA?
YOU OKAY?
YEAH. I'M JUST A LITTLE SHOOK UP!
I'M LETTING GO, SEE?
I SEE.

HERE'S YOUR "THANK-YOU"!

The HOI-POLLOI RING has been **smashed!** The CHOW-PLUK'RS sweep in to grab the CHOW while the HOI-POLLOI are reeling from their injuries.

PLUK'N WANDS filled, the CHOW SOL'JER ARMY withdraws...

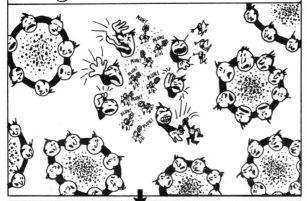

PLUK!

THE **NEW** SPEAR-FLING'R TACTICAL MANEUVER PERFORMED **WAY TOO WELL.**

THE FLING INTO THE SOFT PART CREATED TOO MUCH BLIND THRASHING!

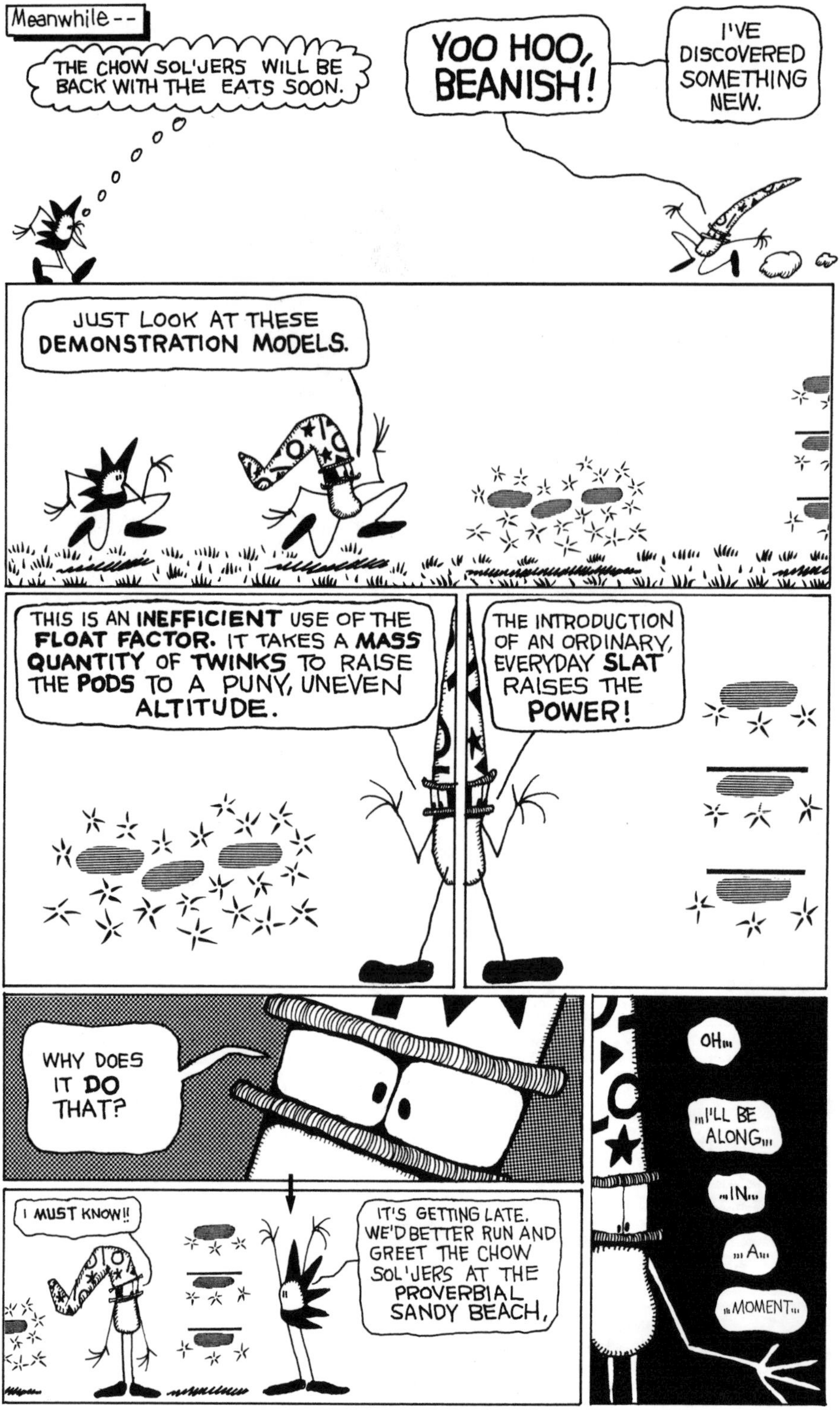
Meanwhile --
THE CHOW SOL'JERS WILL BE BACK WITH THE EATS SOON.
YOO HOO, BEANISH!
I'VE DISCOVERED SOMETHING NEW.
JUST LOOK AT THESE DEMONSTRATION MODELS.
THIS IS AN INEFFICIENT USE OF THE FLOAT FACTOR. IT TAKES A MASS QUANTITY OF TWINKS TO RAISE THE PODS TO A PUNY, UNEVEN ALTITUDE.
THE INTRODUCTION OF AN ORDINARY, EVERYDAY SLAT RAISES THE POWER!
WHY DOES IT DO THAT?
I MUST KNOW!!
IT'S GETTING LATE. WE'D BETTER RUN AND GREET THE CHOW SOL'JERS AT THE PROVERBIAL SANDY BEACH,
OH...
...I'LL BE ALONG...
...IN...
...A...
...MOMENT...

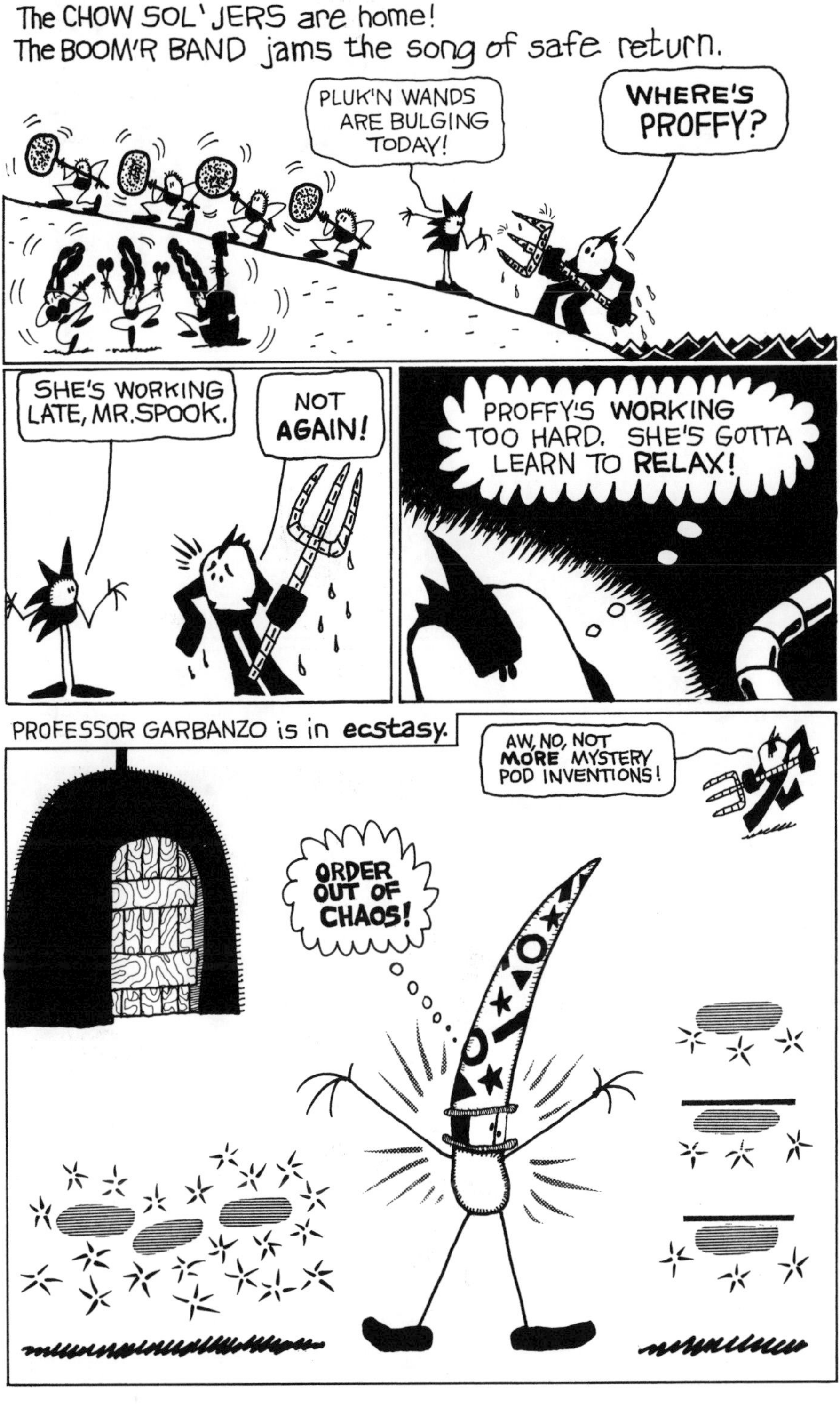
The CHOW SOL'JERS are home!
The BOOM'R BAND jams the song of safe return.
PLUK'N WANDS ARE BULGING TODAY!
WHERE'S PROFFY?
SHE'S WORKING LATE, MR. SPOOK.
NOT AGAIN!
PROFFY'S WORKING TOO HARD. SHE'S GOTTA LEARN TO RELAX!
PROFESSOR GARBANZO is in ecstasy.
AW, NO, NOT MORE MYSTERY POD INVENTIONS!
ORDER OUT OF CHAOS!

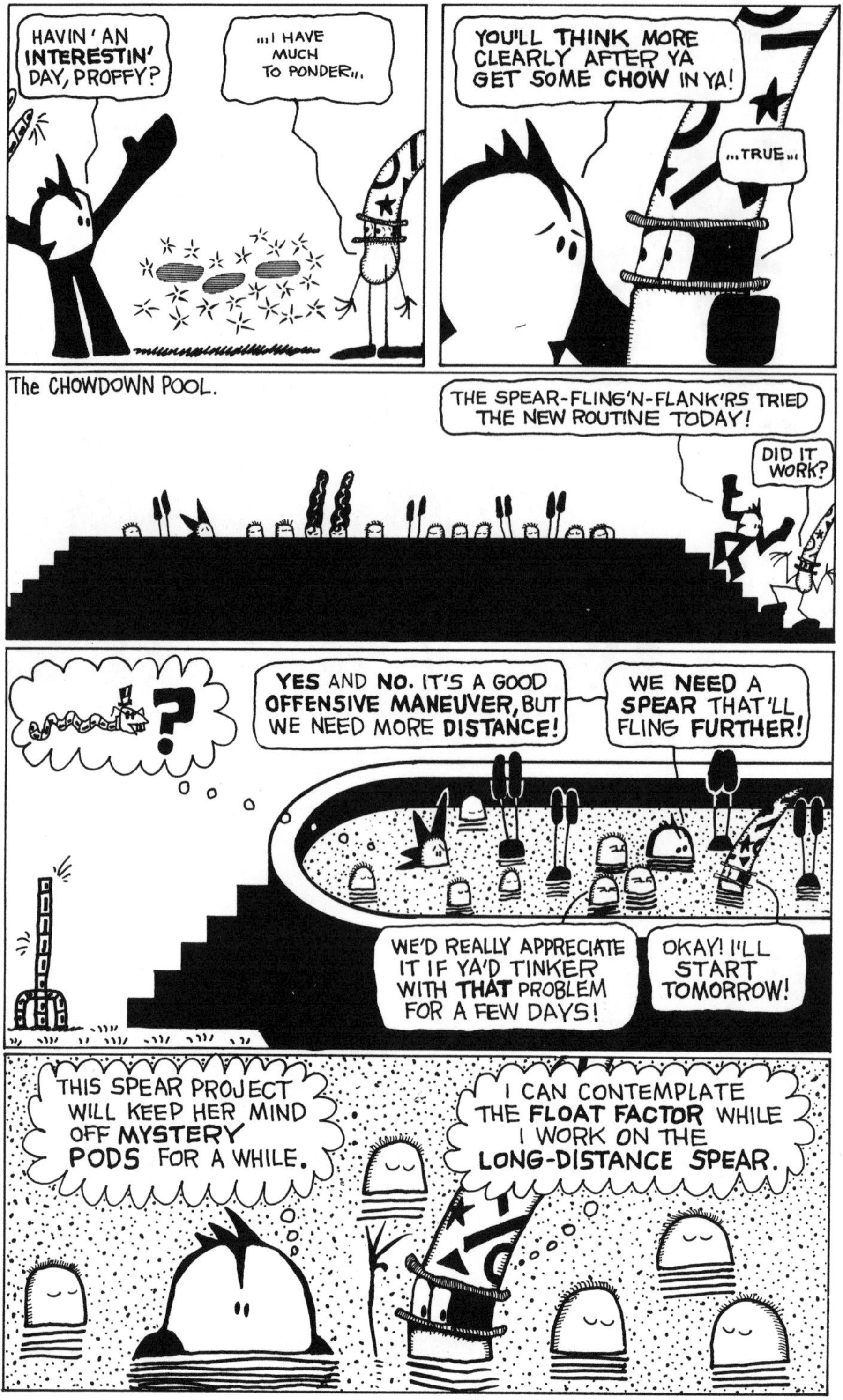
HAVIN' AN INTERESTIN' DAY, PROFFY?
...I HAVE MUCH TO PONDER...
YOU'LL THINK MORE CLEARLY AFTER YA GET SOME CHOW IN YA!
...TRUE...
The CHOWDOWN POOL.
THE SPEAR-FLING'N-FLANK'RS TRIED THE NEW ROUTINE TODAY!
DID IT WORK?
YES AND NO. IT'S A GOOD OFFENSIVE MANEUVER, BUT WE NEED MORE DISTANCE!
WE NEED A SPEAR THAT'LL FLING FURTHER!
WE'D REALLY APPRECIATE IT IF YA'D TINKER WITH THAT PROBLEM FOR A FEW DAYS!
OKAY! I'LL START TOMORROW!
THIS SPEAR PROJECT WILL KEEP HER MIND OFF MYSTERY PODS FOR A WHILE.
I CAN CONTEMPLATE THE FLOAT FACTOR WHILE I WORK ON THE LONG-DISTANCE SPEAR.

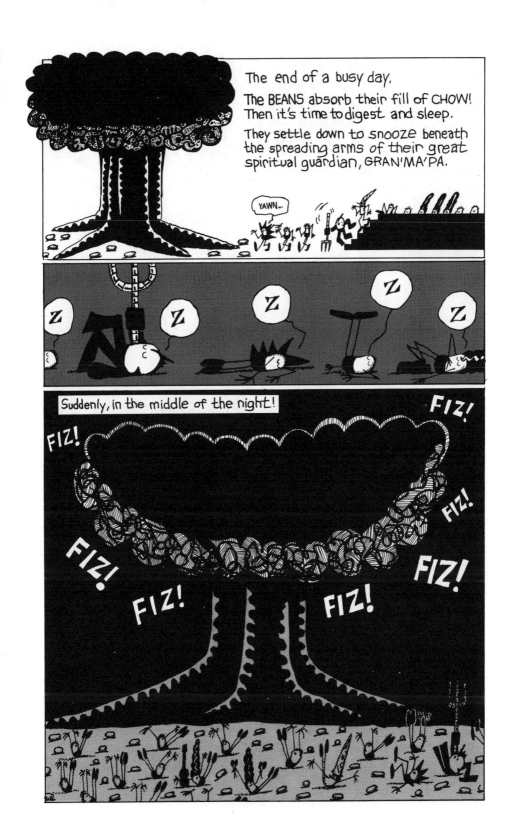

The end of a busy day.

The BEANS absorb their fill of CHOW! Then it's time to digest and sleep.

They settle down to snooze beneath the spreading arms of their great spiritual guardian, GRAN'MA'PA.

YAWN...

Suddenly, in the middle of the night!

FIZ! FIZ! FIZ! FIZ! FIZ! FIZ! FIZ!

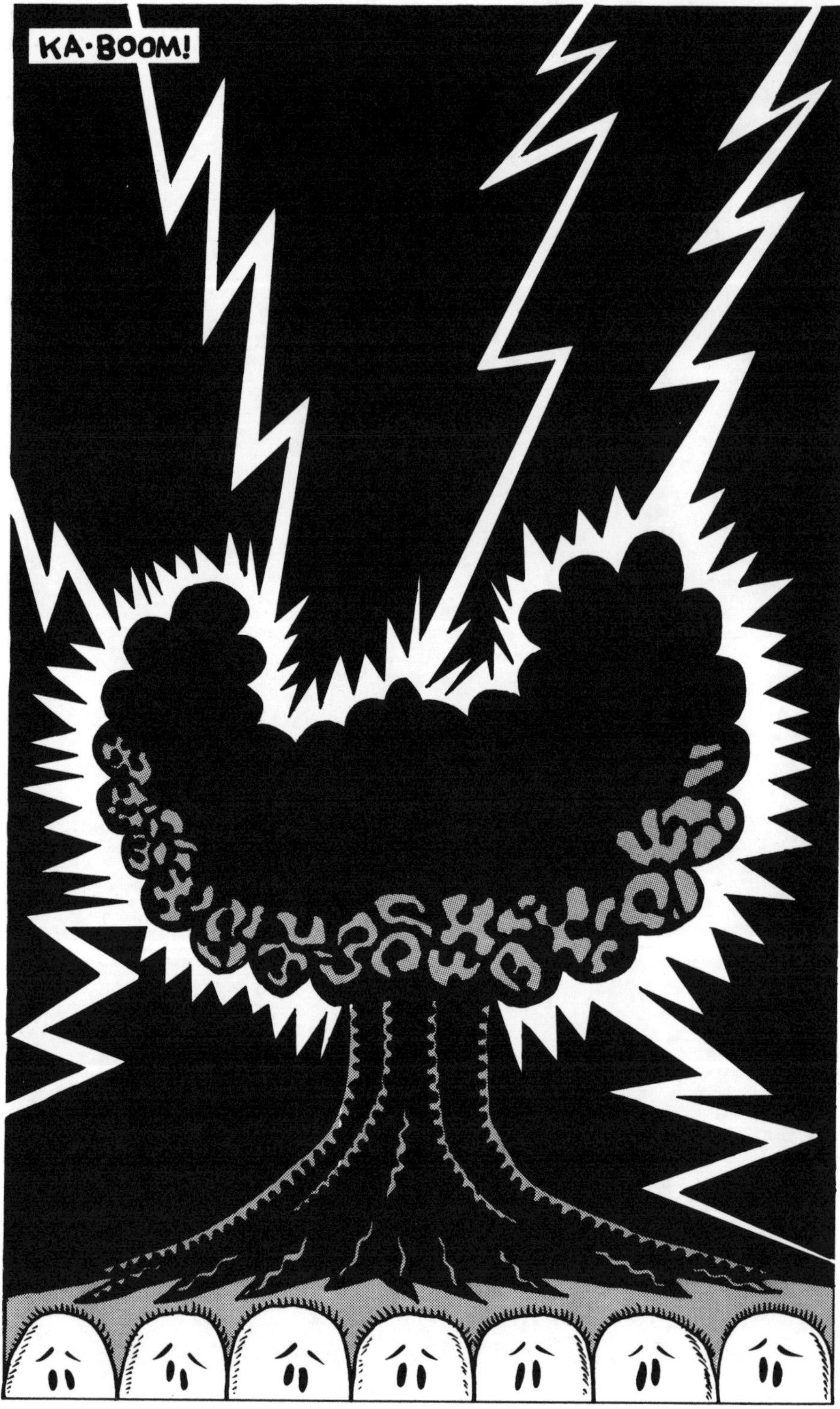
KA-BOOM!

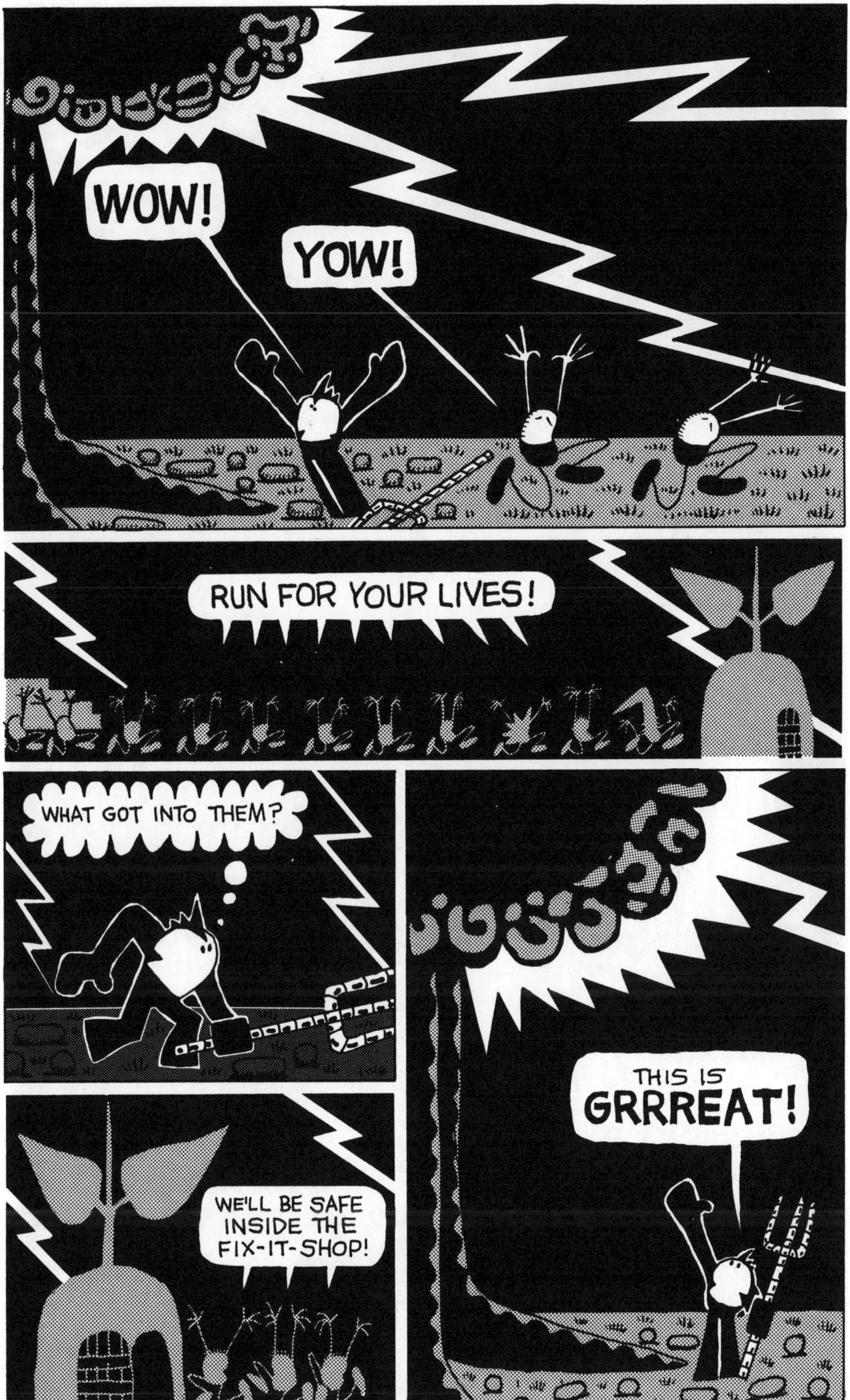
WOW!
YOW!
RUN FOR YOUR LIVES!
WHAT GOT INTO THEM?
WE'LL BE SAFE INSIDE THE FIX-IT-SHOP!
THIS IS GRRREAT!

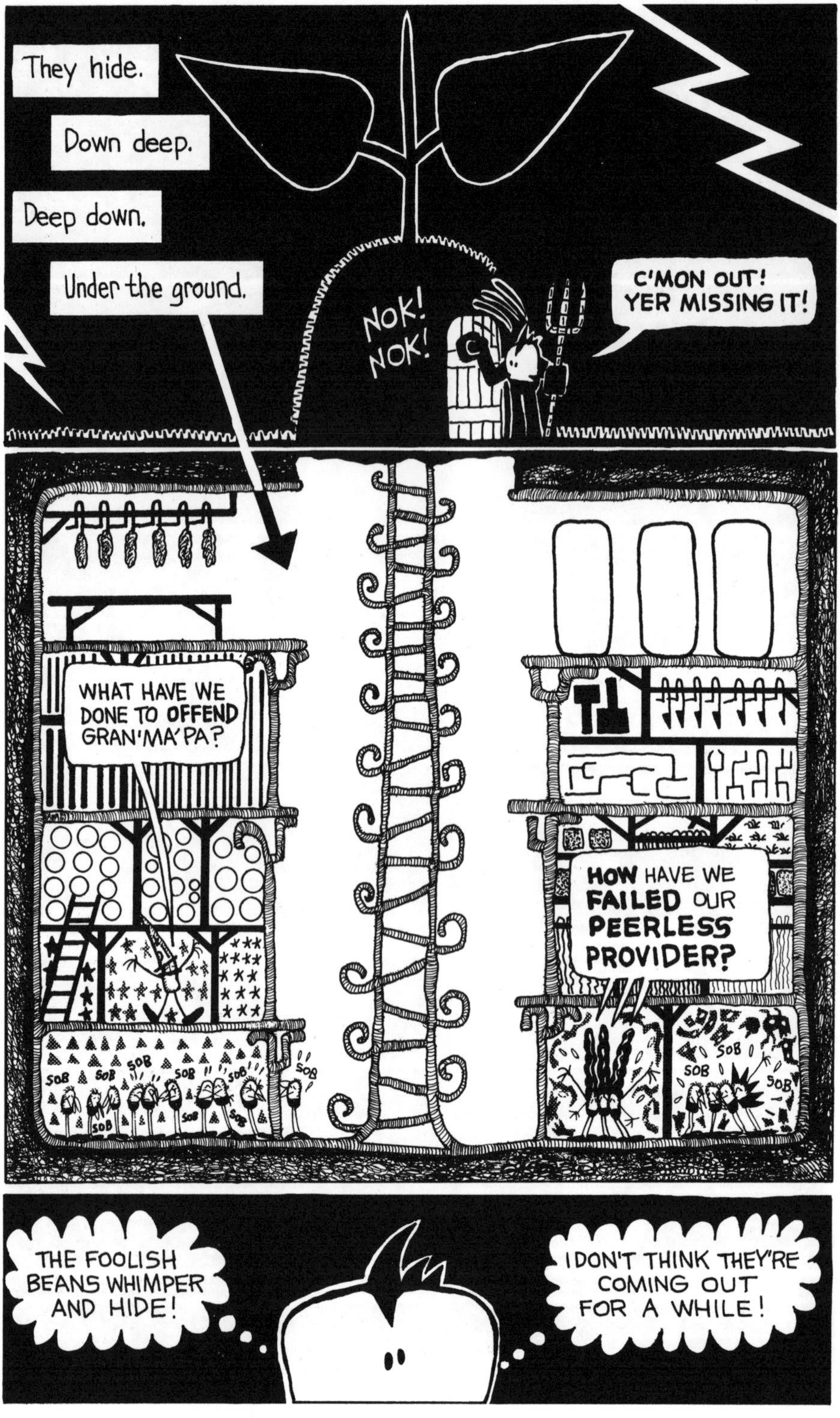
They hide.
Down deep.
Deep down.
Under the ground.
NOK! NOK!
C'MON OUT! YER MISSING IT!
WHAT HAVE WE DONE TO OFFEND GRAN'MA'PA?
HOW HAVE WE FAILED OUR PEERLESS PROVIDER?
SOB SOB SOB SOB SOB SOB SOB SOB
SOB SOB SOB
THE FOOLISH BEANS WHIMPER AND HIDE!
I DON'T THINK THEY'RE COMING OUT FOR A WHILE!

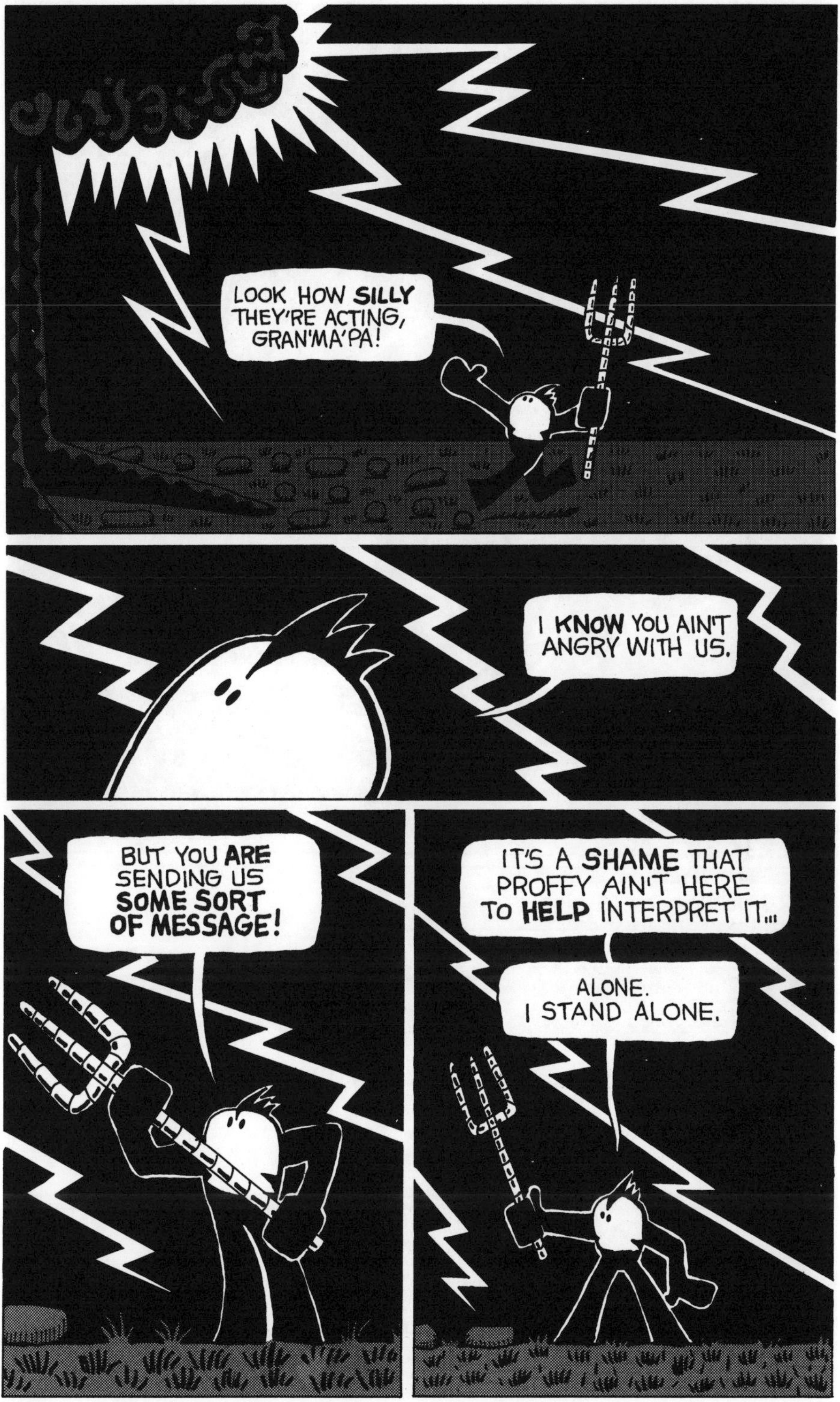
LOOK HOW SILLY THEY'RE ACTING, GRAN'MA'PA!
I KNOW YOU AIN'T ANGRY WITH US.
BUT YOU ARE SENDING US SOME SORT OF MESSAGE!
IT'S A SHAME THAT PROFFY AIN'T HERE TO HELP INTERPRET IT...
ALONE. I STAND ALONE.

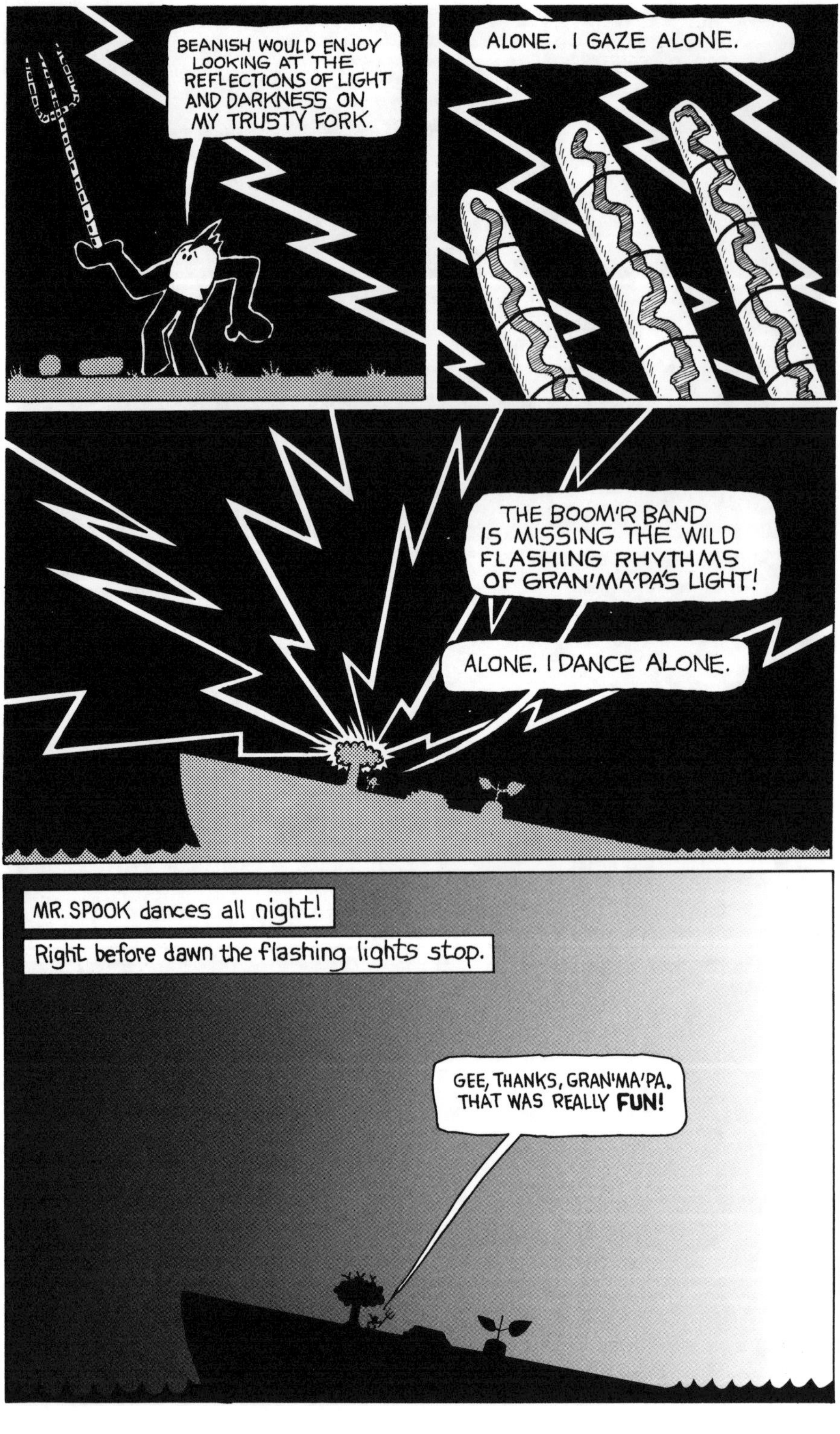
BEANISH WOULD ENJOY LOOKING AT THE REFLECTIONS OF LIGHT AND DARKNESS ON MY TRUSTY FORK.
ALONE. I GAZE ALONE.
THE BOOM'R BAND IS MISSING THE WILD FLASHING RHYTHMS OF GRAN'MA'PA'S LIGHT!
ALONE. I DANCE ALONE.
MR. SPOOK dances all night!
Right before dawn the flashing lights stop.
GEE, THANKS, GRAN'MA'PA. THAT WAS REALLY FUN!

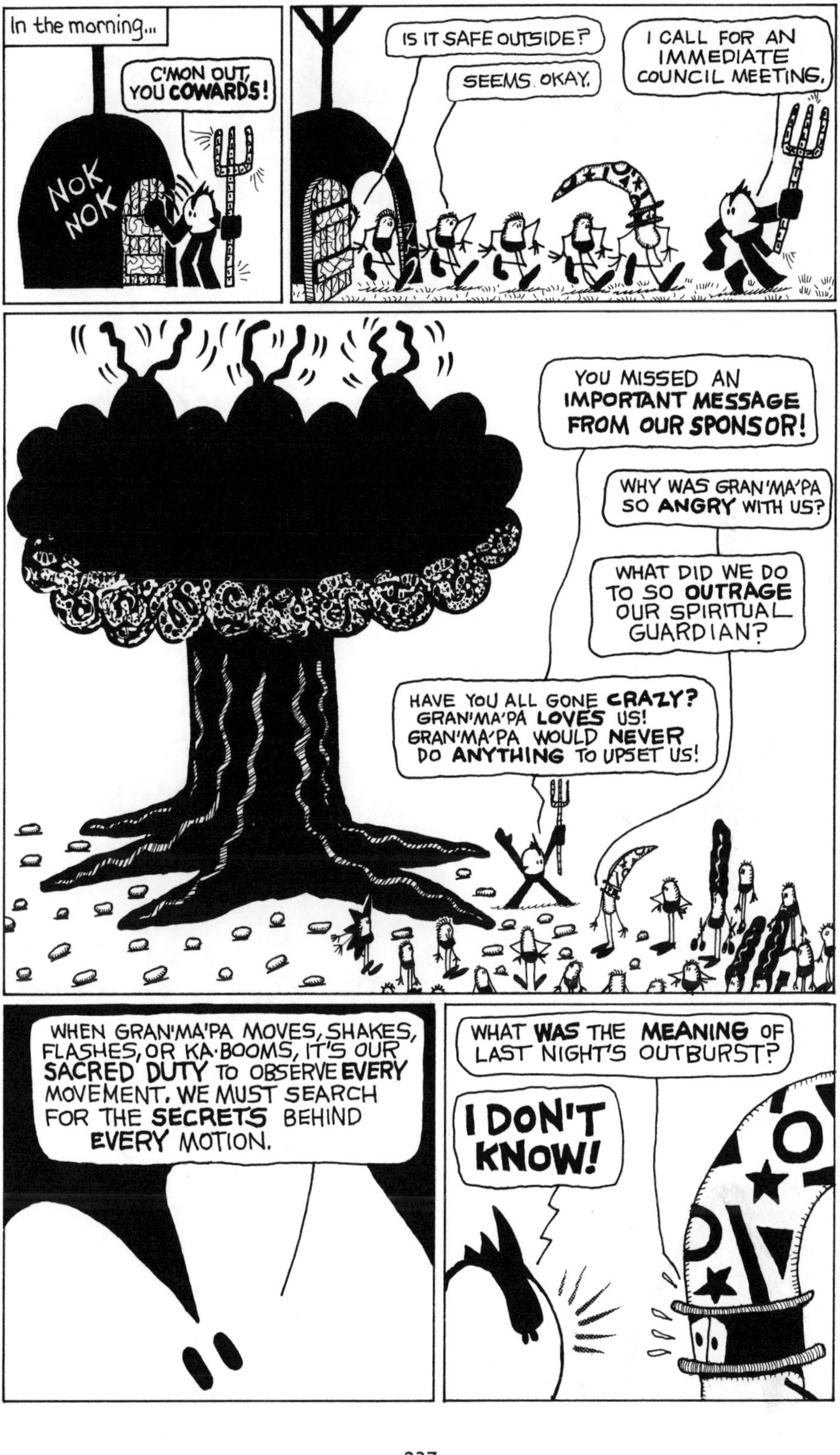
In the morning...
C'MON OUT, YOU COWARDS!
NOK NOK
IS IT SAFE OUTSIDE?
SEEMS OKAY.
I CALL FOR AN IMMEDIATE COUNCIL MEETING.
YOU MISSED AN IMPORTANT MESSAGE FROM OUR SPONSOR!
WHY WAS GRAN'MA'PA SO ANGRY WITH US?
WHAT DID WE DO TO SO OUTRAGE OUR SPIRITUAL GUARDIAN?
HAVE YOU ALL GONE CRAZY? GRAN'MA'PA LOVES US! GRAN'MA'PA WOULD NEVER DO ANYTHING TO UPSET US!
WHEN GRAN'MA'PA MOVES, SHAKES, FLASHES, OR KA·BOOMS, IT'S OUR SACRED DUTY TO OBSERVE EVERY MOVEMENT. WE MUST SEARCH FOR THE SECRETS BEHIND EVERY MOTION.
WHAT WAS THE MEANING OF LAST NIGHT'S OUTBURST?
I DON'T KNOW!

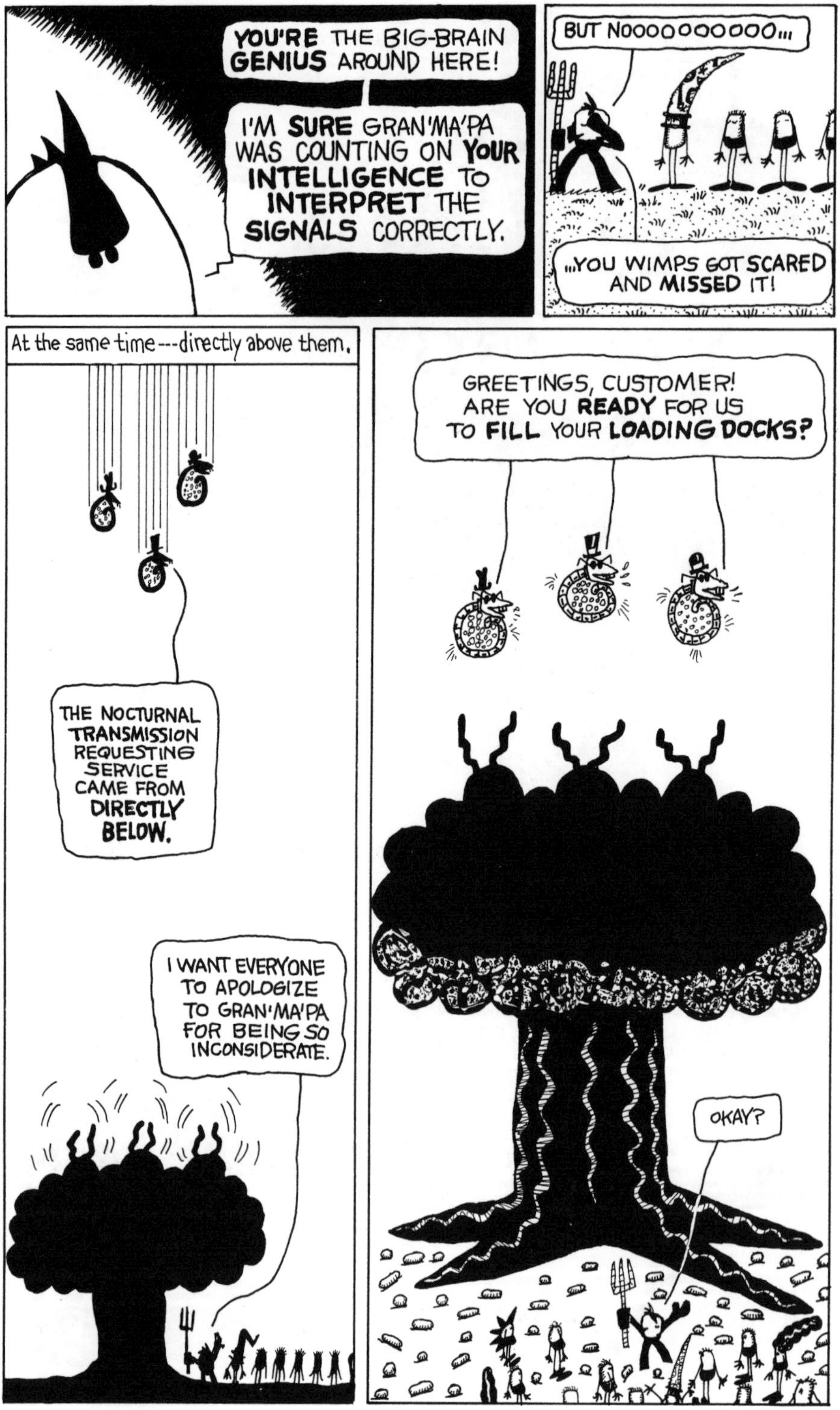
YOU'RE THE BIG-BRAIN GENIUS AROUND HERE!
I'M SURE GRAN'MA'PA WAS COUNTING ON YOUR INTELLIGENCE TO INTERPRET THE SIGNALS CORRECTLY.
BUT NOOOOOOOOOOO...
...YOU WIMPS GOT SCARED AND MISSED IT!
At the same time---directly above them.
THE NOCTURNAL TRANSMISSION REQUESTING SERVICE CAME FROM DIRECTLY BELOW.
I WANT EVERYONE TO APOLOGIZE TO GRAN'MA'PA FOR BEING SO INCONSIDERATE.
GREETINGS, CUSTOMER! ARE YOU READY FOR US TO FILL YOUR LOADING DOCKS?
OKAY?

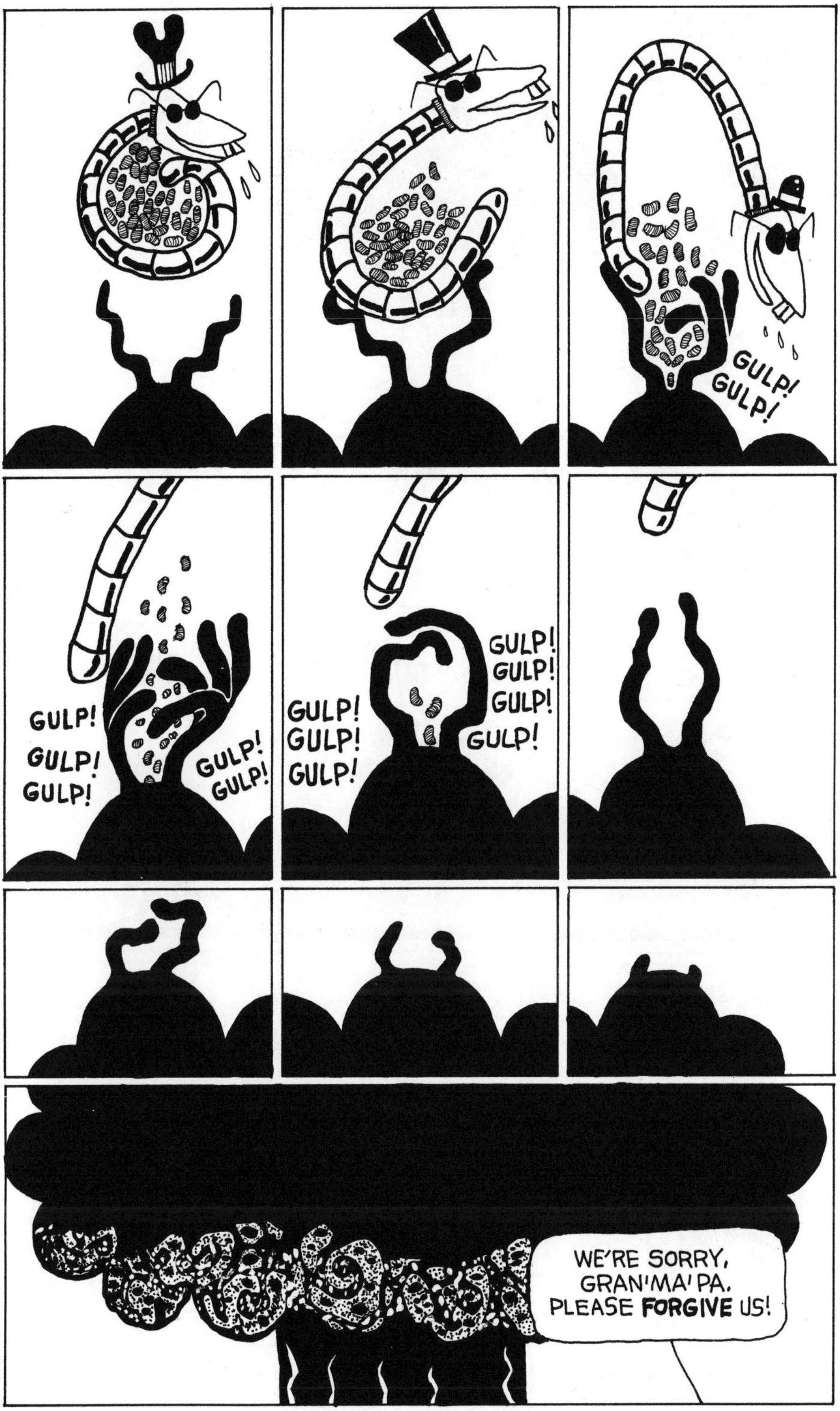
GULP!
GULP!
GULP!
GULP!
GULP!
GULP!
GULP!
GULP!
GULP!
GULP!
GULP!
GULP!
GULP!
GULP!
GULP!
WE'RE SORRY, GRAN'MA'PA. PLEASE FORGIVE US!

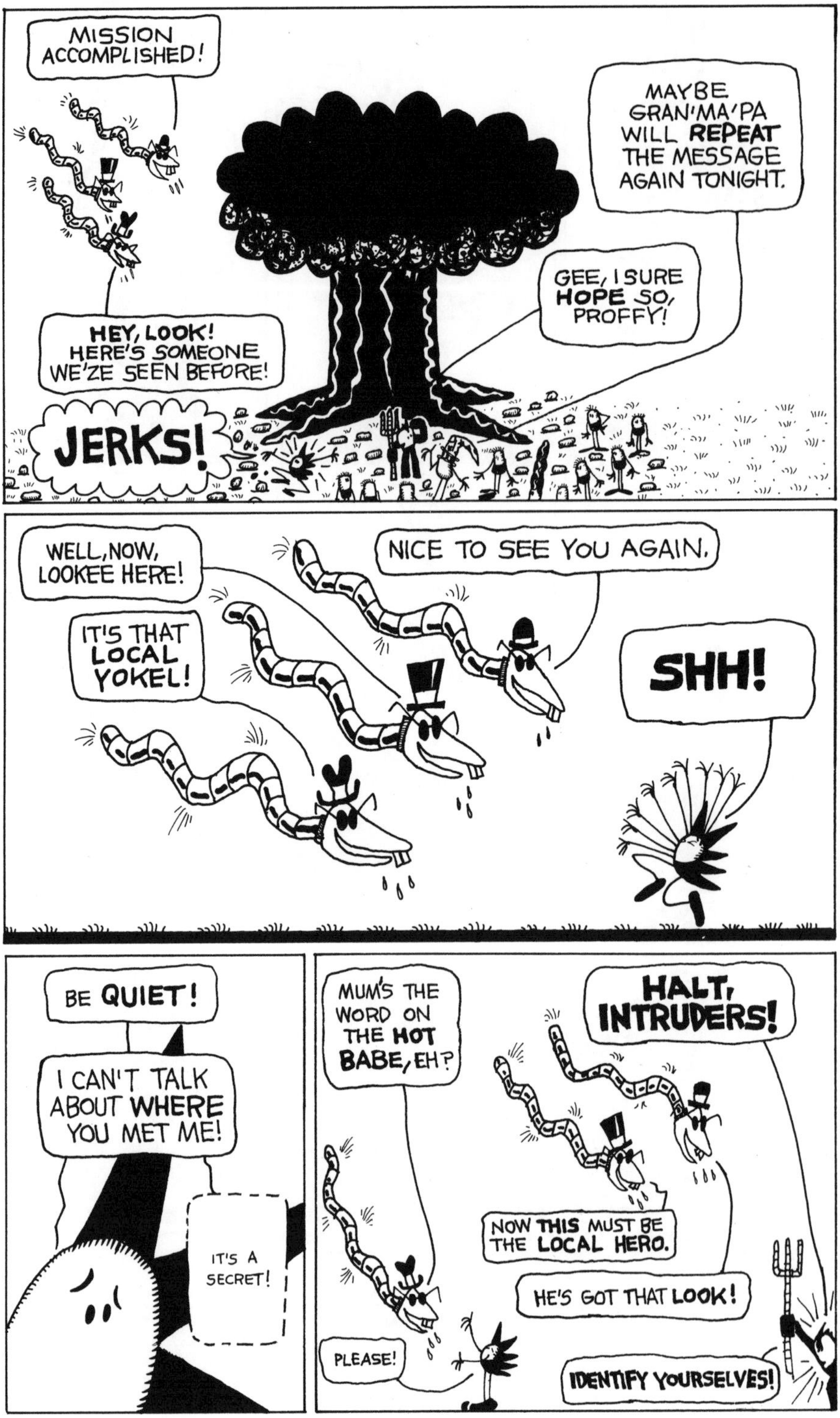
MISSION ACCOMPLISHED!
MAYBE GRAN'MA'PA WILL REPEAT THE MESSAGE AGAIN TONIGHT.
GEE, I SURE HOPE SO, PROFFY!
HEY, LOOK! HERE'S SOMEONE WE'ZE SEEN BEFORE!
JERKS!
WELL, NOW, LOOKEE HERE!
NICE TO SEE YOU AGAIN.
IT'S THAT LOCAL YOKEL!
SHH!
BE QUIET!
I CAN'T TALK ABOUT WHERE YOU MET ME!
IT'S A SECRET!
MUM'S THE WORD ON THE HOT BABE, EH?
HALT, INTRUDERS!
NOW THIS MUST BE THE LOCAL HERO.
HE'S GOT THAT LOOK!
PLEASE!
IDENTIFY YOURSELVES!

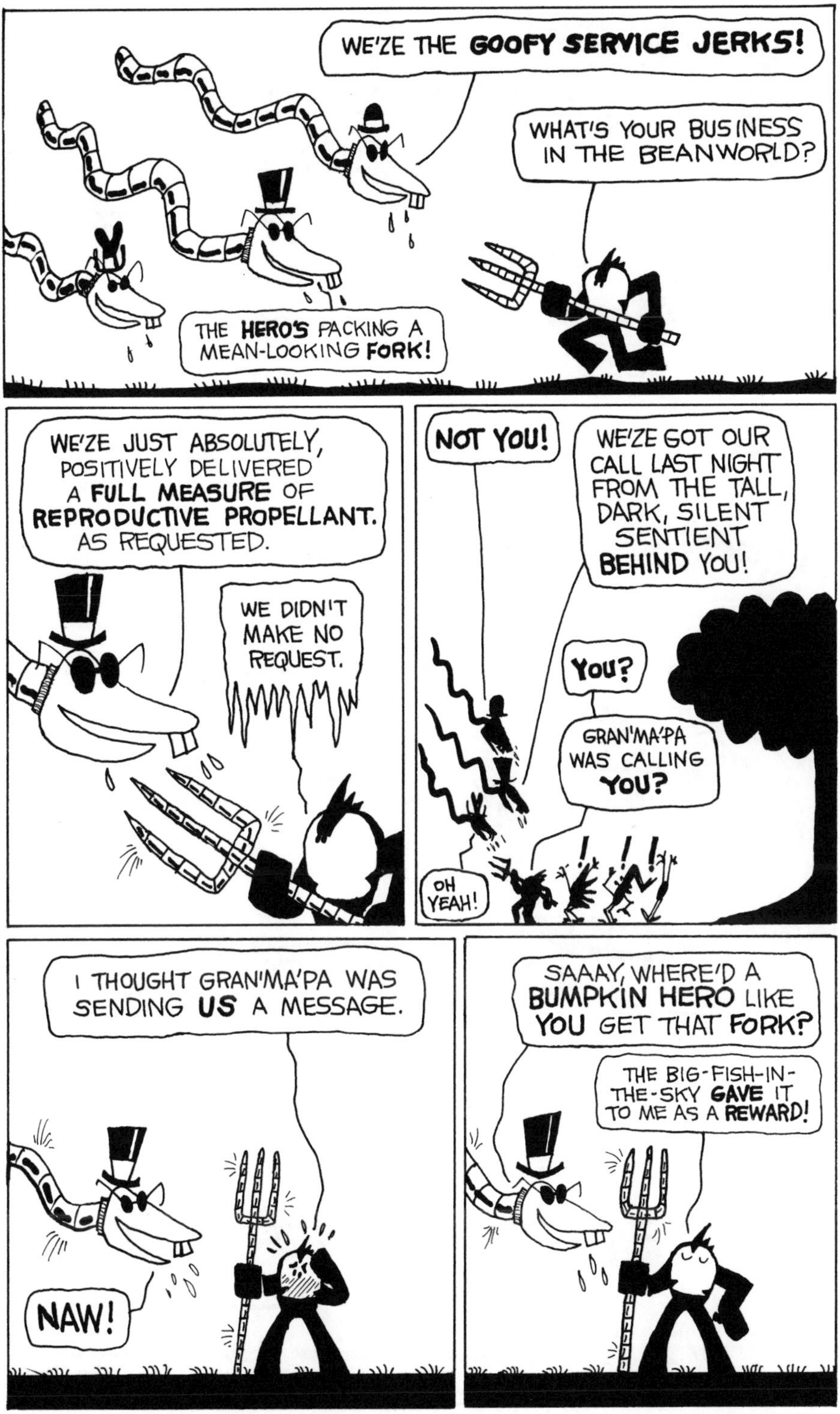
WE'ZE THE GOOFY SERVICE JERKS!
WHAT'S YOUR BUSINESS IN THE BEANWORLD?
THE HERO'S PACKING A MEAN-LOOKING FORK!
WE'ZE JUST ABSOLUTELY, POSITIVELY DELIVERED A FULL MEASURE OF REPRODUCTIVE PROPELLANT. AS REQUESTED.
WE DIDN'T MAKE NO REQUEST.
NOT YOU!
WE'ZE GOT OUR CALL LAST NIGHT FROM THE TALL, DARK, SILENT SENTIENT BEHIND YOU!
YOU?
GRAN'MA'PA WAS CALLING YOU?
OH YEAH!
I THOUGHT GRAN'MA'PA WAS SENDING US A MESSAGE.
NAW!
SAAAY, WHERE'D A BUMPKIN HERO LIKE YOU GET THAT FORK?
THE BIG-FISH-IN-THE-SKY GAVE IT TO ME AS A REWARD!

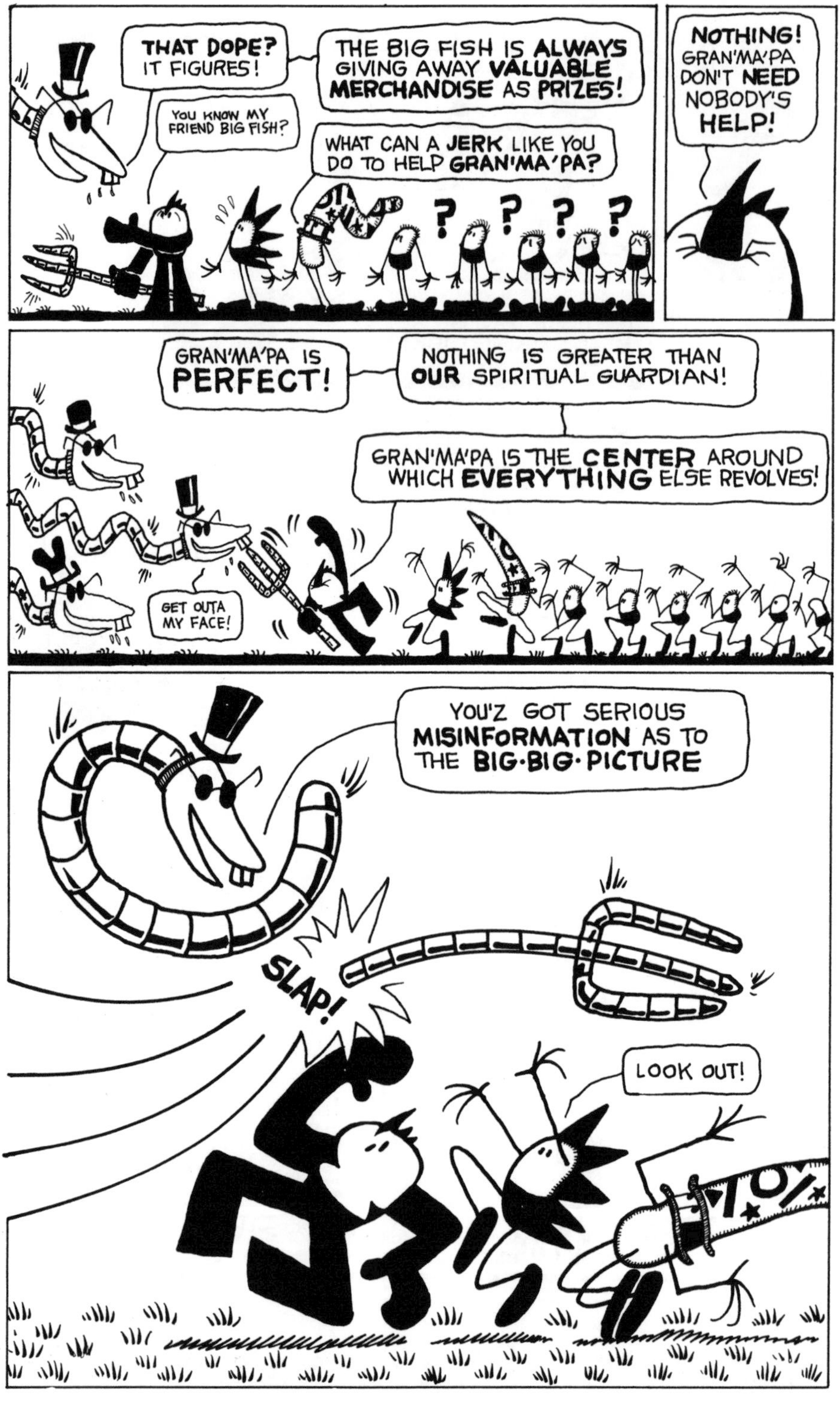
THAT DOPE? IT FIGURES!
THE BIG FISH IS ALWAYS GIVING AWAY VALUABLE MERCHANDISE AS PRIZES!
YOU KNOW MY FRIEND BIG FISH?
WHAT CAN A JERK LIKE YOU DO TO HELP GRAN'MA'PA?
? ? ? ?
NOTHING! GRAN'MA'PA DON'T NEED NOBODY'S HELP!
GRAN'MA'PA IS PERFECT!
NOTHING IS GREATER THAN OUR SPIRITUAL GUARDIAN!
GRAN'MA'PA IS THE CENTER AROUND WHICH EVERYTHING ELSE REVOLVES!
GET OUTA MY FACE!
YOU'Z GOT SERIOUS MISINFORMATION AS TO THE BIG·BIG·PICTURE
SLAP!
LOOK OUT!

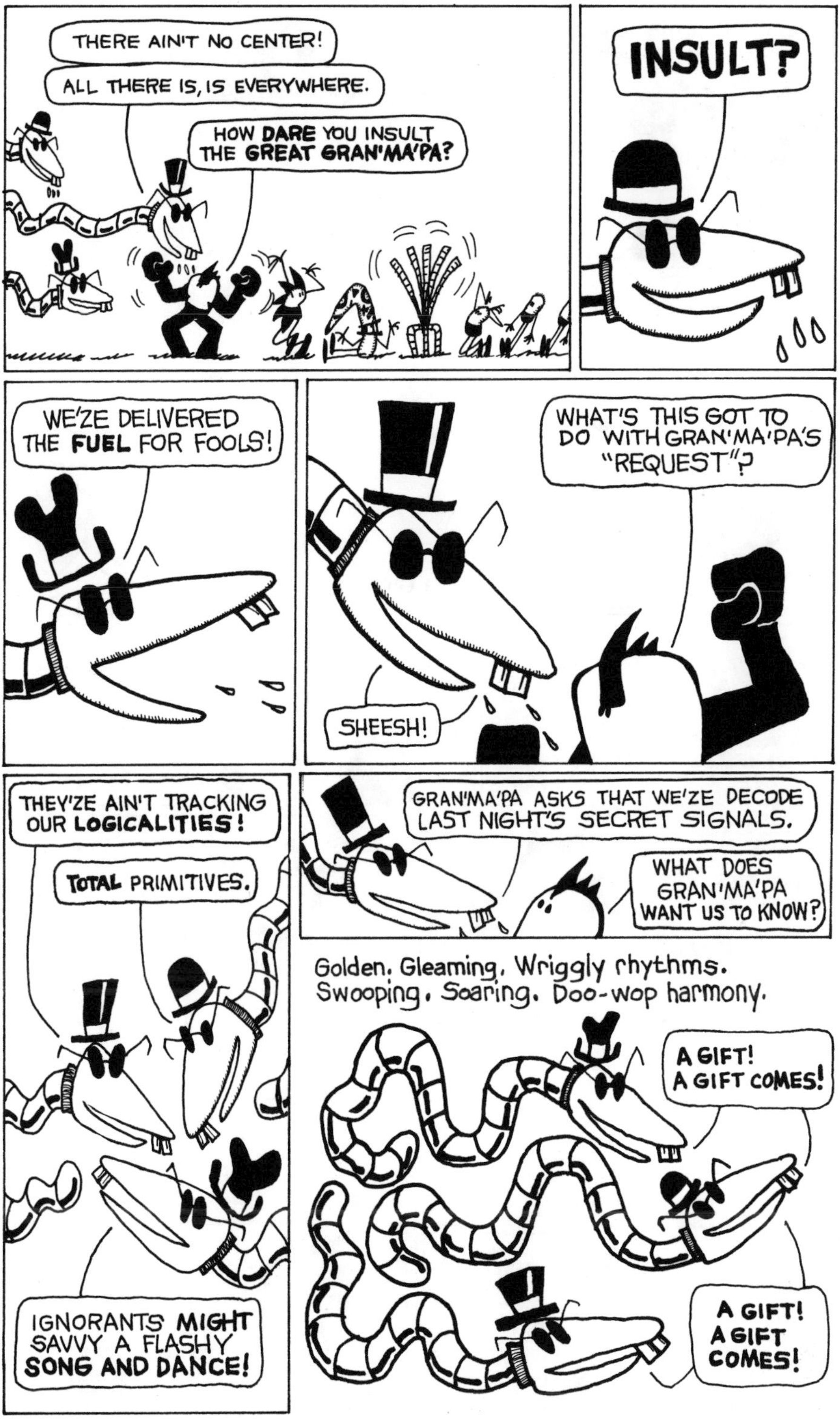
THERE AIN'T NO CENTER!
ALL THERE IS, IS EVERYWHERE.
HOW **DARE** YOU INSULT THE **GREAT GRAN'MA'PA?**
**INSULT?**
WE'ZE DELIVERED THE **FUEL** FOR FOOLS!
WHAT'S THIS GOT TO DO WITH GRAN'MA'PA'S "REQUEST"?
SHEESH!
THEY'ZE AIN'T TRACKING OUR **LOGICALITIES!**
**TOTAL** PRIMITIVES.
IGNORANTS **MIGHT** SAVVY A FLASHY **SONG AND DANCE!**
GRAN'MA'PA ASKS THAT WE'ZE DECODE LAST NIGHT'S SECRET SIGNALS.
WHAT DOES GRAN'MA'PA WANT US TO KNOW?
Golden. Gleaming. Wriggly rhythms.
Swooping. Soaring. Doo-wop harmony.
**A GIFT! A GIFT COMES!**
**A GIFT! A GIFT COMES!**

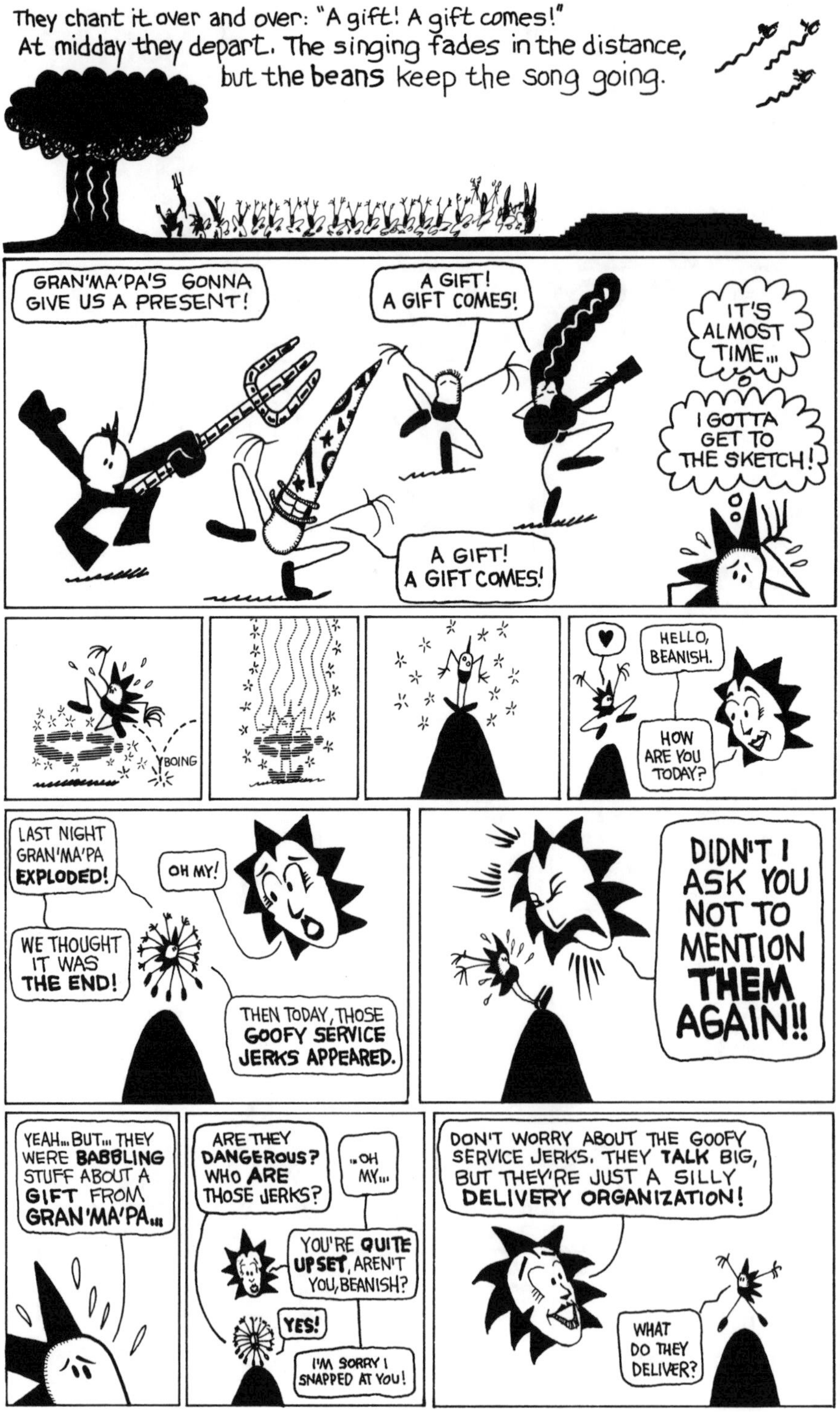
They chant it over and over: "A gift! A gift comes!"
At midday they depart. The singing fades in the distance, but the beans keep the song going.
GRAN'MA'PA'S GONNA GIVE US A PRESENT!
A GIFT! A GIFT COMES!
A GIFT! A GIFT COMES!
IT'S ALMOST TIME...
I GOTTA GET TO THE SKETCH!
BOING
HELLO, BEANISH.
HOW ARE YOU TODAY?
LAST NIGHT GRAN'MA'PA EXPLODED!
OH MY!
WE THOUGHT IT WAS THE END!
THEN TODAY, THOSE GOOFY SERVICE JERKS APPEARED.
DIDN'T I ASK YOU NOT TO MENTION THEM AGAIN!!
YEAH... BUT... THEY WERE BABBLING STUFF ABOUT A GIFT FROM GRAN'MA'PA...
ARE THEY DANGEROUS? WHO ARE THOSE JERKS?
...OH MY...
YOU'RE QUITE UPSET, AREN'T YOU, BEANISH?
YES!
I'M SORRY I SNAPPED AT YOU!
DON'T WORRY ABOUT THE GOOFY SERVICE JERKS. THEY TALK BIG, BUT THEY'RE JUST A SILLY DELIVERY ORGANIZATION!
WHAT DO THEY DELIVER?

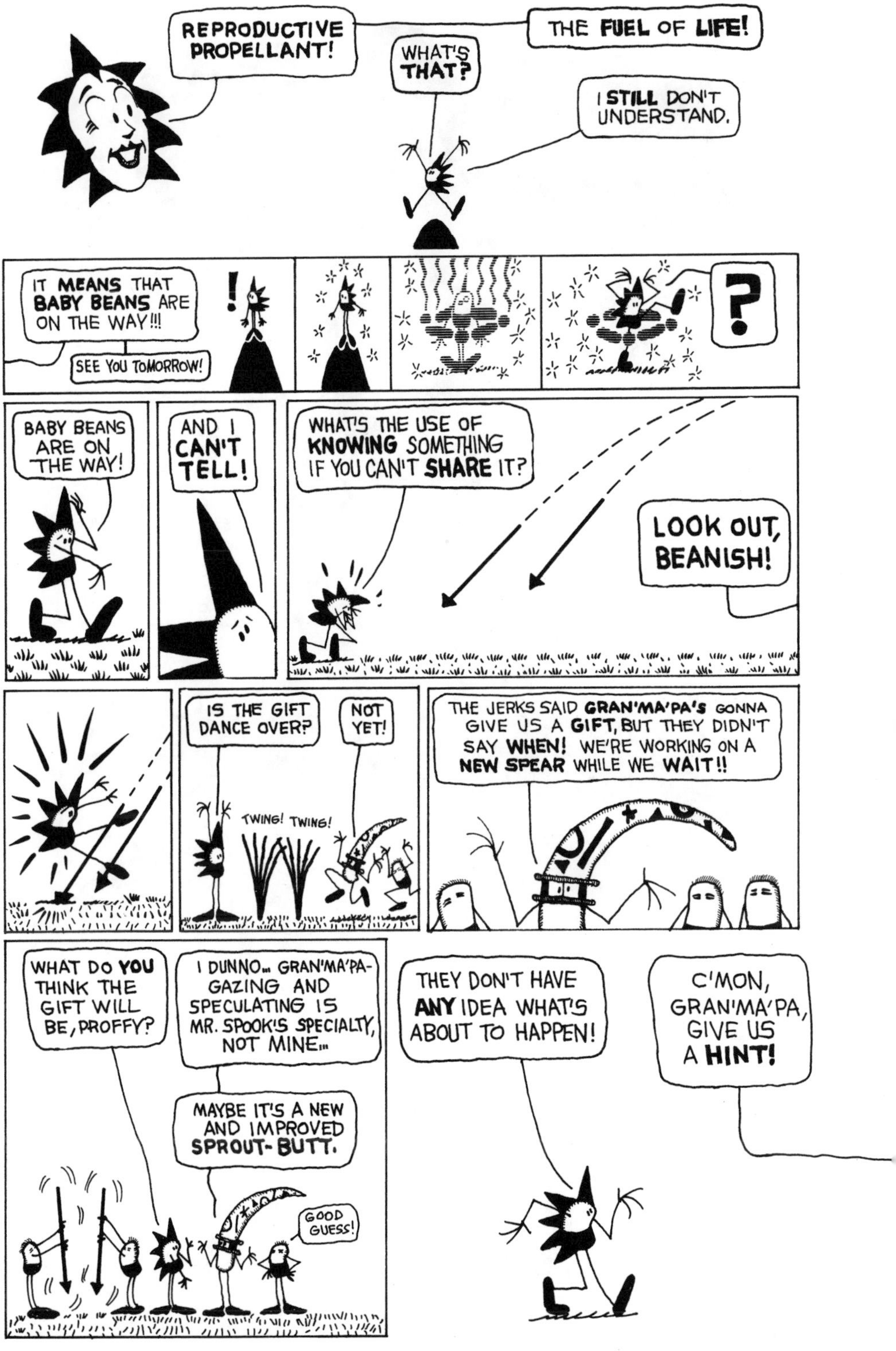
REPRODUCTIVE PROPELLANT!
WHAT'S THAT?
THE FUEL OF LIFE!
I STILL DON'T UNDERSTAND.
IT MEANS THAT BABY BEANS ARE ON THE WAY!!!
SEE YOU TOMORROW!
!
?
BABY BEANS ARE ON THE WAY!
AND I CAN'T TELL!
WHAT'S THE USE OF KNOWING SOMETHING IF YOU CAN'T SHARE IT?
LOOK OUT, BEANISH!
IS THE GIFT DANCE OVER?
NOT YET!
TWING! TWING!
THE JERKS SAID GRAN'MA'PA'S GONNA GIVE US A GIFT, BUT THEY DIDN'T SAY WHEN! WE'RE WORKING ON A NEW SPEAR WHILE WE WAIT!!
WHAT DO YOU THINK THE GIFT WILL BE, PROFFY?
I DUNNO... GRAN'MA'PA-GAZING AND SPECULATING IS MR. SPOOK'S SPECIALTY, NOT MINE...
MAYBE IT'S A NEW AND IMPROVED SPROUT-BUTT.
GOOD GUESS!
THEY DON'T HAVE ANY IDEA WHAT'S ABOUT TO HAPPEN!
C'MON, GRAN'MA'PA, GIVE US A HINT!

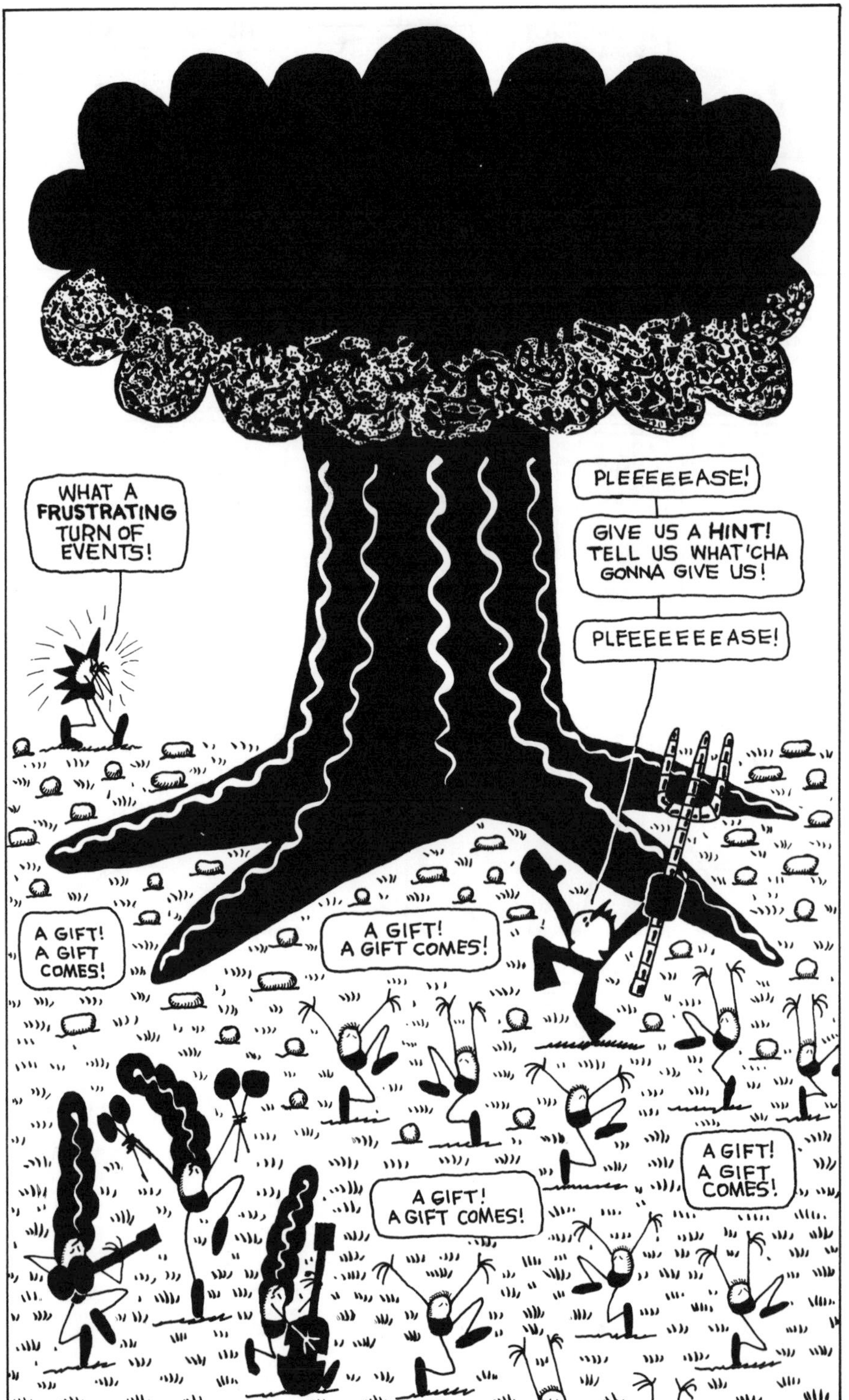
WHAT A FRUSTRATING TURN OF EVENTS!
PLEEEEEEASE!
GIVE US A HINT! TELL US WHAT'CHA GONNA GIVE US!
PLEEEEEEEEASE!
A GIFT! A GIFT COMES!
A GIFT! A GIFT COMES!
A GIFT! A GIFT COMES!
A GIFT! A GIFT COMES!
A GIFT! A GIFT COMES!

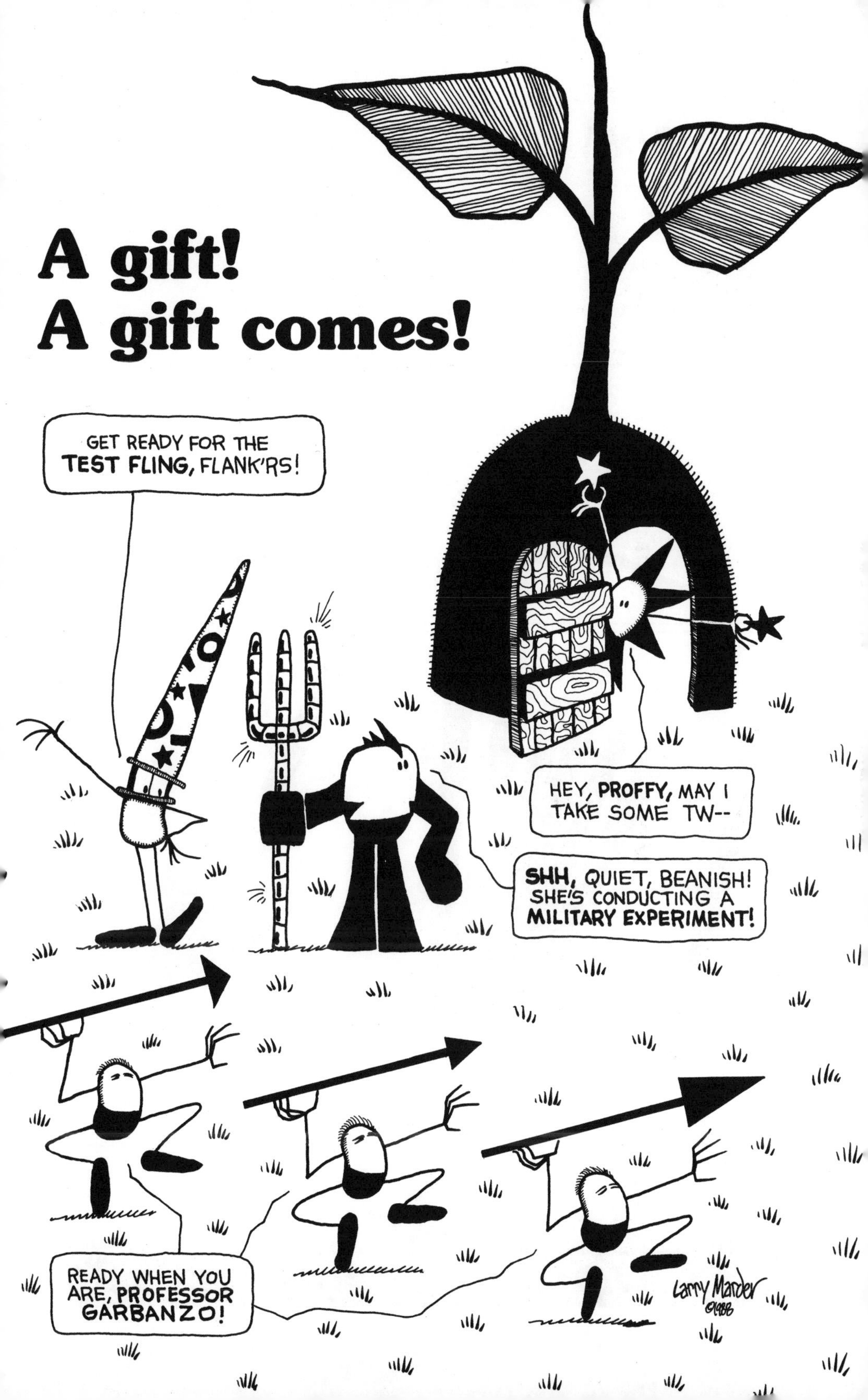
A gift!
A gift comes!
GET READY FOR THE TEST FLING, FLANK'RS!
HEY, PROFFY, MAY I TAKE SOME TW--
SHH, QUIET, BEANISH! SHE'S CONDUCTING A MILITARY EXPERIMENT!
READY WHEN YOU ARE, PROFESSOR GARBANZO!
Larry Marder ©1988

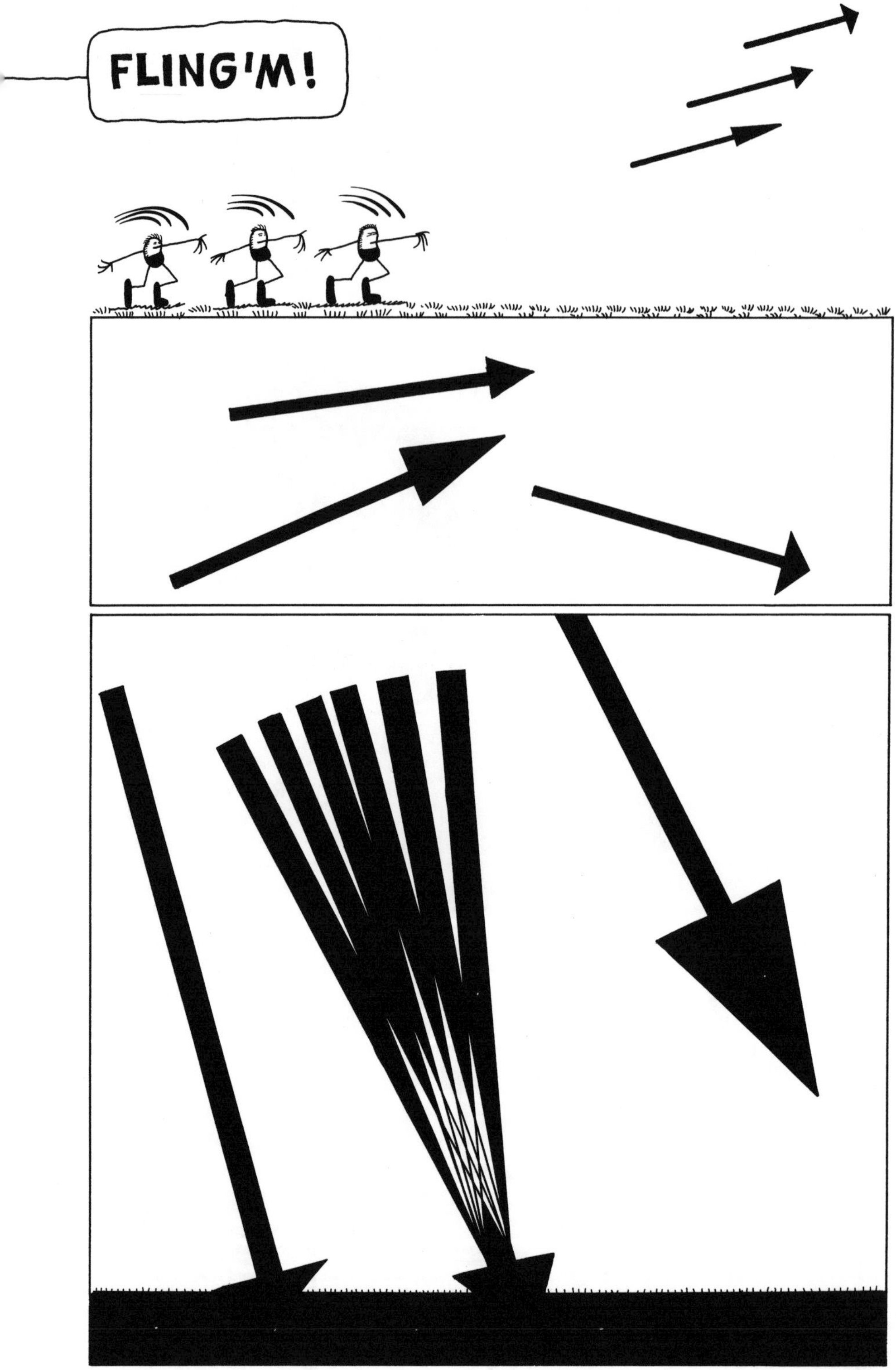
FLING'M!

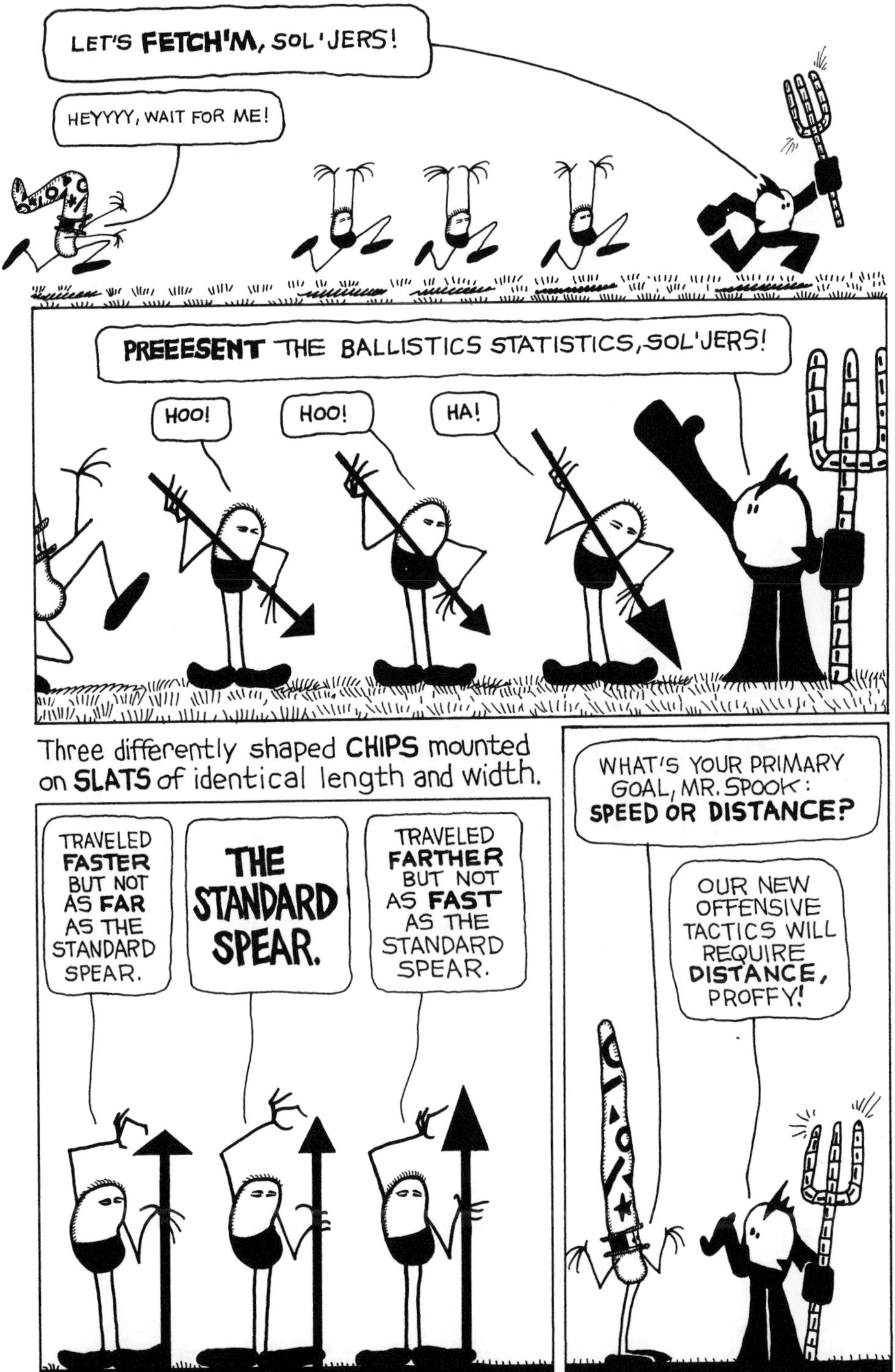
LET'S FETCH'M, SOL'JERS!
HEYYYY, WAIT FOR ME!
PREEESENT THE BALLISTICS STATISTICS, SOL'JERS!
HOO!
HOO!
HA!
Three differently shaped CHIPS mounted on SLATS of identical length and width.
TRAVELED FASTER BUT NOT AS FAR AS THE STANDARD SPEAR.
THE STANDARD SPEAR.
TRAVELED FARTHER BUT NOT AS FAST AS THE STANDARD SPEAR.
WHAT'S YOUR PRIMARY GOAL, MR. SPOOK: SPEED OR DISTANCE?
OUR NEW OFFENSIVE TACTICS WILL REQUIRE DISTANCE, PROFFY!

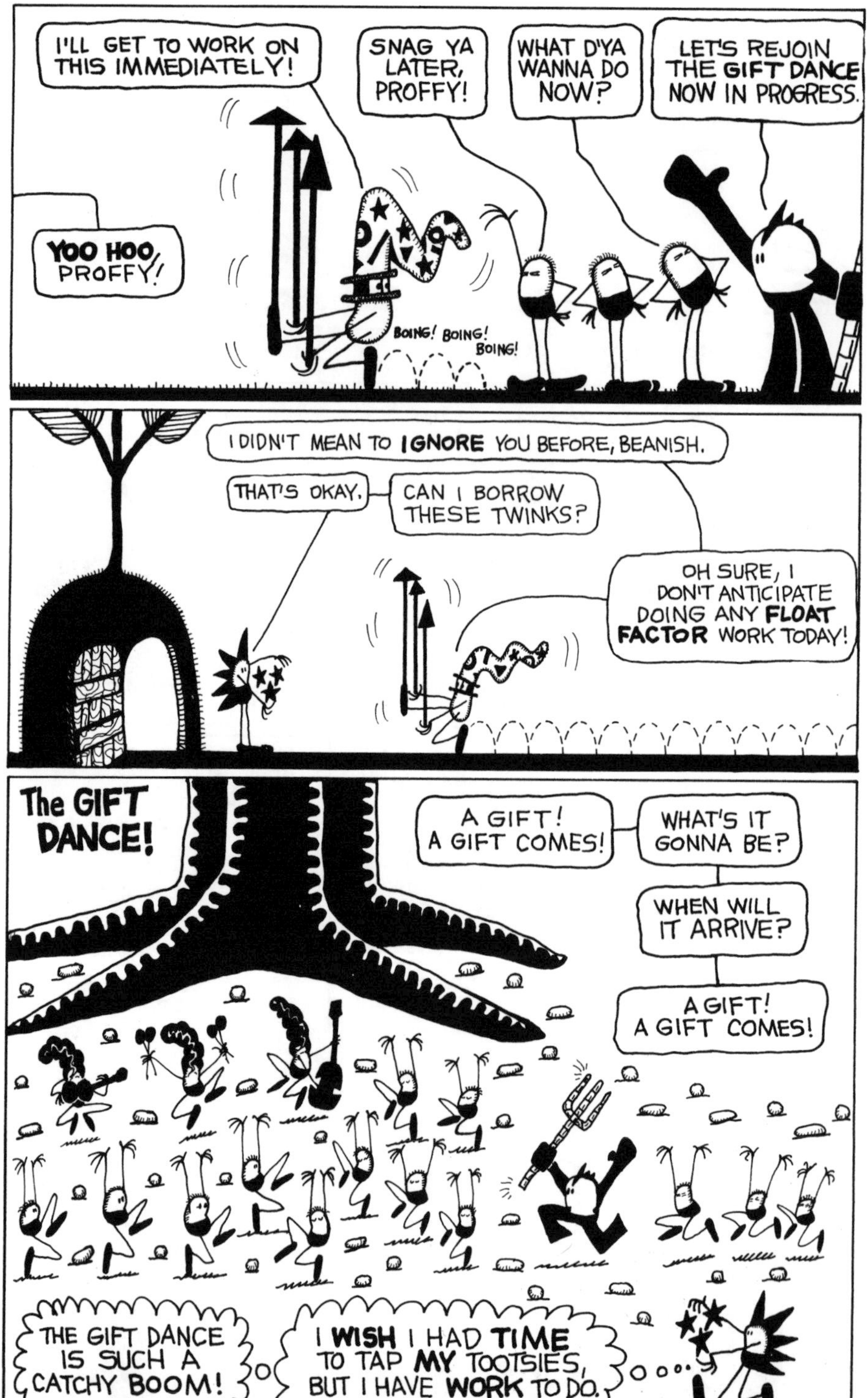

I'LL GET TO WORK ON THIS IMMEDIATELY!
SNAG YA LATER, PROFFY!
WHAT D'YA WANNA DO NOW?
LET'S REJOIN THE GIFT DANCE NOW IN PROGRESS.
YOO HOO, PROFFY!
BOING! BOING! BOING!
I DIDN'T MEAN TO IGNORE YOU BEFORE, BEANISH.
THAT'S OKAY.
CAN I BORROW THESE TWINKS?
OH SURE, I DON'T ANTICIPATE DOING ANY FLOAT FACTOR WORK TODAY!
The GIFT DANCE!
A GIFT! A GIFT COMES!
WHAT'S IT GONNA BE?
WHEN WILL IT ARRIVE?
A GIFT! A GIFT COMES!
THE GIFT DANCE IS SUCH A CATCHY BOOM!
I WISH I HAD TIME TO TAP MY TOOTSIES, BUT I HAVE WORK TO DO.

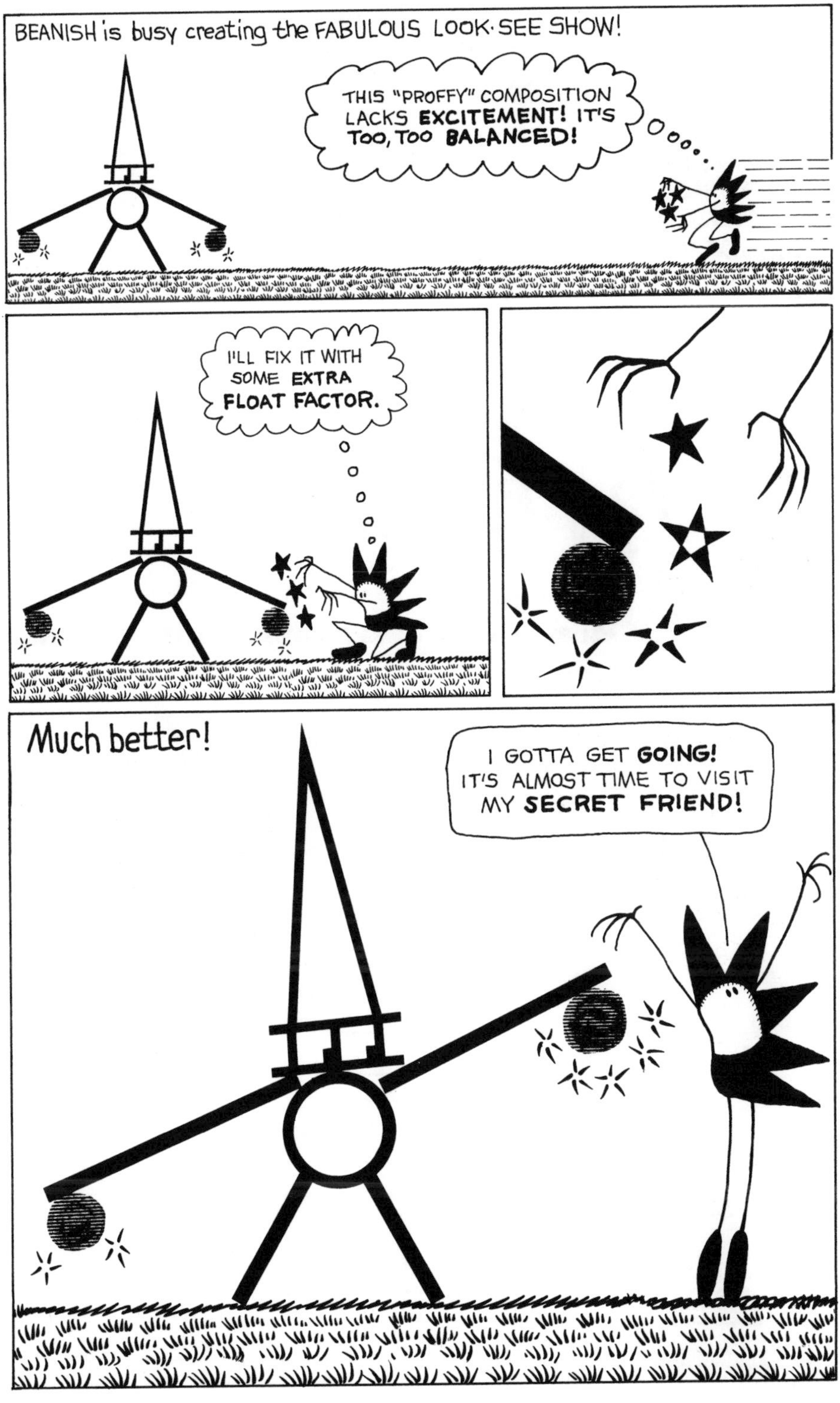
BEANISH is busy creating the FABULOUS LOOK·SEE SHOW!
THIS "PROFFY" COMPOSITION LACKS EXCITEMENT! IT'S TOO, TOO BALANCED!
I'LL FIX IT WITH SOME EXTRA FLOAT FACTOR.
Much better!
I GOTTA GET GOING! IT'S ALMOST TIME TO VISIT MY SECRET FRIEND!

Every day, at midday, **BEANISH** stands inside the "secret sketch" and travels to an unknown territory where he meets a secret friend.

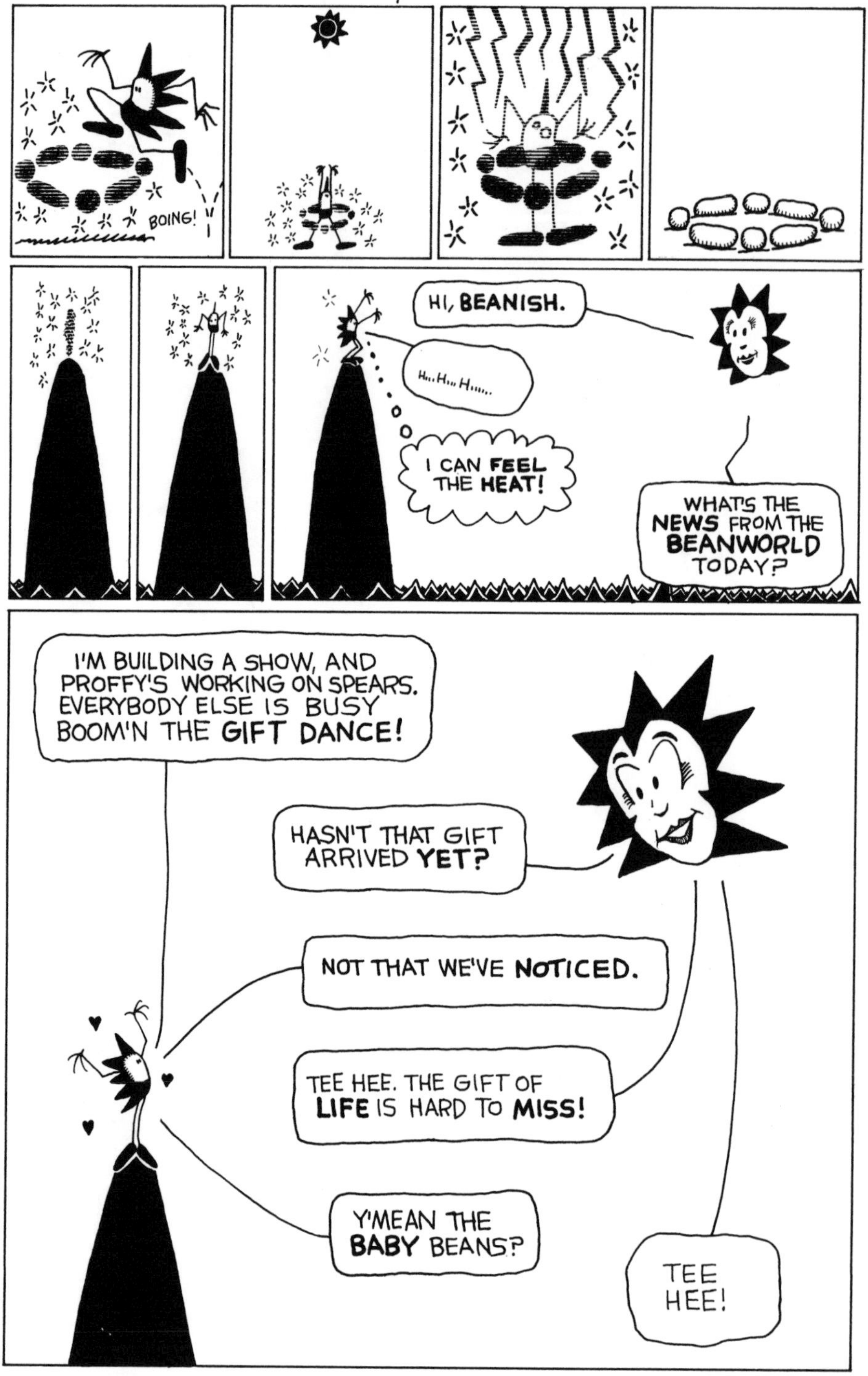
BOING!
HI, BEANISH.
H... H... H.....
I CAN FEEL THE HEAT!
WHAT'S THE NEWS FROM THE BEANWORLD TODAY?
I'M BUILDING A SHOW, AND PROFFY'S WORKING ON SPEARS. EVERYBODY ELSE IS BUSY BOOM'N THE GIFT DANCE!
HASN'T THAT GIFT ARRIVED YET?
NOT THAT WE'VE NOTICED.
TEE HEE. THE GIFT OF LIFE IS HARD TO MISS!
Y'MEAN THE BABY BEANS?
TEE HEE!

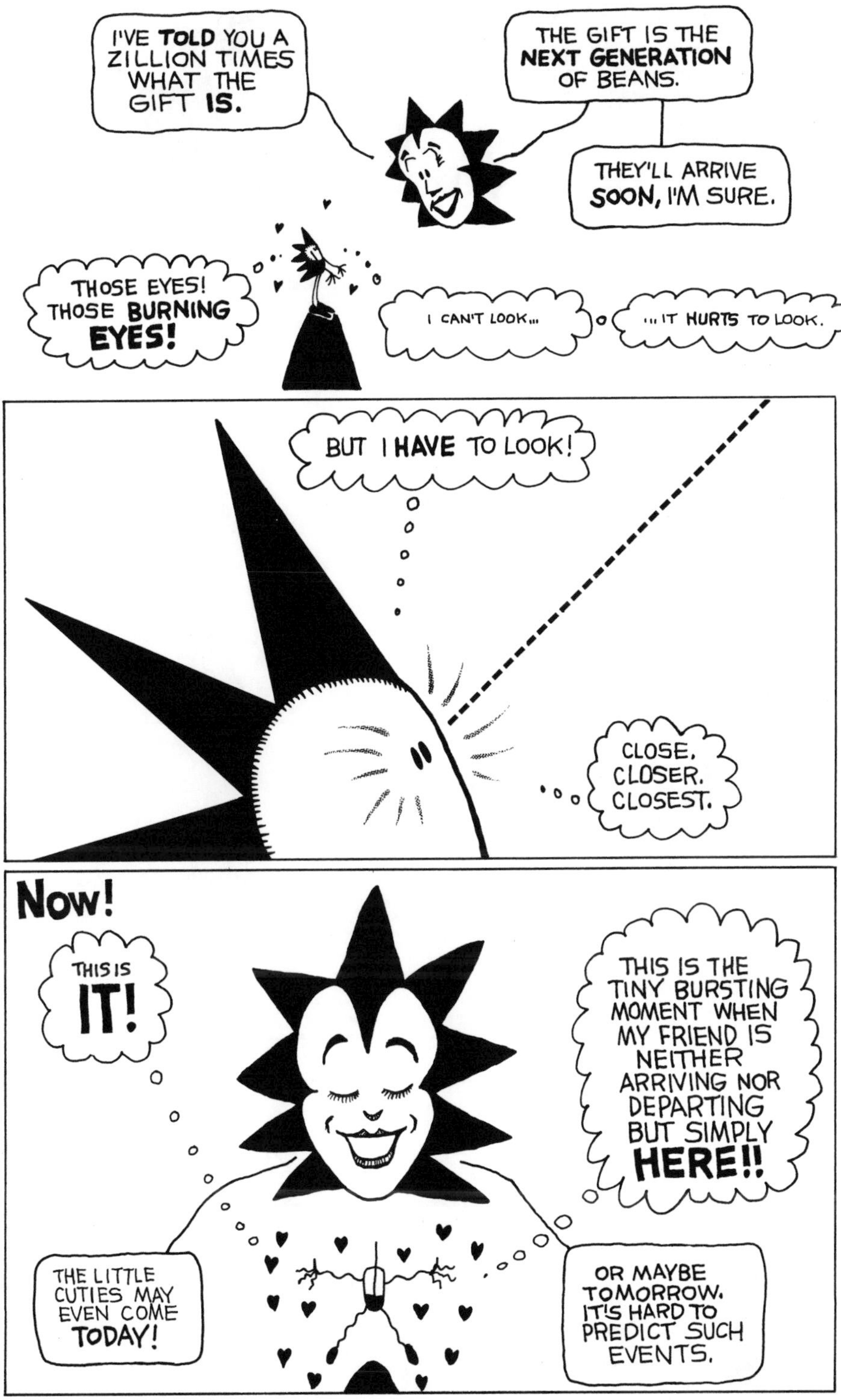
I'VE TOLD YOU A ZILLION TIMES WHAT THE GIFT IS.
THE GIFT IS THE NEXT GENERATION OF BEANS.
THEY'LL ARRIVE SOON, I'M SURE.
THOSE EYES! THOSE BURNING EYES!
I CAN'T LOOK...
...IT HURTS TO LOOK.
BUT I HAVE TO LOOK!
CLOSE. CLOSER. CLOSEST.
Now!
THIS IS IT!
THIS IS THE TINY BURSTING MOMENT WHEN MY FRIEND IS NEITHER ARRIVING NOR DEPARTING BUT SIMPLY HERE!!
THE LITTLE CUTIES MAY EVEN COME TODAY!
OR MAYBE TOMORROW. IT'S HARD TO PREDICT SUCH EVENTS.

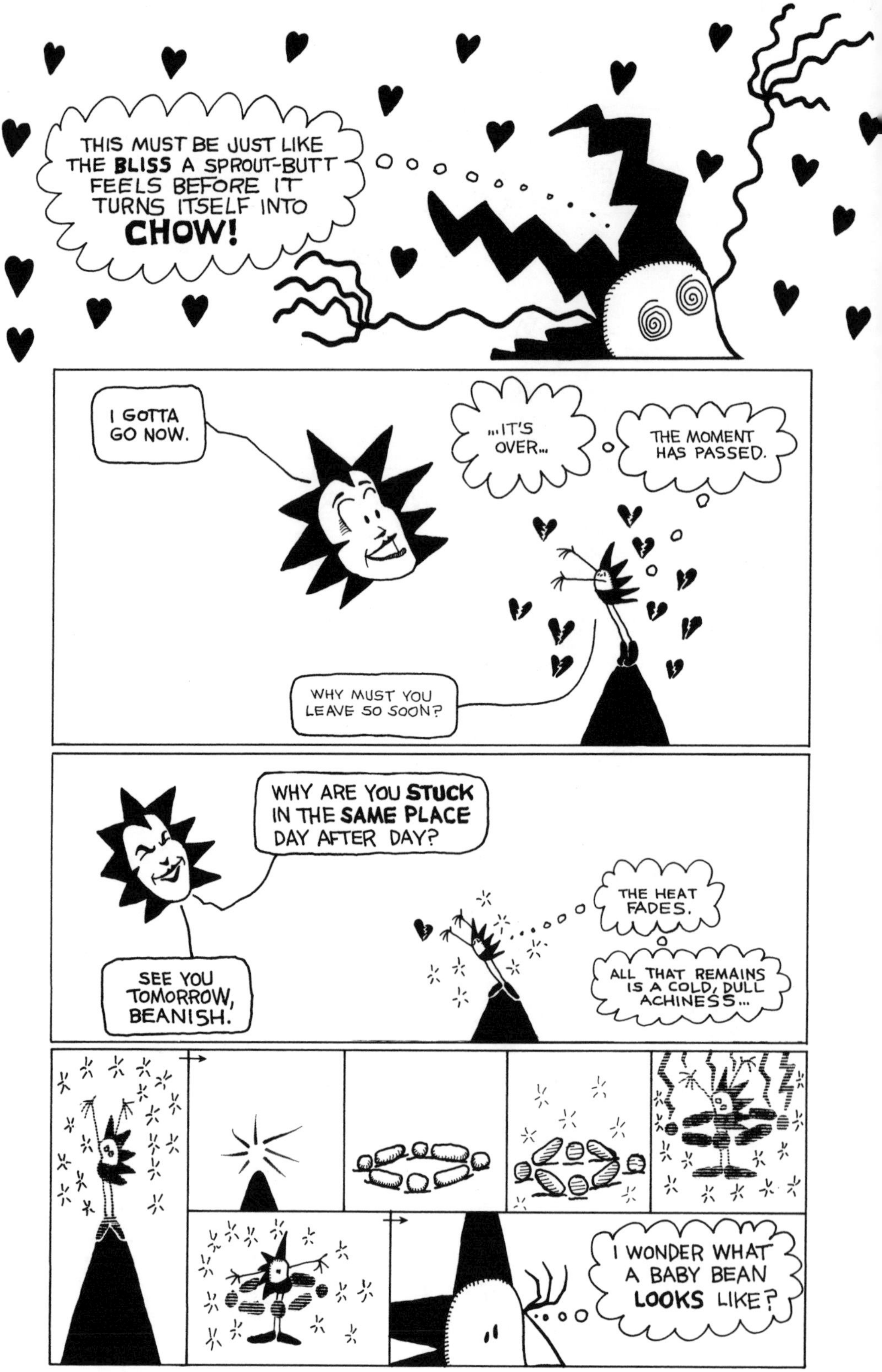
THIS MUST BE JUST LIKE THE BLISS A SPROUT-BUTT FEELS BEFORE IT TURNS ITSELF INTO CHOW!
I GOTTA GO NOW.
...IT'S OVER...
THE MOMENT HAS PASSED.
WHY MUST YOU LEAVE SO SOON?
WHY ARE YOU STUCK IN THE SAME PLACE DAY AFTER DAY?
SEE YOU TOMORROW, BEANISH.
THE HEAT FADES.
ALL THAT REMAINS IS A COLD, DULL ACHINESS...
I WONDER WHAT A BABY BEAN LOOKS LIKE?

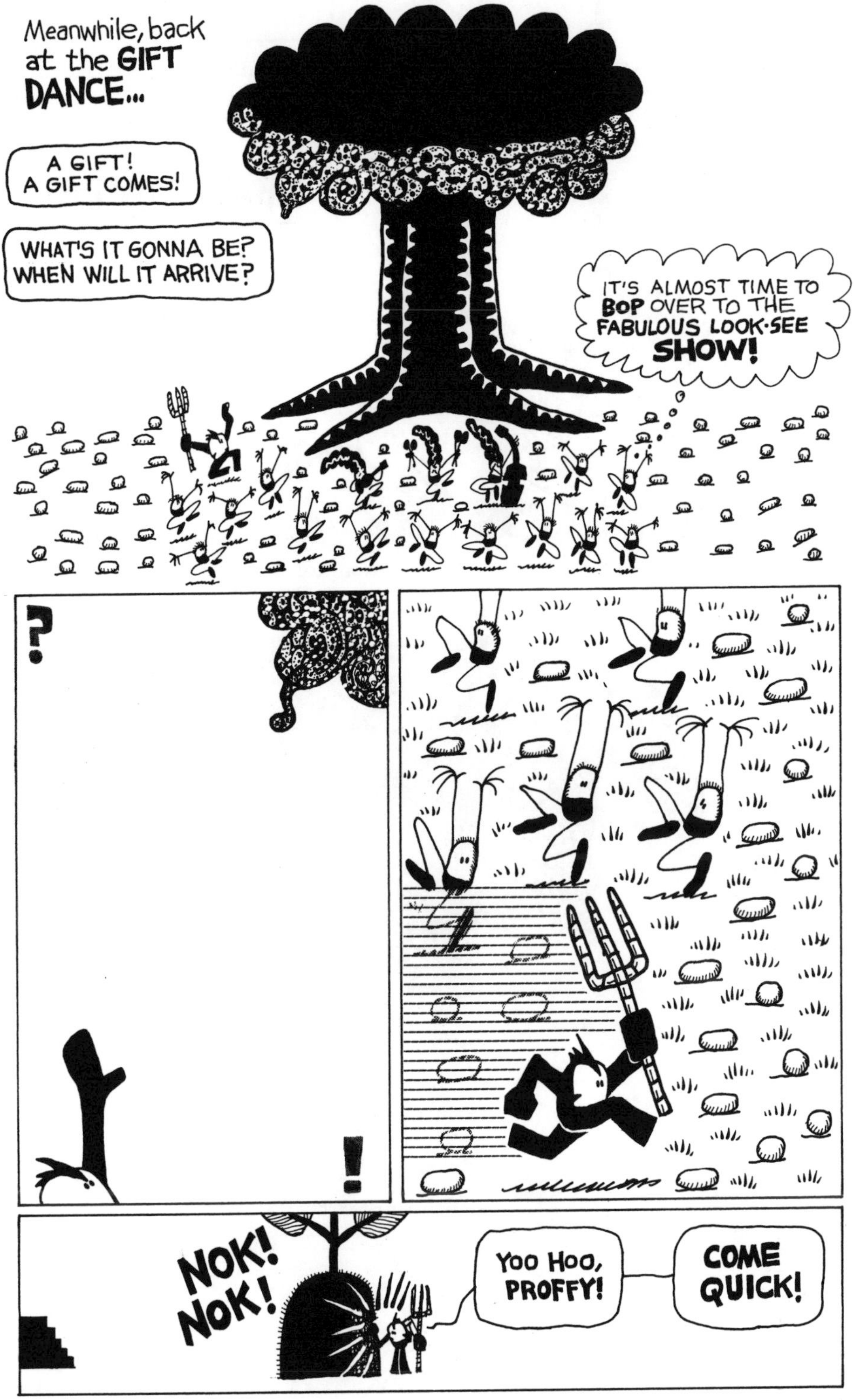

Meanwhile, back at the GIFT DANCE...
A GIFT! A GIFT COMES!
WHAT'S IT GONNA BE? WHEN WILL IT ARRIVE?
IT'S ALMOST TIME TO BOP OVER TO THE FABULOUS LOOK-SEE SHOW!
?
!
NOK! NOK!
YOO HOO, PROFFY!
COME QUICK!

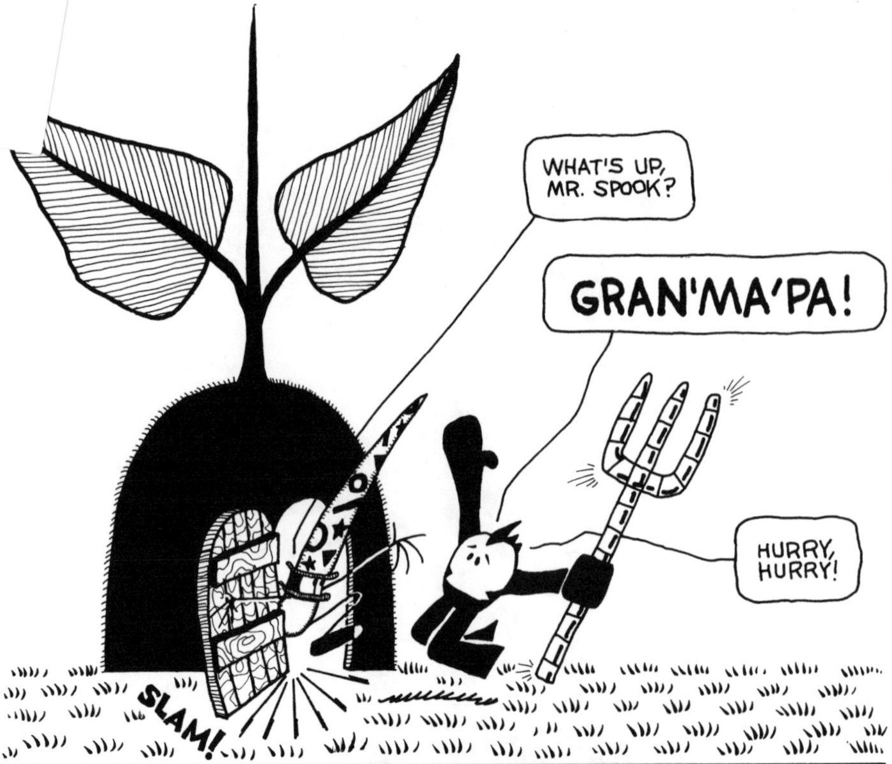
WHAT'S UP, MR. SPOOK?
GRAN'MA'PA!
HURRY, HURRY!
SLAM!

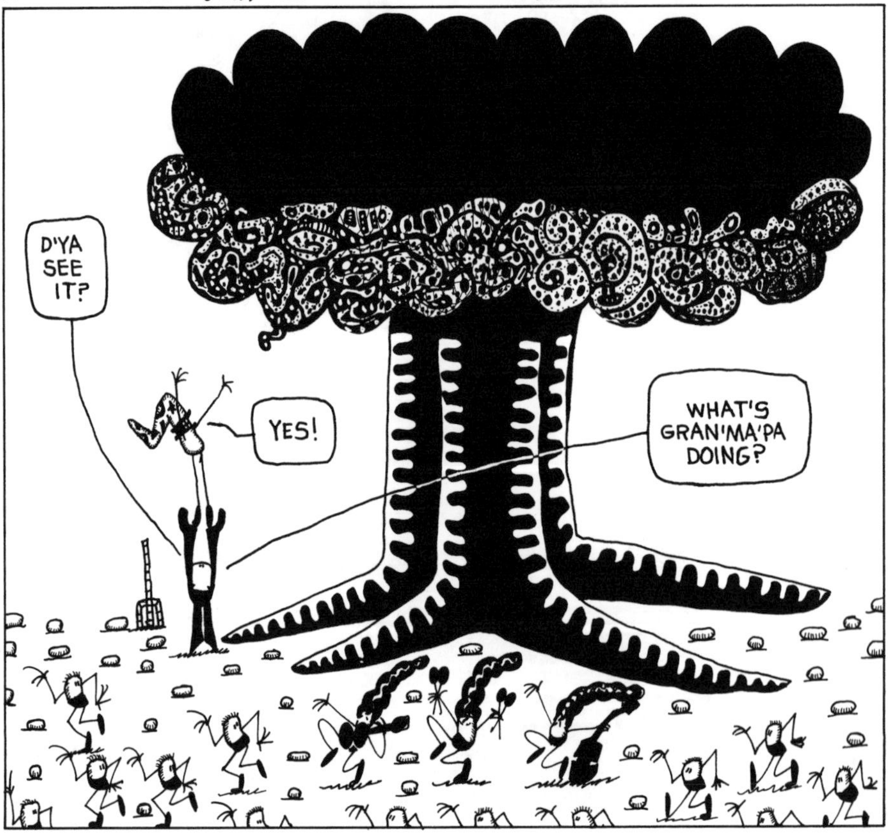
D'YA SEE IT?
YES!
WHAT'S GRAN'MA'PA DOING?

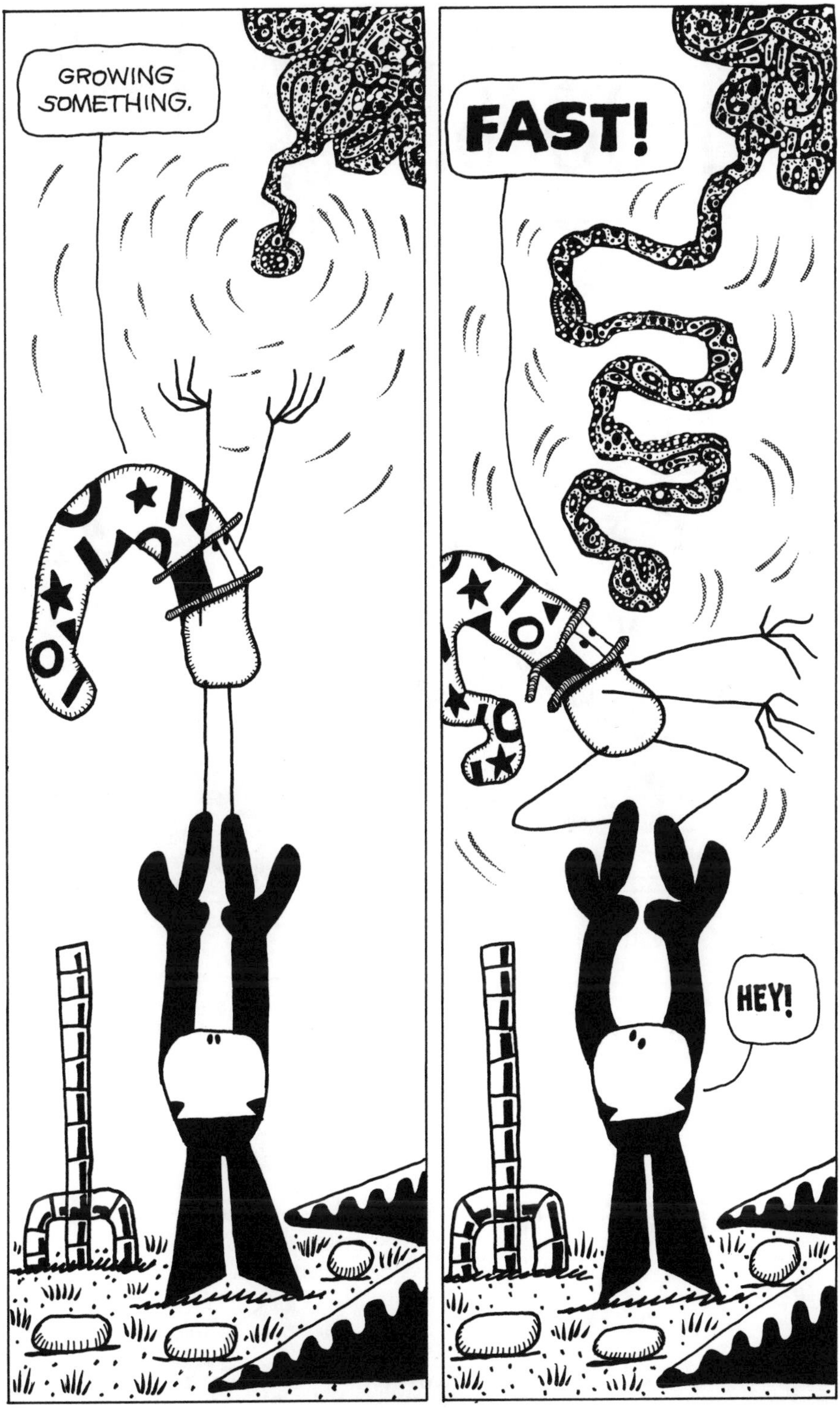
GROWING SOMETHING.
FAST!
HEY!

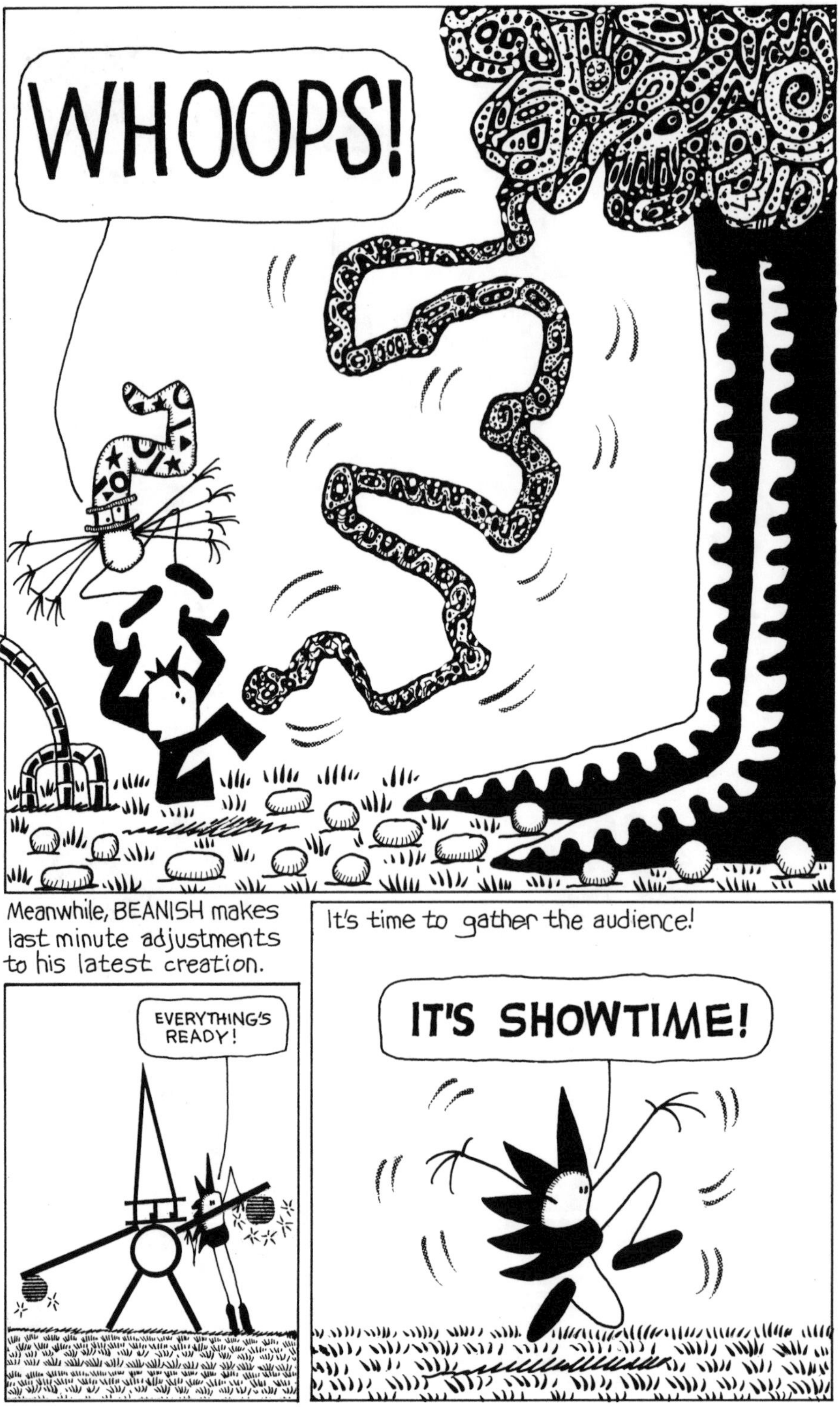
WHOOPS!
Meanwhile, BEANISH makes last minute adjustments to his latest creation.
EVERYTHING'S READY!
It's time to gather the audience!
IT'S SHOWTIME!

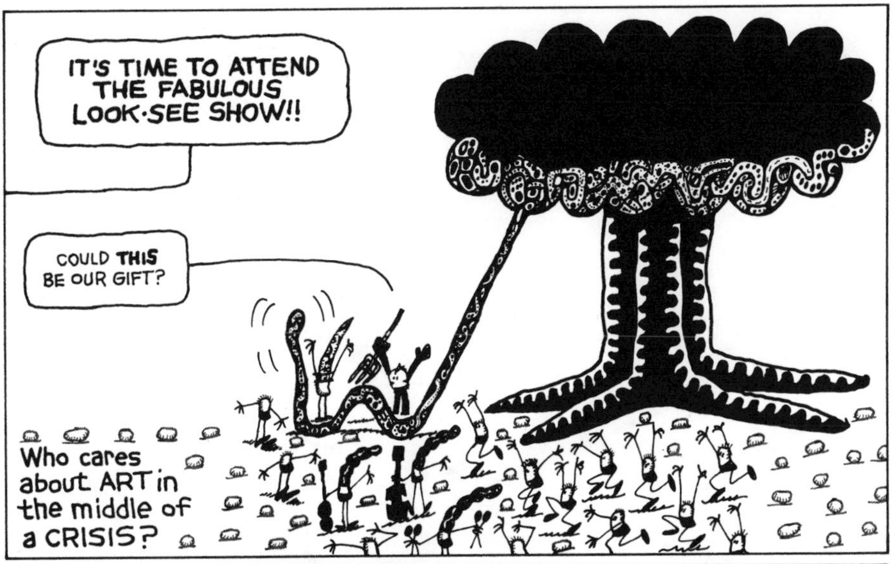

IT'S TIME TO ATTEND THE FABULOUS LOOK-SEE SHOW!!
COULD THIS BE OUR GIFT?
Who cares about ART in the middle of a CRISIS?


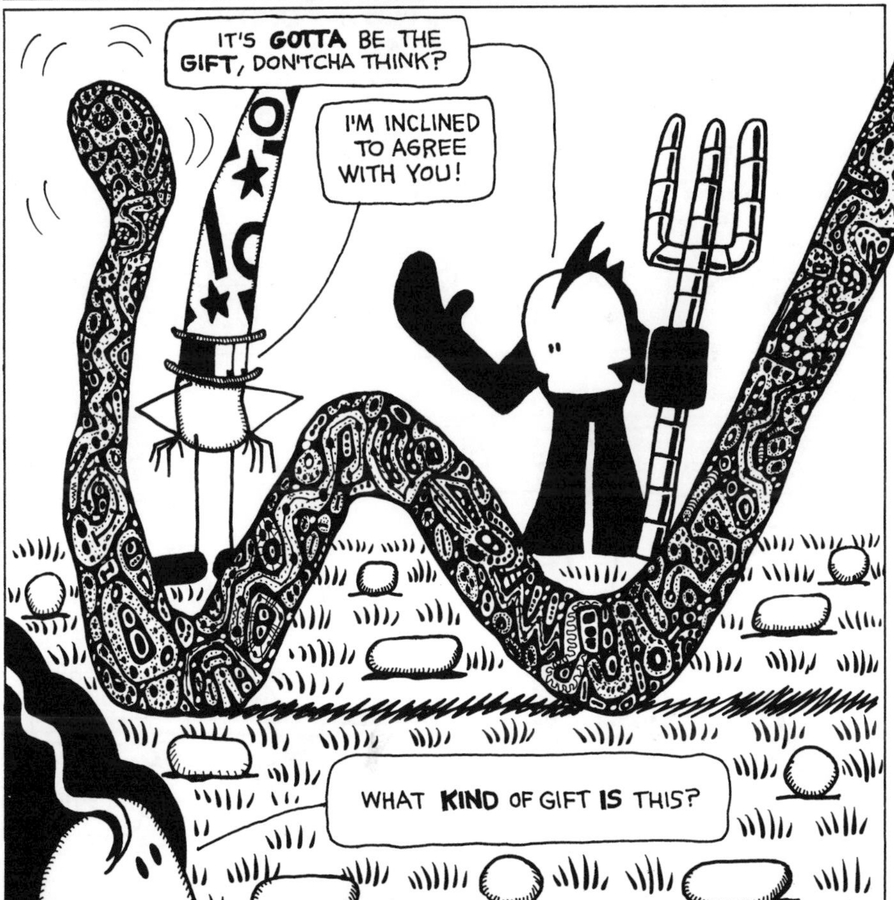

IT'S GOTTA BE THE GIFT, DON'TCHA THINK?
I'M INCLINED TO AGREE WITH YOU!
WHAT KIND OF GIFT IS THIS?

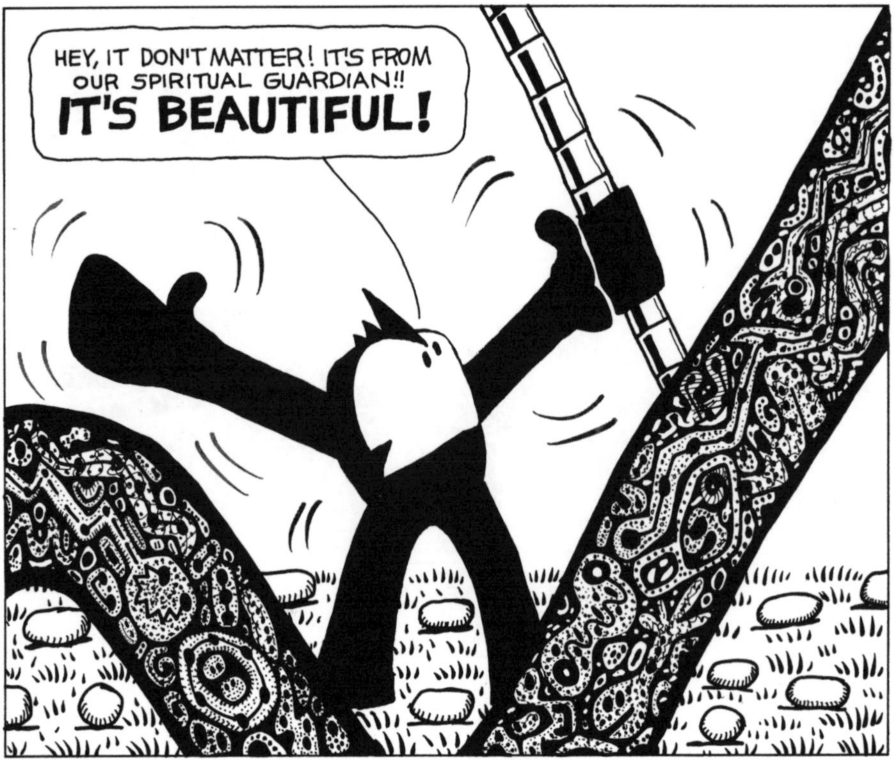
HEY, IT DON'T MATTER! IT'S FROM OUR SPIRITUAL GUARDIAN!! **IT'S BEAUTIFUL!**

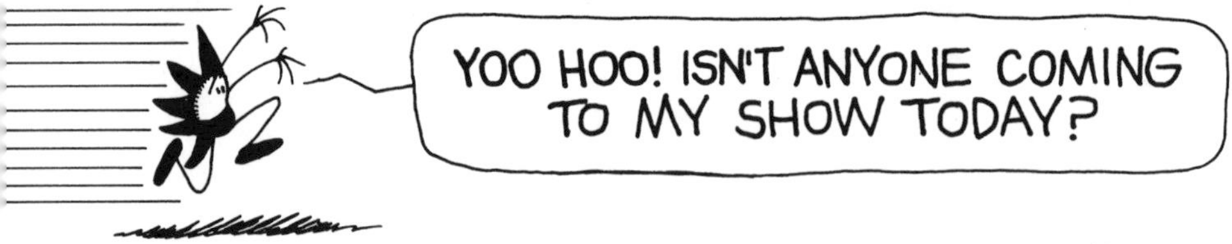
YOO HOO! ISN'T ANYONE COMING TO MY SHOW TODAY?

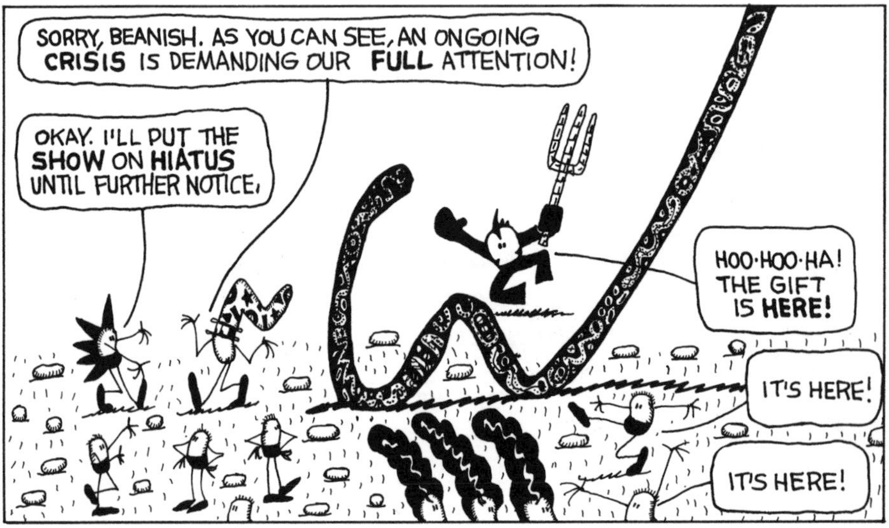
SORRY, BEANISH. AS YOU CAN SEE, AN ONGOING **CRISIS** IS DEMANDING OUR **FULL** ATTENTION!
OKAY. I'LL PUT THE **SHOW** ON **HIATUS** UNTIL FURTHER NOTICE.
HOO·HOO·HA! THE GIFT IS **HERE!**
IT'S HERE!
IT'S HERE!

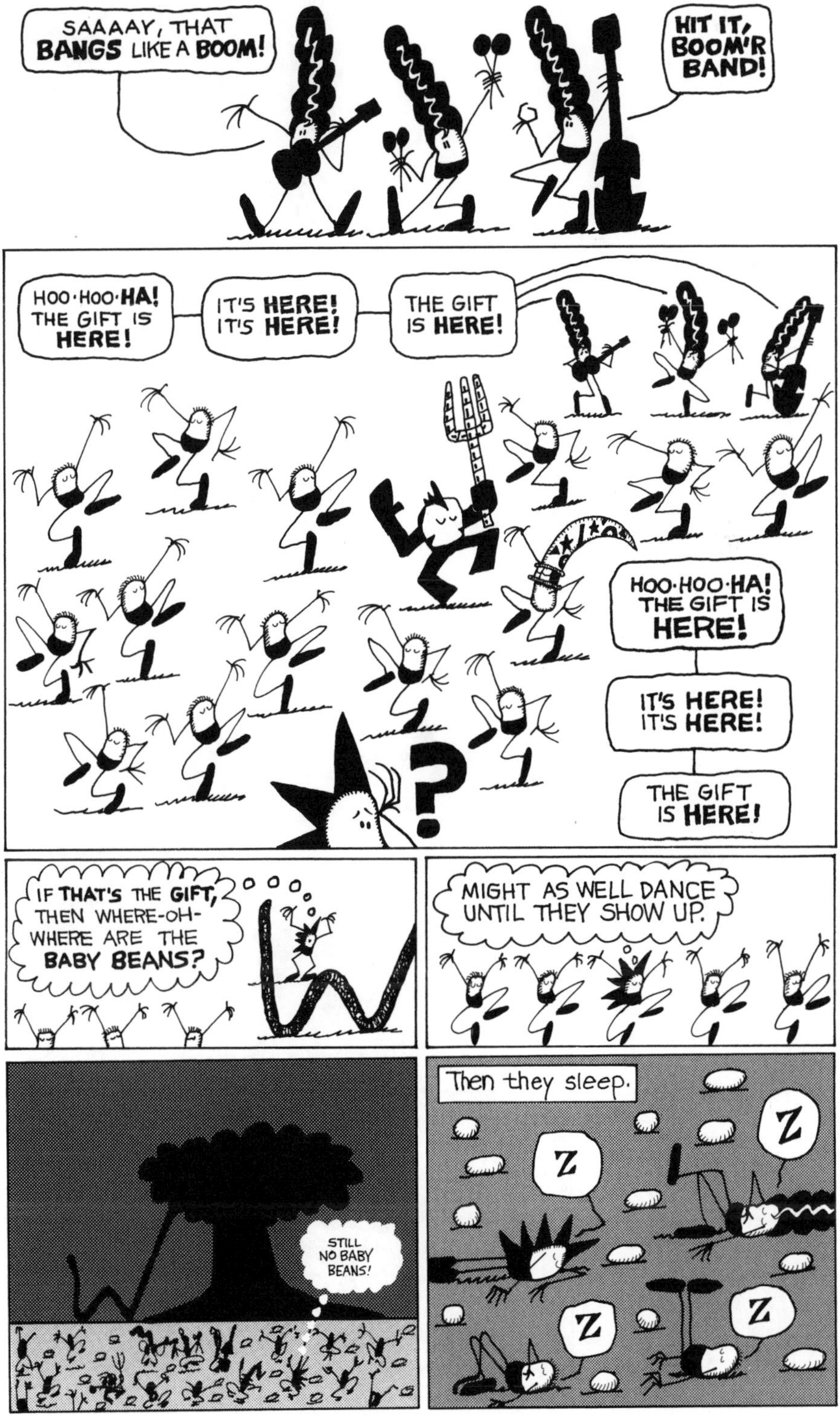
SAAAAY, THAT BANGS LIKE A BOOM!
HIT IT, BOOM'R BAND!
HOO·HOO·HA! THE GIFT IS HERE!
IT'S HERE! IT'S HERE!
THE GIFT IS HERE!
HOO·HOO·HA! THE GIFT IS HERE!
IT'S HERE! IT'S HERE!
THE GIFT IS HERE!
IF THAT'S THE GIFT, THEN WHERE-OH-WHERE ARE THE BABY BEANS?
MIGHT AS WELL DANCE UNTIL THEY SHOW UP.
STILL NO BABY BEANS!
Then they sleep.
Z
Z
Z
Z

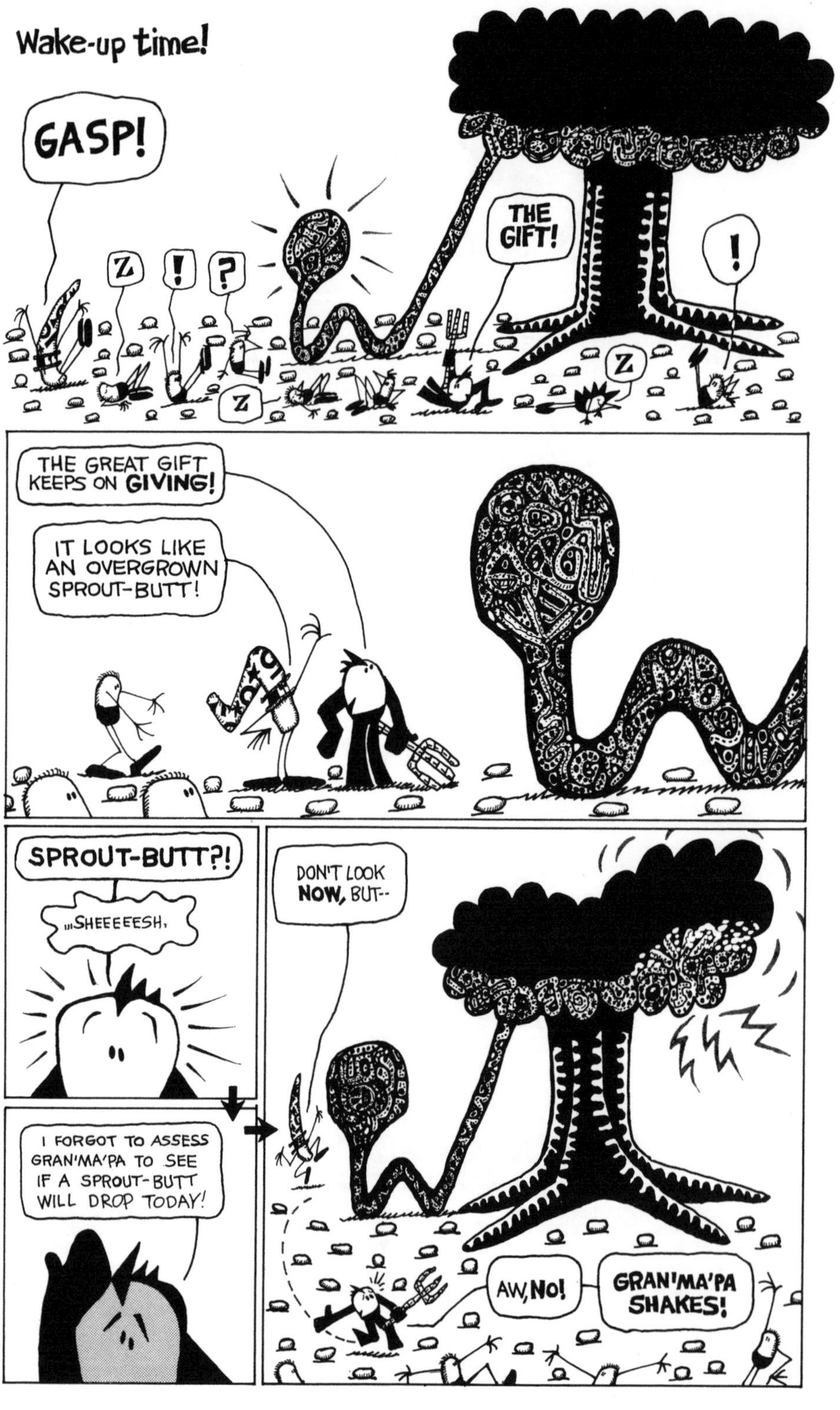
Wake-up time!
GASP!
Z
!
?
Z
THE GIFT!
Z
!
THE GREAT GIFT KEEPS ON GIVING!
IT LOOKS LIKE AN OVERGROWN SPROUT-BUTT!
SPROUT-BUTT?!
...SHEEEEESH...
I FORGOT TO ASSESS GRAN'MA'PA TO SEE IF A SPROUT-BUTT WILL DROP TODAY!
DON'T LOOK NOW, BUT--
AW, NO!
GRAN'MA'PA SHAKES!

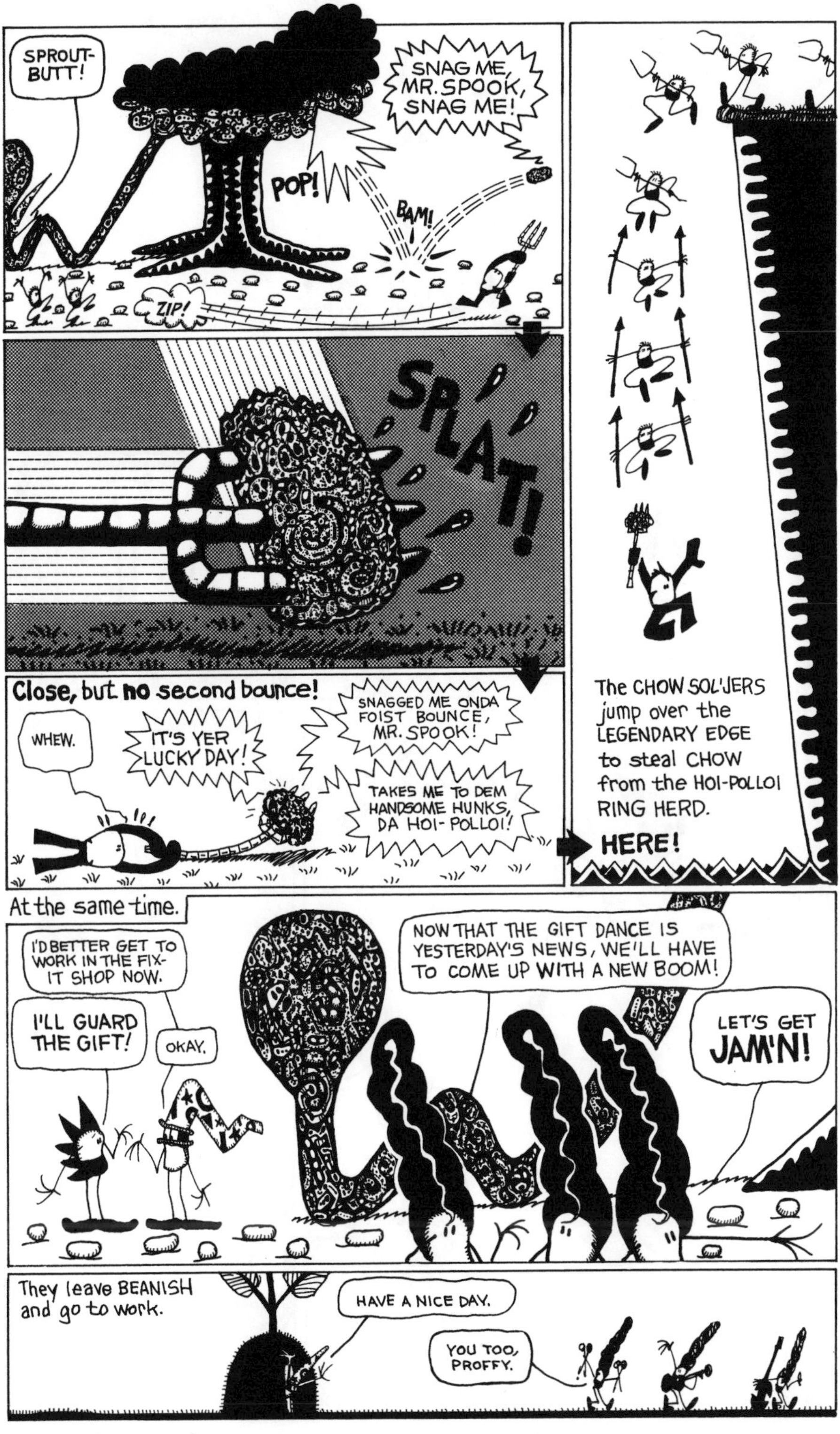
SPROUT-BUTT!
SNAG ME, MR. SPOOK, SNAG ME!
POP!
BAM!
ZIP!
SPLAT!
Close, but no second bounce!
WHEW.
IT'S YER LUCKY DAY!
SNAGGED ME ONDA FOIST BOUNCE, MR. SPOOK!
TAKES ME TO DEM HANDSOME HUNKS, DA HOI-POLLOI!
The CHOW SOL'JERS jump over the LEGENDARY EDGE to steal CHOW from the HOI-POLLOI RING HERD.
HERE!
At the same time.
I'D BETTER GET TO WORK IN THE FIX-IT SHOP NOW.
I'LL GUARD THE GIFT!
OKAY.
NOW THAT THE GIFT DANCE IS YESTERDAY'S NEWS, WE'LL HAVE TO COME UP WITH A NEW BOOM!
LET'S GET JAM'N!
They leave BEANISH and go to work.
HAVE A NICE DAY.
YOU TOO, PROFFY.

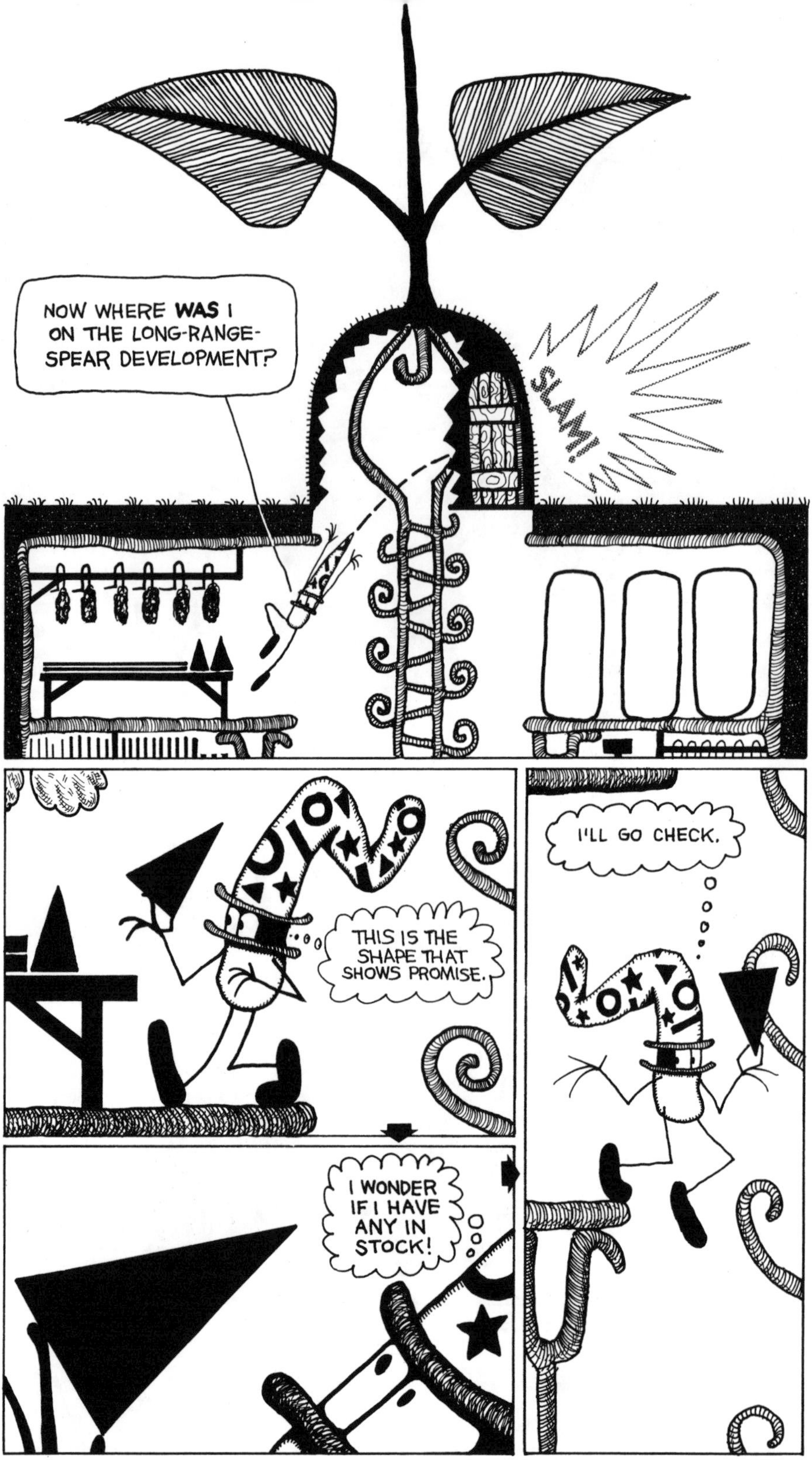
NOW WHERE WAS I ON THE LONG-RANGE-SPEAR DEVELOPMENT?
SLAM!
THIS IS THE SHAPE THAT SHOWS PROMISE.
I WONDER IF I HAVE ANY IN STOCK!
I'LL GO CHECK.

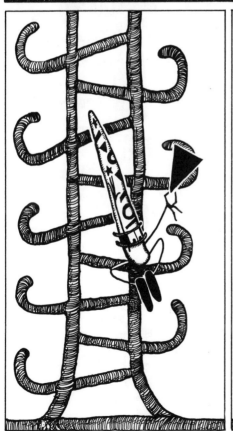

TWING!
A thorough search reveals:
NOTHING IN STOCK.
I'LL HAVE TO MAKE A TRIP TO THE FOUR REALITIES.
TWING!

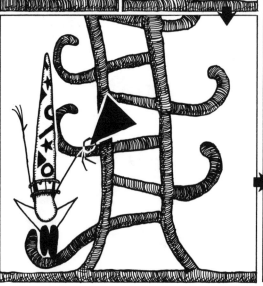

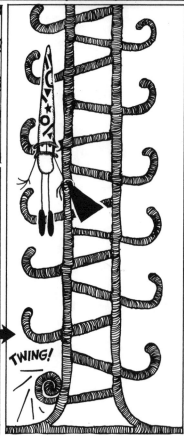

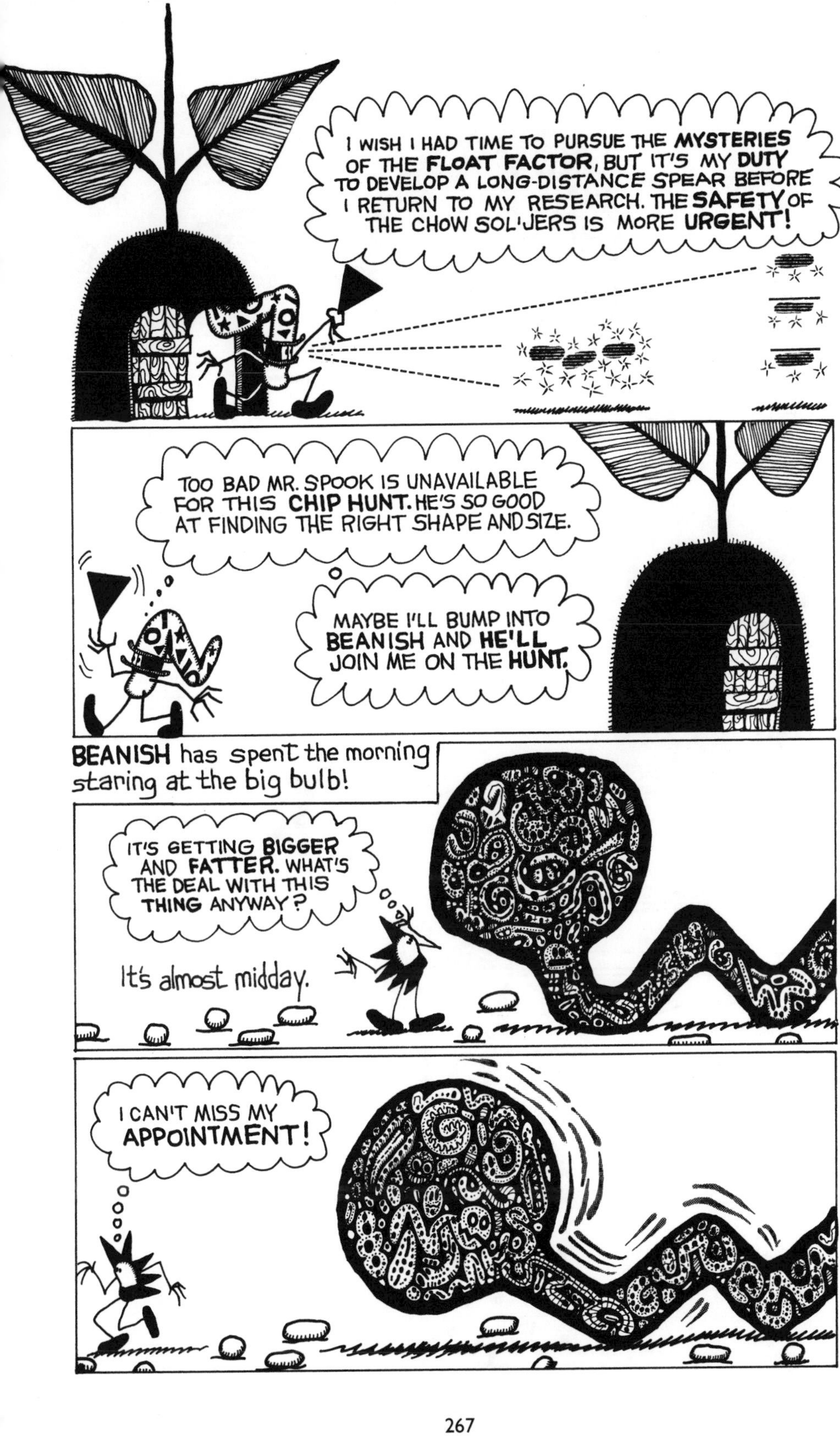
I WISH I HAD TIME TO PURSUE THE MYSTERIES OF THE FLOAT FACTOR, BUT IT'S MY DUTY TO DEVELOP A LONG-DISTANCE SPEAR BEFORE I RETURN TO MY RESEARCH. THE SAFETY OF THE CHOW SOL'JERS IS MORE URGENT!
TOO BAD MR. SPOOK IS UNAVAILABLE FOR THIS CHIP HUNT. HE'S SO GOOD AT FINDING THE RIGHT SHAPE AND SIZE.
MAYBE I'LL BUMP INTO BEANISH AND HE'LL JOIN ME ON THE HUNT.
BEANISH has spent the morning staring at the big bulb!
IT'S GETTING BIGGER AND FATTER. WHAT'S THE DEAL WITH THIS THING ANYWAY?
It's almost midday.
I CAN'T MISS MY APPOINTMENT!

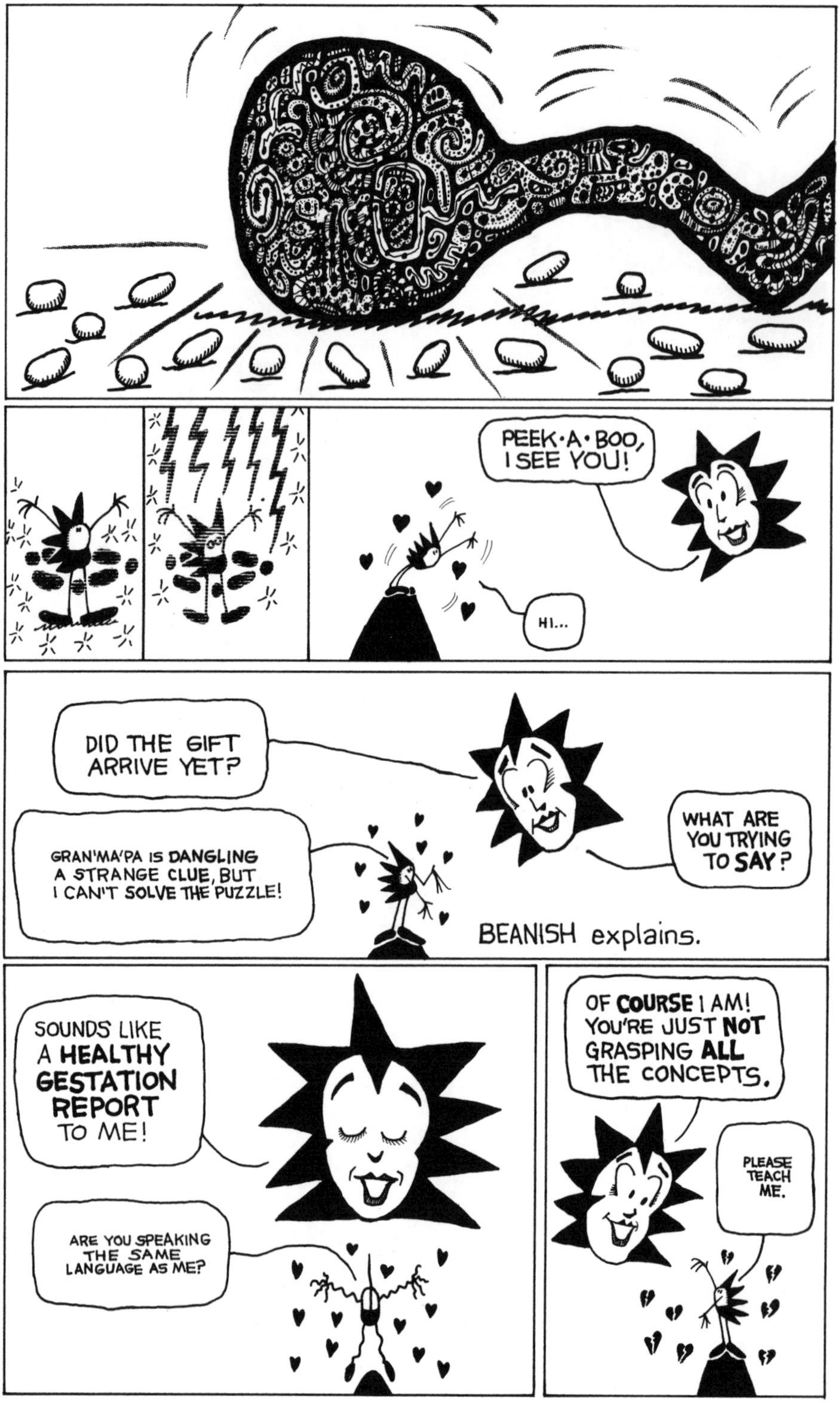
PEEK·A·BOO, I SEE YOU!
HI...
DID THE GIFT ARRIVE YET?
GRAN'MA'PA IS DANGLING A STRANGE CLUE, BUT I CAN'T SOLVE THE PUZZLE!
WHAT ARE YOU TRYING TO SAY?
BEANISH explains.
SOUNDS LIKE A HEALTHY GESTATION REPORT TO ME!
ARE YOU SPEAKING THE SAME LANGUAGE AS ME?
OF COURSE I AM! YOU'RE JUST NOT GRASPING ALL THE CONCEPTS.
PLEASE TEACH ME.

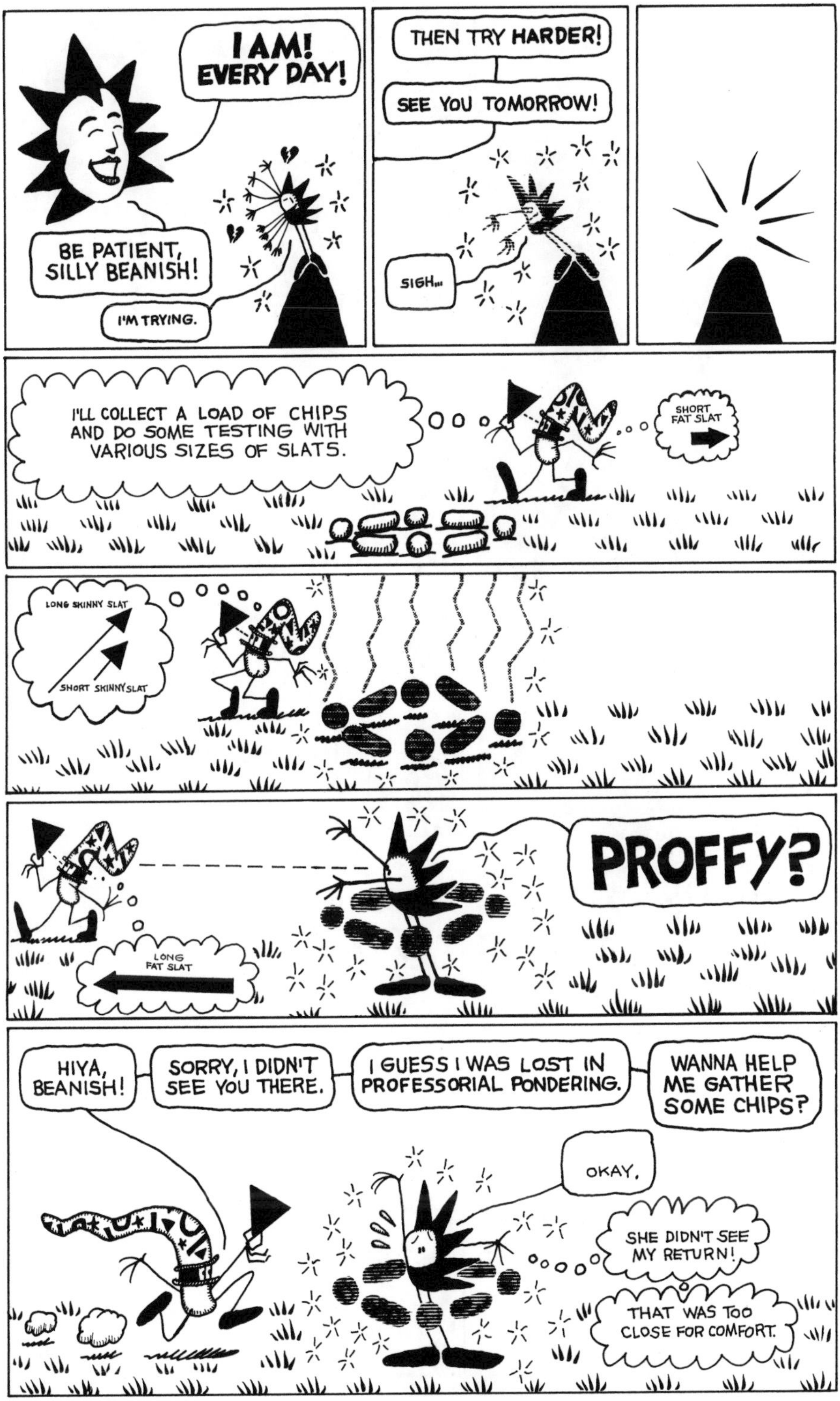
I AM! EVERY DAY!
BE PATIENT, SILLY BEANISH!
I'M TRYING.
THEN TRY HARDER!
SEE YOU TOMORROW!
SIGH...
I'LL COLLECT A LOAD OF CHIPS AND DO SOME TESTING WITH VARIOUS SIZES OF SLATS.
SHORT FAT SLAT
LONG SKINNY SLAT
SHORT SKINNY SLAT
PROFFY?
LONG FAT SLAT
HIYA, BEANISH!
SORRY, I DIDN'T SEE YOU THERE.
I GUESS I WAS LOST IN PROFESSORIAL PONDERING.
WANNA HELP ME GATHER SOME CHIPS?
OKAY.
SHE DIDN'T SEE MY RETURN!
THAT WAS TOO CLOSE FOR COMFORT.

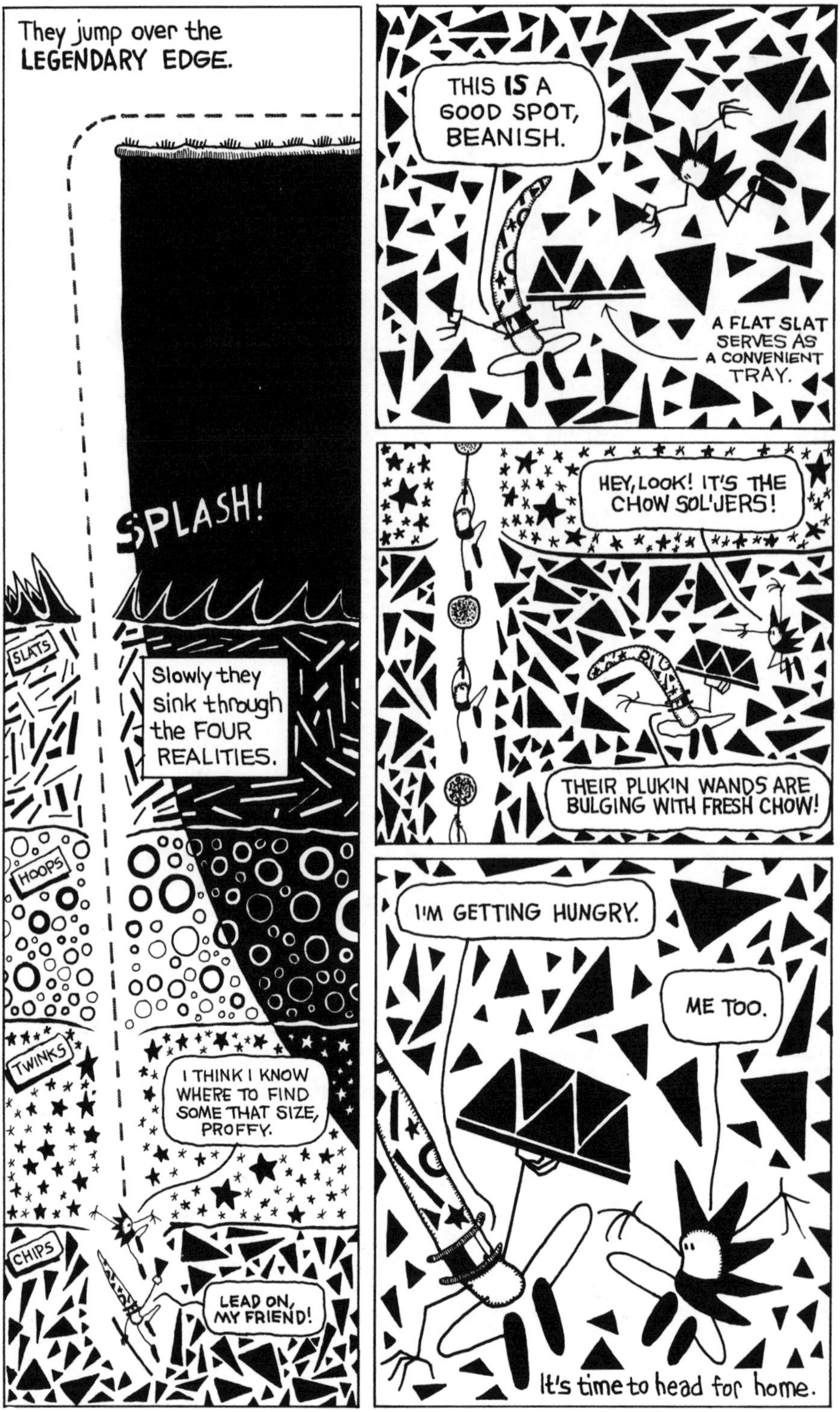
They jump over the LEGENDARY EDGE.
SPLASH!
SLATS
Slowly they sink through the FOUR REALITIES.
HOOPS
TWINKS
I THINK I KNOW WHERE TO FIND SOME THAT SIZE, PROFFY.
CHIPS
LEAD ON, MY FRIEND!
THIS IS A GOOD SPOT, BEANISH.
A FLAT SLAT SERVES AS A CONVENIENT TRAY.
HEY, LOOK! IT'S THE CHOW SOL'JERS!
THEIR PLUK'IN WANDS ARE BULGING WITH FRESH CHOW!
I'M GETTING HUNGRY.
ME TOO.
It's time to head for home.

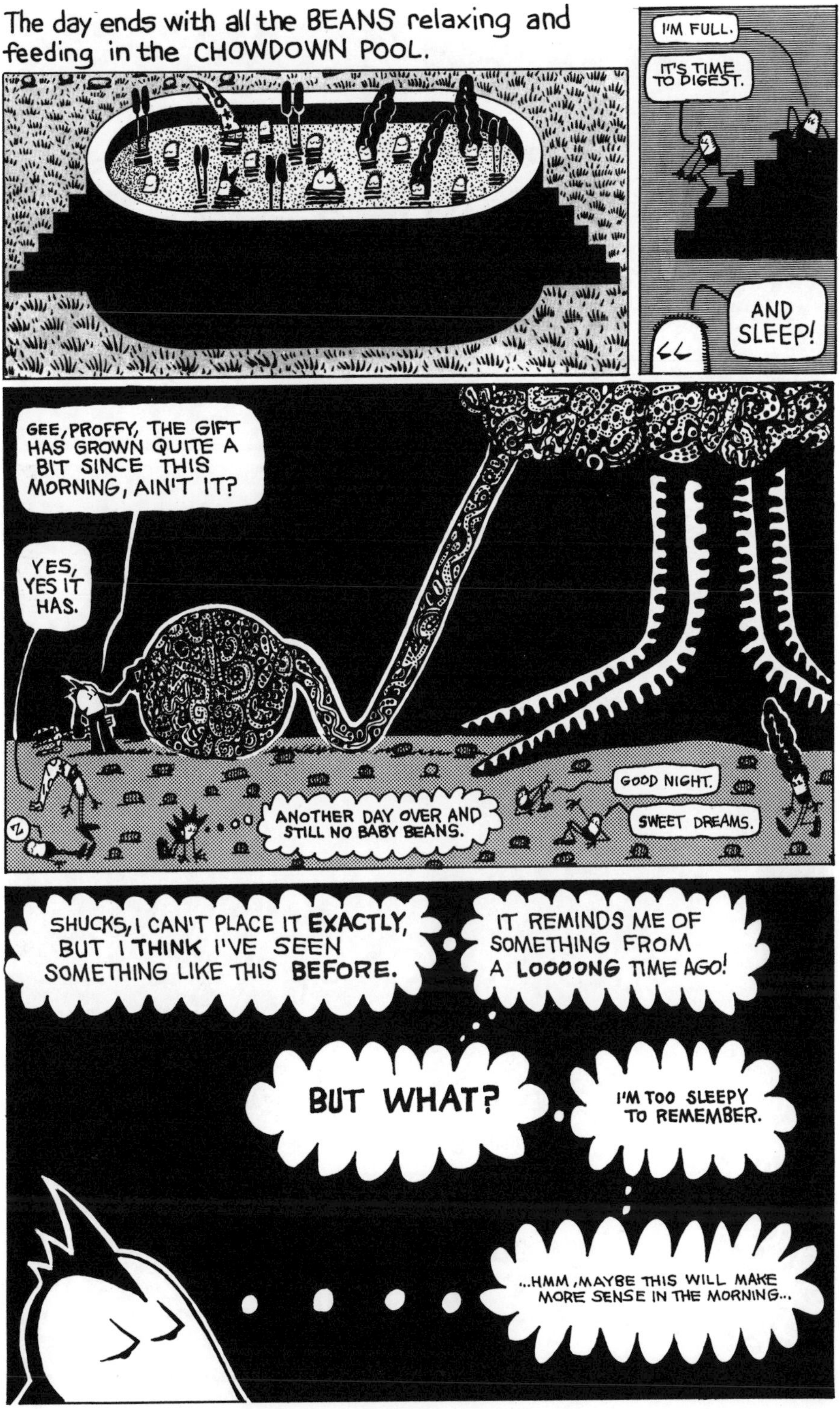
The day ends with all the BEANS relaxing and feeding in the CHOWDOWN POOL.
I'M FULL.
IT'S TIME TO DIGEST.
AND SLEEP!
GEE, PROFFY, THE GIFT HAS GROWN QUITE A BIT SINCE THIS MORNING, AIN'T IT?
YES, YES IT HAS.
Z
ANOTHER DAY OVER AND STILL NO BABY BEANS.
GOOD NIGHT.
SWEET DREAMS.
SHUCKS, I CAN'T PLACE IT EXACTLY, BUT I THINK I'VE SEEN SOMETHING LIKE THIS BEFORE.
IT REMINDS ME OF SOMETHING FROM A LOOOONG TIME AGO!
BUT WHAT?
I'M TOO SLEEPY TO REMEMBER.
...HMM, MAYBE THIS WILL MAKE MORE SENSE IN THE MORNING...

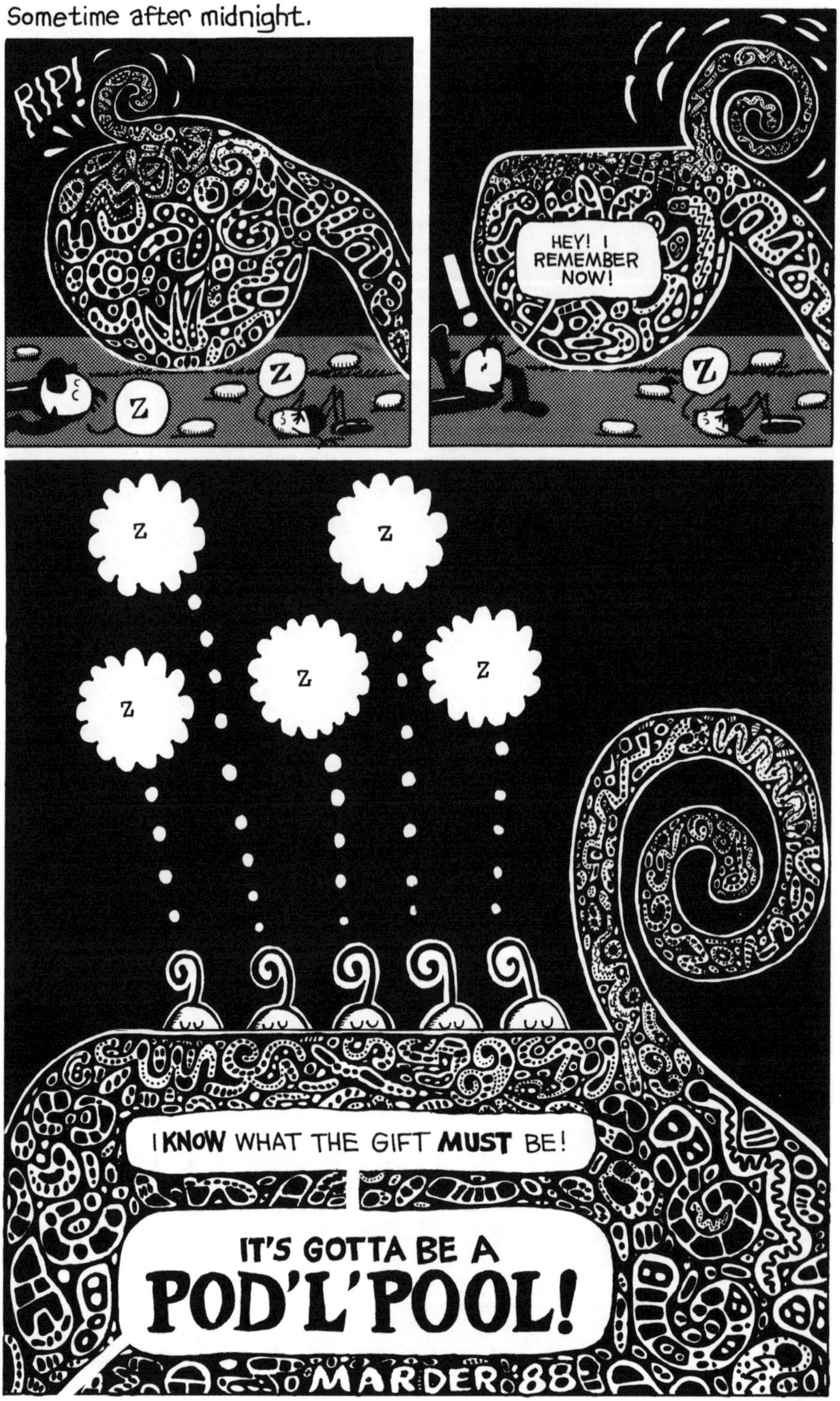
Sometime after midnight.
RIP!
Z
Z
!
HEY! I REMEMBER NOW!
Z
Z
Z
Z
Z
Z
I KNOW WHAT THE GIFT MUST BE!
IT'S GOTTA BE A POD'L'POOL!
MARDER 88

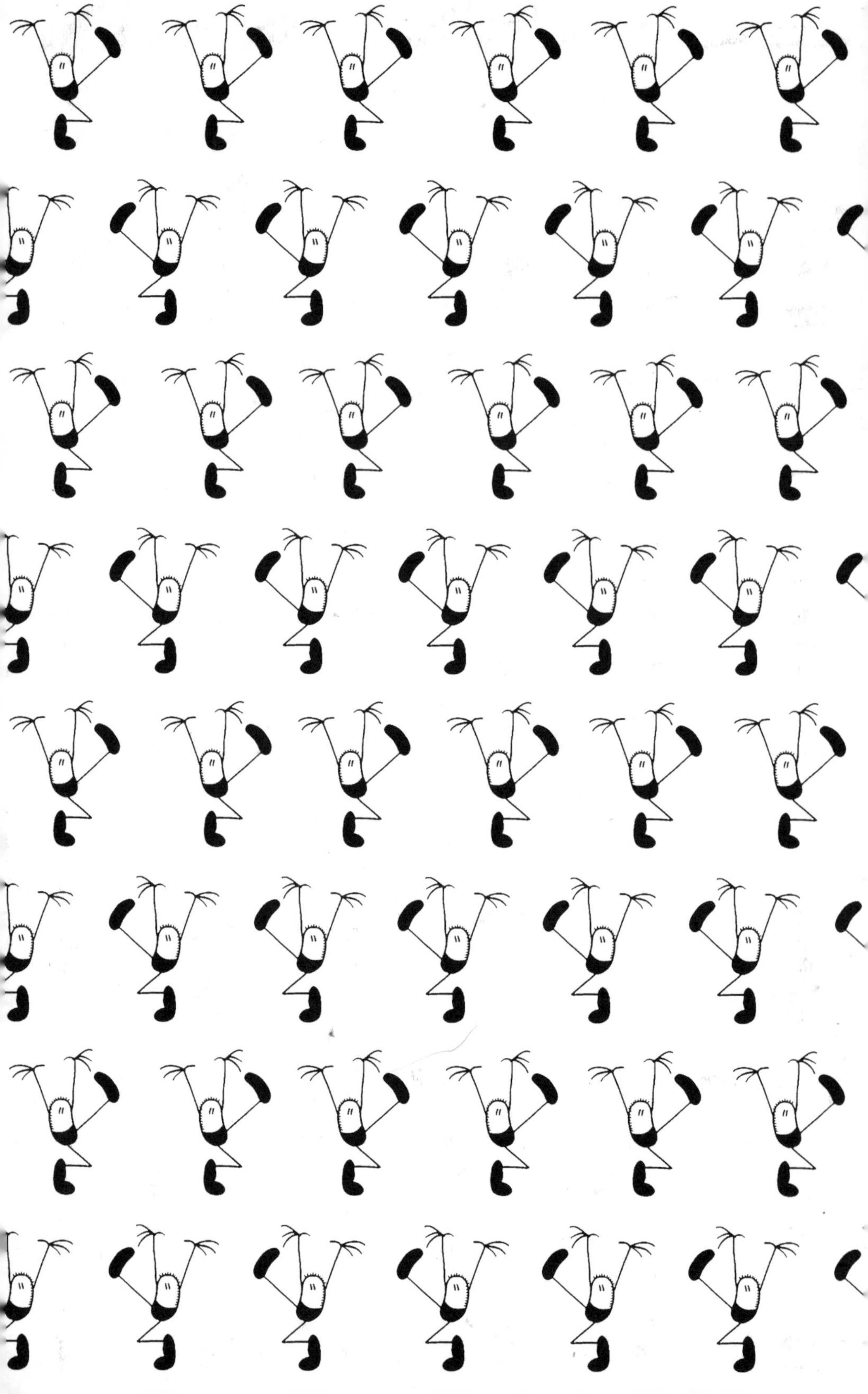